Translated Texts for His

This series is designed to meet the needs of student_ ....u ..i.uivai history and others who wish to broaden their study by reading source material, but whose knowledge of Latin or Greek is not sufficient to allow them to do so in the original language. Many important Late Imperial and Dark Age texts are currently unavailable in translation and it is hoped that TTH will help to fill this gap and to complement the secondary literature in English which already exists. The series relates principally to the period 300–800 AD and includes Late Imperial, Greek, Byzantine and Syriac texts as well as source books illustrating a particular period or theme. Each volume is a self-contained scholarly translation with an introductory essay on the text and its author and notes on the text indicating major problems of interpretation, including textual difficulties.

Front cover drawing: Portrait of Avitus with his signet ring, stylus and waxed writing tablets, drawn by R. S. O. Tomlin. The background shows the 6th-century manuscript of his *Homilies* (Bibliothèque Nationale, Paris).

A full list of published titles in the Translated Texts for Historians series is available on request. The most recently published are shown below.

Bede: The Reckoning of Time
Translated with introduction, notes and commentary by FAITH WALLIS
Volume 29: 582 pp., 1999, ISBN 0-85323-693-3

Ruricius of Limoges and Friends: A Collection of Letters from Visigothic Gaul
Translated with notes and introduction by RALPH W. MATHISEN
Volume 30: 272pp., 1998, ISBN 0-85323-703-4

The Armenian History attributed to Sebeos
Translated with notes by R. W. THOMSON, Historical commentary by JAMES HOWARD-JOHNSTON. Assistance from TIM GREENWOOD
Volume 31 (in two parts): 240 pp., 224 pp., 1999, ISBN 0-85323-564-3

The Chronicle of Pseudo-Joshua the Stylite
Translated with notes and introduction by FRANK R. TROMBLEY and JOHN W. WATT
Volume 32: 240pp., including 3 maps and 2 plans, 2000, ISBN 0-85323-585-6

The Ecclesiastical History of Evagrius Scholasticus
Translated with an introduction and notes by MICHAEL WHITBY
Volume 33: 454pp., 2000, ISBN 0-85323-605-4

Antioch as a Centre of Hellenic Culture, as Observed by Libanius
Translated with an introduction and notes by A. F. NORMAN
Volume 34: 224pp., 2000, ISBN 0-85323-595-3

Neoplatonic Saints: The Lives of Plotinus and Proclus by their Students
Translated with an introduction and notes by MARK EDWARDS
Volume 35: 224pp., 2000, ISBN 0-85323-615-1

Politics, Philosophy and Empire in the Fourth Century: Select Orations of Themistius
Translated with an introduction by PETER HEATHER and DAVID MONCUR
Volume 36: 384pp., 2001, ISBN 0-85323-106-0

A Christian's Guide to Greek Culture: The Pseudo-Nonnus *Commentaries* on *Sermons* 4, 5, 39 and 43 of Gregory of Nazianzus
Translated with an introduction and notes by JENNIFER NIMMO SMITH
Volume 37: 208pp., 2001, ISBN 0-85323-917-7

For full details of Translated Texts for Historians, including prices and ordering information, please write to the following: **All countries, except the USA and Canada**: Liverpool University Press, 4 Cambridge Street, Liverpool, L69 7ZU, UK (*Tel* +44-[0]151-794 2233 *Fax* +44-[0]151-794 2235, Email J.M. Smith@liv.ac.uk, http://www.liverpool-unipress.co.uk). **USA and Canada:** University of Pennsylvania Press, 4200 Pine Street, Philadelphia, PA 19104-6097, USA (*Tel* +1-215-898-6264, *Fax* +1-215-898-0404).

Translated Texts for Historians
Volume 38

Avitus of Vienne
Letters and Selected Prose

Translated with an introduction and notes by
DANUTA SHANZER and IAN WOOD

Liverpool
University
Press

First published 2002
Liverpool University Press
4 Cambridge Street
Liverpool, L69 7ZU

British Library Cataloguing-in-Publication Data
A British Library CIP Record is available.
ISBN 0-85323-588-0

Set in Times by
Koinonia, Manchester
Printed in the European Union by
Bell and Bain Limited, Glasgow

TABLE OF CONTENTS

x CONTENTS

MAPS AND GENEALOGIES

ABBREVIATIONS

Avitus,	*CA*	*Contra Arrianos*
	CCL	*De consolatoria castitatis laude*
	CE	*Contra Eutychianam haeresim*
	SHG	*De spiritalis historiae gestis*
AASS		*Acta sanctorum*
ACO		*Acta conciliorum oecumenicorum*, ed. E. Schwartz (Berlin, 1965–)
ALL		*Archiv für lateinische Lexikographie und Grammatik*
AV		Authorised version
Blaise		A. Blaise, *Dictionnaire Latin–Française des auteurs chrétiens* (Turnholt, 1967)
Boissier		G. Boissier, 'Le *Carmen paschale* et l'*Opus paschale* de Sedulius', *Revue de Philologie* 6 (1882), pp. 28–36
Burckhardt		M. Burckhardt, *Die Briefsammlung des Bischofs Avitus von Vienne*, Abhandlungen zur mittleren und neueren Geschichte, Vol. 81 (Berlin, 1938)
Bury, *LRE*		J. B. Bury, *History of the Later Roman Empire* (London, 2nd edn, 1923)
CA		Avitus, *Contra Arrianos*
Carm.		*Carmen* (poem)
CCL		Avitus, *De consolatoria castitatis laude*
CCSL		*Corpus Christianorum, Series Latina*
CE		Avitus, *Contra Eutychianam haeresim*
Charaux		A. Charaux, *Saint Avit, évêque de Vienne, en Dauphiné, sa vie, ses oeuvres* (Paris, 1876)
Chevalier		Ulysse Chevalier, *Oeuvres complètes de Saint Avit, Évêque de Vienne* (Lyon, 1890).
Clavis		*Clavis patrum latinorum*, ed. E. Dekkers and A. Gaar (Turnhout, 2nd edn, 1961; Steenbrugge, 3rd edn, 1995)
Cod. Theod.		*Codex Theodosianus*, ed. T. Mommsen, P.M. Meyer and P. Krüger, *Theodosiani libri XVI cum constitutionibus*

sirmondianis et leges novellae ad Theodosianum pertinentes, 3 vols (Berlin, 1905; repr. 1970–71)

CP	*Classical Philology*
CR	*Classical Review*
CSEL	*Corpus scriptorum ecclesiasticorum latinorum*
DACL	F. Cabrol, *Dictionnaire d'archéologie chrétienne et de liturgie* (Paris, 1907–53)
Daremberg –Saglio	C. Daremberg, E. Saglio, E. Pottier and George Lafayé, *Dictionnaire des antiquités grecques et romaines d'après les textes et le monument*, 5 in 10 vols (Paris, 1877)
Delisle	L. V. Delisle, *Études paléographiques et historiques sur des papyrus de VIème siècle … renfermant des homélies de Saint Avit* (Geneva, 1866)
Denkinger	H. Denkinger, *Alcimus Ecdicius Avitus, archévêque de Vienne 460–526 et la destruction de l'arianisme en Gaule* (Geneva, 1890)
DHGE	A. Baudrillart, A. D. Meyer and R. Aubert, *Dictionnaire d'histoire et de géographie ecclésiastiques* (Paris, 1912–99)
Divjak	J. Divjak, ed., Augustine, *Epistulae*, *CSEL* 88 (Vienna, 1981)
DOP	*Dumbarton Oaks Papers*
EME	*Early Medieval Europe*
Ep.	*Epistula* (letter)
Epist. imp.	*Epistulae imperatorum pontificum aliorum inde ab a.CCCLXVII usque ad a. DLIII datae avellana quae dicitur collectio*, ed. O. Günther, *CSEL* 35, 1–2 (Vienna, 1895–98).
FHG	*Fragmenta historicorum graecorum*, ed. C. Müller (Paris, 1874–85)
Goelzer	H. Goelzer, *Le Latin de Saint Avit* (Paris, 1909)
Greg. Tur.	Gregory of Tours
DLH	*Decem Libri Historiarum*
GC	*Liber in Gloria Confessorum*
GM	*Liber in Gloria Martyrum*
LVJ	*Liber de Virtutibus sancti Juliani*
LVM	*Liber de Virtutibus sancti Martini*
LVP	*Liber Vitae Patrum*

Hil. Pict.	Hilary of Poitiers
Jones, *LRE*	A. H. M. Jones, *The Later Roman Empire A.D. 284–640: A Social, Economic, and Administrative Survey* (Oxford, 1964)
Jord. *Get.*	Jordanes, *Getica*
JRS	*Journal of Roman Studies*
Loyen	A. Loyen, ed., *Sidoine Apollinaire: Poèmes et Lettres* (Paris, 1960–70)
MÉFR	*Mélanges de l'école française de Rome*
MIÖG	*Mitteilungen des Instituts für oesterreichische Geschichtsforschung*
MGH	*Monumenta Germaniae historica*
AA	*Auctores antiquissimi*
Epp.	*Epistulae*
Leg.	*Leges*
Poet.	*Poetae latini*
SRM	*Scriptores rerum merovingicarum*
OLD	*Oxford Latin Dictionary*
Peiper	R. Peiper, ed., *Alcimi Aviti opera quae supersunt*, *MGH AA* 6.2 (Berlin, 1883)
PL	J.-P. Migne, ed., *Patrologia latina*
Pliny, *NH*	Pliny, *Historia Naturalis*
PLRE 1	A. H. M. Jones, J. R. Martindale and J. Morris, eds, *The Prosopography of the Later Roman Empire. Volume I. A.D. 260–395* (Cambridge, 1971).
PLRE 2	J. R. Martindale, ed., *The Prosopography of the Later Roman Empire. Volume 2. A.D. 395–527* (Cambridge, 1980)
PLRE 3	J. R. Martindale, ed., *The Prosopography of the Later Roman Empire. Volume 3. A.D. 527–640* (Cambridge, 1993)
PLS	*Patrologia latina, supplementum*
PWRE	Pauly–Wissowa–Kroll, *Real-Encyclopädie der klassischen Altertumswissenschaft*
RB	*Revue Bénédictine*
RBPH	*Revue Belge de Philologie et d'Histoire*
Rilliet	A. Rilliet, *Conjectures historiques sur les homélies préchées par Avitus, évêque de Vienne dans le diocèse de Genève* (Geneva, 1866)

SbBAW   *Sitzungsberichte der Bayerische Akademie der*
  phil.-hist. Kl. *Wissenschaften*, phil.-hist. Klasse
SC   *Sources chrétiennes*
Schanz–Hosius M. Schanz, C. Hosius and G. Krüger, *Geschichte der*
                     römischen Literatur, Vol. 4.2 (Munich, 1920)
Sid.Ap.   Sidonius Apollinaris
Stein–Palanque E. Stein, *Histoire du Bas-Empire: 476–565*, ed. and trans.
                     J.R. Palanque, Vol. 2 (Paris–Brussels–Amsterdam, 1949)
Sirmond   Iacobus Sirmondus, *Sancti Aviti Archiepiscopi Viennensis*
                     Opera (Paris, 1643). Reprinted in Migne *PL* 59, cols 202–
                     382
TAPA   *Transactions of the American Philological Association*
Ter. *Eun.*   Terence, *Eunuchus*
Thiel   A. Thiel, *Epistulae Romanorum pontificum* (Brunsberg,
                     1867)
TLL   *Thesaurus Linguae Latinae* (Leipzig, 1900–99)
WS   *Wiener Studien*

GLOSSARY

Bonosus, *Bonosiaci* Bonosus, a bishop in Illyricum in the late fourth century, emphasised the fact that the Virgin Mary continued to bear children after the birth of Christ, and was further believed to have regarded Christ himself as having been born to Mary and Joseph, and adopted by God: Pseudo-Isidore, *Indiculus de haeresibus, PL* 81.646.

Comes patrimonii Count of the imperial patrimony: one of the officials charged with the oversight of imperial estates. See the comments in Barnwell, *Emperor, Prefects and Kings*, pp. 148–50.

Dux Military leader, sometimes associated with a particular province: see the comments in Barnwell, *Emperor, Prefects and Kings*, pp. 38–40: also Lewis, 'The Dukes in the *Regnum Francorum*, AD 550–751', *Speculum* 51 (1976), pp. 381–410.

Eutyches Constantinopolitan monk who denied the human nature of Christ: his theology, known as Monophysite, after its contention that Christ had a single, divine nature, was condemned at the Council of Chalcedon in 451.

Mag. Off., Magister officiorum Master of the Offices, associated with the supervision of personnel, especially imperial agents, and of elements of provincial administration: see the comments in Barnwell, *Emperor, Prefects and Kings*, pp. 23–24.

MM, Magister militum Master of the soldiers. In the West, the leading commander of the infantry (*Magister peditum*) or of the cavalry (*Magister equitum*), or of both combined: *MVM: Magister utriusque militiae*.

MM per Gallias, Magister militum per Gallias Master of the soldiers in Gaul: the senior military commander in Gaul.

MVM, Magister utriusque militiae Master of both forces (cavalry and infantry): see the comments in Barnwell, *Emperor, Prefects and Kings*, pp. 41–44.

Nestorius, Nestorianism Nestorius, bishop of Alexandria (428–31), upheld the dual nature of Christ, divine and human, but in so doing implied that

Christ had two separate natures. The doctrine was condemned at the Council of Ephesus in 431.

patricius Patrician: a title, which could be used to identify the *MVM*, although it was clearly not confined to that one office: see the comments in Barnwell, *Emperor, Prefects and Kings*, pp. 44–47.

Photinus, Photinians Photinus was bishop of Sirmium in the mid-fourth century, and believed that Christ was conceived through the carnal intercourse of Mary and Joseph: Pseudo-Isidore, *Indiculus de haeresibus*, *PL* 81.644.

v.i., vir illustrissimus Title identifying the highest ranks of senators: see the comments in Jones, *The Later Roman Empire, 284–602*, pp. 528–30.

PREFACE

The works of Avitus of Vienne are a major source for the kingdom of the Burgundians, and more generally for the history of the post-Roman West in the early sixth century, yet they are little read. In large measure as a result of the difficulty of his Latin style, the bishop of Vienne has received less than his due. This is the first complete translation of Avitus' letters into English, or indeed into any language. A limited number have been translated, and where translations into any modern language are available, we have noted the fact; but it will become readily apparent that even these letters look somewhat different when considered within the context of the bishop of Vienne's total oeuvre. To the letters we have added translations of two of Avitus' homilies, and have noted where other translations can be found. His poetic works, by contrast have been rather better served, and have recently been translated in their entirety into English.

ORGANISATION

Since what is called Avitus' 'letter-collection' was not assembled by its author in the order transmitted by the manuscript, and since indeed the manuscripts do not transmit all the letters in the same order, we have rearranged the collection into what we call 'dossiers', groups of related letters. A dossier can be a group of letters to one significant individual, e.g. Avitus' letters to his cousin or brother, or to a class of individuals, e.g. his suffragan bishops. Dossiers sometimes contain groups of letters with common concerns or topics, e.g. letters related to the Acacian schism and affairs of the Eastern Empire, or letters that deal with the ransoming of captives. While in some cases our decisions may be disputed, and some letters are susceptible to classification in more than one category, this system will provide historians using the translation with the quickest way to find both the letters they are looking for and the material that is closely related. Peiper's numbering is retained for convenience of reference, and at the start of each letter we have provided the Peiper page and line reference for those who wish to follow along with the Latin. Within dossiers, where a relative chronology can be established, we have tried to put earlier letters first. Otherwise we have tended to retain the relative order of Peiper's edition, although there are exceptions. The table of contents lists the letters as they appear in their dossiers, but for those who would prefer to read the collection in Peiper's order, we provide another finding-list complete with page-numbers.[1] In addition to the letters from the letter-collection, we have translated the dedicatory letters which preface Avitus' poetry, since they provide an important insight into his cultural attitudes. We have, moreover, translated two of Avitus' sermons: one (*Hom.* 25) survived in the papyrus which contained Avitus' letters, and is therefore an indication of the nature of the papyrus collection. The other (*Hom.* 6) was probably part of Avitus' lost homiliary: as an account of the origin of Rogations it is also an important historical document. We have used the Authorised Version of the Bible to translate Avitus' biblical quotations. When there are variations in his text, we have noted them.

GRATIAS

This has been a long and complicated project, carried out over email across the Atlantic between Ithaca and Leeds and Ithaca and the Netherlands, and between Leeds and Cambridge. We are grateful to the Society for the Humanities at Cornell for a grant for Collaborative Research that enabled us to work together in January 1997. We owe special gratitude to Corpus Christi College, Oxford, for providing its two former Corpuscles with space in the Fraenkel Room and hospitality in the SCR, and to Michael Winterbottom who came and read some of the more rebarbative letters with us and helped us make sense of their (often highly corrupt) text. As a result of our collaboration we can feelingly say that there is no greater scholarly luxury than to read an ancient text in the company of someone who comes to it from a different discipline. We have benefited immeasurably from being able to put together an historian and a philologist.

This particular text, with its many technical problems (ranging from echoes of ancient comedy, to Natures and Persons, incestuous adultery, kilns, slurry pits, rings, debased coinage, escaped slaves, candles for the dead, sanctuary, fish and wine) sent us in dismay to many experts for the help we needed. It is a pleasure to acknowledge their generous help and

---

1 See Appendix 3, p. 416 below.

support. Gillian Clark, Peter Heather, Ralph Mathisen, and Roger Wright were our acute referees. We have done our best to face their objections squarely and mend our ways as necessary. We owe thanks to the many kind friends and colleagues whom we have consulted over problems encountered in the Avitan corpus: Sam Barnish, Jay Jasanoff, Roald Hoffmann, Paul Hyams, Robert Markus, Leslie Webster and Mary Whitby, our vigilant editor. Two of Danuta Shanzer's then graduate students, Greg Hays and Stuart Koonce suffered through far more Avitus than anyone should be expected to and have left their mark on *Ep*. 86. The librarian at the Bibliothèque Municipale de Lyon gave Danuta Shanzer the chance to work directly from L in May 2000 and provided a microfilm. We would like to acknowledge our special gratitude to Roger Tomlin who brought the bishop of Vienne to life for our cover and was willing to get involved in innumerable queries and tenaciously help puzzle them out. Both of us owe our inspiration, sanity, and *stabilitas* to the patience of our respective partners, Ralph Mathisen and Ann Christys, who have probably seen as much of our bishop as they would like!

We wish, in ending, to dedicate our work to the memory of the person who started and edited this series and originally commissioned our project, but did not live to see 'this deserving chap', as she wryly called the bishop of Vienne, receive his philological and historical due – Margaret Gibson.

Danuta Shanzer
Ian Wood
29 June 2001

INTRODUCTION

CHAPTER 1

AVITUS OF VIENNE: THE HISTORICAL CONTEXT

Alcimus Ecdicius Avitus, bishop of Vienne is one of the less well-known figures of Late Antiquity, despite a flurry of interest in him in the nineteenth century, when he was picked up by opposing factions in debates between French Catholics and Protestants.[1] More important, two significant editions of his works were produced in 1883 and 1890.[2] In 1909 Goelzer embarked on a massive analysis of his Latin,[3] while Burckhardt wrote what remains the best analysis of the letter-collection immediately before the Second World War.[4] Otherwise, with the exception of the famous letter to Clovis (*Ep.* 46), Avitus' prose has been remarkably little considered. Recently, however, some attention has been paid to his poetry, which is of considerable merit.[5]

The reason for the neglect of Avitus can, no doubt, be linked directly with the difficulty of understanding his Latin, and of teasing out the implications of his letters, which are often oblique. One frequently has to infer the context in which a letter was written in order to unlock its meaning. Few scholars have been prepared, or have been able, to set aside the time necessary to tackle the bishop of Vienne's works. Yet Avitus is a figure of considerable interest, both in his own right, and in terms of what he reveals about the Burgundian kingdom, which, albeit short-lived, allows numerous

---

1 E.g. A. Charaux, *Saint Avite, évêque de Vienne en Dauphiné, sa vie, ses oeuvres* (Paris, 1876). Much of this introduction is culled from I. N. Wood, 'Avitus of Vienne: religion and culture in the Auvergne and the Rhône valley, 470–530' (unpublished DPhil thesis, Oxford, 1980) although work for this current volume has prompted numerous revisions of detail.

2 R. Peiper, *MGH AA* 6.2 (Berlin, 1883); U. Chevalier (Lyons, 1890).

3 H. Goelzer, *Le Latin de saint Avit* (Paris, 1909).

4 M. Burckhardt, *Die Briefsammlung des Bischofs Avitus von Vienne* (Berlin, 1938).

5 E.g. M. Roberts, *Biblical Epic and Rhetorical Paraphrase in Late Antiquity* (Liverpool, 1985); D.J. Nodes, *Doctrine and Exegesis in Biblical Latin Poetry* (Leeds, 1993); G. W. Shea, *The Poems of Alcimus Ecdicius Avitus* (Tempe, 1997); A. Arweiler, *Die Imitation antiker und spät-antiker Literatur in der Dichtung 'De spiritalis historiae gestis,' des Alcimus Avitus* (Berlin, New York, 1999). Also the new edition by N. Hecquet-Noti of the first three books of poetry: *Avit de Vienne. Histoire spirituelle, Tome 1 (Chants i–iii), SC* 444 (Paris, 1999).

insights into the political and social structures of a large part of Gaul in the
last years of the Western Empire and immediately thereafter. Consideration
of the bishop can usefully be divided into some comments on his family, and
its position within the senatorial aristocracy of fifth- and sixth-century Gaul,
a brief account of his life, in so far as it can be reconstructed, a few
observations on his theology and his place within the theological developments of his time, and finally a discussion of the Burgundian kingdom itself,
for which the information provided by the bishop of Vienne is crucial.

THE FAMILY OF AVITUS

Some of Avitus' close family can be identified with precision. His father,
Hesychius, is named in Ado of Vienne's *Chronicle*,[1] as well as the *Vita
Aviti*.[2] He is, in all probability, to be identified with the Hesychius *tribunus
legatus* whom the emperor Avitus sent to the Visigothic king Theodoric in
455–56,[3] and he was certainly Avitus' predecessor as bishop of Vienne,
succeeding Mamertus.[4] Of Avitus' mother, we known no more than her
name, Audentia, and the fact that she had four children, two sons and two
daughters.[5] His brother, Apollinaris of Valence, in addition to being the subject
of a work of hagiography, also features prominently in the bishop of Vienne's
letter-collection. He explicitly names one sister, Fuscina, who is the subject
of a liturgical saint's Life preserved in a manuscript of the twelfth century,
where she miraculously escapes rape, having been dragged from the monastery of SS Gervasius and Protasius in Vienne.[6] It was for Fuscina that he wrote
his hexameter poem on chastity, *De consolatoria castitatis laude* – a work
which clearly illustrates the extent to which the late Roman aristocracy was
concerned about family sanctity – long before the Germanic aristocracy had
developed a concern with their own *Adelsheilige*: indeed the *Adelsheilige*
should be seen as a continuation of a Gallo-Roman senatorial tradition.[7]

---

1   See Peiper, p. 177, n.

2   *Vita Aviti* 1, ed. Peiper, *MGH AA* 6.2.

3   Hydatius, (170 [177]), ed. R. W. Burgess, *The Chronicle of Hydatius and the Consularia
Constantinopolitana* (Oxford, 1993): R. W. Mathisen, 'Epistolography, Literary Circles and
Family Ties in Late Roman Gaul', *TAPA* 111 (1981), p. 100.

4   For the death of Mamertus, Sidonius, *Ep.* 4.11.

5   Avitus, *De consolatoria castitatis laude* 19. Henceforth *CCL*.

6   *Catalogus codicum hagiographicorum latinorum in bibliotheca nationali parisiensi* 3
(Brussels, 1893), pp. 563–65.

7   The tradition is not exclusively Gallo-Roman; see D. R. Shanzer, 'Review of G.W. Shea,
The Poems of Alcimus Ecdicius Avitus', *CR* 49.2 (1999), p. 405.

Subsequently he circulated the poem more widely, with a prefatory letter addressed to his brother. It is possible, but unlikely, that his other sister is to be identified with Aspidia, who also appears in the poem.[1] Fuscina entered the monastic life at the age of ten: Aspidia, had already done so at the age of twelve, but was dead by the time that Avitus composed the *De consolatoria castitatis laude*. The poet makes no mention of male relatives becoming monks: but a number of them are known to have become bishops. Apart from Avitus himself, his father and his brother, relatives from subsequent generations can be traced from the episcopal epitaphs of Vienne.[2]

Avitus was also related to Sidonius Apollinaris, and hence to the world of the Gallic senatorial aristocracy meticulously charted by Stroheker.[3] Avitus uses the words *meus* and *communis* to refer to Sidonius,[4] and he was on very close terms with Sidonius' son Apollinaris, who appears regularly in the letter-collection, not least as an arbiter of taste.[5] That the families of Avitus and Sidonius were closely connected, perhaps through more than one marriage, is also indicated by the recurrence within both kin-groups of the names Apollinaris, Avitus and Ecdicius – the last two names being attested in the family of Sidonius' wife, Papianilla. The exact nature of the connection between Avitus and Sidonius is, however, uncertain. Mathisen has suggested that Avitus' mother, Audentia, was Sidonius' sister, which is possible, but unproven.[6]

Regardless of the detail, the general picture is clear and important. Avitus belonged to the social world of Sidonius, but to the following generation – that is the generation which came to maturity after the collapse of the Western Empire. This generation is remarkably well evidenced, because of the survival of three letter-collections, those of Avitus himself,[7] Ruricius of Limoges[8]

---

1 Avitus, *CCL* 87–89. See R. W. Mathisen, 'PLRE II: Some Suggested Addenda and Corrigenda', *Historia* 31 (1982), p. 367. See also the discussion of *Ep.* 13, below.

2 The epitaphs are edited by Peiper, *MGH AA* 6.2. For a discussion, M. Heinzelmann, *Bischofsherrschaft in Gallien* (Munich, 1976), pp. 220–32.

3 K. F. Stroheker, *Der senatorische Adel im spätantiken Gallien* (Tübingen, 1948).

4 *Ep.* 51.

5 *Ep.* 51.

6 Mathisen, 'Epistolography', p. 100.

7 I. N. Wood, 'Letters and Letter-Collections from Antiquity to the Early Middle Ages: The Prose Works of Avitus of Vienne', in M. A. Meyer, ed., *The Culture of Christendom* (London, 1993), pp. 29–43.

8 See now the translation by R. W. Mathisen, *Ruricius of Limoges and Friends: A Collection of Letters from Visigothic Gaul* (Liverpool, 1999).

and Ennodius of Pavia.[1] Comparison of these collections with those of
Symmachus, Ausonius and Sidonius reveals a continuity of social communication, with all its implications for aristocratic influence and class solidarity,
through the exercise of friendship.[2] At the same time the comparison shows
something of the discontinuities, as well as the continuities, within the world
of the southern Gallic aristocracy at the end of the fifth and start of the sixth
centuries.[3] The great senatorial families of Gaul had survived the arrival and
settlement of the barbarians, and continued to have considerable prestige: the
absence of an imperial court, however, dramatically changed the career
possibilities available to senators, depriving them of the possibility of holding any of the great offices of the Roman state – an absence of opportunity
which seems to have prompted an increasing number of aristocrats to enter
the Church.

In addition to ending the traditional *cursus honorum* available to
enthusiastic senators, the barbarian kingdoms had the equally important
impact of setting up frontiers between the new states. The old empire-wide
connections of the aristocracy could no longer be relied upon, or exploited
as a matter of course. Avitus deliberately avoided writing to Sidonius' son,
his cousin Apollinaris, when the latter was under suspicion of treason.[4]
Contacts across borders could make one suspect, as Caesarius of Arles also
discovered.[5] Despite the biological continuity of the senatorial aristocracy,
its sixth-century members had to work in very different circumstances from
their predecessors: their wide networks could still be useful, but in certain
circumstances they could also be dangerous. Although members of the great
senatorial families of the fifth century can still be traced in the late sixth
century, in the poems of Venantius Fortunatus and in episcopal epitaphs,
aristocratic networking is less in evidence after 520 than it once had been.

---

1 See H. Kirkby, 'The Scholar and his Public', in M. Gibson, ed., *Boethius, his Life,
Thought and Influence* (Oxford, 1981), pp. 44–69.

2 Compare J. F. Matthews, 'The Letters of Symmachus', in J. W. Binns, ed., *Latin Literature
of the Fourth Century* (London, 1974), pp. 58–99; I. N. Wood, 'Family and Friendship in the
West', in *Cambridge Ancient History*, ed. A. Cameron et al. (Cambridge, 2000), 14, pp. 416–36.

3 Wood, 'Letters and Letter-collections', and 'Family and Friendship in the West'.

4 *Ep.* 51.

5 I. N. Wood, 'Gregory of Tours and Clovis', *Revue Belge de Philologie et d'Histoire* 63
(1985), p. 257.

THE LIFE OF AVITUS

Of Avitus' career prior to his election as bishop nothing is known, although it has been thought he might be identified with Alcimus, the author of certain lost works, 'Against a young man who laughed in public when his father fell down, and who gave a love-potion to an ill maiden', and 'About the debate of the fuller or the bald man'.[1] On the other hand Sidonius knew of another Alcimus, who was a rhetor in Bordeaux, and who is perhaps a more likely author.[2] That Avitus himself underwent rhetorical training is, in any case, likely. His was perhaps the last generation for which the full Roman pattern of education was available in Gaul, and he certainly took immense pride in the correctness of his pronunciation.[3]

Unfortunately we do not know when Hesychius died, or when his son succeeded him in office. Nevertheless Avitus was already in post by 494/6, when he contributed towards the ransoming of Italian captives requested by bishop Epiphanius of Pavia, following a Burgundian raid on northern Italy.[4] Ennodius, in recounting the episode, describes Avitus as 'the most outstanding Gallic bishop, in whom wisdom enclosed herself as if in a shining abode'[5] – a description which deserves some attention, not least because Caesarius of Arles is usually portrayed as the most impressive Gallic bishop of the period.[6] Ennodius' praise suggests that the bishop of Vienne's judgement and perhaps his theology was highly regarded in his own time. Emphasis on the bishop's *peritia* also suggests that his preeminence was not dependent on the status of his see – which alongside Lyons was one of the two metropolitan sees within the Burgundian kingdom. Vienne had indeed once been the senior see in southern Gaul, but had lost that position to Arles in the course of the fifth century, although Pope Anastasius II (496–98) briefly reversed matters in Avitus' favour. This intervention, however, was

1 *In adolescentiam (sic) qui in publico patre cadente rississet (sic) et languenti puellae amatorium dedit* and *De controversia fullonis vel calvi*, Peiper, *MGH AA* 6.2, p. lii. See below p. 256 n. 6.

2 Sidonius, *Epp.* 5.10.3; 8.11.2.

3 Avitus, *Ep.* 57.

4 On Avitus' importance in ransoming captives see D. R. Shanzer, 'Dating the Baptism of Clovis: the Bishop of Vienne vs. the Bishop of Tours', *EME* 7.1 (1998), pp. 47–50 and 'Two Clocks and a Wedding: Theodoric's Diplomatic Relations with the Burgundians', *Romano-barbarica* 14 (1998), pp. 228–31.

5 Ennodius, *Vita Epifani* 173, ed. F. Vogel, *MGH AA* 7 (Berlin, 1885) *Praestantissimus inter Gallos … episcopus, in quo se peritia velut in diversorio lucidae domus inclusit.*

6 For Caesarius, W. E. Klingshirn, *Caesarius of Arles: The Making of a Christian Community in Late Antique Gaul* (Cambridge, 1994).

overturned by Pope Symmachus (498–514), who restored the authority of Arles in 499/500. In fact the question of precedence between Arles and Vienne was largely academic, since the two cities belonged to different kingdoms, which made it difficult for one bishop to exercise jurisdiction over the other. As a result, a more important relationship was that between Vienne and its neighbouring metropolitan see, that of Lyons. Here relative status depended on which bishop had been consecrated first – though Lyons was to also to gain prestige from the sanctity of a number of its sixth- and seventh-century bishops.[1]

Despite Ennodius' comment there is little other evidence for Avitus' episcopate outside the bishop of Vienne's own writings.[2] He must have been affected by the siege of Vienne in 500, when the Burgundian king Gundobad cornered his brother Godegisel;[3] indeed an exchange of letters with the rhetor Heraclius may refer to his experiences at this time.[4] It is also possible that the bishop lost some of his writings in the course of the siege: he refers in his prologue to his poems *De spiritalis historiae gestis* to a 'very well-known disturbance' (*notissima perturbatio*), in the course of which various works were mislaid.

Avitus' own letters show him subsequently to have been closely attached to Gundobad and to the king's son Sigismund, advising and even writing letters for both of them – the letters written to the emperor Anastasius on behalf of the two kings can be compared directly with letters to various emperors written by Cassiodorus for Theodoric and his successors.[5] The bishop of Vienne tried hard to convert Gundobad to Catholicism, and his correspondence over the issue provides a remarkable insight into the learning of the king himself.[6] Although Gundobad himself did not publicly

---

1 R. W. Mathisen, *Ecclesiastical Factionalism and Religious Controversy in Fifth-Century Gaul* (Washington, DC, 1989); Klingshirn, *Caesarius of Arles*, pp. 65–69. For the actions of Anastasius and Symmachus, Symmachus, *Epp.* 2–3, ed. A. Thiel, *Epistolae Romanorum Pontificum Genuinae* (Brunsberg, 1868). For the confirmation of this position after 508, see also Symmachus, *Epp.* 14, 16, as well as *Epistulae Arelatenses Genuinae* 25, 28–9, ed. W. Gundlach, *MGH Epp.* 3 (Berlin, 1892).

2 Gregory of Tours' comments clearly derive from Avitus' works: Greg. Tur, *DLH* 2.34.

3 Marius of Avenches, *s.a.* 500, ed. J. Favrod, *La Chronique de Marius d'Avenches (455–581)* (Lausanne, 1991); Greg. Tur. *DLH* 2.32–33.

4 Avitus, *Epp.* 46A, 95 and 96.

5 E.g. Avitus, *Epp.* 93, 94. Nevertheless he was clearly not the political figure postulated by P. N. Frantz, *Avitus von Vienne als Hierarch und Politiker* (Greifswald, 1908).

6 See also the discussion in G. Kampers, 'Caretena – Königin und Asketin', *Francia* 27 (2000), pp. 1–32.

abandon Arianism, despite the possibility that he privately accepted the strength of the Catholic position,[1] his son did convert. Not that Avitus was directly responsible for Sigismund's conversion, which was prompted by a visit to Rome.[2] Nor was Avitus the main local religious influence on the prince – who, albeit subject to his father, had a separate residence in Geneva, where he was most likely advised by the local bishop, Maximus.[3] But Avitus did preach the dedication homily for the prince's monastic foundation of Agaune, in the upper Rhône valley, established in 515, while Gundobad was alive.[4] Such homilies could be important public statements, and those delivered by Avitus before Gundobad's death, which include plenty of comments on both Arianism and on the secular hierarchy, are important indications of the old king's tolerance.[5]

Sigismund's conversion seems to have had some impact on the position of the Catholic Church – the unfortunately fragmentary letter of Avitus which appears to deal with the prince's change of religion hints at the cessation of persecution, although this may be an allusion to events somewhere other than the Burgundian kingdom.[6] Sigismund's accession as sole ruler of the kingdom in 516 opened up new horizons for the Catholic Church within Burgundy. The removal of royal support for Arianism also presented the Catholic episcopate with a number of dilemmas, and Avitus as one of the two metropolitan bishops of the kingdom played a leading role in dealing with the changes caused by the collapse of the Arian Church. He wrote a major letter on the subject,[7] and presided in 517, alongside Viventiolus of Lyons, over the Council of Epaon. Comparison between Avitus' letters

---

1 Greg. Tur. *DLH* 2.34.

2 Avitus, *Ep.* 8.

3 This might be deduced from Avitus, *Hom.* 20.

4 *Hom.* 25.

5 See also *Hom.* 20 and 24: for the latter see the edition, translation and commentary by C. Perrat and A. Audin, 'Alcimi Ecdicii viennensis episcopi homilia dicta in dedicatione superioris basilicae', in *Studi in onore di Aristide Calderini e Roberto Paribeni*, 2 (Milan, 1957), pp. 433–51. A less successful attempt to reconstitute an Avitan homily is E. L. Borrel, 'Étude sur l'homélie prêchée par saint Avit, au commencement du Vie siècle dans la basilique de Saint-Pierre de Moutiers en Tarantaise (Savoie) à l'occasion de sa consécration', *Bulletin du Comité des travaux historiques et scientifiques, Section d'histoire, d'archéologie et de philologie* (1883), pp. 46–55. In general on Avitus' dedication homilies, see I. N. Wood, 'The Audience of Architecture in Post-Roman Gaul', in L. A. S. Butler and R. K. Morris, eds, *The Anglo-Saxon Church* (London, 1986) pp. 74–79.

6 Avitus, *Ep. 8*. Gregory of Tours does, however, suggest that Gundobad did institute *leges mitiores* after the conflict with Godegisel: *DLH* 2.33.

7 *Ep.* 7.

and the canons of Epaon indicate that his was indeed the dominant voice at the council.[1]

Epaon seems to have been the last great public act of Avitus' episcopate. His feast is celebrated on 5 February, which would normally be an indication of the day of his death.[2] The *Vita Aviti*, a late text known from an eleventh-century manuscript, claims that he died during the reign of Anastasius:[3] the imperial dating may suggest access to sixth-century documentation. Since Avitus was alive in September 517, when the Council of Epaon took place, and since Anastasius died in 518, the implication must be that the bishop died either late in 517 or in the same year as the emperor: taken together with the February feast day, this implies that the bishop of Vienne died on 5 February 518. If the evidence of the *Vita Aviti* is rejected as being too late to be reliable, one can only note that Avitus was no longer in post at the Council of Lyons, held at some point between 518 and 522.

AVITUS' THEOLOGY

Just as Avitus' works help chart the changes in the society of the Gallic aristocracy, so too they illuminate the theological developments of the late fifth and early sixth centuries. Gaul in the fifth century had been a centre of theological debate. Augustine's theology, particularly over predestination, had divided opinion, with John Cassian taking a critical and Prosper a favourable line.[4] Later in the century Faustus of Riez continued a line critical of Augustine – but was himself subject to a major onslaught, on the question of the nature of the soul, from Claudianus Mamertus, brother of the then bishop of Vienne.[5] This conflict was a matter of some embarrassment to Sidonius Apollinaris, who regarded Faustus as his religious mentor, but was also closely connected to Claudianus.[6] Avitus' position in this debate was

1 On one aspect of the Council of Epaon, see I. N. Wood, 'Incest, Law and the Bible in Sixth-Century Gaul', *EME* 7.3 (1998), pp. 291–303.

2 For the entry in Ado's *Martyologium*, see Peiper, *MGH AA* 6.2, p. 177, n. More recently, J. Dubois and G. Renaud, *Le martyrologe d'Adon* (Paris, 1984), p. 80.

3 *Vita Aviti* 6.

4 On this see R. Markus, 'The Legacy of Pelagius: Orthodoxy, Heresy and Conciliation', in *The Making of Orthodoxy*, ed. R. D. Williams (Cambridge, 1989), pp. 214–34.

5 E. L. Fortin, *Christianisme et culture philosophique au cinquième siècle* (Paris, 1959) and C. F. Brittain, 'No Place for a Platonist Soul in Fifth-Century Provence? The Case of Mamertus Claudianus', in D. R. Shanzer and R. W. Mathisen, eds, *Culture and Society in Late Antique Gaul: Revisiting the Sources* (Ashgate, 2001), pp. 239–62.

6 Sidonius, *Carm.* 16; *Epp.* 4.11.3; 9.3; 9.9. See the comments on Avitus, *Ep.* 4, below.

more clear-cut, and not surprisingly, since Mamertus, brother of Claudianus, and predecessor of Hesychius in the see of Vienne, stood as godfather at his baptism.[1] Avitus may, nevertheless, have found Faustus' work embarrassing. When asked by Gundobad to comment on the bishop of Riez's notion of penitence, he assigned the ideas in question to Faustus the Manichee, the opponent of Augustine.[2] Heterodox theological ideas were best not associated with Catholic bishops.

Much of Avitus' surviving theology was written in response to Gundobad, or at least with an eye on the Arianism of the king and his clergy. From Avitus' comments it appears that Burgundian Arianism, at least, was concerned with the precise reading and interpretation of the Bible – even of little-known passages: on one occasion the bishop of Vienne can be seen to have wrongly identified a passage under discussion.[3] Gundobad's position in the Arian–Catholic debate is a particularly interesting one. Although an Arian himself, surrounded by Arian clergy, he seems to have had an independent turn of mind, and apparently consulted the bishop of his own accord. Avitus' letters, which may only relate to the period after 500, reveal the king as remarkably liberal in his attitude towards theological debate, and show him as being quite capable of keeping up with theological arguments himself. In addition to discussing issues relating to Arian theology, the king also commissioned from Avitus the rather curious, 'Against the Eutychian Heresy', *Contra Eutychianam Haeresim*, a work written in the aftermath of the *Trishagion* riots in Constantinople in 511, indicating that his theological interests were not limited to local questions. In dealing with the Constantinopolitan crisis the bishop of Vienne's information and assumptions were such as to lead him totally to misunderstand the nature of the conflict between monophysites and orthodox, and indeed to confuse the two parties. As a guide to the *Trishagion* debate, Avitus' treatises are, therefore, of little value, but as contemporary documents they are of considerable importance in illustrating the confusion and misinformation that dogged theological debate.

Despite the confusion in his understanding of the *Trishagion* riots, and the misidentification (deliberate or otherwise) of Faustus of Riez, Avitus' own theological position is clear and conforms closely to what was being established as Catholic orthodoxy in the opening decades of the sixth

---

1 Avitus, *Hom.* 6. See below p. 381.

2 *Ep.* 4.

3 *Ep.* 22. Peiper in his edition made the same mistake as Avitus.

century. There is some slight indication that Avitus knew the writings of Hilary of Poitiers – an obvious source in combating Arianism.[1] It is also likely that the family of Hesychius held Ambrose in high regard. The nunnery which Fuscina entered, and which may have been founded by Hesychius, was dedicated to Gervasius and Protasius, martyrs clearly associated with Ambrose.[2] Avitus' chief theological inspiration, however, was undoubtedly Augustine. This is abundantly clear in the bishop of Vienne's versification of the book of Genesis, for close inspection of the first three books of the 'Epic Deeds of Spiritual History' (*De spiritalis historiae gestis*) instantly shows that Avitus was very much dependent on Augustine's literal commentary on Genesis (*De Genesi ad litteram*); indeed he even versifies the bishop of Hippo's excursus on the Marsi, a people of Latium who practised a snake cult.[3] He had no such guide when it came to versifying Exodus: the resulting poem, 'On the Crossing of the Red Sea', *De Transitu Maris Rubri*, has been seen as inferior to the bishop's other books of biblical verse,[4] but it should perhaps be seen, rather, as a more independent work, in which the bishop of Vienne attempted his own reading of an Old Testament story.[5] Like Caesarius of Arles, Avitus marks the consolidation of the Gallic theological tradition into a single Augustinian position – a position which turns its back on the theological richness of the fifth century, especially in rejecting what is now lumped together under the single unhelpful title of Semipelagianism.

It may well be that the presence of Germanic peoples in Gaul played a major role in stifling theological debate. Gundobad's sharp questions may

1 *CA* 30 (= *Ep*. 1). See below p. 183 n. 6.

2 *Vita Fuscinulae* 6. The Life also claims that the monastery was founded by Isicius (=Hesychius). There are problems in this claim, in that a fourth-century epitaph of the religious Foedula, baptised by Martin, was found on the site. Hesychius may have refounded the monastery, or have been a major benefactor.

3 Augustine, *De Genesi ad litteram*, 11.28 (*PL* 34); Avitus, *Carm*. 2.303 ff. See also I. N. Wood, 'Avitus of Vienne, the Augustinian Poet', in Shanzer and Mathisen, eds, *Culture and Society in Late Antique Gaul*, pp. 263–77.

4 G. Vinay, 'La poesia di sant'Avito', *Convivium* 9 (1937), pp. 453–56, and A. Roncoroni, 'L'epica biblica di Avito di Vienne', *Vetera Christianorum* 9 (1972), pp. 321–29, are representative of scholars in underestimating the importance of the *De Genesi ad litteram* for Avitus, and its impact on the relative quality of the first three books. For the general influence of Augustine on Avitus, see D. J. Nodes, 'Avitus of Vienne's Spiritual History and the Semipelagian Controversy. The Doctrinal Implications of Books I–III', *Vigiliae Christianae* 38 (1984), pp. 185–95.

5 The comments of Shea, *Poems of Alcimus Ecdicius Avitus*, pp. 45–55 are more sympathetic than many.

have made the variety within the Gallic theological tradition something of an embarrassment to the Catholic episcopate, who wished to put on a show of religious unity – and the presence of Clovis in the wings, also considering which version of Christianity to follow, is likely to have added to the need to close ranks.

The need for unity also coloured Avitus' comments on the papacy. He was firmly of the opinion that the pope could be judged by no one, and felt himself compelled to complain that the synod which was summoned to investigate the charges made against Symmachus in the course of the Laurentian schism was extremely damaging: papal failings should be left to God alone to deal with. In addition, the bishop of Vienne considered that the accusations brought against the pope were all the more damaging because they were being made at a time in which heresy – by which he meant Arianism – was a considerable threat.[1] A papal schism meant weak leadership at a time of theological crisis: it also gave the Catholics a bad image.

Avitus' theology was very much in tune with the orthodoxy which was being established in his own day. In the ninth century he was excerpted alongside such figures as Cyprian, Hilary, Ambrose, Pope Leo, Fulgentius, Paulinus of Nola and Augustine,[2] hence the survival of fragments of the 'Treatise against the Arians' (*Contra Arrianos*) and other of his theological works. He was praised by Florus of Lyons and by Ado of Vienne for his faith, industry, doctrine and erudition.[3] This, however, marked the highpoint of his theological reputation. His use of the term *assumptus* ('adopted'), seems already to have been taken by Felix of Urguel as support for his own adoptionist theology,[4] and this unwanted attention may have been a factor leading to the neglect of Avitus' theological writings, and as a result to their survival in no more than excerpted fragments – leaving his ever-popular versification of the opening books of the Old Testament as the surest guide to his theological position.

AVITUS AND THE BURGUNDIAN KINGDOM

Avitus provides important evidence for changes within the senatorial aristocracy and for the emergence of orthodoxy in the closing years of the fifth and opening years of the sixth centuries. In both cases, however, there

---

1 *Ep.* 34.
2 Peiper, p. xxx, n. 46.
3 Dubois and Renaud, *Le martyrologe d'Adon*, p. 80.
4 Agobard, *Liber adversus Felicem Urgellitanum*, 39 (*PL* 104).

are alternative sources which at least point in the same direction. With regard to the history of the Burgundian kingdom itself, his evidence is unique. He does not, admittedly, provide us with a narrative, which must be found in various chronicle sources – and which is, in any case, fragmentary. Nor does he shed much light on matters of secular legislation within the Burgundian kingdom, for which one must turn to the law codes. The laws apart, however, he is our only major source – and the evidence he provides is infinitely greater than that of the chronicles, and arguably more important that that of the laws. At a rough estimate he is responsible for almost half the written documentation to have come out of the Burgundian kingdom.

Like the kingdoms of the Ostrogoths and the Vandals, that of the Burgundians lasted a relatively short time: all three came to an end in the 530s. Yet simply because they collapsed so quickly, these three kingdoms force us to consider the nature of successor states as they evolved out of the west Roman Empire. Unlike the kingdoms of the Franks or the Visigoths, they do not raise questions about developments into the late sixth century and beyond. The Ostrogothic kingdom in Italy has attracted the attention of numerous scholars, not least because of the voluminous works of Cassiodorus – and the architectural glories of Ravenna. The Vandals and the Burgundians have not been as fortunate.[1] Like the Ostrogothic kingdom, however, these last two illustrate a very precise period of development, before the political map of the early Middle Ages stabilised.

The Burgundian kingdom originated in a settlement of Burgundians who had survived Aetius' onslaught against that people in the mid-430s. They were placed in *Sapaudia*, a region now identified as stretching approximately from the Lac Léman to Windisch.[2] The date of the settlement, which is usually given as 443, is unfortunately uncertain: our sole evidence comes from the *Chronicle of 452*, whose chronology, where it can be checked against other sources, is often demonstrably wrong, and cannot, therefore,

---

1 For the Vandals, C. Courtois, *Les Vandales et l'Afrique* (Paris, 1955) remains the classic work, despite more recent studies, notably by F. M. Clover. See his collected studies in *The Late Roman West and the Vandals* (Aldershot, 1993). For the Burgundians, the nineteenth-century works of K. Binding, *Das burgundisch-romanische Königreich* (Leipzig, 1868) and A. Jahn, *Die Geschichte der Burgundionen und Burgundien bis zum Ende der 1. Dynastie*, 2 vols. (Halle, 1874) still have much to commend them, despite the recent book by J. Favrod, *Histoire politique du royaume burgonde (443–534)* (Lausanne, 1997) which is certainly a considerable advance on its French-language predecessors (R. Guichard, *Essai sur l'histoire du peuple Burgonde* [Paris, 1965] and O. Perrin, *Les Burgondes: leur histoire, des origines à la fin du premier royaume (534)* [Neuchâtel, 1968]).

2 Favrod, *Histoire politique*, pp. 100–17.

be taken to be reliable.[1] Without corroboration from elsewhere, its dates, and therefore that for the Burgundian settlement, have to be ignored, or at best taken as a rough indication. In any case Aetius' policy seems to have had some success, since Burgundians fought on the imperial side against Attila at the battle of the Catalaunian Plains in 451.[2]

The history of the ensuing years is far from clear. The *Continuatio Havniensis Prosperi* states that the Burgundians, dispersed throughout Gaul, were driven back by the Gepids.[3] On the other hand, they fought under their leaders Gundioc and Chilperic alongside the Visigoths in the imperially sanctioned attack on the Sueves of Galicia in 456.[4] In the same year, according to Marius of Avenches, they occupied part of Gaul, making a division of land with the senators.[5] This expansion was not officially sanctioned, or if it was, approval was almost immediately withdrawn by the new emperor Majorian.[6]

Despite Majorian's intervention there were those among the Gallo-Romans who continued to believe in division of land with the Burgundians,[7] and in any case Gundioc and Chilperic secured for themselves places within the official hierarchy, the former appearing as *vir illustris magister militum* (*per Gallias*?) – the leading military official in Gaul – in the record of an episcopal election at Die in ca. 462/3,[8] and the latter exercising power, also as *magister militum* (*per Gallias*?) and *patricius* (that is, holding the honorific position of patrician), from Lyons and Geneva in the 460s and

1 For the problems of the chronology, see I. N. Wood, 'The Fall of the Western Empire and End of Roman Britain', *Britannia* 18 (1987), pp. 253–56; *idem*, 'Continuity or Calamity? The Constraints of Literary Models', in J. Drinkwater and H. Elton, eds, *Fifth-century Gaul: A Crisis of Identity* (Cambridge, 1992), pp. 14–15. Favrod, *Histoire politique*, pp. 187–88, unfortunately persists in using the Chronicle's dates. A. C. Murray refers to the problem of the chronology in his introduction to his translation of the Chronicle in *From Roman to Merovingian Gaul: A Reader* (Peterborough, 2000), pp. 76–85.

2 Jordanes, *Getica* 36 (191), ed. F. Giunta and A. Grillone, *Fonti per la Storia d'Italia* 117 (Rome, 1991).

3 *Continuatio Havniensis Prosperi* 574 (=455), ed. T. Mommsen, *Chronica Minora* 1, *MGH AA* 9 (Berlin, 1892). It would make more sense if the Gepids rather than the Burgundians were the subject of the verb *repelluntur*.

4 Jord. *Get.* 44 (231).

5 Marius of Avenches, *s.a.* 456. This episode is usually equated with that described by Fredegar 2.46, ed. B. Krusch, *MGH SRM* 2 (Hanover, 1888) where it is wrongly dated to 372.

6 Sidonius, *Carm.* 5. 564–71.

7 Sidonius, *Ep.* 1.7.

8 *Epistolae Arelatenses Genuinae* 19, ed. W. Gundlach, *MGH Epp.* 3 (Berlin, 1892).

70s.[1] Chilperic's authority, however, was not well regarded by all, and it was undermined by the change of emperor, from Glycerius to Julius Nepos.

The end of Glycerius' reign had other, more significant, implications for the Burgundians. He had been elevated to imperial office by the *magister militum* (*praesentalis*, 'attendant on the emperor'?) Gundobad, son of Gundioc and nephew of Chilperic.[2] Gundobad had come to the fore largely as the protegé of the previous *magister militum praesentalis*, Ricimer, to whom he was related: the evidence for this family relationship is unfortunately contradictory, but one possibility is that Gundobad's mother was Ricimer's sister.[3] Gundobad's activities as *magister militum* (*praesentalis*?) and *patricius* meant that, more than any other barbarian king, he was involved in the west Roman court before its collapse – a point of some significance when assessing his later history. Although Theodoric the Great looked down on the Burgundian kingdom,[4] he had little reason to do so: Gundobad had had a career within the Roman Empire every bit as illustrious as his own, and he appears to have been a good deal better educated.[5] With the failure of Glycerius, who had indeed been his appointee, Gundobad abandoned imperial politics for those of the Rhône valley.[6]

Exactly when and how Gundobad took over power from his uncle are unclear. He had three brothers,[7] with whom he seems to have been at loggerheads.[8] The body of one of them, Chilperic II, the father of Chrotechildis, who was to become Clovis' queen, is said by Gregory of Tours to have been thrown down a well on Gundobad's orders,[9] although this may be a doublet for the fate of Sigismund, who certainly suffered in this way at the hands of

---

1 Sidonius, *Epp.* 5.6; 5.7; 6.12.3; *Vita Patrum Iurensium* II 10 (=92), ed. F. Martine, *Vie des Pères du Jura, SC* 142 (Paris, 1968). See P. S. Barnwell, *Emperor, Prefects and Kings: the Roman West, 395–565* (London, 1992), p. 83.

2 John of Antioch, fr. 209, 1, 2: see C. D. Gordon, *The Age of Attila* (Ann Arbor, MI, 1960), pp. 122–23.

3 John of Antioch, fr. 209, 2. See Favrod, *Histoire politique*, p. 211, n. 85. It should be noted that John of Antioch is inconsistent in his account, and, therefore, that the exact relationship between Gundobad and Ricimer is uncertain: Gordon, *The Age of Attila*, p. 205, n. 15.

4 Cassiodorus, *Variae* 1.45 and 1.46 (where Gundobad's Italian career is acknowledged), ed. T. Mommsen, *MGH AA* 12 (Berlin, 1894). The letters in question are included in S. J. B. Barnish, *Cassiodorus: Variae* (Liverpool, 1992).

5 See Shanzer, 'Two Clocks', pp. 241–42 and 251–54.

6 The most recent discussion of this is Favrod, *Histoire politique*, pp. 263–64.

7 Greg. Tur. *DLH* 2.28.

8 Avitus, *Ep.* 5.

9 Greg. Tur. *DLH* 2.28.

the Merovingian king Chlodomer.[1] The only brother whose history is clearly attested is Godegisel, who allied himself with Clovis in 500 in an ill-fated attempt to overthrow Gundobad.[2] Previously Godegisel certainly had a powerbase in Geneva, where he was visited by Epiphanius of Pavia in 494/ 96. Ennodius, in describing the bishop's visit, does not call Godegisel *rex*, but rather 'the king's brother', *germanus regis*,[3] implying that, although he had a court of his own, his power was subordinate to that of Gundobad. A similar set-up seems to have been instituted subsequently, since Gundobad's son Sigismund also appears to have had a royal residence in Geneva, even though he was unquestionably subject to his father, on whom he had occasionally to attend – indeed Avitus refers to him as being junior to some in the seat of judgement (*in tribunali aliquibus iunior).*[4]

Gregory of Tours describes the kingdom of Gundobad and Godegisel as including the valleys of the Rhône and Saône, as well as the province of Marseilles.[5] Mention of Marseilles is problematic. It is possible that Gundo-bad lost land in the south to the Ostrogoths in 508, but it is fairly clear from the relatively abundant evidence relating to Caesarius that Arles was never in Burgundian hands. A letter of Avitus which refers to Sigismund making a journey to Provence[6] might, however, support Gregory's statement. Perhaps one should envisage Gundobad claiming some rights in the Provençal port, but if that were the case, it is unclear how he might have exercised them.[7] Elsewhere the boundaries of the Burgundian kingdom are somewhat clearer, not least because of the witness-list from the Council of Epaon, which may be taken to illustrate the boundaries of the kingdom in 517.[8] North of

1 Greg. Tur. *DLH* 3.6.

2 Marius of Avenches, *s.a.* 500; Greg. Tur. *DLH* 2.32–3.

3 Ennodius, *Vita Epifani* 174.

4 Avitus, *Hom.* 25. Avitus' letters also imply that Sigismund was subordinate to his father: see esp. *Ep.* 77. See I. N. Wood, 'Kings, Kingdoms and Consent', in P. H. Sawyer and I. N. Wood, eds, *Early Medieval Kingship* (Leeds, 1977), p. 22. Favrod, *Histoire politique*, pp. 156– 57, misunderstands and misrepresents the argument, reiterating the traditional view that there were geographically distinct kingdoms – an assertion which flies in the face of the evidence provided by Ennodius and Avitus. He assumes that a subordinate position would mean that Godegisel 'n'a donc ... aucun pouvoir', which is an unsubtle reading of the possibilities.

5 Greg. Tur. *DLH* 2.32.

6 *Ep.* 79.

7 Favrod, *Histoire politique,* pp. 292–94, argues that Gregory was reading back the situation of his own day into that of Gundobad, but does not deal with the problem raised by Avitus, *Ep.* 79.

8 Epaon, ed. J. Gaudemet and B. Basdevant, *Les Canons des conciles mérovingiens (VIe– VIIe siècles)* 1, *SC* 353 (Paris, 1989), pp. 120–25.

Avignon the frontier appears to have followed the Rhône as far as Viviers. Thereafter it must have lain to the west of the river. Beyond Lyons and its hinterland it stretched northwestwards to take in Nevers. Although Auxerre was Frankish, Autun was in Burgundian hands, as were Langres, Avenches, Geneva and Sion. The southern and eastern sides of the Alpine passes belonged to Ostrogothic Italy, but Tarantaise, Grenoble, Embrun, Gap and Vaison were Burgundian. Gundobad's preferred royal centres appear to have been Lyons and Chalon-sur-Saône. In the last years of the kingdom Godomar, the second of Gundobad's sons to come to the throne, is known to have legislated from Ambérieux-en-Bugey.[1]

Epiphanius' visit in 494/96 provides the earliest clear date for Gundobad's reign, as for Avitus' episcopate. The *Vita Epifani* also seems to imply that the marriage of Gundobad's son, Sigismund, to Theodoric's daughter, Ostrogotho Areagni, took place at approximately the same period as the bishop of Pavia's mission.[2] The marriage itself is mentioned additionally in the *Anonymus Valesianus*.[3] Avitus reveals that Sigismund visited Rome in the context of his marriage, and made a further visit in the time of Pope Symmachus (498–514).[4] More important, the bishop of Vienne apparently places Sigismund's conversion from Arianism to Catholicism in the context of this second visit. In addition, he seems to indicate that it took place before the conversion of Clovis, and to place it ca. 501/02.[5] It appears that according to Avitus, Sigismund was 'the only one of the kings who was not ashamed to convert' (*de regibus solus ... quem in bonum transisse non pudeat*) although strictly speaking he was not the first Catholic Germanic king – that honour must go to Rechiarius, king of the Suevi.[6]

The Italian context of Sigismund's conversion is interesting: on the one hand the prince had married an Arian Ostrogothic princess; on the other the marriage had brought him into contact with the papacy. As a result of this the prince abandoned Arianism – and developed a particular enthusiasm for the

1 For Ambérieux, *Liber Constitutionum, Constitutiones Extravagantes* 21, ed. L. R. de Salis, *Leges Burgundionum, MGH, Leges* 2.1 (Hannover, 1892).

2 Ennodius, *Vita Epifani* 163; see also the comments on Avitus, *Ep.* 29 below and Shanzer, 'Two Clocks', pp. 225–32, 249–51, and 255.

3 *Anonymus Valesianus* 63, where Ostrogotho Areagni is wrongly called Theodogotha: see the commentary by I. König, *Aus der Zeit Theoderichs des Großen* (Darmstadt, 1997), pp. 154–56.

4 Avitus, *Epp.* 8, 29.

5 See the commentary on *Ep.* 8 below. Favrod, *Histoire politique,* pp. 377–80, prefers a date of 506, but he provides no reason other than a need to place the conversion before the baptism of Clovis, which he places in the same year.

6 Hydatius (129 [137]).

cult of Peter, and for relics of the Apostle.[1] His children, and one may guess his wife, did not immediately follow suit.[2] Rome and the papacy, together with the Catholic clergy of the Rhône valley, were not the only influences weighing on Sigismund. It is also important to note the strength of Catholicism among the Burgundians of Gundobad's kingdom. Sigismund's mother, Caretene, was unquestionably a Catholic,[3] and one might assume that she had some influence on her son's ultimate choice of religion. This is at least implied by her epitaph, which may be dated to 506.[4] Another Catholic was Sigismund's cousin, Chrotechildis, as was his great-aunt, the unnamed wife of Chilperic I, who according to Sidonius was a fervent admirer of bishop Patiens of Lyons.[5] In fact it is difficult to find named Burgundian women who were Arian, although an unnamed daughter of Sigismund, who may or may not have been Suavegotha, remained Arian long after her father's conversion.[6] Gundobad and, initially, Sigismund were clearly Arian, as was the latter's son Sigistrix – who certainly did not abandon Arianism until after his father's accession[7] – and, one assumes, Godomar. Further, Gundobad was unquestionably surrounded by an Arian priesthood. The doctrinal position of other of their male relatives, however, is open to question.[8] Since Chilperic II's daughter Chrotechildis was a Catholic one might reasonably ask whether he or his wife shared her religious position. So too Chilperic I is not portrayed as a heretic by Sidonius.[9] The Burgundians, therefore, do not appear to have been staunchly Arian, despite Gregory of Tours' attempt to portray them as such.[10] Indeed, fifth-century writers saw them as Catholics,[11] and it is possible that Gundobad's religious affiliation came not from his father but from his mother, who has been identified as the sister of the Arian Ricimer. As a people the Burgundians seem

1 Avitus, *Ep.* 29: one might also associate the relics mentioned in *Hom.* 21, 28/9 with Sigismund. For Peter as the *peculiaris patronus* of Sigismund, see *Ep.* 31.

2 Avitus, *Ep.* 7 and *Hom.* 26.

3 *Vita Marcelli* 9 (*compar regis*), ed. F. Dolbeau, 'La Vie en prose de Saint Marcel, évêque de Die', *Francia* 11 (1983), p. 124. See also Kampers, 'Caretena – Königin und Asketin'.

4 Ed. Peiper, *MGH AA* 6.2, p. 185.

5 Sidonius, *Ep.* 6.12.3.

6 Avitus, *Hom.* 26.

7 Avitus, *Ep.* 7 and *Hom.* 26.

8 I. N. Wood, 'Ethnicity and the Ethnogenesis of the Burgundians', in H. Wolfram and W. Pohl, eds, *Typen der Ethnogenese unter besonderer Berücksichtigung der Bayern* (Vienna, 1990), p. 60 – though this needs modification in the light of Avitus, *Hom.* 26.

9 Sidonius, *Ep.* 6.12.3.

10 Greg. Tur. *DLH* 2.32.

11 Wood, 'Ethnicity and the Ethnogenesis', pp. 58–59.

to have been of mixed religious affiliation, although Arianism was apparently
in the ascendant in the time of their most successful king, Gundobad.

If Sigismund's conversion is rightly placed in 501/2, it took place shortly
after Godegisel's attempt to seize the throne from his brother. The attempt
itself was backed by Clovis, who after Godegisel's initial success withdrew
from the conflict.[1] Despite, or perhaps because of, Clovis' support for
Godegisel, Gundobad subsequently worked together with the Franks, to
whom he was initially tributary.[2] At some point, probably after his return to
power in 500, he may have proposed a marriage between his own daughter
and Clovis.[3] Her death, however, which is recorded by Avitus,[4] may well
have led to the substitution of Gundobad's niece, Chrotechildis, the daughter
of Chilperic II, as a bride for the Frankish king. In the ensuing years
Gundobad collaborated with Clovis, despite Theodoric the Ostrogoth's
attempt to use him as a check on the Frank's ambitions.[5] Although he did not
take part in the 507 campaign against the Visigoths, Gundobad did join in the
dismemberment of Alaric II's kingdom in the following year.[6] The association of Burgundians and Franks at this moment in time may well account
for Avitus being invited to attend the baptism of Clovis.[7] Gundobad's support
for the Franks in 508, however, proved to be costly, since the Burgundians
were to suffer at the hands of the avenging Ostrogoths as a result.[8]

Much of our evidence for the Burgundian kingdom in the last few years
of the fifth and the first decade of the sixth century concerns relations with
the Ostrogoths and Franks. With regard to the internal history of the kingdom, the most significant developments relate to the position of Sigismund.
Fredegar recounts that Sigismund was elevated to royal office, *sublimatur in
regnum*, at the villa of Carouge, just outside Geneva, on Gundobad's orders.[9]
He provides no date for the episode, but since Avitus apparently uses the
word *rex* to describe Sigismund at the time of his conversion to Catholicism,
probably in ca. 501/2, it may well be that he was elevated to a position of

1 Greg. Tur. *DLH* 2.32.

2 Greg. Tur. *DLH* 2.32–33.

3 See Shanzer, 'Dating the Baptism of Clovis', p. 55.

4 Avitus, *Ep.* 5. See also Favrod, *Histoire politique*, pp. 355–57.

5 Cassiodorus, *Variae* 3.2.

6 Isidore, *Historia Gothorum, Wandalorum, Sueborum*, 36–37, ed. T. Mommsen, *Chron.
Min.* 2, *MGH AA* 11 (Berlin, 1894); *Chronicle of 511*, s.a. 508, ed. T. Mommsen, *Chron. Min.* 1.

7 For the chronology see Wood, 'Gregory of Tours and Clovis', and Shanzer, 'Dating the
Baptism of Clovis', pp. 29–57.

8 Favrod, *Histoire politique*, pp. 400–06.

9 Fredegar 3.33.

subordinate kingship immediately before that date.[1] This would place his elevation hard on the heels of Gundobad's defeat of Godegisel, and would suggest that Sigismund was being installed in the position vacated by his uncle.

Elevation *in regnum*, that is to the subkingship, apparently with a royal seat at Geneva, was only the first stage in Sigismund's preparation as his father's successor. Here the detail of Avitus' correspondence reveals a more complex pattern of royal grooming than is known for other early medieval rulers, and one which was more concerned than any other to demonstrate legitimacy within a Roman tradition. In a letter of 515, written to the patriarch of Constantinople, in the course of some complex negotiations relating to at least two hostages, Laurentius and his son(s), the bishop of Vienne refers to Sigismund as *patricius*.[2] This was a title that Gundobad had assumed in 472,[3] and one that his uncle Chilperic I had used at the same time.[4] The patriciate was not the only Roman position held by Gundobad. Two letters written by Avitus in the name of Sigismund, on either side of Gundobad's death, reveal that the old king may have hung onto his title of *magister militum* (*praesentalis*?), apparently since 474 (unless one is to assume that it had subsequently been regranted), and that his son was now petitioning for the same office.[5] They also show that Theodoric the Ostrogoth caused difficulties for one set of legates responsible for delivering Sigismund's request to Anastasius. Finally in 516, on Gundobad's death, his son was elevated as king, in this instance to full kingship over the Burgundian kingdom, as opposed to his previous subordinate role.[6] Interestingly, although he had a brother, Godomar, who would succeed as king of the Burgundians in his turn, no post appears to have been created for him either before or after Gundobad's death. He may, like the young Sigistrix, have remained an Arian up until this point, for Avitus shows considerable concern that the Catholic Sigismund might be followed by another Arian king.[7] Additionally, or

---

1 Favrod, *Histoire politique*, pp. 373–76, rightly separates Fredegar's account from that of Marius of Avenches, *s.a.* 516, but places the episode in ca. 505. See also the comment in *PLRE* 2, Sigismundus: 'He already bore the title "rex" during his father's lifetime; Avit. *Ep*. 29, 45.'

2 Avitus, *Ep*. 9. The title is confirmed by the *Vita Abbatum Acaunensium absque epitaphiis* 3, ed. B. Krusch, *MGH SRM* 7 (Hanover, 1920).

3 *Fasti Vindobonenses Priores*, p. 306, ed. Mommsen, *Chron. Min.* 1. In general on the Burgundian use of Roman titles, Barnwell, *Emperor, Prefects and Kings*, pp. 82–89.

4 *Vita Patrum Iurensium* II 10 (=92).

5 Avitus, *Epp*. 93, 94; see also *Ep*. 47.

6 Marius of Avenches, *s.a.* 516.

7 See Avitus, *Ep*. 7.

alternatively, Godomar, who may have been Gundobad's son by a second wife, may have been a good deal younger than Sigismund, and may not have been of age to hold office at the time of his father's death.[1]

Sub specie aeternitatis Sigismund's succession does not appear to be of great moment. At the time, however, it was. Since Clovis' death in 511 Frankish power had been on the wane, not least because three of his four sons were still minors. Gundobad must have appeared to be the leading figure in Gaul for the next five years. In 516 Sigismund may have looked yet more impressive than his father had done. He could boast not only that he was a Catholic, as well as Gundobad's son, but also that he was Theodoric's son-in-law – and the Ostrogoth certainly seems to have been interested in the fate of his grandson, Sigistrix, who was a plausible heir to the Ostrogothic throne.[2] In addition, Sigismund's daughter, Suavegotha, was married to Clovis' eldest son, Theuderic.[3] Since the date of this marriage is uncertain, however, its political significance is unclear.

Sigismund was well placed to establish himself as the leading secular figure in Gaul, but his succession also meant the end of public support for Arianism within the Burgundian kingdom. His commitment to Catholicism had already been marked not merely by his conversion, but also by his foundation of the monastery of St Maurice at Agaune in 515, on the site of the martyrdom of the Theban legion, one of the great cult sites of fifth-century Gaul. The dedication ceremony had been graced by a sermon of Avitus (*Hom.* 25). Although Gundobad had been remarkably tolerant of the Catholic Church, Sigismund's accession had immediate implications for its standing in Burgundy.

As the senior of the two Catholic metropolitans in the kingdom, having been consecrated before his colleague Viventiolus of Lyons, Avitus took a lead in addressing the problems and seizing the opportunities presented by the removal of royal support for the Arian Church. He was instantly faced with questions relating to whether Arian churches and liturgical vessels could be taken over by the Catholics.[4] His ruling was stricter than that followed by the Aquitanian bishops at Orléans in 511, after Clovis' kingdom

1 Kampers, 'Caretena – Königin und Asketin', p. 19, argues that Godomar was Gundobad's son by a second wife: he also implies, on the evidence of the Carolingian *Passio Sigismundi*, that Godobad was converted to Catholicism at the same time as Sigismund. This inference may be contradicted by Avitus, *Ep.* 7.

2 Greg. Tur. *DLH* 3.5. Also Shanzer, 'Two Clocks', pp. 252 and 255.

3 Greg. Tur. *DLH* 3.5.

4 Avitus, *Ep.* 7.

had expanded southwards to include their dioceses.[1] The bishop of Vienne's position was subsequently enshrined in the canons of the Council of Epaon, called by Avitus and Viventiolus in 517.[2] Nor was the fate of the Arian Church the only significant topic dealt with by the council. Also of importance, and, once again, deriving from earlier rulings by Avitus, was the legislation on incest[3] – which was to be extremely influential in later canonical rulings.[4]

Epaon reveals the Catholic episcopate active in the aftermath of Sigismund's succession. Earlier in the same year, at the royal Easter court, another, secular, legislative gathering had taken place. Sigismund was intent on making his mark across the board. Perhaps he had in mind the model of Alaric II, who had both issued the *Breviarum Alarici* and at approximately the same time authorised the Catholic Council of Agde (506). It was at the Easter court of 517 that the compilation of law, later known wrongly as the *Lex Gundobada*, was issued.[5] Quite apart from gathering earlier laws, Sigismund issued some edicts of his own. Already in 516 he had legislated on foundlings, following a request from bishop Gemellus of Vaison.[6] There is, however, no indication that Avitus himself had any direct influence on Sigismund's secular legislation.

Although Sigismund's reign began with a flourish, it ended almost immediately in catastrophe. Avitus himself died, probably in 518, before the crisis broke, but the canons on incest which he had masterminded were to play a crucial role in events, as was his brother Apollinaris. Despite the fact that he came down heavily against the crime in his own legislation of the Easter court of 517,[7] Sigismund attempted to ignore a case of incest involving his own treasurer, Stephanus.[8] The case may have been discussed at Epaon, or perhaps more likely at a subsequent council whose canons do not

---

1 Orléans (511) *can*. 10, ed. J. Gaudemet and B. Basdevant.

2 Epaon, *can*. 33, ed. J. Gaudemet and B. Basdevant.

3 Epaon, *can*. 30; Avitus, *Epp*. 16–18.

4 Wood, 'Incest, Law and the Bible'.

5 For the date of the *Liber Constitutionum*, I. N. Wood, 'Disputes in Late Fifth- and Sixth-Century Gaul: Some Problems', in W. Davies and P. Fouracre, eds, *The Settlement of Disputes in Early Medieval Europe* (Cambridge, 1986), p. 10.

6 *Liber Constitutionum* 20.

7 *Liber Constitutionum* 52.

8 Lyons (518–22), ed. J. Gaudemet and B. Basdevant, who suggest a date of 518–23, but 523 is impossible, following Marius of Avenches, *s.a.* 522; *Vita Apollinaris* 2–6, ed. B. Krusch, *MGH SRM* 3 (Hanover, 1896).

survive.[1] It was certainly taken up by the bishops at a separate council held at Lyons between 518 and 522, by which time Avitus' successor, Julianus, was in post.[2] The bishops, led, according to his *Vita*, by Avitus' brother, Apollinaris of Valence, threatened to go on strike if the king continued to ignore the law.[3] In the end a compromise was reached, but not before the shine had been wiped off the new Catholic monarch's standing.

Matters were soon to degenerate further. Sigismund, according to Gregory of Tours, was convinced by his second wife that his son Sigistrix posed a threat to him, and in 522 he had the boy strangled.[4] This was not just a matter of local importance, for the prince was a direct descendent of Theodoric the Ostrogoth, who seems to have considered the boy as a possible successor, and may have sent troops to avenge the murder.[5] The Franks also took advantage of the crisis.[6] Sigismund himself withdrew to his foundation of Agaune, where he was tracked down, seized by the Franks and taken to the Merovingian king, and son of the Burgundian Chrotechildis, Chlodomer, who had him killed and his body thrown down a well.[7] Nevertheless, the Burgundians rallied under the leadership of Sigismund's brother Godomar, who defeated the Frankish army at Vézeronce, killing Chlodomer in the process.[8] The Burgundian kingdom thereafter struggled on until 534, when it was destroyed by Chlodomer's two brothers, Childebert I and Chlothar I.[9]

THE AGE OF AVITUS

Sigismund's reign started in a blaze of glory, but lasted only seven years, ending in catastrophe. The Burgundian kingdom itself survived for another eleven years. The future, however, lay with the Franks. Nevertheless, the fact that the kingdom of the Burgundians failed should not blind us to its importance for understanding developments in the period immediately following the collapse of the west Roman Empire. The kingdom was

1 Wood, 'Incest, Law and the Bible', p. 299. The canons of the Council of Lyon *can.* 1 state that the bishops had gathered together again (*iterato*) to discuss the case of Stephanus.

2 Lyons (518–22).

3 *Vita Apollinaris* 3–6.

4 Greg. Tur. *DLH* 3.5; Marius of Avenches, *s.a.* 522.

5 I. N. Wood, *The Merovingian Kingdoms (450–751)* (London, 1994), p. 53.

6 Greg. Tur. *DLH* 3.5.

7 Greg. Tur. *DLH* 3.5; Marius of Avenches, *s.a.* 523.

8 Greg. Tur. *DLH* 3.6; Marius of Avenches, *s.a.* 524.

9 Greg. Tur. *DLH* 3.11; Marius of Avenches, *s.a.* 534.

fashioned by three members of the Gibichung family, Gundioc, Chilperic I and Gundobad, each of whom held significant Roman office within the western Empire. In this it contrasts with the kingdoms of the Visigoths under Euric and of the Vandals. It is more directly comparable with that of the Ostrogoths, although Theodoric's state was the product of an invasion of Italy. The leaders of the Burgundian and Ostrogothic kingdoms more than their counterparts, wished to remain within an imperial commonwealth.

Most, if not all, western kings of the period continued to show some deference to the Empire. One indication may be found in the pseudo-imperial coinage, which is the norm for the successor states of the early sixth century. Gundobad, for instance, minted solidi and tremisses bearing Anastasius on the obverse and a Victory on the reverse with only his monogram GUB (for 'Gundobadus') to identify it as Burgundian. So too, Sigismund's coins bore Justin I on the obverse and a letter 'S' at the end of the legend.[1] Interestingly, Avitus took a keen interest in the coinage, apparently referring to the legend 'Pax et Abundantia', which appeared on one issue, in one of his dedication homilies.[2] He also noted the poor quality of the Visigothic coinage, and its economic consequences.[3]

It was, indeed, taken for granted that gold coinage should bear the image and name of the emperor. When the Frankish king Theudebert I (534–48) broke the taboo to issue gold coins in his own image, there was an outcry in Constantinople.[4] The same Merovingian king was also prepared to argue with Justinian over titles.[5] Whether Clovis, in Gundobad's day, was as respectful of the Byzantine emperor as his Burgundian colleague is unclear, but his recognition by Anastasius, marked by the reception of imperial diplomas (*codecilli*) in Tours in 508 make it clear that the Byzantines saw the Franks as being within their hegemony.[6] They also saw Clovis at that precise moment as a useful counterbalance to Theodoric in Italy. No doubt Theodoric looked with suspicion on Clovis' recognition by Byzantium,[7] and

1 This S is interpreted as a modest 'Sigismundus' by P. Grierson and M. Blackburn, *Medieval European Coinage 1, The Early Middle Ages (5th–10th Centuries)* (Cambridge, 1986), pp. 74–77 and p. 460 with plate 17.

2 *Hom.* 24.

3 *Ep.* 87. Perhaps to be compared with *Liber Constitutionum, Constitutiones Extravagantes* 21.8.

4 Grierson and Blackburn, *Medieval European Coinage*, pp. 115–66.

5 *Epistulae Austrasiacae* 20, ed. W. Gundlach, *MGH Epp.* 3 (Berlin, 1892).

6 Greg. Tur, *DLH* 2.38. For the meaning of the episode, see M. McCormick, *Eternal Victory* (Cambridge, 1986), pp. 335–37.

7 J. Moorhead, *Theodoric in Italy* (Oxford, 1992), pp. 184–86.

one may guess that Gundobad, proud as he was of his Roman titles, would not have been overjoyed at the grant. Avitus, however, in writing of the Merovingian king's baptism at exactly this moment, placed it in a Byzantine context.[1]

Gundobad, Theodoric and Clovis all looked to the East. Clovis' Byzantine connections are the hardest to fathom, although links between the eastern Empire and the Franks may already have begun in the days of Clovis' father.[2] Contact with and recognition by the Byzantine court, however, was central to the ideals of both Gundobad and Theodoric – and of the two, it seems as if the Burgundian was the more simply deferential. Byzantine recognition was a logical desire, given the significance of Gundobad's early career in Late Roman politics.

Gregory of Tours' lack of interest in the politics of the last years of the western Empire, and even in the influence of Byzantium thereafter, has obscured the extent to which the kingdoms of the Burgundians and of the Franks of the late fifth and early sixth centuries need to be considered in a Mediterranean-wide context . At the same time, his interpretation of Arian–Catholic conflict has led to a reading of the same period which is in no way supported by the writings of Avitus.[3] In so far as the conflict caused any major problem in the successor states of the period before 534, it seems to have been confined to Vandal Africa.[4] Despite his Arianism, Gundobad worked closely with the Catholic episcopate, notably with Avitus. Unlike his Vandal counterparts, the king seems to have taken theological rebuffs in good part. When he died, to be succeeded by his long-Catholic son, the episcopate led by Avitus acted cautiously, determined to ensure the purity of their Church, and also to avoid unnecessary offence which might backfire in future years. As it was, the Catholic kingship of Sigismund did not turn out as the bishops must have hoped: a Catholic monarch could provide more headaches than an Arian one had done.

In strict theological terms the Age of Avitus also has its particular flavour. The presence of an Arian Church and of a heretical, but open-minded, and, above all, non-persecuting king seems to have been a factor in the development of orthodoxy. Gone was the intellectual excitement which had characterised Gaul for much of the fifth century, and in its place, in the

1 *Ep.* 46.
2 Fredegar 3.11.
3 Wood, 'Gregory of Tours and Clovis', pp. 255–60.
4 Even allowing for the bias of Victor of Vita.

writings of both Avitus and Caesarius of Arles, there was an increasing concern with theological uniformity, which came to mean dependence on Augustine. Gallic writers would not contribute much to theological thought for the next two centuries.

Avitus and Ruricius of Limoges also mark a change in the letter-writing tradition which had been a distinctive aspect of Gallic culture. Such a statement needs to be hedged round with disclaimers. Letter-writing continued: Ferreolus of Uzès produced a collection of letters in the manner of Sidonius,[1] which has not survived, and there were later collections, notably the *Epistulae Austrasiacae* and the letters of Desiderius of Cahors, as well as the books of verse epistles by Venantius Fortunatus.[2] Nevertheless the collections of Sidonius, Ruricius, Avitus and Ennodius form a compact group, not least because they overlap in geography, and all four collections come from men who were related – Ennodius rather less closely than the other three. The existence of the collections suggests that letters had an importance for the society which produced them.[3] The Late Roman aristo-cracies of Gaul and indeed of northern Italy used epistolary communication to maintain their position in the changing world of the fifth century. Arguably, as the frontiers of the new kingdoms became more firmly fixed, letters and friendship lost some of their social importance.

The Age of Avitus was, in effect, a short-lived one. Squeezed in between Late Roman and Merovingian Gaul, it casts light on the developments between the two periods. Yet it also deserves consideration in its own right. No longer fully part of the imperial Roman world, the Burgundian kingdom was not yet part of the Merovingian world as portrayed by Gregory of Tours. Its liminal position should be recognised, and the crucial evidence supplied by Avitus should be given the attention it demands.

---

1 Greg. Tur. *DLH* 6.7.
2 Wood, *The Merovingian Kingdoms*, pp. 24–27 and 241–42.
3 Wood, 'Letters and Letter-Collections'; *idem*, 'Family and Friendship in the West'.

CHAPTER 2

MANUSCRIPTS, PAPYRUS, AND EDITIONS OF AVITUS' LETTERS

Avitus' letters were first edited by Jacques Sirmond in 1643 from an unknown and probably now lost manuscript of uncertain date and provenance.[1] His preface reveals that the manuscript divided the letters into five books (he erased these distinctions in his edition) and that he emended its text freely.[2] Thus, when modern editors cite the readings of the Sirmond edition as 'S', the siglum does not necessarily represent a manuscript reading. The text provided could be one of Sirmond's (often excellent) emendations. Each passage must be evaluated individually. In 1661 Johannes Ferrandus edited four Avitan letters (*Epp.* 6, 50, 58, and 64) not found in S using a Lyons codex that had been lent him by Laurent de Leusse.[3] To him belongs the credit for finding an alternative source to S.[4] These same four letters were subsequently re-edited by Stephanus Baluzius in vol. 1 of his *Miscellanea* (1678). The Lyons manuscript (L = Lyon, Bibliothèque de la Ville 618 [535[5]]) is dated to the eleventh/twelfth century by Peiper and is currently the only known close-to-complete manuscript of Avitus' letters.[6]

The first complete edition of the letters based on the Lyons manuscript was Peiper's.[7] It has become standard, and we will at all times use its numbering and refer to its text. In 1890 Avitus was re-edited by Ulysse

---

1 Iacobus Sirmondus, *Sancti Aviti Archiepiscopi Viennensis Opera* (Paris, 1643). Reprinted in Migne *PL* 59.

2 See Peiper, p. v and also pp. xii and xiv.

3 Johannes Ferrandus, *Sancti Alcimi Aviti Viennensis Episcopi epistolae quatuor nunc primum in lucem editae et notis illustratae* (Cabilone apud Philippum Tan, 1661). On the loan, see Chevalier, p. liv.

4 Peiper damns his editing on p. vi, however.

5 No. 535 in A. F. Delandine's, *Manuscrits de la Bibliothèque de Lyon* (Paris, 1812), vv. 1–3.

6 For descriptions see A. Molinier and F. Desvernay, *Catalogue général des manuscrits des bibliothèques publiques de France*, v. 30 (= Lyons) (Paris, 1900), pp. 164–65, no. 618 (535). Peiper gives the manuscript's shelfmark as 111.

7 R. Peiper, *Alcimi Ecdici Aviti opera quae supersunt* (Berlin, 1883) = *MGH AA* 6.2.

Chevalier.[1] Unfortunately copies of his edition are virtually impossible to find, and we have not been able to consult it seriously and collate it.[2] Chevalier's edition has the same manuscript basis as Peiper's.[3] Chevalier mentioned a *CSEL* edition under preparation by one Kunz, but it failed to appear.[4] Some individual letters are transmitted separately in other MSS.[5] The fragments of the *Contra Arrianos* and of the *Libri contra phantasma* are transmitted in the works of Florus of Lyons (F).[6]

In many ways the most interesting and famous manuscript of the works of Avitus is the group of sixth-century papyrus leaves in the Bibliothèque nationale (MSS. BN Lat. 8913–14), first published and described in detail by L. Delisle.[7] The papyrus alone transmits *Ep.* 8, and is an extra and usable witness for *Epp.* 9, 18, and 19.[8] Sirmond used it for editing the latter three;[9] surprisingly he failed to edit *Ep.* 8. It also transmits minute fragments of *Epp.* 51, 55, and 56.[10] Thus in some cases the papyrus' text can reliably be compared with L's. Peiper points out that it shares archetypal errors with L[11]

1 Ulysse Chevalier, *Oeuvres complètes de Saint Avit, évêque de Vienne* (Lyon, 1890).

2 Burckhardt, p. 1, notes that despite the fact that Chevalier did not use Peiper's edition, the differences between their texts are insignificant. Yet on p. 5 he notes Chevalier's preference in ca. 150–200 places for S's readings.

3 Namely Sirmond's edition, the Lyons MS 618 (111, 535); Paris, BN Lat. 8913 and 8914; Rome, Vat. Pal. Lat. 574 (for *Ep.* 7), Rome, Vat. Lat. 4961 (*Epp.* 41 and 42), and Paris, BN Lat. 1920 (for *Ep.* 34). Chevalier, p. xiv, mentioned a *CSEL* edition of Avitus being prepared in 1890 by one Kunz. It never appeared.

4 Chevalier, p. xiv.

5 See Peiper, p. x, for the transmission of *Epp.* 34, 7, 41, 42. The letter from Pope Symmachus (*Ep.* 33) is one of Vignier's forgeries. See H. Rahner, *Die gefälschten Papstbriefe aus dem Nachlasse von Jérôme Vignier* (Munich, 1935), pp. 24–66.

6 See his work on the Pauline epistles in *PL* 119 col. 279–420. See Peiper, pp. ix and xviii. That Florus used the papyrus codex is clear from marginal annotations in the manuscript: C. Charlier, 'Les manuscripts personnels de Florus', in *Mélanges E. Podechard* (Lyons, 1945), p. 83. By extension Agobard's (*Liber adv. Felic. Urguell.* 39 and 41 in *PL* 104) may come from the papyrus codex. Peiper, p. xix maintains an agnostic position.

7 L. V. Delisle, *Études paléographiques et historiques sur des papyrus du VIème siècle ... renfermant des homélies de Saint Avit* (Geneva, 1866). For more accessible illustrations, see also E. A. Lowe, *Codices Latini Antiquiores. France: Paris*, vol. 5 (Oxford, 1950), no. 573; J.-O. Tjäder, *Die nichtliterarischen lateinischen Papyri Italiens aus der Zeit 445–700* (Lund, 1955), p. 39; P. Gasnault 'Fragment retrouvé du manuscrit sur papyrus des Homélies de saint Avit', *Comptes-rendus de l'académie des inscriptions et belles lettres* (1994), pp. 315–23.

8 It contains minute fragments of *Epp.* 51, 55, and 56. See Peiper, p. 154.

9 Delisle, p. 12.

10 See Peiper, p. 154.

11 Peiper, p. xvii and p. xxviii. On p. xviii he points out that in some instances it is hard to tell whether it or L is right.

but otherwise evinces little interest in it, concluding that its testimony is inferior to L's. Its orthography is poor, as might be expected from a Merovingian document: confusions of e and i and o and u are rife.[1] The cursive script likewise caused sufficient difficulties for one sixteenth-century reader to mistake it for Greek.[2] Even though the papyrus contained letters as well as homilies, there is no sound basis for Peiper's assertion (p. xix) that it was originally more complete (*plenior*) than L or S.

Its history since the sixteenth century can be traced from Lyons, whence it reached the library of de Thou before 1617. There it was used by Sirmond for his edition before 1643 and was copied by Bignon. Before 1689 it had made its way to the Bibliothèque du Roi. By 1704 it was known to Mabillon, who mentioned it in the supplement to his *De re diplomatica*. In 1865 one more fragment (also traceable to Lyons) turned up in the Bibliothèque nationale in Paris.[3]

The transmission of the corpus of Avitus' letters is difficult to untangle. Uncertainty surrounding the testimony of S does not help, for although S's readings *may* represent testimony with manuscript authority, they do not *necessarily* do so. The relationship between S, L and the papyrus is likewise not straightforward. S is clearly not a copy of L because it contains letters that are missing from L, e.g. *Epp.* 20, 22, [41, 42], *Ep.* 74, p. 91.15–17, the end of 87, p. 97.1–16, and 94. Whether Sirmond's codex contained these letters, or whether he supplied some or all of them from another source, remains unclear. L is not a copy of S, because it contains various letters missing in S: *Epp.* 6, 50, 58, 64, and 65. Both manuscripts are missing *Ep.* 8, which is transmitted in the papyrus alone. Since the latter contained not just the epistles, but also homilies written for specific occasions, it differed in that respect from both the collection represented by S and that by L.[4]

One way to approach the question of what, if anything, L and S represent is to compare them with existing letter-collections, and search for signs of overall order, e.g. groupings of subjects, types of letters or recipients, or chronological order. The last possibility can be easily eliminated. S's texts are clearly not grouped in chronological order, nor are L's. Both intersperse later with earlier letters in seemingly random fashion. In order to make sense of the collection, a table is necessary. Peiper's conspectus, a finding-list

1 See, for example, the text of *Epp.* 8 and 19 *passim*. Peiper, p. xviii, calls it *vulgaris litteratura*.

2 Delisle, p. 14.

3 The details of its provenance are distilled from Gasnault, 'Fragment retrouvé', pp. 319–23.

4 See Wood, 'Letters and Letter-Collections', pp. 34–35.

designed to compare his numbers with those of Sirmond's edition, does not give a ready visual sense of what appears in L.[1] Accordingly we have created a table that shows the Chevalier numbers and the arrangement of L in parallel with that in S, but makes use of the Peiper numbering system.

For archaeologists, allegedly, one stone is a stone, two stones a coincidence, and three a wall. We have applied an even more generous standard in our attempt to discern any sort of order in L and S. Accordingly, even two letters sharing a recipient, or a letter and its reply, constitute a meaningful unit in our calculations. The seventh column, 'Classification', makes some attempt to guess at how the grouping got where it did, e.g. by addressee, type of addressee, location of addressee.

Conspectus of Letters in L and S

Bold type indicates a break in the sequence shared by L and S

Chevalier number	Order in L	Order in S	Recipient	From Elsewhere	Meaningful Unit?	Classification
1	**89**				**Floater**	
2	**90**				**Floater**	
		1	Gundobad		Gundobad	Addressee
		2	Gundobad		Gundobad	
		3	Gundobad		Gundobad	
3	4	4	Gundobad		Gundobad	
4	5	5	Gundobad		Gundobad	
	6	X	Dominus Rex		Gundobad	
5	**34**	X	Faustus & Symmachus	Also in Paris BN lat. 1920	Floater	
6	7	7	Victorius	Also in Vat. Pal. lat. 574	Bishops	Class of addressee
	X	X		8 from the papyrus codex[2]		
7	9	9	Papa Const.		Bishops	
8	10	10	Eustorgius		Bishops	
9	11	11	Caesarius		Bishops	
10	12	12	Maximus		Bishops	
11	13	13	Avitus		Apollinaris	Addressee

1 His explanation on p. xx using the Sirmond numbering is difficult to visualise.

2 It is unclear why Peiper (p. xx) believes that the letter fell out of LS: *excidit in LS epistula quam papyrus habet ante Ep.* 7.

Chevalier number	Order in L	Order in S	Recipient	From Elsewhere	Meaningful Unit?	Classification
12	14	14	Apollinaris		Apollinaris	
13	15	15	Contumeliosus		Floater	
14	16	16	Avitus		Sex Docket	Addressee (and topic)
15	17	17	Victorius		Sex Docket	
16	18	18	Victorius		Sex Docket	
17	19	19	Viventiolus		Floater	
20c	X	20	Symmachus	Peiper (p. xx) suspects it was missing from Sirmond's manuscript and was supplied from a lost papyrus[1]	Floater	
18	21	21	Avitus		Floater	
18b	X	22	Gundobad	Peiper (p. xx) suspects it was missing from Sirmond's manuscript	Floater	
19	23	23	Sigismund		Floater	
20	24	24	Apollinaris v.i.		Floater	
21	25	25	Papa Hieros.		Floater	
22	26	26	Lugdunensis Episcopus (Stephanus)		Floater	
23	27	27	Apollinaris		Floater	
24	28	28	Stephanus		Floater	
25	29	29	Symmachus papa		Floater	
26	30	30	Gundobad		Floater	Related in subject to the CA
27	31	31	Sigismund		Sigismund	Addressee
28	32	32	Sigismund		Sigismund	
29	35	35	Liberius		Floater	
30	36	36	Apollinaris v.i.		Floater	
31	37	37	Aurelianus		Floater	
32	38	38	Helpidius		Italian	All to the Ostrogothic Kingdom
33	39	39	Senarius		Italian	
34	40	40	Petrus		Italian	

1 Burckhardt, p. 7, thinks it was in Sirmond's manuscript.

Chevalier number	Order in L	Order in S	Recipient	From Elsewhere	Meaningful Unit?	Classification
32d	X	41	Hormisdas	From the papal archives[1]	Hormisdas	Addressee
34e	X	42	Avitus	From the papal archives[2]	Hormisdas	
35	43	43	Euphrasius		Floater	
36	44	44	Gundobad		Floater	
37	45	45	Sigismund		Floater	
38	46	46	Clovis		Floater	
38f	46A	46A	Anastasius		Laurentius	Topic
39	47	47	Vitalinus		Laurentius	
40	48	48	Celerus		Laurentius	
41	49	49	Sigismund		Laurentius	
42	50	X	Arigius		Floater	
43	51	51	Apollinaris	Appears after 55 and 56 in the *Schedulae Parisinae*. See Peiper, p. 154	Apollinaris	Addressee
44	52	52	Apollinaris		Apollinaris	
45	53	53	Heraclius		Heraclius	Addressee
46	54	54	Avitus		Heraclius	
47	55	55	Ansemundus	Appears in the *Schedulae Parisinae* before 56. See Peiper, p. 154	Floater	
48	56	56	Messianus	Appears in the *Schedulae Parisinae* after 55. See Peiper, p. 154	Floater	
49	**75**		**Victorius**		Floater	
50	**76**		**Sigismund**		Floater	
51	57	57	Viventiolus		Bishops	Type of addressee
52	58	58	Stephanus		Bishops	
53	59	59	Viventiolus		Short festal to Bishops	Genre of letter and type of addressee
54	60	60	Gemellus		Short festal to Bishops	
55	61	61	Apollinaris		Short festal to Bishops	

1 Peiper, p. xx.
2 Peiper, p. xx.

Chevalier number	Order in L	Order in S	Recipient	From Elsewhere	Meaningful Unit?	Classification
56	62	62	Victorius		Short festal to Bishops	
57	63	63	Claudius		Short festal to Bishops	
58	64	X	Gregorius		Short festal to Bishops	
	65	X	Alexandrinus		Short festal to Bishops	
59	66	66	Maximus		Short festal to Bishops	
60	67	67	Viventiolus		Short festal to Bishops	
61	68	68	Avitus		Short festal to Bishops	
62	69	69	Viventiolus		Short festal to Bishops	
63	70	70	Constantius		Floater	
64	71	71	Avitus		Apollinaris	Addressee
65	72	72	Apollinaris		Apollinaris	
66	73	73	Viventiolus		More festal to Bishops	Genre of letter and type of addressee
67	74	74	Maximus		More festal to Bishops	
	See above after 56	75	Victorius		Floater	
	76	76	Sigismund		Sigismund	Addressee
68	77	77	Anastasius		Sigismund	
69	78	78	Sigismund		Sigismund	
70	**88**		**Apollinaris**		Floater	
71	**91**		**Sigismund**		Floater	
72	79	79	Sigismund		Sigismund	
73	80	80	Ansemundus		Festal letters to laymen	Genre of letter and type of addressee
74	81	81	Ansemundus		Festal letters to laymen	
75	82	82	Valerianus		Festal letters to laymen	

Chevalier number	Order in L	Order in S	Recipient	From Elsewhere	Meaningful Unit?	Classification
76	83	83	Ceretius		Festal letters to laymen	
77	84	84	Helladius		Festal letters to laymen	
78	85	85	Ruclo		Festal letters to laymen	
79	86	86	Sapaudus		Festal letters to laymen	
80	87 defective at end	87	Apollinaris		Apollinaris	Addressee
	See after 78 above	**88**	**Apollinaris**		Apollinaris	
	See before 1 above	**89**	**Quintianus**		Floater	
	See before 1 above	90	Amandus		Floater	
	See before 79 above	**91**	**Sigismund**		Sigismund	Addressee
81	92	92	Sigismund		Sigismund	
82	93	93	Anastasius		Sigismund	
82g	X	94	Sigismund	Peiper p. xx thinks this letter was likewise introduced by Sirmond.	Sigismund	
83	95	95	Heraclius		Heraclius	Addressee
84	96	96	Avitus		Heraclius	
85	1	See 1 above	Gundobad		Gundobad	Addressee
86	2	See after 1 above	Gundobad		Gundobad	
87	3	See after 2 above	Gundobad		Gundobad	

Here is an attempt to classify the letters as they appear without breaks in the Lyons manuscript:

Avitus *Epistulae* as in the Lyons Manuscript (L)

Gundobad: *Epp.* 4, 5 and 6 (also a unit in S, except that 4 is missing)
Bishops: *Epp.* 7, 9, 10, 11 and 12 (also a unit in S)
Personal docket: Apollinaris of Valence: *Epp.* 13–14 (also a unit in S)
Incestuous adultery docket: *Epp.* 16, 17 and 18 (also a unit in S)
Two to Sigismund: *Epp.* 31 and 32 (also a unit in S)
Three letters to Italy: *Epp.* 38, 39 and 40 (also a unit in S)
The Laurentius docket: *Epp.* 46A, 47, 48 and 49 (also a unit in S)
Personal docket: Apollinaris, *v.i.*: *Epp.* 51 and 52 (also a unit in S)
Heraclius docket: *Epp.* 53 and 54 (also a unit in S)
Letters to Bishops: *Epp.* 57–70 (also a unit in S)
comprising also
Short festal letters to Bishops: *Epp.* 58–69 (also a unit in S which, however, lacks 58, 64 and 65)
Personal docket: Apollinaris of Valence: *Epp.* 71 and 72 (also a unit in S)
More festal letters to bishops: *Epp.* 73 and 74 (also a unit in S)
Two to Sigismund: *Epp.* 77 and 78 (contains four items in S)
Festal Greetings to laymen: *Epp.* 80–86 (also a unit in S)
Two to Sigismund: *Epp.* 92 and 93 (contains four items in S)
Heraclius Docket: *Epp.* 95–96 (also a unit in S)
Longer theological pieces: *CA*, *CE* 1 and *CE* 2

We have applied the same criteria to the collection as it appears in Sirmond. Here is an analysis of the letters as they appear without breaks in his edition. Where a letter is missing, it means that there is a segment with 'no apparent order', comprising what appear to be 'floaters', i.e. letters with no apparent connection to what comes before or after them in the manuscript. Meaning-ful units that are unique either in nature, position or completeness in each collection have been highlighted in boldface.

Avitus *Epistulae* as in Sirmond (S)

Gundobad: *Epp.* 1, 2, 3, 4, 5
Bishops: *Epp.* 7, 9, 10, 11 and 12 (also a unit in L)
Personal docket: Apollinaris of Valence: *Epp.* 13–14 (also a unit in L)
Incestuous adultery docket: *Epp.* 16, 17 and 18 (also a unit in L)

Micah docket: *Epp*. 21 and 22: (L is missing 22)
Two to Sigismund: *Epp*. 31 and 32 (also a unit in L)
Three letters to Italy: *Epp*. 38, 39 and 40 (also a unit in L)
Hormisdas: *Epp*. 41 and 42 (not in L)[1]
The Laurentius docket: *Epp*. 46A, 47, 48 and 49 (also a unit in L)
Personal docket: Apollinaris, *v.i.*: *Epp*. 51 and 52 (also a unit in L)
Heraclius docket: *Epp*. 53 and 54 (also a unit in L)
Letters to Bishops: *Epp*. 57–70 (also a unit in L)
comprising also
Short festal letters to Bishops: *Epp*. 58–69 (S lacks 58, 64 and 65) (also a unit in L)
Personal docket: Apollinaris of Valence: *Epp*. 71 and 72 (also a unit in L)
More festal letters to bishops: *Epp*. 73 and 74 (also a unit in L)
Four to Sigismund: *Epp*. 76, 77, 78 and 79 (L has only 77 and 78 consecutively)
Festal Greetings to laymen: *Epp*. 80–86 (also a unit in L)
Four to Sigismund: *Epp*. 91, 92, 93 and 94 (L has only 92 and 93 consecutively; it lacks 94)
Heraclius Docket: *Epp*. 95–96 (also a unit in L)

If one compares the order of the letters in L and in S, the following salient facts emerge. There is a virtually complete overlap of meaningful units between the two collections. The meaningful units occur in the same relative order in both collections. The differences are minor, e.g. L is missing one item in the Micah docket; S alone has the Hormisdas docket (almost certainly transcribed from another manuscript).[2] S has fuller versions of both the Sigismund dockets that follow the festal letters, while lacking some items among the short festal letters to bishops. Some of the longer theological letters to Gundobad appear at the beginning of the collection in S as opposed to at its end in L. There are areas of apparent disorder, particularly the long string of 'floaters' from *Ep*. 19 to *Ep*. 30.

Burckhardt rightly observed that systematic arrangement played little or no role in the creation of the Avitan letter-collection.[3] The very concept of

1 Although *Epp*. 41 and 42 appear in S, they were imported by Sirmond from another manuscript, and did not appear in L's and S's archetype, since they share an independent transmission. They come from the papal archives, a collection of Hormisdas' letters and decretals, transmitted in Vat. lat. 4961.

2 See Peiper, p. x.

3 Burckhardt, pp. 8–9.

'systematic arrangement', however, needs to be examined. Why does this 'collection' seem to lack order? There is no chronological organisation (one might contrast the Ennodius collection, as edited by Vogel). There are no introductory or dedicatory epistles or any envois.[1] There seems to be no artistic structure or hierarchy of recipients (contrast Cassiodorus who puts letters to important recipients at the beginnings and ends of books),[2] except for the fact that some of the theological letters to Gundobad appear either at the beginning or the end of the collection.[3] Nor are all letters to notable recipients grouped together[4] (contrast Symmachus' collection).[5] There is no consistent attempt to separate public and private letters. Instead, the parallel islands of order in the 'collection' permit a glimpse of the docketing system used either by Avitus or his secretaries. The meaningful units are primarily small groups of letters with one addressee, or pairs consisting of letter plus reply. Some letters seem to address particular topics (e.g. Laurentius' son), but at least one of these dossiers (incestuous adultery) could also be classified according to addressee, bishop Victorius of Grenoble. More interesting are the generic and addressee groupings at the end of L, which contains two separate groups of festal letters, one to bishops, the other to laymen. These generic classifications recall poetic collections, e.g. Martial's *xenia* or *apophoreta*, or epigrams in similar metres,[6] but may simply represent ancient groupings not unlike our piles of Christmas cards or RSVPs for a given wedding or party. But even this noticeable generic grouping appears amid political letters for Sigismund that are completely unrelated.

Although there are many parallels between the orders in L and S, the sequence of letters is not identical, and it is thus by no means clear that they represent genetic branches of an archetypal book.[7] Both S and L lack important letters found in its brother-witness. In some respects S seems the more orderly and structured. The collection begins with letters to Gundobad, an important royal correspondent. Its Sigismund dossiers are more complete. It does not seem to reflect the same evident breaks in sequence apparent in L, particularly at the end of the manuscript. The clear signs of order shared

1 Burckhardt, p.12.

2 See *Var*. 1.1, 1.46, 2.1, 2.41, 3.1, 4.1, 5.1, 5.44, 8.1, 9.1, 10.1.

3 See Burckhardt, p. 19.

4 Burckhardt, p. 13, saw some sort of arrangement by Addressat.

5 E.g. to Praetextatus 1.44–55; 1.13–43 2.1–91 to Flavianus; 6.1–81 to his daughter and son-in-law, etc.

6 Within the 'festal groupings' one finds sub-dockets that may have been filed by addressee, e.g. *Epp*. 67–69 to Viventiolus, *Epp*. 71–72 to Apollinaris, and *Epp*. 80 and 81 to Ansemundus.

7 *Pace* Peiper, p. xxviii and p. xx *uno volumine*.

by L and S, however, must go back to some sort of ancestral common order, and the shared sequences vindicate the closely parallel order in Sirmond as authentic, not as a structure he imposed on his material. There is no tidy explanation of what caused the breaks and variations in sequence, some of which seem very unlikely if the ancestors of S and L had been copied from a bound collection.[1]

THE STRUCTURE OF AVITUS' WORKS: EARLY *TESTIMONIA* ABOUT HIS WHOLE OEUVRE

As we have seen, the corpus of Avitus' letters is problematic. So too are the early *testimonia* about his collected writings: the number of books Avitus is said to have written varies. Gregory of Tours says he wrote nine books;[2] the *Vita Aviti* mentions three books of epistles.[3] The lost manuscript used by Sirmond (S) was apparently divided into five books.[4]

Peiper attempted to reconstruct the lost codex from which L and S (or their ancestors) were allegedly copied and to reconcile his vision of the Avitan corpus with the testimony of the *Vita Aviti* and Gregory of Tours. He (p. xxiii) considered Gregory's and the *Vita's* testimony to be independent, and suggested that both had the works of Avitus in front of them, but that Gregory described 'novem epistularum libros' and the *Vita* 'novem scriptiones epistulares', i.e. nine works in epistolary format. The *Vita* counted as 'epistolary works' the *CA*, *CE* 1, *CE* 2, *Ep.* 4, *Ep.* 5, and *Ep.* 6, plus three books of letters *ad diversos*. If the anti-heretical tracts and *Epp.* 4–6 are all counted as 'books', then indeed the total reaches 'nine books'. Peiper suggested that Gregory was doing something similar, i.e. counting the *CA* among the anti-heretical works listed as 'epistolae admirabiles' (so three books) and then working on similar assumptions to those of the author of the *Vita* (*Epp.* 4–6 are each 'books'), and then counting the three books *ad diversos* for a total of nine. This is certainly a possible, and indeed likely, reconciliation of the apparent discrepancies in testimony (though it is odd that anyone would have described *Epp.* 5 and 6 as 'books', given that they are so short).

---

1 *Pace* Burckhardt, p. 8 who imagines leaves falling out of a codex and being restored in the wrong place.

2 *DLH* 2.34. The count includes *CE* 1 and *CE* 2.

3 *Vita Aviti* 1, Peiper, p. 2.

4 Peiper, p. v cited Sirmond on the *librorum etiam quinque partitionem* and on his removal of the book-divisions: *omisso librorum discrimine*.

'Book' Count	Identity of Surviving Work	Gregory	*Vita Aviti*
3 Books	*CA* (both dialogue and epistle, see fr. 30) *CE* 1 *CE* 2	*Epistolae admirabiles … haeresim oppresserunt*	*Dialogum haeresim illam (Arrianam) oppugnans + libellos duos contra Nestorium et Eutychem* (+ the *CA* per Peiper, p. xxiii)
1 Book		*Homiliarum librum unum*	*Homilias de diversis temporibus anni*
6 Books	SHG + CCL	*De mundi principio etc. libros sex versu*	
9 books (including 3 above), so 6 books in all, as detailed below:		*Epistolarum libros novem inter quas supradictae continentur epistolae.*	
1 Book to Gundobad			*De subitanea paenitentia*
1 Book to Gundobad			*Consolatoria de transitu filiae Gundebadi*
1 Book to Gundobad			*Item epistolam …* (= Ep. 6)
3 Books			*Epistolarum ad diversos libros tres*

But Peiper went further. He noted that the order of the letters in L is disturbed and defective. *Epp.* 74 and 87 are defective at the end. *Ep.* 91 has been split in two. *Epp.* 34 and 90 have been displaced, and *Ep.* 90 wrongly placed at the beginning of the book. He reconstructed an original corpus that contained: the '*Dialogus Contra Arrianos*,'[1] *CE* 1, *CE* 2, *Ep.* 4, *Ep.* 5, *Ep.* 6,

---

1 He claimed (p. xxv) that the *CA* (an epistolary dialogue) began the corpus and was therefore lost at the beginning of the codex. He assumed that Fr. 30 of the *CA* was the end of the dialogue, and that another letter to Gundobad preceded it — hence the heading in L, *Item beati Aviti Viennensis episcopi epistula*, which does not make sense following directly on *Ep.* 96, a letter of Heraclius. But again there is no clear reason why Fr. 30 could not indeed be a separate letter on an anti-Arian topic, not necessarily part of the fragmentary *CA*. *Ep.* 30's topic is very close to that of the *CE*, but is not part of it.

and 'three books of letters *ad diversos*' with their *incipit* at the beginning of *Ep.* 7 (where there is no heading in L). The 'three books of letters' are based on the testimony of the *Vita*. Peiper acknowledged that there were no book-divisions in L.[1] Nonetheless he reconstructed a title 'Epistularum ad diversos Libri tres' (p. 35), a first book that ran until *Ep.* 32, a second book that began at *Ep.* 33 (spurious in fact), and a third book that started with *Ep.* 57.

The *Ur*-oeuvre, according to Peiper (p. xxvii) contained the *CA* in one fascicule plus the *CE* 1 and 2, and *Epp.* 4–6 as a second one addressed to Gundobad. He does not say so explicitly, but he may have intended this arrangement to explain the five-book structure found in S. The *CA* as '*Liber primus ad Gundobadum*', *CE* 1 and *CE* 2, and *Epp.* 4–6 as '*Liber Secundus ad Gundobadum*', and the final three as '*Ad diversos*' for a total of five? Possible, but unproven.

FORMAT AND TRANSMISSION

At least one manuscript of some of Avitus' letters also contained his homilies for special occasions (*ad hoc*, i.e. 'one-offs', not reusable for standard liturgical feasts). The now fragmentary papyrus manuscript may represent such a line of their transmission.[2] Both Gregory and the author of the *Vita* had certainly seen his homilies. Peiper suggested that, because Gregory mentioned them *before* the letters, he must have had the works in separate codices.[3] The author of the *Vita* on the other hand had used a manuscript such as the papyrus-codex, because he mentioned the homilies *after* the letters. But Peiper's argument makes little sense. Indeed, given that the author of the *Vita* refers to sermons *de diversis temporibus anni*, it would appear that he means quite different homilies from the *ad hoc* ones in the papyrus. Furthermore there is no reason for Peiper to make any assumptions whatsoever about what sort of 'codex' or 'codices' both Gregory and the author of the *Vita* saw Avitus' writings in. All we can safely say is that they had seen, or knew of, certain of his works. About format one can draw no conclusions.

---

1 Peiper, p. xxv.
2 Wood, 'Letters and Letter-Collections', p. 34.
3 Peiper, p. xxvii and p. xxviii. The logic makes little sense.

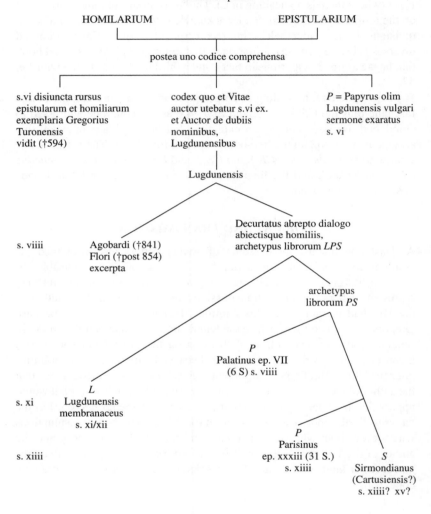

Peiper's Stemma
(Peiper p. xxviii)

Critique of Peiper's Stemma[1]

1. There is no evidence that all the homilies and the letters were ever combined in one codex. All one can safely is say that one particular existing manuscript, the papyrus, contained some homilies and some letters.
2. There is no evidence that the author of the *De dubiis nominibus* had seen a codex with letters and homilies. One cannot tell where the Avitan phrase he quotes, namely *squalore vicino*, came from, except that it was not from the hexameter verse.
3. While it would appear that both Agobard and Florus saw the *CA* in complete form in the ninth century, it is not certain that there ever was one codex with the *CA* (= *dialogus*) and the letters and the homilies (Peiper's lost *Lugdunensis*).[2]
4. Peiper argues for this hyparchetype, a lost *Lugdunensis*, by suggesting that *CA* 30 (clearly called a letter by L) is the (epistolary) end of the *CA*, and that it is a ghost in L, a vestige of the rest of the *CA* that existed in the 'lost Lugdunensis'. It is not, however, clear that *CA* 30 is indeed part of the *CA*, any more than that *Ep.* 30 is. Both could be independent theological epistles. The literary form of the *CA* remains unclear.[3]

Counter-proposal for the *Epistles*

1. The evidence suggests that L and S both go back not to an ordered and structured collection, but to a bundle of miscellaneous letters containing various meaningful dockets within it, dockets being an obvious way of storing papyrus.[4]
2. S's order looks better,[5] and L's can more easily be conformed with it than vice versa, so it would appear that S's order represents some vague arrangement, and that L's is a subsequent *dis*ordering.[6] One might hazard a guess that S represents the primal state of the exemplar and that some of the individual letters had come loose or been filed out of sequence by the time L was copied. For example, some of the Gundobad

---

1 Peiper, p. xxviii.

2 For more on Agobard's fragments and the lost *Dialogus*, see below p. 187.

3 For a detailed discussion, see below p. 187.

4 Letters were written on papyrus. See Sid. Ap. *Ep.* 4.3.1.

5 See Burckhardt, p. 15.

6 Peiper, p. xx, rightly observes that it is easier to reduce L's order to the S order than S to L's, and that where L's order differs it shows clear signs of disturbance.

material may have failed to emerge at the top of the pile, where it belonged,[1] and instead been left at the bottom.

3. The disordering in L is extremely hard to account for if it was copied from a bound book. It shows no clear signs of any intent or purpose.

4. Conclusion: The 'archetype' of the *Epistles* was an unbound one, from which epistolary material was copied at least three times (S's and L's ancestors and the papyrus or its ancestor). S's ancestor copied them first. They were then somewhat disarranged. Thereafter they were copied by L's ancestor.

This is not, however, to say that individual letters did not have archetypes, ultimately the exemplars[2] retained by Avitus in his *armadium* or *scrinium*. There are clear errors shared by S and L, particularly nonsense or lacunae that point in that direction. There are also clear archetypal errors shared by the papyrus and L.[3] But reconstructing the order of any 'original letter-collection' on the basis of the current manuscript evidence is impossible.[4] The letters existed as dockets or bundles that may well already in the sixth century have been copied twice, independently, in somewhat different order. L, S and the papyrus[5] may well then go back to separate copyings, not to one copying of a fixed bound corpus. We can reconstruct much of the state of this bundle in the sixth century, but a bundle it remains.

Letters from unique sources:

From the papyrus only:
8 To the pope

From S only:
20 Avitus to Pope Symmachus,
22 Avitus to Gundobad,
87 fin. Avitus to Apollinaris of Valence,
94 Sigismund to the Byzantine emperor

From L only:
6 Avitus to either Gundobad or Sigismund
50 Avitus to Arigius, *vir illustrissimus*

1 Letters to kings rightly adorn the heads of collections. Cf. Cassiodorus' *Variae* above p. 38 n. 2.

2 Did Avitus send the original or the copy to the recipient?

3 Peiper, pp. xvii–xviii.

4 See Burckhardt, p. 21.

5 The papyrus *schedulae* give *Epp.* 55, 56, and 51 in that order. See Peiper, p. 154.

58 Avitus to Stephanus, bishop of Lyons
64 Avitus to Gregorius, bishop of Langres:
65 Avitus to 'Elexandrinus', bishop: Missing

From the papal archives:[1]
41 Avitus to Pope Hormisdas:
42 Pope Hormisdas to Avitus and all of the suffragan bishops of the Viennensis

PEIPER'S EDITING

Peiper's preface justifies his editorial procedures and attempts to reconstruct the relationship between his manuscripts. Its *Leitmotiv* is dissatisfaction with Sirmond, particularly with his conjectures. Since Sirmond, unlike a modern editor, did not distinguish his conjectures from readings of his manuscript, Peiper (and indeed all scholars) had to decide which of its readings were likely to be manuscript testimony and which conjectures. It is in this tricky area that there can be considerable difference of opinion.[2] *Hinc illae lacrimae*.

Sirmond (1559–1651) was a first-rate scholar who had edited Ennodius (1611) and the *Concilia Galliae* before he brought his considerable talents and knowledge to Avitus. He could and did produce excellent and accurate conjectures. For this reason, where there is patent nonsense, one may be reasonably sure that it was in the manuscript. Where there seems to be solid information not provided in L and not conjecturable by ready comparison of another source, one is likewise probably seeing the manuscript, not Sirmond. But neat *lectiones faciliores* and elegant cleanings-up are much more likely to be Sirmond's own work.[3]

Despite Bédier's witty and paranoid observations,[4] most editors still prefer more than two manuscripts from which to constitute their texts.[5] But in almost all cases the editor of Avitus is denied this luxury. Only for *Ep.* 7,

---

1 Burckhardt, p. 6. There is no reason for thinking that these letters were preserved in the dossiers. They might never have been part of the text as transmitted from Vienne.

2 For more on the problem, see Burckhardt, pp. 4–5.

3 For more on this sort of problem, see Shanzer, 'Dating the Baptism of Clovis', p. 38.

4 Joseph Bédier, *La Tradition manuscrite du Lai de l'Ombre* (Paris, 1970), pp. 10–12, esp. p. 12, 'Un arbre bifide n'a rien détrange, mais un bosquet d'arbres bifides, un bois, une forêt? *Silva portentosa*.'

5 S. Timpanaro, *Die Entstehung der Lachmannschen Methode* (Hamburg, 2nd edn, 1971), pp. 116–17 discusses Bédier on editors' desire to maintain editorial free will.

which enjoys a separate transmission in a Lorsch manuscript (P),[1] can the editor use another codex to help understand the readings of S, i.e. conjecture or manuscript? Peiper took advantage of the opportunity and did a detailed comparison of the readings in his introduction and came to the following conclusions: common errors demonstrate that P and S shared a common hyparchetype not shared by L; in places where P and S share evident errors, one can often see the springboard for Sirmond's corrections; places where L and P agree with one another against S represent authentic readings of the archetype of LPS.[2] Peiper used his findings as a licence consistently to devalue unique readings of S.

This rationale is open to question. For example, first it is not clear that all the readings of L against SP that are identified by Peiper as unquestionably correct are valid. If this is not the case, then the 'stemma' doesn't hold; all three, for example, could have been copied from one exemplar. Even though shared readings of L and P are indeed likely to be archetypal, if Peiper's stemma is correct, this does not give licence to use it mechanically as a tool for editing. Sirmond's reading, emendation or not, may well be correct. Secondly, nothing is known about the nature of Sirmond's manuscript, which may well have contained variants from other sources or corrections, i.e. items that *could* be correct, but were not transmitted to P.

Peiper was an accurate collator, who noted variations in his manuscripts scrupulously.[3] His main fault lay in consistently undervaluing S (presumably out of a regrettable *odium philologicum*) and in being prepared to print clearly incorrect readings of L without noting that they are questionable or using the obelus. We have noted all our variations from Peiper's text. What emerges from our editorial decisions is more obeluses, greater recourse to S, and more conjectures, both our own and others'. This is just the beginning. Avitus' Latin is difficult, his text corrupt and the manuscript transmission inadequate. While we have not produced an edition or new collations as such, a substantially different text (based on Peiper) lies behind our translation. We have noted all our deviations from Peiper's text in textual footnotes and provided a textual appendix.[4] We have not been shy about expressing dismay or incomprehension, or drawing the obelus, when we felt it was warranted, in the hope that others may be motivated to rethink this rather challenging Later Roman author with fresh eyes and open minds.

---

1 Vat. Pal. Lat. 574.
2 Peiper, pp. xiv–xvii.
3 We have had the opportunity to check his collations in many places against the Lyons MS.
4 Below p. 407.

SHORT DESCRIPTION OF L, LYON, BIBLIOTHÈQUE MUNICIPALE MS 618 (535 DELANDINE) (111 PEIPER AND CHEVALIER) AND ANALYSIS OF ITS HEADINGS

Collation:[1]

$i^8+ii^8+iii^8+iv^8+v^8+vi^8+vii^8+viii^8+ix^8+x^8+xi^8+xii^8+xiii^8+xiv^8+xv^8+xvi^8+xvii^8$
$+xviii^8+xix^8+xx^8+xxi^8+xxii^8+xxiii^8+xxiv^8+xxv^8+xxvi^5$

Vellum. 206 leaves. 224 x 136 mm. Pricked in both margins; ruled in lead; one scribe; written above the top line in a large clear proto-Gothic book hand (s. xii rather than xi?)[2] in dark black ink. Abbreviation is very limited, e.g. no ampersand or Tyronian *et*. Contemporary quire numbers up to quire xxiv.

The manuscript contains a collection of letters written by bishops born in Gaul: Paulinus of Nola (ff. 2–133^r), Eucherius (f. 133^r), Avitus (ff. 133^v–189^v), and Agobard (f. 189^v *Epistula Agobardi episcopi Lugdunensis de sacerdotii dignitate ad Barnardum Viennensem archiepiscopum*). For fuller descriptions from editions, see Peiper, pp. vi–viii; Chevalier pp. liii–lv; *Paulini Nolani Epistulae*, ed. G. von Hartel, *CSEL* 29.1, pp. ix–xi. Previous scholars have described the date, provenance and transmission of the manuscript in some detail. Here we will devote ourselves exclusively to features of its presentation (chapters, rubrics and marginal annotations) that have not received sufficient attention in the past.

f. 1v Scribal capitula for Paulinus I (*Sancto et Amando*) -xl (*Epistula Eucherii episcopi. Expliciunt capitula*)
There are no (and probably never were any) chapters (*capitula*) for the Avitus collection.[3] The Eucherius letter must have travelled with the Paulinus collection in L's exemplar, since it is included in its capitula, 'Expliciunt capitula.' Thus it seems a reasonable supposition that the Paulinus and the Avitus letters were copied from different sources.

There are no book-divisions. But each letter of Avitus is distinguished by a rubricated *littera notabilior* (more elaborate ones appear on ff. 133^v, 134^r, 159^v (to Celer) f. 160^r (to Sigismund), f. 169^v (to Apollinaris), f. 178^r (*Contra Eutychen*), and f. 189^v (*Epistula Agobardi*)). Almost all also have rubricated headings that were clearly fitted into the spaces left between the letters after

---

1 Roman numerals indicate the gathering; superscripts the number of leaves.

2 S-longa medially and initially, but round S finally. Hair-strokes over double 'I's.; e-caudata; or-ligatures; both upright and uncial d's.

3 Peiper, p. vii notes 'desunt capitula epistularum Aviti', which seems to imply that there had been *capitula* for Avitus, but that they are missing from L. There is no evidence that there ever were such *capitula*.

the scribe had written the text. They never start on the left, but are inserted in gaps in the middle of the page and in the right margin. In the margins appear contemporary annotations that appear to duplicate the text of the rubricated headings. They were not, however, notes for the rubricator,[1] but indexing aids for an interested and awake reader:[2] note that on f. 168^v the heading, 'ad elexandrinum episcopum', that does not correspond to any letter in the manuscript was *not* reproduced by the marginal annotator. The annotator has likewise corrected *dicta* in the heading of *Ep*. 29 to *dictata*. For *Ep*. 86, the rubricator has 'Epistula ad Usapaudum dictata ab Avito episcopo', where the marginal annotator has 'ussapaudum', which seems to be a correction, i.e. 'v.s. Sapaudum'. It is unclear what happened in the case of *Ep*. 48, where both rubricator and annotator seem to have bungled and corrected themselves. In many places, however, these annotations have been clipped by the binder and are now only half-visible. They also adorn the letters of Paulinus.

What are the rubricated headings? It seemed worthwhile to transcribe and analyse them.

Headings in L

Chevalier number	Order in L	Order in S	Recipient	Meaningful Unit?	Rubricated heading in L	
1	89		Quintianus?	Floater	Incipiunt epistulae Aviti Viennensis episcopi. Epistula ad Amandum	133^v
2	90		Quintianus?	Floater	Epistula ad Amandum	133^{v}6– 134^{r}18
		1	Gundobad	Gundobad		
		2	Gundobad	Gundobad		
		3	Gundobad	Gundobad		
3	4	4	Gundobad	Gundobad	Incipit epistula Aviti episcopi ad Gondobadum regem de subitanea paenitentia	134^{r}19– 136^{r}3
4	5	5	Gundobad	Gundobad	Epistula consolatoria Aviti episcopi de transitu filiae regis	136^{r}4– 137^{r}16

1 *Pace* Peiper, p. vii, *eam atramento praescripserat librarius in margine* and Chevalier, p. liii, 'les titres indiqués en minuscule sur la marge n'ont pas été toujours exactement reproduits par le rubricateur.'

2 The annotations also appear in the Paulinus collection.

Chevalier number	Order in L	Order in S	Recipient	Meaningful Unit?	Rubricated heading in L	
	6	X	Dominus Rex	Gundobad	Epistula Aviti episcopi ad domnum regem facta	137^r17–138^r6
5	34	X	Faustus & Symmachus	Floater	Avitus episcopus ad Faustum et Symmachum senatores	138^r7–139^v10
6	7	7	Victorius	Bishops	Ad Victorium episcopum	139^v11–142^r16
	X	X				
7	9	9	Papa Const.	Bishops	Ad Constantinopolitanum episcopum	142^r17–142^v17
8	10	10	Eustorgius	Bishops	Ad Fortugium episcopum	142^v18–143^r13
9	11	11	Caesarius	Bishops	Avitus Viennensis episcopus ad Caesarium episcopum	143^r14–143^v18
10	12	12	Maximus	Bishops	Ad Maximum episcopum	143^v19–144^r10
11	13	13	Avitus	Apollinaris	Apollinaris episcopus ad Avitum episcopum	144^r11–144^v1
12	14	14	Apollinaris	Apollinaris	Avitus episcopus ad Apollinarem episcopum germanum	144^v2–145^r7
13	15	15	Contumeliosus	Floater	Aviti epistula ad Contumeliosum	145^r8–145^r21
14	16	16	Avitus	Sex Docket	Victorius episcopus ad Avitum episcopum	145^r22–145^v12
15	17	17	Victorius	Sex Docket	Aviti Viennensis episcopi ad Victorium	145^v13–146^r9
16	18	18	Victorius	Sex Docket	Item ad eundem	146^r10–146^v21
17	19	19	Viventiolus	Floater	Avitus episcopus ad Viventiolum episcopum	146^v22–147^r23
20c	X	20	Symmachus	Floater		
18	21	21	Avitus	Floater	Gondobadus rex ad Avitum Viennensem episcopum	147^r24–147^v4
18b	X	22	Gundobad	Floater		
19	23	23	Sigismund	Floater	Epistula Aviti ad domnum Sigismundum regem	147^v5–148^r29
20	24	24	Apollinaris, *v.i.*	Floater	Aviti epistula ad virum illustrem Apollinarem	148^r30–148^v10
21	25	25	Papa Hieros.	Floater	Aviti epistula ad papam Hierosolimitanum	148^v11–148^v30

Chevalier number	Order in L	Order in S	Recipient	Meaningful Unit?	Rubricated heading in L	
22	26	26	Lugdunensis Episcopus (Stephanus)	Floater	Ad Stephanum Lugdunensem episcopum	149^{r}1– 149^{r}24
23	27	27	Apollinaris	Floater	Avitus episcopus ad Apollinarem episcopum	149^{r}25– 149^{v}17
24	28	28	Stephanus	Floater	Avitus episcopus ad quendam episcopum Lugdunensem	149^{v}18– –150^{r}29
25	29	29	Symmachus papa	Floater	Epistula ab Avito episcopo dicta[1] sub nomine domini Sigsimundi ad Symmachum papam urbis Romae	150^{v}1– 151^{v}1
26	30	30	Gundobad	Floater	Aviti epistula ad domnum Gondobadum regem de divinitate filii dei	151^{r}1– 152^{v}9
27	31	31	Sigismund	Sigismund	Aviti epistula ad domnum Sigismundum	152^{v}10– 153^{r}6
28	32	32	Sigismund	Sigismund	Item ad eundem	153^{r}7– 153^{r}30
29	35	35	Liberius	Floater	Avitus Viennensis episcopus ad Liberium praefectum	153^{v}1– 153^{v}28
30	36	36	Apollinaris, *v.i.*	Floater	Avitus Viennensis episcopus ad virum illustrem Apollinarem	153^{v}28– 154^{v}1
31	37	37	Aurelianus	Floater	Avitus Viennensis episcopus ad virum illustrem Aurelianum	154^{v}2– 154^{v}25
32	38	38	Helpidius	Italian	Avitus episcopus ad Helpidium diaconem	154^{v}26– 155^{v}5
33	39	39	Senarius	Italian	Epistula beati Aviti episcopi ad virum illustrem Senarium	155^{v}6– 156^{r}3
34	40	40	Petrus	Italian	Epistula beati Aviti Viennensis episcopi ad Petrum episcopum Ravennatem	156^{r}4– 156^{r}30
32d	X	41	Hormisdas	Hormisdas		
34e	X	42	Avitus	Hormisdas		

1 The marginal annotator has corrected this to *dictata*.

Chevalier number	Order in L	Order in S	Recipient	Meaningful Unit?	Rubricated heading in L	
35	43	43	Euphrasius	Floater	Epistula beati Aviti episcopi ad Eufrasium episcopum	156^{r}30– 156^{v}22
36	44	44	Gundobad	Floater	Epistula beati Aviti episcopi ad Gondobadum regem	156^{v}23– 157^{v}5
37	45	45	Sigismund	Floater	Epistula beati Aviti episcopi ad Sigismundum regem	157^{v}6– 158^{r}7
38	46	46	Clovis	Floater	Epistula beati Aviti episcopi ad Chlodovechum regem	158^{r}8– 159^{r}12
38f	46A	46A	Anastasius	Laurentius		159^{r}12– 159^{r}28
39	47	47	Vitalinus	Laurentius	Epistula Aviti episcopi ad Vitalinum senatorem	159^{r}29– 159^{v}18
40	48	48	Celerus	Laurentius	Avitus episcopus ad /// senatorem /// ad Celerum[1]	159^{v}19– 160^{r}9
41	49	49	Sigismund	Laurentius	Epistula beati Aviti episcopi ad domnum Sigismundum	160^{r}10– 160^{r}24
42	50	X	Arigius	Floater	Epistula beati Aviti episcopi ad illustrem virum Arigium	160^{r}25– 161^{r}28
43	51	51	Apollinaris	Apollinaris	Avitus Viennensis episcopus ad virum illustrem Apollinarem	161^{r}29– 162^{v}17
44	52	52	Apollinaris	Apollinaris	Item ad eundem	162^{v}18– 163^{r}20
45	53	53	Heraclius	Heraclius	Avitus episcopus ad virum illustrem Eraclium	163^{r}21– 164^{r}15
46	54	54	Avitus	Heraclius	Heraclii rescriptum ad Avitum episcopum	164^{r}16– 164^{v}29
47	55	55	Ansemundus	Floater	Epistula beati Aviti episcopi ad virum illustrem Ansemundum	165^{r}1– 166^{r}6
48	56	56	Messianus	Floater	Avitus episcopus ad virum illustrem Messianum	166^{r}7– 166^{r}18
49	75		Victorius	Floater	Epistula beati Aviti episcopi ad Victorium episcopum	166^{r}19– 166^{v}10

1 The marginal annotator has 'Avitus episcopus ad Celerum ~~senatorem~~ atorem [sic]'.

Chevalier number	Order in L	Order in S	Recipient	Meaningful Unit?	Rubricated heading in L	
50	76		Sigismund	Floater	Epistula beati Aviti episcopi ad domnum Sigismundum	166^{v}11– 166^{v}26
51	57	57	Viventiolus	Bishops	Epistula beati Aviti episcopi ad Viventiolum rhetorem	166^{v}27– 167^{v}24
52	58	58	Stephanus	Bishops	Epistula beati Aviti episcopi ad Stephanum episcopum	167^{v}25– 168^{r}1
53	59	59	Viventiolus	Short festal to Bishops	Avitus episcopus ad Viventiolum episcopum	168^{r}2– 168^{r}9
54	60	60	Gemellus	Short festal to Bishops	Avitus Viennensis episcopus ad Gemellum episcopum	168^{r}9– 168^{r}15
55	61	61	Apollinaris	Short festal to Bishops	Avitus episcopus ad Apollinarem episcopum	168^{r}16– 168^{r}21
56	62	62	Victorius	Short festal to Bishops	Epistula beati Aviti episcopi ad Victorium episcopum	168^{r}22– 168^{v}2
57	63	63	Claudius	Short festal to Bishops	Epistula Aviti episcopi ad Claudium episcopum	168^{v}3– 168^{v}9
58	64	X	Gregorius	Short festal to Bishops	Epistula Aviti episcopi ad Gregorium episcopum	168^{v}10– 168^{v}17
	65	X	Alexandrinus?	Short festal to Bishops	Epistula beati Aviti episcopi ad elexandrinum episcopum	168^v
59	66	66	Maximus	Short festal to Bishops	Epistula beati Aviti episcopi ad Maximum episcopum[1]	168^{v}18– 168^{v}26
60	67	67	Viventiolus	Short festal to Bishops	Epistula beati Aviti episcopi ad Viventiolum episcopum	168^{v}27– 169^{r}9
61	68	68	Avitus	Short festal to Bishops	Epistula Viventioli episcopi ad Avitum episcopum	169^{r}10– 169^{r}13
62	69	69	Viventiolus	Short festal to Bishops	Item Avitus ad Viventiolum episcopum	169^{r}14– 169^{r}19
63	70	70	Constantius	Floater	Epistula beati Aviti episcopi ad Constantium episcopum	169^{r}20– 169^{v}5
64	71	71	Avitus	Apollinaris	Apollinaris episcopus ad Avitum episcopum	169^{v}6– 169^{v}11

1 Marginal only. A correction of the marginal annotator.

Chevalier number	Order in L	Order in S	Recipient	Meaningful Unit?	Rubricated heading in L	
65	72	72	Apollinaris	Apollinaris	Item Avitus ad Apollinarem episcopum	169v12–169v30
66	73	73	Viventiolus	More Festal to Bishops	Ad Viventiolum episcopum	170r1–170r10
67	74	74	Maximus	More Festal to Bishops	Epistula beati Aviti episcopi ad Maximum episcopum	170r11–170v1
	See above after 56	75	Victorius	Floater		166r19–166v10
68	77	77	Sigismund	Sigismund	Epistula Aviti episcopi ad domnum Sigismundum	170v2–170v16
69	78	78	Anastasius	Sigismund	Epistula Sigismundi regis ad domnum imperatorem	170v17–171r12
70	88		Apollinaris	Floater		171r13–171v2
71	91		Sigismund	Floater		171v3–171v11
72	79	79	Sigismund	Sigismund		171v12–171v22
73	80	80	Ansemundus	Festal letters to laymen	Epistula ad virum illustrem Sigismundum	171v23–172r7
74	81	81	Ansemundus	Festal letters to laymen	Epistula Aviti episcopi ad Ansemundum	172r8–172r17
75	82	82	Valerianus	Festal letters to laymen	Epistula ad virum illustrem Valerianum	172r18–172r26
76	83	83	Ceretius	Festal letters to laymen	Epistula ad virum illustrem Cerecium	172r27–172v9
77	84	84	Helladius	Festal letters to laymen	Epistula ad virum illustrem Hilladium	172v10–172v21
78	85	85	Ruclo	Festal letters to laymen	Epistula ad virum illustrem Ruclonem	172v21–17v30
79	86	86	Sapaudus	Festal letters to laymen	Epistula ad Usapaudum dictata ab Avito episcopo	173r1–173v12
80	87 defective at end	87	Apollinaris	Apollinaris	Epistula beati Aviti ad Apollinarem episcopum	173v13–174r7
	See after 78 above	88	Apollinaris	Apollinaris	Epistula beati Aviti episcopi ad Apollinarem episcopum	171r13–171v11
	See before 1 above	89	Quintianus	Floater		

Chevalier number	Order in L	Order in S	Recipient	Meaningful Unit?	Rubricated heading in L	
	See before 1 above	90	Amandus	Floater		
	See before 79 above	91	Sigismund	Sigismund	Epistula Aviti episcopi ad domnum Sigismundum	$171^{v}12$– $171^{v}22$
81	92	92	Sigismund	Sigismund	Epistula ad domnum Sigismundum	$174^{r}20$– $174^{v}11$
82	93	93	Anastasius	Sigismund	Epistula Sigismundi regis ad domnum imperatorem	$174^{v}12$– $175^{v}4$
82g	X	94	Sigismund	Sigismund		
83	95	95	Heraclius	Heraclius	Epistula beati Aviti episcopi ad illustrem virum virum Eraclium	$175^{v}5$– $175^{v}20$
84	96	96	Avitus	Heraclitus	Rescriptum Heraclii ad Avitum episcopum	$175^{v}21$– $176^{v}7$
85	1 (=CA fr. 30)	See 1 above	Gundobad	Gundobad	Item beati Aviti Viennensis episcopi epistula	$176^{r}8$– $177^{v}30$
86	2	See after 1 above	Gundobad	Gundobad	Incipit liber primus beati Aviti Viennensis episcopi contra eutychianam haeresem	$178^{r}1$– $183^{r}16$
87	3	See after 2 above	Gundobad	Gundobad	Incipit secundus ... no explicit	$183^{r}17$– $189^{v}9$

Four of the headings (*Epp.* 2, 3 [=*CE* 1 and *CE* 2] *Ep.* 90 and *Ep.* 4) take the more formal shape of *incipits*. The headings of two letters (*Epp.* 54 and 96, both from Heraclius) describe them as *rescripta*. Parallel examples where letters come in pairs are not so designated in the case of other correspondents, e.g. Apollinaris of Valence, Viventiolus and Victorius of Grenoble.

The headings are clearly based on the *incipits* of the letters. When the letter has a patent error (e.g. *Ep.* 10 *ad Fortugium* [*sic*], *Ep.* 80 *ad Sigismundum* [*sic*]), so does the heading. When the addressee is unclear, the heading does its best, e.g. *Ep.* 28, f. 149ᵛ *Avitus episcopus ad quendam episcopum Lugdunensem*. They never retail information independent of what is found in the text of the letters.

Ep. 90 presents special problems. It is entitled 'epistula ad Amandum' by the rubricator. The marginal annotator, however, has 'Epistula beati Aviti ad

Quintianum episcopum' which follows the MSS's salutation to *Ep*. 90, the invitation to the Council of Epaon, 'Diu est ...' 'Avitus episcopus Quintiano episcopo'. Peiper (pp. 97–98) rightly suspected that the rubricator picked the name up from the Paulinus collection, since no 'Amandus' signed the canons of Epaon.[1] A problem still remains: are we still missing a letter to the banished Quintianus, bishop of Clermont?[2] That is, is there a lacuna consisting of the body of the lost letter? Or was *Ep*. 90 indeed addressed to Quintianus, strictly speaking an extra-territorial bishop, rather than being transmitted as a circular[3] without a specific addressee?[4] Since the heading to *Ep*. 90 is the only evidence for Quintianus being invited to Epaon, and since he was never a bishop of the Burgundian kingdom, it is difficult to know whether he was invited to attend the council. There is, however, evidence that bishops could participate in councils and ecclesiastical decisions outside their dioceses.[5] So there is no reason to reject the possibility that Avitus, for political reasons, may have invited the bishop of Clermont to Epaon, which was in some sense a 'super-provincial council' like Agde. Here, however, as elsewhere, the annotator has corrected a mistake of the rubricator.

Were these headings inserted by the scribe of L, or do they reproduce something that was already in L's exemplar? They cannot have been created for L, since they are not sufficiently uniform in format. More importantly, however, they were clearly available to Sirmond in his manuscript too.[6] In a critical case S's reading is right and L's (and its heading's) erroneous:

---

1 E.g. from *Ep*. 1 *Sancto et Amando*.

2 See Greg. Tur. *DLH* 2.36 for his exile from Rodez and the charity he received from the bishop of Lyons. See L. Duchesne, *Fastes épiscopaux de l'ancienne Gaule* (Paris, 1910), vol. 2, p. 35, for his episcopate at Clermont from ca. 515–525/6.

3 A form-letter to bishops, in fact.

4 Perhaps the file-copy of his circular that Avitus retained was one addressed to Quintianus.

5 Our gratitude to Ralph Mathisen, who drew our attention to three cases: 1) Agrestius, bishop of Lugo, who in 441 attended the council of Orange and subscribed: 'ex provincia Gallecia civit. Lecentium Agrestius episcopus, Deudatus diaconus' (*CCSL* 148.87). 2) Euphronius of Autun – in Lugdunensis I – who ca. 470 was asked by Sidonius, in Aquitania I, to confirm the choice of Simplicius as bishop of Bourges, and invited to participate in the ordination, a rather irregular request, because only intra-provincial bishops were supposed to attend under ordinary circumstances. In this case, Euric had been preventing ordinations in other cities of the province. See Sid. Ap. *Ep*.7.8. 3) Euphronius of Autun (Lug. I) and Lupus of Troyes (Lug. IV), who in the 450s presumed to send a joint letter to Thalassius of Angers (Lug. III) instructing him on bigamous clerics (*CCSL* 1.140–41).

6 Note that Heraclius' answers, and his alone, are also called *rescripta* in Sirmond's edition.

'Ansemundus' S vs. 'Sigismundus' L in *Ep.* 80.[1] In another case, *Ep.* 43, S
failed to copy 'Eufrasio', but Sirmond guessed correctly about the addressee
documented in L. In some shape or form the headings adorned the common
exemplar of L and of S.[2] Since we have suggested above that L and S were
not copied from a bound exemplar, but from unbound, grouped dockets, it
would appear that the dockets may have carried labels or tickets (like
modern 'Post-its') identifying their contents. It would seem that the
headings visible in L are based on these *ad hoc* labels, probably written by
different cataloguers of Avitus' *Nachlaß* with different perspectives and
intentions. Some are minimal (*Epistula Aviti* or just *Epistula*: those on the
festal letters to laymen (*Epp.* 82 to 85) are good examples); others more
formal (*Epistula Aviti Viennesis episcopi*);[3] others more pious (*Epistula
beati Aviti*).[4] Two stand out, namely Heraclius' answers, *Epp.* 54 and 96,
labelled *rescripta Heraclii*. One might hazard a guess that these two were
labelled by Avitus himself: *Rescriptum* is a word he used in his own
correspondence.[5]

To summarise: the headings in L are not uniform, nor were they created
exclusively for this manuscript. They are authentic, though not (except
perhaps in the case of the *rescripta*) authorial, and most probably represent
notes made by others in classifying the original dockets in the Avitan
'collection'. They thus provide a unique glimpse into early medieval filing-
systems.

The unique and very formal heading of the letter to Hormisdas (*Ep.* 40)
*Domino sancto, meritis praecellentissimo, in Christo gloriosissimo et
apostolica sede dignissimo, papae Hormisdae Avitus* shows us how Avitus'
official correspondence was actually addressed. But, as we have seen, this
letter is missing from L and was almost certainly missing from S too.
Sirmond copied it from a papal manuscript. Many other official letters in the
Avitus collection would have required formal headings or salutations, but
none have them.[6] In this we may see proof that the letters we have (aside

1 L may have remembered the previous letter, which was indeed addressed to Sigismund.

2 These are the work not of Avitus, but of a third party. See Burckhardt, p. 22, who rightly
discusses the one exception, *Ep.* 41, which carries an appropriate formula of address.

3 *Epp.* 1, 2, 11, 17, 35, 36, 37, 40, 51, 60 and 90.

4 *Beatus* features in *Epp.* 1, 39, 40, 43, 44, 45, 46, 49, 50, 55, 57, 58, 62, 65, 66, 67, 70, 74,
75, 76, 87, 88 and 95.

5 E.g. *Ep.* 32, p. 62.28.

6 One could contrast the elaborate headings used by Ruricius.

from *Epp*. 41, 42 and letters addressed to Avitus by other people) were all 'file copies' from his own desk, not a formal publication or fair copies with full headings.[1]

---

1 For more on salutation-headings, see M. Zelzer, 'Der Brief in der Spätantike. Überlegungen zu einem literarischen Genos am Beispiel der Briefsammlung des Sidonius Apollinaris', *WS* 107–108 (1994–95), p. 543.

CHAPTER 3

LITERARY ASPECTS OF AVITUS'
LETTER-COLLECTION

Literary historians traffic in change and continuity, in zeniths and nadirs.
They judge and evaluate their dead prey. They damn their authors, apologise
for them[1] and indulge in special pleading on their behalf. Many who
consider the literary history of Later Roman Gaul dwell on Sidonius as a
high point, the 'last of the Romans', and their main exhibit, and then make
their way to the decadence and *rusticitas* of Gregory of Tours, who marks
the onset of the Middle Ages. Avitus of Vienne allows us to see some of what
happened between these two towering (or alternatively abject and ridiculed)
figures. All three of these Gallic authors came from the highest social class
and can reasonably have been expected to have had the best education
available.[2] They are thus fit subjects for comparison. Sidonius and Gregory
have always attracted the attention both of literary scholars and of historians.
Not so Avitus. Every author on trial has the right to an advocate, and the
bishop of Vienne should prove no exception. Manitius omitted him. Brunhölzl
relegated him firmly to the patristic age.[3] Schanz-Hosius have so little to say
about his prose that one might justifiably wonder whether they had read any
of it.[4] The poetry has always had its admirers.[5] The prose is another matter:
the homilies are largely fragmentary, the letters and theological tractates

---

1 Take the avant-propos of A. Loyen, *Sidoine Apollinaire et l'esprit précieux en Gaule aux
derniers jours de l'empire* (Paris, 1943), where he informs us that a writer of a decadent period
may be of great interest to the literary historian provided that one regard his writings as a stage
or the culmination of the general evolution of language or style.

2 For expectations of both rhetorical prose and verse of the provincial Gallic nobility see
Sidonius, *Ep.* 3.3.2 *tuae personae quondam debitam quod sermonis Celtici squamam
depositura nobilitas nunc oratorio stilo, nunc etiam camenalibus modis imbuebatur.*

3 F. Brunhölzl, *Histoire de la littérature latine du moyen âge*, v. 1 (Louvain-la-neuve, 1990),
p. 116.

4 M. Schanz, C. Hosius and G. Krüger, *Geschichte der römischen Literatur*, v. 4.2 (Munich,
1920), pp. 386–88.

5 See above p. 3.

obscure and often corrupt. As a result the prose has remained largely unread.

Avitus is far more of a theologian than Sidonius.[1] He is well acquainted with the Bible.[2] He is neither apparently as well versed in classical literature as his senior relative,[3] nor as much the *homo urbanus* as Ennodius. Nor is he the précieux, merely interested in piquant ornaments, historical and literary exempla, and learned tidbits. Outside of his poetry his visual imagination fails.[4] In his favour is the excellence of much of his five-book biblical epic, the *De spiritalis historiae gestis*. He shows little awareness of philosophy or of philosophical debate. Here one might well contrast Claudianus Mamertus or Faustus of Riez. Avitus must be judged on what survives. But much of his oeuvre has been lost, including letters,[5] homilies[6] and all of his early occasional poetry.[7] Our subject, however, is his letters, and it is these which must be set in a general historical and literary context.

THE FUNCTION OF LETTERS

An oddly self-reflexive letter of Avitus' contemporary, Ruricius, bishop of Limoges, describes the epistolary genre:

> We who seek an opportunity to write in accordance with our close relationship must not let one pass us by once it presents itself, so that language, as mediator, may give us some share of [your] presence: it (*sc.* language) is emitted, but not lost, it is granted, yet still possessed; it seems to depart, but it does not leave; it is sent off by me, but received by you; written by me, yet read by you – but all the same it is not divided, since it is preserved whole in each of our hearts as if it had been divided, because it does not go forth, but is handed on like the divine word; it is conferred upon him who needs it, yet it is not taken away from its author; it is a gain to the receiver without being an expense to the giver; it enriches him who was

---

1 On Sidonius and theology see the damning comments of Loyen, pp. 34–37.

2 For a quick conspectus of citations see Peiper, pp. 297–99.

3 Loyen, p. 30, points out that Sidonius primarily imitates Pliny the Younger and Symmachus among prose authors and Lucan, Statius and Claudian among poets. Ovid, Apuleius, Fronto and Ausonius figure further down the list. On p. 34 he discusses borrowings from Plautus, Terence, Petronius, Juvenal and Martial.

4 Or as G. Vinay said of the prose works, 'Sulla loro soglia muore il poeta'; 'La Poesia di sant'Avito', p. 456.

5 The only lost letter explicitly attested is the epistle to Remigius mentioned by Flodoard. See Peiper, p. 103.9–12.

6 Most are fragmentary or attested by title alone.

7 See the dedicatory epistle to the *SHG*, p. 201.7–12.

without it, but does not diminish the possessor. (Ruricius, *Ep.* 2.5 to Namatius)[1]

All of this is one sentence: one letter – with no other function than to glorify the act of letter-writing. The passage has a certain internal wit: it is a letter about letters, but it has none of the characteristics that we would expect of modern letters: it conveys no news; it is not even particularly polite: it extols the largesse of the writer, the *inopia* of the recipient and the miracle of the letter itself. Pompous bombast it may be, but there is no need to assume that the text is incomplete; what mattered was not *what* one wrote, but *that* one wrote.[2] In some ways the friendship epistles of antiquity are not unlike the modern Christmas card. The content is minimal, it is the thought that counts.[3] With a wry smile one observes that Ruricius plagiarised himself in *Ep.* 2.36, where the sentence is shamelessly recycled as an exordium of a letter to Caesarius of Arles, serving to recommend Ruricius' grandson, Parthenius.[4] The bishop of Limoges would have appreciated the 'cutting and pasting' capabilities of modern word-processors.

Virtual vs. Actual Praesentia

There is eloquent praise of the power of the pen in Sid. *Ep.* 7.14.2 to Philagrius. In a discussion about whether the man of letters was better

---

1 *Qui occasionem scribendi pro necessitudinis iure perquirimus, oblatam praetermittere non debemus, ut reddat nobis quandam praesentiae portionem sermo mediator, qui emittitur et non amittitur, tribuitur et non habetur, videtur discedere nec recedit. a me dirigitur, a me scribitur, a te legitur nec tamen dividitur …*

2 H. Hagendahl, *La Correspondance de Ruricius* (Gothenburg, 1952), p. 23, thinks that the letter must be fragmentary in light of its subsequent reuse as an *exordium*. This conclusion is not inevitable. There are numerous examples of one-sentence letters in Later Roman correspondence. Furthermore, Hagendahl himself (p. 10) drew attention to *Ep.* 2.51 where Ruricius says that he is happy to hear from Censorius, *even though* there is an occasion. He goes on to say that it makes no difference whether it be out of necessity or of one's free will, as long as those who love one another speak together.

3 For more charitable assessments see Mathisen, *Ruricius*, p. 53 and Wood, 'Letters and Letter-Collections', p. 39: 'strategic documents rather than the frivolous creation of an idle aristocracy'. M. Wagner, 'A Chapter in Byzantine Epistolography: the Letters of Theodoret of Cyrus', *DOP* 4 (1944), p. 130, discusses letters written not only for 'purposes of necessity, but also for display and emulation'.

4 Ruricius made the minimum change necessary, namely the alteration of *pro necessitudinis iure* (appropriate for his son's in-laws) to *pro mutua caritate* (for the bishop of Arles). For more on his plagiarisms see Hagendahl, *La Correspondance*, pp. 12–31.

known to his rustic neighbours or to his readership far away, Sidonius stuck to his guns.

> I persisted in maintaining that it is difficult for eloquent friends if they never get to see one another, but tolerable, because they can stretch forth their intellects with the help of the pen to those who long to read them in distant provinces. In their presence their own countrymen are strangers. Through the pen more affection is formed amongst those who are separated – provided they are educated – than is generated by constant presence and attendance. Therefore, if this is true, let those who tout faces rather than true character cease to say bad things about the necessity of being apart from one another.[1]

In Sulpicius Severus' *Vita Martini* 19 a letter of St Martin's cured Arborius' daughter in the absence of the saint himself.[2] But even in less pressing matters, when travel was difficult, and wars or political contretemps interrupted communications, letters assumed great importance in maintaining the bonds of *amicitia*. It was through them that one made oneself present.[3] Avitus, like all letter-writers, recognised the importance of regular correspondence and employed the traditional epistolographic *topoi*, though not with Ruricius' monotonous effusion.[4] In this, he was no different from most formal letter-writers of the Later Roman Empire of whom M. Wagner[5] wrote with understanding:

> The fact that they rang the changes of a sometimes fulsome hyperbole upon this basic note by means of fictions invented to preserve the illusion of an actual meeting does not weaken its validity in their regard. Nor are their epistolary colloquies less truly named because they often possessed a kind of pompousness peculiar to a rhetorical age or becomes sometimes, like a formal bow, they merely complied with the decrees of courtly etiquette. The extravagant and ceremonious phrase was the mode among the learned of the day and an artless and naïve epistolary style, a later touchstone, might, from their pens, have seemed an affectation.

---

1 *Constanter asserui, si eloquentibus amicis numquam agnitio contemplativa proveniat, esse asperum utcumque, tolerabile tantum, quia praevaleant ingenia sua, coram quibus imperitia civica peregrinatur, ad remotarum desideria provinciarum stilo adminiculante porrigere; per quem saepenumero absentum dumtaxat institutorum tantus colligitur effectus, quantus nec praesentanea sedulitate conficitur. igitur, si ita est, desistant calumniari communis absentiae necessitatem vultuum mage quam morum praedicatores.*

2 Sulpicius playa on *praesentia* and *absentia* in the passage.

3 Cf. Ennodius, *Ep.* 1.8 and 1.11.

4 E.g. *Epp.* 64, 66, 84 and 85.

5 Wagner, 'A Chapter in Byzantine Epistolography', p. 140.

Structure of Letter-Collections

Epistolography was a genre with its own conventions that governed both the structure of collections and the nature of the material included in them. A number of treatises have come down from antiquity that describe and catalogue different types of letters and, in some cases, provide samples.[1] Ancient as well as later Roman letter-writers echoed both the contents and the structure of the letter-collections of their predecessors.[2] Pliny wrote nine books of letters; so eventually would Symmachus, Sidonius and Cassiodorus.[3] Some letter-collections clearly were edited by their authors, e.g. those of Ambrose,[4] Symmachus and Sidonius, who brought his letters out book-by-book in response to the encouragements of various friends, processes reflected in the dedicatory epistles themselves.[5] In the case of other writers the authorial *summa manus* or formation of any sort of collection is far less clear, e.g. for Jerome, Ruricius or Ennodius.[6]

Sidonius as Model

Sidonius' letters were acclaimed by his contemporaries, who called for their publication. They achieved the status of epistolary classics within one generation, aided no doubt by the commemorative efforts of his son Apollinaris, who corresponded both with Ruricius and with Avitus. Although Apollinaris, surprisingly, seems to have needed to borrow from Ruricius a

1 See, for example, A. J. Malherbe, *Ancient Epistolary Theorists* (Atlanta, 1988); S. K. Stowers, *Letter Writing in Greco-Roman Antiquity* (Philadelphia, 1986); for *topoi* see K. Thraede, *Grundzüge griechisch-römischer Brieftopik* (Munich, 1970).

2 See Loyen, p. 31, for a list of common types of letters shared by Sidonius and Pliny: description of a villa, lamentation over the death of a friend, praise of the ancients, praise of friendship, compliments about writings received, political journal to inform a friend. There are other similarities: both think that a letter should treat only one topic (*Ep.* 6.11.2; 7.18.4.). If there is more than one, they apologise; both guide their readers through their topics: *quod restat*; *hoc restat unum*. Both love parallelism or parallelism with chiasmus. Almost all of Sidonius' Greek words come from Pliny.

3 See Sidonius *Ep.* 1.1 for explicit homage to Pliny and Symmachus. For the ninth book, see *Ep.* 9.1.

4 See Zelzer, 'Der Brief', p. 545.

5 For more on this see Loyen, pp. 124–25.

6 Jerome's collection was not compiled by its author. See J. Schwind, 'Hieronymus' Epistula ad Innocentium (epist. 1) – ein Jugendwerk?', *WS* 110 (1997), pp. 175–76. For Ruricius, see Mathisen, *Ruricius*, pp. 56–61 who suggests that some of the letters of Book 2 may have been thrown together by a compiler. For convincing evidence that Ennodius' collection was not compiled by its author, see F. Vogel, p. xxix.

copy of Sidonius' works for transcription,[1] he is said to be the 'translator of his father's speech, able to produce everything that he wrote not so much from a parchment codex, but from the page of the heart'.[2] Ruricius, *Ep.* 2.26 to Apollinaris has some significant hints. To Ruricius, Sidonius is 'our lord and our common father' (*nostrum domnum patremque communem*). Even though it restores his former affection to read Sidonius' work, the obscurity of his phrasing makes him difficult for Ruricius to understand.[3] This is interesting, because it may be testimony to a slipping in standard of Latinity: the bishop of Limoges had difficulties with the affected style of the previous generation. Open acknowledgement appears in Avitus' *Ep.* 43, p. 73.5 'the son of our lord Sidonius who, amongst the delights of his father's eloquence, will be nauseated at our times' (*domni Sidonii filio inter facundiae paternae delicias meis temporibus nauseaturo*), as well as a hint that writing has got worse. Nonetheless Gregory of Tours suggests that Sidonius may have been the model for Ferreolus of Uzès as late as 553-581.[4] And Sidonius certainly exercised influence on Avitus.[5]

AVITUS' LETTER-COLLECTION

Although the Avitan epistolary corpus is commonly called a 'collection', Avitus did not compile the assemblage of material that has come down to us.[6] There is no trace of any dedication. There are no self-conscious statements about his own prose (other than those in the prefaces to the poetry) and no modesty *topoi*.[7] There are few signs of the authorial *manus*, other than, perhaps, the inclusion side-by-side of certain (fairly trivial) types of

1 See Ruricius *Ep.* 2.26.3, *quem transcribendum sublimitati vestrae dedisse me dixeram, legendum recepi.*

2 *Ep.* 2.26.7, *ut ipse sis paterni interpres eloquii, qui universa quae ille conscripsit non tam de codicis membrana quam de cordis potes pagina proferre.*

3 Ruricius *Ep.* 2.26.3, *cuius lectio sicut mihi antiquum restaurat affectum, ita prae obscuritate dictorum non accendit ingenium.*

4 Greg. Tur. *DLH* 6.7. The *quasi* probably indicates Gregory's interpretation (nine books in both) rather than fact.

5 See Peiper's *apparatus fontium*, pp. 300–01 for clear cumulative evidence of imitation. Note, however, that Peiper's criteria for an imitation are often rather lax. Goelzer, p. 695, agrees: 'on pourrait effacer presque la moitié des passages cités'.

6 *Pace* Chevalier, p. xi, 'Malgré l'absence d'un témoignage direct, nous pouvons affirmer que Saint Avit avait pris soin lui-même de publier une édition de ses lettres.'

7 Avitus knew perfectly well how to frame such remarks. See *Ep.* 43, p. 73.2–3, *qualecumque est opusculum ipsum, nec ante editum, nec omnimodis emendatum ... publicate atque excusare dignamini.*

letters, e.g. the festal greetings to various bishops and laymen.[1] That both these sets of letters appeared together in the manuscript may suggest that they survived as dockets in Avitus' bottom drawer, whence they were pulled by the compiler(s) of the collection.[2] A few letters written by Avitus' correspondents are included in the collection.[3] The inclusion of simply silly[4] and bad-tempered[5] material likewise may not bespeak the considered choice of the bishop. The bishop disliked having his work circulated in unemended form.[6]

It has been suggested that the collection was used as a model book to provide patterns for certain types of letters, the closest analogy being the *Variae* of Cassiodorus. The inclusion of the letters written for Sigismund to the Byzantine Emperor might point in this direction[7] as might the quasi-chancery script of the papyrus codex: *notarii* formed part of later Roman bishops' entourage.[8] It is worth noting, however, that in the case of Cassiodorus the model letters often had the circumstantial details and names removed and *ille et ille* 'so-and-so' inserted instead. The collection was almost certainly assembled from the dead bishop's *Nachlaß*,[9] perhaps as a portrait or compilation of his oeuvre, but more probably out of that all-too-human urge not to throw out written material. There was no doubt the occasional Gallic Genizah for episcopal ephemera. It is thus impossible to speak of an 'audience' for Avitus' letter-collection.[10]

1 See *Epp.* 58–69 and 80–85.

2 See Chapter 2 above.

3 Epp. 13, 16, 21,42, 54, 68, 71 and 96.

4 E.g. the comic correspondence about fish with Maximus and Apollinaris. None of it, however, could be censured as *turpis* or *scurrilis*. Cf. *Statuta ecclesiae antiquae* can. 73 *clericum scurrilem et verbis turpibus iocularem ab officio retrahendum*.

5 E.g. some of the irritated letters to Viventiolus, such as *Epp.* 58 and 59, also *Ep.* 96. Would Avitus have included a letter that openly accuses him of cowardliness in face of an invasion? Similarly would Ennodius have wanted to parade his begging-letters and passive-aggressive complaints to Boethius and Maximus? Similar arguments are valid in the case of Ruricius whose 'collection' includes a rebuke from Caesarius of Arles, 'Dum nimium' (see Mathisen, *Ruricius*, pp. 192–93), and also a rather nasty letter with an attack on his colleague Volusianus' wife (*Ep.* 2.65).

6 See *Ep.* 43, cited above p. 63 n. 7.

7 Wood, 'Letters and Letter-Collections', p. 39.

8 Wood 'Letters and Letter-Collections', pp. 40–41. See *Ep.* 51 for the *notarius*.

9 Greg. Tur. *DLH* 10.19 mentions a *puer familiaris* in Egidius' episcopal household who kept shorthand (?) copies of his letters. Hence another possible source of outgoing correspondence.

10 It (or part of it) was indeed copied at least three times, but, unlike the poetry, it was not extensively read or used in the Middle Ages. The only exception is the Carolingian reception of the *CA*. See above p. 13.

SALIENT CHARACTERISTICS OF THE AVITAN COLLECTION

Miscellaneous Nature

The collection is heavily miscellaneous: it ranges from the personal to the official, hence both *epistulae negotiales* and *familiares*. Most of it is business correspondence, both political and ecclesiastical: chancery letters for Avitus' kings, Gundobad and, eventually, Sigismund, theological correspondence with them, and business correspondence with bishops, both suffragans and colleagues in other bishoprics. There is much of political importance in these letters, the best-known of the collection unquestionably being *Ep.* 46, Avitus' letter of congratulation to Clovis on his baptism.[1] In this respect the collection differs greatly from that of Ruricius.[2]

Notable Absences

Little Personal Material

There is extremely little private material in an openly personal voice. Avitus' letters to his brother, bishop Apollinaris of Valence, and to his cousin, Apollinaris, *Vir Illustris*, are the only exception. The tone of the festal letters to Maximus of Geneva (see below p. 276) also indicates that the latter had the status of a *familiaris*, not a mere clerical colleague.

Daily Life

Avitus provides few colourful images of everyday life in fifth/sixth-century Gaul. In this respect his letters may seem disappointing compared to those of Sidonius, whose details of meals, descriptions of villas (e.g. Sidonius, *Ep.* 2.2 in which he gives his friend Domitius a tour of his villa, including baths and dining-room) and dramatic accounts of events have far more to offer in that department.[3] The best Avitus provides here is *Ep.* 87, but its description of an episcopal ring he is commissioning and the kiln he also needs are as close to undecipherable as can be. He also fails to provide us any narrative accounts of notable political events, except for his imagined description of the baptism of Clovis. One contrasts the accounts of the misdeeds of

---

1 In contrast to those of Ruricius, see Hagendahl, *La Correspondance*, p. 7.

2 See Hagendahl, *La Correspondance*, p. 7 and Mathisen, *Ruricius*, pp. 3–4.

3 See Loyen, p. 43, for Sidonius' fine eye and ability to see and tell. More on the same topic on pp. 119–22.

Arvandus and of Seronatus in Sidonius *Epp*. 1.7 and 2.1, 5.13, and 7.7. Likewise there are no vivid descriptions of events such as episcopal elections. Contrast Sidonius, *Ep*. 7.5 and 7.9 with its transcription of his own *contio* in support of Simplicius. Instead one finds a genuine documentary item such as *Ep*. 75 with its vaguely worded disgruntlement about the role of the *plebs* in such elections.

Classical Reading

Here further disappointments are in store. In the letters one cannot go much further than Vergil,[1] Lucan[2] and the occasional unknown source.[3] Only in *Ep*. 51 to Viventiolus are Avitus' education, knowledge of metrics, and sensitivities all on parade. In comparison to the work of Sidonius, Avitus' letters contain surprisingly few allusions to classical authors. What few exist are seldom integrated in a literary way. One might contrast Ruricius, *Ep*. 2.4, where Ruricius compares the grief for his daughter-in-law that made it difficult for him to write a letter of consolation to Daedalus' grief in *Aen*. 6.32–33. There are no allusions to pagan mythology.[4] In this respect Avitus differs both from Sidonius and from Ennodius. The latter certainly stands out, even from Sidonius, as the rare ecclesiastical *homo urbanus* who wrote obscene epigrams as well as frankly pagan poetry.[5] Avitus was, however, well acquainted with his own kinsman, Sidonius' letters. In one notable instance one can emend his text because he wrote an homage to a literary showpiece of Sidonius'.[6] The *apparatus fontium* for the poems is far wider.[7] It is unclear why Avitus, who clearly was well read, limited his classical allusions so strictly in his letters. He might have felt chill winds of change in the generation after Sidonius. Episcopal (and other) culture in Gaul may have been subject to ascetic influences emanating from Lérins.[8] The *Statuta*

---

1 *Aen*. 11.283 cited in Ep. 5.

2 Lucan 1.1 is cited in *Ep*. 23.

3 Unidentified quotations: *Ep*. 26, p. 57, 15; *Ep*. 51, p. 80.12; *Ep*. 52, p. 81.5–6; *Ep*. 55, p. 84.31–32. The latter however seems to be a paraphrase of Ezek. 33.2–3.

4 In the verse one can find mythological material as *recusatio*, e.g. *SHG* 4.3–8 (Deucalion).

5 On some possible reasons for this see D. R. Shanzer, 'Literary Obscenity in the Later Roman West' (forthcoming).

6 See Sidonius *Ep*. 3.13 and Avitus *Ep*. 86. Also below p. 280.

7 See Peiper, pp. 302–08. Now also Arweiler, *Die Imitation*.

8 See R. Bartlett, 'Aristocracy and Asceticism: The Letters of Ennodius and the Gallic and Italian Churches', in Shanzer and Mathisen, eds, *Culture and Society in Late Antique Gaul*, pp. 201–16.

Ecclesiae Antiquae, for example, sought to prevent the bishop from reading secular works.[1] Later in the century, the classical reading and teaching of a subsequent bishop of Vienne, Desiderius, would elicit a papal reprimand.[2]

Books

There is less in the Avitus correspondence about books (even the politesses of their arrivals, loans and returns) than might be expected. Only in *Ep.* 43 is a 'book-bandit' (*praedo*) alluded to, and Emeterius is asked to pass on a copy of the *SHG* to Apollinaris, *v.i.* and in *Ep.* 51 Avitus mentions the incident directly to Apollinaris. One can contrast Ruricius (*Epp.* 1.6, 1.7, 1.8, 2.17 requesting the return of a copy of the *City of God*, 2.26 to Apollinaris about the works of Sidonius) and Sidonius, where books travel and are freely exchanged. In *Ep.* 5.15 Sidonius arranges for his bookseller to deliver a Heptateuch and a copy of the Prophets to Ruricius. In other Sidonian epistles appear allusions to other texts, e.g. *Ep.* 8.3 Philostratus' *Vita Apollonii*; 8.6.18 Varro's *Logistorici* and Eusebius' *Chronographia*; 9.9.6 a work of Faustus of Riez is copied on the fly; 9.11.6 Sidonius' own *Liber Epistularum*. Ennodius too wrote verse on book-loans (*Carm.* 2. 144 and 145). The paucity of such material in Avitus is almost certainly a function of the nature of the collection. There are few non-festal or non-pastoral letters to men of Avitus' own class and interests.

Gifts and Services[3]

Avitus does not apparently send valuable gifts such as the horses Ruricius sent to Sedatus (*Ep.* 2.35) and to Celsus (*Ep.* 1.14). Nor are there such comparatively curious items as the fir trees (*abietum plantae*) sent by Ruricius to Freda (*Ep.* 1.11)[4] or the columns apparently sent to Ruricius in exchange for *vehicula* (*Ep.* 2.64.3–4). But he does, like Ruricius, touch on the exchange of skilled craftsmen. Paulinus of Pella had emphasised the importance of speedy and handy workmen on a well-run estate.[5] But by the

---

1 Can. 5, *Ut episcopus gentilium libros non legat, haereticorum autem pro necessitate et tempore.*

2 Greg. Mag. *Ep.* 54, *PL* 77.1171 C.

3 For more on this interesting topic, see I. N. Wood, 'The Exchange of Gifts among the Late Antique Aristocracy', in M. Almagro-Gorbea, ed., *El Disco de Teodosio* (Madrid, 2000), pp. 301–14.

4 The letter looks like a pretext for an elaborate ekphrasis.

5 *Eucharisticon* 210–11, *et diversae artis cito iussa explere periti/artifices.*

early sixth century it is clear that even the wealthy needed to go far afield for services. Ruricius sent a *vitrarius* to Celsus (*Ep.* 1.12) and a painter and apprentice to Ceraunia (*Ep.* 2.15) to produce wall-paintings. Avitus asked his brother for a master-potter to build a brick-kiln (*Ep.* 87). He also sent and received gifts of fish.[1]

Women Correspondents

There are no letters to or from women in the Avitus collection.[2] In this he is not unlike Sidonius, whose collection contains only one letter addressed to a woman, namely *Ep.* 4.16 to his wife Papianilla. Pliny published four letters to Calpurnia (4.19, 6.4, 6.7, 7.5) plus five to other women (1.4, 2.4, 3.3, 7.14 and 8.11). Fronto wrote to Domitia Lucilla (*Ep. Graec.* 1 and 2). Symmachus wrote *Ep.* 9.108 to a Vestal Virgin, and there is a block of letters in Book 6 to 'Nicomachi filii', i.e. his daughter and son-in-law, *Ep.* 6.67 being expressly addressed to 'domina filia'. Jerome had numerous and distinguished female correspondents, but none of their letters appear in his collection.[3] Among Avitus' close contemporaries, Ruricius has two (*Epp.* 2.15; 2.50), but Ennodius' collection contains twenty-three letters to eleven different women[4] including seven to his sister Euprepia.[5] Given Avitus' affection and regard for his dead sister (*Epp.* 13 and 14) and his interest in the holy females of his own family, demonstrated by the *CCL*, we may reasonably assume that there was indeed correspondence between him and them. But it is quite possible that even had he collected and published his own letters, he would not have included items written to women family-members. In the dedicatory letter to the *CCL* he expresses concern about its private nature and the need to keep it only for family-members and for those

1 See below p. 250. Also D. R. Shanzer, 'Bishops, Letters, Fast, Food, and Feast in Later Roman Gaul', in Shanzer and Mathisen, eds, *Culture and Society in Late Antique Gaul*, pp. 217–36.

2 Letters written by women are rare at all times. Some may be of questionable authenticity, e.g. the letters allegedly written by Cornelia, the mother of the Gracchi that were accepted as authentic by Cicero and Quintilian. See P. Cugusi, *Epistolographi Latini Minores* v.1.1 (Turin, 1970), pp. 110–13.

3 E.g. Asella, Laeta, Demetrias, Eustochium, Fabiola, Furia, Marcella, Paula and Principia.

4 To Speciosa, *Ep.* 2.3; to Helisea, *Ep.* 5.4; to Dominica, *Ep.* 6.18; to Archotamia, *Ep.* 6.24; 7.14; to Domnina, *Ep.* 6.35; to Firmina, *Ep.* 6.38; to Barbara, *Epp.* 8.16 and 8.27; to Stephania, *Ep.* 8.17, 9.15, and 9.18; to Camella, *Ep.* 9.9; to Apodemia, *Ep.* 9.17; and to Agnella, *Ep.* 9.25.

5 To Euprepia, *Epp.* 2.15, 3.15, 3.28, 5.7, 6.3, 6.26, 7.8 and (perhaps) *Ep.* 4.4: *sorori* (*exemplar epistulae quam ipse dictavit*).

with comparable (?ascetic) religious commitments.[1] We may also surmise
that he wrote to Gundobad's wife, the pious Caretene and to her daughter,
the princess, for whose death he wrote a consolatory letter (*Ep*. 5).

Moralising

There are no examples of extensive Christian moralising, followed by one
sentence that contains the nub of the letter. Ruricius *Ep*. 2.17 is a good
example of that construction: 35 lines of fluff; 2 lines of request for a copy of
the *De Civitate Dei*; 8 lines of coda. The collection has very little preaching
directed to a one-person audience, except for *Ep*. 37 to Aurelianus. Those
letters that concern moral matters are nearly all pastoral, not personal. In this
respect the collection differs from that of Ennodius also.

Letters of Recommendation

Letters that introduce or recommend an acquaintance of the writer to the
addressee are extremely common in other letter-collections, e.g. Symmachus'.
Avitus' collection contains remarkably few of this type, only *Ep*. 11 to
Caesarius of Arles and *Ep*. 38 to Helpidius. Both, interestingly enough, are
referrals of patients. *Ep*. 43, however, acknowledges receipt of a letter of
recommendation. The metropolitan of Vienne would have mediated many
contacts both within Gaul and abroad. There must have been many more
ephemeral letters of this sort that failed to survive the dispersal of Avitus'
effects after his death.

Some Unexpected Features

Humour and Food

Episcopal good humour is on display in the various thank-yous to
Apollinaris and Maximus of Geneva, and in the Leonianus correspondence.
These are unusual enough to merit detailed discussion, for much of it centres
around food and fish in particular. This topic is not quite so prominent in
other preserved Later Roman private correspondence (though Symmachus
did touch upon fish in his letter to Ausonius about the *Mosella* and there are

---

1 P.275.2–4: *illis tantummodo legendum dare, quos revera nobis aut vinculum
propinquitatis aut propositum religionis adnectit.*

some parallels in Sidonius).[1] Ruricius' correspondence attests gifts of vegetables (*Ep.* 2.42), birds and a boar's loin (*tergus aprunum* in *Ep.* 2.43), *legumina marina* (*Ep.* 2.44), unspecified fishy *deliciae* from the river Dordogne (*spolia Doroniae* in *Ep.* 2.45), fish (*Ep.* 53) and pears (*Ep.* 2.60). The Avitan group includes *Epp.* 71, 72, 74, 83 and 86. It is fortunate that these ephemera have been preserved, for had they been omitted from the collection, one would have had little sense of Avitus' more intimate personality, classical reading and sense of humour.

Fictitious Letters sub persona alicuius

Such exercises can take many different forms. Petrarch wrote to Cicero (*Epp. Ad Fam.* 24.3 and 4). Jerome's collection contains at least one item apparently written to a dead correspondent and a letter that is a pure rhetorical exercise.[2] There are also literary epistles such as the *Heroides* of Ovid or the *Epistula Didonis ad Aeneam*[3] that were never intended to deceive and presuppose a broad literary audience. Sidonius mentions letters, perhaps works in a similar vein, of Iulius Titianus *sub nominibus illustrium feminarum*.[4] Some rhetorical exercises posing as letters of famous men eventually found their way by mistake into authentic collections.[5] Avitus wrote at least one letter in someone else's name – the comic epistle (*Ep.* 86) purporting to have been written by 'Leonianus' to 'Sapaudus', but rightly described in both L and S as *dictata ab Avito*.[6] It forms part of the food sequence mentioned above.

AVITUS' STYLE

There is a splendid 767-page study of Avitus' style by Henri Goelzer, remarkable both for the common features it notes and for those that are

---

1 See Shanzer, 'Bishops, Letters'.

2 *Ep.* 78 seems to have a dead addressee. So may *Ep.* 1: see Schwind, 'Hieronymus' Epistula ad Innocentium', pp. 171–86. Ep. 117 is an exercise, *ficta materia*. See Jerome, *Contra Vigilantium* 3.

3 G. Solimano, *Epistula Didonis ad Aeneam* (Genoa, 1988).

4 Sidonius, *Ep.* 1.1.2.

5 Dziatzko, *PWRE* 'Brief', p. 841.

6 Sirmond never saw L, so his words 'Epistola ab Avito Viennensi episcopo dictata, sub nomine Leoniani archidiaconi ad virum spectabilem Sapaudum' cannot be an invention or a guess. The information that the letter was composed by Avitus is archetypal.

prominent by their rarity or absence.[1] But it hardly makes pleasurable reading for the non-specialist: it is primarily concerned with the morphological and syntactic description ('pathology' might be a better word) of Avitus' poetic and prose style.[2] Goelzer is a philologist writing for philologists. One of the greatest difficulties involved in using his work is that he seldom translates any words or passages discussed. As one rapidly discovers, some attempt to translate Avitus is crucial to understanding him. Goelzer does not really provide an informal narrative description of the qualities of Avitus' style.[3] He characterises it instead as excessively 'pretentious', 'crafted', 'stilted', 'twisted' ('prétentieux',[4] 'travaillée', 'guindée', 'entortillée').[5] Most discussion takes the form of detailed lists of specified features rather than of accessible analyses of them.

The following is a multinational chorus of modern press-releases on Avitus' prose: 'Every instant one is made aware of how declamation had ruined his style, and, unfortunately, the reading he must have done failed to inspire more healthy ideas.'[6] 'Added to this was the patchy style of the author which he (i.e. Sirmond) failed to take into account sufficiently: in one place bumpy, convoluted, and knotty; in another flowing like a smooth river; yet soon excessively vague, hindering the reader's comprehension. Add to this those stains and wounds that no book of any somewhat more ancient author completely lacks. All of this brings it about that absolutely no sentence can be deciphered by the editor without a serious struggle.'[7] 'But neither Pliny nor Cicero inspired this strange prose, which is further disfigured by the deplorable state of its transmission. There are perhaps more bizarre features in Avitus' letters than in what remains of his

---

1 E.g. examples of Avitan *brevitas*, for which see Goelzer, p. 715.

2 I.e. items such as the syntax of agreement, regimen, coordination and subordination; the parts of speech; and morphology.

3 Pp. 692–726 go part of the way.

4 Goelzer, p. 10: 'On sent à chaque instant combien l'exercice de la déclamation avait gâté son style et malheureusement les lectures qu'il avait dû faire ne lui ont pas inspiré des idées plus saines.'

5 Goelzer, p. 11.

6 Goelzer, p. 5.

7 Peiper, p. xii: *Accedebat, quem non satis perspectum habebat, sermo auctoris inaequalis, qui passim salebrosus intricatus nodosus, alibi placido flumine decurreret, mox diffusus nimis intellectum impediret; denique labes atque vulnera illa, quibus nullus paulo antiquioris auctoris liber prorsus caret. Unde factum est, ut nulla omnino sententia sine gravi luctamine ab editore explicaretur.*

homilies.'[1] 'One is astonished to see Latin prose degenerate into this sort of language. To the strained preciousness that characterises periods of literary decadence is joined an impoverishment of idiom; to the use of abstract terms and periphrases is joined subtlety of ideas and clattering antitheses.'[2] 'Only his poetry is estimable. His prose-works, as the following study will show, are only interesting in that they show how far bad taste can go.'[3] 'From time to time he even tries to free himself from barbarism and to rise aloft to urbanity and elegance. But almost invariably he mourns the failure of his attempts that are overwhelmed by his common rusticity. I find him not dissimilar to the man who feels that he has fallen into a muddy swamp and tries to extract his feet from the slime: while he raises one foot up, he immerses the other all the more profoundly, and is overwhelmed on all sides by bushes and reeds. If things turn out well for him and he manages to get out of the swamp, he makes it out with difficulty, muddied all over and coated throughout with slime.'[4] In short, 'Avitus writes in a tortuous and turgid way that approaches the incomprehensible.'[5]

The critical consensus is far from positive. Avitus' style has been destroyed because of his taste for declamatory rhetoric. His text is corrupt and his writing must be deciphered, not read. The language of the letters has become more bizarre than that of the homilies, sporting an impoverished vocabulary and a hyperabundance of abstract language and periphrases,

1 A. Rilliet, *Conjectures historiques sur les homélies préchées par Avitus, évêque de Vienne dans le diocèse de Genève* (Geneva, 1866), p. 38: 'Mais ni Pline, ni Cicéron n'ont inspiré cette prose étrange, que l'état déplorable des textes contribue encore à défigurer; et dont les lettres de saint Avit présentent peut-être plus de traits bizarres que ce qui nous reste de ces homélies.'

2 Rilliet, p. 5: 'On s'étonne de voir la prose latine devenue un tel langage. A la recherche prétentieuse, qui charactérise les époques de décadence littéraire se joint l'appauvrissement de l'idiome; à l'emploi des termes abstraits et des périphrases, la subtilité des idées et le cliquetis des antithèses.'

3 Goelzer, p. 10: 'Seuls ses poèmes ont de réelles qualités. Ses oeuvres en prose, comme le démontrera l'étude qui va suivre, ne sont intéressantes qu'en se qu'elles montrent jusqu'où peut aller le mauvais goût.'

4 V. Cucheval, *De Sancti Aviti Viennae Episcopi Operibus Commentarium* (Paris, 1863), p. 14: *Etiam interdum contendit, ut e barbarie sese expediat et ad urbanitatem et elegantiam sese evehat, at saepissime irritos cecidisse conatus suos luget, communi rusticitate obrutos. Non absimilem eum misero cuidam esse dicas qui in paludes lutosas 'sensit delapsus' et e caeno plantas evellere nititur; at dum alteram sublevat, alteram altius immergit, virgultisque et arundinibus undique premitur. Cui si res ita bene feliciterque evenit, ut paludem egrediatur, limosus totus et luto circumstante horridus, aegre excedit.*

5 Schanz-Hosius, p. 388: 'Avitus schreibt geschraubt und schwülstig bis zur Unverständlichkeit ...'

joined to tinny antitheses. His poetry has virtues, the prose demonstrates extreme poor taste. He is a man prone to barbarism,[1] attempting unsuccessfully to wade through a marsh. His writing is contorted and oppressively stifling to the point of incomprehensibility.

In the following section we aim to give a somewhat fuller and more accessible description of Avitus' style. 'Style' is not limited to lexical, morphological or syntactic features, nor just to broader rhetorical features and sentence-structure; our treatment will also survey other elements of the bishop of Vienne's writing that contribute both to its difficulty and to its more positive features. We'll begin with the former.

Lexical and Rhetorical Features

Avitus' fine writing does not consist of vivid parallelisms, colourful details, all the enticements of the literary *locus amoenus* (cf. Ruricius *Ep.* 3 with its *topoi*, classical plumage and repeated word-plays, or Ruricius *Ep.* 5 for an overloaded and pretentious description of spring). Occasionally a classical allusion is used pointedly[2] for emotive effect.[3] Avitus fails to exploit some of the opportunities he had, e.g. to wax lyrical about Easter in *Ep.* 76 to Sigismund. All of this is what he is not.

One can approach Avitus through his Gallic forbear, Sidonius. For this purpose one might use Loyen's convenient stylistic shopping-basket for the would-be précieux: recherché and poetic vocabulary, archaism, Greek words, neologisms[4] and abstractions. Asianist authorial tics should include *copia verborum* (diverse vocabulary), *tumor* (using three words when one will do), and puns and word-plays. 'Grandiloquence and coquetry', we are told, are hallmarks and twin poles of Asianism.[5] All of the above are features of Sidonius' style.

Although Avitus clearly admired and quoted his elder relative's writings, his own style is different.[6] Herewith a swift survey of some of its lexical features. Avitus is not, on the whole, a coiner of neologisms or *sectator* of

---

1 This is simply incorrect. Aside from some influence from VL and the developing vernacular in the deployment of pronouns, i.e. *eius* and *suus*, Avitus is shows no 'barbarism' or *rusticitas* whatsoever. For sound criticism of such views, see Goelzer, p. 729 n.1.

2 *Aen.* 2.560 in *Ep.* 51.

3 Cf. Ruricius, *Ep.* 2.4.2 which quotes *Aen.* 6.32–33.

4 E.g. adverbial monstrosities, such as *cocleatim.*

5 Loyen, p. 152

6 For detailed information see Goelzer.

archaic,[1] recherché or poetic[2] vocabulary. *Copia*, however, shows up in the form of the persistent redundancy that makes him difficult to translate into lucid and economical English: e.g. *CE* 1, p. 15.10, *Inter regias ordinationes gloriosissimi principatus vestri*, 'the [many] matters of royal business in/of your glorious princedom'; *Ep*.10, p. 44.21, *emanans e largiendi thesauro insignis fontis ubertas*, 'the abundance of an outstanding fountain that emanates from the treasure of your largesse'; *Ep*. 51, p. 79.24, *obstaculi praepediente obice*, 'with the impediment of an obstacle getting in the way'. His most distinctive traits are rhetorical ones: for example, the antithesis characterising an ageing adulterer, *Ep*. 18, p. 49.28, *aevo friget, adulterio calet*, 'shivering with age, hot in adultery'. Avitus can ironise about his declining intellectual faculties in antithetical gerunds, rhyming feminine abstracts and alliterative finite verb forms: *Ep*. 57, p. 85.24, *Si sciendi in me facultas minuitur, discendi cupiditas non mutatur.*[3] Examples are innumerable.

He relishes puns, both in humorous and in serious contexts. For the latter, see the pun on *pedes* and *scandere* in *Ep*. 95, p. 102.18, *plus quam poeticis pedibus innitentes montium scandendorum magis moveat cura*, and on p. 202.12 *salubrius totius artis pede quam veritatis vestigio claudicatur*. He will, likewise, make a word-play (*figura etymologica*) on Vincomalus' name in a pastoral letter: *Ep*.18, p. 49.26, *utinam vincat malum*. The puns on *marinis copiis* and *duo paria solearum* in *Ep*. 72, p. 90.7 and 16 are, on the other hand, playful.

The letters are also full of far less loaded (and hence more dispensable) word-plays that are little more than 'points' or 'fillips': word-plays that emphasise a point, i.e. paronomasia. We see examples in *Ep*. 7, p. 39.12, **ob**lata ... **ab**lata; *Ep*. 18, p. 49.22, *non minus* **honorare** *quam* **onerare**; *Ep*. 10, p. 44.17, **pretiosius** *factum est* **pretium**; *Ep*. 35, p. 65.26, *dignitas* vs. *dignatio*; *Ep*. 76, p. 95.25, **conclu**sus **exclud**it; *Ep*. 81, p. 94, 8-9, *vota ... votiva*. Some, as Goelzer, points out, are in questionable taste, e.g. (of the Annunciation): *CE* 1, p. 17.35, *Hic unius mulieris* **salutatione** *omnem mundum* **salute** *complevit*. But Avitus may have thought that paronomasia in some sense profound, like Gregory the Great's 'non Angli, sed angeli', or the famous paradox 'Eva' fit 'Ave!'

Avitus was fond of metaphors. One thinks of short expressions such as *Ep*. 16, p. 48.12, *ordinationis vestrae ventilabra*, 'the winnowing-fan of

---

1 Goelzer, p. 702.

2 Goelzer, p. 705. Note, however, that the poeticisms were nearly always found earlier in another late Latin prose author.

3 'Even if my intellectual abilities are shrinking, my eagerness to learn is unchanged.'

Your Ordination'; *Ep.* 54, p. 83.10, *amputato aequore prolixitatis,* 'after the sea of prolixity has been cut off'; *Ep.* 78, p. 93.15-16, *desiderii prosiliente compendio,* 'a short-cut to what is desired leaping forth'. There are also far more extended efforts such as *Ep.* 64, p. 88.18, *Festivitatem nostram pleno vos desiderio sitientem, etiamsi non satiastis praesentia, refecistis expensa,* 'Even if you have not sated by your presence our feast that thirsts for you with full desire, you have restored it through your outlay', or *Hom. Rog.* p. 108.5, the *flumen irriguum* of Rogations.

Prose Rhythm

Writers of classical Latin artistic prose frequently used metrical *clausulae* to round off the endings of their cola and sentences. In the Later Roman and medieval period, distinctions in quantity, particularly blind quantities, began to be lost, and authors gradually switched from metrical prose-rhythm based on quantity to an accentual system based on ictus. The latter is known as the cursus. In its simplest form it consists of four basic types of accentual patterns, employed at significant breaks in the sentence: the planus (óooóo derived from the cretic spondee), the tardus (óooóoo derived from the dicretic), the velox (óooooóo derives from the cretic ditrochee), and the trispondaicus (óooooóo derived from the paeon spondee [*esse videatur*]).[1] Avitus consistently employs the cursus throughout his letters. In some cases he tolerated awkward hyperbaton in order to achieve it.[2] In many places one can use it as a criterion to judge between readings or to identify lacunae or corruptions.[3] Reading the prose out loud so that the cursus can be heard often helps in translating: one can use it to tell whether a word should be construed regressively (with what went before) or progressively (with what comes afterwards). The cursus punctuates and modulates the lengthy but often nicely balanced structures in Avitus' prose. It is a positive feature of his style that calls for attention.

As we have seen, however, the critical consensus is negative. After discussing some of the more successful effects he sought and achieved, it is time to turn to the stylistic features that have aroused his readers' impatience or ire. The first point to be considered will be the apparent disparity between the quality of Avitus' verse and his prose.

1 S. Oberhelman, 'The Cursus in Late Imperial Prose: a Reconsideration of Methodology', *CP* 83 (1988), pp. 136–49.

2 Goelzer, p. 725, gives some examples where the natural word-order is violated in order to achieve *cursus.*

3 Such criteria can be seen put to work in *Epp.* 46 and 87, for example.

Verse vs. Prose

That the verse should be easier to understand than the prose is hardly
surprising.[1] Most of Avitus' letters are official and routine business
correspondence, not items written for pleasure. In his chancery documents
he sought the formality and dignity befitting the official correspondence of a
Burgundian monarch.[2] These works are no more pompous or difficult than
corresponding letters of Cassiodorus. Some of them (in particular *Ep.* 93)
seem to be written in a somewhat less convoluted style, employing a more
natural word-order, no doubt with oral delivery before non-native speakers
of Latin in mind. In similar places in the *CE*, Avitus may have recycled
material from sermons intended for oral delivery, and eschewed his usual
intricate and lapidary interlace.[3]

That his verse should be judged *better* than his prose is an observation
familiar from critical reactions to other later Latin writers, e.g. Ennodius[4]
and Caelius Sedulius.[5] In the case of the latter's *opus geminatum*, G.
Boissier made a precise and illuminating comparison between the same
author's prose and poetry on identical topics.[6] The same could be done to
similar effect with an author such as Aldhelm.

Verse

Then, as now, Latin verse, particularly the dactylic hexameter and elegiac
distich, was written by a process involving the combination and recom-
bination of two- to three-word metrical units, often drawn from earlier
writers, e.g. Vergil, a process that reached its *reductio ad absurdum* in the
Vergilian *Centone*s. But it ensured recognition, familiarity and a certain
degree of quality-control over the units: reused units had been successfully

1 *Pace* Goelzer, p. 693: 'En vain peut-on dire que dans certains de ces poèmes Avitus a
échappé aux défauts qui nos choquent dans sa prose.'

2 *Epp.* 29, 46A, 47, 78, 93 and 94.

3 E.g. *CE* 2, p. 25, with its questions and exclamations.

4 A. Dubois, *La Latinité d'Ennodius. contribution à l'étude du latin littéraire à la fin de
l'empire romain d'occident* (Paris, 1903), p. 13.

5 Alan Cameron, *Claudian: Poetry and Propaganda at the Court of Honorius* (Oxford,
1970), p. 318, mentions the greater difficulty involved in writing prose to explain the apparent
differences in achievement of Claudian and Ammianus. There were, however, exceptional
Greek-speakers such as Evagrius of Antioch who could write excellent idiomatic and literary
Latin.

6 G. Boissier, 'Le *Carmen paschale* et *l'Opus paschale* de Sedulius', *Revue de Philologie*
n.s. 6 (1882), pp. 28–36.

employed by a previous writer, after all.[1] In the hands of a good poet the process could yield superb results, where the metrical *spolia* served a genuine poetic function and resonated with overtones from their original context.[2] Even in the case of a mediocre poet the very derivative nature of the poetic production served to render the language of poetry less permeable to change and to authorial weaknesses and idiosyncrasies. Avitus would have studied verse-composition in the usual fashion. But, to his credit, he was a more than competent *artifex* able to 'do a grove', *ponere lucum*,[3] to write an attractive, learned, but derivative digression,[4] to paint a fine psychological moment (*SHG* 2.204–19). His poetry has a serious doctrinal and exegetic dimension, yet only in it do his visual sensuality and pleasure in the objects of the senses come through.[5]

Prose

Prose *per se* (which must here be distinguished from literary prose) was the medium of everyday speech, and, as such, was far more susceptible to various types of change. Boissier[6] rightly detailed the way prose vocabulary is more likely to undergo semantic change (e.g. usages so weakened that the word seems to end up having no precise meaning whatsoever),[7] syntactic change[8] and intrusions from the spoken language.[9] He rightly emphasises the increase in abstraction in prose and the quest for periphrasis.[10] All of these observations prove helpful when describing Avitus' prose styles. Peiper himself provided an index of items in Avitus' Latinity that are symptomatic of the language of a later (and implicitly inferior!) period.[11]

The very fact that Avitus' letters have not been translated till now shows how difficult they are. Isolated letters, yes,[12] but the whole *corpus*, important

---

1 Goelzer, p. 694, calls it 'travail de marqueterie'.

2 See Goelzer, p. 697 for such imitations.

3 Persius 1.70; *SHG* 1.193–257.

4 *SHG* 1.258–98.

5 See now Arweiler, *Die Imitation antiker und spät-antiker Literatur* and Wood, 'Avitus of Vienne, the Augustinian Poet'.

6 Boissier, p 31.

7 Boissier, p 33.

8 Boissier, p 31.

9 Boissier, p 32.

10 Boissier, p 33.

11 Peiper, pp. 324–53.

12 Where there are existing translations, we have noted the fact.

as it is for Later Roman history and for the history of the second Burgundian kingdom in particular, no. It is no exaggeration to agree with Peiper that one does not read Avitus' letters; one deciphers them.[1] With this in mind, we will turn to some of the reasons (not entirely Avitus' fault) that his prose is difficult for modern readers. We will end with a sample analysis of a typically difficult Avitan sentence in order to show how ambiguity, convolution and pretentiousness (with some help from textual corruption) all contrive to make Avitus difficult to read and interpret.

Allusiveness

Letters can be either literary productions (epistles), or documents (letters), or both simultaneously. Those that are one-audience documents, i.e. 'real letters'[2] are often difficult by their very nature. One encounters them and their principals *in mediis rebus*. They are not heard, but *over*heard. Not a legal or historical narrative that aims to lay out facts for outsiders, Avitus' collection, consisting largely, as it does, of 'real letters', is particularly difficult to penetrate. One may fail to figure out what is being discussed. In writing a commentary one must devote special care to reconstructing the putative scenario behind a letter or to reconstructing the lost letter that elicited a given response (e.g. the difficulties with *Ep.* 19).

Ambiguities

Innumerable pitfalls await the unwary reader. When a 'brother' is mentioned, is it Avitus' blood-brother, the bishop of Valence, or merely a brother-in-the-Christ, or some anonymous fellow bishop?[3] And what of Avitus' 'children'? The semisomnolent reader of *Ep.* 55 might well think that Avitus had begotten some children and lost one.[4] But if he looked at *Ep.* 52, p. 81.13, he would clearly see that Avitus had no children and that the *filii*

---

1 Their own editor knew this very well. See Peiper, above p. 71.

2 I.e. letters that were not written with an eye for publication or doctored prior to publication.

3 The problem is illustrated by *Ep.* 19. Sirmond thought Avitus referred to his own blood-brother, Apollinaris of Valence.

4 The mistake is made at great length by Cucheval, *De Sancti Aviti*, pp. 4–5, who thought him married but with an unknown wife. He read the borrowed rhetorical *dissuasio* of *CCL* 163–96 as the words of a man who had married, but lived to repent his deed. Chevalier, p. iii, also believes in a marriage.

referred to in *Ep.* 55 are *spiritual* offspring. The rapist is the one who has perished: he has died a *spiritual* death.

Intentional Vagueness

Even though many letter-writers are used as historical sources for their times, and some even explicitly discussed writing history themselves, the risks were great.[1] Avitus lived in Interesting Times and needed to exercise caution with what he committed to papyrus. In a later period there would be the case of bishop Aegidius of Rheims and his treasonable letters about Brunichildis.[2] Avitus had to be vague when alluding to political circumstances in the Burgundian and Visigothic kingdoms. Throughout his letters appear maddeningly and deliberately vague allusions to circumambient troubles, in some cases wars and invasions,[3] in others vaguer political difficulties.[4] Avitus' *Ep.* 37 says, 'Write, if it is permitted': p. 67.4 *si licet scribe. Ep.* 29 to Pope Symmachus hints at what may have been constraints imposed on the pontiff by the Laurentian schism: 'as often as the chance arises or your freedom permits, please shower us with letters'.[5] There were clear signs of caution in Sidonius' correspondence too.[6] See, for example, *Ep.* 6.11.2 (the case of the Jew): 'He himself more appropriately will make clear to you in person how his troubles have unfolded, for it is very unwise to extend the terseness fit for a letter with various conversational details.'[7] Another allusion to a verbal message appears in *Ep.* 4.12.4.[8] Sidonius, *Ep.*

1 See Zelzer, 'Der Brief', pp. 548–49 on this topic. She suggests that dispersing historical material in a letter-collection enabled the wary author to provide a portrait of his age without running the risk of censure that a history would have entailed.

2 Greg. Tur. *DLH* 10.19: *post haec epistulae prolatae sunt in quibus multa de inproperiis Brunichildis tenebantur*, 'After this letters were brought forth in which there was much reproach of Brunichildis.'

3 E.g. *Ep.* 95, p. 102.22: *incursibus formidandis.*

4 E.g. *Ep.* 51, p. 79.33: *omnia tuta esse*; also *Ep.* 37.

5 *Ep.* 29, p. 59.25–26: *Litteris nos, in quantum possibilitas patitur aut libertas … frequentate.*

6 But passages like *Ep.* 6.10.1, *depraedationis Gothicae turbinem vitans*, are far more explicit than Avitus ever could be. Likewise his free use of the word *barbarus* in, for example, *Epp.* 3.5.2 and 3.7.3. Ruricius was likewise cautious in *Ep.* 2.65 with its possible allusions to the Franks.

7 *Quae sit vero negotii sui series, ipse rectius praesentanea coram narratione patefaciet. nam prudentiae satis obviat epistulari formulae debitam concinnitatem plurifario sermone porrigere.*

8 For examples from Ruricius see Hagendahl, *La Correspondance*, p. 10 n. 1. There do not, however, seem to be issues of security in these cases.

9.3 to Faustus, describes the searching of couriers,[1] and *Ep*. 9.5 reveals more
of the tensions between the Visigoths and Romans. There are likewise
explicit allusions to bad times and difficulty of travel in Ruricius *Ep*. 2.41.4
to Apollinaris, 'tumults and dire straits'[2] and in Ruricius *Ep*. 64.4, 'fear of
the enemy'.[3] The ever-present danger that treasonable correspondence
might be discovered permits occasional arguments *ex silentio*, such as the
ones *in re Ep*. 46, namely that because the letter is openly written to the King
of the Franks and concerns the possibility of an official visit to Frankish
territory, it must have been written at a time when the Franks and the
Burgundians were allies, or at least on friendly terms.

Formality

Honorifics

Honorifics may be defined as two-element expressions consisting of an
(often abstract) noun and an adjective[4] that is functionally equivalent to a
pronoun, e.g. 'I', 'me', 'you', 'he', 'him', 'her'. Like all Later Latin epistolo-
graphers Avitus used them when he addressed his correspondents, however
intimate. He does not, however, in his extant letters use the sort of elaborate
salutations that Ruricius does,[5] and never employs the customary *vale* or
valete at all. But the letters are peppered with abstract nouns used as titles,
e.g. 'Your Sublimity', or 'Your Keen-sightedness'. These have not been
translated with the more idiomatic-sounding 'you' (or whatever other pronoun
could be substituted) but generally retained to give a more accurate
impression of the formality of the text. There is, furthermore, some evidence
that a system is involved. Some honorifics were used with some sorts of
addresses, e.g. laymen vs. ecclesiastics, acquaintances vs. intimates, differing
ranks both of ecclesiastical and lay officials.[6]

---

1 The problem continued. Cf. Greg. Tur. *DLH* 7.30 for the searching of the abbot of Cahors
and the discovery of hidden treasonable letters.

2 *Ut, tumultibus temporis huius vel necessitatibus aut deletis in perpetuum aut parumper
oppressis, citius fructus faciat de nostra capere praesentia.*

3 *Quod scribis te metu hostium hebetum factum.*

4 Usually a possessive adjective.

5 A. Engelbrecht, 'Titel und Titulaturen in den Briefen des Ruricius und seiner Genossen',
Patristiche Analecten (1892), pp. 48–83.

6 See Appendix 1, below p. 391 on the honorifics.

Pluralis Maiestatis ('formal plural')

Avitus regularly employs the *pluralis maiestatis* and the *vos* and *vester* forms. Throughout the letters one finds both some oscillation between *vos* and *tu*[1] and sudden sources of confusion where a plural honorific must refer to a singular addressee.[2]

Periodicity

In classical Latin well-crafted periods aided comprehension and were used extensively both in history (Caesar, Livy and Tacitus) and in oratory (Cicero). Classical periods aimed to deliver circumstantial information to the reader in the right chronological and logical order: either concision or fine abundance, and anticipation followed by closure were the proper goals in that age of this elegant construction. In Later Roman Latin, however, many writers lost a sense both of the appropriate use and of the purpose of periods. Gildas is a notable abuser of the construction.[3] Avitus too offended in this regard, though not invariably. Many of his festal letters consist of one or two fully[4] or partially[5] periodic sentences. These are readily comprehensible, as are most of his elegant efforts in his official writings.

But the private epistles are another matter. There one frequently finds a long and would-be periodic sentence that can barely be understood, let alone readily translated. The average human brain can only hold so many grammatical suspensions (causal, temporal, conditional, concessive, correlative or coordinate) embedded in its memory bank without becoming confused. Avitus' worst sentences resemble onions with layers and layers of material that the reader is required to keep in a holding pattern. All too frequently one loses track of the beginning (and indeed the purpose) of the thought. Often there is an insufficiency of helpful adverbs to pinpoint the nature of the circumstantial relationship.

One can illustrate the problem effectively from *Ep.* 36 with what Burckhardt called 'dieses Muster von einem verschlungenem Avitus-Satz'.[6]

---

1 *Ep.* 50, p. 80.22: *sinceritate vestra* juxtaposed with *tuo iudicio*. Here *sinceritas* has honorific force and requires *vestra*.

2 See *Ep.* 44, p. 73.27: *pii domni*; *Ep.* 50, p. 78.30: *mutastis, viri fortes*; *Ep.* 92, p. 99.27: *piissimi domni*.

3 See *De Excidio* 17.2 and 18.1–2 for an example.

4 *Epp.* 68 and 69.

5 *Epp.* 58, 64, and 85.

6 Burckhardt, p. 33 n. 1.

He wisely fought shy of translating it. Here is the text of the problematic sentence and the one before it:

> Avitus, *Ep*. 36, p. 66. 13–22 Nam ecce mihi testis deus est, quanto lumine praefatus carissimus noster in ipsa contenebrati recessus nocturnali habitatione respersit, cum dulcissimi pignoris nostri reditus, ante quem nescieram, nuntiato, resolidatam Christo propitio familiam meam ab eo quem misissem, inventam esse firmavit. Quocirca nec vos iam de nobis aliquid semiplenum putetis: quorum contubernio divinitate propitia etiam oculi mei per praesentiam paginae satis facientes adcrescunt, tum videlicet sinceritate perfecta hilaris diei gratiam recepturi, si me rescribere hactenus vestra dulcedo sic ignoscens quamlibet infirmum atque anxium ad votivam tamen frequentiam litterarum in dei nomine Arcadio iam dictante solis subscriptionibus occupanda compellat.

The sentences are obscure for several different reasons.

1. Syntax: The first sentence is a full period, containing an indirect question with an indicative verb, a mannered *cum-inversum* main clause, and an indirect statement. The second sentence starts with an introductory relative, contains a main clause with a jussive subjunctive, a relative clause (whose antecedent is not instantly transparent), a participial clause (*recepturi*), and a conditional clause with the subjunctive broken by an ablative absolute. The subject of the conditional is, exceptionally, modified by a gerundive in the nominative.

2. Periodicity.

3. Punctuation. Sirmond placed a full stop after *adcrescunt*. Peiper chose not to, because he was aware that to do so would create a dangling participle, *recepturi*. In our English translation we have chosen to break the unit up into several separate sentences.

4. An obvious textual error: *reditus* for *reditu*.

5. Eccentric word-order, e.g. *ante quem nescieram* . Should one take *quem ante nescieram* (a *lectio facilior*) with S? Persistent hyperbaton: **ipsa** contenebrati recessus nocturnali **habitatione; reditu**, ante quem nescieram, **nuntiato; resolidatam** Christo propitio **familiam** meam ab eo quem misissem, **inventam** esse firmavit.

6. Lack of transparency: what does *oculi adcrescunt* mean? This may point to a textual problem. One might suggest the addition of *valetudine*.[1]

---

1 *Quorum contubernio divinitate propitia etiam oculi mei per praesentiam paginae satis facientes <**valetudine**> adcrescunt, tum videlicet sinceritate perfecta hilaris diei gratiam recepturi.*

What is the force of the *iam* in *iam putetis*? What is the force of the *sic* in *sic ignoscens*? What is the force of the *tamen* in *votivam tamen*? What is the force of *iam* in *iam dictante*?

7. The end of the last sentence is tortuous. What is to be construed with what? Does *hactenus* modify *ignoscens*? Or is it the ghost of a missing participial construction such as *cunctanti* or *haesitanti*?[1] And what is *ad frequentiam* to be construed with? With *rescribere* (as it must now be)? Or should one delete *rescribere* and construe *ad frequentiam* with *compellat*?[2]

We decided to make the minimum number of changes necessary to make sense of the text and have hence settled for correcting *reditus* and supplying *valetudine*, yielding the following text:

> Avitus, *Ep*. 36, p. 66.13-22. Nam ecce mihi testis deus est, quanto lumine praefatus carissimus noster in ipsa contenebrati recessus nocturnali habitatione respersit, cum dulcissimi pignoris nostri **reditu**, ante quem nescieram, nuntiato, resolidatam Christo propitio familiam meam ab eo quem misissem, inventam esse firmavit. Quocirca nec vos iam de nobis aliquid semiplenum putetis: quorum contubernio divinitate propitia etiam oculi mei per praesentiam paginae satis facientes **<valetudine>** adcrescunt, tum videlicet sinceritate perfecta hilaris diei gratiam recepturi, si me rescribere hactenus vestra dulcedo sic ignoscens quamlibet infirmum atque anxium ad votivam tamen frequentiam litterarum in dei nomine Arcadio iam dictante solis subscriptionibus occupanda compellat.

> For lo! God is my witness to how much light our dear friend[3] shed in the night-filled habitation of my beshadowed retreat! After he announced the return[4] of our beloved child[5] (which I had not known about before) he confirmed that our family, had been found reunited – Christ being propitious!

---

1 *Tum videlicet sinceritate perfecta hilaris diei gratiam recepturi, si me rescribere hactenus* **<cunctanti vel. haesitanti>** *vestra dulcedo sic ignoscens quamlibet infirmum atque anxium ad votivam tamen frequentiam litterarum in dei nomine Arcadio iam dictante solis subscriptionibus occupanda compellat.*

2 A suggestion of Michael Winterbottom's. *Si me [rescribere] hactenus vestra dulcedo sic ignoscens quamlibet infirmum atque anxium ad votivam tamen frequentiam litterarum in dei nomine Arcadio iam dictante solis subscriptionibus occupanda compellat.*

3 I.e. Domnulus.

4 Emending to *reditu*, as subject of the ablative absolute, *reditu ... nuntiato*. This seems preferable to construing *nuntiato* substantivally.

5 Arcadius, son of Apollinaris, see below. For *nostri*, see *Ep*. 52, p. 81.12: *spes reparandae prosapiae.*

– by the man I had sent. Therefore do not now entertain any incomplete[1] information about me. In your company, God willing, my eyes too, as they make amends through the present page, grow <in health>. But they will for certain only receive the grace of joyful day in perfect health, if Your Sweetness, who up till now have so forgiven[2] me [for not writing], now compels me to write back, however ill and anxious I am, in answer to[3] the frequent correspondence that I nonetheless[4] long for, while you need only worry about signing letters written now in God's name by Arcadius.[5]

The sentence is a coded communication, complex because Avitus is trying to convey his message without making anything too explicit to the individual to whom he dictated the letter. He takes refuge in his characteristic metaphors and nominalisations. The significant words are highlighted in boldface: *iam ... semiplenum* is euphemistic: 'do not entertain any incomplete thoughts about me *now*'. *Sic ignoscens* alludes to the fact that Apollinaris has not written (presumably because he could not). *Votivam ... frequentiam* makes it clear that Avitus would *very* much like to hear from Apollinaris. *Tamen* emphasises the fact that Avitus cannot read. *Iam* reminds Apollinaris that Avitus knows that he finally has his son back. The young man had evidently been in danger.

In short some of the difficulties in reading Avitus' Latin are the result of his style (unnecessary and often awkward periodicity, excessive abstraction), some the result of the modern reader's imperfect command of the language and slow intake rate, but others (obscurity, ambiguity) are purely situational. Each letter demands a fresh start and a fresh process of reading oneself in to what it is about. The process takes time, but is well worth the effort required

1 I.e. because my letter is in coded speech. The use of *semiplenum*, 'half-complete', is significant. The word occurs in Sidonius, *Ep.* 4.22.5, where Sidonius describes the perils of writing history: *praecipue gloriam nobis parvam ab historia petere fixum, quia per homines clericalis officii temerarie nostra iactanter aliena, praeterita infructuose praesentia semiplene, turpiter falsa periculose vera dicuntur.* Present circumstances can only be written about allusively, i.e. by leaving much unsaid. Apollinaris is not to be excessively worried because of the cryptic nature of Avitus' communication: it does not portend dire circumstances.

2 The use of *ignoscens*, 'forgiving', is analogous to the common Latin use of *parco*, meaning both 'to spare', and 'not to do x'. But it is also pregnant: Apollinaris has 'spared' Avitus' poor sight by not writing to him. In the economy of epistolographic cliché a letter demands a reply. He may also have 'spared' Avitus by not forcing him to put anything potentially dangerous in writing.

3 Construing *ad frequentiam* with *rescribere*.

4 Avitus' eyes are still weak, but he longs to hear from Apollinaris.

5 Arcadius was Apollinaris' son, who had been separated from Apollinaris, the child whose return was alluded to above. He appears in Greg. Tur. *DLH* 3.9.

to make such an important source for the history of Later Roman Gaul more accessible.

Sidonius' letter-collection has long been quarried for the social and literary history of Later Roman Gaul. Ruricius' has recently been translated and is now accessible to the general historical public.[1] Ennodius still awaits a sufficiently chalcenteric devotee. Avitus differs in many ways from the other three. His collection arguably casts more light on political dark places than any of the others, given that he is often the only source for the second Burgundian kingdom. While his literary interest may be less than Sidonius', he documents an important phase where one may begin to see the compartmentalised early medieval bishop rather than his more urbane late antique confrère. Avitus' poetry reveals the depth of his classical reading as well as his knowledge of Augustine. But the letters that have survived are not literary in a learned way. Instead they are largely the working pastoral and political correspondence of an important Gallic bishop, and are thus of inestimable historical value. Almost all may be unrevised, or indeed may be the 'file copies' rather than the full 'fair copies' of outgoing letters.[2] In his works, we see a man who confined his classical literary allusion to his verse, but wrote carefully and bombastically to impress his correspondents. He had a specially close and friendly relationship with both his barbarian kings. Tantalising glimpses are provided of his brother, sisters and cousin. An ability to laugh and joke can be seen in the letters to Maximus of Geneva. Snobbery and insecurity show in the letters to Viventiolus. But the greatest value of the collection will continue to lie (as long as one can interpret it accurately) in the political and theological correspondence. It is here that Avitus can change preconceptions about matters such as relations between minor barbarian kingdoms and Byzantium, the comparatively friendly conversation between Catholics and Arians in Burgundy, the educational level of barbarian kings, and the chronology of the baptism of Clovis.

---

1 See Mathisen, *Ruricius*.

2 Hence the lack of elaborate salutations and valedictions. *Ep.* 41 (preserved in the papal archives) is the only exception. See Burckhardt, p. 22.

EASTERN QUESTIONS

1. THE ACACIAN SCHISM

Contents

Epistula 2 *Contra Eutychianam haeresim* 1.

Epistula 3 *Contra Eutychianam haeresim* 2 (date 512/3).

Epistula 39 Avitus to Senarius, *vir illustrissimus*: Avitus asks Senarius to intercede with the pope (Hormisdas), and ensure that an official account of Roman–Byzantine ecclesiastical relations be sent to Vienne. Compare *Epp.* 40–42 (date 515/6).

Epistula 40 Avitus to Peter, bishop of Ravenna: Avitus writes to Peter to get an official letter about the state of the Acacian schism (date 516/7). Perhaps to be linked to *Ep.* 41.

Epistula 41 Avitus to Pope Hormisdas: not in the Lyons MS: from papal archives. Avitus writes to the pope acknowledging a previous letter sent to him and the province of Vienne, via clerics from Arles, about the condemnation of Eutyches and Nestorius and the transfer of the bishops of Dardania, Illyricum and Scythia to communion with Rome. He has not, however, been told of the outcome of negotiations between the papacy and Constantinople and has sent two of his own clergy for information. Date ca. 516.

Epistula 42 Pope Hormisdas to Avitus and all of the suffragan bishops of the Viennensis: not in the Lyons MS: from papal archives. Hormisdas' reply to *Ep.* 41. Date Feb 517.

Contra Eutychianam haeresim, Book 1: Introduction

Eutyches was the archimandrite of Constantinople, whose Monophysite teachings[1] were condemned at the Council of Chalcedon in 451.[2] Despite this condemnation Monophysitism continued to survive, especially in Syria but also in Constantinople.[3] In 482, to try to end the divisions within the eastern church, the emperor Zeno issued a compromise statement of faith known as the Henotikon. This pleased neither the Monophysite nor the orthodox party in the East, and in the West Pope Felix III responded by excommunicating the patriarch of Constantinople, Acacius, in 484, thus beginning a rupture between papacy and patriarchate known as the Acacian schism.[4]

---

1 I.e. that Christ had only one, divine, nature.

2 For Eutyches, see J. N. D. Kelly, *Early Christian Doctrines* (Edinburgh, 4th edn, 1968), pp. 330–34. E. Schwartz, 'Der Prozess des Eutyches', *SbBAW* phil.-hist. Kl. (1929, 5), p. 14.

3 W. H. C. Frend, *The Rise of the Monophysite Movement* (Cambridge, 1972).

4 For a convenient historical survey, see E. Stein, *Histoire du bas-empire: 476–565*, ed. and trans. J. R. Palanque, vol. 2 (Paris–Brussels–Amsterdam, 1949), pp. 20–27, 31–39, 165–71,

Curiously, the fact that Rome regarded both emperor and patriarch as heretical does not seem to have reached Avitus until ca. 512. It was only as a result of the so-called *Trishagion* riots that he learnt something (somewhat inaccurately) of the theological situation in Constantinople. In 496 the patriarch of Constantinople, Euphemius, was deposed for his hostility to the Henotikon of Zeno, and replaced by Macedonius, who agreed to the Henotikon, but who seems otherwise to have upheld the Chalcedonian position.[1] Despite this he seems to have remained on good terms with the Monophysite emperor, Anastasius, at least until Severus, patriarch of Antioch, arrived in Constantinople, accompanied by a large group of Monophysite monks in 508. Severus appears to have strengthened Anastasius' resolve against his Chalcedonian patriarch.

Matters came to a head when ca. 510 some of Severus' monastic supporters attempted to introduce the phrase 'who was crucified for us' into the Mass, at the *Trishagion*, the liturgical doxology 'Holy, Holy, Holy'. This phrase was something of a Monophysite battle-cry, because it was associated with the Monophysite patriarch of Antioch, Peter the Fuller. Macedonius, however, had the support of the people of Constantinople, and in the riots that followed Anastasius very nearly had to flee the city.[2] Having survived the crisis, he turned against Macedonius, using the *magister officiorum* Celer.[3] The latter, who features among Avitus' correspondents, persuaded the patriarch to sign a confession of faith which mentioned the councils of Nicaea and Constantinople, but made no reference to Ephesus, which had condemned Nestorius, or Chalcedon, which had condemned Eutyches. Failure to mention Ephesus left Macedonius open to the charge of Nestorianism in the eyes of the Monophysites, and failure to mention Chalcedon lost him the support of the Catholic monks. As a result Anastasius was able to arrest and depose his patriarch in 511, exiling him to Pontus, where he joined his predecessor Euphemius.[4] He was replaced as patriarch by another Chalcedonian, Timothy. It would appear to be news of this first crisis prompted by the alteration of the *Trishagion* that reached Avitus, since he refers to the exile of a patriarch in *CE* 2, p. 23.5.

The victory of the Monophysite party also registered in Rome. When a group of Eastern bishops wrote to Pope Symmachus in 512 asking for a reconciliation for the Acacian schism,[5] Symmachus responded on 8 October 512 with *Ep.* 13.3,[6] in which he alluded to a renaissance of Monophysitism.[7]

182–92, 224–28. The evidence for the schism is gathered by E. Schwartz, *Publizistische Sammlungen zum Acacianischen Schisma* (Munich, 1934).

1 Stein-Palanque, pp. 166–67.
2 On the *Trishagion*, Schwartz, *Publizistische Sammlungen*, pp. 239–44.
3 *PLRE* 2, Celer 2.
4 Stein-Palanque, pp. 168–71.
5 Symmachus, *Ep.* 12, Thiel.
6 Thiel, p. 719.
7 *Adversus hos, si patrum dogmata ratio suadet esse servanda, cogitate, si possunt ea*

There was, however, a second *Trishagion* crisis, which was in some ways more significant, and which is also relevant for understanding Avitus' later letters concerning contacts with Constantinople.[1] In 512 Anastasius officially approved the introduction of the *Trishagion* into the Mass in Santa Sophia.[2] Again there was a riot, which was forcefully suppressed on the orders of the emperor. The next day, however, orthodox monks turned on the Monophysites, massacring them: they then drove out Anastasius' counsellors, among them Celer. The riots were only brought to an end when Anastasius himself went to face the rioters in the Hippodrome, without his diadem. It was, however, one thing to end the crisis in Constantinople and quite another to prevent the Chalcedonian backlash from gathering strength outside the city. In particular the crisis played into the hands of the Chalcedonian *comes* (*?foederatorum*) Vitalian,[3] who was already aggrieved at the treatment of his federates. After an initial uprising in 513, Vitalian was able in 514/5 to force the emperor to agree to open a dialogue with Pope Hormisdas to end the schism. In the event negotiations failed, and although Vitalian rebelled for a third time, he was forced to retreat to Thrace.[4] The two years of Anastasius' reign when Vitalian dominated Constantinople are, however, well represented in Avitus' collection.[5]

News of the first of the *Trishagion* riots reached Gundobad, apparently in 511, and, given his desire to maintain good relations with Anastasius, he must have asked Avitus to inform him so that he might respond. Gundobad was unlucky in his adviser:[6] Avitus turned out to be ignorant both about the contemporary doctrinal situation in the East and about Christology. In one place he confuses Eutyches with Nestorius,[7] and he mistakenly believed that the addition to the *Trishagion* was orthodox, and that its omission was Eutychian.[8]

We should, however, beware of attributing too much to Avitus' incompetence. Much of the problem may well stem from the information reaching the Burgundian

---

majori transgressione calcari, quam nunc per eos, qui in partibus vestris Eutychetis dogmata recidiva resuscitant.

1 Stein-Palanque, pp. 177–81.

2 See H. Chadwick, *Boethius: The Consolations of Music, Logic, Theology and Philosophy* (Oxford, 1981), p. 185.

3 *PLRE* 2, Fl. Vitalianus 2. The query over *foederatum* is Martindale's.

4 Stein-Palanque, pp. 182–85.

5 *Epp.* 9, 46A–49.

6 See Burckhardt, pp. 66–70. Also Stein-Palanque, pp. 187–88.

7 *CE* 1 p. 16.24–29. 'Christotokos' was Nestorius' term. Chadwick, *Boethius,* overstates Avitus' errors on p. 184: 'At least he (Gelasius) wrote with better information at his disposal than Avitus of Vienne, whose treatise explaining the Christological controversy for the Burgundian king ascribes Nestorius' doctrines to Eutyches and vice versa.' Such confusion is, however, standard in Merovingian Gaul: cf. *Epistulae Austrasiacae* 7, and Columbanus, *Ep.* 5, 10, 16. No doubt the stringing together of heretics in lists of anathemas encouraged confusion.

8 *CE* 2, p. 22.21–29.

kingdom. Here the fact that papal information regarding the Acacian schism seems not to have reached Avitus – perhaps because of problems within Rome and Italy – will have been significant. As for information from Constantinople, there appears to have been direct contact with the imperial court.[1] A letter may have come directly from the emperor, or from an official such as the *magister officiorum* Celer.[2] It is worth noting that Celer appears later as a correspondent of Avitus.[3] Since he was also the man who wrong-footed Macedonius into a confession of faith which ignored both Ephesus and Chalcedon, he is likely to have had a very biased view of events. Were he to have been the man who passed on information on the first *Trishagion* riots to the Burgundian kingdom, then it would not be surprising to find that it was misleading. Further, while Avitus' information is remarkable as a very early witness to events in Constantinople in 511, it would be even more valuable if one could see it as being perverted by imperial propaganda.

Book 1 of the treatise is loosely organised around a series of scriptural passages, most of which have been chosen to illustrate and emphasise the divine nature of the Incarnate Word. An earlier example of a diphysite patristic *florilegium* is preserved with Gelasius' Third Tractate against Eutyches and Nestorius.[4] Interestingly enough there are only two places in Book 1 where there is any overlap between passages cited by Avitus and those cited by previous authorities.[5] Avitus does not allude to discussions by his theological precedessors. It would appear first that he had no convenient scriptural *florilegia* (Gundobad asks him to assemble such a document, and he shows a somewhat disingenuous reluctance to do so) and second that he did not have access to theological polemic against Eutyches. He knows very little about the man himself, or about his theology; for example, he does not discuss Eutyches' catchphrase, 'One nature after the union'. He argues against a theology that denies divinity and/or divine characteristics to Christ Incarnate. The technical terminology of nature and person that dominates Boethius' *Contra Eutychen* is barely visible here. In this treatise we are seeing Avitus' own work, achieved with poor research-tools in unfavourable circumstances – hence, no doubt, the somewhat haphazard nature of the passages he has chosen, and the poorly delineated structure of the treatise.

---

1   *CE* 1, p. 16. 2–3: *Cum se ad tenendam veritatem vobis reddiderit docilem.*

2   On the duties of a *Mag. Off.*, see Jones, *LRE*, pp. 368–69; Barnwell, *Emperor, Prefects and Kings*, pp. 23–24.

3   In the second half of *Ep.* 48, Avitus speaks of Celer's *fideles*, and indicates that he awaits Celer's commands. Avitus clearly had correspondence with the man about religious matters – specifically ones relating to orthodoxy.

4   See Thiel, pp. 544–57. See also Vigilius of Thapsus, *Contra Eutychen libri quinque*, PL 62.95–154.

5   In the Gelasian florilegium: John 1.1 (p. 550); Mt. 1.1 (p. 551).

Outline of Book 1[1]

1. Praise of Gundobad for his interest in orthodox doctrine; gratitude for the commission; allusion to the error of Anastasius.

2. Eutyches the heresiarch.

3. He claimed that God could not have been confined in a human womb. Mary was not the *Theotokos*.

4. God does not suffer pain: such expressions are figurative: Judg. 10.16; Eph. 4.30.

5. The Incarnate Word has divine attributes: John 1.1; Isa. 9.6.

6. The text of the Annunciation: Lk. 1.35.

7. God was in Christ reconciling the world to himself: 2 Cor. 5.19.

8. A mediator must partake of two natures in order to mediate: Gal. 3.19–20.

9. The Law of Christ is the same as the Law of God: 1 Cor. 9.21.

10. The OT Lawgiver and Christ are one and the same: Ps. 83.8.

11. A man came down from heaven and a god left earth: John 3.13.

12. Jesus told the Jews that he was alive before Abraham: John 8.58.

13. Eutychians stubbornly refuse to believe that human characteristics can be fused with divine ones. In effect they are denying the possibility of redemption.

14. Avitus refuses to collect masses of scriptural *testimonia* to support his argument.

15. Jesus will come in judgement, i.e. as God. He will come with his own angels. They are his subordinates. He cannot therefore be purely human in nature: Mt. 25.31–34.

16. In the NT Abraham said that he who will not listen to Moses and the prophets will likewise be deaf to a witness come back from the dead. Christ is the witness. Therefore Abraham alluded to the doctrinal unity of the OT and the NT: Lk. 16.31.

17. Abraham is the father of both testaments.

18. Abraham asked his servant to take an oath by God, touching his (A's) genitals. Since Abraham was the Christ's ancestor, He was present in the seed in Abraham's genitals. Therefore God can be identified with Christ in this passage: Gen. 24.2–3.

Contra Eutychianam haeresim 1, *Against the Eutychian Heresy*, Book 1

Avitus the bishop to his lord, Gundobad the king

1.{15.9 Peiper} A gift both unique and manifold has been granted to us[2] by the dispensation of the Divinity – namely that, among the many matters of

---

1 The chapter-divisions are our own. Peiper has none.

2 Lit. 'our age'.

royal business in your glorious princedom, you take special care to preserve the orthodoxy of the Catholics.[1] It is because of this pious concern of yours that, in a recent and clement authorisation-[letter], you have ordered me to divert waves of examples[2] from the sacred fount of heavenly scripture [to quench][3] the renewed madness of Eutychianism that is pullulating as if from the dead tinder of a rising conflagration.[4] A worthy undertaking indeed that such a great ruler commands – provided that someone be chosen who is worthy to perform the task; if the power of his eloquence match the author of the subject; if our tongue should thus happen to do as much good in speaking[5] to increase the [spiritual] salvation of the people as Your Benignity has clearly[6] done in ordering me to do so. For you love the country and person of the emperor (Anastasius I), who is bound to you, not exclusively for the convenience of political peace, as other kings usually are, but, because you fear that someone dear to you is being deceived by error, you wish that all the friendship[7] between you serve this [one] useful purpose – to prevent him from committing a sin. Who could have any reason to be surprised that you trumpet his praises and commend him for being faithful and devoted to God, since special[8] and all-conquering[9] forgiveness[10] comes in abundance from him.

I, however, {16.1 Peiper}beg God with all my strength that this very man we are talking about, the Caesar of the Greeks,[11] if he is faithful to you, and honourable towards us, be persuaded by our ruler[12] to persuade his own people.[13] Since he has made himself your student in order to maintain the

---

1 Since Gundobad was an Arian such theological concern is particularly noteworthy. One might compare Theodoric's deliberate avoidance of theological issues.

2 There is a nice parallel to this request of Gundobad's in *Ep.* 23 (55.30–33) and in *Ep.* 30 (60.20–22), both of which ask for lists of scriptural *auctoritates* or *testimonia*.

3 Lit. 'against'.

4 Avitus self-consciously employs imagery of water used to quench a fire.

5 Peiper has mispunctuated. There should be no period after *proloqui*, since the *sic* is balanced by the *ut* that follows.

6 Rendering *abunde*.

7 Burckhardt, p. 68 n. 1, mysteriously translated 'Feindschaft!'

8 There is a typo in Peiper's text. It clearly should read *praecipua*.

9 Lit. 'triumphal'.

10 *Venia,* 'forgiveness' for Anastasius' heresy.

11 I.e. the Eastern emperor.

12 Gundobad.

13 I.e. to follow orthodoxy.

truth,[1] he should rejoice that he has become one who helps[2] your preaching[3] in order to fight the [heretical] diseases of his own land.

2. Eutyches, the deadly author of the pernicious disease that we are discussing, was [just][4] a priest in the church of Constantinople, but was [still] in charge of many monks. (The bishops of the East call such persons 'archimandrites'.) Since he was all eagerness, aflame for the highest priesthood that must be acquired with the support of a reputation in his zeal to introduce whatever new [theological] ideas he had, he is said to have promulgated the doctrine that we abhor in his followers through whisperings rather than writings. There was no sign of distinguished learning[5] in the man that could buttress his outrageous arguments[6] with any semblance of the truth. After he had initially infected the souls of his monks with this poison and exposed them to shipwreck under the nefarious colours of his 'guidance'; once he had become the heresiarch of a considerable company, as I said above, a large council of bishops judged him – including bishops from Rome sent for the purpose – and he was interrogated, exposed and condemned.[7] But because no schism was ever able be abrogated in this fashion along with its author – so that the death of the teacher entirely dispelled his pernicious teachings – what had been cut down by the just oversight of the pontiffs arose, as if from earth infected by weeds, because it was nursing contagion from seeds that it had taken in long ago.

3. Listen now to the teaching of the heresy against which we speak. They deny that the Son of God who remained with the Father before time, who, as

1 This suggests that the instruction and exempla were destined to go East. It is possible that Anastasius preferred to seek instruction in Catholic doctrine from neutral Burgundy rather than from Rome itself.

2 Peiper's text and the MSS read *adiutorem*, 'helper', but another possibility is *auditorem*, a minor emendation that may work better with the genitive and matches *docilem*: people who permit themselves to be taught are bound to *listen*.

3 This could conceivably be an honorific with an ecclesiastical flavour intended to flatter Gundobad.

4 Rendering *quidem*.

5 Pope Leo I's judgement was not dissimilar. See *Ep.* 5 (*Collectio Novariensis*, ed. E. Schwartz, *Acta Conciliorum Oecumenicorum* 2.2.1), p. 24: *multum inprudens et nimis inperitus ostenditur*, and pp. 24–25: *quid autem iniquius quam impia sapere et sapientioribus doctoribusque non cedere?*

6 A free rendition of *sensum conceptae animositatis*.

7 I.e. at the Council of Chalcedon.

orthodox opinion compels us to believe, came down from heaven for this reason, to take on a body, could have been crammed[1] into a woman's womb. The son of God, *qua* God, who said, 'I fill heaven and earth',[2] could not have gone where he was,[3] unless he were content by taking on flesh to be what he had not been.[4] Our[5] Eutyches, since he feared this conclusion, when, during the synod I mentioned above, he was urgently begged by those who were hearing him[6] to call the Virgin Mary 'Theotokos',[7] since she had given birth to God, and to sign the opinion, turned deceitfully to wicked and sophistic distinctions, and confessed her as 'Christotokos',[8] i.e. one who seemed to have given birth only to the Anointed One.

4. This he did in order that the person who keeps his divine nature might be kept separate from the one who suffered the indignity of the Passion.[9] While avoiding the left which must be checked on its treacherous and precipitous edge, yet not accepting the right, in fearing each side to an equal degree, the safest way lies in the middle[10] – namely when we say that the twofold nature of the Redeemer can be discerned, but not divided.[11] Nor do we try [to make people think] that the inviolable Godhead be believed to have suffered bodily pain, even though all pain felt by any body in some fashion naturally precedes the death that will ensue. Whence, just as our very own flesh, when it has received the gift of resurrection, will be impassible after death, so too God, who cannot feel death, once he had taken on a body and been joined to it and made one with it, suffered with it, though without the bitterness of

1 Translating *contrudi*. Avitus deliberately uses a disrespectful and dissonant word to heap ridicule on his opponent.

2 Jer. 23.24.

3 The Virgin's womb.

4 I.e. human.

5 Rendering *de quo loquimur*.

6 His judges?

7 'Mother of God'.

8 'Mother of Christ', i.e. of the Anointed One. Here Avitus goes badly astray: he is ascribing to Eutyches the views of Nestorius.

9 There are a number of parallel discussions in Faustus, *Ep.* 3 and Claudianus Mamertus, *De Statu Animae*: Avitus shares a number of words and phrases with *De Statu Animae* 1.3 (esp. at pp. 33–37): *inviolabilis divinitas, duplex substantia, adsumptus*.

10 For similar imagery of the *via media*, see Symmachus, *Ep.* 12.8 (p. 714 Thiel): *Et inter duas diabolici vias erroris, Eutychetis atque Nestorii, tertiam immo mediam nobis ostendens expressius veri rectique dogmatis viam* and 12.9 *viam mediam reperiri … viam mediam veritatis*.

11 See Nodes, *Doctrine and Exegesis*, p. 69.

suffering: He neither failed [us] during the glorious agony of our salvation, nor did He feel pain. Against the sense of this distinction, the heresy, our opponent, raising itself up, does not allow even Christ to be polluted by real physical anguish, even though in the case of the Godhead itself,[1] who feels no bodily affliction, from time to time one finds the experience of pity. For we read of the Israelites, 'they called out to God ... and his soul was grieved for the misery of Israel',[2] {17.1 Peiper} and the apostle orders us, 'grieve not the holy spirit of God'.[3] These and other similar passages listed in the sacred books are a sign of goodness and mercy rather than of any necessity enforced by nature.

5. In the meantime in what follows, I will put off any statement about the two [persons],[4] and will develop the theme of the unity of the double substance in Christ. Where are the great mysteries about the truth in heavenly scripture, which have no other intent than to persuade us that the Word was incarnated in a divine man? 'In the beginning was the Word. And the Word was with God. And the Word was God.'[5] Now we know what there was that had no beginning. Let us now try to understand what was begun and what followed. 'And the Word was made flesh.'[6] Since God was at the beginning with God, he lacks both a beginning and an end; since the Word was clothed in flesh, it lacks an end, but had a beginning. Let that Emmanuel who was foretold of old by the voice of the prophetic oracle come to the aid of my discussion: for, as Isaiah said, He was the son of God, 'born to us and given to us',[7] so that He could be God among us.[8] It is in vain to divide corporality from the sacred nature of divinity, if the prophet was correct in stating that the Son of God proceeded [from the Father] as a boy. He says, 'And He will be called "wonderful", "Counsellor", "the mighty God", "the everlasting Father", "the Prince of peace".' As far as the name is concerned, it is enough that the boy is called 'Emmanuel'. But when he says, 'He will be called

1 The Father.

2 Avitus' quotation *exclamaverunt ad deum* picks up the beginning of Judg. 10.10, *et clamantes ad dominum, dixerunt* in a form that is slightly different from that of the Vulgate. He combines it with Judg. 10.16.

3 Eph. 4.30.

4 *Duorum* is S's conjecture for *quorum* L, but it is not entirely clear to what it refers – possibly persons.

5 John 1.1.

6 John 1.4.

7 Isa. 9.6.

8 'Emmanuel' means 'God with us'. See Mt. 1.23 and Isa. 7.14.

"wonderful", "Counsellor", "the mighty God", etc.' what other reason, I ask, is there for him to list so many epithets, other than so that you might realise that the truthful prophet, expressing what is appropriate for man and for God in one and the same person, has listed the benefits that will follow from the mediator's actions rather than his names [alone]? I shall compel the heretic now to answer: Who is it that can be understood to require the titles 'the mighty God', 'the everlasting Father', 'the Prince of peace'? If it is the Son of God who existed before time,[1] why will he be given these epithets [only] still[2] in the future, if he has always been what he is? If it is the son of man who is being born, the fullness of time guards the secret of how two different beings are to be joined to one another. It was to this that the apostle referred when he said, 'But when the fullness of time was come, God sent forth his Son, made of a woman.'[3]

6. The Father sent what the woman brought forth. His corporeal birth is the same as his divine coming. God does not want him whom He sends to lie hidden. Let the world notice the signs of the coming of the Lord. He whom the Father begat without a mother, and the mother conceived without a father, will be just as much the son of God as[4] of man. Let us consult Gabriel about the sacrament of that unity. He is the prince of ministers. Because he stands in the presence of eternal brightness and untiringly serves it, the ineffable secrets of [God's] visible majesty are revealed to him, not only for his understanding, but also for his contemplation.[5] He was the first to lead an embassy from heaven to earth. He promised a divine offspring to the virgin who had been impregnated by the Word. It was he who by greeting[6] one woman, filled the whole world with salvation. He said, 'The Holy Ghost shall come upon thee, and the power of the Highest shall overshadow thee: therefore the holy thing which shall be born of thee shall be called the Son of God.'[7] Since no process of reasoning suggests that it was merely a man who was born from the heavenly spirit , since the psalmist says that every man is conceived in iniquity and born in sin,[8] {18.1 Peiper} here through an angel,

1 Cf. Hil. Pict. *Hymn* 1.1: *Ante saecula qui manens.*

2 The Latin is *adhuc*, 'still', but the sense of the passage seems to require an 'only'.

3 Gal. 4.4. Avitus has *natum* 'born'.

4 Emending *ut* to *ac*.

5 *Intellegenda* and *contemplanda* should probably be reversed. The sentence makes more sense if Gabriel not only contemplates, but also understands.

6 *Salutatione.* Avitus puns on *salutatio*, 'greeting', and *salus*, 'salvation'.

7 Lk. 1.35.

8 Ps. 50.7.

on account of the power of the Holy Spirit poured into the limbs of a woman, we see the sacred thing that had to be the product of such a mystery.

7. The apostle now defines this by separating what had been joined, on the grounds that 'God was in Christ'[1] for our redemption. But perhaps the cunning adversary will wish to abuse this testimony of the apostle in the following fashion: namely he will agree that 'God is in Christ',[2] but by grace, not by nature – as is the case with the hearts of the saints whose minds, free from sin, are made glorious by the divinity dwelling in them. Let us now see whether this erroneous notion perishes or not, if the sentence is finished. 'God,' he says, 'was in Christ, reconciling the world to himself.' Let our rival theologian here choose who at the end of time will reconcile to himself the world that caused offence at its very beginning to our most generous Creator through the sin of our first parent. If it is God alone, why should he make an excuse to himself, since it would have been sufficient for him to have forgiven himself? If, on the other hand, it is the man alone, how (= *quo effectu*) can a mortal reconcile to himself what the divinity does not release? God and man, therefore, are one, who himself commends the world to himself, and who as son of the mother begs himself as the Son of the Father for the life of the world. This is why the apostle did not say 'reconciling the world to God', but 'to himself'. He did not want you to think that man alone prayed for the redemption of the human race. For if [Christ as] man were not to be transformed, taken up into the nature of divinity,[3] not only would he not dissolve the slavery of the human race by intercession, but he himself would bear the burden of our common debt according to the bond[4] binding our parents.[5]

8. The same apostle (i.e. Paul) says that this remedy has been arranged 'by angels in the hand of a mediator'.[6] And by showing the reason for which he

---

1 2 Cor. 5.19: *quoniam quidem deus erat in Christo.*

2 2 Cor. 5.19.

3 Words such as *assumptus* later left Avitus open to charges of Adoptionism: Agobard, *Liber Adversus Felicem Urgellitanum*, 39 (*PL* 104. 65). The most recent discussion of Adoptionism, J. C. Cavadini, *The Last Christology of the West. Adoptionism in Spain and Gaul 785–820* (Philadelphia, 1993), does not discuss Felix's use of Avitus.

4 For the bond see Col. 2.14.

5 On the necessity of the two natures see also Claudianus Mamertus, *De Statu Animae* 1.3, pp. 34 and 36.

6 Gal. 3.19.

offered himself as a middleman,[1] taken up from below, bending down from on high, he says, 'a mediator is not a mediator of one, but God is one'.[2] Since this is the case, just as it makes no sense to speak of mediation unless it be between two people, so he, whom we call the mediator, if he took on only one, whichever it were, of the two substances, would then have no middle ground from which to approach the office of mediation.[3] And he draws this conclusion with one statement of a sort that cannot be tainted by any trickiness like this: 'For He is our peace who hath made both one.'[4] That is to say that he, evidently the peace both of the humble and of the mighty, having been made one out of two, gave back one [made] out of two.

9. Certainly, as I explained above, either the evidence seems to require an exposition or the example proof. But what could be clearer than that statement of the apostle where, when adapting himself to many different types of men, he said that he had 'been made all things to all men',[5] so that as an eager doubler of celestial wealth[6] he might acquire everyone's souls? He said, 'I have become to them that are without the law, as without the law, being not without law to God, but under the law to Christ.'[7] Surely there cannot be anyone sunk so low as to think that this point should be explained this way: namely that he is under the law of Christ without divine law?[8]

10. It is clear that there is one law-giver, who, one and the same, as the psalm says, embracing both past and future, gives blessing in baptism, and gives law through his command.[9] That such different characteristics are brought together in one person offends minds weighed down by carnality and made sluggish by the habit of living with the conjecture and uncertainty that characterise the human state: {19.1 Peiper} namely that the fullness of divinity and the state of being human, the humbleness of the servant and the majesty of the master, the power of the creator and the slavery of the creature, all seem to have created one person out of all of these. But neither

---

1 Translating *medium*.
2 Gal. 3.20.
3 Compare Claudianus Mamertus, *De Statu Animae* 1.3, pp. 36–37.
4 Eph. 2.14.
5 1 Cor. 9.22.
6 Lit. 'talents'. The allusion is to the good servant of Mt. 25.20–21.
7 1 Cor. 9.21.
8 I.e. the law of the Father.
9 A loose allusion to Vulg. Ps. 83.8: *etenim benedictionem dabit legislator.*

is the reason for this cohesiveness entirely unconnected with the unity of opinion among the wise,[1] which seems to be especially in force among [their] heirs – namely that he alone who formed him from the mud can reform the fallen state of man. Hence what the most blessed Paul says, 'The first man is of the earth, earthy; the second man heavenly[2] from heaven.' He said that he was a real man to be sure, but an earthly one because of the contagion of pollution, and a heavenly one, because of his contact with divinity.[3]

11. I am asking now, since the apostle says that a man came down from heaven, who is there who would dare to deny that a god came back from earth? Still if what the chosen vessel[4] said was insignificant, let us ask him who filled the mind of that most chosen and precious vessel. 'No one will[5] ascend up to heaven, but he that came down from heaven, the Son of man who was first in heaven.'[6] And if God himself, who is truth, thus is so much in harmony with his incarnation that before time he united in his foreknowledge what he had already arranged to take on in his nature at the end of time, see whether he be God, when he rises after the triumph of the resurrection, if he was said to be a son with the father before he took on flesh. Look at what cohesiveness he had in the past, whose unity is proclaimed to be so great in the future. And lest we have any hesitation concerning that inseparable nature, the apostle still goes on to add a testimony from the psalms: 'Wherefore he saith, "When he ascended up on high, he led captivity captive, and gave gifts unto men. Now that he ascended," he says, "what is it but that he also descended[7] into the lower parts of the earth?"'[8] It is no great thing for him to say that God came down to earth, unless he confirm also that, because of the unity of the person he assumed, he also descended into hell.

1 *Sapientum soliditate* is difficult to interpret. *Soliditate* may be *Perseverationsfehler*. Or perhaps Avitus intends the cohesiveness (unity of testimony) found among the wise men, i.e. biblical authorities.

2 1 Cor. 15.47. Avitus' text differs slightly from the AV; instead of 'the Lord', he has 'heavenly'.

3 Avitus is misinterpreting this passage. Paul referred to Adam and to Christ. Avitus takes the passage to refer to Christ's two natures.

4 Paul. See Acts 9.15.

5 Avitus' text has a future here rather than the perfect *ascendit*.

6 John 3.13.

7 Avitus' text omits the 'first' present in the AV.

8 Eph. 4.8–9; Ps. 67.19.

12. When the Jews were murmuring on all sides and brandishing the naked darts of blasphemy against our Lord, who do we think answered, 'Verily, verily, I say unto you, before Abraham was, I am',[1] unless it was he, who[2] through a concord of father and of race, himself through the stock of his maternal ancestors descended from the seed of Abraham, who preceded Abraham countless years before eternity? Abraham, the greatest of the patriarchs, even though he saw the day in which God exists eternally,[3] still longed to see that one in which man is united to God.[4] 'He saw,' he says, 'and he was glad.'[5] Because he once had a chance to see him in whom there was true majesty,[6] so too he greatly desired to see the one in whom a humility that was adopted shone clearly. 'Then took they up stones,' he says, 'to cast them at him.'[7] Why should we be at all surprised that the Eutychians are murmuring against the Catholic faith, when we see our own head[8] putting up with lack of belief from his own people, those for whose sake he had come, and about to return their indignation with interest?[9] Is it any surprise that the Jews raged in the past in the same contumelious fashion that the heretics do now? That they threw stones at the Lord then was a parricidal act, but you would think that these people now in their own time are [still] throwing [figurative] stones at the self-evident truth with their hard and stubborn minds.

---

1 John 8.58.

2 *Quia* makes no sense. The structure of the sentence demands *qui*: *quem respondisse credimus, nisi qui* ...

3 The Latin reads *sine fide*, but the trust and trustworthiness of God are not at issue. *Sine fine* is a simple emendation and fits perfectly with *permanet*. For *sine fide* to make sense one would have to see it as describing Abraham who lived before the coming of Christ; the tense of *permanet* still poses a problem.

4 Abraham looked forward to the coming of the Messiah.

5 John 8.56.

6 Abraham saw God at Gen. 18.1.

7 John 8.59.

8 I.e. Christ. See 1 Cor. 11.3.

9 Peiper's text *pertulisse redditurumque perfidiam indignatione una cum faenore* cannot be correct. There can be no question of Christ's 'tolerating *and returning* perfidy/lack of faith in indignation and with added interest too'. One minimal correction would involve transposing *perfidiam* to before *pertulisse*, and changing *indignatione* to *indignationem*: *perfidiam pertulisse redditurumque indignationem una cum faenore*. Another possibility would be to insert a lacuna between *redditurumque* and *indignatione, yielding perfidiam pertulisse redditurumque < ...> indignatione una cum faenore*. But even here what is the precise allusion? In John 8.59 Jesus merely hides when the Jews try to stone him and passes by them out of the Temple. The passage should probably be obelised.

13. {20.1 Peiper} The madness of two sets of people[1] conspires to see to it that man and God not be believed to be one. Could it be the case, I ask, that we were created to become something better?[2] Could matter mixed with mud be permitted to be exalted with the honour due to divine beings? Why are you making such an effort against your best interests, O Man, so as not to believe that you are capable of becoming a god? Divine majesty is inviting you to participate in its being. Why do you reject its offer? Why do you despise the one who brings it (sc. the offer)? Cultivate the truth in order to become like it; love orthodoxy in order successfully to imitate it. If Christ is our head, when they are elevated, let the limbs then take on a partnership of however limited a kind with the head.

14. Therefore let other people ask for a mass of examples from the body of both testaments for their instruction to enable them to protect their affirmations;[3] for this job, the tendency of both libraries[4] is such that if we should wish to confirm what we are saying with a [scriptural] testimonium, it would seem necessary to gather together all the oracles of the canonical scriptures into one work. Out of the multitude of such passages, it is quite right to set down certain chosen excerpts in order to avoid excessive lengthiness. Just as those [sayings] are of little effect that are not supported by scripture, because they come exclusively from us,[5] so too equally ineffective is he who disdains to take in few passages, but throws together his argument, emphasising quantity rather than quality. For because he is afraid of being defeated, yet is unwilling to be instructed, and because he wants a [whole] roll [of citations] rather than some individual proofs to teach the truth, he believes that the weight of an argument consists not in facts, but in the number of pages.

15. Our Lord and Redeemer revealed the coming of his Glory to his disciples in this passage above all,[6] where he says: 'When the Son of man shall come in his glory, and all the holy angels with him ... and before him shall be

1 Jews and Eutychians.

2 *Rogo* suggests that both sentences that begin with *liceat* are questions and should be repunctuated as such. Cf. 20.25 below. The questions are potential and could receive a positive answer.

3 This paragraph addresses the original terms of Gundobad's request to Avitus.

4 I.e. the Old and New Testaments.

5 I.e. from Avitus or patristic authorities. Avitus might be alluding to collections of patristic doxography on the nature of Christ. See above p. 92.

6 Representing *specialius*.

gathered all nations: and he shall separate them one from another ... and he
shall set the just like lambs on his right hand, but the unjust like goats on his
left.[1] Then shall the King say to them on his right hand, "Come ye blessed of
my Father, inherit the kingdom prepared for you from the foundation of the
world." ... Then shall he say unto them on the left hand that they should
depart[2] from him into everlasting fire, prepared for the devil and his angels.'[3]
What contemptible thing is there here in Christ, I ask, for human pride to
disdain? What could be so worthy of fear? What so clear in its honour? What
so worthy to be venerated in terror? Let the heretic put his mind to this
question: whether he is to ascribe this to the glory of the Father or of the Son.
In connection with the topic that we are discussing, it is sufficient for me to
hear, 'When the Son of man shall come in his glory.'[4] In the present world
'learn of me, for I am meek and lowly of heart';[5] in the world to come be
warned that lofty and terrible in his brightness 'He will come in his glory
with his holy angels.'[6] Let him who divides the unified mediator[7] state
whence can there be any majesty in a body that was bowed down by insult,[8]
if there be no divinity? I will not mention that he is sent by the Father,
whether to kingdoms or to peoples, according to their individual merits; it
might seem more terrifying that he decree the appropriate punishments as a
man than that God the Father have prepared the instruments of judgement
for the sentence of the Son of Man. 'For the Son of man shall come in the
glory of his Father with his angels, and then he shall reward every man
according to his works.'[9] He did not say that he would come with the angels
of his Father, but with his own angels, because whatever his Father has is his
also. Therefore, when as son of his mother he receives on high what as Son
of his Father he had rejected in his humility,[10] what heretic could there be so
rebellious {21.1 Peiper} as to be unwilling, though himself mortal, indeed

1 Our own translation here. Avitus' text differs from the AV.

2 The AV has been adapted to match Avitus' indirect command construction.

3 Mt. 25.1. Compare the use of this same quotation in Faustus, *Ep.* 5, ed. A. Engelbrecht,
CSEL 21 (Vienna, 1891), p. 187.

4 Mt. 25.31.

5 Mt. 11.29.

6 Mt. 16.27. Avitus' text differs from the Vulgate and from the AV. He reads *in gloria sua*
instead of *in gloria patris sui*. See below n. 9 for the conventional form.

7 I.e. Christ, both human and divine.

8 The diphysite *florilegium* in Thiel (p. 545) cites the mocking of Christ as a sign of his
human nature. See Mt. 27.27–30 and 39–44.

9 Mt. 16.27, this time in its usual form.

10 I.e. celestial honours in heaven. S's *contemptus* must be right.

already dead, to think him, to whom he sees the immortal nature of angels subordinated, to be God?

16. But the patriarch[1] already said what we mentioned above, when he was begged by a certain individual (sc. Dives) for relief from the burning heat, with prayers both in vain and belated: namely that if someone was unwilling to take in Moses or the prophets, he would not be any more willing to listen even to someone who came back from the dead.[2] Who is the preacher who was brought back from the dead, if not Jesus Christ, into whose nature, double, as we call it, the unity of the double testament is gathered together from diversity?[3] For those things are narrated in the gospels that were foretold in the prophets. And of necessity[4] the newness of the testament consists not in its being different, but in its coming later. What is come to pass today is recent, but what was awaited for a long time is ancient.

17. For because a chance has come to talk about Abraham, who we read was established as the father of both testaments – of the old in introducing circumcision, of the new in pleasing [God] through faith[5] (in the former he was father of the Jews alone, in the latter of all peoples) – let us see whether he agrees with the gospels about the genealogy of Christ, through whom (i.e. Christ) he recognises that he is the father of peoples. Does[6] he understand the eternal nature of the very offspring that he was to beget?[7] Does he recognise himself in his great-great-great grandson?[8] Does he himself also agree with the Redeemer who put himself before Abraham? Without any parental pride has he respectfully paid the seed he owes as service to the corporeal birth of the Creator?

---

1 Abraham.

2 Paraphrase of Lk. 16.31 Dives and Lazarus. The story was one which Avitus treated at length in *Carm.* 3.220–310.

3 Compare Claudianus Mamertus, *De Statu* 1.3, p. 34.

4 Guessing at the meaning of *ex viribus*, based on its legal use. See *OLD* 'vis' 25c. An alternative is to emend *viribus* to *veteribus*: 'The transition from the old to the new testament is not a matter of difference, but of date.'

5 See Heb. 11.8–17.

6 The following four sentences have been changed in translation from indirect questions to direct questions.

7 Mt. 1.1ff. establishes Christ's paternal descent from Abraham.

8 Lit. 'grandson', but in this context 'nth great-grandson'.

18. Let me briefly here mention that solemn witness, where an oath was demanded, but which also prefigured the sacraments, adjuring the treasurer of his house, not without the mystery of future grace: 'Put, I pray thee, thy hand under my thigh ... and swear by the Lord, the God of heaven ... that thou shall not take a wife unto my son of the daughters of the Canaanites.'[1] Let someone explain to me, I ask, what is the special respect implied by swearing using the thigh? If this were happening merely to him as a person, the man who had been asked to swear might more easily have touched his head. But what is the reason for the thigh, along with an allusion to swearing by the Lord our God, other than that the oath was taken on that very Lord and God of Heaven, whom subsequently the ages seemed to have brought forth? For he knew, beyond a doubt he knew, what offspring it was that he did not so much overshadow[2] as serve. He knew for certain what he ought to worship in his own body; he understood what limbs contrary to human habit should be venerated with special honour.[3] After these indicators of what happened before and the miracles that happened subsequently, even though we have brought out many testimonia from the gospels and the apostles, in the final analysis I am afraid that, since the Eutychians are not awakened either by the deeds of the patriarchs or the words of the prophets, 'if they hear not Moses and the prophets, neither will they be persuaded, though one rose from the dead'.[4]

Contra Eutychianam haeresim, Book 2: Introduction

Even more than *CE* 1, *CE* 2, reveals the limited knowledge of religious developments in Constantinople and Rome since 476. Although this renders the *CE* unusable as a source for the events of the Acacian schism, it makes it a very significant document for understanding the constraints with which some of the parties were acting.

Avitus' confusions in *CE* 2 are as follows: first he does not know that Acacius was ever condemned, even though he thought he ought to have been: second he assumes that the addition to the *Trishagion* of 'qui crucifixus es propter nos' was already in place in Constantinople, and that it was orthodox – this suggests that some of his information was from a source favourable to the Monophysites, and that he interpreted it, very reasonably, in the light of his assumption that there was no fixed form of the Mass: third he portrays the patriarch as being in league with the emperor:

---

1 Gen. 24.2–3.
2 Lit. 'overshadow', but used here as a biblical euphemism for 'cover', 'beget'. See Lk. 1.35.
3 I.e. the genitals. *Femur*, 'thigh' is, of course, a biblical euphemism.
4 Lk. 16.31: returning to the story of Dives and Lazarus.

although Anastasius certainly supported the *Trishagion*, Macedonius and his supporters in Constantinople did not.[1]

The mixture of precise detail and confusion is instructive. Avitus knows well enough that the *Trishagion* was an issue, that it caused riots, and that it led to the deposition of the patriarch. He does not know that the Constantinopolitan church had been schismatic since 484,[2] that Emperor Anstasius was more committed to Monophysitism than was the patriarch (Macedonius), who had only gone so far as to accept the Henotikon of Zeno,[3] or that the *Trishagion* was regarded as heretical not by the Monophysites, but by the orthodox.[4] His confusions may stem in part from Western assumptions (e.g. that there was no fixed liturgy and that the addition of the 'qui crucifixus es propter nos' at a particular point in the liturgy, after the word ἀθάνατος (Immortal) was more than a pious utterance).[5] There may have been an additional factor: Avitus' information may originally have come from Imperial circles, most probably from the *magister officiorum* Celer, with whom he is known to have corresponded subsequently.[6] Celer's success in making Macedonius look like a Nestorian to the Monophysites (because he failed to approve the Council of Ephesus in his profession of faith) and like a Eutychian to the orthodox (because of his failure to cite Chalcedon)[7] may have further contributed to Avitus' theological confusion.

It should also be noted that *CE* 2 in its final form seems also to have another audience: the Arian bishops of Gundobad's court. It is possible that, for Avitus, the king's commission to reply to the Monophysites was primarily an opportunity to deal with heretics nearer to home. This meant not just the Arians, but also the Bonosiaci, who are presented as semi-Monophysite. It is also worth noting that when Avitus turns directly to Gundobad's clergy he uses the slightly mean *sectatores*, a word which he otherwise uses to describe heretics when he addresses Catholics (*Ep*. 23, p. 55.35 and *Ep*. 46, p. 75.1). Clearly by this time in Gundobad's reign, with Sigismund having professed Catholicism perhaps ten years earlier, Avitus could be openly critical of the king's clerical advisers.

---

1 Stein-Palanque, p. 169.

2 Stein-Palanque, p. 33.

3 Stein-Palanque, pp. 166–67.

4 Stein-Palanque, p. 169.

5 One might here compare the later problem over the 'filioque' clause, which was regarded as heretical in the East, but caused no such trouble in the West: see F. Dvornik, *The Photian Schism: History and Legend* (Cambridge, 1948), p. 122.

6 *Ep*. 48.

7 Stein-Palanque, p. 170.

Outline of Book 2

1. Acacius' position on Eutychianism
2. The *Crucifixus*-addition to the Trishagion, allegedly orthodox in the East (Avitus is misinformed by Celer?)
3. The removal of the *Crucifixus*-addition in Constantinople
4. Avitus inveighs against erring clergy
5. The divine and the human cohabit in Christ's incarnate body: witness the Crucifixion
6. The Canaanite woman attested the two natures in the Incarnate Christ
7. So did Mary at the marriage at Cana
8. 'My hour is not yet come' has nothing to do with astral fatalism
9. Peter identifies Jesus as the Christ and the Son of God (Mt. 16.16)
10. Varying *testimonia* at the Crucifixion
11. The Good Thief believed in Christ's divinity
12. Isa. 53.4–5
13. Biblical evidence for Christ's human nature
14. Christ, not a phantasm, was crucified
15. Doubting Thomas
16. The Eutychians claim that the apostles were deceived by the appearance of a resurrected Christ
17. Christ borne bodily to heaven
18. Peroration: Avitus hopes that Gundobad's bishops will find his treatise useful

Contra Eutychianam haeresim 2, *Against the Eutychian Heresy*, Book 2

[Avitus the bishop to his lord, Gundobad the king]

1. {22.3 Peiper} I consider it a significant and worthwhile effort briefly to mention in my present writing the recent moment when[1] the deadly poison broke out into sharp difference [of theological opinion]. Belief in the evil spawned by Eutyches[2] that we have undertaken to combat had lain quiet after the death of Acacius, the former bishop of Constantinople.[3] This same Acacius, as Your Highness may know, was more[4] a hesitant lover of the doctrine than its public champion;[5] for he praised the sayings of Eutyches that he found, but did not dare to preach them to a then devout and

---

1 Peiper's text is untranslatable. Mommsen's *qua* is the simplest correction.

2 The archimandrite of Constantinople whose theology was condemned at Chalcedon in 451.

3 Acacius died in 489: Stein-Palanque, p. 37, esp. n. 2.

4 The second part of the sentence shows that S's *magis trepidus* must be right.

5 Acacius, although he had resisted Zeno's anti-Chalcedonian encyclical, was not an enthusiastic supporter of Chalcedonian theology.

unpolluted people. For his dissimulation of a false and imaginary doctrine, thanks to the favour of the reigning emperor of his day (*sc.* Zeno), he died not only unpunished, but uninvestigated.[1] Hence the opinions of the people, and – worse still – those of the clergy diverged concerning the outrageous fact that the dead man had still been in communion. Just as each one had right or wrong theological opinions, so likewise did each feel [differently] about memory of the dead preacher. And, in this (sc. the memory) secret disagreement was prolonged in the meantime, not so much in [open] schism as in pretense [of unity].[2] The issue was raised[3] with the Eastern emperor and thereafter with[4] the patriarch of Constantinople,[5] in the hope that he could take advice in peaceful discussion and with mollifying appeasement.[6]

2. It is customary in the East in the churches of important cities for a supplication to be made at the beginning of the mass to accompany the praise of the Lord.[7] The voice of the plebs raises this acclamation as one[8] with such religious enthusiasm and alacrity that they believe – not without reason – that any plea made in the subsequent liturgical celebration will find favour [with God] as long as this dutiful expression of devotion is added at the beginning. Even though Your Piety is very familiar with it, I decided that it would be a good idea to cite the end of this supplicatory prayer here, since my argument requires it:

---

1 This is a very strange and erroneous account of Acacius, who was certainly condemned by Pope Felix III: see Stein-Palanque, pp. 24–27, 33–35, 37–39.

2 There had, of course, been a schism between the papacy and Constantinople since the excommunication of Acacius in 484: Stein-Palanque, p. 27.

3 *Agitur* (L) cannot be right, given *anno superiore*. *Actum est igitur* S is preferable.

4 Taking *cum* as a preposition in parallel to *cum rege*. The meaning of the sentence is not entirely clear, and the possibility remains that *cum* should be taken as a conjunction governing *conferret* and that there is a lacuna after *conferret* that contained the main verb, i.e., 'The issue was raised with the Eastern emperor in the previous year; thereafter, when he (the emperor) was bringing ... to the bishop of his own city in peaceful discussion and with mollifying appeasement' < ...>

5 Translating *urbis suae*: *Suae* (= *eius*) refers to Anastasius.

6 *Blanda meditatio*, 'soothing practice', does not make much sense. One could emend to *mediatio* 'mollifying appeasement'.

7 There was no fixed canon of the Mass in Avitus' day: thus he could perfectly well approve of an invocation which he found theologically meaningful. For the fact that the *Trishagion* was already used in Syria, see Chadwick, *Boethius*, p. 185

8 Rendering *consonae*.

'Holy God, Holy Powerful One, Holy Immortal, have mercy on us!
You who were crucified for us, have mercy on us!'[1]

And just as it had been whispered[2] to the emperor, so he too made it known
to the bishop: that nothing should be a cause of dissension,[3] and that there
would be[4] no mention of dissension,[5] if the bishop, once he had been asked
to do so by the emperor, were to order or allow what used to move the souls
of some in the prayer to be removed.[6] Allegedly[7] some were not content that
at the end of the prayer itself they called out: 'You who were crucified for us,
have mercy on us!'[8] You know that this means in Latin 'You who were
crucified for us, have mercy on us!'

3. He managed to convince the bishop of this, who was careless and in no
way learned enough to be the patriarch of so great a city and, through it,
patriarch of the whole East. Through an ill-advised definition of this solemn
prayer,[9] he thought up and arranged a loss that had so great an effect, that the
clause, because it had not been handed down in the canonical scriptures or
instituted at the time of the apostles, seemed easily susceptible of alteration
– even against the will of the people. But where the hymn was customarily
first sung in church, {23.1 Peiper} because the end of the prayer had been
deleted, it did not please its audience. Whatever was considered the product
of Eutychian heretics clearly seemed to be the [theological] message of this
patriarch.[10] What one of the faithful would not rightly be upset, if he heard
that one ought not to pray to him who had been crucified for us? What more
need I say? A storm of riots swelled up.[11] While the people insisted, and the

1 Avitus supplies the text in Greek.

2 Note the over-determined form *insussuratum fuerat*.

3 *Veniret* seems to imply an indirect command.

4 The text reads *fieri*, but it must be used in a future sense here. Note the awkward switch to
accusative-infinitive indirect statement.

5 Since Avitus seems not to have known about the Acacian schism, *de scismate* must refer to
division within Constantinople.

6 I.e. the *crucifixus*-clause of the *Trishagion*. Macedonius was, of course, opposed to the
Trishagion. Where Avitus is wrong is in assuming that it needed removing.

7 Rendering the *oratio obliqua* of the original.

8 The quotation is given in Greek.

9 By stating that the *Trishagion* referred to the Trinity rather than to Christ? This was the
interpretation of the Syrian Monophysites, Chadwick, *Boethius*, p. 185.

10 The patriarch in question, Macedonius, was certainly not Monophysite, although he had
subscribed to the Henotikon of Zeno. Avitus has mixed up his parties.

11 These are probably the riots of ca. 511, as is suggested by Avitus' description of the

emperor did not stand in their way, the patriarch was expelled from his ancient see, and – to make matters worse – he was not innocent.[1]

4. Just as we read in a certain place in scripture (1 Sam. 2.25) 'If one man sin against another, a priest shall judge him: but if a priest sin against the Lord, who shall entreat for him?'[2] But above all other sins, that man especially sins against God, in contradicting apostolic teaching and deviating from the rule of truth. Just as nothing is more serious than when a blind man, in arrogantly taking the initiative to lead, becomes a destroyer of the faith, after being its preacher, judge the madness of this whole heresy by its rejection of one sentence. To be sure, it might seem as if little had been taken away from the *ears*, but, along with that one phrase, the full meaning of Catholic truth is excluded. They do not wish us to pray to him who was crucified in order that it should appear that just as the person of a human should not be able to grant anything, in exactly the same way the substance of the [divine] majesty should not be able to suffer any punishment. And what is this other than to pay back love with hate, and a good turn with abuse?

5. For the dignity of divine beings was placed in a human body. God, to be sure, is not subject to torture, but the divinity *was* involved in the passion. The daylight, darkened by the shadows of night, showed terror at the harm done to God at the time of the Crucifixion.[3] And the earth bore witness, as it trembled, that the Jews had sinned against heaven. There are no uncertainties, no guesswork:[4] the truth shines of necessity. It expects us to affirm what is necessary, since it alone on its own authority is sufficient unto itself. Let us pay attention to the apostle who protests: 'for had they known it, they would never have crucified the Lord of glory'.[5] But even that prophet who is

---

subsequent deposition of the patriarch (see Stein-Palanque, pp. 169–70) and not the more famous riots of 512: Stein-Palanque, p. 177.

1 Macedonius was indeed exiled, with the emperor's connivance, and he had effectively been exiled as a result of his own stupidity in signing a profession of faith which ignored both Ephesus and Chalcedon: Stein-Palanque, pp. 169–70. Since the emperor's chief agent in all this, Celer, was a correspondent of Avitus (*Ep.* 48), we should probably understand Byzantine propaganda as causing some of the bishop of Vienne's difficulties.

2 The AV text reads: 'If one man sin against another, the judge shall judge him: but if man sin against the Lord, who shall entreat for him?'

3 Mt. 27.45.

4 See Goelzer, p. 106, for the archaic and unusual use of *careo* plus genitive.

5 1 Cor. 2.8.

nicknamed 'the angel' for his foreknowledge,[1] had said this before[2] 'whether a man will crucify his God, because you rob me'.[3] I ask, would he so openly contrive obstacles[4] for his own purpose?[5] If the Lord of Majesty hung on, or was nailed to, a cross, let the opposition say why we should not call upon a man in heaven.

6. For up to that point he had still laid away his heavenly glory in a body as hiding-place; he still owed a death because of the womb [he came from]; he was still performing acts of humility to teach us, even among his acts of glory. When a certain Cananite woman, devout as the Israelites, but of a foreign race – her strength befitted a man; her prayer was commendable; her stubbornness prevailed – begged Christ to be propitious, saying, 'Have mercy on me, O Lord, thou Son of David',[6] the inner wisdom of her perceptivity, surpassing the biological sex of her flesh,[7] detected something

1 Malachi. See Aug. *Civ Dei* 20.25.

2 Mal. 3.8.

3 Mal. 3.8. The Vulgate reads *Si affiget homo Deum, quia vos configitis me?* AV 'Will a man rob God? Yet ye have robbed me.' Avitus' text reads *Si affiget homo deum suum, quoniam vos adfigitis me?* Jerome, *In Malachiam* 3.8 (*CCSL* 76 A) provides some clarification of the problem in translation. The word that is translated as *affigo* is the Greek πτερνίζειν, 'to trip up, supplant'— hence also 'to cheat'. Of the verb Jerome says: *Verbum Hebraicum, quod scribitur haiecba LXX interpretati sunt, 'si supplantat,' pro quo Aquila, Symmachus, et Theodotio posuerint 'si fraudat,' ut sit sensus: 'si fraudat homo Deum, quia vos fraudatis me?' revera secundum historiae ordinem, quia decimas et primitias Levitis populus non reddebat, seipsum fraudem, dicit Dominus, sustinere, cuius ministri, fame coacti et penuria templum deseruerint ... Hoc quod dicimus 'haiecba,' lingua Syrorum et Chaldaeorum interpretatur, 'Si affiget;' unde et nos ante annos plurimos ita vertimus, magis ad mysterium Dominicae passionis, in qua homines crucifixerunt Deum, quam ad decimas ac primitias, quae sunt scripta referentes. Quaerat prudens lector quomodo nostra interpretatio cum his congruat, quae sequuntur: 'In decimis et in primitiis,' et videat an possimus haec dicere: 'ut me affigeretis cruci,' ut sceleratas manus iniceretis deo vestro, multarum ante rerum meditatione fecistis, subtrahendo decimas et primitias ... hoc de verbo uno a nobis dictum sit, lectoris arbitrio intelligentiae iudicium relinquentibus.* In connecting the passage in Malachi with the Crucifixion, Avitus is following Jerome's exegesis which interprets *affigo* as an allusion to the nailing of Christ to the cross. We have translated the text accordingly.

4 *Obstinacula* is a hapax. See *TLL* s.v. *obstaculum* 238.25. See Goelzer, p. 461, who does not translate it.

5 The subject of this sentence is unclear. Perhaps Malachi?

6 Mt. 15.22.

7 *Sexu carnis* cannot be translated, and was rightly obelised by Peiper. Hence the following diagnostic conjecture: *sexu<m> carnis <superante>*. The woman has already been character-ised as surpassing her sex in her *virtus virilis*. Here the inner wisdom of her mind might well have been said to have surpassed the outward womanly form of her flesh.

superhuman in the man. The Eutychian learned men do not agree that it is right to pray to him who was crucified for us.[1] She proclaims that both divinity, which could not die, and humanity, which could be brought back to life, should be fixed to that cross: 'Son of David' echoes back the flesh; 'Have mercy on me,' declares the god. He was called 'the Lord God of Heaven' because of his power, but 'the Father of Man' through his stock. A long sequence of time, I believe, after the death of David, {24.1 Peiper} from whose seed Christ shone upon earth through Mary, has now been drawn out from the lineage of the royal stock.[2] I am asking now, from these generations of great-grandfathers and grandsons, from the father I mentioned down to the offspring of the virgin, with all that accrues from heredity, is the lineage of a phantasm to be traced or one of a graft?[3]

7. Let us see whether Christ tasted[4] the words of the aforesaid Canaanite in his response, or whether he was exasperated at the foolishness of the supplicant: 'O woman, great is thy faith: be it unto thee even as thou wilt.'[5] If that faith is truly great, what does not agree with it will not be correct. It was quite a different answer that he gave his mother when he had been invited to a wedding celebration along with his disciples, and the wine ran out, and he was asked to perform a miracle. To her he said: 'Woman, what has this concern of yours to do with me?[6] Mine hour is not yet come.' It is as if he were to say, 'why do you think that I am merely what you gave birth to?'[7] If you think that all I consist of is flesh, then I cannot carry out what you are asking. This exalted [favour] that you ask of me, I inherited from my Father, I did not derive it from my mother. Do you teach a body that was formed in you what is owed to infirmity, yet at the same time enjoin acts of power? You do well to think that I can do what you want, if you understand that, just as you are the mother of my body, you are also the mother of your

1 Avitus' confusion might reflect some knowledge that in Constantinople the phrase 'qui crucifixus es propter nos' was attached not to Christ but to the Trinity: Chadwick, *Boethius*, p. 185.

2 Taking *stemmate* Peiper.

3 See Prudentius, *Apoth.* 915 for *tradux*.

4 I.e. 'took in'.

5 Mt. 15.28.

6 John 2.4. *Quid mihi et tibi est mulier?* The AV which reads 'Woman, what have I to do with thee?' But Avitus seems to read the passage differently. See R. E. Brown, *The Gospel According to John (i–xii)* (Garden City, NY, 1966), p. 97 for the translation and p. 99 for an explanation of the Semiticism.

7 I.e. a human being.

Creator. For if you would have it that you gave birth to a mere human being, 'Mine hour is not yet come.'

8. None can be thought such a fool as to apply his phrase, 'Mine hour is not yet come', as if he were a pagan, to astral fatalism.[1] To understand the mystery of that hour, it is right to look for a means of drawing a distinction rather than a [fixed] decree. Since the very condition of our mortality itself is not bound to it (*sc.* any decree), but every necessity of our state is the will of him who governs us eternally, how much the more unwilling to entangle himself in any fixed decrees of fate is Christ, who has the power of laying down his life[2] and of gaining it back. But when the time arrives to undergo execution, both the divine traits, which came from the Father, and the fleshly ones, which the womb brought forth, will appear. Therefore, since the Lord himself here in carrying out a miraculously divine action has not rejected his mother, but taught her in her ignorance, let us see what he discussed with his disciples in a more lengthy treatment.

9. In a certain place in scripture, he was asking them what the varying opinion of the crowd was about his identity. When they had suggested that the people had different ideas, and some believed that he was one of the ancient prophets, or Moses, or at least Elijah, he said 'But whom say ye that I am?'[3] Then the chief of his disciples took the initiative in answering, and said, 'Thou art the Christ, the Son of the living God.'[4] What Peter admits here clearly could have sufficed, even if Christ too had not confirmed it in an indirect fashion in his answer. 'Blessed art thou, Simon Bar-jo-na: for flesh and blood hath not revealed it unto thee, but my Father which is in heaven.'[5] 'Blessed art thou', I say, who, to recognise the son of God, have judged not merely in the flesh and in blood, nor have the lineaments of the body[6] that I took on offered you my glory to be revealed to you. You by gazing with your noble mind did not take account of what came from flesh and blood. Instead

---

1 *Constitutis fatalibus (sc. horis)* means lit. 'fixed, fateful hours'. For the debate on whether Christ was subject to the stars, see Augustine, *Contra Faustum* 2.5 *CSEL* 25 p. 259; also Augustine, *Sermo* 199.3 (*PL* 38.1027ff.). The Manichees claimed that he was subject to astral necessity.

2 John 10.17.

3 Mt. 16.15.

4 Mt. 16.16.

5 Mt. 16.17.

6 *Lineamenta corporis*: compare Gelasius, *De Duabus Naturis,* p. 18.

my Father, who is in heaven, revealed his son to you, to whom he is joined
on earth, whose glory is not concealed by poverty, nor his honour by insults.

10. {25.1 Peiper} The body of our mediator hung raised up on the lofty tree
of salvation in triumphal eminence,[1] and the power of the salvation-bearing
trunk drew forth an opinion from deep within the heart of each person
[present]. That derisive man [offered] insult: 'Here is the man who was
destroying the temple of God in order that he might raise it up in three
days.'[2] Another one held out a drink of vinegar fouled with animal-gall on a
sponge instead of in a cup.[3] All the same, among the tortures undergone by
the man, he preserved the mercy appropriate to the Creator, and since he
grieved [to see] that they, for whose sake he had come, were still in error,
even at the very moment of redemption, he cried out, 'Father, forgive them;
for they know not what they do.'[4] What does 'They know not what they do'
mean, except that they believe that they have executed someone who is only
a man? He who does not perceive the majesty in the tortured body does not
know what he is doing. And if, because they believe that they were killing
merely the son of his mother, they did not know what they were doing, why
does Eutyches today still pretend that he does not know? For 'had they
known it' at the time, with Christ and the apostle making it clear, 'they
would never[5] have crucified the Lord of glory'. Therefore even though here
the Lord would like us to forgive those who did not know [what they were
doing], it is clear that forgiveness cannot be granted to the conscience of
those who know [what they are doing.] Or are we perhaps surprised that
Christ deigns to explain his passion so clearly?

11. I would venture to say that we have further evidence here of what is
worthy of admiration. The joint crucifixion of a pair of thieves, suspended
on either side of him, accompanied the death of our Lord. It was, however,
the cruelty of the judgement, not the fact that they deserved their servile
death that made them partners of an innocent man. For the horror of nearby
pollution was unable to affect the pure radiance of the sacred seed, just as the
sun too, if it shines on what is gross, is in no way aware of the contagion it
has entered. Therefore one of these thieves, changing a long life of crime by

---

1 Cf. the imagery of Fortunatus' Cross-hymns, *Carm.* 2. 1–6.
2 Mt. 26.61, but different from the AV.
3 Mt. 27.48 contaminated with Mt. 27.34.
4 Lk. 23.34.
5 1 Cor. 2.8. The AV reads 'not' for 'never'.

a shortcut taken near its end, became a doctor after having been a murderer, a martyr after having been a thief. His limbs were bound, but he was loosed from his crimes; attached by nails, but free with his love, he said, 'Lord, remember me when thou comest into thy kingdom.'[1] O happy circumstance that he bore witness! What inexpressible courage in belief! It was not portents that overcame his [disbelief] to make him sense the divinity in the man; instead he picked up his sense of virtue through a sign of weakness: he wished to pray to one who was bound like himself. Yet even now Eutyches disdains to pray to him who was raised on high [on the Cross]. The thief trembled before Christ when he died, yet Eutyches scorns him even when he reigns. Eutyches did not fear death at the hands of him who will judge him, while the thief sought life from a man who was dead. But once he had suffered with his Redeemer in a death of abominable slowness, he joined his own cross to the Lord's. He adored him, free of guilt, yet a participant in his punishment, and finally, eager to make an onslaught,[2] he changed his prayers by preaching and armed with nails from the Cross, he brought force to bear against the kingdom of heaven. He understood that it was in Christ, the poor man, that the rich neighbour was to be found. He found what he could 'lift' from a naked man.[3] He took full forgiveness and seized the portion of innocence. He gazed upon God on the Tree and followed a man into heaven. And furthermore, now that the martyrdom that He suffered teaches us that he[4] was a real man, tortured by pain, likened to thieves, killed by execution, buried in a sepulchre – through all of these things, the true fact that he took on a body contradicts all who claim that he was a phantasm. Even though the clear unity of both substances[5] convinces them with the clear light of proof, they disturb the whole sequence of the Lord's passion that will be fulfilled in what follows with the fantastic construction of a contumelious office.[6] They claim {26.1 Peiper} that there was a sort of wraith, a cloud-like body that was put out to endure the injuries, punish-

---

1 Lk. 23.42

2 Lat. *invadendi*. Avitus may be punning on the idea of onslaught in theft or burglary. He repeats this idea in the *SHG* 3.416–19 *martyrium de morte rapit. cui fine sagaci/maxima cura fuit tales non perdere poenas./ praeripuit scandens aditum caeloque levandus/ardua sublimi tenuit compendia saltu.* A similar treatment of the good thief's thievery can be found in Sedulius, *Carmen Paschale* 4.231.

3 For the proverb, see Juv. 10.22 and A. Otto, *Die Sprichwörter und sprichwörtlichen Redensarten der Römer* (Leipzig, 1890), 1250.

4 *Quam* in Peiper seems to be a typo for *quem*.

5 I.e. natures, human and divine.

6 Obscure. Perhaps because it is paradoxical. An honour that is an insult.

ments and pain instead of our Redeemer – that it was a lifeless being in the trumped-up shape of a man, because [divine] majesty cannot undergo tortures, and because it was not true flesh that the people harassed, that the judge tortured, and blows struck, that they made a mockery of with insults, that thorns pierced, at whom a reed was poked, on whom a nail fixed and from whom blood was extracted.[1] But because we place all our hopes in the mystery of our redemption alone, and our being brought back to life has no foundation other than our Lord's having suffered death,[2] it is false [to say] that he saved us with his Incarnation, if what he took upon himself to tolerate for us in the flesh also is called into doubt.

12. Instead, come, holy Isaiah, a prophet in your own time, yet an evangelist of ours! Come swiftly to protect the salvation of Christians against the lies of Eutyches! It would be no hardship to say, indeed to swear of Christ, 'Surely he hath borne our griefs, and carried our sorrows … and with his stripes we are healed.'[3] While the ability to heal was not certain, it was a fact that he took upon himself willingly to suffer for us.[4] If indeed he himself truly 'carried our sorrows', then we too are now secure that it was not a trumped-up phantasm that tolerated real pains. And if we have been healed with his stripes, in vain does lying envy begrudge me the health brought to me.[5] Furthermore by any definition it is only reasonable to conclude that a fabrication, because it was faked, could not be alive. But even in these words of the prophet clear evidence of the double nature of his substance is found. 'Surely he hath borne our griefs, and carried our sorrows … and with his stripes we are healed.' These things are two, of which God alone could not do both, nor man alone. God could do one, man the other. When the prophet says 'Surely he hath borne our griefs, and carried our sorrows', he was clearly alluding to one being that consisted both of godhead and of a body. He alone healed the diseases that the wounded descendants of Adam caught from the wound that was their corrupt origin. He alone healed who had made the healthy being in the first place. He carried our sorrows who could not sweat through the battles of the Passion except by enduring tortures and

---

1 For a similar series of indignities in asyndeton, see Fortunatus, *Carm.* 2.2.19.

2 S's *dominum necem* is correct. Cf. Rom. 6.4–10.

3 Isa. 53.4–5.

4 As punctuated by Peiper, this is a sentence fragment consisting of two ablative absolutes. Peiper's period after *sumus* should be replaced with a comma.

5 Avitus puns here on the two meanings of *livor*: 'bruise' or 'stripe', and 'envy'.

pain. Therefore that we have evil in nature, God bore it; that we suffer evil in our body, Christ bore it to the bitter end.[1]

13. Therefore we should look and see how the Eutychians are submerged in an even deeper abyss than were the Bonosiacs.[2] The latter take away only the honour due him as a divinity; the former take away the truth of his body too. Photinus laughs at us for worshipping the person of a man; Eutyches for worshipping a cloud. Is it perhaps that the heretics draw the inspiration for this illusion from the very celebrations that accompanied Christ's nativity? Will it be equally false that he lay in swaddling-clothes? That he appeared to the wise men? That he wept in his cradle? I will refrain from saying anything about what occurred later on in his life, when, because he embraced both a divine and a human nature, our Refreshment suffered fatigue, our Consolation poured forth tears, our Light slept, our Bread hungered, and the Fountain thirsted. I will not mention how he initially displayed the tender feeling appropriate to the human condition in a lament over the dead Lazarus {27.1 Peiper} before showing himself to be God by bringing him back to life. If he who did so much is being called into doubt, it follows that his deeds too must be considered questionable.[3] The paralytic who believes that he has been healed is in error; the lame man falsely thinks that he walks upright; the ray of the sun is invalidated[4] that the man blind from birth beholds after the shadows of his native prison. Was Lazarus himself deluded by this phantasm so that as he slept among the dead he already thought that he had been resurrected?

14. If they believe all these things to be true, and take umbrage only at the indignities of the Passion, let them tell [us]: where was the Son of the Virgin when, offering in place of himself the shadow that deceived people with its tenuous cloudlike appearance, which we thought was being offered for us, he was deceiving both the faithful and the persecutors with an empty image of himself?[5] He made his Father a liar too by this trick, since the apostle said of him, 'He that spared not his own Son, but delivered him up for us all.'[6]

---

1 Avitus makes a word-play on *tulit* and *pertulit*.

2 For Bonosiaci see *Ep*. 31, p. 62.16 and Gennadius, *Liber sive definitio ecclesiasticorum dogmatum* 21, ed. C. H. Turner, 'The *Liber Ecclesiasticorum Dogmatum* Attributed to Gennadius', *JTS* 7 (1906), p. 94.

3 Cf. Prudentius, *Apotheosis* 1020.

4 A curious legal use of *circumscribo*.

5 Cf. Prud. *Apoth*. 952ff. for similar argumentation against the phantasmatics.

6 Rom. 8.32.

What 'son', if he was not real? How did he 'deliver him up', if he confined him? How did he 'not spare' him, if he prevented him from feeling pain? What death finished off Our Lord, if he could not fail to owe even the smallest death because of his mother's mortal nature to dissolve his slavery according to the law of dying, even if he was not going to see corruption, because he would be resurrected immediately? The gall that he did not want to drink, once he had tasted it,[1] signified this law that governed both natures. For he did not want to drink of the death that we all owe as part of our heritage from Adam, but he had to taste it, because of the dispensation. But when what the apostle said, happened, when 'Christ being raised from the dead dieth no more; death hath no dominion over him',[2] let the heretic want either a Christ without God or God without man, if he can.

15. Holy Thomas had been away when the Saviour returned from the dead, and was fulfilling the prayers of the disciples by his visible presence and was steadying the wavering faith of his own followers by coming back from the dead [and appearing] alive. The disciples say that they have seen the Lord. Thomas states that he does not believe them, and will not trust under any circumstances, unless he has a chance to see [for himself]. After a while Jesus appears for a second time – this time to all of them at once. After giving the sign of peace, he very gently reprimanded the slowness of the reluctant apostle. At the command of our Lord, in case sight alone was too little, the sense of touch explored faith. He said, 'Reach hither thy finger ... and thrust it into my side: and be not faithless, but believing.'[3] [Just as inexcusably you will persist in not believing, even when you have received proof through touching.][4] He explored the traces of the Passion with his finger. The healing wound remained just where it had been inflicted, and the life-giving cut happily preserved a gaping entry-way where the side had been pierced. Then finally he came to his senses, and, illuminated by touching his holy body, said 'My God and my Lord.' [5]

16. What understanding of the heavenly did the Holy Apostle gain from the flesh? What divinity did he feel in the wound by touching it with his curious hand, unless he had already learnt that Christ could not exist without God

1 Mt. 27.34.
2 Rom. 6.9.
3 John 20.27. Avitus has omitted the middle of the the quotation.
4 This sentence fragment should be excised. It looks like an intrusive marginal comment.
5 John 20.28.

and that these very wounds he was touching had conquered the man, but yielded to the victor? They would not have been able to put him to death unless he was a man, nor would they have been able to have been defeated, except by God resurrecting [Him].[1] {28.1 Peiper} Here, confounded by the great and astonishing miracles, when they hear, let them recognise that our Lord, visible to [their] eyes where his body was buried[2] and palpable to fingers, had entered the room where the apostles were seated, even though the door was shut. They complain about the darkened gaze of men being fooled into lending credence to a well-known trick with a phantasm, through deceptive contrivances and a false semblance of empty clouds. For they sense something divine in the magnitude of what happened, the force of the subtle nature by which a body entered the secret room, even though the doors were bolted and no access was available. They trump up a tale of uncertainty lest they be forced to admit a marvel. See what a discredit to divinity it is, if the master of truth who forbade us even lies in words alone,[3] be thought to have lied in his deeds. There is no doubt but that it would be a sort of lie, if he wished his apostles to believe that he had done something that he had not done, and were Christ thought to have done something that no Christian is allowed to do. < ... > He (= Thomas)[4] was both instructed in understanding a mystery by sight (which was enough for a healthy man) and convinced by touching (the additional faculty required by the blind). An ailment that is sought voluntarily cannot be cured. Whatever sort of medicine is put on his ailing eyes, the man who takes pleasure in being blind[5] cannot be healed. What use are eyes anyway in the case of such a stubborn man[6] who rejects the truth that his very eyes proclaim? As if it were no less a miracle for God to penetrate closed spaces than for the heavens to lie open to a man. He who often bore witness to his disciples after the resurrection: 'Handle me and see; for a spirit hath not flesh and bones, as ye see me have.'[7] What could be so invisible to Eutyches? What could militate so clearly against phantasms?

1 Goelzer, p. 455.

2 Translating *situs* as 'place'. Avitus is apparently alluding to the first sightings of Christ after the resurrection. See John 20.1–23.

3 Mt. 12.36; John 8.44.

4 The *qui* must refer to Thomas, yet he is not mentioned in the preceding passage. There may be a sentence missing between *Christiano* and *qui*.

5 Taking Mommsen's *caecutire*.

6 A *constructio ad sensum*: *obstinatione* refers to a stubborn *person*; the relative pronoun is hence masculine.

7 Lk. 24.39.

17. It is as if he were to say, 'An apparition, insubstantial as the wind, does not have the bulk of bones and flesh.' He does not wish himself to be called a spirit alone (i.e. one without a body), even though he is a true spirit. He would prefer that you recognise him by your judgement to be just the man that you saw return from the tomb. Now that he has triumphed after the struggles of the Passion, he has nothing earthly for the needs of a resuscitated body to demand. For it is not there (i.e. in heaven) that hunger demands food, thirst drink, labour rest, or activity sleep. All of these things[1] have been made to vanish[2] not only in our head which is Christ[3] with his brief, nay momentary death, but also in our case they will have dominion [only][4] up till the time of death, because they will cease with our resurrection. Nonetheless, as I had begun to say, even though those limbs of our Lord were no longer subject to any [mortal] needs, he was seen with his apostles so as to remove any suspicion that he was a ghost from the minds of his followers. He ordered food to be put on the table and deigned to eat it after giving thanks. What they were still doing to fortify their bodies, the good teacher did to bear witness to truth. Unless perhaps the man who preaches the doctrine of the phantasm were to say that the shadow, an appearance of limbs intended to deceive, was eating what was put before it, and that the food taken by the sacred offspring [i.e. Christ] did not enter the body of the Lord without burdening it with corruption,[5] but that it weighed down empty wind with a mass of food of uncertain nature.[6] The deceptive image certainly either spirited this food away, if it snatched it, or else is not insubstantial, if it ate it. I know however that none other than Christ among the records of that supper says, 'All things must be be fulfilled, which were written in the law of Moses, and in the prophets, and in the psalms, concerning me.'[7] And we are looking for a [only a] few examples, when he says that scripture is altogether fulfilled in its unity? And 'after this, while he blessed them, he was carried up into heaven'.[8]

---

1 Human beings' subjection to the needs of the body.
2 See Goelzer, p. 577, for *decoquere*.
3 1 Cor. 11.3.
4 One would have expected a *tantum* to make the sense clearer.
5 Avitus seems to exhibit concern about the digestive processes of the risen Christ.
6 Alternatively 'some sort of food'.
7 Lk. 24.44.
8 Lk. 24.51. AV adjusted to match Avitus' syntax.

18. {29.1 Peiper} Go far away, Eutyches, with the tricks that you have thought up! He alone has no blessing who rejoices that he is blessed or redeemed by a phantasm. In the meantime the Son of Man, who had long been in heaven through his foreknowledge, was being carried there in his person.[1] Nor did he need the help of any angel's hand, even though he is said to be carried. The Son of the Father carried the son of the mother: he went, because he was God; he was carried, because he was man. The gate of heaven lay open to him as he returned, and the glory of his original fatherland welcomed its god as he returned, this time with a body. Once he had been received, two angels, he (i.e. Luke) said, stood by, and said the following to the apostles: 'Ye Men of Galilee, ... this same Jesus, which is taken up from you'.[2] That is to say, He, whom the Father received on his throne and whom you received in faith, 'shall so come in like manner as ye have seen him go into heaven'.[3] Those to whom what happened seems to be an illusion[4] have something to hope for from these words, if 'he shall so come in like manner as ye have seen him go into heaven'.[5] When the Catholics see the One they worship and the enemy see the one they crucified, when at the sight of those same visible traces of the nails, < ... >[6] let Eutyches perhaps cease to think those fires counterfeit, with which, after the smoke from the phantasm, the ever-lasting fire-brand will burn in delayed penance.

19. Let it suffice for [your] sectaries[7] to have absorbed these few things to stigmatise his ingrained doctrine or to correct it for a while, as is desirable, so that from the example of the testimonies that I have adduced, they themselves may seek out both examples that are necessary for themselves[8] and more numerous [ones]. If by chance, because of the old wickedness of their dogma they either persist in their heresy,[9] or else add some new

1 The Latin word used is *natura*.
2 Acts 1.10–11.
3 Acts 1.11.
4 Lat. *phantasma*.
5 Acts 1.11.
6 The *ubi* which starts this phrase in Avitus seems rhetorically sound, so there appears to be a verb missing.
7 Avitus intends Gundobad's Arian bishops, whom he calls *sectatores* both at *Ep*. 46, p. 75.2 and at *Ep*. 23, p. 55.35.
8 Avitus is clearly hoping that his words will also be significant in bringing Arians to his understanding of the faith.
9 Translating *infidelitas*.

contrivance,[1] if indeed it is the characteristic of those who err always to wish to speak in their perverse obstinacy, so that they perish, God will grant that when I carry out your command [this] wickedness, which so far has been kindled by argument, may be cast out by the magisterial authority of heavenly scripture that is one and always the same.

Epistula 39: Introduction

This letter seems to have been written in the context of negotiations which took place between Pope Hormisdas and the emperor Anastasius in 515, relating to the question of Monophysitism (see also *Epp*. 31–32).[2] The letter implies that there had been at least one previous request for information that had gone unanswered. Since he does refer to a papal letter in *Ep*. 41 it is possible that *Epp*. 39 and 40 belong to an group of correspondence earlier than that represented by *Epp*. 41 and 42 (which may never have been part of the Avitus letter-collection). Avitus' tone is distinctly tetchy (e.g. 'or whoever he is',[3] *seu quicumque nunc ille est*). Nevertheless, the letter contains one of the earliest and clearest expressions of papal primacy in doctrinal matters to be found outside Rome. This, despite the elevation of Arles above Vienne, and the consequent downgrading of connections between the latter city and Rome. The lack of reply may reflect papal inefficiency,[4] but may also reflect continuing hostility between Arles and Vienne,[5] and between the Ostrogothic and Burgundian kingdoms, which, for instance, led to the failure of a legation sent by Sigismund ca. 518, to reach the imperial city (*Ep*. 94). That Avitus resorted to appealing to a man high in Theodoric's favour may suggest that he feared that political conflict was getting in the way of ecclesiastical communication.

Senarius was *comes patrimonii*[6] (Italy 509–10) and a frequent ambassador of Theodoric. It was perhaps as a result of one such embassy that Avitus knew Senarius (see p. 68.2, 'having frequently experienced your favour', *gratiam frequenter*

---

1 I.e. there is a danger that the Arians will combine their own doctrine with that of the Monophysites.

2 For the date of Hormisdas' legations to Constantinople in 515 see Hormidas, *Epp*. 7–8 (Thiel). On the negotiations, Stein-Palanque, pp. 182–84.

3 Of the pope.

4 See the excuses offered by Hormisdas in *Ep*. 42.

5 Though it is clear that the papal letter which Avitus received in 514/5 was passed on by Caesarius (*Ep*. 41). That letter may have borne some resemblance to the letter sent to Caesarius by Hormisdas: Hormisdas, *Ep*. 9 (Thiel). See also *Epp. Arelatenses Genuinae* 30.

6 See Cass. *Var*. 4. 3, 4, 7, 11, and 13: more generally on Senarius see *PLRE* 2: T. Mommsen, 'Ostgotische Studien', *Neues Archiv* 14 (1889), pp. 464ff: indices to Cassiodorus (*MGH AA* 12, p. 499 including his verse epitaph) and Ennodius (*MGH AA* 7, p. 359).

expertus), and was in a position to write to him.[1] He is here coopted as a go-between between Avitus and the pope. At the end of the letter Avitus makes it clear that Senarius' answer alone would establish the facts, but that he needs an official notification. Senarius was already established as someone both discreet and 'in the know' in 509/10, when in his appointment letter (*Var.* 4.3.3) Cassiodorus says of him: 'another aspect of your life was praiseworthy, namely that you kept our secrets hidden through your honesty, even though you were privy to many, and were not arrogant even though you knew many things'.[2]

Avitus the bishop to Senarius, vir illustris *{68.1 Peiper}*

Since I have frequently experienced the favour of Your Magnificence, and because you kindly entertain such communications, I am sending my greeting in this letter.[3] Since you know that it is routine in synodal law that, in matters related to the state of the church, if any doubt or hesitation arises, we, the obedient limbs, as it were, have recourse to the highest priest of the Roman church, as if to our head,[4] I have, with all due care, in accordance with the will of the bishops of the province of Vienne,[5] sent my humble obedience to the holy Hormisdas,[6] or whoever now is pope.[7] I wish to hear from the papal authority what he knows about the outcome of the embassy he sent to the Eastern empire.[8] Therefore, as I said, when I am consulted by my provincials, even I do not take it upon myself to answer, unless I have taken advice from my superior. I have need of Your Ordination's[9] help to conclude

1 For more on Senarius' ambassadorial activities and their possible relationship to events in the Burgundian kingdom, see Shanzer, 'Two Clocks', pp. 248–49.

2 *Fuit quoque in te pars altera vitae laudabilis, quod arcana nostra probitate claudebas, multorum conscius, nec tamen, cum plura nosses elatus.*

3 Lit. 'with the page playing the part of servant'.

4 This is one of the earliest, if not the earliest, surviving expression of papal primacy to have come from outside Rome.

5 Technically only Vienne, Geneva, Grenoble, Tarantaise and Valence (Duchesne, *Fastes épiscopaux* v. 1, p. 124), although Avitus was, of course, writing for all the bishops of the kingdom.

6 Hormisdas, pope 514–23. Avitus' comment suggests that communication between the papacy and the province of Vienne was at best intermittent, despite the previous expression of papal primacy. This may reflect the rise of Arles, but may also reflect the continuing hostility between the Burgundian and Ostrogothic kingdoms, which is also visible in Avitus *Ep.* 94.

7 Avitus' formulation, 'or whoever now is pope', is irritated and somewhat dismissive.

8 Stein-Palanque, pp. 189–91.

9 The honorific *ordinatio vestra* is unusual for a laymen. Avitus uses it to Viventiolus (*Ep.* 19) and Victorius uses it to Avitus (*Ep.* 16). *TLL* s.v. *ordinatio* 936.80–937.3 gives a minimal number of examples where it is used of non-ecclesiastical offices. It is not discussed by M. B.

this matter satisfactorily from both sides: namely that our question arrive, and that an answer be forthcoming from an authority. The state of the church is not a matter for bishops alone: it is a common cause for concern to all the faithful. Whoever we are, and in whatever way we are seen to run the church, we are handling your business in the Catholic faith. When something in the rule of faith is either ill or is healed, you ought either to rejoice or to groan with us. I cannot therefore believe that there is anything about this affair that lies hidden from you. If I were acting on my own behalf, a note from you alone would be a sufficient answer to my question: I could not hear any greater truth from the pope than from you. But the interests of the church demand that the teacher tell us what you yourself know. I therefore, your special friend, ask the special favour of a reply from you, so that, as I said, the truth can be made known to me to the extent that it will please the Roman pontiff by virtue of his authority to tell those who are waiting for an answer.

Epistula 40: Introduction

This letter provides an important insight into the difficulty of obtaining information in the post-Roman period. Avitus appears not to have known that there was a breach between Constantinople and Rome at the time he wrote to Clovis (*Ep.* 46). The *Trishagion* riots of 511, at the latest, brought him to understand that there were theological differences between Rome and Constantinople even if he did not fully understand them (*CE* 1 and 2). During the period (c. 515) in which Vitalian controlled Constantinople it seemed that the schism might be settled.[1] This hope soon faded.[2] The current letter seems to be a pair with *Ep.* 39, and may date to 515, when negotiations between the papacy and Constantinople opened up again, although it is possible that it, and *Ep.* 39, goes with *Epp.* 41 and 42, which can be firmly dated to 516/7.

A number of factors were significant in causing the breakdown of communication within the church. The divisions within the church, that is the Acacian schism itself, and also the Laurentian schism within the Roman church (498–514),[3] were factors in preventing the distribution of information. It is possible that disagreements between Arles and Vienne over their relative status were also factors in preventing quick dissemination of information. At the time that this letter was written, however, there was the additional problem that relations between

---

O'Brien, *Titles of Address in Christian Latin Epistolography to 543 A. D.* (Diss. Catholic University of America, 1930).

1 Avitus, *Ep.* 9: Stein-Palanque, pp. 178–84.

2 Stein-Palanque, pp. 189–92.

3 Stein-Palanque, pp. 134–39.

Theodoric and Sigismund were bad. Perhaps in the same year, or a year after Avitus wrote enquiring about the Acacian schism, Theodoric prevented Sigismund's envoys from travelling to the court of the emperor Anastasius (*Ep.* 94). It is in this context that one needs to understand Avitus' comment that his letters may not reach the pope. Given the poor relations between the Ostrogothic and Burgundian kingdoms, all significant embassies to Rome would have needed permission from Theodoric – they may have needed permission at any time. It is at least clear from *Ep.* 42 that a mission was allowed to proceed to Rome in the winter of 516/7.

Peter of Ravenna would have been a useful ally for Avitus in his search for information. First he was bishop of Ravenna, Theodoric's seat of government. Second, he was closely associated with some aspects of Theodoric's religious policies, notably towards the Jews,[1] and he was involved in dealing with the Laurentian schism.[2]

Avitus, the bishop of Vienne to Peter, bishop of Ravenna {68.23 Peiper}

Even if there were no other reason for which my devotion might seek Your Beatitude in a dutiful letter, it would be right for you to be cultivated by all, since you cause everyone to want to meet you because of your holy reputation. Therefore it is no less right that you be sought out than the see of Rome,[3] for it is no more distinguished for power than you for charity. Omitting the greeting due to its reverence (i.e. the Papacy's),[4] I therefore confess to Your Apostleship, though it be with shame, the ignorance of those of us in Gaul. Nor do I think it better for someone to pretend that he knows, than to have learned, if he does not know. We have not heard from any authority what is happening between the churches of Rome and Constantinople, but we get our information from rumours instead and from a variety of different messengers. And therefore, in order that we not be thought both to be boorish and negligent, the whole province[5] is now making

1 Anonymus Valesianus 14.81; Moorhead, *Theodoric in Italy*, pp. 98–99.

2 *Praeceptio Regis* III, ed. Mommsen, *MGH AA* 12, pp. 419–20: *Acta Synodi* (502), ed. Mommsen, *MGH AA 12*, pp. 444–55: see also Cassiodorus, *Var.* 3.37.

3 For the use of the ablative of comparison rather than *quam* Goelzer, p. 113 compares *CE* 2, p. 26.27 as a parallel.

4 Or 'yours'. The antecedent of *cuius* is not entirely clear, but it is most likely to refer to the *sedes Romana*.

5 This might be read as a challenge to Caesarius: in 450 Leo had assigned the whole province of the Viennensis to Arles, except for Vienne itself and its suffragans of Valence, Tarantaise, Geneva and Grenoble: *Epp. Arelatenses Genuinae* 13; Duchesne, *Fastes épiscopaux* 1, pp. 123–24. In fact the political divisions between the Burgundian and Gothic kingdoms effectively rendered this ruling void, and Pope Anastasius appears to have made some

an official inquiry of the pope and of Your Beatitude through [these] clerics from the Viennensis.[1] We would like you to make clear to us through the health-bringing light of a reply what your understanding is about the state of the faith with the Eastern church. Even with teachers who are far away, it is right to ask for teaching of one's own accord: for the sake of the unity of the body we must see to it that the limbs are reassured about the health of their head. Therefore, if my sons, your servants, whom I have sent for that purpose, are granted the opportunity to reach Rome itself, it will be a wealth of information for Gaul to be informed through two princes of the church.[2] If those whom we have sent should return from your see,[3] the faithful response of Your Apostleship, which may come back to everyone,[4] will be more than adequate information.

Epistula 41 = *Hormisdae Epistula* 22, Thiel, pp. 781–83: Introduction

Epp. 41 and 42 are not preserved in any of the extant Avitus manuscripts, and neither may have formed part of the Avitus collection; they do, however, relate to *Epp.* 39 and 40 and have therefore been included. Although Sirmond edited them, it is not clear whether they appeared in his (now lost) manuscript of Avitus. But since *Ep.* 41 ends with a note of its reception by the papacy, it is virtually certain that Sirmond saw the letter in a papal MS and inserted it into the Avitus collection. The oldest MS containing the letter is Vat. lat. 4961 of the tenth century. Since the reception of *Ep.* 41 at Rome is dated 30 January 517, and Hormisdas' reply (*Ep.* 42) is firmly dated to 15 February 517, *Epp.* 39–41, which belong to the same group of letters in which Avitus sought information on the state of the Acacian schism, must have been written at the end of 516.

---

modification in Vienne's favour: Symmachus, *Epp.* 2, 3, ed. Thiel; *Epp. Arelatenses Genuinae* 23. Symmachus himself temporised in 500–1 (*Epp. Arelatenses Genuinae* 24) and then restated the position of Leo (*Epp. Arelatenses Genuinae* 25). Avitus might be seen as offering further criticism of Caesarius for not passing on any information about the Acacian schism.

1 Assuming that Avitus refers to the bearers of the letter.

2 I.e. the bishop of Ravenna and the pope. Avitus is flattering Peter by putting him on a par with the papacy.

3 I.e. not be permitted to travel to Rome.

4 Again this may be a snide dig at Caesarius – or perhaps at Hormisdas who has not passed on information to all.

Avitus to his most holy lord, the pope, most outstanding in his merits, most glorious in Christ, and most worthy of the Apostolic See {69.7 Peiper}

Since you know that it is appropriate for the status of our religion and all the rules of the Catholic faith that your alert care and exhortation inform the flock entrusted to you through all parts of the universal church, you visited[1] the Viennensis last year, if you remember, in that you sent letters to your humble servant. They reached me as the opportunity afforded itself through clerics of the church of Arles, yet they were full of a sense of paternal care. In them, just as you summon us to share in your joys in the conversion of the provinces of Dardania, Illyria and Scythia,[2] at the same time you instruct us with a very delicate admonition, lest something deceive us in our ignorance. The condemnation of Eutyches and Nestorius, whom the authority of the Holy See under your predecessors had crushed in the past, had already been made known to us some time ago through apostolic diligence. But this has now made us very unsure and anxious, that, even though you ordered us attentively to wait for the outcome of the second embassy sent to Constantinople, your son, my holy brother Ennodius[3] has told me nothing, nor have you informed us whether it returned having achieved its goal, and you left your promise hanging with a such a long silence[4] that the taciturnity of the preacher now astounds us no less than the delaying of the embassy had already made us suspicious. Whence, for this reason alone,[5] I have sent with this dutiful letter your servants, my sons Alethius the priest and Viventius the deacon, in the name of the whole province of Vienne[6] which was committed to my church by all of your predecessors and by the Apostolic See. I hope to learn through them – your answer will be my oracle! – whether the fervour of the aforesaid schisms, which had burnt in vicious obstinacy at Constan-

---

1 For the *topos*, see the opening of *Ep.* 35. An indication of the contents of the letter may be found in the one sent to Caesarius on 11 September 515: Hormisdas, *Ep.* 9 (Thiel).

2 See Hormisdas, *Epp.* 1 (on Scythia), 3, 5 (on Thessalonika), and 9: and for subsequent developments Hormisdas, *Epp.* 15–20.

3 Ennodius, bishop of Pavia, post 513–521: *PLRE* 2, Ennodius 3. He headed the 515 legation, Hormisdas, *Epp.* 7, 8, 10 (Thiel), and he would lead the 517 legation, Hormisdas, *Epp.* 27, 33, 34, 37. Since the letters carried by the 515 legation were written on 11 August 515, it must be this legation that Avitus counted as the second. In *Ep.* 42 Hormisdas counts it as the first, although he had already sent messengers to the emperor in 515: Hormisdas, *Epp.* 4, 6 (Thiel).

4 *Tanta silentii diuturnitate*: Lit: 'with so great a length of silence'.

5 Taking *sola hac causa* with S.

6 Technically only Vienne, Geneva, Grenoble, Tarantaise and Valence (Duchesne, *Fastes épiscopaux* 1, p. 124; see *Epp. Arelatenses Genuinae* 25), although Avitus was, of course, writing for all the bishops of the kingdom.

tinople and to which – a greater cause for sorrow – you say that Alexandrian and Antiochene churches are bound, has been extinguished at your teaching, Christ willing, by the appropriate measures, or whether the embassy, once returned, has brought back something to show that can easily be read, or perhaps brought back in an announcement some means whereby whatever suspicion you have about this may be maintained.[1]

For we are afraid that the pope, when he does not indicate that things are going well, may have sensed that something was going wrong. To this is added the fact that we have heard from different and reliable sources that Greece is boasting about its reconciliation or concord with the Roman church.[2] This is the most welcome of news, if it is true, but we must also be on our guard lest it be a cunning falsehood. All of us therefore ask through me that you instruct me in what I should say to my sons your brothers if I am asked for advice.[3] For, secure not just of the devotion of the church of Vienne, but of that of all of Gaul, I promise you that all of us are seeking your decree about the state of the faith. Pray that just as the false profession of the damned may not deceive us, so too, once we have found out the truth, it may not separate us from the unity that you rule. Received 30 January 517. By the priest Alethius and the deacon Viventius.

Epistula 42 = Hormisdas Epistula 2, Thiel, pp. 783–86

Hormisdas to Avitus the bishop and to all the bishops of the province of Vienne who are in your diocese.[4] {70.13 Peiper}

He who wishes to be instructed, even though he knows a great deal about matters that have to do with the Catholic faith, has clearly shown what zeal he has for the divine commandments. There can be no such care except where [a man's] faith is genuine. For this reason we rejoice in the Lord about

---

1 Peiper's text reads (p. 70.2–3) *unde vobis ad hoc qualiscumque suspicio reservetur.* But *reservetur* seems to be the wrong word. One would have expected something meaning 'allayed'. Goelzer, p. 676, does not comment on the usage here.

2 This would reflect the attitudes of Vitalian's party, which was in power in 515 (Stein-Palanque, pp. 182–84), and with which Avitus was in correspondence (*Ep.* 47). See also *Ep.* 9, where Avitus congratulates the patriarch of Constantinople on the ending of the schism.

3 *Id est Gallicanis* has the air of a gloss, and should be bracketed.

4 I.e. suffragans of Vienne. The phrase *sub tua diocesi* clearly has a sting to it: Hormisdas is specifically limiting Avitus' authority to the dioceses of Geneva, Grenoble, Tarantaise and Valence: *Epp. Arelatenses Genuinae* 25; Duchesne, *Fastes épiscopaux*, vol. 1, p. 124; Klingshirn, *Caesarius of Arles*, pp. 70–71.

the sincerity[1] of your proposal, most beloved brother, when we see through
the letters sent with Alethius the priest and Viventius the deacon, that you
both recall the decisions of the Apostolic See concerning the impious sinners
Eutyches and Nestorius and are making inquiries as to whether we have
admonished them and taken any measures against those by whom the
churches of the East are confounded. It is certainly a worthy source of
concern to the faithful that they bemoan the fall of wretched men, yet see to
it that they themselves not be polluted by someone else's disease. But do not
think that we have been suppressing things, preventing accurate information
from reaching you about what has been done. We [will] make quick work of
eliminating the silence that [so] hurts you.[2] For because we do not often have
to advise you, we have trust in the stability of your conscience and faith.
Care would perhaps have to be paid to those who waver: it is enough to have
made clear what has to be avoided to those who are perfect.

If the longed-for arrival of the embassy (i.e. from Rome to Constantinople) that we sent once (not twice,[3] as you write) had occurred, we would
eagerly have shared with you the news you want. For we know that this is
only reasonable and in accordance with our plan, namely that to those whom
we caused to share in our worry, with them we should join the joys of the
return of unity. As far as the Greeks are concerned they offer wishes for
peace with their mouths rather than their hearts and they say just things
rather than do them. Their boastful words imply that they desire what their
actions proclaim them unwilling to do. What they claim, they fail to
demonstrate, what they have condemned, they follow.

For how did it come about that when they had promised through
Ennodius our brother and fellow-bishop[4] that they would send clerics to

---

1 A *sinceritate* cannot be right. One could emend to *in* or bracket *a*. But S (Sirmond's
Concilia Galliae) reads *in domino de sinceritate* which seems preferable.

2 Lit. 'by which your affection is bitten'.

3 Clearly there had been some misunderstanding, in that Hormisdas appears to have told
Avitus to await the outcome of a second embassy when he wrote in 515 (*Ep*. 41). Furthermore
Hormisdas was splitting hairs as it was, for there had been a considerable exchange of letters
since Hormisdas' appointment in 514. Further, although there had only been one full papal
embassy in 515, a legation had come from the emperor in 516, and Hormisdas had sent a reply:
Hormisdas, *Ep*. 13 (Thiel). The politeness of his reply suggests that Hormisdas realised that he
had not kept Avitus adequately informed. There would be a second papal legation in 517. Stein-
Palanque, pp. 182–85, 189–91 and Chadwick, *Boethius*, p. 42.

4 Ennodius, bishop of Pavia, post 513–521: *PLRE* 2, Ennodius 3. He headed the 515
legation (Hormisdas, *Epp*. 7, 8, 10 [Thiel]), and would lead the 517 legation (Hormisdas, *Epp*.
27, 33, 34, 37).

confirm what the Apostolic See had requested, and also made many promises to emend their wickedness – as they had been requested to do by us – not only did they not as *per* their own agreement send men of religion with full authority to handle the matter, but also, by sending laymen and people who were not part of the church,[1] as if something insignificant were at issue, they did not at that time make an effort to extricate themselves from the mud in which they were immersed, but instead tried to darken through obfuscation[2] the Catholic faith in all its brightness? This was the reason that we were silent, as you too saw through the revelation of spiritual prudence. What could I explain to you about this matter by sending letters, stubbornly stuck in its own wickedness as it was? Let those who are concerned about an unexpected outcome ask for a careful account of what is happening:[3] he who makes no indication of what he knows is declaring that previous things are staying entirely the way they were.

For this reason, most beloved brother, we both encourage you with this missive and through you too, since now we have the opportunity, we warn the others in Gaul who share the same faith with us. Keep the constancy in the faith that you have promised and that is pleasing to God, and refuse the company of transgressors. Show your constancy 'to Christ, a virgin to one husband',[4] as you have promised. Beware, 'lest just as the serpent beguiled Eve through his subtility, so too the minds of some may be corrupted away from the simplicity and chastity that is in Christ Jesus'.[5] The blandishments of harmful people are pernicious and for that reason you should be alert, because 'the adversary' of human salvation, 'as a roaring lion walketh about, seeking whom he may devour. Whom resist, steadfast in faith.'[6] Because those who follow his footsteps and love [him] have this special characteristic of their father, who was cast down from the citadel of heaven:[7] that because they have been deprived of that light of truth, they rejoice that others are benighted in their darkness, and even though they know that they will pay the penalty for their perversity, they rejoice, if they can acquire some miserable companions in their damnation. For how does it happen that, even

---

1 The legates were the *viri illustres,* Theopompus and Severianus: Hormisdas, *Epp.* 11–14.

2 *Satietate* (Peiper) makes no sense. *Obscuritate* (S), 'darkness', is better.

3 *Novi exitus* makes no sense as a nominative. It must be a genitive, and the simplest emendation is to change *sollicite* to *solliciti.*

4 Alluding to 2 Cor. 11.2.

5 Alluding to 2 Cor. 11.3.

6 1 Pet. 5.8.

7 I.e. Lucifer.

though on the whole they are being deserted by their neighbours, the Thracians, Dardanians and Illyrians,[1] now that their perversity is known, in the hope that they will be ignorant, they try to entice those who live far away[2] by deceit and various tricks – unless it be in order to stain for others too by wicked contagion the light that they themselves do not have?

So that you may recognise the goals of these factions – many of the people in Thrace, even though they are ground down by the attacks of persecutors, keep communion with us, since they know that faith becomes brighter in adversity. Dardania and Illyricum,[3] both near to Pannonia, have asked that bishops be appointed by us for them where necessary, and we have already done so. They have thus joyfully separated themselves from the company of the damned, with the result that they seek remedies, provided that they have nothing to do with the transgressors. The metropolitan of Epirus, that is the bishop of Nicopolis, who has recently been set apart from the wicked along with his synod, has made the necessary profession of faith and restored himself to apostolic communion.[4]

We thought we should put this information in the present letter, in order that, just as it is right that we mourn the fate of those who are perishing in pain, so too we rejoice in the safety of those who are returning, and in order that the faithful who live rather far away may be instructed in it (sc. the letter) in the precautions necessary to avoid the poison of those whom they see are rightly being shunned even by their own people. And we too ought to remember our arrangement to seek them out with one embassy after another, so that, even if they are not moved in their desire for salvation by respect for God, or by the considerations of reason, at least they may give way, if we keep on knocking importunately and stubbornly, and either reject their errors and return to the straight path, or be judged incorrigible by all because of their stubborn spirit, since, even though they had been warned, they persisted in their obstinate perfidy. Pray and join your prayers to God and entreaties to ours, that through his charitable efforts our action, working for the stability of the Catholic faith, may make progress, keeping you pure and whole, separated from any contact with transgressors in order that we may

1 For Hormisdas and Dorotheus of Thessalonika, Hormisdas, *Epp*. 3, 5 (Thiel), and John of Nicopolis and the bishops of Epirus, Hormisdas, *Epp*. 15–19 (Thiel): Stein-Palanque, pp. 183–84, 190.

2 A hint that proselytisers have been sent to Gaul? Or a reference to Avitus' Constantinopolitan informants?

3 V's *Illyricus* must be wrong. Read *Illyricum*.

4 Hormisdas, *Epp*. 15–19.

either join our hearts and senses with those who have been reformed, or else that we be fortunate enough to be free from the poisons of those [who are evil]. For we who know (just as you too testify that it is not unknown to you) that Eutyches and Nestorius were condemned by apostolic, i.e. official Catholic authority, how can we be saved, if we cling in any form of communion to their followers and successors, since Belial can share nothing with our Christ?[1] We believe that it is in the interest of your authority that we inform you through a reading of the documents about what was done before us by the Nicopolitans or the Dardanians,[2] or in what order they were taken back into communion. Given 15 February 517.

1 2 Cor. 6.15.
2 Hormisdas, *Epp.* 15, 16 (Thiel).

2. THE LAURENTIUS FILE

Contents

Epistula 9 Avitus to the patriarch of Constantinople: Avitus congratulates him on negotiations to end the Acacian schism (date post-March 515).

Epistula 46A [Sigismund to Anastasius] a fragmentary letter, written to accompany the son(s) of Laurentius back from Burgundy.

Epistula 47 Sigismund to Vitalinus, Senator: Sigismund negotiates the return of the son(s) of Laurentius from the imperial court.

Epistula 48 Avitus to Celer, Senator: Avitus negotiates the return of the son of Laurentius from the imperial court.

The dossier on Laurentius and his son touches on a number of major issues. First, the letters appear to relate to the year 515, though they seem to concern more than one embassy. The context appears to be the expected ending of the Acacian schism, during Vitalian's dominance in Constantinople (*Ep.* 9). Whether Vitalinus (*Ep.* 47) and Vitalian are the same person is unfortunately unclear. In the event, the schism was to last another three years. Second, apart from the Acacian schism, the letters are also concerned with the return of the son of the *vir illustrissimus* Laurentius, who is being sent to join his father in Constantinople, at the request of the emperor. Laurentius himself had already been allowed to return (*Ep.* 47), and it appears that father and son had both been hostages of some kind at the Burgundian court. Exactly under what circumstances such hostages were held is unclear, although there is a further reference to such a situation in *Ep.* 49. Since the hostages seem in some way to have been connected to Vitalian, one might perhaps guess that they were effectively exiles sent abroad after Vitalian's initial revolt in 514.[1] Whatever the explanation, the presence of hostages suggests a complicating factor in any relations between Byzantium and the West. At the same time, the embassies seem to have been involved in negotiations for Sigismund to take over the office of *MVM*, which his father had been granted in 472 (*Epp.* 46A, 47, 48: see also 78, 93, 94),[2] and which he may well have continued to claim thereafter. Since Gundobad was still alive, this must have been an attempt to ensure the continuation of good relations between the Burgundian kingdom and the Empire after Gundobad's death, and perhaps to strengthen Sigismund's position in preparation for his succession to the senior position in the Burgundian kingdom. In all this there is the added complication that Sigismund appears to have angered

---

1 The Chronicle of Marcellinus *comes* provides an important contemporary account for Vitalian's revolt, especially *s.a.* 514, 515. He is known to have held Hypatius as a captive, *s.a.* 515.4.

2 See *PLRE* 2 'Gundobadus 1'.

Avitus in initially choosing someone else to write the diplomatic correspondence to the imperial court. Unfortunately this multi-layered correspondence is, as usually with Avitus, both allusive and elusive, and by no means easy to interpret.

Epistula 9: Introduction

This letter must be dated to 515, because of its association with *Epp.* 46A, 47, 48. It reflects the expectation that the Acacian schism would be ended, following the success of Vitalian's rebellion against Anastasius.[1] Sigismund has sent a legation to the emperor, perhaps reflecting his elevation to the patriciate,[2] and Avitus has taken advantage of it to send a letter to the patriarch of Constantinople. Because of the date we can be sure that the patriarch was Timotheus.[3]

See D. Norberg, 'Alc. Avit. *Ep.* 9 (Peiper p. 44,1)', *Eranos* 36 (1938), pp. 129–30, and Burckhardt, pp. 109–11, who translates the letter.

Avitus the bishop to the patriarch of Constantinople[4] *{43.5 Peiper}*

Since my master, your [spiritual] son, the patrician Sigismund[5] sent out an embassy to the most glorious *princeps*,[6] he provided[7] for me as well a doubly sacred chance to pay my respects to you. When I was thirsting for you as our foremost priest, with justified longing, Laurentius, *vir illustris*,[8] increased our respect for you by indicating in his letters[9] that everything

---

1 Stein-Palanque, pp. 181–84.

2 Sigismund clearly received the patriciate while his father was alive. This is the first (and only) clear mention of the office. Since Vitalian seems to have been responsible for Sigismund's elevation to some office other than that of *MVM* in 515 (*Ep.* 47), it is likely that he received the honour immediately before this letter was written. Martindale, *PLRE* 2, is sadly imprecise over the chronology of Sigismund's office-holding.

3 Stein-Palanque, pp. 170–71 and 190–91: although Vitalian had demanded the restoration of Macedonius, he died in exile, pp. 179 and 184. In the complicated theological politics of Constantinople, Avitus may not have known who the patriarch was. One should compare *Ep.* 39, p. 68.7 where Avitus, if he is not being snide, clearly does not know the name of the pope, and *Ep.* 25 where he does not know the name of the patriarch of Jerusalem. Charaux wrongly identifies the bishop as John of Cappadocia, but provides a translation of the letter on pp. 103–04.

4 For Avitus' use of *papa* for 'patriarch', see Goelzer, p. 429 n. 1.

5 See above p. 21.

6 The emperor Anastasius.

7 *Prospexit.*

8 See *Epp.* 46A–48 on the return to Constantinople of Laurentius' son.

9 *Apicibus suis*, the actual written characters of the letter, is here used *per synecdochen*, see Goelzer, p. 600.

clouded that had darkened the peace of the Eastern peoples with its obfus-
cating lies had been cleansed by the serenity of peace restored, and that you
now have the sort of peace with the pope at Rome that befits, as it were, the
twin princes of the Apostles[1] to offer to the world. What Catholic would not
rejoice at the peace of two such great churches, ones which the world looks
at, as if they were a sign[2] of the faith placed in heaven, as if upon a double
star. Who does not rightly rejoice in the return of the weak, the safe state of
those who are unharmed, when, once the other sheep are safe within the
fold, the one who has wandered off because of a mistake of her erring keeper
is called back to the heavenly fold with rejoicing?[3] Guard like fathers the
disciplinary power of the church – even over us! – that is entrusted to you.
Your concord is required as much to enforce [religious] authority as to serve
as an example.[4] What charity will we be able to enjoin upon our people, if
we cannot find it in our rulers? What stability can there be in a body whose
head nods? In unity of spirit give an abundance to those returning.[5] See to it
in your preaching that no one perish intentionally, that the thieving beast not
prey upon the assigned watch-tower,[6] if Rome should depart from your
consensus. Our grief, should the sun go down upon your dissension,[7] is a
loss for the East.[8] Since we have received the happy news that I mentioned
above from a most reliable source,[9] confirm my information in your own
hand, so that the eager Western church may rejoice that the gift of a heavenly
oracle that it is happy to have received through a fellow-student[10] may be
multiplied for it by a master.

1 Peter and Andrew. Constantinople was popularly supposed to have been founded by Saint
Andrew.

2 *Signum*, the word used here, could mean either 'military standard' or else 'constellation'.

3 Mt. 18.12.

4 See Goelzer, p. 129, who construes *concordia* as ablative with *opus est*, and *magisterio* as
dative.

5 L has a nonsensical reading *unam ergo copiam*. Norberg, 'Alc. Avit. *Ep.* 9', pp. 129–30,
finds Peiper's emendation *unanimi* too far removed from the *ductus litterarum*, and suggests
vestram ergo copiam, where *vestram copiam* = *vestri copiam*.

6 Isa. 21.8: *et clamavit leo super specula Domini ego sum stans iugiter per diem et super
custodiam meam ego sum stans totis noctibus. Adsignatam*, 'assigned', may refer to Isa. 21.6:
vade et pone speculatorem: et quodcumque viderit, annunciet.

7 Eph. 4.26: *sol non occidat super iracundiam vestram.*

8 This is, of course, an inversion of the imperial imagery of the eastern sun, which is to be
found in Avitus' diplomatic letter *Ep.* 93 and in *Ep.* 46A.

9 I.e. from Laurentius.

10 Metaphorical. Avitus is probably referring to Laurentius. The patriarch is the master.

Epistula 46A: Introduction

Although this appears as the conclusion to *Ep*. 46 in the Lyons MS and in Sirmond's edition, it is clearly another item in the Laurentius dossier.[1] That it is addressed to the emperor is clear from the language, which more closely resembles that of *Epp*. 78, 93 and 94 than it does *Ep*. 46, although Clovis himself is treated to some panegyrical imagery.[2]

Interestingly, the letter seems to have been penned in the name of Sigismund, since the supposed author is clearly distinguished from the *rex*, who must be Gundobad.[3] This would seem to imply that the letter was written at a moment when Gundobad had transferred some power to Sigismund: this could suggest a date after Sigismund's elevation as *rex* at Carouge. This elevation, however, may have taken place shortly after the turn of the century,[4] although there is no indication that Sigismund exercised much authority for a while thereafter. He was, however, certainly acting independently of his father by 515, as is most obvious in his foundation of Agaune. Having become *MVM* in 472 Gundobad was certainly an elderly man by the second decade of the sixth century. At all costs, Sigismund may well have been exercising considerable power by the time of the Laurentius episode in 515.

[Sigismund to the emperor Anastasius] {76.15 Peiper}

< ... > Let no country claim you as if it were your special seat. It is clear that you are shared by all to whom you grant office.[5] All enjoy the brilliance of one sun: what is nearer, to be sure, rejoices in more light,[6] but what is further away does not have to do without [any] brightness. Accordingly, let your diadem shed light on those who are present; your majesty on those who are absent. Let the news of the number of joyful triumphs that adorn that land

1 *Epp*. 46A, 47, 48 and 49.

2 *Pace* F. Vogel, 'Chlodwigs Sieg über die Alamannen und seine Taufe', *Historische Zeitschrift* 56 (1886), p. 398.

3 If the headings of Avitus' letters are not sufficient proof that he regarded Gundobad as *rex* (and it is true that some of the headings may not be authorial), this passage is uncontrovertible, *pace* G. Scheibelreiter, '*Vester est populus meus*. Byzantinische Reichsideologie und germanisches Selbstverständnis', in E. Chrysos and A. Schwarz, eds, *Das Reich und die Barbaren* (Vienna, 1989), pp. 206–08.

4 Fredegar 3.33. On the various elevations of Sigismund, see above p. 21.

5 This sentence confirms the identity of the addressee, the Eastern emperor. See the opening of *Ep*. 47, esp. p. 77.1, *communi principi*. Sigismund is clearly alluding to *honores* granted to Burgundian rulers by the Byzantine emperor. At this point Gundobad is still alive (see below), so Sigismund had not yet been made *MVM* (see *Ep*. 93, p. 100.9), but he may be referring to his own patriciate (*Ep*. 9).

6 Compare the imagery in *Ep*. 46.

thanks to you be known everywhere. Your happiness affects even us. As often as you fight there, we are the victors here. But even among these [victories] the desire to be merciful burns in you with [all] the feeling inspired by Catholic faith, and your holiness is in evidence at the summit of the imperial government as much as your power is. This is why it came about that you gave a command in a princely pronouncement[1] that the son of your servant, the *vir illustris* Laurentius, be sent to you. I submit that I have managed to bring this about with my master,[2] the king of his people,[3] but your soldier.[4] There is no matter in which he would not be eager to serve you; he sends the boy and commends him [to you]. I rejoice that he has been sent and envy him because he will see you. It is less important that he be restored for the convenience of his own father than that he be presented to the father of all.

Epistula 47

Sigismund to Vitalinus[5] the senator[6] {76.28 Peiper}

As far as it pertains to your worthy integrity of judgement, those whom you adorn and elevate with the privileges of office,[7] you should consider Romans.[8] Since we are therefore confident, it is not appropriate that they be thought altogether absent, who, even though they are separated by the

1 Lit. 'oracle'.

2 Gundobad, cf. *Ep*. 47 p. 77.3.

3 See above p. 137.

4 Doubtless there is a reference here to the claims of Gundobad to be *magister militum*.

5 *PLRE* 2, Laurentius 9 and Fl. Vitalianus 2 identify 'Vitalinus' as Vitalian, which is the name in the edition of S. There are arguments both for and against the identification of the recipient of the letter with Vitalian. In favour is the clear indication of influence over the emperor which the man is assumed to have: against is the title 'senator', which seems inappropriate for the most powerful military figure in the East.

6 The manuscripts differ widely over the rubric at the head of this letter: L has *Epl'a aviti epi ad vitalinum senatorem*, while S has *Epistola ab Auito episcopo dictata sub nomine C.S. ad Vitalianum senatorem*, and he glosses C.S. as *Comitis Sigismundi*, while Binding, *Das burgundisch-romanische Königreich*, p. 242, glosses it as *gloriosissimi Sigismundi*. The heading in L is simply *Avitus episcopus vitalino senatori*.

7 This appears to link Vitalian with the negotiations surrounding the concession to Sigismund of the title of either *patricius* or *MVM*. Since this letter must date to 515, because Vitalian was still in power, and since Sigismund did not receive the office of *MVM* before Gundobad's death in 516 this must refer to title of *patricius*, which is mentioned in *Ep*. 9.

8 *Romanus*, as used by Byzantines, meant 'Byzantine'. They considered themelves the successors of the Roman Empire.

location of their fatherland, are represented by their office.[1] Therefore, since it is the one thing I can do, showing my devotion of spirit through my attentive and dutiful behaviour (or because I have the chance), I state what I would very much like. Tell our common and most clement prince[2] what I desire.[3] Make known to him in greater detail the service that I am actually performing for him now, but always am willing to. Let him know, and represent favourably to him the fact that the order his Princely Reverence gave was carried out by your admirer and my father and lord[4] through my mediation. Let the son of your client, the *vir illustris* Laurentius, be given back to his father and to his country by my efforts. Some time ago we had sent a servant in the person of the father,[5] now we are adding in the person of the son a retinue.[6] Let us know, once this one man has been sent to you, how things are going with the others.[7] It remains [only] for the aforementioned soldier[8] of yours, whose offspring[9] is both to be offered to Your Grace there and is being kept safe here[10] for his fatherland,[11] once he has been commended to you by my effort, himself to commend <us to you by his>,[12] because he[13] is both now certain that he will get that son of his[14] back, and confident that the other son[15] who is coming back with our party[16] is safe.

1 Peiper's text and punctuation do not make sense. The *ut* clause is not dependent on anything. He has inserted a question mark despite the lack of any interrogative word in the sentence. S's text, *ex hac ergo fiducia non convenit ut*, solves the problem. Sigismund refers to himself.

2 I.e. Anastasius: the envisaged closeness of Vitalinus and the emperor further supports the identification of Vitalinus as Vitalian.

3 Could this be the office of *MVM*?

4 I.e. Gundobad.

5 Taking *in parente* as a fore-runner of Fr. 'en', 'acting in the capacity of'.

6 The sentence is very difficult to interpret. The clear parallel structure suggests that S rightly supplies <*in filio*> to parallel in *patre*.

7 Or 'how the others are being dealt with'.

8 The *militia* could be *militia civilis*. The identification of the individual is unclear, though it could be Laurentius.

9 The son of the *miles*, perhaps being sent as a hostage, or the son of Laurentius being returned.

10 *Hic* rather than *hinc* is needed to parallel *illic*.

11 I.e. Byzantium

12 *Commendet* seems to be missing an object. A *nos* may have fallen out, or better still a more elaborate balanced phrase such as <*nos studio suo vobis*>*ipse commendet*.

13 Again the *miles praefatus*.

14 *Illius* is here used as a demonstrative.

15 Laurentius may have two sons, and they are perhaps being swapped.

16 *Nobiscum* must mean 'with our party'. Sigismund cannot be going to Constantinople since he is sending a *famulatus* to accompany the boy.

Epistula 48

Avitus the bishop to Celer(us) the senator[1] {77.11 Peiper}

It is clearly not just my desire, but my duty that the good services that you have rightly and devotedly paid to that great and glorious city,[2] be especially appreciated by me, who have long seemed beholden to its kindness. This is all the more true since divine favour now has offered me a good opportunity devotedly to comply with the command of his Highness.[3] For this reason, after first mentioning the generous gift of safety, I commend to Your Magnificence the son of your admirer, Laurentius the *vir illustris*, whom an august command ordered to be sent to his father, to be promoted by your effort and to be protected because you so kindly[4] wanted it. In this land he sought a father, in you let him find paternity. Protect also the man[5] who has been taken up along with his son, who even though he is very much your debtor for his office,[6] began to be even more in your debt because of his son. For through you he will find solace for his own affections and will pay you back by loving you the more.

As for the rest, regarding your faithful,[7] we continually await and desire an order. We wish to have a chance to obey you. If the divinity is propitious, grant us a chance to recognise, both in the serenity of his speech and in a letter from Your Dignity, Roman prosperity under our most glorious leader,[8] at the peak of whose [government][9] you shine in the citadel of an office that is worthy of you.[10]

---

1 Avitus called him '*Celerus*' (*sic*). See *PLRE* 2, Celer 2. He was one of Anastasius' leading officials, and was *Mag. Off.* (East) 503–18.

2 I.e. Constantinople.

3 I.e. Anastasius.

4 Translating *animo pietatis*.

5 Presumably Laurentius.

6 Or 'through your office'?

7 Presumably the word is deliberately chosen, to include the Chalcedonians, even if at face value it might only seem to refer to followers, since Celer seems to have had Chalcedonian leanings: *PLRE* 2, Celer 2, citing Severus of Antioch, *Ep. Sel.* 1.24.

8 I.e. Anastasius.

9 Lit. 'at whose peak'.

10 Referring to Celer's position as *Mag. Off.* (East).

3. SIGISMUND AND THE EMPEROR

Contents

Epistula 49: Introduction

This letter has much in common with those of the Laurentius file. The *adulescens* mentioned here, however, although he clearly is a Byzantine hostage in Burgundy, cannot be the son of Laurentius. The final sentence's parallelisms and use of *quasi* make it certain that he is not being returned to a biological father, but to a figurative one, no doubt the Byzantine emperor. In all probability, this does, nevertheless, belong to the same period as *Epp.* 9, 46A, 47 and 48.

Although it may seem unlikely, given the bishop's age,[1] Sigismund appears to have asked Avitus to go to Constantinople to deliver a message to Anastasius. Avitus refuses. Sigismund asked a fellow-bishop (*conservus*) of Avitus to rewrite (or translate) the letter. He seems to have turned to Avitus again. The latter demurs, with the excuse that simpler, less florid Latin is more comprehensible for foreigners: the stylistic errors of the other writer will not matter. Indeed Avitus finds the usual formalities expressed in Latin more polite than an amateur's attempt at translation, and guesses that they are Sigismund's own words. In the event, Avitus may have written the letter requested.[2]

Ep. 49 provides an interesting glimpse into the problems of translation in international diplomacy. One might compare Avitus' refusal to go to Byzantium on

---

1 And given the illnesses he refers to in other letters which cannot be much later in date, viz. *Epp.* 36, 61, 74, 88. He died in 518.

2 *Ep.* 46A may be a fragment of a letter that was written on this occasion.

this occasion with the information in *Ep*. 94, p. 101.24, that Sigismund had sent 'one of his counsellors who, given Gallic ignorance, is considered more educated than the rest' (*unus de consiliariis … qui, quantum ad ignorantiam Gallicanam, ceteros praeire litteris aestimetur*). The passage in *Ep*. 94 has an ironic tone: it may represent Avitus' judgement on the colleague he alludes to here. Fortunately perhaps, thanks to the intervention of Theodoric, the man never made it to Constantinople to discredit Gallic literacy. Avitus tells us that foreigners find less polished Latin easier to understand.[1] Avitus' own highly artificial and convoluted periodic style obviously set his standard for 'polished'. Yet he was prepared to write more simply and directly for foreign audiences and especially for oral delivery. See *Ep*. 93 p. 144 and his many sermons, including perhaps sections of the *CE*.

Avitus the bishop to (his) lord, Sigismund {77.27 Peiper}

Even if I *could* speak[2] as well as you are kind enough to believe, my Latin speech[3] would be demanding and discordant[4] to Greek ears. But as it is, since in our language[5] they (the Byzantines) will consider something *less* polished more intelligible, in the letter which you ordered my colleague to compose, [stylistic] faults can be dictated without anxiety.[6] Let them to be sure work out for themselves with whatever translator they like[7] what we are trying to say. In the standard salutation,[8] I, with [my own] experience to [help] translate, recognised the favour of my – dare I say it? – more than most pious master (i.e. Sigismund).

For the rest,[9] may Christ repay you in kind for the continuing favour which you reserve for your special servants.[10] [Your] favour is shown to be such even in the case of this young man in particular whom you are sending, in that while having an eye to convenience in this case to be sure, but in

1 His modern Anglophone translators concur.

2 *Loqui*: this seems to imply oral rather than written delivery.

3 'Sermo Latinus' could mean either 'Latin speech' or else 'Latin accent', but appears to mean the former.

4 'Would be a trial to ...'

5 I.e. Latin.

6 The other bishop's 'stylistic faults' are ones that would tend to make the letter easier to understand.

7 I.e. the Byzantines.

8 Presumably in the opening of the letter that had been written by the other bishop and submitted to Avitus for approval.

9 I.e. new paragraph, new subject.

10 *Gratia* in two senses: Sigismund's favour towards the young man, Christ's Grace to Sigismund.

neither to a reward:[1] as if for yourself, you nursed[2] a son[3] and as if to a father[4] you gave a son[5] back.

Epistula 78: Introduction

The letter is written in the overblown language of diplomacy, and serves merely to introduce Sigismund's ambassadors.[6] Note the frequent and varied honorifics: 'Your Loftiness', *celsitudo vestra*, 'Your Glory', *gloria vestra*, 'Your Everlastingness', *vestra perennitas*, 'Your Prosperity', *vestra prosperitas* as well as the light imagery that matches the language of *Ep.* 46. Avitus lays it on with a trowel, taking special care to emphasise Burgundy's subject status in relation to Byzantium.[7] The reason for this subservient tone must lie in the fact that Sigismund is a petitioner, but the Burgundian is also harping on about a title he has received from Anastasius, presumably that of *MVM per Gallias*.[8] This letter is associated in some way with a *gratiarum actio*. As a result it can be dated later than *Ep.* 93, when Sigismund seems still to have been seeking the title, and must be roughly contemporary with *Ep.* 94.

Sigismund the king to his master, the emperor [of Byzantium] {93.1 Peiper}

Even if obstacles of time and space[9] do not permit us to present to you in person the devotion with which we serve[10] you in our spirit, we will try to make the content of our prayers clear through the duties [we offer]. For we believe that we are admitted to the sacred gaze of Your Glory as often as we pay our debt of concern through the zealous offices of the written page. For

1 Taking *in neutro* S.

2 *Nutristis.*

3 I.e. not a real son, but a hostage.

4 I.e. not to a real father but to the Byzantine emperor, figurative father to his subjects.

5 *Nutritum*, picking up *nutristis* above.

6 Burckhardt, p. 96.

7 p. 93.10 *subiectorum* and p. 93.11 *possidemur*.

8 Stein-Palanque, pp. 188–89, with n. 6: 'à cause des locutions *devotionem nostram, qua vobis animo militamus* et *quos militiae fascibus sustollitis*, je crois que dans cette lettre Sigismond remercie l'empereur de l'avoir nommé maître des milices.' *Ep.* 94 seems to thank the emperor for an office soon after Gundobad's death, and since he was clearly *patricius* in 515, the office in question must be the *MVM*, which should be distinguished from the patriciate: *Ep.* 78 might, therefore, be a letter of introduction to *Ep.* 94, or might be a later letter making a passing reference to Sigismund's elevation. One notes that Martindale (*PLRE* 2) distinguishes between Gundobad as *MVM* and as *patricius*.

9 That these obstacles could be very real is made clear in *Ep.* 94.

10 The word used is *militare*, 'to fight', used with reference to the *militia civilis*, the civil service.

although your prosperity is unable to lie hidden from the gaze of the world, and it illuminates the orb with clear shining rays, it is still a pleasure, if those whom you have promoted with military insignia[1] and with the piety of a special favour, those whom you have made rich in the most distant parts of the world by granting membership in your court and participation in the venerable Roman name, especially recognise the joys of Your Eternity that rumour celebrates to all the world. That your subjects are far away is testimony[2] to the size of your imperial power, and that we are possessed from afar reaffirms the [broad] diffusion of your republic. Therefore be favourable to the dutiful bearer of this letter. And although it is the height of honour for all petitioners [merely] to have looked upon you, those whom we presume to commend to you,[3] will bring us also into your presence. Since we believe that these dear members of our household by acting as our messengers will be of use to us too, in taking an eager and hasty short-cut to what we want, we will meet you in the persons of our ambassadors.[4] We beg, above all, that, because the dignity of Your Highness cannot forget good deeds, in return for the thanks we offer, we may receive a response from Your Most Serene Countenance as soon as possible.

Epistula 93: Introduction

The date of this letter is uncertain, although it is fairly clear that it should be placed before Gundobad's death in 516.[5] Despite the emphasis on Sigismund's ancestors,[6] there is no clear statement that Gundobad had died: by contrast Sigismund is quite open about his father's death in *Ep.* 94, which must date to the period between 516 and Avitus' death in 518. It is clear from *Ep.* 47 that Sigismund negotiated directly with the Byzantines during his father's lifetime, and indeed it seems from that same letter that he was already angling for the office of *MVM*: a letter asking for such an office before 516 is therefore perfectly possible. Since Sigismund was elevated to the kingship on Gundobad's orders,[7] there is nothing to suggest that a date for *Ep.* 93

---

1 The implication is surely, following Stein-Palanque, pp. 188–89, n. 6, that Sigismund has been granted the office of *magister militum*, which his father held before 476 (Martindale, *PLRE*, dates Gundobad's holding of the office to 472) and must have continued to claim: see also *Epp.* 93, and 94.

2 Lit. 'adorns'.

3 Sigismund's ambassadors. See *Ep.* 9.

4 Peiper needed a comma after *occurrimus* on p. 93.16.

5 Marius of Avenches, *s.a.* 516.

6 E.g. *Parentalia debita, proavis generis mei, cunctisque auctoribus meis, a patribus.*

7 Fredegar 3.33.

between Sigismund's elevation as king and the death of his father in 516 is impossible. An early date might help explain the exceptionally smarmy language of the letter, which is different in tone from *Ep.* 94.

Despite its epistolary trappings, this is a panegyric. The style is somewhat different from that of Avitus' other writings. While the vocabulary and concepts are similar, he has avoided his usual extremely convoluted and artificial periodicity. This text was written to be taken in by ear. It would have been delivered before the emperor. Many of its *topoi* are similar to those of *Ep.* 78, but this letter must antedate *Ep.* 78. Here Sigismund hints to Anastasius that he would like to be accorded his father's title of *MVM per Gallias*, whereas there he refers to the title as a fact. Similarly, he seems to imply that he has received the title in *Ep.* 94. In many ways the style of this letter (and of the other letters to the emperor) can be compared to those letters of Cassiodorus' *Variae* addressed to the emperor,[1] suggesting compliance with well-established conventions of literary address.

The letter is also important for what it implies of the political success of Anastasius in the East during the closing years of his reign. Although other sources do not help directly in filling out Avitus' allusions, it may be that this letter refers to a renegotiation of the seven-year peace of 506 between Byzantines and Persians, which ought to have taken place ca. 513.[2] The other possibility, which may perhaps have stronger support from Procopius, is that the reference is to Anastasius' success in fortifying Dara without incurring Persian reprisals.[3] If this interpretation is accepted, Avitus may provide some help in dating Anastasius' dealings with the Persians, following the fortification of Dara, since it would seem that he is writing about relatively recent events.

Ep. 93 exploits geographical *topoi*. Sigismund begins by invoking West, North and East, Gaul, Scythia and Byzantium, to claim that Anastasius' Eastern sun sheds its rays on the West and North too. Although Sigismund cannot meet Anastasius in person, he can enjoy his presence through letters. He awaits Anastasius' command. Sigismund then continues to survey the points of the compass. Now points east of Constantinople await conquest: first the Persians, and then the peoples of the Indus. The burning South (*axis meridianus*) awaits *refrigerium* ('cooling relief') from Byzantium too.

---

1 Compare *Variae* 1.1; 2.1; 8.1; 10.1, 2, 8, 9, 15, 19, 22, 25, 26 and 32.
2 Cf. Jones, *LRE*, vol. 2, p. 232. For the original peace: Procopius, *BP* 1.9.24.
3 Cf. Procopius, *BP* 1.10.17.

*Sigismund king [of the Burgundians] to his master, the emperor
[Anastasius] {100.1 Peiper}*

It is known to all that Your Highness measures not the impediments caused
by circumstances,[1] but the desires of his subjects. Since we are secure in this
happy trust, we are present in spirit to our most glorious ruler, even though
we are absent in body.[2] And even though my race, who are your servants,
have discharged their duty out of devotion, the debt that my father owed
[you][3] no less than the kindnesses you have done me make me beholden to
your favour. For my people are yours,[4] and it gives me more pleasure to
serve you than to be in charge of them. The devotion to the Romans that they
have always felt in their hearts[5] has seen to it that the great-grandparents of
my race[6] have felt – as far as you and your predecessors are concerned – that
the glory that Your Highness has offered us in titles of military honour[7] has
been considered the greater glory by us, and, for all my ancestors, what they
received from emperors has always been worth more than what they had
derived from their own fathers.[8] Even though we may seem to rule our own

1 Rendering *temporum*. Not *mare clausum*, but presumably an allusion to Theodoric's
hostile behaviour. See *Ep*. 94 and. *Ep*. 78 p. 93.3 *obex temporum*.

2 This idea of spiritual contact despite bodily separation is, of course, also a *topos* in letters
of friendship.

3 Taking *parentalia debita* as equivalent to *parentis debita*. Sigismund may be referring to
the title of *MVM* held by Gundobad.

4 See Scheibelreiter, '*Vester est populus meus*', pp. 206–08, although the comments on
Avitus' relations with the Burgundian kings are simply inaccurate. The term *populus noster* is
used frequently in the *Liber Constitutionum*, almost always with the clear implication that the
Burgundians alone, and not the population of the kingdom in general, are meant, although
occasionally the context seems to imply a broader usage: e.g. *Lib. Const.* 79.1.

5 *Romana* means 'devotion to the Romans', i.e. Byzantines. Cf. *Ep.* 78 p. 93.8 where Avitus
speaks of the *veneranda Romani nominis participatione* accorded Sigismund. Peiper's
suggested emendation, *Germana*, is unnecessary.

6 Four generations back from Sigismund would go back to the second quarter of the fifth
century and to Gundahar: see *Lib. Const.* 3: *auctores nostros* (*sc.* of Gundobad), *id est Gibicam,
Gundomarem, Gislaharium, Gundaharium, patrem quoque nostrum* (i.e. Gundioc) *et patruum*
(i.e. Chilperic I). The generation which lived through the 430s, the crushing of the Burgundians
in the 430s and the settlement of the Burgundians in Sapaudia would seem to be significant. It
should also be noted that Gundahar was the first Burgundian king to be involved in imperial
politics: Favrod, *Histoire politique*, p. 46.

7 Sigismund had been named *patricius* by Anastasius in or by 515. See *Ep*. 9. Gundobad
had been *MVM* after 472. See *PLRE* 2 'Gundobadus 1'.

8 The syntactic construction of this sentence is not quite parallel. In *illa* (*sc. claritate*) *nobis
magis claritas putaretur quam* (*sc. claritatem*) *vestra per militiae titulos porrigeret celsitudo*,
the *quam* is the relative pronoun. In the second part of the sentence *quam* introduces an explicit
second term of comparison after *magis*.

people, we think of ourself as nothing other than your soldiers. Your prosperity fills us with the gift of joy. Whatever you care for over there on behalf of the safety of all is ours too. Through us you administrate the [vast] areas of remote regions; our country is your sphere; the light of the East touches Gaul and Scythia, and the ray of light that is believed to rise there, shines here.[1] We do not take in the brilliance of your countenance with our own eyes, but in our longing we possess the light of serenity that you radiate in every direction. No obstacle cuts you off from the domination that has been granted to you by God, nor is the jurisdiction of your happy sceptres limited by any provincial boundaries. Saving the honour of the Deity, let it be said that it in no way diminishes your majesty that all [your subjects] are not able to run to [serve] you; it suffices the reverence owed to you that all adore you from their own native lands. You reign over the Eastern orb through your power; in your happiness you reign over the Western one. You can be loved everywhere, even though not all are granted the privilege of gazing upon you. But since this is rightly said of everyone, imagine now how much [more] those people owe, whom you have ennobled with offices, whom you make companions in all of your triumphs and successes by giving them honorific titles. The result is that the adornments of Your Virtue are ours, and whatever the source of honours wears becomes part of the ornamentation of those who hold office [under you]. O renowned among princes, I long for the honour of a letter,[2] for expressions of favour; I am waiting for an oracle from the Royal Lips; I am eager to perform whatever you may deign to command, because, even if Your Dignity cannot be believed to need my services, whoever deserves to serve such a happy one [as yourself], fights on his own behalf. Let distant Oriental peoples too beg you[3] as suppliants, and let the leader of Persia in his cruelty ask for our Prince to lord it over him.[4] For this reason, if he rejoice to come under the jurisdiction of Roman (i.e. Byzantine) power for the sake of peace, let the

1 The letter to Clovis, *Ep.* 46, of course, takes similar language, putting it to very different ends by combining it with the imagery of Epiphany.

2 Cf. *Ep.* 78 p. 93.18. Again the idea would be equally at home in the context of the exchange of friendship letters.

3 Or 'mercy'. For the text of this vexed passage, see appendix below p. 148.

4 The object of this allusion is unclear: given the date of the letter, which would seem to be shortly before the death of Gundobad in 516, there is no obvious episode in Eastern sources to which this may refer, except possibly the building of Dara. More likely this is a reference to an otherwise unattested renegotiation of the seven-year peace of 506: since renegotiation ought to have taken place in 513, this would be appropriately close in time to Sigismund's letter.

Indus itself, tame after what it has undergone,[1] choking its shrill tongue, recognise, with your favour[2] as a interpreter, the laws that it is ordered to obey. If there is any heat burning in the southern sphere,[3] temper with coolness and defeat through your respect whatever before your time had been unconquered through its [very] nature. Whoever wishes to reject the sceptres of unconquered faith that hang over him, let him accept them.[4] Through you let religion be promoted by the exercise of power too – both to strengthen the truth[5] and to provide the freedom to those people who serve you to venerate both the heavenly and the earthly.[6] And through this freedom may it long be our honour to serve you, supported by the cult of eternal salvation, not only in the capacity of our human rank, but also with divine love.

Appendix on p. 100.29

Peiper reads *Me exposcat,* **supplico***, Orientalium quoque gentium distantia, crudelitate exposcat* **principari** *sibi praesulem nostrum Parthicus ductor*, 'Let the distant Oriental peoples too, I beg, ask for me. Let the leader of Parthia in his cruelty ask that our emperor rule over him.' The opening of the sentence is difficult. Why should distant peoples of the East demand or make demands of *Sigismund*? The parenthetical *supplico* is likewise meaningless. Why should he *implore* them to?

The manuscripts provide some help. L reads *me exposcat* **supplicio** *Orientalium quoque gentium distantia, crudelitate exposcat* **principali** *sibi praesulem nostrum Parti. quos doctor*. Here neither *supplicio* nor *principali*, nor *Parti. quos doctor* is satisfactory. S reads *offerat ergo supplex Orientalium quoque gentium distantia* **cruditatem***. Exposcat principari praesulem nostrum Parthicus ductor*. Here *cruditatem* is unsatisfactory, but S's *principari* is a clear improvement on L's *principali* and *Parthicus ductor* is an easy correction for *Parti. quos doctor*.

There is clearly something wrong with the opening of the sentence (though the repeated *exposcat* is consonant with the oratorical style of the passage).[7] It seems best to obelise *me* and *supplicio*. *Supplicio* could easily represent *suppliciter*, which

1 It is unclear whether *post experimenta mansuetus* refers to an event that has actually happened, or whether it forms part of the wish implied by *cognoscat*.

2 S reads *Graeco*, 'with a Greek interpreter'.

3 This may be a reference to Abyssinia: see A. H. M. Jones and E. Monroe, *A History of Abyssinia* (Oxford, 1935), pp. 26–31, 35–38.

4 *Religio invicta* is more likely to refer to Christianity itself rather than to orthodoxy. Avitus ended *Ep.* 46 (as it survives) with a similar call for conversion of the pagans.

5 Presumably religious orthodoxy.

6 For a similar association of power and the spreading of religion see *Ep.* 46.

7 L's repeated *exposcat* is likely to be more reliable than Sirmond's *offerat*, etc., the latter very probably his own emendation.

would make good sense: †Me† *exposcat suppliciter Orientalium quoque gentium distantia, crudelitate exposcat principari sibi Parthicus ductor. Me* is a more difficult problem. A direct object is missing and there are two slightly different lines of emendation: a personal pronoun, i.e. *vos* or else a noun like *misericordiam*, both of which might be put forward as diagnostic conjectures: 'Let the distant Oriental peoples too ask for mercy as suppliants; Let the warlord of Persia in his cruelty ask our emperor to rule over him', or else 'Let the distant Oriental peoples too ask for you (i.e. Anastasius) as suppliants.'

Epistula 94: Introduction

Sigismund tells Anastasius of the death of his father Gundobad and his own succession to the Burgundian throne. Clearly the Byzantine had heard of these events in Burgundy, and had sent a messenger to Sigismund before Sigismund's message could reach Byzantium. The Burgundian makes it clear that he had sent an embassy, but that its passage had been blocked in Italy by Theodoric. He apologises earnestly, underlining both his own respectful and faithful intentions and the *invidia* of the King of the Ostrogoths. Despite this, the letter is much more forthright than *Ep.* 93, suggesting that it is the later of the two letters, and that Anastasius has granted Sigismund what he was petitioning for in the former one.

The letter is of great interest because of its implications for understanding Sigismund's career. He appears to have been given some recognition by the emperor while Gundobad was alive: 'the beginning of my command that you fostered [even] when my father was alive':[1] this is best understood as the title *patricius*, which he is known to have held before 515.[2] He subsequently received a title not conferred by the emperor, *non me quidem legistis officii mei compotem,* which must therefore be the full kingship of the Burgundians.[3] Thereafter the emperor added something to his status, which is most plausibly seen as the *MVM*.[4]

The letter also provides a close-up view of the later phases of Burgundian–Ostrogothic–Byzantine diplomacy. Despite Theodoric's care to establish a family link with the Burgundians by marrying his daughter Ostrogotho Areagni[5] to Sigismund in

1 p. 101.21 *Meae militiae rudimenta quae genitore quidem meo superstite nutristis.*

2 *Ep.* 9. On Burgundian *patricii*, see Barnwell, *Emperor, Prefects and Kings,* pp. 82–83. That Sigismund was already negotiating directly with the emperor in ca. 515 is clear from *Ep.* 47.

3 *Ep.* 94, p. 101.15. On the initial conferment of the kingship to Sigismund by Gundobad see Fredegar 3.33: *Gundebadi filius Sigymundus apud Genavensim urbem villa Quatruvio iusso patris sublimatur in regnum.* On the elevation of 516 see Marius of Avenches, *s.a.* 516: *Hoc consule rex Gundobaudus obiit et levatus est filius eius Segismundus rex.*

4 *PLRE* 2: Sigismundus sees the title mentioned in *Ep.* 78 as being the *MVM per Gallias.*

5 On Areagni, see *PLRE* 2; on the marriage, Anonymus Valesianus 12.63; Jord. *Get.* 297; Greg. Tur. *DLH* 3.5. There may be an allusion to this marriage in *Ep.* 29: cf. the use of the word *familiaritas.* See Shanzer, 'Two Clocks', pp. 250–51.

the late 490s, he was more than willing to compromise his son-in-law's relations with
Anastasius, at a time when Anastasius seems to have been playing the Burgundians
off against the Ostrogoths.

*Sigismund king [of the Burgundians] to his master, the emperor
[Anastasius] {101.5 Peiper}*

How insignificant in the judgement of Your Pious Majesty are the impediments caused by circumstances, and how much Your Serenity values the
intentions of your servants is clear; for in offering holy correspondence from
afar, you satisfy the prayers of those in longing without waiting for
suppliants to dance attendance on you. The hearts of all are eager to meet
you. It is not so much a source of renown that few are able to see you, but that
all want to. But because the communiqué, in which Your Majesty compels me,
has now arrived *ahead* of the devoutly dutiful letter I owed you, do not, kind
judge, impute this occurrence to lack of devotion or to procrastination. Had
an impediment not prevented our efforts, you may be sure that by now [your]
word, worthy of worship throughout the world, would have been able to
send an answer rather than an oracular decree.[1] But the delay did not do me
as much harm as the envy of rivals hoped [it would]. For although, to be sure,
you did not choose me to hold my office,[2] you made me happy with a
command from your kind lips. It makes no difference whether the official
recognition[3] of the emperor receives us (i.e. once we have been chosen) or
awaits us (i.e. before we are chosen). It is as important that our [concerns]
not be looked down upon by Your Most Lofty Dignity as that yours be
granted. My father [was] your most devoted and faithful courtier: among the
most happy successes of his intact prosperity he was accorded, by divine
favour, a longed-for boon, namely that he knew a republic that was happy
and prospered, while you ruled the world, and that he left you as master of
nations, when he died his peaceful death. Therefore, after his death < ... >[4]
To tell you these things[5] and also to commend to you the beginning of my

1 I.e. you would have something to respond to, and would not have to have issued a
unilateral statement.

2 I.e. Sigismund's elevation to the kingship was not dependent on Anastasius.

3 *Sermo* really signifies 'official recognition' through diplomatic relations, i.e., speech.

4 There may be a lacuna here. There is no main clause describing whatever happened after
Gundobad's death. What *haec* (p. 101.21) refers to is unclear. It cannot refer to Gundobad's
death alone. The sentence, as it stands, runs on for 11 lines.

5 The precise reference is lost in the lacuna.

command[1] that you fostered [even] when my father was alive,[2] but will increase after his death by lavishing more [favour] of your Sacred Good Opinion, as was only proper and expected of me, I was offering one of my counselors to the ears of your venerable entourage,[3] a man, who, in light of the ignorance endemic in Gaul, is thought to be far more skilled in letters than the others,[4] especially once the assurance had been received that the ruler of Italy[5] was publicly applauding your peace and, once the [false] rumour had been dispersed, was pretending[6] that the favour of the East had been given back to him. Therefore the road that had been taken by the embassy sent to you was closed off and forbidden.[7] He will certainly see for himself what the appearance[8] of truth can expect[9] from your August Happiness. It seems but a mean indication of friendship not to wish him, whom one (i.e. Theodoric)[10] claims to be cultivating, to be honoured by

---

1 Taking *militiae meae rudimenta* as 'the start/early stages of my command': the word *militia* cannot refer to the office of *MVM* because it was offered before Gundobad's death, and Sigismund seems to have been angling for the title thereafter. The obvious solution is that it referred to the title of *patricius*, which he clearly had during Gundobad's lifetime: see *Ep.* 9.

2 Sigismund was accorded the title *rex* while Gundobad was alive. Cf. Fredegar 3.33: see also *Epp.* 29 and 45.

3 Or does *comitatus* mean 'council', 'court', or something more precise here?

4 See above p. 142.

5 Theodoric, Sigismund's father-in-law. Burckhardt, p. 97, characterises *rector Italiae* as 'contemptuous'. M. Reydellet, *La Royauté dans la littérature latine de Sidoine Apollinaire à Isidore de Séville* (Rome, 1981), p. 91 n. 12, disagrees. Note that the phrase is used neutrally of Theodoric at Ennodius, 263 = *Pan.* 92 *Italiae rector*.

6 For this use of *colorare*, see Goelzer, p. 576.

7 Theodoric had stopped a Burgundian mission to Byzantium.

8 Reading *species* for *series*. Goelzer, p. 606, glosses *series* as *contextus*, 'suite, enchaînement, ensemble de fait ou d'idées qui se succèdent et s'enchaînent', citing Salvian, Claudianus Mamertus and Cassian. But see Burckhardt, p. 98, n. 1, 'Zum Text: "series veritatis" ist trotz Goelzers Hinweis (S.604) unwahrscheinlich. Der ganze Satz (101, 28f.) will den Grund angeben, warum Theodorichs Verhalten anders hätte ausfallen müssen (Gegensatz: *certe ipsum – tamen*).'

9 *Spectet*, here in the sense 'expect'.

10 The second person singular seems odd, as noted by Burckhardt, p. 99 n. 1: 'Formen wie "te," "adseras" (101, 29 und 30) sind in einem Schreiben an den Kaiser stilistisch unmöglich, im Unterschied zu Ähnlichem in den Briefen an die Apollinares. Wir würden an obriger Stelle im Text etwa setzen: "cum quem se colere adserat nolle a ceteris honorari."' He is right to note that Avitus almost always uses the second person plural in addressing people. The point here, however, is that the 'te' is Theodoric, to whom Sigismund suddenly alludes, and the choice of the word is either neutral (*te* = 'you' = English 'one') or deliberately over-colloquial. Avitus soon moves back into his standard honorifics.

everyone else: for all of us who look up to you (Anastasius) and worship you as you deserve ought to wish everyone else to do the same. He shows little duty of his own who, by denying open access, strives hard to make other people also [seem] undutiful, even though the holiness of a heavenly mind[1] would not be able to judge one guilty whom his own intentions proclaimed innocent. This is clearly why you see him claiming [to know] what my intentions[2] were, even though he carefully tried to prevent me from being able to carry them out. Therefore because the letters that arrived were both sacred and timely, thanks to God and to you, even though there is a difference of opinion,[3] those to whom you offer new things pray that your kingdom be increased, and those whose customary interests you maintain, desire your protection. Thus under your kind guidance,[4] one side sought for remedies, even though neither had suffered a rebuff.

Among these people I especially am in your debt, because, by doubling the effect of the petition offered to my respect, and by offering it for free, you have shown how much favour you accorded your special servant, and for this convenient reason alone – once the reward has been laid away among your treasures – namely that you wished what you gave to the poor to be a prize, not a price.[5] And you – let it be appropriately recorded with tact – preferred to return the very thing that had been offered by servants rather than to spurn it, and, to make the gift a more happy one, you were unwilling to sadden the givers.[6] And since[7] whatever comes into your hands is turned over to the poor, and for that reason perhaps he, who is reluctant to make charitable payments,[8] might discourage your acceptance, lend your aid to divine charity, and give alms when those without resources are in need, and grant [payment], when those in debt entreat you. For this reason forge

1 Avitus refers to the commonplace that God knows the secret of men's hearts. The implicit comparison is both flattering to the emperor and helpful for Sigismund.

2 Lit. 'what I wanted'.

3 *Quamquam discrepat* Peiper does not really make sense. S had *quam*, and noted that the passage was corrupt. We translate the impersonal *quamquam discrepat*, but note that there is almost certainly something missing that would have clarified who had the disagreement with whom about what.

4 Lit. 'Steersmanship'.

5 The Latin plays off *pretium* against *praemium*. For the same pun, see *Ep.* 25, p. 56.28.

6 Translating *obsequium*.

7 The text reads *licet*, a concessive conjunction governing *vergatur*. This cannot be right. A causal relationship is demanded by the sequence of thought and by *idcirco*. It could provisionally be emended to *cum*.

8 Translating *erogare*.

ahead,[1] Most Pious One, on the right path, in the singleness of your purpose.[2] If you have faith, there will never be a lack of resources for such a spirit. Since He himself grants the possibility for it to be offered, you have [it] from him, who put the suggestion in your heart,[3] not to deny anything.

1 Lit. 'run'.

2 In the light of the involvement of Gundobad and Avitus in the theological disputes surrounding the *Trishagion* and the Acacian schism it is reasonable to read theological overtones into this and the following sentence.

3 Lit. 'poured it into your will'.

4. RELICS OF THE TRUE CROSS

Contents

Epistula 20: Introduction

Avitus[1] has sent a messenger to the pope at Rome to ask him to write to the patriarch of Jerusalem and request a relic of the True Cross. Since there is a letter of Avitus thanking the patriarch for some unspecified religious gift (*Ep*. 25), it is reasonable to assume that the pope complied in providing Avitus' messenger with a letter of introduction. Further, since Theodoric regulated communications between the Burgundian kingdom and the Empire in 516 (*Ep*. 94), it is likely that Avitus' letter predates that crisis. This would tend to make Pope Symmachus (499–513) the most likely recipient of the letter.

<Avitus the bishop to Pope (Symmachus)> {53.20 Peiper}

...> [The letter is defective at the beginning] Whence, even though we think that you have one of the relics of the Holy Cross in Rome, we still believe that this generous favour should be sought from the venerable patriarch of Jerusalem. In fact, by maintaining the true and inviolable purity of that sacrament within his jurisdiction of the pilgrimage-place,[2] he is able to present us with a share in the desirable gift in such a manner as to free us from any hesitation and doubt.[3] Therefore in this dutiful letter I beg a great favour: that Your Apostleship entrust a letter addressed to the patriarch of the said church to my letter-carrier, so that support may come to me with your

1 Since the opening of the letter is missing this letter could conceivably have been written in Sigismund's name, but the fact that there is a letter of Avitus thanking the patriarch of Jerusalem for some holy gift (*Ep*. 25) suggests that this letter to the pope was also written in the bishop's name.

2 Until the reign of Heraclius the True Cross was preserved in Jerusalem.

3 Avitus can scarcely have intended to imply that the pope's relic was a forgery.

joint blessing, because <to the ...>¹ of the world's preeminent churches either the authority of your see, once consulted, will respond, or his (i.e. the patriarch's) kindness, once implored, will offer.²

Epistula 25: Introduction

This letter to the patriarch of Jerusalem³ should be considered in connection with *Ep.* 20. In the former letter Avitus asked the pope to provide his messenger with letters of introduction to the patriarch. That the messenger went on to secure relics from the Holy Land is apparent from this letter of thanks. See Charaux, pp. 105–06.

Avitus the bishop to the patriarch of Jerusalem {56.23 Peiper}

Your Apostleship exercises a primacy granted by God, and seeks to show not by your privileges alone, but also by your merits that you hold pride of place in the universal church of God. Your see adorns our law⁴ and your person your see.⁵ I am bound to your worthy self by the debt I owe your generosity, and I offer you thanks through the messenger who brought the gifts, gifts that are to be valued not in price, but in the rewards of salvation.⁶ You have enriched the poverty of the end of the earth with your holy resources, and you have touched the darkness of the setting sun by sharing the light of its rising with us.⁷ The brightness of your gift has cleaned the rust of devotion grown sluggish from our provinces, and by watering it with a stream of goodness has granted a gift for our faith to contemplate. On the occasion when, once the inner regions of the celestial treasure-houses had been opened by Your Piety,⁸ we gazed upon what we, as Catholics, are ordered to

---

1 *Respondebit* requires a dative (there is none), and the parallelism between *consulta* and *obsecrata* seems to guarantee that both must be nominatives modifying *auctoritas* and *humanitas* respectively. It would seem that a dative noun on which *ecclesiarum praeminentium mundo* depended has been lost. A word meaning 'prayers' or 'requests' seems a likely candidate.

2 *Porrexerit* still seems to be missing an object.

3 Probably Elias 1, patriarch of Jerusalem 494–516 d. 518 on whom see R. Janin, 'Élie 1er', *DHGE* 15.189–90.

4 *Lex nostra* = Catholicism. Perhaps in contrast to the heresy of the Monophysites: for the theology of Elias, *Cyril of Scythopolis: the Lives of the Monks of Palestin*e, trans. R. M. Price (Kalamazoo, 1991), pp. 149–51.

5 The parallelism demands S's *cathedramque persona*.

6 Avitus puns on *premium* and *pretium*, cf. *Ep.* 94, p. 102.6.

7 Avitus lives in the West; the patriarch in the East.

8 Taking S's *a pietate*.

worship. All that remains is for you to pray that you have sent the gifts to worthy recipients; commend us to the mystic objects that you have seen fit to entrust to us. Let our devotion be built on them; let our region be defended by them, so that, once the life-giving token has been granted to us, you render us, whom you have not deemed unworthy to share in the company of the earthly Jerusalem, fit to live in the supernal and celestial one.[1]

1 Avitus employs some of the same rhetoric at the end of his letter (*Ep.* 8) to the pope asking for relics to celebrate Sigismund's conversion.

THE WEST

THE PAPACY

5. THE LAURENTIAN SCHISM

Contents

Epistula 34 Avitus to Faustus and Symmachus. Avitus makes a plea for an end to the
Laurentian schism and expresses his support for Pope Symmachus (date 502).

Epistula 34: Introduction

The Laurentian schism was caused by a disputed papal election in 498/9, as a result
of which both Symmachus and Laurentius claimed to have been elected pope. Each
candidate had substantial support within the city of Rome. The divided election,
which caused ongoing problems, resulted in an appeal to Theodoric, and was only,
officially, ended as a result of a synod in 502.

Avitus was unable either to travel to Rome himself or to convene a synod in Gaul
to support Pope Symmachus. Instead he writes to Faustus,[1] leader of the party that
supported Pope Symmachus,[2] and to the senator Symmachus[3] on his own to
condemn the procedures used against the pope in the synod of 502.[4] Mixed in with
Avitus' genuine concerns about the unity of the church was a concern that division
would not help the Catholics in their dealings with the Arians: hence his allusion to
the *haeresum tempestates* towards the end of the letter. The question of schism must
have been particularly awkward at the time of Sigismund's conversion, which seems
to have occurred at the turn of the century: that it was an issue may be indicated by
Epp. 8 and 29.

Avitus' picture of the implied attitude of Faustus Niger and Symmachus to Pope
Symmachus is interesting. The Laurentian schism is often discussed as if Symmachus
was a pope supported by the *populares* and Laurentius by the senatorial party.[5] Yet
the *Liber Pontificalis* 53.5 states that Faustus alone 'fought for the Church', i.e., that

---

1 *PLRE* 2, Fl. Anicius Probus Faustus iunior Niger 9.

2 *Liber Pontificalis* 53.5.

3 *PLRE* 2, Q. Aurelius Memmius Symmachus iunior 9.

4 Moorhead, *Theodoric in Italy*, pp. 114–23. The Roman synods of the Laurentian schism
are most fully covered by G. B. Picotti, 'I sinodi romani nella scisma Laurenziano', in *Studi
Storici in onore di Giacchino Volpe* 2 (Florence, 1958), pp. 743–86.

5 C. Pietri, 'Le Sénat, le peuple chrétien, et les partis du cirque à Rome sous le pape
Symmaque', *MÉFR* 78 (1966), pp. 128–29, and Caspar, *Geschichte des Papsttums* 2, p. 88.

he was one of Symmachus' chief supporters. Both Faustus, an Anician, and Symmachus belonged to two of the most distinguished Roman senatorial families.[1] Is the case really that clear-cut? This letter only seems to make matters more complicated, because it is far from clear, as Chadwick rightly noted,[2] that Avitus regards Symmachus and Faustus as Pope Symmachus' supporters.

The text of this letter is printed in E. Caspar, *Theoderich der Grosse und das Papsttum* (Berlin, 1931), pp. 58–59, a useful collection of Latin texts pertaining to the Laurentian schism.

Avitus the bishop to Faustus and Symmachus, senators of Rome {64.1}

At first it would have been desirable that we in person visit the city that is revered throughout the world[3] to pay our respects both to God and men. But because, in light of present circumstances, for a long time this has ceased to be possible,[4] we would like, we must admit, at least to approach with the confidence that your Highnesses might learn in a communiqué from a synod[5] of Gallic bishops what we ought to beg for in our common cause. But because our province, since it is bounded by the fixed limits of kingdoms,[6] does not grant this wish either, above all I humbly beg you[7] not to be in any way annoyed by this communication, on the grounds that it appear to come from an individual. I have taken it upon myself, weighed down both with

---

1 Pietri, 'Le Sénat', p. 132 n. 1, however, acknowledges the high rank of these two senators and their support of Pope Symmachus.

2 Chadwick, *Boethius*, p. 287 n. 27: 'I do not think that Avitus is asking Faustus and Symmachus to do something that they are committed to doing already. The letter is an essay in persuasion, not congratulation.'

3 Avitus makes a somewhat trite pun on *urbs* and *orbs*.

4 Matters were not just difficult in Rome with the Acacian schism, but also in Burgundy in the aftermath of Clovis' invasion of 500. On the other hand Sigismund's second visit to Rome, which culminated in his conversion to Catholicism (see *Ep.* 8 below), seems to have taken place at almost exactly this time. Apparently a prince could travel (perhaps to secure political support), while a bishop could not.

5 *Congregatorum sacerdotum* translates *synodos*.

6 Two factors may have impinged here: first, although Avitus presented himself as bishop of the whole of the Viennensis, his claim was vitiated by the reality of the political geography of Gaul – something that he openly admits here: second, although Pope Anastasius had supported Avitus' metropolitan claims (*Epp. Arelatenses Genuinae* 23), Symmachus had shown some support for the position of the metropolitan of Arles in 500 (*Epp. Arelatenses Genuinae* 24), which he fully restored in 513 (*Epp. Arelatenses Genuinae* 25): see Klingshirn, *Caesarius of Arles*, p. 71.

7 *Celeberrima ordo*, lit. 'your distinguished order'.

verbal and written instructions from the rest of my Gallic brethren,[1] alone to suggest to you what we would all like to ask you. When all of us were extremely anxious and fearful about the state of the Roman church, since we felt that, when the head was injured, our own stability was wavering, for one charge would have struck all of us equally †without the hatred/envy of many,†[2] if it had overwhelmed the stability of our leader, there was brought in < ... > copies from Italy[3] to our care-ridden attention the episcopal decree, which the Italian bishops assembled in Rome had put out concerning Pope Symmachus.[4] Even though the agreement of a large and venerable council renders this constitution worthy of respect, we still understand that if the holy father Symmachus had first been accused in a civil court, he would have more appropriately enlisted the sympathetic support of his fellow-bishops than received their judgement. For just as God orders us to bow down before earthly powers and says that we will have to appear before kings and princes whatever the charge,[5] it is not easy to understand what rationale or law permits the more eminent individual to be judged by his inferior.[6] For since it is well known that the apostle proclaims that an accusation should not be entertained even against a priest, what license is there for accusations against the leader of the whole church? The venerable synod, praiseworthy in its constitution, when it looked into a matter that it had taken upon itself – please forgive the presumption! – somewhat rashly, exercised greater discretion and reserved it for divine dispensation.[7] It concluded as briefly as it could that none of the charges that had been levelled against the pope had been clearly substantiated either in its eyes or in those of that most glorious man, King Theodoric. Since this is known, if longed-for prosperity ensue in your times as a gift of the divinity you worship, if the dignity for which you are renowned throughout the world maintain the

1 Avitus has presumably canvassed the opinions of the episcopate of the Burgundian kingdom, if not from elsewhere.

2 Burckhardt, p. 43 n. 2, is likewise puzzled by this phrase.

3 The text is probably corrupt. *Ab Italiae exemplaribus*, 'from copies of Italy' makes little sense. With *perlata* one would have expected a place whence the decree came. S has tried to remedy the text with *ab Italia in exemplaribus*, but *exemplaribus* without qualification seems trivial. An adjective may have dropped out. One could suggest *ab Italia exemplaribus <multis>*.

4 The Council concluded on 23 October 502: for the text, *MGH AA* 12, pp. 426–32.

5 Tit. 3.1; Mt. 10.18; Mk 13.9.

6 1 Tim. 5.19.

7 Moorhead, *Theodoric in Italy*, p. 119. Avitus refers to the dispensation following the Roman synod of the 23 October 502.

grandeur of the Roman name in a collapsing world, I as a Christian bishop beg from you as Roman senators that the status of the church be no less important than that of the republic in your sight. May the power that God granted you be of use to us too! May you love the see of Peter in your own church[1] no less than you love the peak of the world in the city. If you see the matter clearly in the profound and wise counsel proferred by your tractate, what is going on at Rome does not have to be conceived of in that way alone: if someone among the other bishops has erred,[2] the matter can be repaired, but if the bishop of Rome is called into question, the episcopate itself, not just a bishop, will seem to be wavering. You know very well through what sort of heretical storms we are led in the bark of faith, as if gusts of winds were blowing from all sides. If you are worried about this sort of peril with regard to us, it would be well for you to take up your share of the burden and look after your own steersman. What other recourse is there, if the sailors have no leader? One cannot give in to this sort of danger without risk to the crew. Let him who is in charge of the sheepfold of the Lord give a reckoning of how he administers the sheep entrusted to his care. It is not the business of the flock to strike fear into its own shepherd, but that of a judge. Therefore, if you have not already done so, give back to us peace for our leader.[3] For this reason we enjoined this task upon your client, the venerable priest Symmachus,[4] namely that he bring back to us through the restoration of peace a concrete result of our plea in the form of a letter from you.[5]

---

1 Taking *in ecclesia vestra* S to maintain the parallelism with *in civitate*.

2 Lit. 'nodded'.

3 Taking *principalis* as 'pertaining to the *princeps*'.

4 The letter mentions three different Symmachi, the pope, the senator (father-in-law of Boethius), and this man, presumably a connection of Avitus'.

5 Lit. 'in the form of an oracle consisting of your letters'.

GUNDOBAD, KING OF THE BURGUNDIANS

6. THEOLOGICAL LETTERS

Contents

Contra Arrianos: Introduction

Avitus probably never composed a work or works which he entitled *Contra Arrianos*. The fragments known by that title were collected by Sirmond from a commentary on the Epistles of Paul compiled in the ninth century by Florus of Lyons , out of excerpts from twelve Fathers of the Church, among them Avitus.[1] In addition Baluze, who

---

1 The full text of the commentary, which is in what was Phillipps, Cheltenham MS 14036 (see A. N. L. Munby, ed., *The Phillips Manuscripts* (repr. London, 1968), p. 260), remains unpublished. On the commentary see C. Charlier, 'Le Compilation augustinenne de Florus sur l'Apôtre', *Revue Bénédictine* 57 (1947), pp. 132–67. On Florus' working method, and the significance of this for the Avitus fragments, Charlier, 'Compilation augustinenne', p. 159: see also C. Charlier, 'Les Manuscrits personnels de Florus', in *Mélanges Podechard* (Lyons, 1945),

transcribed two of the fragments transmitted by Florus, discovered two further passages of theology by the bishop of Vienne.[1] The current numbering of the fragments largely follows that of the order in which they appear in Florus, taking the commentaries on Paul in their biblical order.[2]

In Florus' compilation the fragments are described as coming variously 'from the books against the Arians' (*ex libris contra Arrianos*) and 'from the letters against the Arians' (*ex epistolis contra Arrianos*).[3] The passages transcribed by Baluze were said to have originated 'in the book about the divinity of the Holy Spirit that he wrote against Gundobad, the Arian king'.[4] These annotations might be thought to suggest that Avitus compiled a number of full-scale works as well as a number of letters against the Arians. There are, however, several objections to such a suggestion. Most significant is the question of what constituted an Avitan *liber*. This is by no means easy to deduce: the bishop of Vienne's epistolary output is varyingly described as being in 3, 5 or 9 *libri*.[5] Nevertheless, there are some clues which help solve this problem. The two letters against Eutyches are described as *libri* in the Lyons MS,[6] while the lengthy *Ep.* 30 is also described in L as constituting a work 'about the divinity of the son of God' (*de divinitate filii dei*), and sections from the same work are said by Florus to come 'out of the book about the divinity of Christ' (*ex libro de Christi divinitate*).[7] It is, therefore, clear that some, if not all, of Avitus' theological *libri* were letters on theological topics, similar in form to those of Faustus of Riez, but contained within the letter collection.[8] Further, since Florus is known to have used the papyrus,[9] it is likely that some, perhaps most, of the fragments of the *Contra Arianos* were drawn from that manuscript.

The title *Contra Arrianos* is misleading in a number of other ways: it obscures the fact that the target of these fragments is not simply Gundobad and his Arian

---

pp. 71–84 and Peiper, pp. xxx–xxxvii. *CA* 4–5, 7–11, 15–29 are described by Florus as coming *ex libris contra Arrianos*, while 6 and 12 are described as coming *ex epistolis contra Arrianos*. Florus describes *CA* 28 as coming *ex libro contra phantasma*, and 29 *ex libris contra phantasma*.

1 Peiper, p. 6, n. Baluze transcribed *CA* 12–14, describing 12 as being found *in illo libro quem de divinitate sancti contra Gundobadum Arrianum regem scripsit*.

2 Peiper, p. 3, n.

3 Peiper, p. 3, n.

4 *CA* 12: Peiper, p. 6, n. *In illo libro quem de divinitate spiritus sancti contra Gundobadum Arrianum regem scripsit*

5 Wood, 'Letters and Letter-Collections', p. 35. Also above pp. 39ff.

6 Peiper, pp. 15, n, and 22, n.

7 Peiper, p. 60, n.

8 *Ep.* 4 *de subitanea paenitentia* is a good example. Gennadius, *De Viris Illustribus* 86.

9 C. Charlier, 'Notes sur les origines de l'écriture dite de Luxeuil', *Revue Bénédictine* 58 (1948), pp. 153–54, n. 14: idem, 'Compilation augustinienne', p. 159; idem, 'Les manuscrits personnels de Florus', p. 83. On the papyrus, see above p. 29.

clergy. Florus himself described two fragments (28 and 29) as coming 'out of the books against the phantasm' (*ex libris contra phantasma*).[1] This title suggests a link with the two letters *CE* 1 and *CE* 2. The fragments *Contra Arrianos* thus bear witness to a very much more complex world than one simply polarised around an Arian–Catholic Trinitarian conflict over the nature of the Son. Those concerned with Arianism provide crucial information on the Arianism of the Burgundian kingdom. They reveal something of the Arian Church, or at least of the court clergy,[2] and of its mode of argumentation. This seems to have been concerned largely with a close reading of the Scriptures:[3] and it is clear that here the Arians were every bit as informed as Avitus himself, who on more than one occasion accuses his opponents of misquoting, when in fact he had misidentified the passage of Scripture (whether deliberately or not we do not know). In one fragment of the *Contra Arrianos*,[4] and in one other instance in his surviving writings,[5] he substituted another passage more amenable to Catholic interpretation. This misidentification of Scripture raises interesting questions concerning the text of the Bible used by Avitus and his Arian adversaries, who, it should be noted, appear to be using a Latin Bible rather than Ulfila's. Avitus' own biblical quotations are close to, but often not the same as, the equivalent passages in the Vulgate, which suggests that he tended to quote the Bible from memory, rather than with an open text before him[6] – a potentially dangerous way of proceeding when precise interpretations of the Bible were at issue. The central point of disagreement with the Arians is, as one might expect, the equality of the persons in the Trinity, with lesser issues such as the question of double baptism also appearing in Avitus' writings.[7]

It is not just Arianism that is an issue at court and in the *Contra Arrianos* fragments. Other Christological heresies were discussed, including ones that questioned Christ's nature and person rather than his position in the Trinity. The passages named by Florus, for example, as coming *ex libris contra phantasma*[8] show concern with the heresy of Eutyches, over and above what can be seen in the *CE* 2. In addition there is a concern with the Photinians and the Bonosiacs,[9] heretics whose ideas Avitus contrasted in the *Contra Eutychianam Haeresim* with those of the Eutychians: the former group seeing Christ as initially man alone, the latter denying

1 Peiper, p. 11, n.

2 *CA* 30 (= *Ep*. 1): compare *Ep*. 30.

3 In *Ep*. 23 Sigismund asked Avitus for a list of scriptural passages discussed so that he might show it to his Arian bishops.

4 *CA* 30 (= *Ep*. 1): Wis. 15.11, Gen. 2.7.

5 *Ep*. 22, where Mic. 4.2–4 is misidentified.

6 Or that he was still using a form of the *Itala*.

7 *CA* 19.

8 *CA* 28–29.

9 *CA* 7, 19. A similar range is apparent in the anti-Arian works of the African Vigilius of Thapsus: *PL* 62.155–472.

his manhood altogether.[1] The Bonosiacs and Photinians seem to have been considered by Avitus as being the same. The second Council of Arles (442/506) described them as 'sharing the same error' (*ex eodem errore venientes*), although it implies that they had differing baptismal rituals.[2] Certainly Avitus' near-contemporary Gennadius of Marseilles thought that the two heresies were identical, since he described a work of Audentius as being 'against the Photinians, who are now called "Bonosiacs"' (*contra Photinianos qui nunc vocantur Bonosiaci*).[3] Jonas of Bobbio was of the same opinion in the mid-seventh century, since he mentioned the presence of *Fotini vel Bonosi error* among the Warasci, who lived close to Luxeuil.[4] Their existence in that region at the end of the sixth century seems to be proven by a reference in Columbanus' penitential.[5] Avitus himself mentions the Bonosiacs as being a problem in Geneva.[6] The Bonosiacs were also to be the subject of legislation at the 538 Council of Orléans,[7] which dealt with Bonosiac bishops, and at the Council of Clichy (626/7).[8]

There are considerable difficulties involved in interpreting what emerges as a collection of Christological 'bites', with no clear literary form. Sometimes one can reconstruct the context behind the fragment. Sometimes not.

---

1 *CE* 2, p. 26.26. For *Bonosiaci*, see also Pseudo-Isidore, *Indiculus de haeresibus*, *PL* 81.646: *De Bonosiacis — Bonosiaci a Bonoso quodam episcopo produntur, qui Christum filium Dei adoptivum, non proprium, asserunt* and col 644 on Photinus: *Photinus ... Ebionis haeresim restaurare conatus est quae dicit Christum a Maria per Joseph nuptiali coetu fuisse conceptum.* See also Avitus, *Ep.* 31, p. 62.16.

2 Arles II (442/506), can. 17, ed. C. Munier, *Concilia Galliae A. 314–A. 506, CCSL* 148 (Turnholt, 1963): on the Photinians, can. 16. See also R. W. Mathisen, 'The "Second Council of Arles" and the Spirit of Compilation and Codification in Late Roman Gaul', *Journal of Early Christian Studies* 5 (1997), pp. 525–26.

3 Gennadius, *Liber de Scriptoribus Ecclesiasticis* (= *De viris inlustribus*) 14, *PL* 58, col. 1068. See also Gennadius, *Liber sive definitio ecclesiasticorum dogmatum* 21, ed. C. Turner, *Journal of Theological Studies* 7 (1906), p. 94: *Sipuri Fotiniaci (qui nunc vocantur Bonosiani)*; but see the seventh-century recension of Gennadius, *De Ecclesiasticis Dogmatibus Liber* (= *Liber ecclesiasticorum dogmatum*) 52, *PL* 58.993, where *Photiniani* are treated separately from *Siphori, qui nunc vocantur Bonosiani*.

4 Jonas, *Vita Columbani* 2.8, ed. B. Krusch, *Scriptores Rerum Germanicarum in usum scholarum* (Hanover, 1905).

5 Columbanus, *Penitential* B 25, ed. G. S. M. Walker, *Sancti Columbani Opera* (Dublin, 1957).

6 Avitus, *Ep.* 31.

7 Orléans (538), can. 34, ed. J. Gaudemet and B. Basdevant, *Les canons des conciles mérovingiens (VIe–VIIe siècles), SC* 353–54 (Paris, 1989).

8 Clichy (626/7), can. 5, ed. Gaudemet and Basdevant, *Les canons des conciles mérovingiens (VIe–VIIe siècles)*.

CA 4.[1] OT Figures (Abraham and Moses) both foresaw the coming of Christ and were saved by him themselves. This fragment could also be construed as an attack on the heretical position refuted by Avitus in *Ep.* 30 which denied Christ divine power before the Incarnation.

I declare Abraham, Moses and the prophets not only to be saved, but also to be highly blessed, and I maintain that they were saved by none other than Christ, as the Lord himself says in the Gospels (John 8.56): 'Your father Abraham rejoiced to see my day: and he saw it, and was glad.' And about Moses (John 5.46): 'Had ye believed Moses, ye would have believed me: for he wrote of me.' Likewise concerning the prophets (Mt. 13.17; Lk. 10.24), 'How many[2] prophets ... have desired to see those things which ye see, and to hear those things which ye hear?' And elsewhere in the Gospel (Lk. 24.44), the Lord himself, pulling together all the items that I mentioned individually, [said] 'that all things must be be fulfilled, which were written in the law ... and in the prophets, and in the psalms, concerning me'. You must guess whether those people believed in Christ who so clearly wrote about Christ! Paul the Apostle too, when he was explaining that those who had been saved before the birth of Christ were redeemed in Christ, set out the reasoning as follows (1 Cor. 15.22): 'For as in Adam all die, even so in Christ shall all be made alive.' Whence, just as no one has died except through the old Adam, so no one is saved except through the one (= Christ).

CA 5. Although there are many patristic passages that cite Rom. 8.26, none of the earlier ones elucidates what Avitus may have been doing with it in his anti-Arian debate. The context supplied here is insufficient; what there is suggests that it had something to do with the paradox of prayer.

'For we know not what we should pray for as we ought.'[3] We should keep it firmly fixed in our minds and conclude that if the Almighty did not create something, he must not have wanted it.

CA 6. The Holy Spirit is not subordinate. Avitus clearly spells out some of the opinions of his (Arian) opponents on this matter.

---

1 The numbering is Peiper's. His *CA* 1 = Greg. Tur. *DLH* 2.34: *CA* 2 = Agobard, *Liber de imaginibus sanctorum*, 9: *CA* 3A = Agobard, *Liber adversus Legem Gundobadi*, 13: *CA* 3B = Agobard, *Liber contra Iudicium Dei*, 6. On these see below, pp. 189ff.

2 Adjusting the AV's 'that' to match Avitus' 'how many?'

3 Rom. 8.26.

'O the depth of the riches both of the wisdom and knowledge of God! How unsearchable are his judgements, and his ways past finding out! For who hath known the mind of the Lord? Or who hath been his counsellor? Or who hath first given to him, and[1] it shall be recompensed unto him again? For of him, and through him, and to[2] him are all things: to whom be glory for ever.'[3] Therefore it is not the depth of wisdom and knowledge of the Father alone, but of *God* – in whom you admit that the person of the Son is included also. No one was privy to his thoughts, nor has any investigator known their meaning – especially one who also insults him who is the highest and cannot be made greater by diminishing his status, even though the apostle himself in his corporeal weakness sighed after the inscrutable depth of God?[4] Who first gives to God in order that 'it may be recompensed unto him', unless it be he who attributes a beginning to the creator so that he [i.e. the misguided man] seems to have obtained his own beginning from the being of God that itself had a beginning?[5] One God is named here and one God is being discussed. Certainly if matters were different – not 'of him, and through him, and to[6] him are all things' – if these are the attributes of three [different individuals], as you would have it, whose, tell me now, is 'the glory for ever'? If it belongs to three, why does it not read to three 'themselves' (*ipsis*)? If it belongs 'to him' (*ipsi*), to which of the three? If, as you wish, the substance of majesty is tripartite, why did he not say 'out of himself, through another, in the third one', unless it was because the one named is one in three? Elsewhere the apostle says about him, 'He is before all things, and by him all things consist.'[7] Furthermore, if, as you said, all things exist in the Holy Spirit and it exists before all things, lest it begin to exist [only] after many other things [have begun to exist], it will not be a created thing.[8] And it since it will not be a created thing, it will owe no service, and, if it is not the servant, it must be the case that it is the master. Let him who is not bound by the ties of service truly be considered the master.

---

1 Avitus' text reads *ut*, 'in order that'.

2 Avitus' text read 'in him'.

3 Rom. 11.33–36.

4 Adjusting Peiper's punctuation. The question mark should come after the *cum*-clause on p. 4.9.

5 Taking *inchoata*, 'begun', as 'initiated' or 'created'.

6 Rom. 11.36. Avitus' text read 'in him'.

7 Col. 1.17.

8 *Creatura.*

CA 7. Christ was raised from the dead and himself had the power to raise the dead. Comparison is made between the doctrine of the Photinians[1] and the Arians.

I openly bear witness that when God inspires the souls of his people, the light of truth shines far. It is enough to recognise in the Redeemer the words of the apostle that you [so] often repeat, 'That if thou shalt confess ...[2] the Lord Jesus, and ...[3] that God hath raised him from the dead, thou shalt be saved',[4] provided that his own (Christ's) divinity be understood along with the Father to have given back life to the man who was crucified.[5] He bears witness to this himself in the Gospel of John (10.18): 'I have power to lay my life[6] down, and I have power to take it again.' It is of no avail to have the right beliefs about Christ the man alone, unless you join to that an [appropriate] opinion about his divinity to your Catholic understanding. For the Photinians too claim that Christ died and was resurrected. And because your orthodoxy,[7] just like ours, abominates their despicable blasphemies, if you are saying that it was only a man who was taken up and died and was resurrected through the power of the father alone, I ask, what in the claims of the aforesaid [heretical] plague (i.e. the Photinians) are you rebutting, since our Lord Himself, as we read, at his own command will raise the temple that has been destroyed by his enemies?[8] It is clear what temple he was talking about, since the restoration of a temple that returns to its original state within two days openly signifies the resurrection of the flesh of the Lord which His divinity inhabits instead of a temple. This same son of God, a god who could not die, raised a dead man, and, restored[9] again [to divinity], in the flesh which he had taken on, the temple[10] that had been destroyed by the hands of enemies, once it had again been made solid in the wholeness of his person.

1 On the theology of Photinus, see above p. 166.

2 Avitus omits *in ore tuo* found in the Vulgate.

3 Avitus omits *in corde tuo credideris* found in the Vulgate. He also reads *quia* for *quod*.

4 Rom. 10.9.

5 Peiper's punctuation is wrong. *Sic tamen*, etc. should be part of the previous sentence.

6 The AV reads 'it'.

7 Avitus' politeness is notable. He uses *lex vestra* and *lex nostra* rather than opposing *lex nostra* to *secta* or *haeresis vestra*.

8 Cf. John 2.19: 'Destroy this temple, and in three days I will raise it up.'

9 Peiper's text is difficult to understand. While *templum* is clearly the direct object of *restituit* and *divinitati* looks like an indirect object, *solidata* cannot be construed with *carne* (the separation is excessive), and the sentence appears to be corrupt. The solution is not clear. We emend *solidata rursus* to *rursus solidatum*, and are tentatively deleting *divinitati*, which might be a gloss explaining *restituit*.

10 I.e. the temple of Christ's body.

CA 8. Christ as God and man.

We are discussing the crucifixion of the Lord of majesty (1 Cor. 2.8), although, if you look at the nature of both his substances,[1] since his divine loftiness was kept apart from all the insults imposed by the cross, only the humble body he took on felt the Passion. For after God, reconciling the world to himself in Christ,[2] was joined to the creature whom he had taken up, 'man' is often signified by 'God' and 'God' by 'man', as it is in 'When the Son of man shall come in his glory',[3] since no one will doubt that majesty befits God rather than man. The psalmist says this too when he speaks about God: 'And he will be seen in his glory.'[4] And the prophet Malachi, known as 'the angel'[5] because of the clearness of his sayings [says], concerning the passion on the cross: 'If a man will crucify his God? Because you rob me,'[6] despite the fact – that no one will deny – that it was not god, but a man who was crucified.

CA 9. The equality of the Holy Spirit with the Father and the Son in the Trinity.[7] If the plural *arbitri* referring to the addressee is not a polite plural, then this text may come from a letter addressed to a group of Arians, presumably Gundobad's bishops or priests, rather than to the king alone.

'But God hath revealed them unto us by his Spirit: for the Spirit searcheth all things, yea, the deep things of God. For what man knoweth the things of man save the spirit of man which is in him? even so the things of God knoweth no man, but the Spirit of God' (1 Cor. 2.10–11). I humbly beg you; judge this passage like judges who have been illuminated by God, and decide whether the Holy Ghost is equal to the Father and the Son on the basis of the depth of its knowledge. No one knows the Son except the Father, nor does anyone

1 *Alternae substantiae.* For *alternus* = *uterque*, see Goelzer, p. 606.

2 2 Cor. 5.19.

3 Mt. 25.31.

4 Peiper identifies this as Ps. 71.19. It is not (though it is close to the English of AV Ps. 72.19, but not to the Latin). The sense is not far from Mt. 25.31 and Lk. 9.26, *cum venerit in maiestate sua.* As it stands, however, this appears not to be a quotation from Psalms, and it raises considerable problems about Avitus' biblical text and his quotations from the Bible.

5 See Aug. *Civ. Dei* 20.25; also *CE* 2, p. 23.22–24.

6 Mal. 3.8. For Avitus' interpretation and use of the passage (which follows Jerome) see above *CE* 2, p. 112 n. 3.

7 The theology of an equal Father and Son, with the Holy Spirit being of lower status was to be upheld by the Visigothic king Leovigild in Spain.

know the Father except the Son. But since neither the Father nor the Son knows anything without the Spirit, for this reason no one knows what is in God other than the Spirit of God: for not even the Spirit can know anything without the Father and the Son. So what do we mean by, 'No one knows other than the Father, no one other than the Son, no one other than the Holy Ghost', except that we cannot find anything in the Trinity other than unity? We read elsewhere: 'Whosoever denieth the Son, the same hath not the Father.'[1] And again elsewhere 'If anyone has not the spirit of Christ he is not His.' How can one divide what cannot exist other than as a whole at any moment?

CA 10. The correct interpretation of 1 Cor. 11.19. Arians had clearly claimed that it justified their existence!

The apostle says (1 Cor. 11.19) 'for there must[2] be also heresies among you'. It is right not for heretics to be what they are, but for Catholics to see to it that they not exist. Just as the Lord said about Judas, his betrayer, 'It had been good for that man if he had not been born',[3] he thereupon said to him that his own birth was an evil for him who was a betrayer, but a good thing for us to whom salvation came out of the betrayal.

CA 11. Glory belongs to all three persons of the Trinity.

When the angels appeared on earth, they cried out, 'Glory to God in the highest'.[4] If the Father and the Son and the Holy Ghost are in the highest, it is well that we say, 'Glory be to the Father and to the Son and to the Holy Ghost'. For we cannot give glory to the Father and not to the Son, when he himself commands us in the Gospel (John 5.23) 'that all men should honour the Son even as they honour the Father'. And the apostle says (1 Cor. 12.3) 'that no man can say that Jesus is the Lord, but by the Holy Ghost'.

CA 12. The Holy Ghost works in all three persons.[5]

---

1 1 *Ep.* John 2.23. For 'denieth' Avitus' text reads *non habet*, 'does not have'.
2 Avitus' text reads *oportet*, 'it is fitting' or 'it is meet'.
3 Mt. 26.24.
4 Lk. 2.14.
5 *CA* 12 is transmitted by both Florus and Baluze; *CA* 13–14 by Baluze alone.

Concerning the divinity of the Holy Spirit who, we read, was neither made nor born nor created, the apostle says (1 Cor. 12.6)[1] 'it is the same God which worketh all in all'. And in the same place (1 Cor. 12.11): 'But all these worketh that one and the selfsame Spirit, dividing to every man severally as he will.' And Peter says in the Acts of the Apostles (Acts 5.3): 'Why did you agree to lie to the Holy Spirit?'[2] and subsequently (Acts 5.4), 'thou hast not lied unto men, but unto God'. Likewise elsewhere (1 Cor. 3.16): 'Know ye not that ye are the temple of God, and that the Spirit of God dwelleth in you?' And in [yet] another place (Rom. 8.9): 'Now if any man have not the Spirit of Christ, he is none of his.' We affirm that the Holy Spirit proceeds from the Son and from the Father.[3]

CA 13. The Procession of the Spirit is eternal. For similar arguments see Faustus, *De Spiritu Sancto* 1.13, *CSEL* 21, p. 128.11–21.

The Lord himself with his own lips certainly mentioned (John 15.26) 'the Spirit of truth, which proceedeth from the Father'. By saying 'proceedeth' rather than 'proceeded' he did not teach of a time when he proceeded, but by removing the past and the future demonstrated the power of his procession, which occurs in an eternity of never-ending present time, so that, just as it is the nature of the Holy Ghost to proceed from the Father and the Son,[4] even if the Catholic Church does not persuade unbelievers [of the truth of] this, it (sc. the Church) not go beyond [this truth] in its own teaching.

CA 14. The Spirit proceeds from the Father *and* the Son.

I confess that the Holy Spirit is equally of the Father and of the Son, and that it is sent forth from the Father and the Son in a similar fashion. The opinion of the apostle that I cited seems to be in agreement, for we read (John 14.26)

1 Avitus' text differs from the Vulgate and does not make noticeable sense: he reads *deus est, deus qui operatur omnia in omnibus* rather than *idem vero deus qui operatur omnia in omnibus*. There may well be a dittography, and the original reading may have been closer to Jerome, e.g. *deus est idem*, etc.

2 Avitus' text reads *Quid convenit inter vos mentiri spiritui sancto*? rather than (as does the Vulgate): *Cur tentavit satanas cor tuum mentiri*, etc. We are using our own translation here.

3 Avitus' discussion here and in *CA* 13–14 effectively prefigures the introduction of the *Filioque* into the Creed, something which is usually associated with the defeat of Arianism in Visigothic Spain.

4 The phrase used is *Filioque*.

'the Comforter ... whom the Father will send in my name', and elsewhere (John 15.26) 'whom I will send unto you from the Father'. Nor is it the case, as I showed in the public discussion[1] that we recently had that Godhead is split when one distinguishes persons. For if the Spirit, as you admit, is sent or proceeds from the Father *and* from the Son,[2] the Sender and the Sent cannot be mixed up nor can the one who proceeds and he from whom he proceeds be confused.

CA 15. Gifts from Father to Son (and vice versa) do not indicate inequality in their relationship.

Because I had cited this passage from the Gospel (Mt. 28.18), 'All power is given unto me in heaven and in earth', to show that the power which he said had been given to him was always intact in his divine nature, I called to mind the words of the apostle (1 Cor. 15.24) that concern the Son, 'when he shall have delivered up the kingdom to God, even the Father',[3] even though for his part the Father could not at any time lack a kingdom.[4] It is not for that reason that the Father who gave power to the Son is greater,[5] since the Son too is said to be about to hand over his kingdom to the Father.[6] For when someone gives another something as a kindness it is right that the giver be considered greater than the receiver. But in the case of the divinity out of whom what is given ineffably to the son is a [gift of] nature, not a favour, the equality of giver and receiver remains [constant].

CA 16. Ps. 8 seems to imply that Christ was God's *creatura* and that he occupies a niche below the angels. Avitus presumably argued that the passage referred to Christ's human nature, as he did below in *CA* 27. The passage shows some of the difficulties presented to Catholic theologians by a literal (Arian) reading of the Bible.

---

1 *Conlocutio*. This probably means 'interview', 'meeting' or 'audience'. Cf. p. 55.11, 55.32, and 98.11. Public discussions are also referred to in *CA* 30, and in *Ep.* 23. Such references prompted Jérôme Vignier's forgery of the *Collatio Episcoporum*, ed. R. Peiper, *MGH AA* VI 2, pp. 161–64: see J. Havet, 'Questions mérovingiennes II, Les découverts de Jérôme Vignier', *Bibliothèque de l'École des Chartes* 46 (1885), pp. 205–71.

2 The phrase used is *Filioque*.

3 Adding a full stop after *patri*.

4 Altering Peiper's punctuation to end the sentence at *potuerit*.

5 The sentence is syntactically confusing, i.e. what generated the accusative construction *nec ideo patrem ... esse maiorem*? A *dixi* may have dropped out, or be implied.

6 Avitus returns to the same quotation in *CA* 27 below.

'When all things shall be subdued unto him, then shall the Son also himself
be subject unto him that put all things under him, that God may be all in all'
(1 Cor. 15.28). The apostle cited that passage from the eighth psalm as an
example. For it is written (Ps. 8.5–6): 'For thou hast made him a little lower
than the angels ... thou has put all things under his feet.' Therefore he has put
all things under the feet of him (Christ) whom he (the Father) made a little
lower than the angels. Nor is it surprising that in that act of creation he be
said to be less than the Father, since in it even blessed angels are greater than
him.

CA 17. Unification of two natures in the Son's person.

The apostle Paul writing to the Galatians (Gal. 4.1) noted the inseparability
of person and said that he whom God sent as his son was born from a
woman, just as elsewhere (1 Cor. 15.47), 'The first man is of the earth,
earthy: the second man is the Lord from heaven.' One and the same mediator
is God from heaven and a man from earth. Born from the womb of a virgin
before he ascended to heaven, he is rightly called heavenly, for, since he has
a component of celestial substance, he was made lord of heaven.

CA 18. The necessity of all the persons in the Trinity.

There is one name for the Trinity, 'For there is none other name', as we read
in the Acts of the Apostles (4.12) 'whereby we must be saved'. If we set the
Son aside, and believe that this refers to the name of the Father alone, we
would have to say that the Saviour does not save, and likewise, if the Father
is set aside, and we are acquired in the name of the redeemer alone, then the
Father has ceased to redeem, even though it was written of him (Ps. 111.9):
'He sent redemption unto his people.' When the apostle says of the Holy
Ghost too (Eph. 4.30), 'whereby ye are sealed unto the day of redemption'
< ... >¹

CA 19. Adumbrations of the Trinity in the Old Testament: the unity in Trinity.[2]

---

1 There may be something wrong with the text. *Cum* ... looks like the opening of a now
fragmentary sentence. Avitus has just shown that salvation comes from the Son and also from
the Father. This sentence began to make a similar argument from scriptural authority about the
Holy Ghost.

2 See Nodes, *Doctrine and Exegesis*, pp. 58–59.

When there seems to be a hint of plurality in divinity it should not be understood as duality, but as the Trinity, as in the tale of the destruction of Sodom (Gen. 18.1–3): 'And the Lord appeared unto him (= Abraham) ... and he sat in the tent door in the heat of the day; And he lift up his eyes and looked, and, lo, three men stood by him: and when he saw them, he ran to meet them ... and bowed himself towards the ground, and said, my Lord, if now I have found favour in thy sight, pass not away.'[1] Clearly none of the three was better-dressed or taller. Yet Abraham, because he understood the sacrament of undivided divinity, prayed to the three by one name, because there are three persons in one, yet one substance in the Trinity.[2] The apostle said about it (sc. the Trinity) (Eph. 4.5), 'One Lord, one faith, one baptism'. Who would dare to disagree with the chosen vessel and confuse that unity with plurality? For Paul knew that the Holy Spirit rules with the Father and the Son, and he consecrated our bodies to it as if they were its home, when he said (1 Cor. 3.16), 'Know ye not that ye are the temple of God, and that the Spirit dwelleth in you?' What more forceful testimony ever to prove the Holy Spirit to be God than [this] – that we are its dwelling-place and that God dwells in us?[3] But Paul has long owed the belief [we accord him] to [his] divine calling. For in the Acts of the Apostles is written (Acts 13.2): 'As they ministered to the Lord, and fasted, the Holy Ghost said, "Separate me Barnabas and Saul for the work whereunto I have called them."' His vocation,[4] in my opinion, was spontaneous, not the result of the command of a superior. He asked [them] to be set aside for himself; He says that they are taken on by Him. It is God beyond a doubt who inspires, chooses, or sends forth apostles. Yet nonetheless the self-same Paul, even though in different places[5] he at one time or another teaches that the Father, Son, or Holy Ghost is God, sums up the high point of faith in the definition I mentioned earlier (Eph. 4.5), 'One Lord, one faith, one baptism'. Thus just as we cannot speak of two baptisms, or of two faiths, so likewise we cannot speak of two Gods. Pagans are eager to name [multiple] gods; the Jew believes that he is washed clean of sins by frequent baths, but neither Truth nor good Latinity permits 'faiths' in the plural, as if there could be many of

---

1 Actually Avitus says, 'did not pass by your servant', *ne transeas servum tuum*.
2 The same example is used by Faustus, *De Spiritu sancto* 1.6, CSEL 21, p. 109.15–17.
3 This sentence ought to be punctuated as a question. Peiper did not do so.
4 *Sc.* Christ summoning Paul.
5 *Distincte.*

them.[1] There is one Lord: we do not divide [him]; one faith: we do not rend [it]; one baptism: we do not repeat [it].[2] We preserve its (*sc.* baptism's) honour, even when we take in Bonosiacs and other heretics, provided that they state that they have been baptised in the name of the Father, the Son and the Holy Ghost.[3] What they did right to admit we receive and preserve; what they believed in error we heal by blessing, and what had been diminished when its name was omitted is supplied once belief has been reinforced.

CA 20–21. Christ was in heaven before the Incarnation and returned thither after his death.[4]

The Psalm (Vulgate 18.7; AV 19.6) says, 'His going forth is from the end of the heaven, and his circuit unto the ends of it.' No one returns except to a place where he has been [before]. But when Christ ascended, the Son of Man, who had previously been in heaven, returned to heaven. Just as Saint Paul, when he was discussing [the matter] said (Eph. 4.8), 'When he ascended up on high, he led captivity captive, and gave gifts to men.' And a bit later (Eph. 4.10), 'He that descended is the same also that ascended up far above all heavens, that he might fill all things.' And although everywhere in his speech he preaches that a god came, but concludes that a man returned, here however he says that the very same person ascended who had come down. Because in Christ [are] both God and Man; not another, but himself; not two [beings] from different [sources], but one mediator out of both: the substance is double, but the person one. If anyone should presume to split this solidity, the first [point] is that he is speaking out in contradiction to the words of the apostle, who says, (1 Tim. 2.5) 'One mediator between God and men, Christ Jesus.'[5] Then he must chose which of the two natures (namely

1 *Fides* is almost never used in the plural in Latin. The point is made by Probus, *GL* 4, p. 88.12: *fides ... pluralem numerum facere prohibetur*. For a few exceptions see *TLL s.v.* 'fides', 662.81–663.5. Asper, *GL* Suppl., p. 47.14, makes Avitus' point: *fides pluralem numerum non habet, quod credo divinitus inspiratum, ut quod una est, quae credi debeat et teneri, et in ratio latinitatis singulariter diceretur.*

2 Arians however did rebaptise.

3 Avitus is supported by the Council of Arles II (442/506), can. 17, but compare Gennadius, *Liber sive definitio ecclesiasticorum dogmatum*, 21, for a different view of Bonosiac baptism. On the other hand Arles II, can. 16 makes it clear that Photinians differed from the Bonosiacs over the particular matter of baptism: Gennadius may have been confusing Photinian and Bonosiac baptismal practice.

4 See Nodes, *Doctrine and Exegesis*, p. 68.

5 The AV reads 'the man, Christ Jesus'.

divine or human) he thinks took on the mystery of mediation. If God alone is the mediator, there is no one else for him to intercede with. If it is man alone, then there is no one strong enough to reconcile. Join them together so that God may be in Christ and [there he is] reconciling the world to himself. Evidently he in whom action must be taken [is] he who acts – hence both the same [being] sent forth and the same returning, just as he both was judged and will judge [himself].

CA 22. The creation of one flesh in human marriage used as an analogy for the Trinity.

When the Lord was consulted in the gospel about the firmness of the bond of marriage (Mt. 19.6), he said, 'They are no more twain, but one flesh. Therefore I say unto you:[1] what therefore God hath joined, let not man put asunder.' This is what the apostle says about marriage (Eph. 5.32): 'This is a great mystery, but I speak concerning Christ and the Church.' The profundity of the mystery comes from the humility of the example. If a coupling of the flesh is said to make one of two, why has not one [shared] substance caused the Trinity to be made one? Or when we say that what God has joined cannot be separated among earthly things, at what risk would we wish what as God has been joined through its nature[2] to be separated in the case of heavenly things? Let me not fail to mention that it is written (Acts 4.32), 'the multitude of them that believed were of one heart and one soul'. Unanimity made their individual hearts one, just as equality unifies and solidifies the individual persons in the Trinity.

CA 23. The Son of God is also the Son of Man, and in his latter capacity he obeyed his earthly parents. This excerpt clearly counters an Arian argument that subordinated Christ to the Father on the grounds that he obeyed Mary and Joseph.

It did not diminish the equality of the Son of God that he obeyed as the Son of Man. How could he not obey the Father, since he was subject [even] to his mother? The evangelist said about his parents (Lk. 2.51), 'and [he] came to Nazareth, and was subject unto them'. Thus it was that he became, as the apostle says (Phil. 2.8), 'obedient unto death'. Even so the Lord himself said (Mt. 26.38; Mk 14.34), 'My soul is exceeding sorrowful, even unto death.'

---

1 An Avitan addition to the quotation.

2 The imprecise parallelism is striking: 'what God has joined' vs. 'what as God has been joined'.

CA 24. The Arians claim that only the Father deserves the title 'dominus'. Avitus contradicts the assertion with a selection of scriptural passages.

Or perhaps only the Father should be called the Lord? In the Gospel Christ says to his disciples (John 13.13), 'Ye call me Master and Lord: and ye say well; for so I am.' And the apostle says (Phil. 2.8–10), that after the death of Christ, 'the death of the cross ...', the Father 'hath highly exalted him, and given him a name ... that at the name of Jesus every knee should bow, of things in heaven, and things in earth, and things under the earth'. That is to say that he should be adored,[1] given that the Lord himself says elsewhere (Mt. 4.10), 'Thou shalt worship the Lord thy God, and him only shalt thou serve.'

CA 25. The glory of the Son is as great as that of the Father.

I said that we teach that the Son has glory and honour equal to that of the Father, because we read (Phil. 2.11) 'that every tongue should confess that Jesus Christ is Lord, to the Glory of God the Father'. If he had said only 'of God', then perhaps one might think, 'So be it, but it was the glory of some God, certainly a lesser one.' But since he said 'in the glory of the God the Father', what can be unequal, insignificant, or divided? He is not in angelic or human glory, but in the glory of God the Father. But elsewhere, in contravention of the Lord's command, not 'all men will honour the Son even as they honour the Father' (John 5.23), unless that glory be thought equal. There is no reasonable way in which the greater can be honoured as the lesser. But whoever has not honoured the Son as he honoured the Father, has insulted Him by detracting from His glory.[2]

CA 26. Ascension and assumption are different. Whereas men can be taken up into heaven (Enoch, Elijah, Paul), only a divinity can ascend thither.

We must understood, as the Son said, that (John 3.13) 'no man hath ascended up to heaven, but that he came down from heaven'. It is only the power of a divinity that can be said to ascend to whence it came. This is not the sense in which the same Lord promised or granted ascent to holy men. Of these, Enoch was translated from the earth for his merits, and Elijah borne to heaven in a chariot (4 Kgs 2.11 = AV 2 Kgs 2.11). I will say nothing

---

1 Peiper reads *adoret*. The sense surely requires *adoretur*, 'be adored'.
2 Lit. 'has used as an insult what was taken away from his glory'.

of him who (2. Cor. 12.2–4) 'whether in the body, or out of the body, I cannot tell: God knoweth' in the third secret region of heaven 'heard ... words, which it is not lawful for a man to utter', because he beheld secret things which mortals are not allowed to see. But perhaps it is not a good idea to go over individual instances[1] of the ascents of the faithful. It is clear that the apostle knew the rewards that were to come, when he promised those to whom he wrote that the conversation of those who live righteously (Phil. 3.20) was already in heaven, where similarly, after the resurrection, the dwelling-place of the body too would be maintained. Our Lord also implies this when he said to his disciples in the Gospel of John (John 14.2–3): 'I go to prepare a place for you. And if I go and prepare a place for you, I will come again, and receive you unto myself; that where I am, there ye may be also.' According to this promise, the righteous will dwell in heaven. Surely they will not enter the heavenly kingdom on high without ascending? And how [does the Apostle come to say] (John 3.13) 'no man will ascend up to heaven, but he that came from heaven?'[2] But because it is just as impossible for the unchanging truth to be deceived about itself when it bears witness as it is for it to deceive when it makes a promise concerning us, although those who are to be glorified will *be* with Him there (i.e. in heaven), he alone *ascended* who did not need the help of another to be raised – he who, when he wanted, could walk firmly on air. When he returned whence he had come, his step, vibrant with celestial power yet fleshly with his earthly nature, was sustained by the breeze that helped him on his path suspended [in the air].[3] Aside from him alone who, as I have already often said, was able to do this because of his double lineage, though many will *be* in heaven, no one will *ascend* thither. For in order that the divine promise made to the faithful be fulfilled, a place on high will be granted not to ones who ascend, but to ones who are taken up.[4] The apostle saw this when he told us (1 Thess. 4.17) that we were to be joined to the Lord and that we would be snatched away in a cloud into the air to be with him for ever after. Furthermore it is clear that

---

1 *Personalia.*

2 Peiper's text reads *Et quomodo nemo **ascendet** in caelum, nisi qui de caelo descendit?* Accordingly we have substituted a future for the AV's 'hath ascended'.

3 As Nodes, *Doctrine and Exegesis*, pp. 55–73, has shown there are indeed ties between the theology of the *Contra Arrianos* and the narrative of the *SHG*. But the ties go further. For a moment one catches a glimpse of the poetic style of the author of the *carmina*. Cf. *SHG* 4.173–186 on Enoch and Elijah's translations to heaven with commentary by Arweiler, p. 50.

4 Avitus distinguishes between ascension (under one's own steam) and assumption (with help from above).

someone who is snatched up and born aloft at someone else's command does not walk of his own free will. You must not think that it is always the unwilling who are snatched up; often grace too shows its own abductions.[1] The gospel tells us both that the Father draws those who come to the Son (John 6.44) and that the kingdom of heaven is taken by force by the violent (Mt. 11.12). This act of violence causes him to achieve his holy desire in such a fashion that he enduces greater generosity on the part of God, from whom this [favour] is forcefully seized.

CA 27. Avitus returns to the crux which preoccupied him in *CA* 16.

'Thou madest him a little lower than the angels' (Heb. 2.7 = Ps. 8.6). The apostle explains that this refers to Christ, even though no one doubts that he is greater than the angels in his divine nature.[2] Concerning him the apostle said to Titus (Tit. 2.12–14), writing, 'denying ungodliness and worldly lusts, we should live soberly, righteously, and godly in this present world; looking for that blessed hope and the glorious appearing of the great God and our Saviour Jesus Christ; who gave himself for us'. Our scripture says about him elsewhere (Rev. 11.17), 'Lord, God Almighty, which art, and wast, and art to come.'[3] If he is almighty, how can he be lesser? Already [right] after his resurrection he uses the concept 'omnipotent' according to Matthew (Mt. 28.18): 'All power is given unto me in heaven and in earth.' If anyone thinks that the receiver is less than him who gives, let him read what the apostle says about Christ too (1 Cor. 15.24), 'when he shall have delivered up the kingdom to God, even the Father' – since just as the Father cannot exist without the kingdom which the Son is said to be about to hand over to him, just so the Son cannot [exist] without all the power which he says has been given to him in heaven and earth.[4] Saint Paul writing to the Colossians prohibits us from having belief 'after the tradition of men, after the rudiments of this world, and not after Christ. For in him dwelleth all the fulness of the Godhead bodily.' (Col. 2.8–9)

---

1 Peiper's text reads *frequenter raptos suos monstrat et gratia*, 'often grace too shows its own [men] snatched up'. This seems to be corrupt. One might emend to *raptus suos*.

2 For a discussion of the same passage, see above *CA* 16.

3 AV text. Avitus' uses the third person singular.

4 Avitus discussed the same passage in *CA* 15 above.

CA 28.–29. According to Florus, these were taken *ex libris contra phantasma*. They contain many parallels with *CE* 2, and may well have been concerned with supposed Eutychian arguments, rather than with Arianism.

28. It is for this reason that scripture on so many occasions[1] commemorates David at the head of the family tree of the Lord, so that, since the truth about the ancestor is clear, there may be no doubt about the offspring – not to mention what the blind men, two in number, but one in the voice of their agreement in faith, called out in the Gospels (Mt. 9.27): 'Thou son of David, have mercy on us.' They knew that one who was born of a patriarch is rightly considered a man, yet that nonetheless supplication for the restoration of sight is made to good effect of a merciful God.[2] Who explains this more clearly than Saint Paul? (Rom. 1.1–3): 'Separated unto the gospel of God,' he said, '(which he had promised afore by his prophets in the holy scriptures) concerning his Son Jesus Christ our Lord, which was made of the seed of David according to the flesh.' In this complete description he affirmed [Christ's] dual nature: one in which according to his godhead he is the maker of all things, and another in which he comes from the seed of David according to the flesh. In neither of the two substances can any suspicion of a phantasm be found.[3] For just as the godhead that came down from heaven was invisible in and of itself, so too, in that it descended from David's stock, the true nature of Christ's flesh can have nothing sham [or deceptive] about it. It goes back not only to David through his [= Christ's] ancestors, but through David himself all the way back to Adam: all the degrees of relationship are cited. For this reason the apostle said that he was 'of the seed of David according to the flesh': in order that he might show that he was consubstantial with his mother, from whom he also inherited death, although a phantasm can neither be born nor die: its beginning is a fraud, its end a vanishing.

29. 'Being in the form of God ... [he] made himself of no reputation, and took upon him the form of a servant ... [and] humbled himself ... unto death, even the death of the cross' (Phil. 2.6–8). He is the true God who deigns to bow down (*inclinari*); he is a true man who is able to die. 'Wherefore God also hath highly exalted him, and given him a name which

---

1 Mt. 1.5; Lk. 3.31.
2 For similar argumentation using a different passage from Matthew, see *CE* 2, p. 23.28–31.
3 See *CE* 2, p. 24.4 for refutation of the doctrine of the phantasm.

is above every name' (Phil. 2.9). Between him who gives honour and him who receives it, every name is triple: the lowest [name is] 'man'; the middle one 'angel'; the highest 'God'. He gave this name 'which is above every name' not to him whom he begat, but to him whom he sent, who 'became obedient unto death' (Phil. 2.8). What is new about believing that he had the form of a servant, since, as the apostle bears witness (2 Cor. 5.21), he did not disdain to tolerate the opprobrium of [being a] sin,[1] 'For he hath made him to be sin for us, who knew no sin?'[2] 'For it is written,' he said (Gal. 3.13), '"cursed is every one that hangeth on a tree".' It was for this reason that he was raised up on high, so that (Phil. 2.10) 'at the name of Jesus every knee should bow' ... that is to say not just men, but also angels [should bow the knee] to him, who, according to the same apostle (2 Cor. 8.9) 'though he was rich, yet for your sakes he became poor'. He was rich from all time,[3] poor because he came from a womb; rich in heaven, poor in his swaddling-clothes.

CA 30 (= *Ep.* 1). This theological letter of Avitus to Gundobad headed the letters of Avitus in the manuscript edited by Sirmond: in the Lyons MS it comes at the end. It is important for showing, along with *Epp.* 22 and 30, the intensity of religious debate at Gundobad's court, and for giving some indication of Burgundian Arianism and the Burgundian Arian clergy. It is above all important for confirming that Gundobad came close to converting to Catholicism, and may even have done so. As such it gives some support to Gregory of Tours' account of Gundobad's religious position,[4] and to the interpretation of homily 24 suggested by Perrat and Audin.[5]

[Avitus the bishop to his lord, King Gundobad]

Christ has been propitious and, despite your many cares of state, truth once ascertained has taught you so much that there is almost no part of the definition of all of divine law[6] that remains hidden from you.[7] Of the things which the piety of Your Highness deigns to ask about, now that it comes from a citadel of full knowledge, this is not the questioning of an ignorant

---

1 The Latin is *maledictum*, 'object of opprobrium'.

2 The sentence was mispunctuated by Peiper. It requires a question mark after *fecit*.

3 *Aeternitate*.

4 Greg. Tur. *DLH* 2.34.

5 Perrat and Audin, 'Alcimi Ecdicii viennensis episcopi homilia', pp. 433–51. Further support might be found in *Ep.* 44.

6 I.e. Catholic orthodoxy.

7 Compare the opening of *Ep.* 46 to Clovis.

man, but of one who analyses,[1] to the extent that the passage of scripture you mentioned in your letter in fact has no ambiguity, but rather demands an explanation of Christ's rebuke to the Jews. This is what the Gospel, which you alluded to in your attached letter says: 'But if ye say, If a man shall say to his father or his mother, it is "Corban" that is to say,' in Hebrew 'a gift,' especially the sort that is offered as a sign of religious devotion, 'thou mightest be profited,' that is the father or mother and 'ye suffer him no more to do aught for his father or his mother.'[2] I believe that you are rankled by this speech, because you indeed alluded to it specially in your letter, asking where the expression 'suffer him no more' comes from. It is nothing other than 'not permit him'. The dismissal is customarily pronounced in churches [palaces and *praetoria*][3] with this verbal formula, when the populace is sent away from the mass. Unless this unaccustomed reading escapes your memory because of your preoccupations, you will find this sort of expression[4] in secular authors also. Therefore 'ye suffer him no more' means 'you do not permit' him to do anything for his father and mother, who ordered that our elderly parents be honoured not in word alone, but by practical attentions.[5] He says (Mk 7.13) that you do many other things of this sort by putting your own traditions before divine decrees. But these things that were said to the scribes and Pharisees alone, who congratulated themselves on the haughtiness of the law, and demanded rewards as if they were owed to their wisdom, have no place in a treatise on faith, as far as I see it. 'Racha', a Hebrew word, means 'empty' or 'void' in Latin.[6] As you know[7] the Greek expresses it more fittingly in one word, 'κένος'. But we are

1 Lit. 'compares'.

2 Mk 7.11–12.

3 These words occur only in Sirmond, and are not present in the Lyons MS. They seem to be intrusive.

4 *Genus hoc nominis.*

5 Taking *rebus obsequiisque* as a hendiadys for 'practical attentions'. The other possibility is that it means 'by gifts and by attentions'. See Mk 7.10 for the allusion to the commandment of Ex. 20.12.

6 This may be a borrowing from Hilary, *In Matthaeum*, 4.17, ed. J. Doignon, *SC* 254 and 258 (Paris, 1978–79). Hilary would seem to have been an obvious source for any anti-Arian diatribe, but this is, curiously enough, the only possible quotation from Hilary identified by Peiper. For a different interpretation of 'racha' as *pannosus* or as a *vox indignantis*, see Augustine, *In Sermone Domini* 8.23, *PL* 34.1240–41.

7 This may indicate that Avitus and, even more surprisingly, Gundobad knew some Greek. If the king did so, one might look to his earlier career as son-in-law of Ricimer and as *magister militum* to find a context for his learning the language. For a further possible indication that Avitus (and Gundobad) knew Greek see the liturgical citation in Greek in *CE* 2, p. 22.21.

prohibited from levelling this abuse at our brother, who is under one God the Father and one mother Church and one faith, for it is not a worthy action to stigmatise someone who is not void of salvation with the opprobrious label of emptiness.

But once these things have been broached through discussion rather than the explanation of doctrine, let us instead think over the objection that, as you write, your bishops made. You were discussing whether the Holy Spirit which claims unity of power in sacred baptism is to be considered creator or creature. For, if it is creator, it cannot be separated from divinity, and if it is a creature, it cannot be joined to God. Since there was no significant response to any of the tricky questions, the other side asked whether our spirit (= the human soul) ought to be conceived of as created or eternal, as if the scriptural passage (Wis. 15.11) had been adduced, in which it is said 'God blew (*insufflavit*) breath (*spiritum*) into the soul of life.'[1] First imagine what those who lie about the passage will do to arrange [this], and how those who alter the words of divine authority pad their inventions with swollen deceptions. Now what they said, 'God blew (*insufflavit*) breath (*spiritum*) into the soul of life', was the product of a skilful fraud. If your Piety decides that the passage should be subjected to analysis, this is what it will find written: (Gen. 2.7) 'And ... God formed man of the dust of the ground and breathed (*inspiravit*) into his nostrils (*faciem*) the breath of life; and man became living soul.'[2] Judge how different the language is. They said, 'he blew into the soul', even though the text reads, 'he breathed (*inspiravit*) into his nostrils (*faciem*)'. An incorporeal being can 'inspire', but no one can 'blow' (*insufflare*), unless he is corporeal. God is not supposed to have blown to add a spirit to a being that was already alive. But as the ancient manuscripts[3] read, he poured the breath of life into matter that was not yet alive, so that it might be raised up as a living being (*anima*). Therefore, if man's soul was made by this inspiration and the human soul is nothing other than spirit, then spirit does not lack a beginning.

They were taken to task by you and sensed that this objection would immediately be raised with them, unless they were to lie and state that the

---

1 Our own translation. On the passage, see also Nodes, *Doctrine and Exegesis*, pp. 59–60

2 Avitus mistakes the original quotation from Wis. 15.11, interpreting it as Gen. 2.7. It is not clear whether he did so knowingly, or whether he knew his Bible less well than his Arian opponents. A similar problem is to be found in *Ep.* 22.

3 It is not clear what is implied by *antiqui codices*. Is Avitus distinguishing different translations of the Bible? Certainly he implies that these codices have more authority than the *adinventiones* of Gundobad's *sacerdotes*.

spirit itself was put in the soul rather than the body, through a physical machination – namely blowing (*insufflatio*). For when they enquire for nefarious purposes, not to find out what is [actually] written, but to contrive that what they preach be thought to have written authority, what do we think their effect is on the uninitiated who have no fear of the reverence of Your Learnedness?[1]

If you will allow [it], let me show with what ineptitude they say,[2] 'If the spirit of God is not a creature, similarly neither can the 'spirit' that God is said to have 'blown in' (*insufflasse*) 'be called a creature in the case of man'. It has often been stated [as axiomatic] that nothing else can exist other than these two: creator and creature. The spirit of God ought to be taken as one that makes, the spirit of man as something that is made. Therefore the spirit that lives in us is understood as the power of God not as [his] nature. For if we believe that the substance of the Holy Spirit has been mixed into us to vivify us – may God and yourself forgive me in order that such a blasphemy may also be refuted! – this can barely be repeated without sin: for, if the human soul overcome by carnality sins, we would have to admit that it was the Holy Spirit that sinned in it, or would certainly be asking for forgiveness for the Holy Spirit, when we supplicate on behalf of the souls of the dead. Up till now has it been so insignificant, I ask, that one is called the Holy Spirit, the other the Paraclete, unless these two names are added as a last refuge, so that as many Holy Spirits as men may be reckoned enslaved to the contagion of sin too? It is skilful the way clerical[3] authority has decided that the spirit of God is poured into all in one and the same way. Perhaps the Holy Spirit enters into the Jew, the heretic and the pagan in the same way that it does into a Catholic? Or perhaps it is crammed[4] at the behest of the Father or the Son into the limbs of guilty beings? But what do we do, since 'the Spirit bloweth where it listeth' (John 3.8)? For, if it sanctifies unworthy bodies of its own will, it refutes the prophet who says that 'it will not dwell in a body subject to sins' (Wis. 1.4). Therefore, while the human spirit begins from creation, the divine one is granted by an act of blessing. For those men on

---

1 Avitus assumed that the Arian bishops will have power to persuade those of the ignorant who do not fear Gundobad's authority.

2 Avitus seems to be quoting one of his Arian rivals' treatises.

3 Avitus uses *sacerdotalis*, which can mean either 'clerical' or 'episcopal'. Here he is referring to interpretations offered by the Arian clergy. For a case against the existence of bishops in the churches of the Germanic Arians see R. W. Mathisen, 'Barbarian Bishops and the Churches "in barbaricis gentibus" during Late Antiquity', *Speculum* 72 (1997), pp. 664–97.

4 *Contruditur* is intentionally disrespectful. Cf. *CE* 1, p. 16.22.

whom hands are laid in the Acts of the Apostles so that they may receive the Holy Spirit did not lack the spirit of their own life. (Acts 8.17; 19.6) If they (i.e. the Arian clergy) wish the Holy Spirit also to become a creature in the degree that it enters the minds of created beings, i.e. the faithful, on the basis evidently of the conclusion mentioned above in which, though saying nothing, they peremptorily say, 'If the Spirit of God is not a creature, similarly it (sc. the Spirit of God) cannot be called a creature in a man',[1] what will they now think about the divinity of the Father or the Son which they cannot pretend was created, and which, because they are frightened by their reading, they will not deny inhabits the bodies of holy men? The apostle bears witness to the faithful (1 Cor. 3.17): 'for the temple of God is holy, which temple ye are'.

But although there are incomparably more things that I could mention in the presence of Your Glory at the end of a discourse to which you not only grant, but command frank speech,[2] depending on yours and God's promise, I beg this of you and God: that you no longer consider those men your bishops[3] who speak against the Holy Spirit, that those who refuse to learn not subsequently be thought to teach before you, that they not persist in blaspheming about what you hear so as to postpone your final conversion[4] somewhat. Do not be kept away from your profession [of orthodoxy] by the tricks of the unskilled and the foolishnesses of the tricksters,[5] when you have long been [orthodox] in confession. For it is [directly] to you that the holy Apostle Paul calls out, 'For what part[6] hath he that believeth with an infidel?' (2 Cor. 6.15), 'What communion hath light with darkness?' (2 Cor. 6.14). 'Wherefore,' he says, 'come out from among them and be ye separate' (2 Cor. 6.17). That is to say lest closeness to the left and the sins of others cause further stain to those who are about to take communion and whom the truth of the right has already acquired.[7]

---

1 The quotation is from Avitus' theological opponents; it was cited above at p. 14.9–10.

2 *Libertas* here refers to freedom of speech, *parrhesia*. An indication of the openness of religious debate at Gundobad's court.

3 Or 'priests': *sacerdotes*.

4 Lit. 'your perfection'.

5 Again, compare *Ep.* 46 to Clovis.

6 Avitus' text read *pax*, 'peace'.

7 Avitus alludes to the biblical commonplace of 'left' and 'right', the goats and the sheep. Cf. Mt. 25.32–33. Avitus seems to imply that Gundobad was on the point of being received into the Catholic church. Compare Greg. Tur. *DLH* 2.34 and Perrat and Audin, 'Alcimi Ecdicii viennensis episcopi homilia'.

Appendix to the CA: *The* CA *and the Lost* Dialogus

Both the *Vita Aviti and Agobard* of Lyons refer to an anti-Arian *dialogus.*[1] Since *Ep.* 30 (which he took as the end of the *Contra Arrianos*)[2] is addressed to Gundobad, Peiper concluded that the *CA* was indeed framed as a dialogue with Gundobad. If one examines the fragments of what is called the *CA*, however, and tries to reconstruct the original work's format, there is no sign of a dialogue. Evidence from the grammatical persons of verbs is ambivalent. Avitus clearly wrote in the first person singular (*CA* 4, 7, 9, 14, 15, 25). There are also examples of the first person plural (*CA* 8, 18, 22, 25, 27), but they are editorial or generalising 'we's. *CA* 21 has a singular imperative, *iunge* (p. 9.6) and *CA* 26 a singular subjunctive, *rearis*.[3] But the latter are substitutes for 'one' that do not elucidate the person addressed. *CA* 6 addresses a plural 'you'.[4] *CA* 9 has a plural vocative *arbitri* (which could well be a *pluralis maiestatis* addressed to Gundobad);[5] *CA* 30 uses the polite plural to the king.

Evidence from the nature of the discourse may be more revealing. *CA* 28 *ex libris contra phantasma* jeers more openly at the combated beliefs. *CA* 30, clearly addressed to Gundobad, is openly hostile about Arian views, not to mention the king's Arian clergy.[6] The rest of the fragments are extremely polite in tone. For example, *CA* 7 refers to *lex vestra* and *lex nostra* and seeks common ground in condemnation of the Photinians. The end of *CA* 19 shows tolerance to heretical baptisms and speaks merely of wrong belief.[7] *CA* 27 refers to *scriptura nostra*.[8] The work, as preserved in fragments, seems to have been written to initiate discussion and convince, not to condemn heresy and exacerbate relations between Arians and Catholics.[9]

There is no positive evidence of dialogue form in any of the existing fragments of the so-called *CA*, any of which could have come from an epistle or theological tractate. *CA* 28 and 30 differ in tone from the rest. The former was excerpted from a different work and the latter is an independent theological epistle to Gundobad written with the *libertas* that characterised Avitus's epistolary intercourse with the

---

1 *Vita Aviti*, p. 177.15 Peiper: *scribit enim dialogum haeresim illam oppugnans fidelissimo et doctissimo immortalique ingenio ad Gundebadum Burgundionum regem* and Agobard, p. 2.8 Peiper, *in dialogo, ubi cum Gundobado rege loquitur* and p. 2.23 Peiper, *qui cum eodem Gundobado frequenter de fide altercans et dialogos in praesenti conficiens et epistulis absenti respondens.*

2 Peiper, p. xxv.

3 P. 10.36.

4 P. 4.13.

5 P. 5.15. Also *Ep.* 23, p. 56.1.

6 Words such as 'lying', 'nefarious', 'ineptitude', 'blaspheming', and 'tricksters' abound.

7 P. 8.29 *perperam crediderunt.*

8 P. 11.10. Since there is no evidence for a different Arian text, it is assumed that *nostra* is conciliatory rather than divisive.

9 Contrast the rioting and disruption at the *disputatio* of 484 in Victor of Vita, *Hist. Pers.* 2.18.52–55. For the *dialogus* form in Vandal Africa see the two works *Contra Arianos* of Vigilius of Thapsus, *PL* 62.155–238.

semi-converted king. The rest of the fragments could all have been addressed either to Gundobad[1] or to an Arian clerical audience.[2] They are not anti-heretical polemic written for internal (i.e. Catholic) consumption, but evidence of a serious theological conversation.

But even if the fragments of the *CA* are not to be identified as Agobard's and the *Vita*'s *dialogus*, Avitus could nonetheless have written a (lost) dialogue in which Gundobad was his interlocutor. The evidence from Agobard seems unambiguous. He cites a work in which Avitus 'speaks with King Gundobad' (*cum Gundobado rege loquitur*).[3] Fr. 3A is even clearer, because it depicts direct speech exchanged between bishop and king.[4]

It is worthwhile to examine the fragments from Agobard and try to determine the subject(s) of the lost *Dialogus*.

Fr. 2 (= Agobard of Lyons, *Liber de imaginibus sanctorum* 9) *His ita se habentibus, est modus divinae, sive angelicae, vel etiam humanae gloriae, sicut Alcimus Avitus episcopus Viennensis in dialogo, ubi cum Gundobado rege loquitur, dicit: Illud tamen quod ab aequalitate coelestis gloriae Patrem et Filium, perinde ut creaturam angelicam secludentes, quamdam mihi invidiam illicite supernis virtutibus delati honoris obtenditis, dicentes: Ergo et angelis atque archangelis, et quaecunque in excelsis sunt, gloriam ferre debemus: licet minime pertinent ad causam, etiam ad praesens non omnino sic renuo, quasi creaturae sublimi atque praestanti gloriam ferre timeamus. Est quippe divinae, est angelicae, est etiam humanae gloriae modus, quem in multis Scripturarum locis invenimus, et sanctorum meritis, et apicibus regum sine vitio assentationis ascribi. Quae enim inter homines prima gloria, gloria haec est omnibus sanctis ejus; et in Evangelio Dominus dicit, quod nec Salomon in omni gloria sua sic vestitus est sicut lilii flosculus specie naturali* (Mt. 6.29).

Fr. 2 (= Agobard of Lyons, *Liber de imaginibus sanctorum* 9) Since this is so, there is a type of divine or angelic or also human glory, as Alcimus Avitus, bishop of Vienne, says in the[5] dialogue, where he speaks with king Gundobad: 'The fact that you, in isolating the Father[6] and the Son, like an

---

1 In which case Florus may have omitted derogatory material.

2 In which case the tone of the sample is representative.

3 Fr. 2, p. 2.8.

4 Fr. 3 A, p. 2.32.

5 Or 'a dialogue'.

6 One would have expected something closer to 'dividing the Son from the Father and isolating him like an angelic creature'.

angelic creature, from equality in heavenly glory, accuse me (*sc*. Avitus) of improperly allotting an honour to supernal powers, and say, "Therefore we (*sc*. Arians) should give glory to angels and archangels and to whatever things[1] are on high?" Although it has little relevance to the matter, even now I do not entirely refuse, as if we should fear to give glory to a sublime and outstanding creature. For there is a measure of divine and angelic and even human glory which we find in many places in scripture and [which we find] being ascribed both to worthy saints and to outstanding kings without any sin of flattery. The prime glory among men belongs to all his saints and in the gospel the Lord says that "even Solomon in all his glory was not arrayed like" the flower of the lily in its natural beauty.'

Fr. 2 seems to concern the doxology and the degree to glory to be assigned to Father and to Son. The Arian Gundobad treats the Son as a *creatura* and does not grant him equal glory with the Father. Avitus argues that scriptures ascribes different sorts of glory to different beings, including kings, such as Solomon, and holy men.

Fr. 3 A (= Agobard of Lyons, *Liber adversus legem Gundobadi* 13)
Quid iste venerandus et sanctus vir saepe dicto Gundebado de supradictis certaminibus responderit, audiat si placet benignitas vestra. Cum de his inter utrumque sermo esset, et beatus Avitus talia certamina reprehenderet, respondit ei Gundobadus: Quid est quod inter regna et gentes, et etiam inter personas saepe singulas, dirimendae praeliis causae divino judicio committuntur, et ei maxime parti cui justitia competit, victoria succedit? Ad quod beatus Avitus intulit dicens: Si divinum, inquam, judicium, regna et gentes expeterent, illud prius quod scribitur formidarent, dicente Psalmista: Dissipa gentes quae bella volunt [col. 299C] (Psal. 67.31). *Et illud diligerent quod perinde dicitur: Mihi vindictam, ego retribuam, dicit Dominus (Rom. 12.19). An forte sine telis et gladiis causarum motus aequitas superna non judicat, cum saepe, ut cernimus, pars aut juste tenens, aut justa deposcens, laboret in praeliis, et praevaleat iniquae partis, vel superior fortitudo, vel furtiva subreptio?*

Fr. 3 A (= Agobard of Lyons, *Liber adversus legem Gundobadi* 13)
May your Benignity (*sc*. Louis the Pious) listen to what that venerable and holy man often said to the aforementioned Gundobad about the combats I spoke of. When the two were having a conversation about them, and the

---

1 Assuming an ellipsis of the antecedent of *quaecumque*.

blessed Avitus was decrying such combats, Gundobad replied to him: 'What about the fact that between kingdoms and peoples or even between individuals cases are entrusted to divine judgement to be decided in battle and that victory comes above all to the party that has justice on its side?' To this blessed Avitus said, 'If either kingdoms or peoples were seeking divine judgement, they would first fear what is written in the words of the psalmist, "Scatter thou the people that delight in war",[1] and correspondingly love what is said, [namely] "Vengeance is mine; I will repay," saith the Lord.[2] Or is it perhaps that divine fairness does *not* judge cases that arise without weapons and swords, even though often, as we see, the part that maintains its position rightly or makes a just request, suffers in battles and either the superior strength of the wicked party or a furtive piece of cunning prevails?'

Fr. 3 B (Agobard of Lyons, *Liber contra iudicium dei* 6)
Haec pie humiliterque considerantibus apparet non posse caedibus, ferro vel aqua, occultas et latentes res inveniri. Nam si possent, ubi essent occulta Dei judicia? Deberet ergo inter catholicos et haereticos tali examine veritas indagari, sicut quidam superbus ac stultus haereticus Gundobadus Burgundionum rex tentabat expetere a beato Avito, egregio et orthodoxo praedicatore, qui ejus vesaniam sapientissime laudabiliterque repressit atque redarguit?

Fr. 3 B (Agobard of Lyons, *Liber contra iudicium dei* 6) It is clear to those who consider these things piously and humbly that things hidden and ones that are hiding cannot be discovered by means of killings, or iron,[3] or water. For if they could, where would the secret judgements of God be? Should truth therefore be sought between Catholics and heretics by this sort of test[4] just as a certain proud and stupid heretic, Gundobad, king of the Burgundians, tried [to solicit] from blessed Avitus, the outstanding and orthodox preacher, who wisely and in most praiseworthy fashion repressed and refuted his madness?

---

1 Ps. 67.31; AV Ps. 68.30.
2 Rom. 12.19.
3 Ordeal by hot iron.
4 Namely the ordeal. The fact that Agobard says *tali examine*, not *hoc examine* makes it clear that he is referring to all three types of ordeal, not just trial by combat, and is attributing them all to Gundobad.

The subject of *Frr*. 3 A and B is the value of trial by combat and ordeal. The king is in favour, Avitus against. In the *Fr*. 3 B Avitus actually mentions not just trial by combat, but ordeal by hot iron and also by water. These are clearly legal questions and relate directly to issues discussed in the *Liber Constitutionum* 8, the second clause of which refers somewhat unspecifically to the *iudicium dei*, and 45, Gundobad's edict of 502, which promoted trial by battle because of the propensity of the Burgundians (*populi nostri*) to commit perjury.[1] Avitus' detail is important in that it makes clear that the Burgundians used all three forms of the ordeal, whereas the *Liber Constitutionum* only makes plain the use of ordeal by battle.

Since it involves the question of the judgement of God, ordeal raises theological issues as well as legal ones. Avitus argues that such ordeals leave no place for the hidden judgement of God and argues from the manifest injustice in outcome of conflicts between peoples and kingdoms decided by war, a topical and efficacious argument to make at a king like Gundobad who had suffered from the *surreptiones* of his own brother Godegisel. The question of the efficacy of war as a means of settling disputes ties in very neatly with *Ep*. 21 where Gundobad had asked Avitus whether the present was the time in which swords would be turned into ploughshares and *Ep*. 22, Avitus' answer. The topic of the letters confirms the credibility of *Frr*. 3 A and 3 B. furthermore, *Fr*. 3 B clearly implies that Gundobad suggested ordeals as a way of settling theological questions.[2] Some support for such an idea might likewise be found in Avitus' use of military terminology when dealing with theological argument: e.g. *Ep*. 23, p. 55.15 for *certamen* and p. 55.17 for *arma*, and *Ep*. 28, p. 58.16 *arma*, although these could, of course, be simply metaphorical.

What is most important about the Agobard fragments is that they show that Avitus depicted himself having legal discussions with his king in a semi-philosophical and legal dialogue. Was this a latter-day *De republica* for a barbarian king? We see thus the shadow of a very classical sort of work in which truth emerged through discourse and dialogue. These fragments clearly need to be considered alongside the *Liber Constitutionum* and in particular in connection with the *leges mitiores* that Gundobad allegedly instituted.[3] Certainly, if Gregory of Tours is right to think that Gundobad did issue such laws after the defeat of Godegisel, Gundobad's edict on ordeal by battle, dated as it is to 502, ought to be linked to the new policy, even if such a means of proof looks to us to be anything but 'mitior'. Avitus' suggested *Dialogus* – which on account of its concern with ordeal would appear to date from 502 shortly after – certainly discussed legal issues in *Frr*. 3 A and B and also seems to have concerned theological issues that touched on Arian and Catholic debate. But *Fr*. 2 need not be purely theological: Avitus alludes to the glory of

---

1 *Lib. Const*. 8.2 and 45, ed. L. R. De Salis, *MGH Leg*. 2, 1 (Hanover, 1892). See also Wood, 'Disputes in Late Fifth- and Sixth-Century Gaul', pp. 14–17 and 242–43.

2 There are clear examples in Greg. Tur. *GM* 80 and *GC* 14 on which see D. R. Shanzer, 'The Origins of the Early Medieval Christian Ordeal by Fire' (forthcoming).

3 Greg. Tur. *DLH* 2.33.

'outstanding kings', and how one can speak of it without being subject to accusations of 'flattery'.[1] The king in question was Solomon, an individual known for the keenness of his judgements.[2] If Charlemagne was Alcuin's David, was Gundobad Avitus' Solomon? The possibility is intriguing. Perhaps the *Dialogus*' central topic was kingship. At any rate, a remarkable picture merges of the intellectual relationship between this exceptional ruler and his bishop.

It has not been noted that the *Vita* and Agobard's testimony bear a certain resemblance to Gregory of Tours, *DLH* 2.34, where Gregory, who admired Avitus, described his efforts to convert Gundobad in some detail, in dialogue form, complete with biblical quotations. One sentence in *CA* 30: 'Do not be kept away from your **pro**fession [of orthodoxy] by the tricks of the unskilled and the foolishnesses of the tricksters, when you have long been [orthodox] in **con**fession' comes very close to the idea and opposition of *DLH* 2.34: 'Although you are king, and have no fear of being caught by anyone, you fear trouble among the people and do not confess the creator of all in public. Leave this foolishness and speak out with your mouth (*ore*) what you say you believe in your heart (*corde*).'[3]

But the question of the historicity of the dialogue[4] may be reconsidered in light of two diptych scenes in Gregory.[5] In *DLH* 5.43 Gregory confutes the Visigothic envoy, Agilano, about Arianism. But, more interestingly, in the next chapter, *DLH* 5.44, he depicts himself in a similar theological dispute about the Trinity with Chilperic who spouts his own private heresy. Both chapters are staged in dialogue form, and the first contains *catenae* of the expected quotations.[6]

The similarities and the dialogue with the king may not be coincidental. If *DLH* 2.34 is based in some way on the now-lost *Dialogus*,[7] Gregory's tableaux are not his literary constructions, but may be fairly realistic depictions of a theological discussion with a highly literate barbarian king. Gregory longed to shine like Avitus, so he put two of his confutation scenes dead centre in the *DLH* (5.43–4). Gregory bettered Avitus. *He* won his dispute. Avitus openly mentioned the *libertas* that

---

1 A court-bishop would be particularly sensitive to accusations of *adsentatio*.

2 3 Kgs 3.16–28, esp. v. 28.

3 *Tu vero cum sis rex, et a nullo apprehendi formides, seditionem pavescis populi, ne Creatorem omnium in publico fatearis. Relinque hanc stultitiam, et quod corde te dicis credere, ore profer in plebe. Sic etenim et beatus Apostolus ait: Corde creditur ad justitiam, ore autem confessio fit ad salutem* (Rom. 10.10). *Sic et Propheta ait: Confitebor tibi, Domine, in Ecclesia magna, in populo gravi laudabo te* (Ps. 34.18). *Et iterum: Confitebor tibi in populis, Domine, psalmum dicam nomini tuo inter gentes* (Ps. 56.10).

4 Which may itself resemble Simplicianus' dialogue with Marius Victorinus in Augustine, *Conf.* 8.3–4, *ergo parietes faciunt Christianos*?

5 Note even the parallel behaviour of Agilano and Chilperic: 5.43 *nescioquid quasi insanus frendens* and 5.44 *ad haec ille frendens siluit*.

6 In fact, it is not unlike the remains of the *CA*.

7 Burckhardt, p. 14, is agnostic.

Gundobad enjoined upon him.[1] Gregory may have enjoyed similar theological freedom with Chilperic, even though he was too mean-spirited to advertise the fact.

Epistula 4: Introduction

This letter to Gundobad is important not only for what it shows of the king's theological interests and the bishop's theology, but also for its information on the problems within the Catholic Church of Gaul at the start of the sixth century.[2] Gundobad has come across a letter in which Faustus bishop of Riez had argued that salvation depended not only on faith, but also on good works.[3] Faced with this argument, Avitus, whose theology was a good deal more Augustinian than was Faustus', suggests that the author of the tract was not the good Catholic Faustus of Riez, but rather Faustus of Milevis, Augustine's famous Manichean opponent.[4] Faustus' interlocutor, a certain Blessed Paulinus, who may indeed have come from Bordeaux,[5] could conveniently be equated with Paulinus of Nola.[6] It is possible that Avitus did not know the true author of Faustus' letter: another of the bishop of Riez's works had circulated anonymously, leading to Sidonius Apollinaris commissioning a reply from Claudianus Mamertus. The result was acutely embarrassing for Sidonius, who was actually Faustus' spiritual protegé.[7] This same episode, however, might point to another interpretation: as the godson of Claudianus, brother of Mamertus,[8] and a relative of Sidonius Avitus may have been only too aware of the difficulties which surrounded Mamertus' attack on Faustus. Rather than attack Faustus directly,

1 *CA* 30, p. 14.37.

2 See for instance Markus, 'The Legacy of Pelagius', p. 221: Avitus 'was more interested in presenting the Gallic Church as united than in assessing Faustus' teaching, about which he may, anyway, have been confused or ill informed.'

3 *MGH AA* 8.275ff. and Engelbrecht *CSEL* 21 p. 181ff. for Paulinus' letter to Faustus and pp. 183–95 for Faustus' answer.

4 For Faustus of Milevis see Augustine, *Conf.* 5. 3.3; 5.6.10; 5.6.11 and *Contra Faustum passim*; also P. Monceaux, 'Le Manichéen Faustus de Milev: Restitution de ses capitula', *Mémoires de l'institut national de France, académie des inscriptions et belles-lettres* 43 (Paris, 1933), pp. 1–111; F. Decret, *Aspects du manichéisme dans l'Afrique romaine* (Paris, 1970), pp. 51–70.

5 *PLRE* 2 (Paulinus 10) raises the possibility that the author of *Ep.* 4 to Faustus may be identical with the Paulinus 10, the son of Pontius Leontius 30.

6 *PLRE* 1 Meropius Pontius Paulinus 21 who came from Bordeaux: Ambrose, *Ep.* 58; Paul. Nol. *C.* 21.397–98.

7 For Sidonius' spiritual links with Sidonius, *carm.* 16; *Epp.* 9.3 and 9.9; for his links with Claudianus, *Ep.* 4.3 and 4.11. On Sidonius and Faustus, see also J. Harries, *Sidonius Apollinaris and the Fall of Rome A.D. 407–485* (Oxford, 1994), pp. 105, 107, 109–10, 169. Fortin, *Christianisme et culture philosophique*, pp. 44–45, suggests that Claudianus at least knew that Faustus was the author of the original letter.

8 Avitus, *Hom.* 6.

he may have found it easier to imply that the author of Faustus' letter was the namesake of Milevis. This subterfuge may explain the rather woolly opening to the *De Subitanea Paenitentia*.[1] Ultimately the Gallic Church would have to condemn the 'semi-Pelagianism' of Faustus outright, which is what happened at the Second Council of Orange, under the leadership of Caesarius, in 529.

Penitence in the late fifth century was a serious matter and could only be undertaken once.[2] It was public, and was frequently postponed till the deathbed. Capital sins requiring penance to free the perpetrator from eternal death were sacrilege (= apostasy), adultery and murder,[3] though some thought that they included any item in the Decalogue. A particular difficulty in translating this letter is caused by Avitus' use of *paenitentia*, by which he signifies both the sinner's *repentance* or contrition (change of spirit, penitence) and the *penance* (action) imposed by the priest and undertaken by the penitent. For the presence of Avitus' notion of penance in his poetry, see Nodes, 'Avitus of Vienne's Spiritual History and the Semipelagian Controversy'. *SHG*.3.220–310 expounded the tale of Dives and Lazarus as a parable of the dangers of an unrepentant death.

See Burckhardt, pp. 71–73.

Letter to King Gundobad on sudden penitence

Avitus the bishop to his lord, King Gundobad {29.23 Peiper}

Your inquiry shows every sign of religious devotion and piety. But because you raised the question of the names of questioner or respondent first when you put the inquiry,[4] I think I should point out that there was a certain Faustus, in Africa, a bishop by sect a Manichee,[5] the author of certain books, execrable indeed, some of which even use vile language.[6] Moreover this

---

1 See D. J. Nodes, '*De Subitanea Paenitentia* in Letters of Faustus of Riez and Avitus of Vienne', *Recherches de théologie ancienne et médiévale* 55 (1988), p. 35. On the linguistic problems see the Appendix below, p. 200.

2 See C. Vogel, *La Discipline pénitentielle en Gaule des origines à la fin du VIIe siècle* (Paris, 1952) and idem, *Le Pécheur et la pénitence dans l'église ancienne* (Paris, 1966).

3 Faustus, *Ep.* 5 p. 187.10: *tria itaque haec capitalia, sacrilegium, adulterium, homicidium.*

4 The letter from Paulinus that Gundobad saw may (like the versions we have) have said no more than *Fausto papae*. Faustus' own reply in our versions has only his own name, 'Faustus', without a title. Gundobad must have explicitly raised the issue of the identities of Faustus and Paulinus.

5 Faustus of Milevis. See Aug. *Conf.* 5 and *Contra Faustum Manichaeum.*

6 The precise allusion is unclear; perhaps Avitus is thinking of words such as the pejorative *scortum* used of the patriarchs' women-folk by Faustus in the *Contra Faustum* 22.15.

man, to all outward appearances professed a most abstinent life,[1] and, by exaggerating a well-advertised cross (i.e. public asceticism) or rather public vanity with a swollen blast of boasting, caused his Hearers[2] to despair of forgiveness[3] as best he could, by posing as an inexorable guardian of the virtues.[4] And because you have read that, when a certain Paulinus of Bordeaux[5] posed this question, he was answered by a bishop of the above-mentioned name (i.e. 'Faustus') (in his day a certain Paulinus – God knows whether he is the one you mention, but anyway he was from Bordeaux – wrote quite a few works of orthodox and irreproachable faith) I mentioned the aforesaid heretic first for this reason,[6] lest the unhappy[7] work of Faustus the Manichee incriminate by a confusion of the name[8] this man closer to home, whom even Your Glory knows, a Briton by origin, but who lived at Riez.[9] < ... >[10] He (i.e. Paulinus) was a man who

1 Avitus may know the slanders in Augustine's *Contra Faustum* 16.30, *An hoc ideo dicis, ut inperitis continentia tua velut ab ineunte aetate miranda videatur?* 'Are you saying this so that your continence seem admirable, as if [you had observed it] from the very beginning of your existence?'

2 *Auditoribus* here refers to Manichaean akousmatics.

3 This is confusing. It sounds much more as if it reflects Faustus of Riez's hardline theology on deathbed penitence than Faustus of Milevis. Paulinus' letter to Faustus (*CSEL* 21 p. 182.18) makes it clear that his master, the hermit Marinus, had terrified him with threats of hellfire for ?sexual? sins: *Nam praedictus vir ita me sub sacramenti etiam interpositione conterruit, quod, qui corporalibus vitiis succumberet, nullam possit veniam promereri, sed in hisdem servetur ipsa resurrectione suppliciis nec possit expiari infernalibus tormentis quod corporalibus <vita> vitiis concreta contraxerat... .* 'For the afore-mentioned man thus terrified me even when the sacrament had been interposed [between me and punishment] on the grounds that one who succumbed to vices of the flesh could not earn any forgiveness, but even in the resurrection would be kept under these same tortures and what a life solidified in vices had contracted could not be expiated by the torments of hell.' Faustus supported this view.

4 Avitus implies that Faustus was not a guardian of virtue. Perhaps he had heard about his *deliciae* (*Contra Faustum* 5.7), including a featherbed (*Contra Faustum* 5.5). Augustine (*Contra Faustum* 5.1) preserves fragments of a rather arrogant sermon of Faustus' in which he held himself up as the embodiment of the virtues taught by Christ in the Gospels.

5 Paulinus' origins are not made explicit in his letter to Faustus of Riez. Avitus may be confusing him Paulinus of Nola. Greg. Tur. *LVM* 1.2, confuses Paulinus Nolanus and Paulinus of Périgueux and thinks them one author.

6 Faustus of Milevis.

7 Avitus puns on *infaustus*, 'inauspicious', and its relationship to Faustus' name. Augustine did something similar in *Conf.* 5.3.3: *Faustus nomine, magnus laqueus diaboli.*

8 Lit. 'on a charge of name'.

9 Narbonensis Secunda.

10 There may be a lacuna. See appendix below p. 201.

at the same time who will have been considered[1] worthy to make inquiries about ambiguous questions[2] and worthy of a written answer to be preserved for posterity.

Regardless of which Faustus is the author of the writings that have come into your hands,[3] they have affected you in a fashion holy, concerned, and royal. To say that the penitence that you properly call 'momentary',[4] that is to say taken on in sickness as if at the moment[5] of death, is of no use to anyone, is a ruling contrary to truth and rather cruel.[6] For in the eyes of divine mercy, even the confession of a humble person ought not to lack fruit. Because, when we read that, once the nature of a person's previous life has been wiped out, where it often is the case that just men sinned or that sinners subsequently grew wise, a man will be judged by the path on which he was found at the moment of his death, even the expression of willingness[7] to be punished – provided it be genuine – must without hesitation be believed to please. The whole (*sc.* of a man's life) is weighed by heavenly mercy in light of the quality of faith. For this reason, also in the case of those hired workers whom you read about in the Gospel,[8] even those who came to the job late were paid a wage equal to that of the first recruits in return for their burning zeal. Likewise the Ninevites bought the whole sum of [divine] indulgence by three burning days of repentance, and used their brief penitence to blunt the sword that was hanging over the neck of their sinning city. The fatal day fixed by the warning of Jonah the prophet, hung ready to fall, its blow destined, but they successfully interposed appropriate penance as a shield.[9] Let those swollen by the pride they affect, carefree because their conscience has never been put to the test, argue against examples of this kind. None-

1 *Potuerit* must be future perfect: 'Will have been able to be considered' literally.

2 Paulinus.

3 *Cuiuslibet* suggests that Avitus may be making a hasty attempt to sweep the identity of 'Faustus' under the carpet.

4 I.e. 'sudden', see Faustus, *Ep.* 5 p. 184.4, *momentanea paenitentia* and p. 195.1.

5 *Momentum*. Avitus is making an etymological connection: *paenitentia momentanea, quasi momento mortis accepta.*

6 *Crudus* means 'cruel' rather than 'unsop histicated'. Cf. *Ep.* 16, p. 49.27. Avitus takes on the first point raised by Faustus in *Ep.* 5 p. 184.3–22.

7 Avitus uses *voluntas* to contradict Faustus (*Ep.* 5 p. 184.12): *circa exsequendam interioris hominis sanitatem non sola accipiendi voluntas, sed agendi expectatur utilitas.*

8 Mt. 20.1–16.

9 Lit. 'As a barrier'. For Nineveh as a model for penitence see also Avitus, *Hom.* 6 and *SHG* 4.357–94 for Jonah.

theless, because you have been kind enough to grant me license to speak, I will here admit what often causes me pain.

We are often saddened by the weakness of our charges, because it is a dangerous test for them to receive such a precious thing[1] as if it were a casual matter. For when they seem to ask for penance with prayers and tears, we say that it is impious to deny it. Yet from time to time it happens that once someone has undertaken it, if he recovers his health, he neglects to perform his penance, and becomes, as in the saying of Solomon quoted by the apostle,[2] 'a dog returning to his own vomit'.[3] A man who bears the tolerable burden of a fragile sin (i.e. one that can be broken by penance), is liable to severe punishment if he abuses the remedy of his sin (i.e. penance). One says to him what was said to Ananias in Acts, 'When you possessed your property unsold was it not yours, and was it not in your power to promise [it]?'[4] 'It is better,' as the prophet says,[5] 'not to make a vow than to vow, but not to deliver.' This is the origin[6] of the idiom that, until one of us fulfil his promise, he is called one who 'owes a vow'. For that reason I admit that penance should not be administered without some sense of trepidation to those who are in trouble. If his last day should find an individual having sexual intercourse that does not entail any capital sin,[7] we think of him as doing something legitimate, not as someone guilty of condemnation, and we do not exclude him from communion. On the other hand, if someone abrogates his penitent compunction, and is drawn back to the world, it is necessary that he be suspended from communion, as if he were already an apostate, that is to say someone who has fallen away from his firm stance. It is better to stay in a state of salvation, however humble and unambitious it be, than to destroy that state by breaking the most important rules. Let it be considered the safer course to live honestly in matrimony than to stain licit dealings with sham chastity. The apostle saw this when he said that widows who 'pledged their first vow in vain'[8] would undergo greater damnation,[9] and allows that people who are bound fast to the peace of a legitimate and irreproachable marriage-

1 I.e. penance offered by the church.
2 2 Pet. 2.22.
3 Prov. 26.11.
4 Acts 5.4. The reading is not that of the Vulgate.
5 Eccl. 5.4. The reading is not that of the Vulgate.
6 Goelzer, p. 676, cites this as an example of *compositus pro simplice*, i.e. *contraxit = traxit*. Lit. 'Whence the idiom brought it about that …'
7 I.e. with a legitimate conjugal partner.
8 1 Tim. 5.12; i.e. widows who wish to remarry. AV 'cast off their first faith'.
9 1 Tim. 5.12 says *habentes damnationem*, i.e. AV 'having damnation'.

bed should have occasional time for prayer,[1] but should go back to the thing itself,[2] lest, as he says, Satan tempt them through their incontinence and make them forget their vows, even though he had not conquered them in the flesh when they were joined.

In regard to the second point, namely where he denies that faith alone can be of use to a man, I strongly disagree.[3] Nor do I profess myself to be one of those[4] who, as the Lord says, 'lay heavy burdens on the shoulders of their disciples, which they themselves are unwilling to move, even with one finger'.[5] For this reason either an outsider could take upon himself such a rigid opinion about faith, or one of our own ought to temper it. If you take this kindly, I will make it clear briefly with a suggestion and with examples.

The elementary doctrines of the Christians, informed from the very beginning by faith, bear witness that it (i.e. faith) is the foundation of all spiritual goods. For, if any small child, either baptised or transferred from some heretical sect, or perhaps someone older is snatched away after baptism by a sudden death, not even the man who boasts of work<s>[6] would deny that a human being had been saved by faith alone. Let us make a judgement concerning secular philosophers, because good deeds alone, whatever they may be, are of no use without faith. Even though they condemned the world, loved wisdom, adopted chastity, despised riches – in short, followed whatever we Catholics preach today, because they lacked faith, it did them no good. Their vain structure was adorned with such tall tottering towers that, because it was built without a foundation, it was unable to stand on its own. What if I now went over examples of different instances of human faith in Holy Scripture, people whose praiseworthy belief always caused their desires to be granted? It was accounted a sign of justice in Abraham that he believed in God alone.[7] The whore Raab through her faith awaited the Israelites and thereby purged her former life, filthy with prostitution though

1 1 Cor. 7.5. Avitus' text differs from the Vulgate which reads *ex consensu ad tempus, ut vacetis orationi*. In his text 'for a time', *ad tempus* modifies *vacare orationi*.

2 *Id ipsum*, Paul's euphemism for sexual intercourse.

3 See Faustus, *Ep.* 5 p. 184.23ff.: *Secundo quaesisti loco, utrum sola sufficiat ad salutem fides et unitae scientia Trinitatis*.

4 I.e. the scribes and Pharisees.

5 Mt. 23.4. Again a non-Vulgate quotation.

6 *Operis*, 'work' or 'a particular deed', is not the word traditionally opposed to *fides*. One would expect *operum*, 'works'. The passage should perhaps be emended. Avitus refers to Faustus of Riez, and ironically calls him 'the man who boasts of works', because Faustus emphasises faith exemplified *in works* in *Ep.* 5 p. 185.1–19.

7 Rom. 4.3.

it was.[1] So too the Cananite woman in the Gospel, even though she had been turned away with a rude word, by persevering in her request, brought it about that the bread meant for children[2] was given to her puppies.[3] Another woman controlled a flux of obscene carnality[4] through her faith in [Jesus'] healing touch. Thus it is clear that devotion, which the faithful should not neglect, ought to be joined to good works.

But when the Apostle says, 'whatsoever is not of faith is sin',[5] you see that even what we consider righteous action, unless it is supported by faith, can be changed into sin. This is what happened to the Pharisee in the Gospel who would boast with swollen and indifferent heart that he 'was not as other men are, extortionate, unjust, adulterers', that he often gave alms and 'that he fasted twice on the Sabbath'.[6] While the Publican, head bowed, though upright in faith, seizing the merits due good works through his humility alone, entered his own house, which he had left as a sinner, a justified man.[7] Why need I cite any more instances? Be patient and listen to one more. That thief, whose body inured to wickedness had been hung as a punishment for his crimes on a gibbet fit for a slave next to the cross of divine purity, sensed the majesty in the body of the dying Christ. He was given over to execution for his past cruelty; for his subsequent confession[8] he was sent to Paradise.[9] He was led downwards through an unjust life, so that he might seize[10] martyrdom through a just death. Lo! There are virtues born of faith; let someone show, if he can, virtue without faith. In the Gospel the Lord compares faith[11] to a grain of mustard, yet promises that it can accomplish whatever it wants. And it is thus that it happens that, although there can be works without faith, there can be no faith without works. 'For with the heart

1 Josh. 2.1.

2 Mt. 15.26.

3 Mt. 15.27. The Canaanite woman obtained obtained Jesus' help for her ill daughter through faith, even though he had (rudely) said that bread meant for children should not go to dogs.

4 Menstrual flux. Mt. 9.20–22.

5 Rom. 14.23.

6 Lk. 18.11–14. Latin *Sabbato* here reflects the *koine* usage of *sabbaton* to mean 'week'. Cf. Mk. 16.9.

7 Lk. 18.14.

8 Confession of faith.

9 Avitus puns on *addictus*, 'condemned', and *additus*, 'added to,' here translated as 'sent to'.

10 Avitus intentionally uses *rapio*, because the man was a thief. Cf. *CE* 2, p. 25–28–31. There is a precise parallel with *SHG* 3.415, *martyrium de morte rapit*.

11 Lit. 'the smallness of faith'.

man believeth unto righteousness, and with the mouth confession is made unto salvation.'[1] In the mind of the Holy Spirit who follows our promises, it is the beginning of good action to have believed whole-heartedly: if, however, as the Apostle says, 'the Spirit itself beareth witness with our spirit',[2] it does not do so, as you have heard claimed above, as a created thing for us, but as a creator: it is the author and the witness of our spirit and is poured into us; it is not [part of our] nature. Look! I have put down those thoughts that I feel are consonant with truth in response to the letter of Faustus (and it does not matter which one). May the fullness of faith be given to me in those whose salvation I thirst for;[3] for them, may their works suffice, as long as they will have been vivified by faith.

Appendix

p. 29.30–30.3 The sentence is tortuous. The Latin reads as follows:

> *Et quia legistis consulenti cuidam Paulino Burdegalensi ab episcopo supradicti nominis (i.e. Fausti) fuisse responsum (cuius [i.e. Fausti] temporibus Paulinus quidam – deus viderit, utrum is quem memoratis, tamen Burdegalensis – non pauca stilo Catholico et inreprehensibili fide conscripsit) praefati haeretici mentionem idcirco praemisi, ne Manichaei ipsius Fausti opus infaustum citeriorem hunc, quem etiam gloria vestra noverat, ortu Britannum habitaculo Regiensem, titulo nominis accusaret. < ... >[4] simul etiam qui aut consulere supra ambiguo quaestionum aut dignus rescripto posteris reservando potuerit inveniri.*

In what sense does Gundobad's reading that Faustus wrote a response to someone called Paulinus provide an explanation for the verb of the main clause? The *quia*-clause appears to be dangling, an effect that is increased by *mentionem* **idcirco** *praemisi:* the *idcirco* clearly looks forward to the purpose-clause, *ne*, which explains why Avitus mentioned Faustus of Milevis at the beginning of his letter: he had wanted to ensure that the epistle on penitence *not* be attributed to Faustus of Riez, its actual author. The apparent duplication of causal subordinate clauses (*quia* and *ne*) may have been caused by the lengthy parenthetical digression about Paulinus. Avitus needed a resumptive *idcirco*. We have therefore repunctuated the Latin sentence above, using both parentheses and dash.[5]

1　Rom. 10.10.
2　Rom. 8.16.
3　Avitus refers to Gundobad himself.
4　A possible lacuna. See below p. 201.
5　Peiper had put only *deus ... Burdegalensis* in parentheses.

The next difficulty comes at the end of the sentence. The most natural interpretation of *simul etiam qui aut consulere supra ambiguo quaestionum aut dignus rescripto posteris reservando potuerit inveniri* is 'He was a man who at the same time will have been considered[1] worthy to ask about ambiguous matters and worthy of a written answer fit to be preserved for posterity.' *Consulere* (as above at *consulenti cuidam*) most naturally means 'take counsel', 'inquire', 'make inquiries'.[2] It suggests the *consultor* (29.25). *Dignus rescripto* should mean 'worthy to *receive* an answer', not 'worthy of the answer he wrote'. Hence the end of the sentence should refer to *Paulinus*, not to Faustus. Either Avitus has made an abrupt transition back to Paulinus, who had dominated the parenthesis, or there may be a lacuna immediately before *simul*.

Epistula 21: Introduction

Gundobad writes to Avitus asking him to comment on Mic. 4.2–4, the passage quoted by Gundobad. In fact Avitus misidentified the passage in his reply (*Ep*. 22), assuming that it was Isa. 2.3–4,[3] followed by a sentence of 2 Kgs 18.31,[4] leaving the last part of the quotation unidentified. Unfortunately subsequent editors and commentators have made the same mistake as Avitus. That Avitus was himself mistaken is enough to dispose of Denkinger's suggestion (p. 42) that this is not an authentic letter, but an introduction written by Avitus to accompany his own *Ep*. 22. More reasonably Burckhardt, p. 74, simply sees the letter as incomplete. This is actually implied by Avitus in *Ep*. 22, where the biblical passage is described as being 'appended at the end of the page directed to me'. The implication must be that the compiler of the letter collection only transcribed the section of Gundobad's letter that was necessary for understanding Avitus' reply.

The context of the request cannot be reconstructed: the implication is that this is a time of peace. Peiper suggested a date of post 509, presumably assuming that it must have followed the Ostrogothic inroads into the Burgundian kingdom. More likely would be some time between the peace treaty with Clovis in 500 and the Frankish campaign against the Visigoths in 507.

---

1 *Potuerit* must be future perfect: 'Will have been able to be considered' literally.

2 Goelzer, p. 535, takes it as 'interroger'.

3 'For out of Sion shall go forth the law, and the word of the Lord from Jerusalem. And he shall judge among the nations, and rebuke many people: and they shall beat their swords into ploughshares, and their spears into pruning-hooks: nation shall not lift up sword against nation, neither shall they learn war any more.'

4 'Then each will lie under his vine and under his fig-tree.'

Lord Gundobad the king to Avitus, bishop of Vienne {54.3 Peiper}

I thought that I should consult Your Holiness about the interpretation of a text from the prophet. I've appended the passage below. Deign to write and tell me whether the times referred to have already occurred, or whether they lie in the future.

'For the law shall go forth of Zion, and the word of the Lord from Jerusalem. And he shall judge among many peoples, and rebuke strong nations afar off; and they shall beat their swords into ploughshares, and their spears into pruning-hooks: nation shall not lift up a sword against nation, neither shall they learn war any more. But they shall sit every man under his vine and under his fig tree; and none shall make them afraid.'[1]

Epistula 22: Introduction

A reply to *Ep.* 21. Since Avitus mixes up Isa. 2.3–4 with Mic. 4.2–3 it is not very surprising that Gundobad elsewhere was unable to identify Avitus' biblical quotations.[2] The style of this letter is terse – for Avitus! – and quite elegant. He may have borne in mind Gundobad's unwillingness to wrestle with overcomplicated writing.

Avitus, bishop of Vienne, to his lord, King Gundobad {54.14 Peiper}

Although you ought to have consulted more knowledgeable bishops – men among whom I would not dare to express an opinion – about the interpretation of the prophet, I wish to satisfy your command by complying, even if my learning is not quite up to the task. The text you would like explained is long in itself and also long in the explaining. It requires more free time for discussion than the exigency of a hasty reply imposes. As briefly as I can, I will answer that the passage from Isaiah,[3] which you appended at the end of the page directed to me,[4] was long ago fulfilled at the time of Our Lord's Incarnation. For when it says, 'the law shall go forth of Sion and the word of the Lord from Jerusalem'[5] think carefully whether the authority of the law has still to be promulgated, which ought hitherto to be waited for. Certainly

---

1 Mic. 4.2–3.

2 Cf. *Ep.* 23.

3 Avitus (with good reason) misidentifies Mic. 4.2–4 as Isa. 2.3 to which it is very close; Peiper's identification is likewise false.

4 This suggests that only the closing section of the previous letter (*Ep.* 21) has been preserved.

5 Mic. 4.2.

after 'the Word of the Lord' that 'became flesh' so that through being born in a body 'it might dwell among us',[1] if *another* Word is to be expected from Jerusalem, the one I mentioned before is not unique. Therefore I do not hesitate to say that the passage you mentioned preaches the Word of the Father, Christ, and the Christian law. Because, since there are two laws, namely the Jewish one that went before, and ours that follows, and the former ancient one was being promulgated long ago even at the time of the prophets, you can see that Isaiah is announcing only the law that arose under Christ's teaching, when he summoned the Gentiles. Whence it follows 'And he shall judge among the nations, and rebuke many people.'[2] Our Lord by judging set up these peoples from all the tribes of the earth within one church and by rebuking them converts them. As to what he says, 'and they shall beat their swords into ploughshares, and their spears into pruning-hooks',[3] to some extent it could be understood as referring to the earthly life of the Lord during which peace, unshaken, flourished throughout the world.[4] But it is more obviously applied to the faithful Christians: even though most of them do not, and will not use the sword: just as the malevolence of the first birth[5] used it as a weapon for the destruction of man, let the second birth[6] convert it to the uses of salvation and the cultivation of living things.[7] For since it is predicted in the gospel: 'nation shall rise against nation and kingdom against kingdom',[8] from these very signs of evil let us understand that the virtual end of the world is upon us. Unless what I said above is taken to refer figuratively to Catholics, I do not know why after the end of the temporal world the blunted edges of weapons should be turned into mattocks and ploughshares. What you asked to be added at the end of the reading, 'But they shall sit every man under his vine and under his fig-tree',[9] is not in the same passage,[10] nor does it, I suggest, have any relevance to the matter. This, however, was frequently granted in former days to the Jews, in accordance with their differing merit, because they had reformed, or taken away from them to punish their renewed sinning.

1 John 1.14.
2 Isa. 2.4.
3 Isa. 2.4.
4 Avitus here offers a historical reading of the text.
5 Cain.
6 The nativity of Christ.
7 Avitus offers an allegorical reading of the text.
8 Mk 13.8.
9 Mic. 4.4.
10 Only because Avitus has misidentified the passage. It is in Micah, but not in Isaiah.

Epistula 30: Introduction

There has been a council of churchmen to discuss doctrine. After it has been disbanded Gundobad asks Avitus to consider a further issue. From Avitus' response it seems that the questions being debated were associated with the Eutychian schism. The theological content of Avitus' letter as well as the scriptural evidence it cites are very close to the *Contra Eutychen* 1 and 2, and it might be read as a trial-balloon, the first letter on the subject that Avitus sent Gundobad. Indeed it is possible to interpret the end of *Ep.* 30 as a promise to deal with the subject at greater length.

This letter was known as the *Liber de Christi divinitate* to Florus of Lyons.[1] It was, unfortunately, one of the sources upon which Vignier drew to forge the *Collatio Episcoporum*, with the result that it was subsequently interpreted in the light of the forgery.[2]

Avitus the bishop to his master, King Gundobad {60.1 Peiper}

When he was coming back from Lyons, where he had settled to deal with some private business when we returned from the council, the holy bishop Cartenius[3] told us that you had posed a question to him, nay indeed to all of us. If this had been made clear with the help of the Holy Spirit when we were present, things could easily have been suggested in answer to your question that were relevant to the matter. Since we must not cheat so worthy an interest by lateness in replying, I take it upon myself to answer your questions with the help of the present letter, knowing that my opinion coincides with that of my brothers in faith, Christ being well-disposed towards me. You order us therefore to show you the reason, or rather the authority by which it is clear that the Son of God had the substance of divinity before taking on human nature at the Incarnation.

Through this let that most dangerous of heresies be refuted which in its contention that the Lord began from Mary, blasphemes God the Father too by diminishing the Son. For according to what they think, it is necessary that something have been added to divine imperfection, if – after so many centuries without a son – he only began to be a father when Mary had a child near the end of the world as it tottered. At the same time, because they are

---

1 Cf. Florus, *Ad Rom.* 9.5.

2 Vignier's forgeries, which he left unpublished at the time of his death, included Avitus, *Ep.* 33, which we have therefore not included. The forgery was published by L. D'Achéry in his *Veterum aliquot scriptorum ... spicilegium* (Paris, 1661): it was exposed by Havet, 'Questions mérovingiennes II', pp. 205–71.

3 Cartenius is otherwise unknown.

bound by their own assertion, they deny that He whom they name 'the Son' is God. For they sense that sane ears will not be able to tolerate the thought that not too many years ago a god took his beginning from a human being.

I have no idea why our Redeemer rose from the dead, unless he *qua* God was the ransom-price for his creation. For a mere man could not redeem man, who, if he is not God, needed redemption in heaven. Your order me to explain with biblical citations what I have thought out on rational grounds. A few examples ought to be enough for Your Keenness, since they are taken from the many that are available for those who wish to know. If a certain number are not sufficient for souls that resist and stick firm in their lack of belief, then [to list] the rest will not be any more useful.

Isaiah therefore, most famous of the prophets, looked ahead to the birth of Christ when the Spirit unveiled it to him, and said: 'For unto us a child is born, unto us a son is given, ... and his name shall be called Wonderful, Counseller, The mighty God, The everlasting Father, The Prince of Peace.'[1] Consider, I say, the power of the word: a Child is born, a Son is given. As if he said 'God and man',[2] the Son of man is born to us, the Son of God is given to us. 'He will be called mighty God': God who created life, strong who destroyed death. The prophet Jeremiah, showing His divinity in the words of his scribe and disciple,[3] said this: 'This is our God, and there shall none other be accounted in comparison of Him. He hath found out all the way of knowledge, and hath given it unto Jacob his servant, and to Israel his beloved. Afterward did he shew himself upon earth and conversed with men.'[4] If there is anyone for whom these words taken from the Old Testament seem obscure, let him read the apostle Paul, who said, when he alluded to the corporeal parents of our Lord: 'Whose are the fathers, and of whom as concerning the flesh Christ came, who is over all, God blessed for ever.'[5] For the apostle Thomas too, when he touched with his finger the holes left by the nails in the body of the resuscitated mediator and the gaping sign that His side had been pierced, putting together his experience of His power and the

---

1 Isa. 9.6. Note the parallel discussion of these lines in *CE* 1, p. 17.15.

2 These words, *ac si diceret deus et homo*, actually appear below in the Lyons MS and in S after *Vocabitur deus fortis*, 'He will be called the mighty God', but there they are clearly intrusive, given that they separate biblical quotation and exegesis from one another with an irrelevancy. They seem to belong here, after *filius datus*, where the words *deus* and *homo* are at issue.

3 I.e. Baruch: see Jer. 36.4ff.

4 Bar. 3.36–38 = AV Apocrypha Bar. 35–37.

5 Rom. 9.5.

signs of His weakness, he called out: 'My Lord and my God'.[1] Here then are
the testimonies by means of which, whether they like it or not, the heretics
themselves, neighbours of the Jews in damnation,[2] are defeated over the
divinity of the Son. You would think that the Jews had challenged the Lord in
the Gospel of John in their words, when they said: 'Thou art not yet forty,
and hast thou seen Abraham?'[3] But he said, 'Verily, ... I say unto you,
Before Abraham was, I am.'[4] Is this, I ask, something that he could veil over,
even if he wanted to? What remains other than that he who is known to be
older than Abraham be known to be younger than the world? And this
statement, even though it is the subject of controversy, can be refuted by
what the Lord himself said in the midst of the insults he suffered at the time
of the Passion: 'Father, glorify thou me ... with the glory which I had with
thee before the world was.'[5] But perhaps they think that this should be added
too, so that we may teach that the Son of God was named in every example
we cite. In the Psalm he says, 'Thou art my son; this day have I begotten
thee.'[6] 'This day' here means 'eternity', which lacks both a beginning and an
end: times to come will not give it days in the future, nor do times that are
past take away the days of yore from it. With us these changes occur with the
coming of the shadows; with God, since he has no night, it is always the
same day.[7] If the heretics themselves wish to understand this in some other
way, it makes no difference to us. For when we are talking about the name of
the Son alone, let them understand whatever sort of 'today' they wish; they
will grant that the Father begat the Son before the mother gave birth to Him.
Solomon also, to be sure, whose exceptional wisdom lends him the greatest
scriptural authority in the Old Testament, openly named the Son and alluded
to him most clearly in Proverbs, when he said: 'Who hath bound the waters
in a garment? who hath established[8] all the ends of the earth? what is his
name, and what is his son's name, if thou canst tell?'[9] Let these words suffice

1 John 20.28. For a parallel and much longer discussion of doubting Thomas, see *CE* 2, p.
27.20–28.18.

2 See John 8.44 for the Jews as sons of the Devil.

3 John 8.57; the AV has 'fifty' not 'forty'. Avitus' text read *quadraginta*, the Vulgate
quinquaginta. The lower age limit is of course less problematic for calculating Jesus' age at the
time of the Crucifixion and the latter's date than John's *quinquaginta*.

4 John 8.58.

5 John 17.5.

6 Ps. 2.7.

7 Lit. 'always today'.

8 Avitus' text reads *suscitavit*, 'awakened'.

9 Prov. 30.4.

about the past; the apostle says: 'But when the fullness of the time was come, God sent forth his Son.'[1] He who was sent existed before he was sent. If he had not existed before Mary, it would have been adoption,[2] not nature, that would have made him a 'son of God' like to the others. Nor would he himself have said in the Gospels: 'For God so loved the world, that he gave his only begotten Son.'[3] Therefore He was not chosen by the Ineffable Fatherhood itself, but begotten; for Him, since He is as much God as man, in each nature faithfully his own, to remain in his divinity comes from his Father; to have had a beginning in a body from his mother. Since you have ordered me to, I have sent over a few small hints about my answer and a few seeds of scriptural testimony to shed light on the truth. Your Keen Intelligence[4] or Eloquence may be able to bring them to fruition in salvation, if Christ waters them. If there is any one of those people against whom I am arguing who, in your judgement you believed to have answered these points completely,[5] even though they may be men who are vigilant in the Catholic [faith] and who deal faithfully,[6] God will nonetheless grant that I too will be able to supply even more examples[7] and an explanation to satisfy you – given that I have the free time to write.

1 Gal. 4.4.

2 Avitus' one use of the technical term 'adoption' in his *Epistles*. He avoids it completely in the *CE*.

3 John 3.16.

4 Cf. *Ep*. 46, addressing Clovis.

5 L reads *ad thorum*, which is clearly wrong. S *ad totum*, if it means 'completely' may be correct.

6 Presumably other bishops who might enter the fray against the Eutychians.

7 See *CE* 1 p. 15.14. It is interesting to observe how much of the Arian–Catholic dialogue centred on the exchange of biblical citations. Cf. *Ep*. 23, p. 55.30–31.

7. PERSONAL AND LEGAL MATTERS

Contents

Epistula 5 Avitus to Gundobad on the death of his unmarried daughter: a letter of consolation.

Epistula 6 Avitus to <Gundobad> (more probably than Sigismund) on the spiritual rewards of conversion to Catholicism.

Epistula 44 Avitus to Gundobad. A letter of exoneration. Avitus has been involved in two problematic cases: a runaway slave took refuge in the church at Vienne and an embezzler claimed that Avitus had encouraged him in his crime.

Epistula 5: Introduction

A letter of consolation of Avitus the bishop on the death of the king's daughter. Another consolation written to a King (Remigius' consolation to Clovis on the death of Albofleda, *Epistulae Austrasiacae*, *Ep.* 1, ed. W. Gundlach in *MGH*, *Epistulae* 3, *Merovingici et Karolini Aevi* 1) provides a more conventional comparison. There are also several personal letters of consolation in Ruricius' correspondence: *Epp.* 2.3–4 and 2.39. On Christian consolation in general, see Peter von Moos, *Consolatio: Studien zur mittelateinischen Trostliteratur über den Tod und zum Problem der Christlichen Trauer*, 4 vols (Munich, 1971–72).

Avitus seems to have been involved in planning a foreign marriage for an anonymous daughter of Gundobad's who died prematurely after 501.[1] If Clovis married Chrotechildis late (i.e. after 501),[2] it is quite possible, as Van de Vyver suggested, that he had been promised this girl first.[3] Indeed Clovis is really the only likely candidate as a prospective son-in-law for Gundobad shortly after 501. Theodoric was already married to Audofleda and had no male heirs. Although Gundobad might have wanted to repay the Visigoths for sheltering him against Clovis, Alaric II had married Theodegotha.[4] Thrasamund was married to Amalafrida. The Warni, Heruli and Thuringians were allies of Alaric's.[5] If Avitus had mediated

1 The *terminus post quem* is provided by the death of Godegisel in 501.

2 See R. Weiss, *Chlodwigs Taufe: Reims 508* (Frankfurt, 1971), pp. 44 and 53.

3 The suggestion was made tentatively by A. Van de Vyver, 'Clovis et la politique méditer-ranéenne', in *Recueil d'études dédiées à la mémoire de Henri Pirenne* (Brussels, 1937), pp. 375–76, followed by Weiss, *Chlodwigs Taufe*, pp. 41–42. For more on the possibilities, see now Shanzer, 'Dating the Baptism of Clovis', pp. 54–55.

4 Moorhead, *Theodoric in Italy*, p. 52, dates the marriage to the early 490s. It may have been connected with the help against Odoacer, extended to Theodoric by the Visigoths. See Jord. *Get.* 297–98; Procopius; *BG* 1.12.22.43; Anonymus Valesianus 12.63 (who reverses the daughters).

5 Cassiodorus, *Variae* 3.3.3.

the marriage of Gundobad's anonymous daughter to Clovis, then we have a meaningful context for Clovis' and the bishop of Vienne's relationship, and specifically for Avitus' interest in Clovis' religious beliefs. The negotiation would have been one of sufficient importance to have involved other bishops too.[1]

While the occasion for this letter is the death of an anonymous daughter of 'Gundobad – Avitus both starts and finishes with this theme – the meat of the letter is in the ostensible digression in the middle. Avitus uses this opportunity to discuss previous providential losses to the Burgundian royal family: the deaths of two of Gundobad's brothers, Chilperic (Greg. Tur. *DLH* 2.28) and Godegisel (Greg. Tur. *DLH* 2.33). As a result the letter is crucial for our understanding of the Burgundian royal family.

According to Gregory of Tours Gundobad was one of four brothers, the other three being Chilperic II, Godegisel and Godomar (*DLH* 2.28). Godomar is only recorded in Gregory; of the other two Godegisel is the better attested. He is said by Gregory to have been an Arian (*DLH* 2.32), and is described as 'brother of the king' (*germanus regis*), and recorded as living in Geneva by Ennodius, *Vita Epiphani* 174; in 500 he deserted Gundobad during Clovis' attack on the Burgundian kingdom, but was killed when Gundobad recovered his power (Marius of Avenches *s.a.* 500; Greg.Tur. *DLH* 2.32–33). Godegisel's death is clearly referred to in Avitus' letter, which emphasises the fact that Gundobad had trusted and been generous to this brother (*vestra natura circumdedit bonis vestris*). The word *malitia* no doubt invokes Godegisel's treacherous pact with Clovis.

The last brother is more problematic: there is an initial difficulty in distinguishing Chilperic from his homonymous uncle.[2] Chilperic I was the brother of Gundioc, and fought alongside the Visigothic king Theoderic II in his attack on the Sueves (Jordanes, *Getica* 231). Chilperic II was the father of Chrotechildis and Chrona (Greg. Tur. *DLH* 2.28; Fredegar 3.18–20). Both Chilperics were apparently Catholic: for Chilperic I this might be argued from Sid Ap. *Ep.* 6.12.3, and for Chilperic II, from the fact that his daughter Chrotechildis seems to have been brought up as a Catholic. Chilperic II's Catholicism also seems to be attested by Avitus' cryptic and perhaps ironic phrase, 'Therein lay what was best for Catholic truth.' What is unclear is which of the two men was *Magister Utriusque Militiae* (*MVM*) and Patricius in 474 (Sid. Ap. *Epp.* 5.6 and 5.7; *Vitae Patrum Iurensium* 2.10), and continued ruling in Lyons and Geneva (Sid. Ap. *Epp.* 5.7 and 6.12). The fate of Chilperic II is also a problem: according to Gregory of Tours he was thrown down a well by Gundobad (*DLH* 2.28). This seems to be at odds with Avitus' comments in this letter. The story

---

1 See the opening of Avitus, *Ep.* 5 from which it is clear that Gundobad sent bishops to console Avitus for what had happened.

2 The entries under Chilpericus I and II in *PLRE* 2 should be treated with extreme care. What is certainly wrong is the identification of Chilperic II's wife as Caretena: she was unquestionably the wife of Gundobad: Cf. *Vita Marcelli* 9, where she is *christiana principis compar*: ed. Dolbeau, 'La Vie en prose de saint Marcel de Die', pp. 97–129.

may have been invented to justify the subsequent throwing of Gundobad's son
Sigismund down a well (Greg. Tur. *DLH* 3.6). It should be noted that Gregory sees
intrafamilial murder as a trait of many of the opponents of Clovis and his sons,
including the Thuringians, Ostrogoths, Visigoths and Burgundians: the accusation
may, therefore, have been an aspect of Merovingian political propaganda.

The letter may have a personal core, to be discerned in phrases such as *experto
credite*, 'trust one who knows', and the curious sentiment, 'Whatever we then
mourned, we now love.' Pain can be transmuted into the sort of love exemplified by
Avitus' yearly commemoration of his sister's death (see *Epp*.13 and 14). Parallels
could likewise be discerned in the sentiments about chastity and the death of young
women that infuse Avitus' *De consolatoria castitatis laude*.

Previously translated by Denkinger pp. 40–41 and Burckhardt, pp. 105–108.

Letter of consolation from Avitus the bishop on the death of the king's daughter

Avitus the bishop to his lord the king {32.14 Peiper}

Since I have experienced your kindness in the past, if I rightly understand
the device Your Dignity employs, I am led to believe that my lords and
fellow-bishops have come to console me at your behest.[1] Indeed – may God
be my witness! – I did not dare to repay my eminent master in accordance
with the respect owed by me in my capacity as a servant. To suggest
consolation, either verbal or written, for the present disaster would be to
detract from your courage. For the prostration that accompanies grief affects
not the mind of a king, but that of a philosopher.[2] It is true that your affection
has prompted everyone to weep with you, but, provided your safety is
granted[3] to the world around you, it is really but a small thing for the father
of all to have lost one child. It is but a short-lived grief when someone dies
who was so innocent that no one contemplated her death. Let each make up
his own mind; as far as I am concerned, nothing happens in your time that is
not inevitably for the best. Consequently I do not think this a chance
occurrence or a harsh one. Rather a secret divine dispensation has arranged
the pain it inflicted. In the past, with ineffable tender-heartedness, you
mourned the deaths of your brothers.[4] The affliction of all followed public

1 Denkinger, p. 32, suggests that this may have been on the occasion of a council, perhaps
even the Council of Lyons.

2 Burckhardt, p. 105, mistranslates 'und überhaupt paßt es nicht zu einem königlichen,
sondern zu einem philophischen Sinn, die Trauer von sich weisen'.

3 *Concedit* makes no sense. We have emended to *conceditur*.

4 See Wood, *Merovingian Kingdoms*, p. 43, suggesting that the grief may have been honest.

grief, yet secretly under the guiding eye of God the trappings of woe were being prepared for joy. The prosperity of the kingdom caused the number of the royal persons to decrease: only those were kept alive who were needed to rule.[1] Therein lay what was best for Catholic truth.[2] We did not know that only what subsequently would not know how to bend was then being broken.[3] What ought we to say of the fate of your brothers? He whom to be called her paternal uncle[4] ...[5] you spontaneously endowed with your worldly goods, conducted himself in a truly evil fashion when he raged without your knowledge,[6] a peril to the people, and, when he was arranging matters, a menace to the region, even though peace would eventually ensue. Trust one who knows:[7] whatever harm he then[8] did, now was made good. Whatever we then mourned, we now love. As far as I am concerned, for those who are unable to know such things ahead of time, it can indeed seem a hard thing that a virgin was snatched away by an attack of illness close to the time of her marriage.[9] She who was courted as if she were a queen, died uncorrupted. In fact, there would have been greater cause for grief, if she had ended her life just after marriage. There, perhaps, there could have been found a place where competitive jealousy would first have employed its envious snare and then fixed its attacking teeth in me.[10] But now who is so

1 See Greg. Tur. *DLH* 2.42 for a grim parallel to elucidate the situation. Clovis had killed all his relatives, and set up a lament that he had no one to help him in his troubles. It was all a trick, however, Gregory tells us, to smoke out any that might remain and kill them.

2 Since, apparently, at least one of Gundobad's brothers, Chilperic, was Catholic, the sentiment may have to be savagely ironic. Alternatively, Avitus has only the Arian brothers in mind.

3 Burckhardt, p. 106, takes this as a reference to the attitude of Gundobad's third and fourth brothers towards Catholicism, although he cautions that we have no precise information. Avitus alludes to Mt. 12.20: *harundinem quassatam non confringet.*

4 Presumably Godegisel, who conspired with Clovis against Gundobad.

5 There is a lacuna in the text. Chevalier's emendation of *Ipse quem vocitari patruum ** vestra natura circumdedit bonis vestris* to *Ipse quem vocitari patruum vestrum natura circumdedit bonis vestris* does not solve the grammar of the sentence, nor does the implication that it was Chilperic I rather than Godegisel who acted wickedly fit the other historical evidence so well.

6 Gundobad is carefully absolved of Godegisel's outrages.

7 A quotation from Vergil, *Aen.* 11.283.

8 Taking *illic nocuit* (Mommsen).

9 See *Epp. Austrasiacae* 1 for Albofledis' death as a consecrated virgin.

10 Avitus presumably had lent his support to this foreign marriage, but his backing must have been unpopular. One may guess that this was because he, a bishop, may have advocated marriage for a princess who otherwise might have pursued the religious life, like Chrotechildis' sister, Chrona. Had the princess died immediately after marriage she would have been denied

barbaric as not to envy[1] the happiness of this virgin? For once she had been
taken into her Father's bosom and that of her homeland,[2] she did not change
her home, or have to journey. Where she was unable to be a princess for a
long time, not even for a short time, did she have to be an alien abroad.[3]
Since everyone is looking forward to your happiness, as if to calm weather,
give yourself back to your people, so that they may rejoice.[4] Your republic
never suffers the plague of being an orphan, as long as mother church with
your support is not bereft.[5]

Epistula 6: Introduction

This letter emphasises the fact of renunciation rather than the thing renounced, the
fact of giving rather than the precise value of the gift. Martyrdom is mentioned *en
passant* as the greatest sacrifice. This leads, almost by sleight of hand, into a discussion of the impact of the Christian life on family relationships. The final paragraph,
which deals with Abraham, was clearly intended to influence an unnamed king:
conversion, the relinquishing of a former life is the new substitute for martyrdom in
a post-heroic age.

   Since the addressee was a king who seems to have converted or to have been
about to convert, and since he seems to be one of a number of kings (*necessitati
principum*), he is most easily identified as Sigismund. The discussion of Abraham at
the end of the letter, given the age of the prophet, however, is more likely to refer to
Gundobad. One possibility is that the letter is addressed to Sigismund, but that he is
provided with arguments to encourage his father to convert. If the letter is to

---

both the rewards of the virgin in heaven and the consolation of having been a useful pawn in her
father's Frankish foreign relations. His interest in a Frankish alliance might also be inferred
from *Epp.* 37 and 46. The image of the tooth of envy is a cliché.

   1 The MSS read *misereatur*. Burckhardt, p. 107, translates 'bewegt würde', 'be moved', but
this may not be legitimate. *Misereor* (*TLL* s.v.) is used with reference to sparing, helping,
indulging and forgiving. Unless the sentence is ironic (i.e. reading 'happiness'), then
misereatur must be corrupt, and what is required is a word such as 'appreciate' or 'envy'.

   2 Translating the uncharacteristic zeugma *paterno regionisque sinu*, which should mean
'her father's bosom and that of her regional homeland', i.e. 'buried and in heaven'.

   3 There is something wrong with the text. To improve the sense and implied parallelism, we
have added a *nec* before *diu*: 'where she was unable to be a princess for long, [i.e. at home], she
did not even for a short time have to be an alien abroad'.

   4 For a similar sentiment see *Ep. Aust.* 1: *meroris torpore discusso, acrius invigilabitis ad
salutem: manet vobis regnum administrandi et, Deo auspice, prosperandi.* 'Once you have cast
off the torpor of grief, you will be more keenly alert to the [general] welfare. You must
administer and, with God's blessing, promote the kingdom.'

   5 The king is a parent both to the republic and to the church.

Sigismund, it is probably the only theological treatise addressed to him, and contrasts with the other, rather saccharine, letters which Avitus sent him. If the letter is addressed to Gundobad,[1] which is perhaps more likely, it is yet another indication of the extraordinary religious dialogue which went on between the king and the bishop of Vienne. It is also worth noting that its position as *Ep.* 6, immediately after *Epp.* 4 and 5 to Gundobad, suggests that he is indeed the addressee. The author of the headings knew that *Ep.* 4 was addressed to Gundobad, and simply continued to refer to him as 'rex' in the headings of *Epp.* 5 and 6.

The terms are very general and the background of the letter difficult to reconstruct. The addressee has clearly posed a question about Lk. 21.2–3, the widow's mite and asked about alms-giving as a sign of belief. The second section of the letter discusses the putting-aside of relatives for the sake of Christ. Those who are not prepared to convert should be abandoned. But those who follow the ascetic life are not to be put aside. Avitus may have had in mind Gundobad's relationship with his Catholic wife, Caretene, whose epitaph suggests that she practised both sexual renunciation and asceticism.[2] Does the allusion to the brothers Peter and Andrew reflect the relationship between Gundobad and his brothers,[3] or to that between Sigismund and Godomar?[4] Who is the *necessitas principum* (p. 34.25)? The addressee? Or a relative of his?

Avitus the bishop to his lord, the king {33.14 Peiper}

The question which Your Piety has asked me to discuss must, when considered in a spiritual light, be interpreted entirely with reference to an inner metaphor. It is not true that what each man will piously bring in the spirit of pity to alms-giving for the poor will certainly be returned with a hundredfold interest. For in the generosity of alms-giving, in which the feelings of the giver are considered rather than his finances, it is not the size of the gift that must be weighed, but the giver's eagerness to give it. This is why in the gospel the small offering of two coins was preferred to infinite gifts of gold and silver.[5] If the gift were to be returned a hundredfold in

1 This is assumed by Kampers, 'Caretena', pp. 12–17.

2 See *Titulorum Gallicorum liber* 6.6., ed. Peiper, p. 185: *iamdudum castum castigans aspera corpus/ delituit vestis murice sub rutilo.* 'Already for a long time she had punished her body: a hair shirt hid beneath the ruddy purple.' In the prose *Vita Marcelli* 9 (ed. F. Dolbeau) she is called the *christiana principis compar.* For an exploration of the implications of the letter for an understanding of Caretene, see Kampers, 'Caretena'.

3 Greg. Tur. *DLH* 2.33, and 3, praef. implies that Godegisel was Arian.

4 Greg. Tur. *DLH* 3, praef. implies that Godomar was an Arian: this might be supported by Avitus' fears of a revival of Arianism in *Ep.* 7.

5 Lk. 21.2–3, the widow's mite.

proportion to its size to the widow who gave it, she would doubtless, because she gave less, have received less than everyone else. Hence also [what] Saint Peter [meant], when he said: 'Behold, we have forsaken all, and followed thee.'[1] Now he, as the book tells us, left behind only his nets, with which he had been gaining a meagre livelihood by fishing. And he was told: 'And every one that hath forsaken houses, or brethren, or sisters, or father, or mother, or wife, or children, or lands, for my name's sake, shall receive an hundredfold, and shall inherit everlasting life.'[2] Since in the sacred scriptures the number one hundred has been sanctified in its complete perfection, you must understand that those things will be returned a hundredfold that were abandoned[3] in the name of Christ, not those that were given in His name. Although generous alms-giving is a great thing and one conducive to salvation, it is a far greater thing to give up everything than to give away many things.

Therefore I hope Your Glory may understand[4] that I am preaching this about martyrdom alone. No human deed, however meritorious, can equal its crown. This is the hundredfold fruit that hopes for eternal life in the future, but also in this world compensates the injuries inflicted on the martyrs with marvellous honour. Thus, in another place in the gospel, the word of our Lord bears witness that the germ of well-nourished seed that fell onto good earth yielded fruit a hundredfold.[5] He condones the abandonment of parents, wife, children or brothers, but for the name of Christ alone, that is to say that to confess His name, we must sacrifice not merely these sorts of relatives,[6] but also our lives and our bodies. The Lord spoke about this separation elsewhere: 'I am come,' he said, 'to set children at variance against their parents, daughter-in-law against mother-in-law.'[7] That is to say that when we are going towards Christ, people, however close their attachment to us,

---

1 Mt. 19.27.

2 Mt. 19.29.

3 I.e. 'foregone'.

4 Goelzer, p. 612, for *definire* meaning 'to determine, decide, stop, declare, etc.'

5 Mt. 13.8.

6 Goelzer, p. 643. If the letter is addressed to Gundobad, this passage must have been intended to recall Caretene: Kampers, 'Caretena', p. 12.

7 Paraphrasing Mt. 10.35: the conflict of daughter-in-law and mother-in-law may have specific force in relations between the Catholic Caretene and the apparently still Arian Ostrogotho Areagni. So too children against parents could refer to the possibility of tension between Sigismund and Gundobad, and indeed to Sigismund's children against their father.

should be left behind, if they are unwilling to accompany us.[1] There is one exception: we gather both by reason and from examples that these relatives must not invariably be dismissed by us as if they were judged guilty in advance.[2] Nor must those relatives be dismissed who hurry to celestial crowns,[3] having trampled death under foot, through their contempt of this world. Nor can we persuade the faithful to cast aside spouses and parents, since the Lord cries out that 'it is not lawful for a man to put aside his wife, and that what God has joined together, let not man put asunder'.[4] And the apostle protests that he who does not provide for his own and for his neighbours denies his faith and is worse than an infidel.[5] Peter followed the Lord, and Peter's own wife followed Peter.[6] When they gave up sexual relations, there remained spiritual solace. And since his brother Andrew accompanied him,[7] he sent away neither his brother nor his wife, and in their company he stayed close in the footsteps of Christ. Therefore we must fear, not lest people of this sort actively obstruct us, but lest they prove handicaps.[8] For even though the word of the Lord claims that the kingdom of heaven can be obtained by any man, whatever his birth, rank, or title, he is a foolhardy preacher if he persuades a close relative of princes,[9] one ruling the kingdom with divine majesty, that all the things I mentioned above must be abandoned. Contempt for the temporal world should be encouraged, and the heavenly kingdom promised even to persons of this high rank, since the apostle, as you may remember, enjoins the rich to be rich in good works, and

1 If this is addressed to Sigismund it might refer to Ostrogotho Areagni and to their children remaining Arian. That Sigismund was converted before his son Sigistrix and his daughter is implied by *Hom.* 26, which would appear to have been preached after their father's accession in 516. Sigistrix seems still to have been Arian in 517: see *Ep.* 7.

2 I.e. the recipient cannot just abandon his heretical relatives, assuming that they will remain heretical.

3 Possibly a reference to Caretene.

4 Paraphrasing Mt. 19.3–6. Possibly implying that the convert cannot put away his wife on religious grounds — in which case the letter would have to have been addressed to Sigismund.

5 Paraphrasing 1 Tim. 5.8.

6 An unusual allusion to Peter's wife.

7 This might be taken to indicate that Godomar converted at the same time as Sigismund. On the other hand *Ep.* 7 might, but does not necessarily, imply that Godomar was still Arian after 516.

8 Presumably a reference to Arian relatives.

9 The phrase *necessitas principum* is difficult to interpret. See Goelzer, p. 519, for *necessitas* meaning 'family-tie'. It suggests that the addressee is a ruler himself who had other relatives who could be called *principes*. Avitus is clearly guarding himself against accusations of trying to convert members of the royal family.

to heap up for themselves a good foundation so as to gain the true life.[1] In accordance with this precept, the use of lands and income can be of service to them – provided the desire for them cause no harm.

There is, however, also another type of holiness, in which, even if persecution ceases, true confession can almost imitate martyrdom. If anyone changes the custom of his ancestors or his sect by following the true belief and is not held by the privilege of custom, since truth challenges him to love salvation, he rightly puts away his relatives, brothers and sisters.[2] The rich man Abraham who enjoyed every celestial gift, children, servants, gold, silver, having used his patrimony and his marriage properly, shook himself clean of the burden of his fatherland and his relatives[3] in the desire to change his religion; when old age was already upon him, he underwent the rite of circumcision (in which Christianity was prefigured), and showed that even the old can become children through conversion. It was to these that the prophet alluded, when he said, 'the child shall die an hundred years old',[4] that is to say that he will receive a hundredfold, because he became a child. Just as a new way of life made a boy of this exceptionally old man (I already mentioned the sacred number of his years) so too the preservation of conversion makes (the convert) perfect in immortal longevity.

Epistula 44: Introduction

This letter deals with two issues: a slave, who has sought asylum in a basilica in Vienne,[5] and a man who denies that he has received a deposit (*depositum: negator depositi: de depositi infitiatione*). The latter claimed that Avitus had told him not to return the property which he is holding, a defence which, as the bishop points out, is on the one hand untrue and on the other an admission of guilt.

By Roman law a slave who sought asylum could only remain in sanctuary for one day, before being returned to his owner, but he could expect a pardon.[6] In this instance, however, the slave is being handed over for further investigation. Ruricius *Ep*. 2.20 to Rusticus[7] deals with a similar problem: he intercedes for a slave called

---

1 Paraphrasing 1 Tim. 6.18–19.

2 On the importance of ancestors and ancestral custom, see also *Ep*. 46 to Clovis. Again Caretene's ascetic life appears to be in Avitus' mind.

3 Taking F's *cognationis suae onere*.

4 Isa. 65.20.

5 For Roman legislation on asylum seekers, *Cod. Theod*. 9.45.

6 *Cod. Theod*. 9.45.5.

7 *PLRE* 2 Rusticus 6 who is perhaps to be identified with Rusticus 5. In Ruricius' letter his status is still lay.

Baxo who has taken refuge in Limoges. For comparative material on bishops and the right of sanctuary in Gregory of Tours, see E. James, 'Beati pacifici: Bishops and the Law in Sixth-Century Gaul. Disputes and Settlements', in *Law and Human Relations in the West*, ed. J. Bossy (Cambridge, 1983), pp. 25–46.

That Gundobad, rather than a *comes* of Lyons, is himself dealing with the trial of the deposit denier (*negator*) is an indication of the severity of the case, and may imply that the *depositum* belonged to a senior figure in the kingdom, or possibly that it was something which had been given by Gundobad to a church in Lyons – this at least would explain the emphasis on how much Gundobad has given to the Catholic church in the closing lines of the letter. Certainly Avitus' appeal to Gundobad, and his pledge of the *substantia* of the church of Vienne, is serious. Like *Ep.* 55 this letter is an indication of the limitations of a bishop's power in the Burgundian kingdom. The letter was translated by Burckhardt.[1]

Avitus the bishop to King Gundobad {73.12 Peiper}

That I have sent back under guard from the church at Vienne to the basilica at Lyons the slave whose presence was vital for the trial is a clear sign of my fear and obedience. For just as I did not take it upon myself to hand him over here,[2] because he had not yet been [formally] arraigned,[3] so I ensured that he be made available for the interrogations that the court was demanding there. Since it is the case both that there is but one rule[4] in force everywhere and that the same scope for action or lack thereof is available to us bishops in accordance with the common regulations governing our ministry,[5] I did not look to the property rights of the church of Lyons or Vienne, but to the dignity of both. The result was that <in a matter>[6] which can affect both of us,[7] the bishop on the spot[8] asserted the claim for intercession that can more

1 Burckhardt, pp. 112–13, although his translation does not deal adequately with all the problems of the text.

2 Presumably a royal messenger had been sent to fetch the man under guard from sanctuary at Vienne.

3 Taking S's *inaccusatum*.

4 Perhaps meaning secular law.

5 Referring to the role of the clergy in sanctuary law.

6 Winterbottom rightly suggests the addition of *in eo* as an antecedent for *quod*.

7 Who is 'us'? Probably the bishops of Lyon and Vienne, although it could be Avitus and Gundobad.

8 *Praesens*: 'present' at Lyon.

easily be provided from nearby.[1] For just as our ministry has the same charity in all places, so too are your royal *imperium* and power the same.[2] I need not mention that the slave who ran away from his master's command ought not to have sought out the church of Vienne[3] and stirred up trouble for me. He was at Lyons; he could have stayed inside the church there.[4]

As for the case in which the cunning man who refuses to return a deposit entrusted to him is arraigned before your Highness, my conscience is as clear as it is shown to be to you and to God in every act of my daily life. But, even if I am silent, the honest plaintiff who, †as to the commands of a gracious master will not hesitate in his charity to deny†[5] will be able to clarify what I intended by consoling him, if he has any thought for Christ. Some of your servants, my citizens, know this already, as they now attest at the present hearing. You are taking judicial action against someone who has caused trouble beyond his station,[6] and is said to be rather unreliable in all his answers. May God and the truth itself tell you whether what he says about me is accurate.[7] Since he was taken to task by me, he is perhaps angry in that very same spirit of falsehood that led him to lie to an honest man and deny the deposit. But with you and God well-disposed, his fabrication was of but little use for his defence: since he said that he had been told by me *not* to give it back, he cannot deny that he took it! This admission of his, even though you might think that it ought to cause *me* trouble, cannot help *him*. I await the instructions of Your Piety. Whatever my small church has, nay all of our churches, is yours in its substance, since up to now you have either guarded it or given it.[8] What you have commanded under God's inspiration, I shall try to obey to the best of my ability. As for the rest, since the gaze of divine majesty sees that there is nothing I fear so much after offending it as

---

1 Burckhardt, however, translates 'by the nearest person'. Presumably, when notifying a master that his slave had sought asylum, the cleric responsible for the church in question was expected to intercede for the fugitive: *Cod. Theod.* 9.45.5.

2 Taking S's *imperio vestro aequa potestas*.

3 Understanding 'basilicam' with *Viennensem*.

4 The slave in Ruricius *Ep*. 2.20 tried a similar trick by running to an out-of-town church.

5 S's *diffiteri*, parallel to *profiteri* below, must be right, but the text of the relative clause still remains hopelessly corrupt. We have obelised it.

6 *Extra ordinem*. Each rank seems entitled to cause a certain amount of trouble. Cf. *Ep*. 55 where Avitus has to lock horns with a troublesome noble rapist.

7 For *certa* reading *recta*, as suggested by Winterbottom.

8 That Gundobad, albeit an Arian, was a benefactor of Catholic churches is clear from Avitus, *Hom*. 24: see Perrat and Audin, 'Alcimi Ecdicii Aviti Viennensis', pp. 442–43.

offending you, I beg this favour as a suppliant: that the unhappy man, whom the very fact that he is making excuses serves to condemn,[1] may not make me the companion of his untrustworthiness in the eyes[2] of your justice, even if he see me punished for upsetting you.

1 Not quite the earliest form of 'qui s'excuse, s'accuse'. For similar puns see Ruricius *Ep.* 1.2. p. 300.19–21, copied apparently from Cassian, *Contra Nestorium* 1.5.2 per Hagendahl, *La Correspondance*, p. 28.
2 Lit. 'spirits'.

SIGISMUND, PRINCE AND THE KING OF THE BURGUNDIANS

8. THEOLOGICAL–RELIGIOUS MATTERS

Contents

Epistula 8: Introduction

This letter is a request for relics written by Avitus on behalf of some recently converted king. The letter would seem to have been addressed to the pope,[1] because of the phrase, 'The people run in crowds, to be sure, to the enclosures <that> you rule' (*catervatim quidem populi ad caularum quas regitis saepta concurrunt*) and the apparently pointed allusion to schisms affecting the *Romani*. Since the letter refers to an early royal conversion to Catholicism ('but he is still the only one of the *kings* who has not been ashamed to come over to the good [side]')[2] it has been taken variously to refer to Clovis and to Sigismund, and has become a point of debate in determining the date of Clovis' baptism. At first sight both identifications are equally possible: Clovis' *caput regni* would be Paris,[3] Sigismund's perhaps Geneva.[4] Further, certain comments, notably those pointing to influence on neighbouring peoples, seem so close to Avitus' comments at the end of his letter to Clovis (*Ep*. 46), that it is tempting to connect the two letters.

---

1 The closing references to relics might seem to be more applicable to Jerusalem than to Rome.

2 *Sed adhuc de regibus solus est, quem in bonum trans<isse>. . non pudeat.*

3 Greg. Tur. *DLH* 2.38.

4 See below p. 222.

Certain points, however, make it far more likely that this letter relates to Sigismund: first, the king in *Ep.* 8 rules over a people many of whom converted ahead of him. This scarcely fits Clovis and the Franks, whereas it is clear that there were many Burgundian Catholics already in the fifth century;[1] second Sigismund went to Rome, as is clear from *Ep.* 29, and made contact with the pope, which fits with Avitus' comment that he might have told the pope personally (*verbo*) about his conversion; third his request for relics which concludes the letter clearly bore fruit, as can be seen in *Ep.* 29, where he acknowledges that he has given almost all his relics away, just as Avitus prophesies in *Ep.* 8. The reference to a *unicum pignus* was also seem to point more obviously to Sigismund, for although Gregory of Tours suggests that Clovis and Chlothild only had one living son at the time of the former's baptism,[2] the king already a son, Theuderic, by another woman. Sigismund's son can easily be identified as Sigistrix.[3]

It is, therefore, necessary to see this letter as referring to Sigismund. Further, the connection with *Ep.* 29 would seem to suggest a date of ca. 501/2, since here Avitus makes a point about a schism, 'the fault of some schism' (*culpa cuiuscumque scismatis*), which could be either the Laurentian or Acacian schism, while in the later letter Sigismund refers to the *libertas* of the pope, which may well be a reference to Symmachus' taking sanctuary in 501/2.[4] This provides a plausible date for Sigismund's conversion, which apparently took place on or as a result of a second visit to Rome.[5]

Although this reconstruction might seem to be ruled out by the fact that the convert is described as *de regibus solus*, since Marius of Avenches claimed that Regismund (sic) became king on Gundobad's death (i.e. 516), it is clear from Fredegar that Sigismund was elevated to the kingship at some unspecified date during his father's lifetime.[6] Furthermore, other letters of Avitus make it clear that Sigismund held some office that could be described figuratively as that of Caesar while Gundobad was still alive.[7] It is, therefore, better to see *Ep.* 8 as helping to define Sigismund's power before 516, rather than to think that the word *rex* was not

1 Wood, 'Ethnicity and the Ethnogenesis', pp. 58–61.

2 Greg. Tur. *DLH* 2.29–31.

3 Greg. Tur. *DLH* 3.5.

4 Moorhead, *Theodoric in Italy*, pp. 115–16.

5 This is clear from *Ep.* 29. A. Van de Vyver, 'La Victoire contre les alamans et la conversion de Clovis', *RBPH* 15 (1936), p. 891, claims that *Ep.* 8 accompanied Sigismund to Rome and that *Ep.* 29 to Pope Symmachus was written after Sigismund's return from pilgrimage to Rome. But this must be wrong. Avitus would never have said that he did not know whether Sigismund had announced his conversion to the pope in writing or in person, had the letter accompanied Sigismund. This letter proves that Sigismund was not officially converted at the time of his first trip to Rome. He must have been converted after the visit to Rome in which he met Symmachus (*Ep.* 29). Subsequently Avitus wrote *Ep.* 8, and *Ep.* 29 represents a continuation of the correspondence.

6 Fredegar 3.33.

7 *Ep.* 77.

appropriate before that time. Since he was initially elevated to the kingship at Carouge,[1] a suburb of Geneva, and since he founded the monastery at Agaune in the upper Rhône valley in 515 (before Gundobad's death),[2] it is likely that it was in Geneva that his household was based. This would explain why Avitus (in Vienne) does not know, and cannot check quickly, whether Sigismund has told the pope in person or by letter about his conversion. If Sigismund's conversion is to be dated to ca. 501/2, then his establishment in Geneva would follow shortly after the death of Godegisel, who is known to have been at least occasionally resident during his period of (sub)kingship.[3]

Strangely enough this letter was not transcribed into L or S, and one must wonder whether it was deliberately omitted, perhaps because it contradicted Gregory of Tours' reading of Clovis as the first Catholic monarch among the Germanic kings. The only witness to its text is the Paris papyrus and the transcription of Jérôme Bignon (1590–1656). Emericus Bigotius collated Bignon's transcription with the papyrus, and his collation is preserved among the Baluziana, vol. 297 ff. 68–78 (Baluze Papiers-Armoires, Paquet 12 no. 1 fol. 69) in the Bibliothèque nationale in Paris.[4]

The papyrus seems to have sustained further damage since Bignon's and Bigot's time.[5] Since the (damaged) papyrus is the only witness for this extremely important letter, and since editorial restorations inevitably involve *petitio principii*, this translation is based, to the extent that it is possible, not on Peiper's edition, but on Peiper's and Bignon's transcriptions (Peiper, pp. 41 and 43). On the whole the variations between the two transcriptions are of negligible significance. We make reference, where necessary, to Peiper's edition and the interpretations it implies (Peiper, pp. 40 and 42).

The letter was previously translated by Burckhardt.[6]

[Avitus to the pope][7] {40.1 Peiper}

< ... > for a long time dogmas of darkness and of (Eastern?) mysteries[8] had closed off the hearts of the (?fierce) barbarians. If the guilt associated with

1 Fredegar 3.33.

2 Avitus, *Hom.* 25; Marius of Avenches, *s.a.* 515.

3 Ennodius, *Vita Epifani* 174 refers to Godegisel only as *germanus regis*, but places him in Geneva: see also Greg. Tur. *DLH* 2.32. That Sigismund was elevated to the kingship in Godegisel's place, in ca. 505, is argued by Favrod, *Histoire politique*, pp. 373–76.

4 See Peiper, p. xxxvii.

5 Peiper, p. 41, notes *quae post Bignonum evanuerunt*, 'that they faded after Bignon's time'.

6 Burckhardt, p. 108 and pp. 77ff.

7 Almost certainly Symmachus.

8 Oriental cults or Arianism?

some sort of schism[1] can cause any offence in the (missing noun abl.) of the Romans and < ... > in precisely the same fashion either the Arian heresy had stained the fearsome spirits of the different tribes or native <feminine abstract pejorative noun>[2] possessed them. But after the prince I mentioned earlier, crossing over from his previous error[3] to your Catholic [Church], like a standard-bearer for the Christians took up the banners of truth to carry them before his people, by enticing everyone by his encouragement, but compelling no one by force, he gained his own people by his own example, and other peoples by the example of his own (*sc.* people).[4] Nor is it worthy for < ... > to be <missing passive verb> to you that truth has. The people run in crowds, to be sure, to the enclosures <that> you rule,[5] but he is still the only one of the *kings* who has not been ashamed to come over to the good [side].[6] Thus those [people] too, whom up to now he has not taken in hand with a [direct] challenge, but controlled by admiration,[7] even if he is not yet able to reckon [it] as salvation, at least he grants that in this fashion < ... > to cease from persecuting.[8] Furthermore, guard by your constant prayer in

---

1 The reference to likely to be an allusion to the Laurentian schism. If so the letter would have had very special force in 501–502, although any time between 498 and 514 would be possible, See Moorhead, *Theodoric in Italy*, pp. 114–26.

2 Some abstract quality, ending in *-itas*, perhaps *feritas*. This seems most likely to be an allusion to paganism.

3 *Error* (*pace* Burckhardt, p. 79 and Reydellet, *Royauté dans la littérature latine*, p. 125) does not *necessarily* imply a heretic. One need only cite Firmicus Maternus' treatise *De Errore profanarum religionum*. For Clovis' paganism described as *error*, see Greg. Tur. *DLH* 2.27: *adhuc fanaticis erroribus involutus*. On the other hand, in this context *error* would seem to refer to the Arianism of Sigismund.

4 Sigismund, the Franks and, perhaps, the Ostrogoths.

5 I.e. the fold of the Catholic church. Avitus speaks of converts to Catholicism.

6 This sentence is crucial for identifying the king of the letter. There is a strong contrast between *people* who run in flocks to Catholicism, and a *king* who is still first among the kings to become a Catholic. The contrast concerns the relative *classes* of the individuals. There is no evidence that Franks were rushing to be converted before Clovis' conversion and the contrast in the sentence is only meaningful if the king in question rules over a people many of whom have been converted. All of the following scenarios are ruled out: *populi* = Burgundians and Franks and *rex* = Clovis, *populi* = Franks and *rex* = Clovis, and *populi* = Burgundians and Franks and *rex* = Sigismund. The king is Sigismund, the *populi* are the Burgundians. The sentence provides an accurate picture of the political and religious *realia* of the Burgundian kingdom: a partially Catholic populace and several kings. It is worth comparing *Ep.* 7, p. 36.13, *si nunc quisquam de vivis regibus legis alienae in regione sua similiter velit*, for the clear way in which Avitus indicates *foreign* kings — in this case Arian ones.

7 I.e. that he inspires in them.

8 For the possibility of persecution by Arians in Burgundy see *Ep.* 7.

these regions[1] his one child[2] for the only devout one,[3] and ask from God that whatever we seek to be preserved for us be granted to other regions.[4] As for the rest, I must admit that I do not know in all truth whether your son, whom we mentioned before, has made known to you either in writing or in person[5] the vow that he took to express his allegiance to you;[6] he has built an orthodox basilica in the city which is the capital of his kingdom.[7] As far as <the external>[8] poverty went, at great expense, < ... > and what ?from the ?powerful is <?rare> he did [it] with the greatest love. And I bless by your gift < ... > the part that is missing, < ... > of him < ... > Know that the man is willing to give to everyone[9] whatever he asked for that he can obtain from you. You add on as much as such a person seems to deserve.[10] For the rest, in his most pious humility he will see that, since all of your city could rightly be called one church, it is right that whatever sacred soil or dust you send[11] be considered heavenly.[12]

1 Where Avitus is.

2 Sigistrix. The reference to one child also rules out Clovis, who, by the time of his baptism had at least two living children, Theuderic and Chlodomer.

3 A possessive dative? Sigismund or, less probably, Gundobad?

4 Catholicism. Avitus may be hinting at the eventual conversion of the Franks, but more immediately, given that he is addressing the pope, that of the Ostrogths.

5 The Latin word used is *verbo*, which, when opposed to *scripto*, clearly implies speech and therefore the king's presence. Clovis never went to Rome, so this sentence provides strong support for the thesis that the letter is about Sigismund. See commentary on *Ep.* 29.

6 Presumably the profession of Catholicism.

7 This would presumably be Geneva. Perhaps Gundobad allowed Sigismund to have his own household there, following the death of Godegisel in 500/1. It may have been this new-found freedom that gave Sigismund the chance to develop his own religious stance; for the problems he had in taking a different religious line from his father, see *Ep.*77.

8 Peiper's supplement *<externam>* still seems to be the only reasonable choice among the possible *-rnus* adjectives. It must refer to the poor external appearance of the church.

9 *Totis* used here for *omnibus*, cf. French 'tous'.

10 I.e. more of the relics. Cf. *Ep.* 29, p. 59.10–16. which must be the follow-up letter to this one. Sigismund did in fact distribute the relics.

11 Stones and earth are familiar Holy Land relics; see J. and L. Robert, 'Bulletin épigraphique', *Revue des études grecques* 71 (1958), pp. 169–363, at p. 329, and B. Bagatti, 'Eulogie Palestinesi', *Orientalia Christiana Periodica* 15 (1949), pp. 126–66 on sacred souvenirs from the Holy Land, including many examples of rocks and earth. Bagatti, 'Eulogie Palestinesi', p. 143 mentions disks made of mud from the grotto of the Nativity and cites an African inscription of 359. But the Roman Christian martyr tourist trade was already being developed by Pope Damasus (see C. Pietri, *Roma Christiana: recherches sur l'Église de Rome, son organisation, sa politique, son idéologie de Miltiade à Sixte III (311–440)* (Rome, 1976), vol. 1, pp. 607–17; *Liber Pontificalis* 39) and it is quite possible that visitors collected dust from the Catacombs, Vatican or Colosseum. Sigismund was fortunate in his compliant pope.

Epistula 29: Introduction

The main subject of this letter, like that of a number of others in the Avitus collection,[1] is the acquisition of relics. Here Sigismund asks Pope Symmachus (498–514) for relics of St Peter, a particular favourite of the prince,[2] explaining that he has distributed most of those that had already been given. The letter is, however, of much greater historical significance, since it refers to a visit of Sigismund to Rome, apparently at the time of his marriage to Theodoric's daughter Ostrogotho Areagni.[3] Ennodius, *Vita Epifani* 163, suggests that this marriage took place around the time of Epiphanius of Pavia's legation to the Burgundian kingdom (494/6),[4] i.e. under either Gelasius (492–6) or Anastasius (496–8).[5] This can be squared with the fact that Sigismund does not indicate that Symmachus was the pope in question at the time of the visit associated with his marriage (referring simply to *pontificalis benignitas*). The prince, however, also indicates a second visit during the pontificate of Symmachus, since he refers to *pontificatus vester ... praesentem monitis docuit* suggesting that a second visit to Rome was in some way linked to his conversion to Catholicism. Since Sigismund's conversion is one of the facts which needs to be taken into account in dealing with the baptism of Clovis, this letter, together with *Ep.* 8, thus has an additional significance.[6] The letter has been translated by Burckhardt,[7] and discussed in some detail by A. Van de Vyver,[8] who, however, envisaged only one visit to Rome.

Hormisdas refused apostolic relics to Justinian and Gregory to Constantina. See Hormisdas, *Ep.* 77 Thiel and Greg. Mag. *Ep.* 4.30 and 9.49 cited in H. Delehaye, *Les Origines du culte des martyrs* (Brussels, 1933), p. 52. In these cases it was the *consuetudo sedis apostolicae* (as opposed to that of the Greeks) not to disturb the bodies of martyrs or part with actual relics. Contact-souvenirs of linen (*brandea*) were prepared instead. See Pietri, *Roma Christiana*, p. 606, 'Ils évitent soigneusement de laisser distraire, si peu que ce soit, des martyres reposant près de la Ville.'

12 For a similar trope see the end of *Ep.* 25, likewise a request for relics.

1 See *Ep.* 25.

2 See *Epp.* 31 and 32.

3 For the marriage see Anon. Valesianus 63 and Shanzer, 'Two Clocks and a Wedding'.

4 Moorhead, *Theodoric in Italy*, p. 53.

5 Since Anastasius is known to have made concessions to Avitus vis-à-vis his metropolitan authority (*Ep. Arelatenses Genuinae* 23), he might seem to be the more likely figure. His attempt to end the Acacian schism (*Liber Pontificalis* 52) might also explain Avitus' assumption that the emperor was orthodox in *Ep.* 46.

6 See A. Van de Vyver, 'La Victoire contre les Alamans et la conversion de Clovis', *Revue belge de philologie et d'histoire* 15 (1936), pp. 890–91.

7 Burckhardt, pp. 111–12.

8 Van de Vyver, 'La Victoire contre les Alamans' (1936), pp. 890–91.

Sigismund the king to Symmachus the bishop of Rome {59.9 Peiper}

As for the sacred relics with which, through me, you have enriched your own land[1] of Gaul with a spiritual gift,[2] since I do not presume to deny them to those who ask for them, I too am compelled to go to the ever-flowing fount of Your Apostleship to ask for the patronage of the saints. Even though[3] there still remains with us some of your gift to be assiduously worshipped by devout Catholics, it is fit that even this be considered a sign of meet devotion,[4] so that, once you have sent letters, we may grasp the instructions by means of which you[5] have either advised me in person, or have added me to your possessions[6] in my absence through intercession. There has not yet been an opportunity for me to deliver this letter in person, but all the same by sending a deacon, the venerable Julian,[7] as messenger, we have hastened to the head of the Universal Church, with the spirit to make us present. Our longing for you grows as we remember your good deeds, nor will I ever forget what pontifical kindness[8] and royal courtesy granted to us in Italy,[9] when, after the family tie[10] that is preferable to all the benefits attendant upon riches < ... >[11] because here he has more generously released <her> to return,[12] there he has surrounded <her> more closely with his affection.

---

1 This does not mean that the pope was Gallic, but that Gaul was under his jurisdiction.

2 The indications of dedications of churches to St Peter in Avitus' homilies (e.g. 21, 29) may reflect Sigismund's distribution of Petrine relics.

3 For redundant *quamquam* with another concessive, see J. B. Hofmann and A. Szantyr, *Lateinische Syntax und Stilistik* (Munich, 1972), p. 603.

4 *Iustae devotionis* is taken as predicative genitive.

5 Literally, 'Your Papacy'.

6 I.e. converted Sigismund to Catholicism. This sentence suggests that while Sigismund was admonished to convert by the pope in person in Rome, the actual conversion took place while Sigismund was in Burgundy.

7 Plausibly Avitus' successor as bishop of Vienne, and therefore, following Heinzelmann, *Bischofsherrschaft*, p. 222, a relative of Avitus.

8 The clear implication of the naked *pontificalis benignitas* (as opposed to *benignitas vestra*) is that the first visit had occurred under one of Symmachus' predecessors.

9 Literally 'your Italy'.

10 An allusion to Sigismund's marriage to Ostrogotho Areagni. Van de Vyver ('La Victoire contre les Alamans' (1936)) thinks this a reference to papal courtesies. But the third-person verbs that follow show that the subject must be someone other than the pope. See Shanzer, 'Two Clocks and a Wedding', pp. 249–51 for an analysis of this passage.

11 There seems to be an extra conjunction here: *cum* has no verb; then comes the *quia-*clause. We posit a lacuna.

12 With Sigismund.

Furthermore pray the more attentively for your people.[1] For the more sheep there are, the greater the responsibility of the shepherd.[2] Since I shall be present [in spirit] at the holy threshold of the apostles through my dutiful commemoration, as long as I live, < ... >[3] your special advocate.[4] Where you have achieved a first step, ask for and gain success:[5] as often as the chance arises or your freedom[6] permits, please shower us with the letters in which your learning and state of moral salvation flourish, and, as we hoped above, grant us the protection of the venerable relics. By worshipping them, may we always deserve to have the most blessed Peter present in his strength and you through your gift.

Epistula 23: Introduction

This important letter is dismayingly allusive. In it Avitus writes to Sigismund, who has presumably already been converted to Catholicism, to tell him the outcome of a religious debate held before Gundobad. The debate has been held in secret, so as not to cause problems either for the king and his Arian clergy or for Avitus. The bishop of Vienne has been successful enough in his argumentation to cause the king to invite him to submit a compilation of the quotations that were crucial to his case, so that Gundobad and the Arians may consider them more closely.

Avitus had been working secretly on a theological rebuttal (*non cessavit ... sed latuit*), waiting for an opportunity to spring it on Gundobad. Sigismund must have accused him of lying low and being non-confrontational.[7] Arian 'arms' (i.e. materials) for the controvery (*ipsa contentionis arma*), Avitus said, had failed as if already facing the Catholic 'arms'. But since Gundobad had not requested outside theological help, Avitus did not have to wait until Gundobad's envoys returned to get practice in controversy. Even though he was on his way back from some unspecified journey and was not thinking about the theological debate at the time, he was able to set his arguments in motion immediately upon his return. The treatise he had

---

1 I.e. Catholics.

2 The *augmentum ovium* must again allude to Sigismund's conversion.

3 The sentence seems to be missing the main verb that governed *specialem praedicatorem*. Something like 'protect' or 'foster' is needed.

4 Sigismund alludes to himself here. He is Symmachus' advocate after his conversion.

5 Peiper mispunctuated. There should be a full stop after *praedicatorem vestri*, and a colon after *profectum*.

6 An allusion to Symmachus' troubles during the Laurentian schism? See Chadwick, *Boethius*, pp. 31–33 for Symmachus seeking sanctuary in St Peter's during 501–502.

7 The charge is addressed indirectly on p. 55.16 *subitam opportunitatem potius quam quietem requirens*.

prepared may be the *Contra Arrianos*.[1] If so, it is interesting to have its author's own assessment of its diplomatic tone.

The letter is of importance for what it shows about the mechanics of theological debate between Arians and Catholics in the Burgundian kingdom. It is also important in that, in Avitus' eyes at least, the king was responsive to his arguments. This might either support Gregory of Tours' view that Gundobad was converted to Catholic doctrine but never dared abandon the Arian church,[2] or it might even have been the source for Gregory's belief. The allusive nature of the letter is presumably to be connected to the fact that discussions had been held in secret, and that Avitus was unable even to commit to paper a proper account of what had taken place.

Avitus the bishop to his master, Sigismund {55.10}

You blame me for not reporting my debate[3] with the king to Your Notice; I had saved[4] the news for my meeting [with you] once the feast was over, because, to tell the truth, the long and complex nature of the proceedings does not permit me to tell you in a letter you everything as it happened. For as much as I think I have sensed < ...>[5] in the soul of my lord, your father, there burns in his zeal a struggle that is concealed under the appearance of leisure. Now as for what I used to believe: once I had set aside my ill will[6] in a period of sensible silence, because I was looking[7] for a sudden opportunity rather than for peace and quiet, [my former beliefs] did not cease after the brief truce in the past,[8] but have lain hidden.[9] The result[10] was that not even the very weapons for the dispute, which, as if they had been lacking in our region, are sought from outside, nor does my eagerness to practice have to wait until his ambassadors return.[11]

1 The letter could also be related to the discussion of Eutychianism that elicited the *CE*.

2 Greg. Tur. *DLH* 2.34.

3 Perhaps even 'audience', depending on the meaning assigned to *collocutio*.

4 Taking *servaveram* as *simplex pro composito* for *reservaveram*.

5 There may be a neuter noun missing, a word meaning something like 'impassibility', 'indifference', 'calm', but the sentence can just about be translated as it stands.

6 I.e. towards Gundobad's Arianism.

7 Avitus is using a singular participle, *requirens*, with his polite first-person plural verb, *credebamus*. For anomalies with the *pluralis maiestatis* see Goelzer, pp. 56ff.

8 The 'truce' must be a pause in theological debate.

9 Avitus indicates that he has been giving the appearance of complying with Gundobad.

10 This sentence is presented as a result of the previous one. Avitus' logic runs as follows: he was so successful in hiding his own controversialist activities that he lulled Gundobad into thinking that outside help with the Arian–Catholic controversy was not required.

11 *Quae* is the subject of *defecerant*. The sense of *quasi iam in nostra* is unclear. S reads *quasi iam in nostra regione*, 'as if already in our region'. *Nostra* anticipates the contrast with *extrinsecus*.

Even though I was coming back from the journey you know about,[1] and had no views in the meantime about these proposals, whatever[2] long-owed work and keen-nosed industry were able to provide through deliberating about these complicated, knotty, and dangerous questions, was set in motion.[3] The treatise[4] seethes rather forcefully with lengthy discussions, but is calm all the same, and adds no turbulent commotion in any pride in dominating.[5] But the chance for the required secrecy saw to it that, whatever might be the result of the dispute, neither would it permit the winner to be puffed up with pride, nor the loser to blush.[6] Need I say more? Without boasting I say openly, what was heaped up against their arguments, so far as I can see, would have pleased you, if you had heard it. I am indeed worried about this and < ... > to satisfy the judgement of the hearer rather than to please because of my zeal. When, God willing, I am fortunate enough to see you, I shall lay out the whole discussion myself. In the meantime deduce the course of our conversation from its end, and judge, from what he asked me to do when I left whether he was moved to answer. He ordered me to send him an annotated and ordered list of all the passages from our scriptures[7] that I had cited in response to questions at the time of the debate, and indeed to add any others, if they occurred to me. When he said that it was largely unknown to him, he added simply that, if I would send him a written text, he would be willing to put it before his bishops,[8] rather his seducers, or, to be even more accurate, sectaries.[9] From this Your Piety[10] can guess that to someone determined to contradict, but a wise arbiter,[11] these matters did not seem invalid or lacking in force. Even though he does not wish his obstinate[12] [bishops] to be corrected in these matters, he longs for them to be

1 More cryptic allusion.

2 Omitting *vel* with S.

3 Avitus here refers to a theological work of his own. *Longa satisfactio* and *sagax industria* are terms too positive to apply to the work of his Arian opponents.

4 Avitus' treatise: possibly the *Contra Arrianos*, or perhaps even the *Dialogus* mentioned by Agobard.

5 Translating *supercilio dominandi*.

6 I.e. the debate was private, so no one lost face.

7 For an allusion to such a list, see *CE* 1, p. 15.13.

8 Translating *sacerdotes*, although Avitus also uses the word to mean 'priests'.

9 Avitus is punning on the similarity between *sacerdotibus* (priests, bishops), *seductoribus* (seducers), and *sectatoribus* (sectaries).

10 Sigismund was presumably already a Catholic.

11 Cf. *CA* 9, p. 5.15.

12 For this use of *intentio*, see Goelzer, p. 590.

kept hard at work on them.[1] Even though I know how frequently people at
the command of God do not give in to those in power, nor for the sake of
truth give in to kings, I was for a long time in two minds about whether to
obey. I knew, and was afraid in my affection for him that I would not be
doing him a favour through this action so much as providing arms to the
enemy,[2] and that I should be under attack no less from fellow-citizens than
from the enemy who disagreed with me, while private hatreds surround
enemy forces in a public siege. Use the power of your high position granted
by God, your religion, and your authority to expel the discord that is firmly
entrenched behind walls and disperse the 'more than civil wars' that rage in
your camp as if 'through the Emathian fields'.[3] Although they have long
been doubled, the complaints of those who are calling out are no closer to
penetrating the deafness of those who listen. It is therefore only right, if you
so deign, that Your Severity too should take thought about those there who
ought to be punished, or feel the pain of those here who are blushing.

Epistula 31: Introduction

Sigismund has established some sort of annual forum, perhaps on the feast of St
Peter, for debate between Arians and Catholics. The Arians seem to have gained
some ground at Geneva. An Arian bishop has been ordained who adheres to the
heresy of Bonosus,[4] and Avitus wants to know whether Gundobad has forgotten
the event or whether he is still suffering from the pain he brought upon the
Catholics by appointing the man in the first place. He evinces delight that the
rival party have been infected by yet another schism.

   Although Peiper dated this letter to 514/6, it is unclear why he should have done
so, other than that Avitus refers to Sigismund's princely office (*principatus*). Since,
however, Sigismund appears to have had some royal authority at the time of his
conversion, which must have predated the death of Pope Symmachus in 514,[5] and

---

1 Bishops should be kept on their toes and thinking, even if their views are not to be
emended! The verb used is *fatigari* which could equally well mean 'worried', 'harassed' or
'importuned'.

2 For this notion, see also *Ep*. 28, *Instruxistis adversarios armis vestris*.

3 Both quotations are from Lucan, *Pharsalia* 1.1.

4 For a Western view of the Bonosiacs, see Gennadius, *Liber sive definitio ecclesiasticorum
dogmatum*, 21, *JTS* 7, p. 94. For Bonosiac bishops in the Merovingian kingdom, Orléans (538),
can. 34, ed. J. Gaudemet and B. Basdevant. See also the introduction to the *Contra Arianos*,
above p. 166.

5 *Epp*. 8 and 29. It should be noted that Fredegar 3.33 supplies no date for Sigismund's
elevation at Carouge, other than to say that it happened in Gundobad's lifetime.

may well have been over a decade earlier,[1] there is no reason to place the letter so late. Indeed the references to the prince's *victoria* would seem to imply a date much closer to the date of his conversion. The letter might, therefore, be dated any time after 501/2.

Avitus the bishop to his master, Sigismund {62.7}

At every time of my life I acknowledge that I am in your debt for < ... >[2] of offering – but especially so on the occasion of the present festivity, which involves you no less in investigating the enterprises of the heretics than in celebrating the rituals of our church. If indeed, by means of a sort of annual contagion[3] at which our opponents are assembled, you have to see to it assiduously that what your victory[4] has already cut down in a glorious show of strength in the name of the Lord does not spring up and flourish through someone else's cunning and deception – however much – Christ willing! – he may keep his distance in your presence. Hence that earlier cause of worry, the assembly at Geneva which, after the fashion of our first ancestors, sounded[5] poison serpent-like into manly souls with a hiss of female speech.[6] Therefore, if I am worthy, I wish to learn as soon as possible whether Your Clemency's royal father has forgotten[7] the ordination that loosed the plague of the Bonosiacs,[8] sent from the confines of hell, upon the Catholics and Arians as they struggled – or if[9] the grief associated

1 *Ep.* 29: the date could be as early as 501/2, if the word *libertas* is taken to be an allusion to the pope taking sanctuary in St Peter's in 501/2. See above in the commentary to *Ep.* 29.

2 Something is wrong with the text. L reads *offerendi factum*, but is clearly missing a noun. Peiper's attempted emendation, *offerendi officii factum*, does not make sense. S reads *asserendi famulatus* which might mean 'claiming my role as your servant'. We obelise *offerendi factum*.

3 Avitus puns on the meaning of *contagium*, both 'contact' and 'contagion'.

4 Presumably Sigismund's conversion.

5 Peiper reads *insonuit*. This should probably be emended to *insinuavit*, 'communicated'. See Goelzer, p. 614, also a similar sequence at p. 22.23, *sic insusurratum fuerat principi, et ipse insinuat sacerdoti*.

6 Avitus alludes to Eve's seduction of Adam at the instigation of the serpent. For *virus*, see *SHG* 2.232, *dulce subit virus*. The precise scene appears at *SHG* 2.252–60.

7 Taking Rilliet's emendation: *exciderit* for *acciderit*. The contrast with *servatur* below requires a verb meaning 'to forget'.

8 Adoptionist heretics, named after Bonosus of Serdica. See Isidore, *Orig.* 8.5.52 and also Avitus, *CE* 2, p. 26.27, *quantum Eutychiani Bonosiacis baratro profundiore mergantur*.

9 At this point Avitus switches from an alternative indirect question *utrum ... exciderit* (after which one would expect *an*) to an indirect question introduced by *si* with the indicative — but the effect is the same. He would like to know whether Gundobad has forgotten, or whether the pain is still in his memory.

with that believing or pretending [to believe] is still preserved [in him], a grief that,[1] not impressed on souls, but written on parchment,[2] †a written promise gradually summons back to [his] former belief in his dogma.†　Indeed, if it is still mixed up, as it started, in the communion of association with the Arians, our triumph will shine the more brightly under your rule, when, once the two heresies have been reduced to one, and we are no less taking over the enemy than convincing them, the number both of schismatics and of schisms decreases. Therefore, please look with favour upon my service and my curiosity, and hurry to me, expectant as I am, from the feast of your special patron the apostle[3] and double the gifts of Your Authority.

---

1 *Dolor* must be the antecedent of the *quem*. Consequently it is very difficult to do anything with the end of this sentence from *paulatim ... promissio*. One would expect a *person* as the object for *paulatim in antiquam sui dogmatis credulitatem revocat litterata promissio*, not *dolor*. There seems to be something wrong with the text.

2 For a similar conceit, see Ruricius, *Ep.* 2.26.7.

3 Probably St Peter: see *Ep.* 29.

9. SECULAR–TEMPORAL MATTERS

Contents

Epistula 45: Introduction

Avitus was summoned back from a festival to see the king. By the time he got back Sigismund had left for war – though for which war is by no means clear. This letter exhibits an ingratiating tone similar to that of *Epp*. 32, 76, 77, 79, 91 and 92. Yet behind Avitus' desire to fawn on Sigismund lies, not routine flattery, but a recent *contretemps*. Avitus was summoned back abruptly. There have been troubles that involved Avitus missing Sigismund through his own fault (p. 74.15 'the malicious agency of sin', *peccato fraudante*) and Sigismund protecting Avitus 'for the sake of protecting his servant in such circumstances' (p. 74.22 *pro tuendo inter talia famulo suo*). There was some question of Avitus losing Sigismund's good regard (p. 74. 24, 'the thought of me will adhere more tenaciously to your senses', *respectum mei sensibus vestris tenacius adhaesurum*), or indeed of his being rejected altogether ('to reject a servant whom you have taken into your care', *quem suscepistis servum reicere*). Sigismund's Catholicism is presented as the factor that will keep him well disposed to his bishop. Some major enterprise is afoot (p. 74.26 *sub cuius occasionis sacro proventu*), which may or or may not be identical with the Sigismund's current campaign. Unfortunately Avitus' language is allusive and opaque, and no more precise interpretation is possible.

Burckhardt, pp. 84–85, ties this letter together with *Epp.* 91 and 92, because in all three Sigismund is away on campaign. Von den Steinen thinks that, because of its enthusiastic tone, this letter must have been written shortly after Sigismund's conversion.[1] This is possible, and can be supported by the text itself (see below p. 235 n. 2). As a result it probably places the letter considerably earlier than 507, and detaches *Ep.* 45 from *Epp.* 91–92. There may, of course, have been regular raids against such neighbours as the Alamans.[2]

Avitus to his master, King Sigismund {74.9}

I returned with the greatest speed from the [religious] festival to which I had gone, to be sure, but you had already set forth under Christ's guidance. Even though I will be cheered, I hope, by your return, I am still very surprised by your departure – namely because, in the return of prosperity that ensued, I did not have a chance to fall down at the knees of my lord (i.e. Sigismund), press his hands with kisses and to adore the seat of our faith in his sacred breast. Nor would I dare to say that this privilege had eluded me through the malicious agency of sin, lest I be rendered ungrateful to the divine grace that has thus offered me yours. For although it is both normal and right for all men to aspire to what is appropriate for the cult of Your Glory, I am especially pleased that I received this [favour] – namely that, †in accordance with the effect of the wills that keep with them,†[3] it is not impossible for the debt of service to be laid out before you,[4] if piety decrees that it [ought] to be paid.

For as often as I am not with my consoler,[5] as often as the kindled heat of tribulations is pent up in me alone and shut out[6] from the cooling refreshment of your conversation,[7] as often as the experienced hand of that doctor[8] fails to soothe my internal pains, I alone am struck by the loss.[9] He,

1 W. Von den Steinen, 'Chlodwigs Übergang zum Christentum: Eine Quellenkritische Studie', *MIÖG* Ergänzungsband 12 (1933), p. 481, n. 2.

2 For an indication of frontier problems, see *Liber Constitutionum, const. extr.* 21.5.

3 *Pro effectu voluntatum tenente secum.* The phrase is almost certainly corrupt. *Tenente* requires an object, but none is present. *Servitii debitum* is clearly the subject of *porrigi*.

4 Peiper has mispunctuated: the comma should go not after *porrigi*, but after *vos*.

5 Taking *consolationi* as abstract for concrete. Avitus means Sigismund.

6 Avitus makes a word-play on *exclusus* ('excluded') and *includitur* ('penned up').

7 Avitus balances heat (*accensus aestus*) and cool refreshment (*refrigerio*).

8 I.e. Sigismund.

9 The phrase *ego solus damno percellor* is repeated in *Ep.* 50.

for the sake of protecting his servant in such circumstances, eager in his piety steadfast in virtue, even though it would be enough if he were willing to offer a patron, deigns to add work.[1] But I assume that, as a favour from God, from this point on, the thought of me will adhere more tenaciously to your senses, since the love of Catholic law has poured it into you.[2] Upon the holy outcome of this matter, it will be no more possible for you to reject a servant whom you have taken into your care than to fail to love the Lord whom you have come to know. It remains to say that, once you have departed happy, go safely and return a victor! Put your faith in your weapons, give warning by promising divine oversight.[3] Pray for help from heaven, arm your missiles with prayers. The Lord will grant that I may magnify[4] the trophies of war that he himself will grant you by making a speech on the occasion of that more precious triumph that I have long expected.

Epistula 76: Introduction

This letter, because of the absence of the word 'king' in the salutation, is dated to before Sigismund's elevation to the kingship, although whether it can be placed before the prince's initial elevation at Carouge, apparently shortly after 500, is uncertain.[5] Sigismund clearly decided to spend Easter at Chalon, and Avitus is writing to express his pique. The prince's absence has caused a prolongation of Lent at Vienne, he says. But the religious feast will really take place when Sigismund arrives, because to have seen their prince is solemnity enough for good Catholics.

This letter seems to show variation in the date of Arian and Catholic Easter of the sort attested in Greg. Tur. *DLH* 5.17.[6] When it was written, Catholic Easter, celebrated by Avitus at Vienne, must have fallen later than the Arian one, celebrated by Sigismund at Chalon. Avitus contrives a 'fastal' letter jokingly to point out the contrast. For more on this conceit, see Shanzer, 'Bishops, Letters'.

1 The meaning of *apponere laborem*, perhaps 'set work before [me]', is unclear.

2 This would seem to suggest that Sigismund has not long been converted.

3 Taking *provisionem* S; *promissionem* looks like an *Antizipazionsfehler*.

4 The verb used is *exaggero*, both 'to exaggerate' and to 'heap up'. Avitus is making a word-play suitable for the royal panegyric he is anticipating.

5 According to Fredegar 3.33 Sigismund was elevated to the kingship before Gundobad's death: this first elevation, which must be distinguished from that in 516 mentioned by Marius, seems to have followed shortly after the failure of Godegisel's rebellion, and should probably be seen as elevation to subkingship with a palace in Geneva: see above, p. 21. A number of references to Sigismund as king belong to this early period: thus the heading of *Ep.* 29, which must be earlier than mid-514, already gives him the title *rex*.

6 See also below p. 236 n. 3.

Avitus the bishop to his master, Sigismund {92.6 Peiper}

While others are feasting on the sacred and serene delights of your presence,[1] I sustain the sterility of my longing more with the slender means of my poor office than with any reasonable excuse. This is why after the feast, a pleasant occasion invariably for all concerned, I am sure, but a special one for the citizens of Chalon,[2] I have sent a letter to express my dutiful worry. If it (= the letter) were to try to touch on even the smallest part of your praises, it would not do justice even to this fact, namely that my humilty is allowed to offer it to you, and your dignity kind enough to accept it. And while I imagine the happiness of so many people (i.e. the inhabitants of Chalon), I frequently ask that, God willing, you may make our Easter a happy one by your return. For, although in your absence some Lenten austerity persists, it is religious occasion enough for all Catholics to have seen their Catholic prince, and for the least of his servants his kind master, even though it be after the date of the [actual] solemnity.

Epistula 77: Introduction

A companion-piece to *Ep.* 76. Avitus trots out more conceits about Sigismund's Easter *in absentia*. The letter is important, however, because it gives clear evidence of Avitus' remarkably candid private religious dealings with Sigismund. Sigismund, it is implied, must have celebrated Easter with Gundobad according to the Arian rite.[3] Avitus even encourages him to go along with his father's Arianism politely until the right moment comes, a point of some significance when looking at some of the more obfuscatory remarks in other letters of Avitus dealing with the prince's Catholicism. The tone of this letter contrasts starkly with the flattery of later letters such as *Ep.* 91.

Avitus the bishop to his master, Sigismund {92.17 Peiper}

We, your poor little people of Vienne, have celebrated the feast of Easter with you, since God was willing: 'with you', I emphasise, *not* in place, but in the spirit. If you were to ask what it was like, I would say that it was difficult to do, since we were not together, but that it went well, because we were [at

---

1 For the king's banquets see also *Ep.* 86.

2 The feast appears, from what follows, to have been Easter.

3 There may also have been a question of celebrating on different days: cf. Greg. Tur. *DLH* 5.17, 6.43, and 10.23: *GM* 23 on the springs of Osset and the calculation of Easter. The phrase *divinitate propitia*, however, would seem to indicate that on this occasion the two groups celebrated Easter on the same day.

least] near each other. Nonetheless, because it would have been easy for you to be present, it was the more annoying that you were absent. But you must not think that I am in disagreement with your decision, when I regret these circumstances. It is my affection, O holy one, I believe, that has long held me back from that (= disagreement), not haughty disdain that prevents it. You love your one church[1] equally in both cities, but you cling to your devout father,[2] to the extent that it is expedient, until such a time as he agrees that you may follow whatever church you like. Therefore, as we have been ordered to do, we first discharge our debt to God regarding this feast, and then to Caesar.[3] To us who are concerned about your happiness and safety, Caesar though you be,[4] give back what[5] we demand from our masters, because we are pious.

Epistula 79: Introduction

Avitus sends greetings for the feast of Saint Vincent to Sigismund. He grumbles that Sigismund did not visit him in Vienne on the way from Sapaudia to Provence.

The reference to Provence at the end of the letter is interesting: before 507 the southern frontier of the Burgundian kingdom lay in the region of the valley of the Durance. As a result of Alaric's defeat by Clovis the Burgundians may have gained land further south: Isidore talks of Gundobad campaigning at Narbonne.[6] Any gains in this region, however, were probably lost in Theodoric the Great's counter-attack.[7] This, however, leaves a considerable problem in identifying what Avitus meant by *provincia*: that it lay in the direction of Provence is clear from the fact that he felt that anyone travelling there from Sapaudia ought to pass through Vienne. There is one further indication that the Burgundians may have had land in Provence, since Gregory of Tours (*DLH* 2.32) says, not necessarily correctly, that they controlled the lands of the Rhône, the Saône and Marseilles. It is possible, therefore,

---

1 I.e. the Catholic church.

2 Note that Avitus calls Gundobad *pius* even though he is an Arian and even though he is discussing Sigismund's Catholicism. On the complexity of Avitus' response to Gundobad's Arianism see especially *Hom.* 24. Compare also Ennodius 437 on Theodoric.

3 Mt. 22.21. For another occasion when Avitus uses the same passage from Matthew, see *Ep.* 53, p. 82.11–13. Caesar here is Gundobad, or possibly Gundobad and Sigismund.

4 Avitus uses the *pluralis maiestatis* here, but the second time round 'Caesar' refers to Sigismund alone. He makes a feeble joke about what Caesar should render unto him. The implication of the term 'Caesar' is that Sigismund has some sort of royal status.

5 I.e. the kings' presence.

6 *Historia Gothorum, Wandalorum, Sueborum* 36–37.

7 *Vita Caesarii* 1.38; L. Schmidt, *Geschichte der Deutschen Stämme bis zum Ausgang der Völkerwanderung: Die Ostgermanen* (Munich, 1934), vol. I, pp. 156–58.

that the Burgundians held a stake in Marseilles, and that that was the object of
Sigismund's journey. The alternative might be to treat the reference as being
chronologically significant, and to date the letter to 508, when the Burgundians may
have had Provençal landholdings, although this might be ruled out by the fact that the
journey took place at the time of the feast of St Vincent, probably 22 January.

Avitus the bishop to Sigismund {93.19 Peiper}

Since I was delayed for two days in the presence of my master, the father of
Your Glory,[1] it was only rather belatedly that I, with my customary concern,
arranged for a messenger to convey my annual respects to you for the feast
of Saint Vincent.[2] I wished that, in the midst of the activity by which your
labour is watchful for our safety, my spirit, always in your debt, might offer
a cult of pure devotion. It suffices to console my longing that the health of all
of us consists (after God) in your welfare. For the rest, it cannot be accepted
without scruple, that, in your carefully chosen stages, we seem to have been
passed by, when you travelled from Sapaudia[3] to Provence.

Epistula 91: Introduction

Even by Avitus' standards the fawning language of this letter is exceptional. That this
is no mere stylistic exercise may be implied by the bishop's concern over the
prince's profession of faith. It seems that Sigismund has only recently converted, and

1 Gundobad.

2 The cult of St Vincent seems to have been particularly significant in Chalon-sur-Saône,
thus raising once again the issue of Sigismund's association with that city. Whether the Vincent
celebrated in Chalon is the same as Vincent of Saragossa is an insoluble problem. The date of
the feast would seem, however, to be that for the Spanish martyr, i.e. 22 January, which might
seem an odd season for Sigismund to be travelling. On the cult of Vincent in the region see E.
Ewig, 'Die Kathedralpatrozinien im römischen und im fränkischen Gallien', in *idem*, ed.,
Spätantikes und fränkisches Gallien (Munich, 1979), vol. 2, p. 306. See also Favrod, *Histoire
politique*, pp. 166–67. On the interest of the Burgundian royal family in the cult one might note
that the church of St Victor built by princess Sedeleuba in Geneva (Fredegar, 3.18; 4.22), was
later known as the church of SS Vincent, Ursus and Victor (L. Blondel, 'Le Prieuré Saint-Victor,
les débuts du christianisme et la royauté burgonde à Genève', *Bulletin de la société d'histoire et
d'archéologie de Genève* 11 (1958), pp. 211–58), though the Vincent in question is more likely
to be Vincent of Lérins.

3 Sapaudia is not to be confused with modern Savoy, lying rather between Geneva and
Neufchatel; cf. P. Duparc, 'La Sapaudia', *Comptes rendus de l'Academie des Inscriptions et
Belles Lettres* (1958), pp. 371–83. For a more recent discussion, Favrod, *Histoire politique*, pp.
100–17. It was the region originally conferred on the Burgundians in the 440s, *Chronicle of 452*
128.

that the security of the Catholics depends, as a result, on his survival. Not surprisingly the Catholics are concerned for his safe return.

The military context of the letter can only be a matter of conjecture. If the expedition undertaken (*suscepta expeditio*) is an aggressive campaign, it is most likely to be the joint Franco-Burgundian campaign against the Visigoths in 508,[1] although there may have been other unrecorded campaigns, for instance against the Alamans. If Sigismund's *expeditio* is defensive it could have taken place in the context of either Clovis' campaign of 500 or Theodoric's counter-attack, following the aggession of 508.[2] Of these possibilities the campaign of 508 may be the most likely, although if the tone of the letter does indicate that Sigismund had only recently been converted, an earlier date might make more sense.

Avitus the bishop to his master, Sigismund {99.1 Peiper}

I know that it is impertinent to suggest that you should write me at a time when you are preoccupied with the cares and concerns over which, with heaven's help, you faithfully keep watch for the safety of our fatherland. But since the Lofty Condescension of Your Piety[3] has been so far from forgetting your special servant that in the very midst of the expedition you have undertaken, you[4] doubled my senses' longing for you through your sweet address, who would not understand that you patiently put up with the very ineptitude that you elicit through your kindness?[5] Therefore in my concern I take it upon myself to inquire whether, with God to strengthen you, you are well, and how the hope of our shared desire smiles upon your undertakings. I do not merely ask this, but pray by the grace that you have received from God and granted to me, that, even though we are rightly secure about the strength of the faith you have declared,[6] we may be the more so when you grant us the gift of being cautious.[7] Please have a thought for our fearfulness and cowardice, and do not think it more important that we all devoutly pray for you than that we are on tenterhooks and fear for you. But even though we are fearful sinners in our own consciences, we assume in our unwavering

---

1 *Chronicle of 511* nn. 689–90: Isidore, *Historia Gothorum, Wandalorum, Sueborum* 36–37.

2 Moorhead, *Theodoric in Italy*, pp. 180–83.

3 All of this is a cumbersome honorific.

4 Avitus used the third person to match the honorific.

5 I.e. you will not be angry that I am writing you, because you addressed me first.

6 This reference to Sigismund's faith seems a little more positive than that in *Ep.* 45, and may suggest that it belongs to the period of a later campaign.

7 I.e. you take care of yourself. The implication is, presumably, that the security of Catholicism in the kingdom depended on Sigismund's patronage, and therefore on his survival.

faith that, since you have Christ to protect you, even though this fear of ours may bring a smile to your lips, at least it will move the ears of God to grant us the joy of a happy outcome[1] for you.

Epistula 92: **Introduction**

This letter presumably refers to the same conflict mentioned in *Ep*. 91, perhaps the campaign against the Visigoths in 508. The religious anxiety expressed in the two letters has also been seen as comparable.[2]

Avitus the bishop to his master, Sigismund {99.15 Peiper}

Whoever worries about your prosperity appears not to trust in what God has promised.[3] But if you consider my feelings with your customary courtesy, you will have no trouble understanding that you ought to forgive my cowardice for its excessive fear. For[4] all who honestly take upon themselves the name of 'Catholic' ought now to entreat God with nightlong prayers, that he faithfully join what is near[5] and with a happy outcome overthrow what is hostile[6] on your behalf, when you convey our prayers to him, untouched and whole, and that thus, in a complicated and difficult situation, with Christ to fight before you, you may gain both the peace you desire and the victory you are owed. Therefore if even this time of great anxiety has not diminished the favour with which you think of me in your spirit, as your special servant, even though I did not dare to send a greeting, but had intended to wait for [news of] your safety from God, it was with a very anxious and alert soul that I sent you this respectful page, worried first about your welfare and then about that of the army. Therefore, even though – thanks be to God! – I may hear the good news from some people who were travelling through, all the

---

1 *Felicitas vestra* could also be construed as an honorific, 'the joy of Your Happiness'.

2 See Van de Vyver, 'La Victoire contre les Alamans' (1936), p. 908, n.1.

3 This could allude to concerns about Sigismund's faith, not just about his personal safety, though the concern does not seem to be comparable to that in *Ep*. 45.

4 Peiper punctuates this as a new sentence, although it is in fact part of the previous one: *deberi, quippe* ... would be better.

5 Neighbouring territory or, more likely, neighbouring people as allies, in which case the reference might well be to the Franks under Clovis, who, even if he was not yet baptised, had certainly made clear his Catholic allegiance in 507. Such a reading might also be supported by the adverb *fideliter*, which could be seen as having a doctrinal implication.

6 Presumably the Visigoths or Ostrogoths.

same you may guess, most pious master,[1] how much sweeter it will be for me if, just as when certain people tell me about it, the knowledge of your kind feelings feeds me, likewise a written answer brings me joy. In your letter, as a substitute for your presence, I may be worthy to possess your words instead of seeing you face to face, and to kiss the signature instead of your hand.

Epistula 32: Introduction

One of Avitus' more flowery, saccharine and supine friendship letters. Addressed to his master, Sigismund, it has no clear content or purpose other than to convey the bishop's respect: overblown and coy rhetoric curries Sigismund's favour and promotes the appropriate hierarchical relations between bishop and prince. It is clearly a follow-up to a letter sent (late) by Avitus to Sigismund for the Feast of St Peter. Sigismund subsequently sent a message to tell Avitus that he had been dilatory in writing, and would keep the messenger who had carried his letter with him a bit longer. Avitus affects misunderstanding. It would be heaven to have been detained at Sigismund's side, and that, if he knew this would be his punishment, he would more frequently delay in answering.

Avitus the bishop to his master, Sigismund {62.25 Peiper}

Recently, I sent the respects that I always owe Your Highness[2] on the occasion of the feast of the Apostle.[3] In a communication (*sermo*) that was no less precious for its politeness than notable for its rhetoric, you told me that you had responded a trifle late for the following reason: namely in order that self-aware humility[4] that rightly seeks to avoid [the appearance of] arrogance in writing would suffer[5] the torture of dryness longer, the more it[6] thirsted for the splendid refreshment[7] of a chance to speak with you.[8] As you deign to reply, it would be a sort of revenge[9] that the letter-carrier, sent by me

1 The honorific is in the plural to match the plural verbs of polite address.
2 *Culmen vestrum.*
3 St Peter.
4 Avitus'.
5 Lit. 'pay'.
6 Taking S's *sitiret*. For the syntax with an honorific compare *Ep.* 91, p. 99.5 *duplicaret*.
7 Lit. 'fountain'. Avitus may be alluding to Ps. 41.
8 Presumably this sentence gives Sigismund's reading of the situation. Avitus was being over-proud in not 'presuming' to write to Sigismund.
9 For a similar playful 'revenge' topos see *Ep.* 72. There are also parallel revenge-topoi in Sid. Ap. *Ep.* 4.2.4. If Sidonius does not write, Claudianus *will*.

a bit late, would tarry a bit longer with you. O sweet punishment! O sentence of longed-for cruelty! Who would <not>[1] tolerate such a punishment calmly? – that locked up the paradise[2] of your presence, he see you on account of a blessed delay. I am quite afraid lest you order me to write frequently, if you are disposed to take revenge in this way upon my delaying. Or if I were certain that I would receive this sort of punishment, I would offer writings that I had written *less frequently* than I ought. Would that I were with you, and were being denied a swift return! The sort of words that I was long allowed to read, I would [then] be permitted to *hear* from their very source for a longer time period.[3] God will certainly see what I deserve in your eyes, both for my boldness in serving you and my fearfulness: all the same I shall be guilty in the eyes of my letter-carriers, if I cheat them of a long stay with you by correcting the crime of which you accuse me.

---

1 The rhetoric of the passage clearly requires a *non* here.

2 Avitus seems to be making a jocular allusion to the expected (and opposite) expression *paradiso exclusus*. For similar word-play on *includo* and *excludo* see *Ep.* 45, p.74.21 and *Ep.* 86, p. 95.25–26.

3 I.e. Sigismund's lips.

CLOSE EPISCOPAL CONNECTIONS

10. APOLLINARIS, BISHOP OF VALENCE, HIS BROTHER

Contents

Epistula 13: Introduction

Apollinaris of Valence writes in contrition to his brother Avitus. He had forgotten to commemorate the death of their sister and experienced a visitation in a dream. A red dove plucked at his hand, and he then remembered what he should have done. The identification of the ghostly visitor as Avitus' and Apollinaris' sister appears in *Ep*. 14, p. 47.12, *necessitudinum praeteritarum* and, especially, p. 47.15 *germanae communis*. This letter is a dreamer's account of an authentic dream, not a standard symbolic literary product.

The dove often represents chastity, simplicity (Mt. 10.16), and innocence. Only in Jeremiah (25.38, 46.16 and 50.16) is it a symbol of vengeance and anger. Since the Holy Spirit appeared in the Gospels as a dove (Mk 1.10; Mt. 3.16), it could represent the soul of a martyr, as in Prudentius, *Per*. 3.161, and here the soul of a dead virgin. The young Virgin Mary in the Temple is described as a dove in the *Protevangelium Jacobi* 8.1 and the the *Barcelona Hymn* 26. More importantly the dove was a common motif on funerary monuments throughout the Later Roman Empire.[1] Doves could also represent men, Greg. Tur. *DLH* 3 15, where they represent Attalus and Leo.

Although Fuscina is not mentioned by name in this letter, it is possible that she is the sister who is the subject of *Epp*. 13 and 14. An argument in favour of this would be the evocation of the colour of blood, which would seem appropriate for a martyr, as Fuscina was later seen to be in a saint's life which recounts (7) an attempt to abduct her from the monastery of SS Gervasius and Protasius.[2] Although Avitus and Apollinaris had one other sister, she is largely ignored in Avitus' works.[3] If this is correct, then letters 13–14 cannot be earlier than 506–07, when Fuscina was still alive, according to the preface to the *CCL*. Concern to commorate her death-day clearly relates to standard commemoration of the dead in Late Antiquity,[4] but this letter also seems to indicate that she had become something of a family saint.

Communication between the living and the dead, whether in visions or in dreams, was a subject of theological concern in Late Antiquity. Augustine discussed whether and how the dead appeared to ask for burial as well as how they found out about the actions of the living.[5] Interestingly this is not the only 'ghost story' involving negligence by the living to appear in letters of this period. Ennodius (161 to Adeodatus and 162 to Beatus) had a vision of his relative Cynegia, harshly reprimanding him for not composing a verse epitaph for her tomb, an omission he remedied instantly. One might further compare Sidonius' anger at the desecration of his grandfather's grave (*Ep*. 3.12).[6]

---

1 See *DACL* 3.2.222–2225, esp. 2222 for Gaul.

2 Ed. *Catalogus codicum hagiographicorum latinorum in Bibliotheca Nationali Parisiensi* 3 (Brussels, 1893), pp. 563–65.

3 Fuscina's sister has been identified alternatively with the Aspidia of *CCL* 87 by Mathisen, '*PLRE* II: Some Suggested Addenda and Corrigenda', p. 376, and with the ?Eusebia of *CCL* 95 by M. Heinzelmann, 'Gallische Prosopographie (260–527)', *Francia* 10 (1982), p. 602: [? Eusebia] 1. But the *quondam* of *CCL* 87 implies that Aspidia was of an earlier generation, and there is no evidence that any of the women of *CCL* 92–96 was a sister of Fuscina. Indeed the Latin of *CCL* 99, *matres*, clearly implies that all three women belonged to an earlier generation. Besides, since the family continued beyond Avitus' generation, and not through direct descendents of Avitus, Apollinaris or Fuscina, it would seem that Fuscina's sister was not a virgin. As a married woman she would not have been an appropriate individual for the *CCL*. That she was not a virgin may explain Avitus' silence.

4 Tertullian (*De exhortatione castitatis* 51 and *De Monogamia* 10) speaks of the *oblationes annuas* that are due a wife.

5 *De Cura pro mortuis* 10 and 15.

6 See also Wood, 'Family and Friendship in the West', p. 423.

Bishop Apollinaris [of Valence] to Bishop Avitus {46.11 Peiper}

My belated repentance has already caused me much pain. All the same, because I failed to show devotion and did not deserve to participate even by proxy, in that feast day fit to be cultivated by angels along with us, I have at least tried to make good my omission. As I confide in you, most reverend master, I was warned to do this by a visitation from the blessed spirit herself. For on the very hallowed evening in question in a vision something stuck to my hands, and, as it sat next to me, a dove that gleamed brightly, but with an unusual red colour, was plucking[1] at it. After awakening, when I recognised the customary cleanness[2] of my hands, but remembered nonetheless that I was undeservedly being absolved, while I turned this curious event sadly and nervously over in my mind, all of a sudden, as if pricked by a goad, I remembered the debt I owed. Your Pious Holiness no doubt can judge what confusion and bitterness overwhelmed me at that point. To some extent, however, I was consoled by the hope that she would forgive what she saw fit to remind me of, so that some chance of serving a saint might be left my unhappy self. My supplication, added to the offices owed her commemorative day, has only one request to make – that she may breathe this part too of her forgiveness into your feelings when you call me to account, which is more than fair to me.[3]

Epistula 14: Introduction

Avitus responds to *Ep.* 13 of Apollinaris. The letter provides an unusual example of the custom of dream-interpretation. Avitus does not take the dove to represent Fuscina's spirit, but Apollinaris' own piety. At the end of the letter Avitus somewhat mysteriously alludes to the lighting of Apollinaris' offering (*oblatio*) *de*

---

1 *Vellere*, 'to tweak, pluck', sometimes denotes actions intended to get someone's attention or remind him of something. See Verg. *Buc.* 6.4, Hor. *S.* 1.9.63.

2 *TLL s.v.* 'horror' 2998.21 lists this as an example of *horror = species squalida vel inculta*. It would be odd, however, for Apollinaris to acknowledge the 'daily dirtiness' of his hands. *Horror* could also mean 'bristliness', 'hairiness'. But there are still difficulties. The dove was plucking or tweaking at whatever was stuck to Apollinaris' hands, but when he awoke, he found that they were as before, i.e. in their day-to-day state. Since this state was presumably one in which nothing was stuck to them, it seems likely that *horrorem* is corrupt, and should be *honorem*. See *TLL*, s.v. 'honor' 2930.16 with the idea of beauty or attractiveness and 2930.49ff. with the idea of brightness. *Honor* in this case would refer to the customary cleanliness and attractiveness of Apollinaris' hands.

3 *Plus iam iusta*, 'already more fair', makes little sense: emend to *plus quam iusta*, 'more than just'.

abundantia superioris anni (because it was so generous last year). He seems to be alluding to a votive candle or lamp used to commemorate the dead. This votive candle should only have lasted for one year's observances; therefore it is a miracle, showing Apollinaris' own holiness, that his votive candle lasted for the second year, thus exonerating him, when he thought he had forgotten his sister's death-day. i.e. there was no sin, because the candle showed he had made enough offerings in times past to compensate. Candles seem to have been used on tombs to commemorate the dead from pagan times.[1] Although their use on tombs was prohibited by the Council of Elvira (c. 34, *cereos per diem placuit in coemeterio non incendi*), they continued to be a common feature of martyr's shrines.[2] It would appear that the tomb of Fuscina was near that of Avitus in Vienne.

Bishop Avitus to Bishop Apollinaris [of Valence] {47.1 Peiper}

Since your very error is so holy, it is clear how much of the grace of God is in you,[3] and the sum of your virtues can be divined. For while a just man accusing himself tries to condemn himself, because he is incapable of sinning, the humility of him who confesses grows in proportion to his merit – not the truth of the confession in proportion to the guilt. I admit that you have gone beyond what is customary – but in devotion. You have always sent a sweet expression of sympathy to me[4] concerning that day which you deign to remember, but not surprisingly forgetfulness supervened. For beyond a doubt, since the commemoration was not carried out, the effect [of the negligence] is apparent.

But you have shown with what high-mindedness it pleases you to observe the day, because it caused you such pain to have forgotten it. Indeed a sacred revelation followed your honourable crime, and the punishment found in the sleeper was the same as the sin of the waking man. Lo! 'I speak the truth in Christ, and lie not.'[5] When I read about the dream you saw, my eyes brimming over with tears, I remembered all our relatives who have

1 Cabrol *s.v.* 'cierges' *DACL* 3.2.1613; J. Marquardt, *Das Privatleben der Römer* (Darmstadt, 1980), vol. I, p. 368, esp. n. 1.

2 Paul. Nol. *C.* 14.100; *De Miraculis S. Stephani* 2.24, *PL* 41.846; Greg. Tur. *GC* 18.

3 Literally 'in Your Merit', taking S's reading *vestro. Vestri*, 'the grace of *you*' is awkward, since *vestri* is usually objective, and creates a jingle with *dei*.

4 L reads *dulcis vobis venit a vobis* (nonsense) and Mommsen emended it to *dulcis vobis venit a nobis*. One suspects that it should be *dulcis nobis venit a vobis*: Apollinaris had always sent a kind expression of consolation, but this year he forgot. Avitus is more likely to be complimenting his brother's behaviour than boasting about his own. The impersonal expression *praevenit oblivio (for oblitus es)* is likewise tactful.

5 1 Tim. 2.7.

been sent on ahead,[1] and thereby understood that I had been warned to pay my respects to them, because of the visitation you received. I will tell you simply what I felt about the revelation.

This is what you say. 'On that very hallowed evening', namely when the burial of our[2] sister used to be celebrated, 'something stuck to my hands, at which, as it sat next to me gleaming with an unusual red colour a dove was plucking'. But when your sense of piety, not having flown away[3] for long, settled down near you in swift recollection, the debt,[4] which you, holiest and dearest of my relatives, sensed, deservedly, I say, in the form of the dove – 'gleaming', because you shone thus in your simplicity, 'an unusual red colour', because although you were innocent, you exceptionally blushed when pricked by your own conscience – you increased, as I said above, the customary interest you owed. Nor was the observance missed, as you thought. For, on the occasion of that very night which, at Christ's instigation, you were not permitted to forget, your gift, plentiful as it was last year, still shone as strongly.[5] Thus from some sort of never-ending fount of divine blessing, what you pay on a given year is sufficient for many. I beg God that some day you may in your kindness make this same payment to me.[6]

Epistula 27: Introduction

Apollinaris has had many visitors from court (*aulici*) living off him,[7] but is still hoping that Avitus will come visit during a forthcoming festival. Avitus replies with

1 Since *necessitudo* is feminine it is impossible to tell whether the dead relatives were men or women. Nonetheless this is the clearest statement outside the *CCL* of the importance of reverence for the family. It is in such developments of traditional Roman reverence for the family that one should see the origins of the early medieval *Adelsheiliger*, usually associated by modern historians with Germanic and not with Gallo-Roman sensitivities. See the discussion in I. N. Wood, 'The Use and Abuse of Latin Hagiography in the Early Medieval West', in E. Chrysos and I. N. Wood, eds, *East and West: Modes of Communication* (Leiden, 1999), pp. 102–04. Avitus' phraseology may be influenced by *Aen.* 2.560 which he quotes in *Ep.* 51 p. 80.6 *animo namque ... subit cari genitoris imago*.

2 *Communis* means 'the sister we share'.

3 Avitus uses imagery to interpret the dream that is in keeping with its substance: the appearance of a dove.

4 There is an anacoluthon in the sentence. *Debitum* which ought to be governed by a verb is left hanging while Avitus executes some exegetical roulades. He instead continues with *ampliastis* several lines down.

5 Referring apparently to some type of votive candle.

6 This would most probably indicate that Avitus is the elder brother; see *Ep.* 88.

7 See the joking *Ep.* 83 for more on the depredations of courtiers given a chance to eat fish.

a barrage of biblical allusions. Clearly one reason why Apollinaris wishes Avitus to visit him is to patch up some difference between his brother and an, unfortunately unnamed, Catholic senator, possibly Heraclius (with whom Avitus is known to have had disagreements).[1]

Avitus the bishop to Apollinaris the bishop [of Valence] {57.25 Peiper}

You command me – and it is your desire – to approach the celebratory rites, both old and new[2] with the zeal of twofold love. But I fear lest the fact that you have held onto the powerful[3] rather [too] long, may hold me[4] back. Pray that an effect may be commensurate with your desire[5] – unless you think that (money) better[6] spent, which is warming your spirit, even though the storehouse is still cold. Therefore, even though you say that you have not paid out a great deal, and even though you heave a sigh of relief now that the assembly of courtiers has been disbanded, if I will have any opportunity to make an excursion, you will invite those extra people who come, even if you are unwilling.[7]

God will provide feasts for the multitude: for you those of a banquet, for himself those of the poor. Oil will be heaped up in a cruse and meal in a barrel.[8] As long as there are even five loaves there, let it suffice to have provided two fishes.[9] May you be confident after experiencing these miracles that Christ is hardly likely to fail a gathering of his poor: when you have gathered together many thousands of people, you will bring back many baskets of leftovers.

You be my guarantor for our son, who, as you write, deigns to beg for his

---

1 Cf. *Epp.* 95 and 96. The description of the man as *filius noster* makes it clear that there was a family connection between Avitus, Apollinaris and the Catholic senator, just as *Epp.* 95 and 96 make clear a family connection between Avitus and Heraclius.

2 Perhaps a reference to a cult of Fuscina. See *Epp.* 13–14.

3 See p. 65.16 for *potestatis vestrae* (of Liberius). The word almost becomes a collective at p. 114.38, *potestatem caelestium ministrorum.*

4 This appears to be a *pluralis maiestatis*, unless Avitus is thinking also of his retinue. A more satisfactory reading, however, might be *vos,* since the impediment affects Apollinaris.

5 Peiper's sentence division at this point is unhelpful: a dash would be preferable.

6 Here *magis* probably means 'better' rather than 'more'. Apollinaris has got his charity to keep him warm.

7 Taking *invitus* L.

8 The allusion is to 3 Kgs 18.12–16.

9 Mt. 14.17–20; Mk 6.38–44.

and my[1] mutual reconciliation. If he wishes to behave in a conciliatory fashion, I will be friendly; if he wishes an end to hostilities, I too wish for perpetual concord – provided that, when a man of my rank, whom it is inappropriate to deceive, intends to trust a Catholic senator, he should not become secure merely to be [subsequently] considered lacking in caution.[2]

Epistula 61: Introduction

There has presumably been some falling-out between the brothers. Avitus is waiting for a letter of forgiveness at Christmas. A good example of the difficulties of interpreting allusive communication. Presumably because of Avitus' comment on his sickness, Peiper dated this letter to 517/18.

Avitus the bishop to Apollinaris the bishop {87.22 Peiper}

After the Christmas service at which I participated, sick and indeed over-exhausted as I was, I am awaiting news of you, the thing that is of the most importance to me after God. If I am fortunate enough to receive it, whatever harshness[3] *I* deserve, will be mitigated, as I trust. As *you* deserve, it will be washed away.

Epistula 71: Introduction

Though this could be the reply to *Ep.* 61, it is more likely that it is a brief and facetious letter in which the *ultio*, the *iniuria* and the *noxa* are all in jest, cf. *Ep.* 32, p. 63.2–3 and *Ep.* 72.

Apollinaris the bishop to Avitus the bishop {90.1 Peiper}

As I carefully pondered with what punishment to strike Your Rudeness, nothing seemed more appropriate than to attend to the imputed injury with alacrity. Therefore you, who see the present wrong instantly expiated, need have no fear for the future.

---

1 Presumably the *filius*' and Avitus'.

2 Avitus is prepared to meet the *Catholicus senator* halfway, but wants to make it clear that it is wrong to make light promises to a bishop, and that he does not want to trust the man, be fooled, and then considered credulous.

3 Taking *asperitas* as the implied antecedent of *qua*. *Asperitas* is also mentioned in *Ep.* 58, p. 87.8.

Epistula 72: Introduction

A 'fish letter' like *Ep*. 84.[1] Behind the heavy-handed jokes of this comic variant on the standard festal-letter lies the following situation: Avitus was unable to attend a festival at his brother's house. Apollinaris presumably said in jest that he would send 'troops' to punish Avitus. Instead he sends him some fish, the promised 'Marines'. As at all periods in the ancient world, from Ennius' *Hedyphagetica* and Plautus' slave-feasts to Ausonius' *Mosella*, fish was a luxury item. There is a parallel (of sorts) to this letter in Symmachus' correspondence to Ausonius (*Ep*. 1.14.5), where the senator cattily protests that he never got served the exotic fish that featured in Ausonius' *Mosella*. Avitus repeats this performance later in *Ep*. 86.

Avitus the bishop to Apollinaris the bishop {90.5 Peiper}

A constraint prevented me from going to the festival, but kindness brought it to me.[2] So, you write that you have avenged[3] my lack of respect with reinforcements from the sea.[4] A fine torture this! May it cause no conflict with the desires of the stomach! I would very much wish to be with you – were it not that you punished the absent after this fashion. May the measures you take against a stubborn offender never stop! In fact nothing alarms me more than the prospect that you may order me not to be afraid in the future. Give your indulgence to him who asks. Forgive him to whom you wish to be niggardly. What is more, now that I have experienced your measures at first hand, it is clear that I long for your displeasure rather than your forgiveness. As for the rest, let God grant to your prayers, that in the future you may after a different fashion make me present through your prayers – who this year partook of the duties rather than[5] the delights of the feast – and that, when I have returned, you may with similar severity believe that I was absent.[6] I have sent your way eight assorted trifles[7] from the marshes and two pairs of

---

1 See Shanzer, 'Bishops, Letters'.

2 The Latin features a mannered interlace of *festivitas–necessitas–festivitas–humanitas*.

3 See A. Klotz, '"Ultuisse": zu Alcimus Avitus', *ALL* 15 (1908), pp. 418–19, though Goelzer, p. 275, followed Peiper's reading, because of the parallel with Cassian, *Conl*. 13.5.3.

4 The Latin has a double-entendre. *Copiae* means both 'troops' and 'supplies'.

5 S's *officiis magis quam* seems necessary.

6 A hideously mannered and contorted sentence. Avitus is saying that this year he could not go, but got sent the goodies. Next year he would like to make his brother's prayers come true and go to the feast, but get sent the goodies *anyway* as if he had not been there.

7 *Quisquiliae* (Haupt's clever emendation) means 'flotsam and jetsam', hence also 'trifles'. Peiper follows Ducange in taking the *quisquiliae* to be quails, while citing Apuleius, *Met*. 1.24, where it clearly refers to fish. Apuleius, *Apologia* 34, p. 40.16, likewise describes fish. Goelzer,

soles[1] for you to sink your teeth into. Since I was somewhat touched, I have not altogether done you a bad turn in return for yours!

Epistula 87: Introduction

One of a number of letters written to Avitus' brother, bishop of Valence. The beginning is another one of Avitus' exercises in coded communication. Note how diplomatically he alludes to Ostrogoths who have been said to have been laying waste to the Rhône valley without mentioning their name. The third sentence seems to be preparing Apollinaris for a further communication that Avitus now feels it is safe to send. The rest of the letter is remarkable because it describes a ring Avitus would like Apollinaris to have made for him, and asks for a master potter and information about preparing clay and constructing a kiln.

The letter is likewise unusual in providing one of the few indications of chronology in Avitus' correspondence. The king of the Goths (*rex Getarum*) is Alaric II, and the 'ensuing disaster' (*secutura ruina*) is therefore his defeat by Clovis in battle at Vogliacum in 507.[2] If this is right, the association of disaster with the debasement of the coinage raises the distinct possibility that the cause of the war between Alaric and Clovis was economic.[3] In all probability it should be linked with the payment of tribute owed by Alaric to Clovis since the meeting at Amboise (Greg. Tur. *DLH* 2.35), which may have been paid in debased coinage in 506/07.[4] This fits well with Cassiodorus' comments on the insignificance of the origins of the war.[5] In short, this letter is possibly of considerable importance for the understanding of the economic origins of an early medieval war.

Avitus' description of his desired signet ring is abstruse, elaborate and pretentious leaving room for surprise perhaps that any craftsman was able to execute it from these instructions. Ekphrases of valuable objects, however, are not unknown

---

p. 559, mistakenly accepted *quisquiliae* as quails — thinking that perhaps that 'cailles' was a French reflex of it. Avitus sent fish, see p. 90.52 *marinis copiis*.

1 The pun on *solea* (sole) operates in Latin as well as English.

2 There is conflict of opinion whether this battle took place at Vouillé or Voulon.

3 See Wood, *Merovingian Kingdoms*, p. 47.

4 For Visigothic currency and its devaluation as a sign of economic crisis, see M. Rouche, *L'Aquitaine: des Wisigoths aux Arabes 418–781* (Paris, 1979), p. 302, esp. n. 371. No examples of such debased coinage have been identified, but the Avitus passage makes it clear that debased coins were issued by Alaric II: see W. J. Tomasini, *The Barbaric Tremissis in Spain and Southern France. Anastasius to Leovigild* (New York, 1964), pp. 51–52 and also Grierson and Blackburn, *Medieval European Coinage*, p. 77, which discusses the strictures of the *Lex Gundobada* against the circulation of *monetas gothium ... qui a tempore Alarici regis adaerati sunt*, but omits this passage of Avitus.

5 *Var.* 3.1; 3.4.

in epistolography. He may have been thinking of the sort of ekphrasis Sidonius produced in *Ep.* 4.8.4–5, a description of a silver shell basin intended as gift for Queen Ragnahild.

The letter is also important as a literary document relating to signet rings. Some of the features of this ring are paralleled, e.g. the swivel mechanism, allowing the face to be turned from public gaze.[1] The material from which the Avitan ring is to be constructed, according to the text as it has come down to us, is, however, unusual: not gold, as one would expect for an episcopal signet ring, but iron.[2] The earliest Roman rings were iron,[3] but iron rings seem to have been used primarily by slaves; ones of lead as ex-votos by the poorest people.[4] Trimalchio's odd ring of gold with iron stars (Petronius, *Sat.* 32) represents his status as a freedman: he would not have been permitted to wear the gold ring of a free man. Avitus emphasises his brother's generosity and taste in offering to have a ring made for him (*amplitudinem elegantiae tuae*) and insists on the high quality of the electrum that is to go into the construction of the bezel, recalling with distaste the debasement of the Visigothic coinage. Iron therefore seems an unthinkable material for this fussily described objet d'art. If Avitus had wished to emphasise the ascetic modesty of his ring's design, he would have made something of it. *Aureo* is an easy correction: the ring was gold. That debased metal was used, fraudulently, by goldsmiths in the Lyons region is attested by Gregory of Tours in the *Gloria Confessorum* (62), and interest is expressed in the purity of gold in *Glor. Mart.* 102 and *Virt. Julian.* 44.

Daremberg-Saglio *s.v.* 'anulus' gives no examples of the type of ring described here. *PWRE* 'Ringe' 825 mentions snake-heads in Later Roman rings, but no dolphins. No. 130 in Dalton's *Catalogue of the Finger Rings* is a possible parallel for Avitus. 'Gold; the hoop hollow and narrowest at the back, where there is a carbuncle in a raised setting; the shoulders are moulded to represent hares. High circular bezel with pierced sides, containing a gold coin of the Emperor Marcian (AD 450–7), showing the obverse.' The ring is fifth century, found in the Seine at Rouen. The illustration shows a large ring (diameter 1.3 inches) in cross-section: a sub-conical bezel supported by a hare either side [dolphins would fit just as well], and below and between them, a projecting cabochon stone. This is not a swivel setting, of course,

---

1 W. Smith, *A Dictionary of Greek and Roman Antiquities* (London, 1890), vol. I, p. 131 'The stone and its setting sometimes revolved on an axis, having on one side a figure in relief, on the other an intaglio.' O. M. Dalton, *Catalogue of the Finger Rings Early Christian, Byzantine, Teutonic, Medieval and Later [in the British Museum]* (London, 1912), p. xxix, cites Avitus' ring 'made with a swivel and engraved with his name in full and in monogram' as an example of a sub-Roman bishop's signet ring, but quotes no comparable example in the collection.

2 *Anulo ferreo et admodum tenui.*

3 F. H. Marshall, *Catalogue of the Finger Rings, Greek, Etruscan, and Roman* (London, 1907), p. xviii, cites Pliny *NH* 33.8ff.

4 *RE* 'Ringe' 832.

but in effect the ring when worn would display the gold-coin bezel, while the cabochon would be out of sight, facing downwards and into the palm of the hand if the fingers were clenched.[1] There has, however, been a recent find of a ring with a swivel setting, from Postwick in Norfolk.[2] The idea of Avitus' name being written in a circle can be paralleled in the contemporary inscriptions on stone sculpture (e.g. columns of Theodoric in Ravenna), and would have a long history, into the Carolingian period and beyond.

Avitus artfully moves from gold and gems to mud: the third item in the letter is a request for a master potter and two pieces of technical information about the preparations needed for preparing and firing clay: (1) how big should the kiln be? (2) how big the pit for preparing the clay? This final section raises various puzzling questions. Why would Avitus at Vienne need to import a master potter from Valence? Surely there was sufficient local expertise. What was Avitus going to fire? The size of the pit described suggests tiles or bricks rather than mere pots. There are parallels for the exchange of craftsmen from the Ruricius correspondence: a *pictor* in *Ep.* 2.15 and a *vitrarius* in *Ep.* 1.12. For more on kilns, see W.F. Grimes, 'Holt: the Works Depot of the Twentieth Legion at Castle Lyons', *Y Cymmrodor* 41 (1930), pp. 24–41 and D. Strong and D. Brown (eds), *Roman Crafts* (London, 1972). Despite Avitus' difficulty in finding a master-potter, there is a fine Roman kiln among the exhibits in the museum at the site of St Romain-en-Gall, across the Rhone from Vienne.

Avitus the bishop to Apollinaris the bishop [96.17 Peiper]

I am completely trusting and have no doubt that it is a gift from God that this common cause for rejoicing has been announced to everyone present. For I suspect that it has also now reached your ears that even those people who were said to be laying waste to our territories have gone back.[3] Therefore because I have been worried I sent you this letter in order that you might

1 There is a close parallel for this in Greg. Tur. *GM* 102, where Anicia Juliana has concealed the emerald on her ring from the emperor Justinian prior to giving it to him as a consolation-prize: *cuius gemmam vola concluserat.*

2 Leslie Webster offered the following comment on the Avitus letter in the light of the new find: 'The account is certainly very interesting as far as the Postwick bezel is concerned, not least because of the idea of concealment which Avitus clearly regards as important. However it raises all sorts of other intriguing issues. The dolphin shoulders, the oval swivel, and the monogram can be readily paralleled; but ... I can't think of an example with a carved stone on one side, and metal on the other. The description of the inscription is also of interest; I wonder what range of meaning might be borne by the original Latin text here translated as 'the sign of my monogram written in a circle?' Could it mean a monogram inscribed in a circle, or simply a monogram in the general shape of a circle, or, like a number of Merovingian examples, a monogram surrounded by a name written in a circle?'

3 The Ostrogoths.

evaluate the things that might reach you later concerning[1] an increase of whatever sort of safety, or,[2] if now the freedom to go back to your city has dragged you away from the habit, perhaps rather, the love of being besieged[3] < ... > Therefore I am hoping that you will order those pastilles[4] that you promised to be sent to me along with brief instructions[5] on how to take them.

So much for family business. Because I'd now like to, in a slightly more cheerful vein, I'll set down for you what remains. The seal-ring, therefore, which Your Piety has deigned not so much to promise as to offer me, I wish to be made in this form: in a fairly thin ring of gold,[6] to end in miniature dolphins joined to each other. Let a revolving double signet be inserted on a pair of pivots, which can be changed at will from hidden to public in the eyes of beholders, in turn, with alternate faces of green stone[7] and pale electrum. And not to be sure the sort of electrum that recently tarnished [even] in the holy and most sincere brightness of an unpolluted hand,[8] as I myself heard.[9] You would have thought present a corrupted mixture of gold that had not yet been purified in a furnace rather than one perfected, or that mixture indeed, the harbinger of ensuing disaster, that very recently, the King of the Visigoths had commanded to the public mints (as) confirming adulteration [of the coinage].[10] But let its colour be of the kind which equally and discreetly

1 Goelzer, p. 183, analyses this *de* as a loose 'point de départ de l'action', but since *quae* is the letter, then it should probably be 'concerning the increase of whatever security'.

2 There is a problem: *direxi* is the main verb; *ut* introduces a purpose-clause which ought to be coordinated to something by *aut*, but nothing is there. This may suggest a lacuna after *extraxit*.

3 This sounds snide. Has Apollinaris been besieged somewhere away from Valence? Compare the exchange with Heraclius in *Epp*. 95–96.

4 *Magdaliolum*, dim. of *magdalium*, is a hapax. The pills that Avitus requests may be connected with the illness he subsequently mentions in *Ep*. 88.

5 For *observatio* = *observantia* see Goelzer, p. 591.

6 The MSS. read *ferreo* 'iron'. For the emendation to *aureo* see above p. 252.

7 Anicia Juliana's ring in Greg. Tur. *GM* 102 likewise featured an emerald, a prized 'Neronianus', so green and bright that it seemed to turn gold green with its reflection.

8 Given this excessively complimentary description of the hand, Avitus cannot be referring to his own. Instead he would seem to be describing some sort of mishap, perhaps involving another virtuous celebrant of the mass and an electrum chalice that oxidised in contact with his hand. Roald Hoffmann informs us that if electrum is imperfectly alloyed, the silver patches can oxidise.

9 For the figurative use of *haurio* to mean 'hear' or 'see', see *TLL s.v.* 'haurio' 2570.49–82 which cites this passage at 70–71. Blümner (PW*RE* 5.2315–17) discusses the formulas for, and the use of, electrum, including in drinking-vessels, jewellery and currency. He does not, however, mention this passage.

10 Grierson and Blackburn, *Medieval European Coinage*, p. 46, who, however, miss the Avitus evidence, and only cite *Lib. Const., const. extr.* 21.7.

draws pinkness from gold, glitter from silver, preciousness from each of them, brightness from torches,[1] and which is given value by an artful pleasantness of green in the middle.[2]

If you ask what is to be engraved on the seal: let the sign of my monogram written in a circle be read as evidence of my name. Furthermore the tails of the dolphins, whose heads I described above, will clasp the middle of the ring near[3] to the closed hollow of my hand.[4] Let the small stone,[5] chosen for the very reason that it is oblong and formed with pointed heads, be set between the dolphin [-head]s.[6] There, you have a sort of mirror – more or less – of the pattern to be followed. However, I do not thereby confine the generosity of your Fine Taste to the example described, as if you were not free to add what seems best. Indeed your surpassing intelligence will be allowed to exceed the limits of the order prescribed.

Finally, at the end of the letter, for that work – muddy, yes, but without which, however the task will not be brought to completion[7] – my dreg-ridden[8] speech requests that you immediately send a craftsman potter to me on a short retainer. He is to teach us the right measurements for the sieve-like[9]

1 *Ceteris* 'others', makes no sense. *Cereis*, candles or wax-torches is a simple emendation. The ring will catch light.

2 I.e. the stone will harmonise nicely with the setting.

3 *Ab ea parte* means 'near/at the place, where'.

4 I.e. the bezel.

5 The oval *lapisculus* is the same as the *vernans lapillus*.

6 The antecedent of *quibus* is not immediately clear. It cannot be *caudae*, for if the stone were set between the dolphin tails, then it would have to be a different stone from that in the reverse of the bezel. The latter would have been joined to the dolphin heads. There do not seem to be any examples of rings with a bezel and a (functionally) invisible stone touching the palm of the hand. The antecedent of *quibus*, therefore, is *delphinorum*. Avitus intended the stone to be set between the dolphins' heads.

7 The subject of *transigetur* is unclear.

8 *Faeculentus* 'unclear', 'dirty', 'impure'. A *paraprosdokian*, perhaps, for the expected *luculentus*: Avitus jokes about the language one needs to hire a craftsman who works with mud, 'the jargon of the trade'.

9 *Cribrati cenaculum furni: cribro* properly means 'to sieve', or 'to sift', and began its existence as a neutral denominative in *-are*. Avitus' usage is unusual. He is analysing *cribrare* as a factitive *-are* verb from the substantive *cribrum*, meaning 'to make into a sieve'. *Cribratus* here clearly means *perforatus*. Appropriately enough this use of *cribratus/criblatus* survives in French. Cf. 'criblé de dettes', 'riddled with debts'. The participle has been transferred from *cenaculum* to *furnus*: it was the upper portion of the kiln that was pierced with holes.

upper section of a kiln,[1] or within what space of excavated clods, < ... >[2] of a pit †enclosed for muck,†[3] the gluey mass of clay for baking[4] can be softened by the feet of animals.[5]

Appendix

Peiper's Latin text of the final sentence:

> In fine autem epistulae luteo operi, sine quo tamen non transigetur, faeculentus sermo deposcit, ut artificem figulum brevi tenendum e vestigio dirigatis, qui nobis qualibus strui mensuris cribrati cenaculum furni vel intra quod spatium fossilis glaebae scrobis, sordibus saeptae animalium pedibus, coctilis caeni glutinum lentari possit.

The final sentence presents considerable difficulties after *glaebae*. Peiper includes *scrobis* in the comma with *glaebae* both against the sense and the cursus: *fossilis glaebae* yields a standard *planus*. At that point no sense can be made of *scrobis*, *sordibus* or *saeptae*. The end of the sentence can indeed be translated from *animalium* to *possit*. It seems probable that there is a lacuna before scrobis ('of the pit') which, if taken as feminine could be modified by *saeptae*, but the construction of *sordibus* ('dung') is still obscure. The obelus seems the best solution.

In fine autem epistulae,[6] | *luteo operi,*[7] | *sine quo tamen non transigetur,*[8] |

---

1 The kiln would be like a bottle lying flat on the ground, half-buried, with its 'neck' as the furnace from which exhaust gases, smoke and heat, are drawn through the body of the 'bottle' and out through a hole in the far end, in other words the chimney which creates the draught; the 'bottle' itself is divided length-wise (i.e. horizontally) by a fired clay floor pierced with holes (the 'sieve') on which the tiles are stacked for firing.

2 For the textual problems, see the appendix at the end of the letter.

3 Before clay can be made into tiles and bricks it has to be washed clean of stones and grit. So the clay, once it has been dug up, is dumped into a pit, water is added, and the filthy mass (Avitus' *sordibus*) is stirred up until the unwanted particles fall to the bottom. Ideally it is screened or sieved, but if the suspended clay can be drawn off, that was good enough. The clay was then allowed to lose water until it became plastic.

4 Even though *TLL s.v. coctilis* lists this passage as an example of *coctilis = torrefactus, ustus*, and Goelzer, p. 522, as 'cuit', it clearly cannot mean 'baked' in this context. For the proximity of clay pits to kilns see Grimes, 'Holt', p. 41.

5 Construing *pedibus* with *lentari*. Peiper's punctuation needs to be altered: the comma after *pedibus* should be moved to before *animalium*. Oxen might have been used, driven around in a very large hole to work the slurry with their hooves.

6 *tardus*

7 *tardus*

8 *planus*

faeculentus sermo deposcit,[1] | *ut artificem figulum*[2] | *brevi tenendum*[3] | *e vestigio dirigatis,*[4] | *qui nobis qualibus strui mensuris*[5] | *cribrati cenaculum furni*[6] | *vel intra quod spatium fossilis glaebae*[7] | < ... > *scrobis,* †*sordibus saeptae*[8] † | *animalium pedibus,*[9] | *coctilis caeni*[10] | *glutinum lentari possit.*[11]

Epistula 88: Introduction

This is a strangely allusive letter. It is ostensibly an expression of thanks for a present Apollinaris has sent to Avitus' church. It is also an expression of regret that Avitus and Apollinaris did not see each other on the occasion of a festival, apparently held in the diocese of Valence. Avitus seems to have been unable to attend because of illness and he seems also to be hinting to his brother that he will soon die and that a new bishop may have to be selected. The selection is apparently to be in the hands of Apollinaris, which would certainly have been uncanonical. Episcopal election was supposedly in the hands of the people and clergy of a diocese – though such legislation was not reiterated at Epaon in 517, being much more obviously of an issue of significance later in the century.[12] Consecration ought to have been in the hands of the metropolitan. Valence was subordinate to Vienne and Apollinaris was not of metropolitan status. The nearest metropolitan would have been Viventiolus of Lyons, who signed second to Avitus at Epaon and first, ahead of Julianus of Vienne and Apollinaris, at Lyons (518/23). Julianus was a relative of Avitus and Apollinaris:[13] he may even have been Avitus' deacon (*Ep.* 29). To judge by the names of bishops the see of Vienne seems to have been dominated by the Aviti,[14] which may suggest that the family had considerable influence in the diocese. It may, therefore, be that Apollinaris did have a say in the episcopal succession of Vienne, even though he should not have done according to the canons. For a detailed account of a slightly

1 *planus*
2 *tardus*
3 *planus*
4 *velox*
5 *planus*
6 *planus*
7 *planus*
8 *planus*
9 *tardus*
10 *planus*
11 pp2p.
12 Councils of Orléans (533) cans. 3, 4, 7; Clermont (535), can. 2; Orléans (538), can. 3; Orléans (549), cans. 10, 11; Paris (561/2), can. 8; Paris (614), can. 2; Clichy (626/7), can. 28; Chalon-sur-Saône (647/53), can. 10.
13 Heinzelmann, *Bischofsherrschaft*, p. 222.
14 Heinzelmann, *Bischofsherrschaft*, pp. 220–32.

earlier election, compare Sidonius *Epp*. 7.8 and 7.9 about the election of Simplicius of Bourges.

Avitus the bishop to Apollinaris the bishop {97.18 Peiper}

Since I am equally bound and burdened by your kind care, the generosity of your gift, and your usual kindness, what adequate expression of thanks – I won't *begin* to mention an appropriate return! – can I give to you? Unless perhaps in many ways < ... >[1] and lacking in strength, I may be sustained in this matter by the very kindness that imposes a burden on me. May God Almighty grant that you adorn the church and console and refresh me, in order that, because you really do not live for yourself alone, you may heap up merit through comforting others. My sins caused a not insignificant constraint to deprive me of the bodily presence of Your Piety and of my own delight on the day when you undertook the celebration of your little feast.[2] But you granted me the chance to behold you through the eye, to hear you in speech, and [experience] your actions in your deed.[3] I believe that through the mercy of our Lord my humble church will honour the gift of Your Oblation[4] not just in my days, but in those to come also. Just as I would like to preserve it as long as I am alive as testimony of your boundless generosity, so may God grant me that Your Authority may specially commend it to him, whom Your Election will decide upon, after me,[5] when God orders you to do so.[6]

1 There must have been an allusion to Avitus' illness in this lacuna. Note that Avitus had asked for *magdaliola*, 'pills' in *Ep*. 87.

2 *Festivitatulae* is Peiper's conjecture for *festitatulae* S and *festivitatae* L. The allusion is unclear: it could refer either to a feast of the church of Valence, perhaps one introduced by Apollinaris (cf. *susceptae*) or to a family feast such as that mentioned in *Epp*. 13 and 14.

3 A literal translation would be highly mannered: 'Your gave back and made present to me the exchange of your aspect in sight, etc.' It is just possible that Apollinaris sent Avitus a portrait of himself. For more on episcopal images, see B. Brenk, 'Mit was für Mitteln kann einem physisch anonymen Auctoritas verliehen werden?', in Chrysos and Wood, eds, *East and West: Modes of Communication*, pp. 155ff.

4 The gift is clearly more substantial than the *deliciae* which feature in so many letters.

5 Avitus is alluding to his own death.

6 Avitus seems to be suggesting that Apollinaris will have some role in choosing his successor as bishop of Vienne.

11. AVITUS' POETRY AND ANOTHER LITERARY CONNECTION

Contents

Dedicatory letter to *De spiritalis historiae gestis*, to Apollinaris, bishop of Valence.
Dedicatory letter to *De consolatoria castitatis laude*, to Apollinaris, bishop of Valence.
Epistula 15 Avitus to Contumeliosus, bishop of Riez.

Dedicatory Letter for *De spiritalis historiae gestis*: Introduction

The following two items are the dedicatory epistles for Avitus' two long surviving poems, the biblical epic *De spiritalis historiae gestis* and *De consolatoria castitatis laude*. The dedicatory epistle for the *SHG* has often been dated *to* 507,[1] apparently because Avitus mentions sending a copy to Apollinaris *vir illustris* in *Ep.* 51, p. 80.28ff. Its date, however, is unlikely to be that precise, because in *Ep.* 51 Alaric is clearly still alive (p. 79.34); strictly speaking the letter must *pre-date* his death in 507.[2] Also relevant to the dissemination of the *SHG* is *Ep.* 43.[3]

Avitus' *Epigrammatum multitudo*: Does this refer to lost epigrams or, as most assume, to the *SHG*? This depends on whether one takes 'certain ... books' (*aliquos ... libellos*) below (p. 201.12) to be part of the same group of writings. If so, why does Avitus call his long hexameter poems 'epigrams' (*epigrammata*)? The usage is anomalous. Pliny, *Ep.* 4.14.9, implies that an *epigramma* is a short poem.[4] Even though Statius describes his *Silvae* as *epigrammata*, and the book in question contains a poem 77 lines long (*Silv.* 2.3), the extension of the term *epigrammata* to books that are 325, 423, 425, 658 and 721 lines long seems highly unlikely.[5] In addition, Avitus says that he was thinking of publishing the *epigrammata* 'maintaining order of subject-matter or date' (*servato causarum vel temporum ordine*). This statement would be nonsensical if applied to the *SHG*. The *epigrammata* are most probably lost shorter poems.[6]

---

1 Roncoroni, 'L'epica biblica di Avito di Vienne', p. 328.

2 Wood, 'Avitus of Vienne', p. 64.

3 See below pp. 340ff.

4 *Sive epigrammata, sive idyllia, sive eclogas, sive, ut multis, poematia ... seu quid aliud vocari malueritis, licebit voces; ego tantum hendecasyllabos praesto.*

5 *Silv.* 2 praef. 17 *leves libellos quasi epigrammatis loco scriptos.*

6 *Pace* Peiper, p. li. A 9th cent. Berlin MS first cited by M. Haupt, 'Analecta', *Hermes* 3 (1889), p. 22, mentions *Libri Alchimi*. *Sic incipit: in adulescentiam (adulescentem* Haupt*) qui in publico patre cadente risisset (risit* Haupt*) et languenti puellae amatorium dedit. De controversia fullonis vel calvi.* These are both improbable topics for a bishop's occasional

Nonetheless a difficulty still remains. Avitus is well aware of the brevity implied by the word *epigramma*. In his preface to the *CCL* (p. 274.6–8) he quotes his brother's opinion that *liber* would be more in keeping with the work's *prolixitas* (666 lines). Yet he still insists that he would more correctly (*rectius*) call the *CCL* an *epigramma* after its *denuntiatum finem*. Given that at the end of the preface of the *CCL* he states that he had been intending to stop writing poetry unless an *evidentis causae ratio* wrung the *necessitas* of an *epigramma* out of him, it would appear that he uses *epigramma* in an idiolectal manner to refer to an occasional piece of writing, something that could have a *causa*, a *finis* and a *necessitas*. The *CCL* qualifies. The *SHG* does not.

On this letter see M. Roberts, 'The Prologue to Avitus' *De Spiritalis Historiae Gestis*: Christian Poetry and Poetic License', *Traditio* 36 (1980), pp. 399–407. For a new translation of this letter, see Shea, *The Poems of Alcimus Ecdicius Avitus*, pp. 71–72.

Dedicatory Letter for *De spiritalis historiae gestis*

To his holy master in Christ, the most pious and blessed Apollinaris the bishop, Alcimus Ecdicius, his brother {201.1 Peiper}

Recently after putting together a few of my homilies into one book at the encouragement of my friends I took on the difficult task of bringing it out. But now that you are still egging me on to yet greater efforts, I steeled myself[1] to proceed to the buskin of yet more frivolous boldness. For you are asking me to dedicate to your name as an *opusculum*,[2] whatever I have written in verse on whatever subject.

For my part I do remember writing some verse, enough so that if the multitude of epigrams were put in order they would comprise a by no means small volume. When I was contemplating doing this, while preserving both order of subject matter and of composition, almost all of those poems were lost in the emergency [connected with that] infamous disturbance.[3] Because it would be either difficult to look for them one by one or impossible to find them, I let the matter drop; since it would have been hard enough to arrange

---

epigrammata. They look more like the stuff of display-oratory or comic poetry. Riese, *Anthologia Latina* 1, p. xxxvi n. 2, goes along with Haupt's ascription (Haupt, 'Analecta', p. 223) to an Alchimus Alethius rhetor, contemporary with Ausonius.

1 *Durata fronte*, i.e. without frowning.

2 *Sub professione opusculi*, i.e. as a small published book.

3 Probably the Frankish invasion of 500. See Burckhardt, p. 39. It may be impossible to tell which siege of Vienne Avitus meant.

them, even if the collection were intact, to restore them once they had been dispersed seemed [even] harder. I subsequently found some of the books at the house of one of my friends. Even though they match their names and titles,[1] when [appropriate] subject matter suggests [itself], they nonetheless touch on other matters too.[2] Therefore, because you order me to, although these writings are obscure *qua* works written by me, at least they will be illuminated by your name.

Although someone be keen and learned, unless[3] he preserve the style appropriate to his religious vocation as much according to the law of metre as that of faith, he can hardly be suited to writing poetry. For the licence to lie that is granted equally to poets and painters must be completely banished from serious matters, for in writing secular verse one is called the more skilled the more 'elegantly' one weaves – no, let's be honest, the more 'ineptly'. I'll say nothing now of those words or names on which we are not allowed to dwell (i.e. read eagerly) even in others' works, let alone write in our own. Because they can signify one thing through another, they provide useful shortcuts for poets.[4] Therefore in the judgement of those who are secular, who will pardon[5] both lack of skill and laziness, < ... > we are not using the licence of poets.[6] Once we have begun a work that is more tasking than enjoyable, we drew a firm distinction between divine censure and human opinion.

Therefore in any sort of assertion or, as available, explanation, if one has to err in some way, it is healthier for a cleric in speaking to fail in grandeur than to go against [his] rule, and he limps more freely in his metrical feet than in tracking truth.[7] For there is no freedom of speech that excuses the

1 E.g. *de mundi initio*, etc.

2 Wood, 'Avitus of Vienne', p. 63 n. 2, sees here a suggestion that books 4–5, the Flood, may have been added later. The tense of *perstringunt*, however, suggests that Avitus may be alluding to the numerous digressions in the *SHG*, e.g. the excursus on the Nile at 1.279.

3 Roberts, 'Prologue', p. 399, translates the passage, but notes on p. 400 n. 2 that he has been unable to avoid a paraphrase in translating the *si*-clause. The MSS read *si*, but the sense clearly requires *nisi*, a negation for the whole protasis. Once this correction is made, the sentence makes perfect sense and says what it ought to say: namely that the *lex fidei* is a *sine qua non*. See the text of the letter below for confirmation.

4 Roberts, 'Prologue', pp. 403–04. Avitus alludes to the metonymical use of the names of the pagan gods, e.g. Ter. *Eun.* 732, *sine Cerere et Libero friget Venus*.

5 *Dabunt* lacks an object. We supply *veniam*.

6 This appears to be the fragment of an indirect statement, and there may be a gap after *poetarum*.

7 For a comparable point about metrical feet and feet, see *Ep.* 95, p. 102.17–18.

perpetration of sin. For if men were compelled to render an account for every idle word they uttered (Mt.12.36–37), it is easy to see that a liberty taken with forethought and practice that puts the law of speech before laws of [righteous] living is the more dangerous.[1]

Dedicatory Letter for *De consolatoria castitatis laude*: Introduction

The dedicatory epistle for the *CCL* clearly postdates the dedication of the *SHG,* so it must have been written after ca. 506/07. Wood identified the dead sister of *Epp.* 13 and 14 as Fuscina, and suggested that she may have been a victim of rape and may have died during the period of Godegisel's rule in Vienne, i.e. ca. 500/01.[2] He also suggested that the description of the poem's contents as *de consolatoria castitatis laude* may have had something to do with the tragic circumstances of her death.[3] There is a difficulty with this suggestion, namely that Fuscina seems to have been alive at the time the *CCL*'s dedicatory epistle was written. Avitus refers to her as *venerabilem Fuscinam nostram* and as *germanae sanctimoniali.* None of the customary epitaphic aggrandisements or sepulchral endearments one would have expected in a public letter appears.[4] Avitus knew how to parody expressions such as *bonae memoriae* (*Ep.* 86, p. 96.8). The poem needs to be set in the context provided by other later Roman ecclesiastical authors who celebrated family saints,[5] specifically religious sisters dedicated to virginity, e.g. Ambrose[6] and Marcella and Gregory of Nyssa and Macrina.

What was the title of this work? The manuscripts call it *De virginitate*, but Avitus describes it in his dedicatory epistle as *versus de consolatoria castitatis laude* (p. 274.5–6), literally 'verses about the praise of chastity intended to console'. What did he mean by this? There is no consolation for death in the poem. What was the praise of virginity intended to console? Teuffel and Schwabe[7] rather vaguely took the phrase to refer to the renunciation of marriage, an interpretation that proceeds along the right lines.

When Jephthah's daughter knew that she was to be sacrificed, she asked permission of her father to mourn her virginity (Jdg. 11.37), the implication presumably being that she had no consolation in the marriage-bed or in the survival of children.

---

1 Compare Augustine, *Conf.* 1.18.29 on divergent attitudes to the sins of dropping aitches (*'omicidium'*) and *homicidium* (murder).

2 Wood, 'Avitus of Vienne', pp. 90–91.

3 Wood, 'Avitus of Vienne', p. 90.

4 In the private discourse of *Epp.* 13 and 14, where both brothers know what they are talking about and 'intent to publish' is by no means clear, such phrases are not necessary.

5 See *CCL* 648 which makes the point explicitly: *te meruit primam cognatio tota patronam.*

6 For Ambrose as a source for Avitus' *CCL*, see A. Roncoroni, 'Note al *De Virginitate* di Avito di Vienne', *Athenaeum* 51 (1973), pp. 122–34.

7 *A History of Roman Literature* (London, 1891), vol. 2, p. 503.

The same ideas appear in the pagan rhetoric of *Aen.* 4.32–33, *solane perpetua maerens carpere iuventa/ nec dulces natos Veneris nec praemia noris?* While Christian authors might like their audiences to think that nuns had no regrets for loss of marriage or children, the written record tells a different tale. In order to sell sacred virginity to the female consumer, all the artifices of rhetoric were required, both persuasory ('you'll be the bride of Christ', cf. *CCL* 65–67), and dissuasory. The latter type of argumentation, also found in texts intended to offer consolation for death,[1] was prominent and often vividly satirical. For examples one can compare Jerome, especially *Ep.* 22 to Eustochium, and *Ep.* 54.4 to *Furia de viduitate servanda* or the *Contra Helvidium.* Such writing enumerated what one should be happy to miss. See Jerome, *Ep.* 22.1 for a snapshot of the *dissuasiones* against marriage: *quomodo uterus intumescat, infans vagiat, cruciet paelex, domus cura sollicitet et omnia, quae putantur bona, mors extrema praecidat*; also *Ep.* 22.22 for more on the *molestiae nuptiarum* and allusions to other authors, including Tertullian, Cyprian, Ambrose and Damasus who treated the topos. Many of these dissuasory points are to be found in the *CCL* vv. 156–95.

Dedicatory Letter for *De consolatoria castitatis laude*

To his holy master and most kind blood-brother Apollinaris the bishop, Alcimus Avitus, his brother in Christ {274.1 Peiper}

After I finished the books which I was unable to dispose of[2] as I wished (you and some of your friends in your affectionate but unthinking haste snatched them away) you also urge me to give specially to you those verses which I wrote to the venerable Fuscina, our sister, in consolation and praise of chastity.[3] Even though I would more correctly call them an 'epigram',[4] after the promised end [and purpose] of the poem, you first called them a book, claiming that this term was appropriate for its length. Therefore in this too consider me the servant of your judgement – nay rather your affection. For it is quite unfair for me to contradict in small matters one whom I obey in greater ones. May Your Piety please remember this very 'little book', as you call it, since it offers a rather personal treatment both of the religious

---

1 The analogy in a consolation for death would be the *De miseriis huius vitae* motif. See P. von Moos, *Consolatio: Studien über Mittellateinischen Trostliteratur* (Munich, 1971), vol. 3, pp. 151–72. Also Menander Rhetor, 2.414.8ff. ed. Russell and Wilson for prescriptions of such arguments.

2 Or perhaps 'arrange'.

3 The allusion to Fuscina suggests that she is alive.

4 See above p. 260 for Avitus apparent use of *epigramma* to mean 'occasional writing'. The passage has been misunderstood by Vinay, 'La poesia', p. 433.

practices of our common relatives and the virgins of our family, must only be given to read to people who are relatives or lead the religious life. You will be able to measure from the quality of the material how and when I would like it to find its way into the hands of strangers:[1] I have difficulty in entrusting even to you (and only after being ordered to frequently) a work written in private for our sister the nun. For since I was certainly intended to cease writing verse and joining foot to foot (unless perhaps there were a clear reason and need for an epigram),[2] nonetheless I promise that it will be so slight that not even you would dare to give it any other name.[3] It has long suited our vocation, and now our age too, if something has to be written to take on the work and occasion in a more serious style instead, and not to linger on writing that sings in verse to few who understand and measures syllables, but on what serves many readers and has measured an increase of faith.

Epistula 15: Introduction

Avitus has sent some of his writings to Contumeliosus of Riez. He makes modest excuses about them, and looks forward to a visit from his fellow bishop that will clearly have political or pastoral implications. Apart from the light it sheds on the way Avitus circulated his writings for criticism,[4] this letter raises interesting questions about the political position of the diocese Riez. It had been part of the Visigothic kingdom under Euric,[5] but no bishop of Riez signed the canons of Agde in 506. This might suggest that the city was taken over by the Burgundians. On the other hand Contumeliosus did not sign the Council of Epaon in 517, but did sign the Caesarian councils of Arles (524), Carpentras (527) and Vaison (529). If the Burgundians did take the city during the reign of Alaric II, they clearly lost it to the Goths again in 508. The implication seems to be that Contumeliosus, like Avitus' other literary arbiter, Apollinaris, lived outside the Burgundian kingdom. In 533 Contumeliosus was deposed at the Council of Marseilles for sexual misdemeanours and appropriation of church property.[6]

---

1 The implication clearly is 'never'.

2 Avitus seems to see an epigram as occasional writing. See above p. 260.

3 Does Avitus mean the *epigram* appended to the *CCL* (p. 694 app. crit.), mentioned by Isidore, *Vir. ill.* 23, *eleganti epigrammate coaptatum*?

4 Compare *Ep.* 51.

5 Duchesne, *Fastes épiscopaux*, vol. 1, p. 284.

6 *MGH, Epp.* 1, pp. 56–57; O. Pontal, *Die Synoden im Merowingerreich* (Paderborn, 1986), pp. 58–60.

Avitus the bishop to Contumeliosus, bishop [of Riez] {48.1 Peiper}

As the days that I prayed for draw near and you intercede for whatever I desire before God, all the more do longing and shame battle in my spirit. For I beg your blessing for work that is less than perfect. There might be some excuse, however paltry, if its size masked and concealed my sin of laziness. But what now could be less attractive than something that is both short *and* unpolished? For this reason, there is one thing that consoles my fearful spirit with its bold encouragement: if God deigns to listen to pious men, when you arrive, everything *must* be improved. For there is nothing that you cannot either set straight through your prayers or excuse through your rhetorical efforts.[1] Only, just as I am sure of the prayer[s] of your incomparable piety, so let me rejoice that a messenger has come to announce your visit for which I have been waiting.

---

1 Avitus makes a word-play on *orando*, 'to pray' and *perorando*, 'to perorate'. There seems to be a hint of some pastoral difficulty here.

12. VIVENTIOLUS OF LYONS

Contents

Epistula 19: Introduction

It seems that the abbot of the Jura monasteries, Eugendus,[1] is very ill and has been unable to perform his duties. There have been quarrels among the monks,[2] perhaps about who ought to take charge in the abbot's illness. The priest Viventiolus, who appears to have been recently elected as the prior of Eugendus' monastery,[3] has ridden to Lyons to visit yet another sick cleric, probably a fellow monk (*frater*). Viventiolus has now left Lyons and sent a gift[4] of a sedan-chair to Avitus.

Viventiolus seems to have been concerned about the propriety of having left his monastery;[5] he may have been questioned about his conduct by his fellow monks; he was put out at the circumstances of his election as prior. Avitus reassures him on this point. In return for the sedan-chair, Avitus tells Viventiolus that he will be

---

1 Eugendus is the subject of the last part of the *Vita Patrum Iurensium* (= 3).

2 *Fraterna dissensio*.

3 See *in secundo gradu*, though this might rather refer to the priesthood. That Condat had a prior is clear from *Vita Patrum Iurensium* 126 (= 3.4).

4 *Transmisso munere*.

5 On Eugendus never having left the monastery, see *Vita Patrum Jurensium* 126 (= 3.4).

recommending him for the episcopal seat at Lyons and hopes that from there he will, perhaps because of his metropolitan status, be able to maintain an affectionate and paternal eye on his former monastery.

Viventiolus was apparently elevated to the episcopate in 513/4:[1] he was certainly in post before 515 (when he appears in the *Vita Abbatum Acaunensium* 7). He presided over the Council of Lyons (518/23), and died possibly before 524,[2] and certainly at some point before 538, when his successor Lupus presided at Orléans III.[3] Viventiolus' succession in 513/4 can probably be used as evidence for dating the last illness of Eugendus,[4] which is said to have lasted for six months.[5] The letter thus becomes an important indication of the abbot's death-date. Further, since the *Vita Patrum Iurensium* was written soon after the death of Eugendus,[6] its date is significant for the composition of the *Vita*. It has even been suggested that Viventiolus was the author of the *Vita Patrum Iurensium*,[7] and as such he may appear in the hagiographical narrative.[8] Certainly there are other indications that Viventiolus may have been a religious author.[9]

Since a Viventiolus did become bishop of Lyons, it is reasonable to equate the priest and the bishop, and to regard at least three[10] if not all four of the letters[11] to or from a Viventiolus (which is in any case an uncommon name) in the Avitus collection as relating to the same man. The case for identifying Viventiolus the priest/monk as the later bishop of Lyons is further strengthened by the description of the bishop as *decus fratrum* in his epitaph, which could imply that he had been a monk.[12] The epitaph also notes that Viventiolus was buried in the same tomb as his brother, who was himself a bishop. Heinzelmann has argued on the grounds of a Procès-verbal of 1308 that Viventiolus' brother was his predecessor-but-one Rusticus.[13] Rusticus had

1 His predecessor Stephanus was still alive in 512: A. Coville, *Recherches sur l'histoire de Lyon du Ve siècle au IXe siècle (450–800)* (Paris, 1928), p. 308; Viventiolus was in post by 515, *Vita Abbatum Acaunensium* 7; Martine, *Vie des Pères du Jura,* p. 55.

2 Coville, *Recherches sur l'histoire de Lyon,* p. 317.

3 Duchesne, *Fastes épiscopaux,* vol. 2, pp. 165–66.

4 Martine, *Vie des Pères du Jura,* pp. 54–55, assumes that Eugendus (Oyend) was already dead because of the phrase *scholam ... praesule viduatam,* but the words *cari communis* suggest rather that he was still alive, but unable to exercise his office.

5 *Vita Patrum Iurensium* 175 (= 3.24).

6 Martine, *Vie des Pères du Jura,* pp. 56–57.

7 I. N. Wood, 'Prelude to Columbanus', in H. B. Clarke and M. Brennan, eds, *Columbanus and Merovingian Monasticism* (Oxford, 1981), pp. 27–28, n.118.

8 *Vita Patrum Iurensium* 175 (=III 24): Martine, *Vie des Pères du Jura,* p. 429, n. 4.

9 Apart from the letter summoning his suffragans to the Council of Lyons (ed. J. Gaudemet and B. Basdevant, pp. 98–101), see *CCSL* 148A pp. 23–24.

10 *Epp.* 67 and 69.

11 *Ep.* 57: see below.

12 Duchesne, *Fastes épiscopaux,* vol. 2, p. 165; Heinzelmann, *Bischofsherrschaft,* p. 115.

13 Heinzelmann, *Bischofsherrschaft,* pp. 117–18.

already had a notable secular career before becoming bishop of Lyons at some point
between 475 and 494/6,[1] and he died in 501.[2]

Avitus' letter to Viventiolus the priest is among his more maddeningly allusive
and corrupt works. The balanced pairing of the opening sentence is by no means
clear. Are *vehendo Lugdunum* and *hucque mittendo* to be taken as a joint unit, 'riding
to Lyons and sending < ...> here, i.e. to Lyons?' Or should they be separated, 'By
riding to Lyons and sending < ... > here, i.e. to Vienne, or wherever Avitus was when
he wrote the letter?' Are the two brothers real brothers? Or spiritual brothers? Or
both? Does *illic* refer to Lyons? *Istic* to yet a third place? Or should *istic* be emended
to *hic* (see n. 6 below)? This is unfortunate, because the letter contains material that
is potentially important for understanding the history of the diocese of Lyons and of
the monastery of Condat in the second decade of the sixth century.

Avitus the bishop to Viventiolus the priest {50.18 Peiper}

You have done a doubly virtuous deed: you have both ridden[3] to Lyons and
have sent word back[4] here.[5] There you took the trouble to seek out one
brother who was ill, here[6] to visit one who was worried.[7] Nor will it be
thought that you have neglected your monastic vows,[8] for even if the sick
man[9] had not asked you to, you would owe[10] more in affection and respect to
a religious brother than < ... >[11] of this spiritual duty, seeing that according
to the rights of a brother [bishop],[12] newness [in office] required encouragement at least, even if anxiety did not require consolation. Please stop making
excuses for a task you took upon yourself with good reason, lest you
continue to appear to have erred in hesitating about whether to undertake
[the task] or draw clear lines concerning the limits of your duties.

1 Heinzelmann, *Bischofsherrschaft*, p. 101.

2 Heinzelmann, 'Gallische Prosopographie (260–507)', pp. 685–86.

3 *Veendo* P, corrected by Peiper.

4 *Mitto* may be used intransitively with an expression of place to where, meaning 'send
word to'.

5 I.e. wherever Avitus is.

6 *Istic* oddly (rather than the expected *hic*) seems to balance *illic*. Emend to *hic*?

7 Avitus himself or some concerned third party?

8 This could be a reference to the expectation that monks of Condat would not leave the
monastery: see *Vita Patrum Iurensium* 126 (= 3.4).

9 Translating *aegrotus* alone. Winterbottom obelises *conventus* L.

10 *Deberetis* Winterbottom.

11 Winterbottom posits a missing ablative noun, and obelises L's *conventus*.

12 Apollinaris of Valence perhaps, as suggested by Coville, *Recherches sur l'histoire de
Lyon*, p. 309, in which case *germanus* is to be taken literally. But it is also possible that Avitus
refers to whichever fellow-bishop of his had jurisdiction over the monastery at Condat.

But now I feel that I can find a better way[1] of thanking you in my prayers than in my letters for the gift you sent. As to the point you make, that such things be brought forth from a wilderness, by some sort of elegance you attract the longings of men to the place where you all dwell together.[2] Thereby, doubtless due to your care, instruction, and learning, although it is in fact a wilderness, it became a paradise.[3] For this reason, in place of the chair that you have sent [me], I earnestly request a change of seat [for you], an episcopal throne,[4] so that you may cherish with spiritual solace and priestly teaching the wavering school of our dear common friend Eugendus.[5] It has been bereft of no mean leader, as far as his status is concerned.[6] Do not let it discourage you from taking pity on them that they did not observe all the due ceremony in their handling of your election.[7] It is not, I think, that they were bent on insulting you, but rather that they are simple and untutored. Thus being promoted to higher posts (as with God's help we desire you will be) and rising to the doubling of five talents with two added,[8] now that you have been tested in the second rank, faithful also in the greatest matters,[9] may you bring to the people this secret knowledge,[10] namely, although among others fraternal dissension had been able to make a desert,[11] among you paternal affection has tried to keep a monastery together.

---

1 Reading *qualiter* for *ut taliter*: Winterbottom.

2 Avitus is referring to the fact that Condat as a monastery was the equivalent of the desert. Even though it was a desert it could also be paradise.

3 Note the anomalous secondary sequence, *fieret*.

4 Avitus is making a joke: in return for a chair, Viventiolus is to get an office (chair).

5 The abbot of Condat and the Jura monasteries. See *Vita Patrum Iurensium*, 118–179 (= 3).

6 Eugendus cannot be dead – *pace* Heinzelmann and Martine (above p. 267 n. 4). Avitus uses *viduatam*, 'widowed', of Eugendus' school, but immediately explains that the word is a metaphor by inserting *quantum ad statum suum adtinet*, 'as far as his state [of health] is concerned'. The school is *functionally* widowed, because Eugendus is ill.

7 *Vestrae ordinationis* is probably not, in this case, an honorific, but an allusion to Viventiolus' promotion within his own monastery.

8 Winterbottom deletes *de*.

9 Echoing God's praise in Mt. 25.21, *qui super pauca fuisti fidelis, super multa te constituam*. Avitus used this parable again in *CCL* 290–337.

10 Presumably Viventiolus' abilities to deal with difficult personalities in closed communities.

11 *Quod in aliis fraterna dissensio nec potuit istic heremum facere* Peiper based on *discessione potuistis* L and *dissinsio ... || potuissita* P. Winterbottom emends to *cum in aliis fraterna dissensio potuisset heremum facere*, which comes close to S's *dissensio potuisset* and has the further virtue of explaining its pluperfect subjunctive and eliminating Peiper's nonsenical *non*.

Epistula 57: Introduction

In the Later Roman Empire, as indeed at all periods, correct Latinity ('integritas Latinitatis' for Avitus, below) marked the educated man. Here Avitus responds indignantly to the charge that he committed a barbarism (in this case an allegedly false quantity *pótitur* for *potîtur)* in a sermon.[1] Avitus does not reproduce the standard grammatical explanation of the anomaly involving *potior.* Instead he boldly claims that it was Vergil, not he, who took the liberty. For further sniping about false quantities, see Ennodius, *Epp.* 362 and 406. Oratory in the pulpit seems to have been as carefully scrutinised as that in the rhetor's school.[2] Even as great a rhetorician as Augustine was prone to anxiety about his speech: Africans apparently had particular trouble with vowel quantities.[3] In the first book of the *Confessions* (1.18.29 where one notes the excessive play with elision in the passage) he bitterly satirises those who care more about aspirations ('human' for ''uman') than about homicide.[4] In the *De Ordine* 2.17.45 he openly speaks of the insecurity he felt because of his accent. Avitus, understandably, takes some care to make a defensive parade of rhetorical tropes in the peroration to his rather 'dignant' response (*attrahere magis quam* **de**trahere[5] */ eloqui potius quam obloqui*).

Avitus' letter is addressed to a certain 'Viventiolus the rhetor'. Is the title used ironically, and is this man to be identified with the recipient of *Epp.* 19, and 59, 67 and 69, and the author of *Ep.* 68, the bishop of Lyons? The venue of Avitus' sermon, Lyons (p. 85.19), would suggest that this is so. Furthermore Viventiolus is an uncommon name,[6] so the burden of proof is on those who would claim that the rhetor and the bishop are two, not one. But it is the tone of the letter that may have the most to contribute to deciding the identity of the recipient. Avitus' response is heavily ironical, huffy and defensive. He even omits his customary salutation and honorifics. There are excellent parallels for both of these features in other letters addressed to Viventiolus. For irony, see *Epp.* 68 and 69, and for omitted honorifics, see *Ep.* 69.

The 'common sons' might have been seen as an impediment to the identification of the 'rhetor', and the bishop – in what sense could he and Avitus be said to 'share sons'? The difficulty might be surmounted by envisaging not shared students, but an

---

1 For a 5th-century discussion of barbarisms and metaplasms, see Consentius in *GL* 5.386–404.

2 See Augustine, *De catechizandis rudibus* 9.13, on priests who perpetrate barbarisms and solecisms. The problem continued in the time of Gregory of Tours. See *LVM* 2.1 for a priest who mispronounced words during Mass in 573.

3 Consentius 392.3–4.

4 *De Catechizandis rudibus* 9.13 picks up the same theme: *discant non contemnere quos cognoverint morum vitia quam verborum amplius devitare.* For ancient evidence about the pronunciation of 'h' in VL, see J. Kramer, *Literarische Quellen zur Aussprache des Vulgärlateins* (Meisenheim am Glan, 1976), pp. 48–57.

5 S's reading *detrahere* preserves a more felicitous concinnity and point.

6 See Heinzelmann, *Bischofsherrschaft*, p. 121 n. 156.

audience (i.e. church congregation) that both of them addressed. In *Ep*. 55. p. 84.36–85.2, Avitus uses 'sons' figuratively of his parishioners. Avitus clearly was invited by Viventiolus to preach in Lyons,[1] and Viventiolus was almost certainly invited for return matches in Vienne.[2] So the 'shared sons' could be the sermon-audiences both at Vienne and Lyons.

Avitus the bishop to Viventiolus, the rhetor {85.18 Peiper}

A rumour originating with you whispers that you say that I fell into a barbarism in a sermon that I recently addressed to the people of Lyons on the occasion of the dedication of a church;[3] indeed you publicly castigated me, because I made a mistake in a public speech. I admit that this could have happened, especially to me from whom 'age has swept away'[4] whatever literary studies I may have pursued in my greener years. I wanted, however, to hear this from you face-to-face, because, even if my intellectual abilities are shrinking, my eagerness to learn is unchanged. But since I found out that you spoke about me when I was away (i.e. from Lyons), absent though I am, I have taken care to respond.

They say that you criticised me because I pronounced 'potítur' with a lengthened medial syllable, and evidently did not follow Vergil in this word, who treated the syllable as short, saying, 'vi pótitur'.[5] But the liberty that we fairly frequently find that Vergil has taken is permissible because of the constraints imposed by verse: it is convenient for the law of metre, if it needs, disregarding barbarism to invert the natural quantity of syllables in certain specific places, ignoring the rules of grammar. Take 'Nos erimus regno indécores', or 'férvere Leucaten', or 'Namque ut supremam falsa inter gaudia noctem/egérimus, nosti.' No cultured person would claim that any of these three words, namely 'fervêre', 'egerîmus' and 'indecôres', should be pronounced with a shortened syllable, but would urge that they be employed

---

1 *Ep*. 57. See *Epp*. 67, 68, and 73 for less firmly defined invitations. The homilies make the point even more clearly. Cf. the venues of *Hom*. 19, 20, 21, 22/3, 24 (Perrat and Audin, 'Alcimi Ecdicii Aviti Viennensis Episcopi Homilia', pp. 433–51).

2 See *Ep*. 59 and *Ep*. 69.

3 On such sermons, see *Hom*. 19, 20, 21, 22/3, 24. Also Wood, 'The Audience of Architecture', pp. 74–79.

4 Vergil, *Buc*. 9.51. Of course Avitus was in his last years at the time this letter was written: Viventiolus was appointed bishop in ca. 513/14; Avitus died in February 518.

5 Vergil, *Aen*. 3.56. Servius *ad loc*. explains that *potior* mixes forms of the third and of the fourth conjugation. For other ancient grammarians' discussions of the question see Probus, *Instituta Artium GL* 4.182.32 and Priscian, *GL* 2.502.16.

with the penultimate syllables long, as they ought to be by nature. Vergil therefore takes advantage of the poetic licence I mentioned above and shortens the middle syllable and dares to write 'pótitur'.

Let us leave aside poetic licence and discuss the word according to the rules of grammar. Since the form 'potîris' has a long medial syllable, it shows that in the third person, i.e. 'potîtur', it is likewise long, since we say 'sortior, sortîris, sortîtur'. Thus too in the perfect tense the first, second and third persons are 'potîtus sum, es, est'. Thus too in the imperative mood in the present tense in the second person we say 'potîre' just as we say 'sortîre'. Likewise in the optative mood in the present and imperfect tenses[1] in all of the three persons the syllable is long: 'utinam potîrer, potîreris, potîretur'. If you were to make the third person 'potîtur' short, you would be compelled to do the same in the second person with the result that you would say 'pótiris'. Proper Latinity in every usage and example forbids this.

So this is the word attacked by you, the word about which I dare to exchange a reckoning! But, now, giving you a polite greeting in good spirits I earnestly pray, just as I in the spirit of friendship set down freely what seemed to me to be correct, that you too in turn lay out for me in your reply the rationale I ought to follow. Please leave the authoritative example of Vergil out of this: because we cannot emulate the dignity of his verse, we should not follow him in daring to use a barbarism, even though the very same Vergil also wrote 'potîtus' or 'potîti' with the syllable lengthened as in 'auroque potîti'.[2] Or if you choose to teach someone who is making a serious inquiry with a précis[3] of someone-or-other's evidence, I hope that you will do your research thoroughly and accurately in the ancient orators instead (whom you are quite right to hand on to your students), and, once you have discovered something, that you will tell us. If this is not to be found in a grammatical treatise or in a rhetorical one, please allow our common children[4] – as far as I am concerned, at the moment I would prefer you to be the *first* rather than the *only* improver of their minds! – to be content with this error alone.[5] Let them nonetheless in their youth drink

---

1 The forms given are imperfect subjunctives. Avitus uses the odd expression 'optatives in the present and imperfect tenses' because his example with *utinam* illustrates a contrafactual wish in *present* time, but employs the imperfect subjunctive.

2 *Aen*. 6.624.

3 Probably not 'profit' here *pace* Goelzer, p. 568.

4 Avitus and Viventiolus share a sermon-audience, see above p. 271.

5 The nature of the error is unclear.

< ... >[1] from that rich fount of flowing learning no less than literature, for one ought to **att**ract a friend through one's efforts rather than **det**ract from his reputation, and it befits an orator to **orate** rather than to **inculpate**.[2]

Epistula 59

Avitus the bishop to Viventiolus the bishop [of Lyons][3] *{87.10 Peiper}*

My joy in the sacred feast that we have passed pleasantly thanks to your intercession has been increased by the kind letter that you sent. And for this reason it has made us all the more happy – that unity in joy embraces a Church that in all places is one.[4] May Christ grant that, just as this year, you have fulfilled our wishes by [giving us your] glad tidings, so in the time to come you may grant a longed-for visit to the church at Vienne.

Epistula 67

Avitus the bishop to Viventiolus the bishop [of Lyons] {89.1 Peiper}

Were it not that our common prayers were often impeded by the obstacle of [our] sins, I [would have] wanted to respond to the customary command of charity by duly complying. But since it would have been a matter of double profit[5] to meet you and be present at the feast, you see that it is purely my loss that I am unable to do as you request. For here with us at any moment

---

1 An object seems to be missing. The students learn something in addition to letters: 'manners' or 'good behaviour', e.g. *prudentiam*? A more theological word is possible if the word *doctrina* is taken to have religious overtones. A religious reading would further strengthen the identification of this Viventiolus with the bishop of Lyon.

2 I.e. to use eloquence rather than insult.

3 Cf. also *Epp.* 19, 67–69, 73, and possibly 57.

4 This would appear to refer to the end of some schism. Identifying the one in question is, however, difficult, since Viventiolus was not appointed until ca. 513/14, while Avitus himself died, apparently, on 5 February 518. Thus Viventiolus did not become bishop until after the end of the Laurentian schism, while Avitus died before the accession of Justin and the ending of the Acacian schism. The reference might be yet another indication that Avitus, being badly informed about the negotiations between Pope Hormisdas and the emperor Anastasius, thought that the Acacian schism was over (cf. *Ep.* 9), or it might refer to the ending of an Arian church in Burgundy.

5 *Compendium* here, exceptionally, means 'profit'. See Goelzer, p. 568, although he is wrong in ascribing this meaning to the word at *Ep.* 57, p. 86.31. Avitus has presumably used it here because it enables him to make a word-play with *dispendium* 'loss'.

we are expecting the arrival of dignitaries[1] with the result that, unless I take special care to be present when they come, even though it would simply be a matter of my having left town, I would be blamed by those who are accustomed to blame me for even the slightest infraction, and my departure would be seen not just as negligent, but as contumacious and provocative.[2] For this reason, look at the circumstances that constrain us both, and be kind, and forgive the fact that I cannot comply, and pray that we may be able to satisfy our longings [for one another] if not for long periods, at least from time to time.

Epistula 68: Introduction

This letter is almost certainly ironic in tone. Even though Avitus and Viventiolus are on close terms with one another (see *Epp.* 19, 57, as well as 59, 67, 69), Viventiolus here overdoes the honorifics, 'Your Deliberation', 'Your Apostleship' (*deliberatio vestra, apostolatus vester*)[3] and compares Avitus' decision to come to Lyons to that of Divine Benignity responding to the petitions of its worshippers. Excessive vocabulary is combined with excessive concision of form to achieve a dry effect.

Viventiolus the bishop [of Lyons] to Avitus {89.11 Peiper}

May Your Deliberation[4] be tempered, like that of the Divine Benignity, by the prayers of its worshippers with the result that a visit from Your Apostleship may grace its beloved little congregation[5] at the time of the feast of Saint Justus.[6]

Epistula 69: Introduction

A testy and terse communication, almost certainly in dialogue with the previous one.[7] The openings of the two are very similar (*Ad similitudinem **divinae** benignitatis*

---

1 *Potestatum*, i.e. Gundobad and Sigismund? See also *Ep.* 27, p. 57.27.

2 For equivalent difficulties in leaving Vienne see *Ep.* 50.

3 Note the absence of honorifics in *Ep.* 67.

4 This may be an ironic honorific implying that Avitus has been vacillating.

5 The diminutive *plebecula* is probably affectionate. Cf. *Ep.* 50, p. 79.30. Viventiolus refers to his own congregation at Lyons.

6 There are four feasts of Justus in the Hieronymian Martyrology, 4 August, 2 September, 14 October and 21 October: Duchesne, *Fastes épiscopaux*, vol. 2, p. 162. For the church of St Justus in Lyon, see Sid. *Ep.* 5.17. For the excavation of the site, see J.-F. Reynaud, *Lyon aux premier temps chrétiens, Guides archeologiques de la France* (Paris, 1986), pp. 54–76.

7 See Wagner, 'A Chapter in Byzantine Epistolography', p. 150 on abrupt beginnings to letters of rebuke. A parallel can be found in Sid. Ap. *Ep.* 4.19 to Florentius.

..., and *Ad firmitatem promissionis **divinae** ...*): Avitus sarcastically compares Viventiolus' promise to a divine one. Viventiolus has reneged on something he had agreed to do, and Avitus ironises at his expense and takes him to task: Viventiolus' 'yea' has not been 'yea' (Mt. 5.37). The use of irony might be compared to *Ep*. 57. Avitus may have invited Viventiolus to Vienne. Viventiolus may firmly have agreed to visit (perhaps even as a guest-preacher?) – and then, equally firmly, reneged, prompting Avitus to fire back this letter. *Ep*. 68 may well be a mock-respectful response to *Ep*. 69.

Avitus the bishop to Viventiolus the bishop [of Lyons] {89.15 Peiper}

Let it have [all the] reliability of a divine promise that you previously conceded, 'yes, yes!' what you subsequently repeated as 'no, no!' For if the nature [of the matter][1] is properly considered in relationship to what we are doing now,[2] even though at that time it ought not to have been broken, it would be especially appropriate now that the agreement between us be fulfilled.

Epistula 73

Avitus the bishop to Viventiolus, bishop [of Lyons] {90.18 Peiper}

You have kept to your usual sweet custom, indeed to tell the truth, you have increased it. You have refreshed our worry about you by telling us that you are thriving. You have visited our feast by seeking to find out about us what you wanted.[3] Among these many foods for the spirit, you, who had fed the church with spiritual delicacies, have adorned our table with ones for the body too![4] For this reason I am unequal to the task of thanking you, and I ask divine mercy for my prayers; may the charity that you so zealously exhibit be a reward for you, a joy for me, and an example to everyone else!

---

1 Taking *qualitas*, unqualified as the subject.
2 Rendering *occupatione praesentium* whose meaning still remains unclear.
3 I.e. 'by inquiring about what you wanted to know about us'.
4 For a similar topos, see above *Ep*. 66.

13. MAXIMUS OF GENEVA'S TABLE

Contents

Epistula 66 Avitus to Maximus, bishop of Geneva: an enthusiastic thank-you for a gift of food on the occasion of a feast.

Epistula 74 Avitus to Maximus, bishop of Geneva: a humorous letter thanking Maximus for a gift of food.

Epistula 86 Leonianus the Archdeacon to Sapaudus, *vir spectabilis*: a joke letter. Avitus writes *sub persona Leoniani* to tease Sapaudus about some recent feasting he has indulged in.

Epistula 66: Introduction

Not the standard formulaic festal letter. Note the lively tricola in asyndeton and the enthusiastic, informal, indeed jocular tone. Maximus kept a good table, and was a man with whom a fellow bishop could let down his hair and play the fool once in a while on the right occasion. See *Epp.* 74 and 86 for further evidence to this effect.

Avitus the bishop to Maximus the bishop [of Geneva]

The delicacies[1] you sent are excellent and worthy of the highest praise – the quantity, the timeliness, the respect! But all the same they do not equal your affection, piety, kind solicitude. They show that it was not Your Worthiness[2] that was lacking to us, but *you*. The feast has now ended happily thanks to the success of your good wishes. At it (*sc.* the feast)[3] food for the body was as much in evidence as food for the soul – contrary to habit – was lacking.[4] If God in the future grants me a reprieve,[5] just as he now deigns to transmit it (*sc.* food for the body) through you, so may he then [in the future] allow me to lay it before you!

---

1 Here *deliciae* refers to food.

2 *Dignatio vestra*. This is almost a joke. Avitus uses an honorific that should properly be rendered 'Your Condescension'. *Dignatio* means 'condescension' or 'deigning' in a positive sense.

3 *Sc. epulae*.

4 For a similar topos, see below *Ep.* 73.

5 *Sc. commeatus*. Since Maximus was only appointed to the bishopric of Geneva in 513 (Greg. Tur. *LVP* 8.1) Avitus was indeed in the last years of his life.

Epistula 74: Introduction

Maximus has sent Avitus some gifts of food via a messenger called Leonianus.[1] The latter is presumably to be identified with the 'author' of *Ep.* 86. The point of the letter seems to be 1) that Leonianus was a greedy person, who had been tempted to taste what he carried, and 2) Avitus could not eat what had been sent, perhaps because it was Lent. This seems to be the implication of 'hungering' (*esuriens*) and 'was not able to devour, however much he lusted after it' (*vorare non potuit concupiscens*) at p. 91.10 and the force of the comparison between Avitus and the prophet Elijah in the desert. It would appear that the present from Maximus consisted of fish and chilled wine, and that it may have been accompanied by instructions about giving Leonianus some of the latter to drink in return for his pains. The letter may shed some light on Gallic Lenten observances.[2]

Avitus the bishop to Maximus the bishop [of Geneva] {91.1 Peiper}

As far as Hell and the End are concerned, there's still some strength in my poor little body.[3] But I am worried that I know nothing about my lord, your son,[4] or the conclusion of this discussion, because I was not in the right place to find out. Since I have been busy at the monasteries at Grigny,[5] I have been away from my house in the city for a while.[6] Nonetheless the tasty treats that

1 See *Ep.* 66 for another occasion on which Maximus sent *deliciae*.

2 See Shanzer, 'Bishops, Letters'.

3 Almost certainly a private joke, as the diminutives in *aliquantulis* and *corpusculi* (used here of a still-living body) seem to indicate. Avitus is responding to a jocular inquiry about his health. Presumably, unlike Jerome *Ep.* 22.30 'the life-giving heat of my spirit was palpitating, now that my whole body was growing cold, in my poor breast that was only lukewarm' (*vitalis animae calor toto frigente iam corpore in solo tam tepente pectusculo palpitabat*). Lenten fasting had not yet brought him to death's door.

4 This must be a reference to Sigismund, whose association with Geneva during Gundobad's reign is well attested: Maximus' association with Sigismund is further attested in *Hom.* 20.

5 See Sidonius *Ep.* 7.17.3: *secundum statuta Lirinensium patrum vel Grinincensium*, and *Gallia Christiana* 16.147. The monasteries of Grigny, apparently a confederation of communities of monks and nuns, seem to have been of considerable importance in the 5th century. Seemingly founded by a bishop of Vienne, possibly to guard the relics of St Ferreolus and the head of St Julian, the principal buildings became unsafe in the days of Mamertus, who had the relics translated: *Vita Clari* 2, Sidonius *Ep.* 7.17.3, Greg. Tur. *LVJ* 2. The monasteries, however, still continued as an important monastic centre into the 6th century. They provided the first abbot of Agaune, in 515, as well as one of the *turmae* of the new foundation: *Vita Clari* 2: *Vita Abbatum Acaunensium absque epitaphiis* 1.4.

6 This implies that Avitus would normally have resided in the city, despite the fact that in *Ep.* 96 Heraclius seems to criticise Avitus as preferring to live in the country.

you sent to me with your usual respect, found me even though I was on the road and still fairly far from the city. Your servant Leonianus[1] – how surprised I am! – complained a great deal, but took very little, and handed them over to me, his stomach greedy, but empty! You would have thought that your gifts, <carried>[2] in a crow's tenacious beak, were being held out by tiny fingers to feed Elijah.[3] The more effectively to excite my justifiable displeasure at you, the one hungering[4] sent what the one who lusted after it[5] could not gobble down. I'd now like to know what good it does, if you are keen on the greed of your special servant, since a desirable excuse to be absent snatches me away from him, and prevents him from grabbing from my mouth or hands[6] the food given by you and God.[7] As far as cold wine[8] is concerned, because you have asked me to, I both surrender my share and multiply his. Let him use whole libation-saucers instead of cups; let him wear down with his lips wide dishes for him to surround with a multitude of labels instead of garlands.[9] For I too shall see to it, and I know that he wants

1 The Leonianus *archidiaconus* who is Avitus' mouthpiece in *Ep*. 86.

2 It is very awkward that both *parvulis unguibus* and *rostro* must be construed with *exhiberi*. A participle is probably missing after *rostro*, e.g. *devectas*.

3 Avitus alludes to the miraculous feeding of 3 Kgs 17.6.

4 Maximus presumably: he is starving because it is Lent.

5 Avitus, also hungry because it is Lent.

6 L's *animus* makes no sense. S's *manibus* provides a natural pairing.

7 Since Avitus is away from his headquarters, he does not have the task of putting up and feeding the insatiable Leonianus.

8 *Recentes*: this appears to be an allusion to wine. Goelzer, p. 559, translates 'rasades de vin à la glace' without explanation. Romans drank *mustum recens* (young wine, see Columella 12.29, *mustum ut semper dulce tamquam recens permaneat sic facito*), but they also drank chilled wine called *vinum recentatum* and attested in the medical writings of Alexander of Tralles 8.2 and 12.1 (ed. Theodor Puschmann, Vienna, 1879), vol. II, pp. 369 and 513) λαμβανέτωσαν ἢ ῥοσάτου ἢ ἀψινθάτου ψυχρίζοντες ὡσαύτως καθάπερ εἰώθασι ποιεῖν οἱ Ῥωμαῖοι τὸ καλούμενον ῥαικεντάτον. There is still a problem with the word, because it is unclear why it is a feminine in Avitus. See p. 91.16 *ad multiplicandas recentes*. Goelzer, p. 649, does not explain what feminine word is to be understood with it.

9 *Circulis* is very odd. Even *TLL s.v.* 'circulus' 1111.50–51 has its doubts about this passage, and Goelzer, p. 601, is unilluminating. Three other texts mention *circuli* in connection with wine, feasting or cups. The reading *circulis* has been questioned at Pliny *HN* 14.2.7.1 *[sc. vinum] circa Alpes ligneis vasis condere circulisque cingere atque etiam hieme gelida ignibus rigorem arcent,* but there may be an allusion to some sort of hoops used to cover wine in barrels and protect it from cold. At Petronius 60 (*ecce autem diductis lacunaribus subito circulus ingens de cupa videlicet grandi excussus demittitur, cuius per totum orbem coronae aureae cum alabastris unguenti pendebant*) the *circulus* seems to be a large round object from which garlands and vials of ointment are hung. The *Leges Visigothorum* (8.3.8 *si quis aliquem*

[me to], that, when I will have excavated[1] something similar[2] from your kind gift in order to multiply[3] glasses of chilled wine for a burning gullet,[4] even if no measure is envisioned for cups, at least it may be enforced for fish.

Epistula 86: Introduction

This letter is clearly a joke, a mock festal letter. But whose? The style and lumbering witticisms are all too familiar, and L's annotation, *dictata ab Avito episcopo*, gives the game away. Avitus impersonates Leonianus, deacon of bishop Maximus of Geneva, the 'servant' (*servus*) mentioned in *Ep*. 74 as the greedy but respectful carrier of edible delights for Avitus.[5] Greed and food dominate both letters.

But who is the addressee 'Sapaudus'? The name is attested, but this individual is hardly to be identified with the rhetor addressed by Sidonius (*Ep*. 5.10) and Claudianus Mamertus (*Ep*. 2)![6] Another line of thought is possible. If Leonianus is an

---

conprehenderit, dum de silva sua cum vehiculo vadit et circulos ad cupas aut quecumque ligna sine domini permissionem asportare presumat, et boves et vehiculum aliene silve presumtor amittat, et que dominus cum fure aut violento conprehenderit, indubitanter obtineat) are closer to Avitus' world, and here *circuli* seem to be cut round sections of wood that can be stolen to be made into wooden drinking-cups. The trouble is that what one would expect here is the opposite of what Avitus' text offers: it should say that Leonianus can use whole *circuli* of wood and wear them down with his lips through use in place of *fialae*. But this would require radical surgery, and a text reading *atterat labris circulos* (rounds of wood), *quos circumdet pittaciorum densitate pro fialis*. A different approach might entail emending *circulis* to *corollis*, 'garlands' (*trispondaicus* for *tardus*). In sympotic contexts Greeks and Romans crowned their cups with garlands. (See *RE* s.v. 'Kranz' 1602 with a frustrating false reference to Athenaeus 10.437e.) Leonianus, who by that time will have made his way through innumerable *amphorae* of wine, is being jocularly asked to string their labels (emblems of the 'empties' or 'dead men') 'instead of garlands' around his oversized *fiala*. For *pittacia* on wine-jars, see Petronius 34.

1 Presumably both the fish and chilled wine must have been packed deep in ice and sawdust for transport, and would require excavation.

2 I.e. more wine.

3 There may be a suggestion of the multiplication of the loaves and fishes in Mt. 14.17–20; Mk 6.38–44. Avitus employed the conceit in *Ep*. 27.

4 For a similar expression, see *Ep*. 86, p. 95.26 *accensis faucibus gula*.

5 Despite this greed it appears that Leonianus has been promoted to the level of archdeacon between the two letters, a point made by M. Besson, 'Maxime de Genève', *Anzeiger für schweizerische Geschichte* 9 (1904), pp. 287–99.

6 See Goelzer, p. 5, for a lengthy footnote that makes a valiant attempt to identity 'Sapaudus' with Sapaudus the rhetorician of Vienne addressed by Sidonius in *Ep*. 5.10.3. But Goelzer acknowledges that Sapaudus died in 474 and that the dating is therefore impossible. Both Sapaudus and Leonianus belong to the time of Maximus of Geneva (i.e. post 511). But it is still possible that Avitus used Sapaudus as a soubriquet for a highly rhetorical friend to whom to send this highly rhetorical letter.

adopted *persona* of the writer Sapaudus might, likewise, be a *persona* of the recipient. The letter mentions a royal feast, so the recipient might be at the court of Gundobad or Sigismund. Since Sigismund sometimes held his court at Geneva, and since Maximus who was bishop of Geneva is the recipient of Avitus' other letter about Leonianus, Sapaudus could perhaps be a pseudonym for Maximus.[1] The name would be appropriate in that Sapaudia is the region between Geneva and Neufchâtel.[2] The letter would then be a comic version of Avitus' standard complaints about not seeing a king during the festal period, but with a moral overlay, dealing with greed. Against identifying 'Sapaudus' with Maximus: 'Sapaudus' is clearly expected to write a verse-panegyric on the feast and is also someone who is expected to be vain about his long hair, a feature that suggests a barbarian rather than a Roman.

Sections of the letter bear a close relationship to Avitus' father-in-letters, Sidonius' *Ep*. 3.13.3ff. a not dissimilar literary exercise and grotesque description of a parasite, or *sector epularum*, called 'Gnatho', whom Sidonius asks his son Apollinaris to avoid. His misbehaviour at the table receives special attention: particularly significant are the phrases 'he starves as often as he is not invited' (*ieiunat, quotiens non vocatur*) (cf. the ultimate fate of Leonianus) and 3.13.4, 'when he has reclined, if there is a delay, he is immediately driven to grab, if he is swiftly satisfied, he is driven to tears, if he is thirsty to complaints, and if he is drunk, to vomitings' (*cum discubuerit, fertur actutum, si tarde comedat, in rapinas; si cito saturetur, in lacrimas; si sitiat, in querelas; si inebrietur, in vomicas*)[3] which is deliberately echoed by Avitus at p. 95.27ff.: 'This is how it came about that by drinking food and by chewing cups, in thirsting after the first part of the meal and complaining, in swooping down and in gobbling the middle part, and, finally stuffed, <in vomiting > with tears the last part ...(*Sicque factum est, ut bibendo cibos, pocula ruminando, primam prandii partem esuriens[4] querelis, medietatem comedens rapinis, ultimam satur <vomitans> lacrimis*). Sidonius' text can be used to emend Avitus and to fill a lacuna. Sidonius described how Gnatho grabbed, if the meal was delayed, wept, if he felt full too soon, complained, if he was thirsty, and vomited, if he was drunk.[5] His greed is organised into two groups of two sorts of loutish behaviour. Avitus takes things a step further in describing surreal greed. Sapaudus is accused paradoxically of gulping (drinking) his

---

1 Maximus sent food to Avitus on at least two occasions, see *Epp*. 66 and 74.

2 The classic discussion of Sapaudia is by Duparc, 'La Sapaudia'. The most recent, and fullest, is by Favrod, *Histoire politique*, pp. 100–17.

3 Certainly corrupt. Read *vomitus*. Vomitings, not pustules, are the natural result of inebriation. Confusion of c/t and a/u are easy in pre-Caroline script.

4 One should emend this to *sitiens* to keep it in line with Sidonius, *si sitiat in querelis*. *Esuriens* is a *lectio facilior*.

5 Sidonius describes the same two poles at the respectable table of Theodoric II: (*Ep*. 1.2.6) *facilius est ut accuset sitis, quam recuset ebrietas*.

food and chewing his cups. Avitus introduces tripartition of dissatisfaction: hungering,[1] grabbing and stuffing oneself, and vomiting. He also merges the eating and the drinking.

The scenario: A king (presumably Sigismund)[2] had invited 'Leonianus'-Avitus to a feast at a time when he was unable to attend. 'Sapaudus', however, was present, and sent 'Leonianus' a description. 'Leonianus' was miffed and wrote back to say that Sapaudus can safely describe what he ate, now that he has gobbled it all up, and is not in any danger of having to give any to Leonianus. Sapaudus, he claimed, was rubbing it in to make him feel bad. Leonianus claims that no one is rightly happy whether he feast or fast. Even in feasting, Sapaudus, eager to eat a peacock, is frustrated by the fact that it is served in a 'chemise' of mincemeat, and his insatiable throat has to wait to get its share until it has been carved. The meal continues as an exercise in frustration: at first Sapaudus is thirsty, then he is greedy, finally he vomits. Leonianus' absence did not help either Leonianus or Sapaudus. Whatever Sapaudus left, however little it was, was enough for everyone. Leonianus goes on to explain that *he* is eating very badly, so badly that he cannot even remember what oysters are like. Even his intake of wine is controlled, and he is using boarding-school techniques to dispose of what he does not want to drink. Presumably the real Leonianus is *chez* Avitus at the episcopal vegetarian table. He would like to be Stoic about it, and he asks Sapaudus to leave him alone. But he wants another invitation to a feast – this time when Sapaudus *cannot* attend.

The letter is a distant cousin both of Roman comedy (the excesses of the parasite) and of satirical texts that juxtapose the fishy and carnivorous excess of the table of the gourmand with the chaste (and dull) vegetables of the virtuous poor man or rustic, e.g. Horace, *S.* 2.2; 2.6; 2.8; Libanius, *Decl.* 28, 'the disappointed parasite', provides an excellent fourth-century parallel. In this case the luxury of Sigismund's court is contrasted with the Lenten fare of the bishop of Vienne's palace. It is perhaps worth recalling that one of the first literary occurences of the *Burgundio* describes him to us as *esculentus*, 'greedy'. See Sid. *C.* 12.6, 'what the greedy Burgundian sings who smears his hair with rancid butter' (*quod Burgundio cantat esculentus/ infundens acido comam butyro*). Sidonius tells us that Chilperic praised bishop Patiens' suppers, his queen the bishop's fasts.[3]

For other 'fish letters', see *Epp.* 72 to Apollinaris and 74 to Maximus; for another 'fastal' letter, *Ep.* 83.

---

1 Or, more probably, thirsting, see above, p. 280 n. 4.

2 The king is almost certainly Sigismund, given that Leonianus was sent by Maximus from Geneva.

3 Sid. *Ep.* 6.12.3, *ut constet indesinenter regem praesentem prandia tua, reginam laudare ieiunia.*

Leonianus the archdeacon to Sapaudus, vir spectabilis *{95.16 Peiper}*

Even though you have described in mouthwatering detail the ceremonial grandeur[1] of the prince's table, shining[2] with the delights of land and sea, it is customary nonetheless that love be declared †without hesitation.†[3] After you have sent the material[4] that was given to you on its way, not in verses,[5] but with your teeth, you can safely recite it! For in one meal one stomach took in what the backs of two mules could barely carry.[6] Paying no attention to your uncombed hair,[7] you combed[8] your gut, stuffed solid with an excess of sea-combs.[9] Even though it might seem clear that you exaggerated in order to make me feel bad, I persist in saying that no one who is like us,[10] whether he feast or whether he fast, can rightly be called happy.[11] Let's start talking about the first course that you detailed. You thought that it was a minor type of punishment that was imposed on you, namely that a peacock,

---

1 *Pompa.* See E. Gowers, *The Loaded Table: Representations of Food in Roman Literature* (Oxford, 1993), p. 39, for the use of *pompa* in banqueting contexts.

2 Cf. Horace, *S.* 2.2.4, *mensasque nitentes* for a similar image.

3 L's *in cuncta* makes no sense. S's *incunctanter tamen,* 'without holding back' is only marginally better, but, as Gregory Hays pointed out, what one really wants here is something like, 'It is customary to declare one's love with some more tangible token of appreciation', i.e. a present, rather than an envy-creating description of a banquet. It seems best to obelise *in cuncta.* Hays' suggested supplement is in keeping with the literary parody involved. This letter inverts the usual type in which thanks are tendered for gifts of food or for invitations. See *Ep.* 66 to Maximus for a straight exercise of this type.

4 A double-entendre: *materia* means 'subject- matter' as well as 'physical material'.

5 A hint that a poem or panegyric was expected? Sapaudus may have been a court poet, or else this may be an allusion to parasitic behaviour such as Sid. *Ep.* 3.13.3, *laudabilem proferens non de bene vivente sed de bene pascente sententiam.*

6 Food too heavy for one person to carry features in Fortunatus *C.* 11.9.7: *portitor ad tantas missus non sufficit unus.* This goes a step further.

7 A cardinal sin for the well-groomed barbarian. See Amm. Marc. 27.2.2 for barbarian hair-dying and drinking. J. Matthews, *The Roman Empire of Ammianus Marcellinus* (London, 1989), p. 322, esp. n. 26, mentions barbarian interest in, and production of bone and antler combs. See also J. Engemann and C. B. Rüger, eds, *Spätantike und frühes Mittelalter* (Bonn, 1991), p. 141, n. 86 B, for a Frank combing his hair.

8 The perfect forms of *pecto* are extremely rare. Note how Sidonius too (*C.* 12.6) mentions the Burgundian's unusual hair-care routines in connection with their eating habits. For barbarian personal vanity, see the description of Sigismer in Sidonius, *Ep.* 4.20.2.

9 The scallop is called 'comb' in Latin. A similar pun appears in Apuleius, *Apol.* 34.6: *si dicas marinum pectinem comendo capillum quaesitum.*

10 I.e. a parasite.

11 A parody of a philosophical gnome.

wrapped in mincemeat,[1] with its devourable shield held off[2] your appetite that salivated after what was inside, and your greed, as it returned with throat aflame,[3] was kept waiting for a little while at the whim of a skilled carver.[4] This is how it came about that by drinking food and by chewing cups, in thirsting[5] after the first part of the meal and complaining, in swooping down and in gobbling the middle part, and, finally stuffed, <in vomiting >[6] with tears the last part, < . . > †by occupation† I would not say that my absence was of any advantage to you.[7] Whatever pitiful amount you left was enough even for all of us. Although you have revelled in the great joy of the feast and were so slow to be sated, since *you* can scarcely prove that you are happy, I venture to ask what you think about poor *me*, who am neither allowed near the abundance of the royal table nor filled by the frugality of the ecclesiastical one? Under the pretext that it is an honour, I am handed over into custody. As if I had been called to a first-rate meal,[8] I am kept from a better one,[9] I am forced to lie still so that I not be able to flee. I am filled with greens and inflated by turnips.[10] I have plenty of vegetables – those the earth produces, not the sea![11] In these [circumstances] I cannot even remember

---

1 A tour-de-force dish. Pliny, *HN* 1.10.23, mentions stuffed peacock. For *isicia de pavo*, see Apicius 2.2.6: *isicia de pavo primum locum habent ita si fricta fuerint, ut callum vincant.*

2 Lit. 'peacock enclosed in mincemeat, shut out an appetite'. Avitus puns on *conclusus* and *excludo*. There is a further possibility that Lenten observance is at issue. Meat is out of the question, but fowl would be acceptable. For more on this see Shanzer, 'Bishops, Letters', p. 231.

3 *Accensis faucibus gula* echoes *gula calenti* in *Ep.* 74. p. 91.16.

4 Cf. the antics of Carpus described in Petronius' *Satiricon* 38.

5 Reading *sitiens*, see above p. 280 n. 4.

6 Given the parallel tricolon in the sentence, there may be is another lacuna *before lacrimis*, which contained a missing trisyllabic proparoxytone participle, something like *vomitans* that would yield a *cursus tardus*.

7 Punctuating with a period after *defui*. Note the word-play on *profuisse* and *defuisse*.

8 *Primam sc. mensam*? Taking *primam* in a somewhat colloquial sense as 'ace', 'super', 'excellent', as the contrast with *meliore* seems to demand.

9 I.e. Sigismund's.

10 French turnips, *napi*, see Martial 13.20.

11 Presumably an allusion to some sort of fish with a 'vegetable' nickname (cf. English 'sea-cucumber', 'sea-tomato'.). Many fish had names derived from their alleged resemblances to terrestrial creatures, see Isidore, *Etym.* 12.6.4 *piscium vero … nomina instituti sunt … ex similitudine terrestrium animalium.* Polemius Silvius, *Laterculus* p. 544.6 (ed. Mommsen, *Chron. Min.* 1, *MGH AA* 5.1) lists the *cucumis* under 'natancium'. *Legumina marina* appear as a gift sent by Ruricius (*Ep.* 2.44).

what certain oysters of blessed memory[1] were like once upon a time! If some small concession is set out, a minute vessel, half-full of pallid wine, even here measure[2] and rule must be obeyed. That is enough about food: [even] greater punishment is entailed in getting hold of chilled wine. When I ask for young wine, I either suffer [wine as bitter as] medicines,[3] or am falsely accused of having stolen something.[4] By dint of being grossly importunate[5] I succeed in getting three lukewarm pipkins.[6] The very bowls that I break by contriving that they fall [to the ground] are shrinking as they are repaired daily.[7] Therefore at least stop adding insult to the injury of those who are suffering: for, since what each of us has drawn as his lot *is* his daily fate, I will eventually be able to forget my customary state of domestic misery[8] – provided our master order me to attend his feast at a time when *you* cannot![9]

---

1 Avitus jocularly employs the sepulchral topos, *bonae memoriae*. See F. Grossi Gondi, *Trattato di Epigrafia Christiana* (Rome, 1920), p. 172.

2 Cf. *Ep.* 74 p. 91.17, *si non excogitatur modus in calicibus*.

3 Something is clearly wrong with *medicina*, which 1) does not scan and 2) would have to be an ablative. The point seems to be that he asks for *mustum*, sweet wine, and gets something he does not want. Stuart Koonce suggested *medicamina*, a change that produces a good *cursus tardus*. One could compare Lucretius 4.11–16 where honey is put by doctors on cups of wormwood to make the bitter medicine palatable to children. Here Leonianus asks for sweet wine, and suffers bitter medicinal draughts. Avitus used *medicamen* in *Hom.* 20, p. 133.26.

4 I.e. because he has asked for too much. For this personal and passive use of *confingor*, see Avitus, *CCL* 6.536–37 of Joseph: *crimine falso/confictus voluisse nefas, quod triste refugit*.

5 Taking S's *importunitate*.

6 *Summa importunitate perago, ut tres †recentes aliis plus† praesumam*. The obelised portion of this sentence is gibberish. It is clear that Leonianus is making some point about putting maximum effort into getting some insignificant quantity of (probably poor) wine. Tomlin conjectures *exempli gratia, tepentes ampullas*, 'three lukewarm pipkins'. The fact that the wine is lukewarm, rather than chilled (like *vinum recentatum*), makes it unpleasant.

7 Leonianus is said to have used *paterae* instead of cups for drinking. See *Ep.* 74, *utatur paterarum capacitate pro cupis*. Here he seems to be trying to get out of having to drink the poor wine by dropping his *patera*. Since it is wide, as its edges break, its capacity is lessened.

8 To be hungry and not to have found food is the superlative degree of misery, as we are told by a Plautine parasite. See *Captivi* 461–63: Erg. *Miser homost, qui ipsus sibi quod edit quaerit et id aegre invenit/Sed illest miserior, qui et aegre quaerit et nihil invenit./Ille miserrumus est, qui, quom esse cupidust, quod edit non habet.*

9 S has the correct reading: *ut te deesse contingat*. The text is guaranteed by a very similar word-play on *sum*-compounds at p. 96.1, *profuisse quod defui*.

PASTORAL LETTERS TO GALLIC BISHOPS

14. SEXUAL CRIMES AND MISDEMEANOURS

Contents

Epistula 16: Introduction

This letter is the first of a group dealing with a case of incestuous adultery. Like two other of the letters to Victorius (*Epp.* 7 and 75) this is concerned with matters of canon law. Victorius seems to have been unusually punctilious in consulting his metropolitan, which may suggest that the letters to and from him date to the first years of his episcopate. Peiper gives a date of 516–17 for *Epp.* 16–18. There is, however, no firm means for dating the letters; although Victorius is attested as bishop of Grenoble at the Councils of Epaon in 517 and Lyons 518/23[1] we have no other indication of the duration of his episcopate. The only reason for dating *Epp.* 16–18 to 516–17 is that Avitus' rulings in *Epp.* 17–18, like that in *Ep.* 7,[2] are closely linked to the canons of Epaon, which suggests a date in the period between Sigismund's accession in 516 and the meeting of the council in 517.[3]

In *Ep.* 16 Victorius appeals to Avitus over the case of a man who had married his dead wife's sister.[4] Although the marriage was long-standing, it had only recently

---

1 Duchesne, *Fastes épiscopaux*, vol. 1, p. 231.

2 For the parallel to *Ep.* 7, Epaon, can. 33.

3 For the rulings on penance: Epaon, cans. 23, 28, 29, 30, 31, 36.

4 This discussion is taken from Wood, 'Incest, Law and the Bible'. See also P. Mikat, 'Die Inzestverbote des Konzils von Epaon. Ein Beitrag zur Geschichte des fränkischen Eherechts', in *Rechtsbewahrung und Rechtsentwicklung: Festschrift für H. Lange* (Munich, 1970), pp. 64–84, reprinted in *idem, Religionsrechtliche Schriften* (Berlin, 1974), pp. 869–88; and *idem, Die Inzestgesetzgebung der merowingisch-fränkischen Konzilien (511–626/7)*, Rechts- und Staats-

become the subject of attention, forcing the bishop to act. Although he suspected that marriage to the sister of one's wife was as heinous as marriage to the widow of one's brother, Victorius did not know whether to separate the couple and enforce penance, and therefore wrote to his superior. Avitus replied (*Ep.* 17) that Victorius was right to see the marriage as wrong, and advised that the sinners be excommunicated until they had separated: thereafter they should be given a public penance, before being received back into the church. In *Ep.* 18 it becomes apparent that the man, now named as Vincomalus, whose unlawful marriage is revealed as having lasted for thirty years, had refused to give up his incestuous wife. Indeed he took his case to Avitus in Vienne, who attempted to persuade him to accept separation and to undergo penance.

Many aspects of this case are worth consideration. First, it is important that Victorius was not certain as to whether Vincomalus' second marriage was incestuous. Indeed, no one seems to have considered it so for thirty years. Second, the issue only came to a head when someone started spreading rumours about the man. Third, at the start of the case Avitus seems not to have known what was the appropriate action. In other words, before the problem of Vincomalus' marriage came to the attention of Avitus, the Burgundian episcopate was ill-informed about the matter of incest. Therefore, although there is no clear date for the Vincomalus episode, it is almost certain that the case underlay the consideration given to incest by the bishops at Epaon, and thus the whole development of incest legislation. The conciliar statement that pardon could only come after the separation of the incestuous couple[1] seems to reflect Avitus' ultimate view of what should happen to Vincomalus. On the other hand the final phrase of Epaon, can. 30, suggests that the episcopate was prepared to be lenient in the case of previously contracted relations.

Leviticus 18.18 prohibited sexual relations with one's wife's sister while the wife was alive, but implies that they are acceptable after her death. The levirate was mandated by Deut. 25.5. when a brother died, to preserve his name. Nonetheless, despite such OT authority, because husband and wife became 'one flesh'[2] such marriages came to be considered incestuous adultery by Christians. This change is reflected by *Cod. Theod.* 3.12.2 (of 355) which mentions the fact that the ancients had considered it proper for a brother to marry his brother's wife, once the previous marriage had been dissolved, or the first wife had died, but explicitly prohibits such marriages.[3]

---

wissenschaftliche Veröffentlichungen der Görres-Gesellschaft. Neue Folge, Bd 74 (Paderborn, 1994), pp. 98, 104–106, 113, 115.

1 Epaon, can. 30.

2 1 Cor. 16.

3 *Liber Constitutionum* 36: adultery with a wife's sister counted as incestuous adultery. The original legislation affected levirate marriage among Jews. See J. A. Brundage, *Law, Sex, and Christian Society in Medieval Europe* (Chicago and London, 1987), p. 107.

Victorius the bishop [of Grenoble] to Avitus the bishop {48.11 Peiper}

I must ask for a ruling from you in your official capacity as a winnowing-fan[1] to separate the grain from the tares on the threshing-floor of the Lord; for he[2] who decided that you should be metropolitan bishop of the royal city[3] wishes for me to carry out your commands, and for you to decree what must be done. One of the citizens, as rumour now has it, has married the sister of his wife, who died many years ago. Because the man who accuses him of this heinous crime, has now been heard in the presence of many people revealing the precise nature of the atrocious deed[4] – not in any secret whispering campaign by his friends, but in the very presence of the perpetrator and proposes, < ... >[5] with precisely the same daring with which he attempted these unlawful actions ...[6] if you will decide the matter, a creature nearly to be pitied, he has not denied the deed. So tell us in what manner he should be kept apart from his wife. Should they both repent? Or should sequestration, or some sort of penance be enforced? Please advise. As far as I am concerned it is no a less a crime to marry the sister of one's wife than the wife of one's brother. But, as I have suggested, decide what seems best to you, for on such a matter, without your advice, I can barely decide what the sentence should be. In my hesitation, I will neither[7] bar him from communion nor allow it to him, unless I am backed up by your authority.

Epistula 17: **Introduction**

The answer to *Ep.* 16. For Avitus the Latin is astonishingly clear, possibly reflecting the judicial nature of the letter: Avitus' ruling could effectively be used as case law. In this it is like *Ep.* 7, *De basilicis haereticorum non recipiendis*, also to Victorius. The case presumably prompted Epaon, can. 30, which also describes marriage to one's dead wife's sister as incest. In its turn Epaon, can. 30, led to the confrontation

---

1 Rendering 'winnowing-fans of Your Ordination'.
2 God – or Gundobad?
3 An interesting indication that Sigismund used Vienne as a royal centre.
4 L reads *a sociis*, which cannot be translated. We take S's *atrocis*.
5 There seems to be another lacuna between *proposuit* and *quique*. We never hear what the accuser proposed.
6 There is a lacuna noted by Peiper.
7 With *nempe* 'certainly', *vel permitto* makes no sense. Victorius is emphasising his dependence on Avitus' judgement. *Neque* is a possibility, but the position of *trepide* still remains a problem. 'In my hesitation I will neither remove him from communion nor let him take it, unless I am backed up by your authority.'

between the bishops of the Burgundian kingdom and Sigismund over the incestuous marriage of his treasurer Stephanus at the Council of Lyons (518/23), can. 1.[1]

Avitus the bishop to Victorius the bishop {49.1 Peiper}

It is a sign of your excellent and tested piety that in matters[2] pertaining to your own bishopric, you think to ask my opinion too. You show that you do this not in the spirit of hesitancy but of affection. I think you are quite right to be upset by the sin you mentioned in your letter. Even a layman cannot fail to be aware that a marriage born of close kinship cannot occur without a great stain. Even though I naturally feel pain and concern at having to discipline the man, he whom we wish to be saved in eternity must for his own good be punished in the temporal world.

Accordingly the husband of two sisters ought not to be afflicted with an irrevocable anathema, but, once religious observations have been enjoined upon him, he ought to be sequestrated from the church for a while.[3] And since you indicate that the wretched fellow himself already long ago drew as his lot an illicit marriage to a second wife, let the crime of incest borne for a long time with impunity suffice.[4] Do not hesitate here out of any fear of divorce. A legitimate separation is in order, where there has been an unlawful union. If it seems best to you, excommunicate both of them as long as they persist in their unhappy obstinacy until they break off their criminal relations with a public profession of penitence.[5] And then, when you take pity on them, once they have been made an example to be feared in their correction, let them receive the grace of reconciliation.[6]

To be sure I have suggested to Your Sincerity what I have believed to be reasonable, because you thought it so important that I issue a ruling. It is a matter for your own authority to mitigate the ordained severity of the punishment – if you see compunction on the part of the sinners. I am sure

---

1 *Vita Apollinaris* 2–3. See also Mikat, 'Die Inzestverbote des Konzils von Epaon', pp. 879–80, and *idem, Die Inzestgesetzgebung*, pp. 106–15.

2 The Latin *causa* has almost become Fr. 'chose'.

3 On the imposition of penance, Epaon, cans. 23, 28, 29, 30, 31 and 36. On the distinction between penance and excommunication in this period, see Vogel, *La Discipline pénitentielle*, pp. 102–06.

4 On the need for moderation in such matters see also Vogel, *La Discipline pénitentielle*, p. 105

5 Epaon, can. 30.

6 On the ending of penitence, Epaon, can. 28.

that, if they are really overcome by remorse, they will obey the conditions imposed on them above.

Epistula 18: Introduction

This appears to be a third letter, following on from *Epp*. 16 and 17. Here, it seems, the man accused of adultery, who is now identified as Vincomalus, has been so outraged by Avitus' judgement that he has followed the deacon who brought the judgement back to Vienne, where the bishop has interviewed him. Presumably, neither Victorius or Avitus had any need to name the man when they were discussing the general principles of his case. Now the matter has become personalised. Although the outcome is happier than in the comparable case of *Ep*. 55, the bishop clearly had difficulty in enforcing canon law against a recalcitrant sinner, not least because of the harshness of public penance.[1] Avitus finds a remarkably humane solution to the problem.

Avitus the bishop to Victorius the bishop [of Grenoble] {49.21 Peiper}

You make the appropriate concessions both to caution and to affection, in deigning no less to honour than to impose an onerous[2] task by consulting me. I am telling you the straightforward truth. You judge correctly, if not my experience, at least my friendship for you: I never suggested any measures in my response to you that I would not want upheld by the church at Vienne. As you have told me, Vincomalus has followed our son the deacon. May God grant that the former 'conquer evil'[3] to his own benefit! I saw a man who was so excessively savage that his own misfortune was never to be able to take pity on anyone.[4] Old in years, yet young in his vices, he deceives himself: he is cold with age, yet hot in adultery. What need to say more? We can only hope that no person of any age perish for vain pleasure. For when we were taking him to task for the crime of incest – more in the spirit of encourage-ment than of harshness – he told us that our severity came too late. He cited as a pretext the fact that only after thirty years had we condemned his illicit sexual relations. At that point, I admit, I stopped making allegations,[5] because

---

1 On the limitations of episcopal power, Vogel, *La Discipline pénitentielle*, p. 102.

2 Avitus puns in Latin on the similar sounds of *honorare*, 'to honour', and *onerare*, 'to weigh down'. The pun may come from his father-figure Sidonius. See Sid. *Ep*. 7.9.7 *multum me honoris, plus oneris accepisse.*

3 Avitus puns again. Vincomalus can be construed as a 'speaking name': 'conquer evil'.

4 More puns: this time on *miseria*, 'misfortune', and *misereri*, 'to take pity'.

5 If we took S's *impudenti*, it would mean 'I gave in to the shameless fellow.'

by deferring the sentence for his sake,[1] we would have preferred to have left[2] the reformation of the man to his own feelings of remorse and to his will.[3] It is quite right that after many years he should at the very least check his *criminal* sexual appetites, since, at the approach of old age, he ought to have reined in his legitimate ones too. When I said this, I am sure that he emitted a groan – not of compunction, but of confusion. He began for a while to promise that that unsuitable woman would forthwith be kept from seeing or approaching him. I answered by persuading him to make a promise to you that, once he had repented of his deed, he should request to be released from the tie by which he had been bound. All the same, because you commanded me to share my opinion with you, let the fact that the two are separated be sufficient punishment in your eyes. Let the ill-omened marriage be broken by a more innocent divorce. Let the end of the wrongdoing be sufficient punishment. Do not trust his 'faithful promise': his whole life has been unfaithful. Let the guarantors themselves[4] believe that improvement will follow, since it is at their instigation that his previous fault will be forgiven. As far as penance is concerned, let him be *advised* in the meantime to do it, but not be *forced* to accept it.[5] Let his crimes suffice for the unhappy wretch, and let there not be brought against him in his misery, when he rejects it, a penance that ought barely to be entrusted to him, had he requested it.[6] Let the duplicity due to weakness stop, and let not the sin of rebelliousness be added to his already considerable love of the flesh. If you order it, I will make one final brief suggestion. Once he has been shaken clear of his wrongdoing, let him be forgiven: let him undergo penance, when he loses the chance to sin; let him admit openly,[7] when he will have lost the desire to do so.

1 Taking S's *sui*: 'for the love of him'.

2 *Servare* is *simplex pro composito* for *reservare*. See Goelzer, p. 679.

3 On the necessity of undergoing penance of one's own free will, Vogel, *La Discipline pénitentielle*, p. 102.

4 This is the first indication that the issue might also have been dealt with in the secular courts.

5 Avitus is probably referring here to public penance, and is only too aware that it ought only to be performed once in a lifetime: cf. Vogel, *La Discipline pénitentielle*, pp. 26–28 and 112.

6 Public penance placed a very heavy burden on the penitent, not least because the sinner was theoretically meant never to sin again, since penance could not be repeated: Cf. Vogel, *La Discipline pénitentielle*, pp. 26–28 and 112.

7 'make confession?'

Epistula 55: Introduction

Avitus writes to Ansemundus, who must, from the contents of the letter, be the Burgundian count (*comes*) of Vienne.[1] He may thus be identified with some certainty with Aunemundus, or with one of the two Aunemundi, who signed the *Prima Constitutio* of the *Liber Constitutionum* of the Burgundians in 517. He may also have been the founder of the monasteries of St André-le-Bas and St Pierre in Vienne.[2] If this is the case, he was still alive in 543, which would tend to imply that the letters addressed to him by Avitus were written relatively late in the bishop's life.

Someone, possibly a Burgundian, from the upper classes has raped an upper-class nun and got her pregnant.[3] The rapist has pleaded in his defence that the woman was not a virgin when he had intercourse with her. Ansemundus had interceded on his behalf. Avitus is forced to comply with the *comes*, but he still wants to voice his disapproval. We may guess that despite his freedom of speech Avitus was worried about the rapist's power. The man had threatened to accuse Avitus of fornication and of having bastard offspring. One can contrast the initial tolerance with which Augustine treated the alleged seduction of a nun by a clergyman in *Ep.* 13* (ed. Divjak). Subsequently, however, (*Ep.* 18* Divjak) he acknowledged that he should be removed from his priesthood.

The issue of the rape of a nun may have been a particularly sensitive one for Avitus, since, according to the *Vita Fuscinulae* (7), the bishop's sister, Fuscina, was forcibly abducted from the monastery of Gervasius and Protasius to satisfy the lust of a man of tyrannical power. Although the *Life* says that she was saved when her abductors killed each other, the exchange of letters between Avitus and his brother, if it relates to Fuscina (*Epp.* 13–14), may suggest that she was thought in some way to have been violated. Other accounts of rape (*raptus*) from the sixth century mention consensual sex with nuns: Greg. Tur. *DLH* 6.16, *Vita Genovefae* 31. It is, of course, possible that a similar situation underlay the episode which concerned Avitus in his letter to Ansemundus.

Perhaps the most important aspect of this letter is the light it sheds on the relative power of the bishop and *comes*. It is common to see the post-Roman period as one in which the power of the bishop, *Bischofsherrschaft*, was more important than that of secular officials.[4] Clearly episcopal power was considerable in a large number of

1 See also *Epp.* 80–81.

2 Ado, *Chronicon, s.a.* 575: For the *Donatio Ansemundi*, ed. J. M. Pardessus, *Diplomata, chartae epistolae, leges aliaque instrumenta ad res Gallo-Francicas spectantia* I (Paris, 1843), pt. 2, n. 140, see P. Amory, 'The Textual Transmission of the Donatio Ansemundi', *Francia* 20.1 (1993), pp. 163–83. See also *PLRE* 2 'Ansemundus'. He was also the recipient of *Epp.* 80 and 81.

3 There is an extraordinary misunderstanding in Denkinger, pp. 74–75, who thinks that Ansemundus has raped the nun.

4 D. Claude, 'Untersuchungen zum frühfränkischen Comitat', *Zeitschrift der Savigny-Stiftung für Rechtsgeschichte*, germanistische Abteilung 81 (1964), pp. 1–79; G. Scheibelreiter, *Der Bischof in merowingischer Zeit* (Vienna, 1983), p. 277.

cities by the mid-seventh century:[1] this letter, however, shows that even the greatest bishop of the Burgundian kingdom could be powerless before the local *comes civitatis*.

Avitus the bishop to Ansemundus, vir illustris *[count of Vienne] {83.32 Peiper}*

I am most astonished that the person for whom you deign to intercede – with the result that while I was at Lyons he[2] alone has denied before me the charge that everyone was bewailing – has come to his senses and that he supplicates for your forgiveness. For if that is all he seeks, let it be clear that the man is also confessing the nature[3] of his guilt. Therefore even though in all affairs, because in return for the respect which you pay me, I am not at liberty to do other than what you order me, I cannot nonetheless, because it seemed best to you, refrain from expatiating on what I so deplore – even though I intend to forgive it.

For Your Piety knows and has often heard read in church, how many degrees of this very sin of adultery[4] divine scripture mentions. The man, who aflame with desire, has lusted after an unmarried woman, has sinned in the first degree – namely of fornication. In the second category is he who by adultery, damnable above all other things, has violated the chastity of the unsullied marriage-bed. Since the human spirit can conceive of no greater wrong than this, imagine how the pure chastity of divine justice would be affected if someone even *gazed* lewdly[5] (I will not dwell on the matter further!) on a consecrated bride of Christ, who had been given a dowry by blessing on the marriage-bed of the sacred altar?[6]

I hear that the young man says that the woman whom he violated was not a virgin, and that, according to him, her body had previously been misused by the desires of many. Therefore, even though nothing but his *own* atonement and your intercession will free the man accused of an evident crime, I cannot say how surprised I am that he takes it upon himself to confess the

---

1 J. Durliat, 'Les Attributions civiles des évêques mérovingiens: l'exemple de Didier, évêque de Cahors (630–655)', *Annales du Midi* 91 (1979), pp. 237–54.

2 Taking *sola* as a feminine in agreement with *persona*. The defendant, however, is a man.

3 The meaning of *ordinem* is unclear.

4 Deut. 22.22; Lev. 20.10.

5 See Mt. 5.28.

6 For another case in which sex with a nun is construed as being adultery, see Greg. Tur. *DLH* 9.39, where both nun and lover are denounced as adulterers.

crimes of *others* as part of his own atonement. In this matter I blame the negligence of our current priests. It is not that I have been hunting for this sort of thing, but that the monstrosity of the crimes, uninvestigated as they are, forces itself upon my attention.

Why does he seek a partner in his crimes? Why does he claim that others are stained? If only his own obscene misbehaviour had held itself in check in such a way as to lie hidden. Let him choose whichever of the two he wants. If he was the first to sin against the girl in the flesh, let him expect what the apostle foretells. 'If any man defile the temple of God, him shall God destroy.'[1] If on the other hand by adding to it, he increased a moral decay that he had not [himself] initiated, what viler, what more horrible thing can be imagined than that not even the very sin, on account of which alone God permits a man to be separated from his wife, kept him away from a whore? If you look at it, it is not I alone who am affected by this matter. Her devout relatives[2] bemoan the acknowledged misdeed and by mourning their child as if she were lost, show their bereavement in beating their breasts. What can I say of her mother's grief, whom his vile life-[style], worse than any death, has already widowed of her debauched husband? Even though he is usually quickly moved, nonetheless this son with no respect put up with it,[3] this husband without offspring, and father without an heir! She is now eagerly nursing what, although it arises from adultery among the upper classes, [must be considered] a noble evil. Thus nonetheless is it that in the birth of a monster,[4] whose safety was despaired of, there is no increase in the stock, but proof of depravity.

Yet, leaving alone the defence that God has offered me in you, I fear the sin of the man more than his uncontrollable rage. But I beg that he not be angry at me when I say, 'I'm a watchman.[5] I hold the trumpet.[6] I am not allowed to be silent.'[7] Would that the sinner, who is accustomed to slip

---

1 1 Cor. 3.17.

2 *Parentes* probably means 'relatives', since the girl's mother is mentioned separately in the next sentence.

3 I.e. the mother's grief.

4 The Latin is *portentum*. It is unclear whether Avitus uses the word as an exaggeration for the necessarily bastard adulterous offspring of a nun or whether the child was deformed.

5 A *speculator* was a military spy. Avitus may be making a bilingual pun on *episcopos* = *speculator.* Cf. Maximus of Turin, *Serm* 93.2 and Isidore, *Orig.* 7.12.12.

6 Reading *tubam teneo*, 'I hold the trumpet', with S. This makes much better sense in light of the following clause.

7 Peiper sees here a poetic quotation: source unknown . The passage is, however, very close to Ezek. 33.2–3, 'if the people of the land take a man from amongst the hindermost and set him

through lack of resistance and to return to gratify himself, would behave with human courage! In the rage of guilt a proud man swells, a bull-like man stinks with lust. Therefore, although he vomit many flames of terror against me, although he summon me to a hearing before the Roman church, and, if he still wants to, may say that I *too* have children,[1] neither will I placate his threats by agreement, nor shrink from the tiring journey, I who am even more exhausted at home by civic accusations.[2] Nor will I deny that I have many children[3] – indeed I now mourn that one of them has died.[4] Grief has indeed wrenched these few [words] from me.

But you, who have greater power to punish because of the power of the law and the privilege attendant on your power, rebuke the man energetically. To conciliate me, vindicate this wrong against me, as you recommend. Lest this evil be renewed through orders or messengers,[5] say that you will remedy it. Thus the opportunity for wrongdoing may be taken away from him, if not with his cooperation through correction, at least by force through imprisonment, if you have not succeeded in convincing him of the health-giving power of repentance.

---

for their watchman: if, when he sees the sword come upon the land, he fails to blow the trumpet, and the sword come and take one life from among the people, I shall seek that man's blood from the hand of the watchman' (*et tulerit populus terrae virum unum de novissimis suis et constituerit eum super se speculatorem. Et ille viderit gladium venientem et non insonuerit buccina, veneritque gladius et tulerit animam unam de populo, sanguinem eius de manu speculatoris requiram*). *Tubam* not *turbam* is the correct reading: the scout holds a trumpet on the watch-tower. The *episcopos*, 'overlooker', is here identified with the *speculator*. Augustine makes a very similar point to justify episcopal chastisement of sin in *CD* 1.9.3 'in this matter (i.e. reproving sinners) an especially weighty responsibility rests on those told through the prophet, "He will die in his sin, but I shall require his blood at the hand of the watchman." For "watchmen", that is those put in charge of people, have been set up in churches so that they not refrain from rebuking sin.' (*Qua in re non utique parem, sed longe graviorem habent causam, quibus per prophetam dicitur, Ille quidem in suo peccato morietur, sanguinem autem ejus de manu speculatoris requiram* (Ezek. 33.6). *Ad hoc enim speculatores, hoc est populorum praepositi, constituti sunt in Ecclesiis, ut non parcant objurgando peccata.*) The same quotation justifies Gregory's speaking out before Chilperic at Praetextatus' trial in *DLH* 5.18.

1 Avitus had no children. See *Ep.* 52, p. 81.11–13.

2 This might be compared with the accusations mentioned in *Ep.* 51. For more on the troubling accusations of sexual misbehaviour faced by bishops, see D. R. Shanzer, 'History, Romance, Love, and Sex in Gregory of Tours' *Decem Libri Historiarum*', in *Gregory of Tours*, ed. K. Mitchell and I. N. Wood (Leiden, 2002), pp. 395–418.

3 Avitus refers to his flock, his spiritual offspring, a common topos. See *Acta Carpi, Papyli, et Agathonikes* 28–32; for the female variant, see Victor of Vita, *Historia Persecutionis* 1.35.

4 Avitus refers to the spiritual death of the rapist.

5 Presumably the letters of summons or accusations about Avitus' own alleged bastards.

15. WHAT TO DO WITH HERETICS?

Contents

Epistula 7: Introduction

In ecclesiastical terms this is one of Avitus' most important letters. It deals with the problem of taking over churches which had been in the hands of heretics. Not surprisingly its conclusions are summarised in canon 33 of the Council of Epaon, the council over which Avitus presided in 517, shortly after Sigismund took over the whole of the Burgundian kingdom. In all probability the letter was written between the king's accession in 516 and the council, which was held less than a year later. Avitus' letter was even thought to have canonical value in its own right, being transmitted not only in the letter collection, but also in a ninth-century Lorsch canon collection, Vatican Pal. lat. 574.

The problem of taking over churches once held by the Arians must have been recurrent in the sixth century, when a number of barbarian kingdoms either abandoned Arianism or were defeated by a Catholic power, which then destroyed the local Arian church (as in Vandal Africa and in Ostrogothic Italy). Avitus' response to the problem is, however, one of the most detailed considerations of the issue to survive. The bishop of Vienne deals with the problem of the churches of the heretics with considerable caution, being more than aware of the possibility of reprisals if the Arians should ever be returned to power. It is possible that Sigismund's brother, Godomar, who was indeed to succeed him, was still an Arian.[1] The new king's son may also have still been an Arian at the time the letter was written.[2] In addition Avitus will have been aware of the reconquest of parts of Aquitaine, and especially the Auvergne, by the Goths, following Clovis' death.[3]

Avitus' caution is all the more apparent when one compares the canons of Epaon

---

1 Greg. Tur. *DLH* 3, *praef*, portrays him as Arian.

2 For his conversion, Avitus, *Hom.* 26.

3 On events in the Auvergne see I. N. Wood, 'The Ecclesiastical Politics of Merovingian Clermont', in *Ideal and Reality in Frankish and Anglo-Saxon Society*, ed. P. Wormald (Oxford, 1983), pp. 34–57.

with those of Orléans (511), in which the Aquitanian Catholic church under Clovis dealt with ex-Arian churches.[1] Orléans, can. 10, states: 'Concerning heretical clerics who join the Catholic religion in total faith and of their own accord, and concerning the basilicas which the Goths have hitherto held in their perversity, we think that, if the clerics are faithfully converted and confess the Catholic faith wholeheartedly and if they live a worthy life of high moral standards and good deeds, they should receive the office of which the bishop thinks them worthy, with the blessing of the laying on of hands.[2] And it is right that churches should be consecrated following the same liturgy as that by which ours are dedicated.' By contrast Epaon, can. 33, following Avitus, states: 'We refrain from setting to sacred uses the basilicas of the heretics, which we hold as hateful with such execration that we cannot treat their pollution as being amenable to cleansing. On the other hand we are able to take back those churches which were taken from us violently.' This information is important not just for what it tells us about the policy of the Catholic church in Burgundy, but also, by implication, what it reveals of the initial seizure of Catholic churches by Arians, when the Burgundian kingdom was set up. This violent seizure is presumably the sort of *persecutio* referred to by Avitus in *Ep.* 8, p. 40.12. Apart from what it tells us about the Burgundian kingdom, the letter is also important for its information on northern Aquitaine (*Gallia superior*), where Arian liturgical vessels were clearly seized, as enjoined by Orléans (511), can. 10.

Avitus the bishop to Victorius the bishop (of Grenoble) {35.6 Peiper}

You requested, indeed advised me, most pious brother, to show you in a letter addressed to your Blessedness, whether the oratories or basilicas of the heretics can be put to the service of our religion, once their founders[3] have corrected their errors and gone over to the Catholic law.

The matter is certainly an important one to ask about – if you had found the right man to answer it. However, since you have ordered me to, I shall unfold in the subsequent pages, what I think follows. Nor will I use a theological formula[4] that precludes the expression of opinion by others, provided they confirm, either by self-evident reason or by authority derived from canonical books,[5] what they decide must be done.

The question you pose about [their][6] oratories or small private basilicas

---

1 See the comments in Pontal, *Die Synoden im Merowingerreich*, pp. 31 and 43–44.

2 On this compare Avitus, *Ep.* 28.

3 An indication of proprietary churches.

4 Goelzer, p. 549.

5 This could be a way of acknowledging the judgement of Orléans (511), can.10.

6 The Arians'. Avitus contrasts proprietary and public churches. On another aspect of proprietary churches see Epaon, can. 18.

is just as difficult to make a decision about as it is in the case of their [larger public] churches. *Persuasion*[1] must be used to convince Catholic kings of what will already have been decided[2] in the case of their subjects.[3] Therefore my first question is, if Catholic prelates should be consulted by the prince of our region, whose cooperation in the true religion God has granted us,[4] may we answer that the churches set up by his father [Gundobad] for heretics ought to be turned over to the Catholics for use?

For if we should persuade him of this, and he should consent, the heretics will not unreasonably object that they have been persecuted.[5] Since it is more fitting for us in our Catholic meekness to put up with, than to provide material for, the calumnies of heretics and pagans, what could be more unfair than that they who die the death of the Spirit in their open perversity should flatter themselves with the titles of 'confessor' or 'martyr'? And because, after the death of our king also[6] – may God grant a long and happy life to him! – if indeed anything in the sequence of the ages can be assumed to be unchanging, some heretic might reign[7] and whatever persecution he instigates against people or places, he will be said to have done it, not out of sectarian bigotry, but as retaliation. Whatever posterity suffers will be accounted our burden of sin, even after our death. And perhaps divine pity may bring it about that the offspring of the prince[8] of whom we speak may follow a Catholic leader[9] in the fullness of received

1 Avitus contrasts the tactful persuasion that must be used on kings with the *faits accomplis* that can be enforced on their underlings.

2 Over-determined future perfect, *constitutum fuerit*.

3 I.e. the owners of the small oratories and basilicas.

4 Sigismund.

5 Peiper has mispunctuated here. There should be a full stop after *causabuntur*. The *cum*-clause goes with the next sentence. That the taking of churches involved *violentia* is clear from Epaon, can. 33.

6 The *quoque* is intriguing. As opposed to the death of which external king, i.e. not *noster*? Avitus might be thinking about the losses sustained by the Franks in Aquitaine after the death of Clovis. The expulsion of Quintianus from Rodez must date to the period between 511 and 515; see Wood, 'Gregory of Tours and Clovis', pp. 256–57: see the narrative of Greg. Tur. *DLH* 2.37, together with Greg. Tur. *LVP* 4.1.

7 The implication seems to be that Sigismund's brother, Godomar, was still Arian at this stage: Greg. Tur. *DLH* 3, *praef.* Avitus will also have been aware that Theodoric the Ostrogoth had reconquered territory from the Franks.

8 Presumably Sigistrix, murdered by his father ca. 522: Cf. Marius of Avenches, *s.a.* 522: Greg. Tur. *DLH* 3.5. It is not clear whether Sigistrix is being portrayed as Arian: on his conversion, see Avitus, *Hom.* 26.

9 *Auctor = dux*, see Goelzer, p. 507. But perhaps better 'father'.

faith. What, however, if one of the neighbouring[1] kings, under another law, should wish to exact vengeance likewise in his own region, one which he would hate to be inflicted upon his own priests here?[2] If someone should scoff at this sort of fear, and break into these words, 'Let me profit from the glory of my times. Let the following age look to its own position!' If anyone cherishes such thoughts in his mind, let him for a moment give me the answer I request: namely that to the extent that heretics acknowledge our truth, so much let them be received by us.[3] Salvation is a most clear and glorious thing, because, as it was written, 'I believed, therefore have I spoken.'[4] Faith precedes speech, and confession follows belief, and through the laying-on of priestly hands the loss of wickedness becomes the fullness of faith.

As for an inanimate object that is first polluted when used again – I confess that I do not know with what sort of sanctification it can subsequently be purified. I say for sure that, if an altar that has been polluted by heretics can be consecrated, so too the bread that was placed on it can be transferred to our rites. This concession is first granted to heretics: he passes over to the divine promise rejoicing in his liberation; he abandons Egypt in migrating in his happy change to the right faith; he leaves behind evils rather than bringing them with him[5] < ... >. When something taboo is brought into contact with an evil that cannot be expiated, polluted things pollute what touches them rather than being purified by the contact. Whence we find in the prophet Haggai,[6] 'Thus says the Lord of Hosts. Ask the priests concerning the law, saying, "If a man remove consecrated flesh and touch bread or anything else with the tip of it,[7] will that thing be made holy?" The priests said in answer, "No." And Haggai said, "If a polluted man touch any one of these things, will it not be polluted?" [That is to say the bread that

---

1 Reading *vicinis* with P and S.

2 Avitus is presumably thinking about Theodoric the Ostrogoth.

3 I.e. taken into our church.

4 Ps. 115.1; 116.10 AV.

5 Note the interesting contrast with Avitus' willingness to use the gold of the Egyptians in *SHG* 5.333–56.

6 Paraphrasing Hag. 2.11–14.

7 There is a textual problem with the biblical quotation. <*In ora vestimenti sui*> is missing in Avitus' text between *sanctificatam* and *et*. In the Vulgate *eius* refers to the *vestimentum*: 'If one bear holy flesh in the skirt of his garment, and with his skirt do touch bread ...' Here *eius* appears to refer to the bread.

recently had been consecrated.]¹ And the priests said, "It will be polluted."'
For which reason we must figure out whether polluted bread can be
sacrificed on these altars, since it would pollute the consecrated bread, if it
touched it. And thus says the prophet Malachi,² 'If ye offer the blind for
sacrifice, is this not evil? And if ye offer the lame, is it not evil?' And a little
later,³ 'Cursed be the deceiver who hath in his flock a male, and voweth, and
sacrificeth unto the Lord a cripple.' What is more pure than this judgement?
What could be more clear than an authority of this sort? The church⁴ which
you wish to adopt and reconsecrate, if it is healthy, why is it being blessed?
If it is sick, why is it being offered? However much you may wish to convert
to the good gifts offered by evil men, since they are – figuratively speaking
– lame, they cannot follow you to sanctity. The apostle says that 'he hath
espoused to one man a chaste virgin to show to Christ',⁵ i.e. the church. A
church which has belonged to heretics, even though it may re-marry a better
man, will not be⁶ a virgin. Why then does a priest, who is utterly denied
contact with the divorced woman and the widow, want what is forbidden?
After incestuous intercourse, marriage comes [too] late.⁷ 'He which is
joined to a harlot is one body. I shall not take the members of Christ, and
make them the members of an harlot.'⁸ See whether a whore can be made
whole, if the limbs of Christ, are joined to her!⁹ For if the limbs of Christ,
that is Christians, are joined to her body they are polluted.¹⁰ Whence in
another place the Apostle says that he wishes to have a church 'not having

---

1 The *id est* is suspicious, perhaps an intrusive gloss intended to make sense of the
somewhat garbled biblical quotation. Avitus appears to have omitted <*inanima*> 'by a dead
body' (the LXX *epi psyche* must be a mistranslation of the Hebrew) after *pollutus* in the
previous sentence, which would have made it clear that *pollutus* referred to the man. The gloss
is intended to clarify the missing object <*quid*> *ex omnibus*, 'any of of these things', i.e. bread,
pottage, wine, etc.

2 Paraphrasing Mal. 1.8.

3 Mal. 1.14.

4 *Fabrica* = church: see Goelzer, p. 432 n. 4.

5 Paraphrasing 2 Cor. 11.2.

6 *Erat* Peiper; the sense demands *erit*.

7 *Post hinc in exitia sera coniunctio est*, L's reading, makes no sense at all. S's *post incesti
nexum sera coniunctio est*. 'after incestuous intercourse, a union comes late', is better. The
similarity to Sidonius, *Ep.* 9.1 *praesentis augmenti sera coniunctio* is noted by Peiper, p. 300.

8 Paraphrasing 1 Cor. 6.16.15.

9 *Adintegrari* is a neologism.

10 *Per pollutionem vertuntur.*

spot, or wrinkle or any such thing'.[1] Could this in any way be said of the churches of the heretics? A blessing pronounced on what lacks faith and is polluted neither cleanses a stain, nor smoothes a wrinkle.

Indeed, if we look a bit more carefully, what is plain in its newness lacks stain; that thing is wrinkled that has been folded twice. Holy purity rejects such a wrinkle, and taking off the old Adam, makes ready[2] what is offered to the new man. The authority of the New Testament through the voice of the Gospels recommends this newness to us. This is why the Lord asked that the very foal that was saddled for him[3] be one that no one before him had mounted, and one that was happily ignorant of worldly use, not subdued by whippings, but gentle because of its sacred origins.

In order that the mystery of our Lord's death not lack the honour of newness, we read that the flesh of the Lord, which redeems us, lay in a new monument that had been cut into the rock. Who could try to persuade me that a sepulchre can be cleansed of the contamination of death after the funereal horrors it has seen? Even though the white bones in a tomb may be removed once the flesh has been consumed and the ooze of corruption dried up, the uncleanness lingers in the memory, even though its outward appearance may be thought absent.[4] You may have thrown out the death-contamination of another man's dogma and have hurled out his vanquished[5] strength from his sepulchre like bones lacking honour, but I believe that the limbs of a sacred body should [still] not be placed among the remains of an age-old stench. You will say perhaps that if they had the opportunity, the heretics would violate our altars. It is true. I do not disagree. When given a chance they rage with filthy nails and invade other peoples' buildings.[6] But to use force, to invade places, to change altars is not for Christians who are simple as doves.[7] I will take care to avoid what a heretic might think himself allowed to do from my example. We ought especially to shun practices embraced by our enemy. It is far from surprising that those who rebaptise

---

1 Eph. 5.27.

2 There is no deponent form of *comparo*, so *comparatur* has been emended to *comparat*. This would be a *Perseverationsfehler* from *offertur*.

3 Mt. 21.5.

4 Death, burial and decay are topics which Avitus returned to on a number of occasions, particularly in his poetry: e.g. *SHG*. 3.252ff. and 5.303ff. See also Greg. Tur. *DLH* 4.12 for a vivid description of the stench of a corpse in a sarcophagus.

5 Emending to *emortuam*. *Sepulchro* is already modified by *suo*.

6 That this had happened is clear from Epaon, can. 33.

7 Avitus actually says *non pertinet ad columbam*, 'is inappropriate for a dove', alluding to Mt. 10.16, *estote ... simplices sicut columbae*.

dare to rededicate.[1] Therefore I will briefly tell you not what I decide, but what I would like.

I would not wish us to invade heretical places of worship; I would prefer them to be avoided, like unused prisons. We must always hope, not that they may be changed and come over to us, but that they rot unused. Let them be eternally widowed, once they have been deserted by a populace now healthily corrected. Nor let our congregations ever take back what in the zeal for conversion is repudiated by its own owners.

As for the vessels of the heretics, which, since they are their products, are judged execrable by us, that is patens and *paterae* – since you ordered me to write down what I believe, a valid example of what one ought to do appears in the Heptateuch in connection with the thuribles of sinners. Those who sacrilegiously presumed to take up fire were consumed in the flames of a temporal damnation that prefigured [signified] eternal [fire].[2]

The censers I mentioned lay mixed with ash and coals, to frighten the living, and as a judgement of the dead; although the vessels were accustomed to the odours of incense, they had caught an abominable contagion from the stench of perverse usage. While Moses wondered what to do, the Lord commanded him to melt the censers down, beat them into plates, and fix them to the sacred altars as ornaments. Thus you see that in this tale, we are likewise taught that evil use of metals, as long as we lack fire, cannot be turned to the good. To make a Catholic comparison, fire offers to metal, what faith offers the senses. As the prophet says in the psalm, 'Try my reins and heart.'[3] Someone might certainly take issue with what I feel in accordance with his own judgement. I, for my part, confess that I am far from pleased about those vessels that have come as booty to churches under our dispensation in Gaul south of the Loire.[4] They brought no voluntary contribution, nothing innocent; if they were seized from people who mourned the loss; they could not be of use to those who offer them as spoils. Why should a victor say to me, 'What I put out on your altars has

1 Avitus refers here to the fact that Arians rebaptised Catholics who joined the Arian church, while Catholics merely administered the laying-on of hands.

2 Num. 16.6–32, the story of the censers of Dathan, which subsequently becomes part of a standard anathema formula.

3 Ps. 25.2; AV 26.2.

4 'Gallia superior' in the Latin. Avitus here refers to the transfer of Arian vessels to the Catholics, which must have taken the injunction of Orléans (511), can. 10, on basilicas as a model. This is important evidence on the events in those areas taken over by Clovis in 507 and subsequently held by his sons.

become mine in some manner or other', if we are enjoined, 'Honour the Lord with the fruit of thy just labours?'[1] It is but little labour, if it is not yours, and it is little of yours, if it is not just. May I never declare something to have been sacrificed, which, before it was offered, was taken away from someone else.[2] But may I always take pleasure that gifts are placed on the altar such as those with which that most devout prince of our land ornaments the churches of his own region. To be sure not only the churches of his own region,[3] because, wherever there is a Catholic church seems his own to him, since, by bringing forth his finest treasures to spend on the Lord, he sees to it that in those things that will serve in sacred rites, not only will their preciousness be pleasing, but also their newness. We must pray for this remaining boon, that for a long time, his wishes achieved, since he will possess the wealth that has been entrusted to him by God not in secret heaps, but in buildings, he, rejoicing in a populace under his control, may always reserve what he has given for the sacred uses of the church.

Epistula 26: Introduction

Stephanus became bishop of Lyons after the death of Rusticus in 501.[4] He was dead by 515, when his successor Viventiolus seems to have been involved in the foundation of Agaune. He was also a correspondent of Ennodius (*Ep.* 3.17). Wood, 'Avitus of Vienne', p. 152; Burckhardt, p. 89; also Avitus, *Ep.* 28.

 This letter, which deals with an African Donatist, raises interesting questions about the nature of Donatism in the early sixth century. Clearly Donatists were still schismatic enough for a ceremony of the laying-on of hands to be required before they could be accepted into the Catholic church. It also documents connections between Vandal Africa and Gaul.

Avitus the bishop to Stephanus the bishop of Lyons {57.7 Peiper}

However much care servants devote to the fields of the Lord, among their repeated efforts to plant, there inevitably spring up things that ought to be cut down. Therefore a fine interest-payment consisting of salvation to be acquired through these works accrues to your vigilant and careful efforts. But among the tares of Arian seed which, to make matters worse, have been

---

 1 Paraphrasing Prov. 3.9.

 2 Avitus puns on 'sacrificed', *oblata* and 'taken away', *ablata*.

 3 Some indication of these churches can be found in the unfortunately fragmentary dedication homilies written by Avitus: *Hom.* 19, 20, 24, 25.

 4 Duchesne, *Fastes épiscopaux*, 2, pp. 164–66.

scattered far and wide in their manifold corruption, I cannot guess whence this enemy seed, far from new to be sure, but, at least, rare, has shown its face, or what wind brought this foreign contagion[1] to a clean world.

But since you are steering the ship,[2] this plague is little to be feared – it has no one to foster it. Because it is insignificant, this tempest makes no headway: 'the merest breeze cannot accomplish a shipwreck'.[3] Therefore in order that the name of the Donatists[4] not be able to live for long in a foreign land, lay it to rest immediately with your life-conferring blessing. Let the fires of this small wandering flame grow cold, even as they begin to grow warm. In order that not even the faintest whiff of a rumour reach the nostrils of innocent Gaul, perform the laying-on of hands[5] on the individual you are writing about, and promise not to mention his name[6] subsequently, should he convert sincerely. It is clear that in his profession of the aforementioned schism he received not only the sacrament of baptism, but also the chrism.[7] It is clear that they follow this observation in that region.[8] In it, may God grant first that people who suffered from this error be corrected, and then, since they differ from us as much in creed as in country, let those who are unwilling to be saved[9] not be able cross over to our side.[10]

Epistula 28: Introduction

Like many of Avitus' letters, this deals with two separate topics: the first is the fact that the bishop of Lyons has passed on some theological information to the Arians. The second, more important, is the question of whether men who had at one time been Arian priests, could subsequently be ordained as Catholic ones.

Although there is nothing to say which bishop of Lyons was the recipient of this letter, it has been usually assumed that the bishop in question was Stephanus, the

---

1 Compare *vomitus transmarinus* in *Ep.* 54.

2 I.e. the ship of the church. For a similar ship of faith metaphor, see *Ep.* 34, p. 65.5, *Nostis bene, inter quas haeresum tempestates, veluti ventis circumflantibus, fidei puppi ducamur.*

3 A poetic fragment, author unknown.

4 On sixth-century Donatism, see R. A. Markus, *From Augustine to Gregory the Great* (Andover, 1983), chs 6–9.

5 Translating *manus impositionem.*

6 I.e 'Donatist'.

7 I.e. there is no need for him to be baptised or to receive the chrism: to rebaptise him would in itself be heretical.

8 Africa.

9 Taking L's *salvari.*

10 Deleting *agnoscendi* which appears not to make any sense.

recipient of *Ep*. 26.[1] It is, however, by no means clear that there is any connection between *Epp*. 26 and 28. Nor is it clear that an Arian cleric would have been allowed to transfer into the Catholic church in Gundobad's day. Ultimately the importance of the letter lies not in any identification of the recipient, but with Avitus' views on the one hand about the extent to which Catholic ideas should be accessible to Arians,[2] and on the other about the possibility of heretical priests holding office in the Catholic church: a subject which is not dealt with at Epaon, but was dealt with at Orléans (511).[3]

Avitus the bishop to the bishop of Lyons {58.11 Peiper}

After a long interval I received your letter. Even though you know that I am severe for the sake of maintaining charity, you ought not thus to think me negligent. For God is my witness that the grief in my spirit is all the greater because of my feeling for you. Nor am I able, without great pain, to explain to you how seriously Your Sanctity has been forestalled in your anticipation of an easy pardon.[4] You have provided our adversaries with your own weapons,[5] you have betrayed our secrets to the uninitiate, you have sung 'the Lord's song in a strange land'.[6] You have brought out, as it were, the vessels of the Lord to be given to the Assyrians for the convivial show;[7] you have, as it were, exposed Noah naked to guffaws that will always be a source of opprobrium.[8] Whether[9] they resist or follow, disease[10] will have crept dangerously close to truth.

If what you decided to make public was precious to you, the wrongful deed of Hezekiah ought to put the fear of God into you. Scripture tells that he

---

1 See Coville, *Recherches sur l'histoire de Lyon*, pp. 305–06.

2 Note, however, that Avitus himself freely sent his lists of scriptural passages to Arian clergy. See *Ep*. 23 and *CE* 1, p. 15.13–14.

3 Orléans (511), can. 10.

4 Although it is attractive to think that there is some link between *venia* here and the restoration of Stephanus mentioned in Ennodius 87, the *venia* in question seems to be associated with Avitus' irritation over his dealings with Arians.

5 Compare the sentiments in *Ep*. 23, where Avitus also uses *arma* to refer to theological arguments.

6 AV Ps. 137.4.

7 The reference is to the vessels taken from the Temple of Jerusalem and used by all and sundry at Belshazzar's feast. See Dan. 5.2–4.

8 Gen. 9.22.

9 Taking *si ... aut* as equivalent to *sive ... aut*.

10 *Aequalitas* 'equality', 'fairness', makes no sense. The word needs to be emended to *inaequalitas*, which is used by Avitus to mean 'disease'. See Goelzer, p. 558.

sinned out of boastfulness.[1] But when you say that all hesitation and fear have been washed away from the soul of the convert, it is right for us to rejoice, and say, 'This is a change effected by the right hand of the Most High.'[2] For, as to the fact that those bestial[3] creatures vainly contradict you, making threats of this sort, with God protecting what each and every weak man †[does?],[4] it is the greater marvel that he can manage without teeth and rages.†[5] When they moan that students of their deadly doctrines are dying, they begin to lose teachers too. It is all to the good that such gains are sought before God and men. There is nothing illegal and violent about receiving a suppliant. Just as the conferral of a blessing confirms the devotion of the man who wants it, it is no theft, but a favour.[6] If Christ sees fit to take someone in, we cannot say that the man in question was an invader.

As for the rest, because you think that I ought to be consulted about the status of the convert, I decree that, with inspiration from God, a man can rise to any level of the priesthood, provided there be no impediment in the nature of marriage,[7] a rule, or his character to debar him from the priesthood.[8] Why shouldn't someone feed the sheep of Christ, who has had the wisdom to see that those he fed before were not sheep at all, one who, because he was not a robber and thief, once he entered the door as a future shepherd, chose the altars? Why should that man not stand erect and tall in our priesthood, who for love of humility wished to be cut off from his own? Let that man become a true priest after being a layman, who was content to become a layman after being a deceitful priest. Let him hold his own people in our church, who condemned an alien people in his own church. With all these great goods, bounty will cause an increase in heavenly grace so that he who once mourned may begin to rejoice once he has acquired them, and this man, each day more richly endowed, may better understand that he has outstripped[9] those he left behind.

---

1 2 Kgs 20.13: Hezekiah showed his riches to the Babylonians.

2 Ps. 76.11 in the Old Latin version.

3 The rare (and highly disrespectful) adjective *beluatus* is found in Plautus, *Pseud.* 147 alone before Avitus.

4 The text begins to degenerate at this point. There is almost certainly a verb missing.

5 The text is obscure. The subjunctive *possit* is currently inexplicable: there may be a *si* missing.

6 Avitus is talking about the reception of an Arian into the Catholic church.

7 Compare Epaon, can. 2.

8 This is more explicit than anything in Epaon: for *conversi*, Epaon, can.16: but compare Orléans (511), can. 10.

9 Or 'gone ahead of'.

16. LEGAL MATTERS INVOLVING BURGUNDIAN BISHOPS

Contents

Epistula 70: Introduction

The cause of the arrest and summons mentioned in this letter is unfortunately unknown. The case may, however, have had repercussions at Epaon, two of whose canons (cans. 11, 24) are at odds with Avitus' opinions expressed here, in that they do concede the right of laymen to summons priests – although the council does concede that the accusations ought to be true. Avitus' view of excommunication is, however, similar to that expressed in Epaon, can. 36. While Avitus' correspondence often betrays traces of pique or tetchiness, this is one of the few letters that expresses true anger.

Avitus the bishop to Constantius the bishop[1] *[of Martigny?]{89.20 Peiper}*

I received Your Holiness' letter at Easter, to be sure, but it was no Easter-greeting, since nothing in it bespoke charity or care. You ordered me to send our brother and fellow-priest Candidianus,[2] whom I had recommended as a special friend, not just to ecclesiastical court, but to the lay-authorities. It appears that his deacon has been handed over in a civil case and locked up as if he were a slave by them.[3] Therefore, if you are under the impression that

---

1 Two bishops called Constantius signed the Council of Epaon, one from Octodurum (Martigny/Sion), the other from Gap.

2 Otherwise unknown. It is not certain whether *consacerdos* means bishop or priest.

3 On clergy appearing before secular courts, Epaon, can. 11: 'Clerics may not presume to appeal to the public authority or institute public proceedings without the permission of the bishops, but if they are summonsed, they should not hesitate to appear before the secular tribunal.' Epaon, can. 24: 'We allow laymen the power of accusing a cleric of any grade against whom they are ready to make a criminal charge provided the charges be true.'

the testimony of laymen is utterly to be believed when it concerns your clerics, write back [and tell me so]. The result will be that we will then ask for information from laymen about every rumour that we hear.[1] Since I love you, I take it upon myself to make this suggestion and warn you that not even laymen, let alone clerics, should be deprived of communion for frivolous reasons, and ones that have to do not with God, but with the temporal world.[2] For unless one suspends someone from communion only with great pain and no personal animus and makes the greatest haste to restore him [to it],[3] one does not understand the worth and honour of communion itself.

Epistula 75: Introduction

It appears that a faction of laymen and priests have elected a cleric – a job which required the involvement of bishops, as, for instance, of Sidonius during the election of Simplicius of Bourges.[4] Avitus tells Victorius to excommunicate the priest who has been elected.

Avitus the bishop to Victorius the bishop [of Grenoble] {91.18 Peiper}

The news that you mention in your letter came to me as a faint rumour before I heard from you. The holy archdeacon[5] told me the bitter tidings: if you believe me, I can only say that I deplore the grief that this upset has caused no less than you do. It is a very sad business that the ordination of clergy[6] is now considered the province of the people. It is for this reason alone that choice in consecrating bishops is reserved for the *plebs*:[7] namely in order that in the matter of subsequent decisions, as they have been given a mandate,

1 Avitus is being openly sarcastic.

2 For excommunication in the Burgundian kingdom, Epaon, can. 36: 'No one should be excluded from the church without the remedy or hope of pardon, nor should the opportunity of returning to pardon be blocked for anyone who repents or corrects himself ...' In general see Vogel, *La Discipline pénitentielle*, pp. 102–06.

3 See *Epp.* 16–18 for Avitus' reluctance to ban offenders from communion.

4 Sidonius 7. 8 and 9. On the canons of episcopal election, see Pontal, *Die Synoden im Merowingerreich*, pp. 228–29, 232–33, and *passim*.

5 Burckhardt, p. 49, suggests that a proper name is missing here. S reads *Archidiam* for *archidiaconum*.

6 *Sacerdotalis* could equally well mean 'episcopal' (Goelzer, p. 428, n.1): Avitus, however, is not describing an episcopal schism within the church of Grenoble: more probably what is at issue is the ordination of a priest without Victorius' approval. *Ordinatio* is the word used in Epaon, can. 2, for the ordination of priests.

7 See, for example, Pontal, *Die Synoden im Merowingerreich*, pp. 1–2.

those who have been appointed may choose what seems best. Do not think it anything new that the insolence of laymen, aided and abetted by the wickedness of priests, is able to contrive to cause us trials and suffering. I think that we should seek the agreement of your sons[1] in the punishment of ecclesiastics on account of those by whose customary malfeasance a decision was taken not to bother with excommunications. I have looked at the letter, which is both pious and quite in order, that you sent to the priest who dared to do what was unlawful. To be honest, you were more patient with the man than he deserved. Therefore, even though a great deal may be permitted to the Devil when such an appalling uprising occurs, go ahead and, without giving it a second thought, punish the injury offered to yourself and God. Lest a similar coup be attempted in the future, see to it that the punishment be duly meted out.

Epistula 90: Introduction

This letter is an invitation to attend the council of Epaon (517): a different text of the letter is preserved in the context of the Gallic councils, and is translated by Gaudemet.[2]

In the canon collection the letter has no named addressee. In L and S, however, the letter is addressed to Quintianus. L also has a rubric *ad Amandum*. Peiper supposed that the invitation followed a missing epistle to Quintianus (*Ep.* 89), and used the rubric to identify the recipient of the letter as Amandus. But no bishop Amandus is attested for the Burgundian kingdom, so there is a problem. Quintianus, however, could perhaps have been invited.[3] He had been bishop of Rodez, but was exiled from that city by the Goths: he was subsequently elected bishop of Clermont, on the death of Eufrasius in ca. 515, but Avitus' kinsman Apollinaris was intruded.[4] The latter died soon after his elevation, and Quintianus did become bishop of Clermont, at the behest of the Frankish king Theuderic. Whether the bishop of a city in Frankish hands could have attended a Burgundian council at this moment is an open question, but one should not rule out the possibility. One might note that Theuderic had better connections with the Burgundians than did his half-brothers, marrying Sigismund's daughter, although exactly when is unclear.[5] A further possibility is that, as in the case of the copy of the letter preserved with the canons of Epaon, the letter originally had no named addressee, and that quite separate letters to Quintianus and Amandus are lost.

1 Possibly implying that Victorius should summon a diocesan council.
2 *Les canons des conciles mérovingiens* (VIe–VIIe siècles), pp. 96–99.
3 For a fuller discussion, see Chapter 2, pp. 54–55.
4 Greg. Tur. *DLH* 3.2. On the date, see Wood, 'Gregory of Tours and Clovis', p. 256.
5 Greg. Tur. *DLH* 3.5.

Avitus the bishop to <Quintianus> {97.31 Peiper}

It has been a long time that we have been putting off a matter that is necessary and that was instituted by the fathers of the church at divine suggestion, either because we forgot about it, or because we have been too busy. But from time to time the chains of constraint must be shaken off, so that at some time we may be able to pay the debts owed by those who teach. The meetings that our careful elders decreed should be held by bishops twice a year – if you think it over well, would that we were holding them assiduously once every two years![1] On occasion harsh and biting letters from the pope at Rome[2] have been brought to me indicating that he has been enraged by my carelessness. Therefore the Province of Vienne begs via me, if you will allow it: a custom that has been stopped,[3] now restored to health, begs that what has up till now grown sluggish be brought back to life. It is appropriate in my opinion that, once the prelates have a chance to be together and once we and our concerns have been dealt with[4] in the order of discussion, we either introduce old things, or, if it is necessary, add our [new] ones too.[5]

Therefore all of us your brothers ask that, God willing, you deign to be present on the 8th day of the Ides of September[6] in the parish of Epaon. It is a central location and a very favourable venue,[7] if one takes into account the hardship of the travel involved for all concerned. Likewise the date permits all to make the trip freely, to the extent that time can be made free from the

1 Taking S's *utinam per singula biennia faceremus*. L's *facerem* is clearly wrong in person, and the mood is likewise inexplicable, unless there had been a conjunction introducing a contrafactual wish. The sentence may well house a deeper corruption. It is not satisfactory as it stands: there is an anacoluthon.

2 Most recently Hormisdas, but probably others are also assumed.

3 Doubtless the fact that Gundobad had been Arian inhibited the holding of Catholic councils, although the fact that the Council of Agde had taken place under Alaric II, who had also authorised the holding of another council, which was aborted as a result of the Visigothic defeat at Vogliacum, must have helped to give the impression that Avitus and the Catholic bishops of the Burgundian kingdom had been remiss in not holding councils.

4 The zeugma is harsh.

5 *Nostra* to make an effective contrast with *vetera* must imply *nova*, new items on the agenda.

6 I.e. 6 September 517. Whether or not this was the date on which the council actually met, the canons show that it concluded on 15 September.

7 This is a rather peculiar description of Epaon, which is now identified as Albon, between Vienne and Valence, and is thus in the south of the kingdom: J. Gaudemet, *DHGE* 15 (1963), col. 524. It was, however, accessible by river. Lying between Vienne and Valence, one may suggest that Epaon was a site chosen by Avitus and Apollinaris.

demands of agricultural labour[1] – even though the business of the church is more important and demands that labours on the land be interrupted, whatever they may be.[2] We beg, we ask, we entreat, we pray that no excuse prove an impediment to anyone in attending such an important religious function, and that no entanglement in day-to-day duties keep anyone away from the bond of such charity. But if perhaps – God prevent it! – [anyone's] severe physical illness should get worse, with the result that spiritual longing be overcome by the ailments of the flesh,[3] let him see to it that two great[4] and virtuous priests attend the brothers on his behalf and that they come strengthened by powers of attorney. And may he deign to choose men who have both the knowledge and the status to take part in a council of bishops, with whom bishops would enjoy conversing, and whom, since they have had the skill to agree to[5] and sign decisions for the bishop, the authority of the law would have chosen.[6] But let this not occur, except under circumstances of the utmost necessity. Moreover, the magnitude of brotherly love and pastoral concern is not demonstrated except through great labour. For your Holiness guesses, after our long and negligent[7] silence, both how the issues that are to be dealt with at God's behest are to be settled, and how what has been decided is to be conveyed to all the ministers of the churches in our province.

1 *Instantia ruralis operis* may seem an odd concern for the higher clergy, but it is clear from the reference to *rurale opus*, the agricultural labour of monks, in Epaon, can. 8, that Avitus does actually mean agricultural labour.

2 Altering Peiper's punctuation. The *quamquam* clause need not stand on its own.

3 See Epaon, can. 1. Of course Avitus himself was ill, cf. *Ep*. 88, and was probably dead less than six months after Epaon.

4 *Magnae vitae* must here refer to ecclesiastical rank.

5 L has the puzzling *continendas*. S's *sanciendas* seems preferable. Gaudemet reads *consentiendas*, 'to agree', but transitive uses of *consentio* are very rare.

6 Taking L's *cum fuerit sollertia, elegisset auctoritas legis*. Peiper, surprisingly, takes S's awkward and even nonsensical *sollertia eligi, sit auctoritas legi*. Gaudemet's 'autant ils seront lus avec autorité' seems unsatisfactory.

7 For *abusio* 'negligence', see Goelzer, p. 599.

17. 'FESTAL' LETTERS, FOR EXAMPLE 'THANK-YOUS', 'REGRETS', TO BURGUNDIAN BISHOPS

Contents

Introduction

Epp. 58–73 belong in a category of their own, and were docketed together in Avitus' bottom drawer. They are all 'festal letters', polite regrets and acceptances, exchanged between bishops on the occasion of major feast-days.[1] Many of the letters consist of no more than one to three carefully crafted sentences. Much of the language is repetitive and conventional. The writer has got through the feast (*transeo/transigo festivitatem/transactam festivitatem*) with the aid of the good wishes and support of the addressee (*interventus* or *suffragium*). The writer's longings (*desideria*) to see his brother-bishop are expressed; whether frustrated or hopeful, he is pleased to have *felicia indicia* of his addressee's prosperity. The festal letters to, and from, Apollinaris of Valence (*Epp.* 61, 71, 72) can be found among Avitus' letters to his brother (pp. 243ff.), those to Viventiolus (59, 67, 68, 69 and 73) in his dossier (above pp. 266ff.), while that to Constantius (*Ep.* 70) subverts formal niceties and is treated separately (p. 306).

Epistula 58

Avitus the bishop to Stephanus the bishop [of Lyons][2] {87.5 Peiper}

After the sacred feast-day, which we passed, even though we were both eager and anxious, thanks to your intervention and to divine protection, in the obligation of service and the spirit of devoted sollicitude, we act the

---

1 For more on festal or festival letters, see Wagner, 'A Chapter in Byzantine Episto-lography', p. 133.
2 Cf. also *Epp.* 26 and 28.

servant, desiring that whatever harshness we deserved[1] there be relieved by hearing that you are thriving[2] – may God continue to cause you to!

Epistula 60

Avitus the bishop to Gemellus the bishop [of Vaison][3] {87.16 Peiper}

The recent feast has made the letters of Your Blessedness, which were something to look forward to as a result of the long time that has elapsed since you last wrote, even more pleasing. We celebrated it successfully in the name of God, and we are happy to hear that it went smoothly for you too. Pray that what the rule of God knows is in accordance with brotherly charity – with peace to all men[4] – may always turn out well with the help of the saints of the Catholic church.

Epistula 62

Avitus the bishop to Victorius the bishop [of Grenoble][5] {88.1 Peiper}

Because with God willing you had obtained a happy start of the feast through your support, you have [in effect] been present through the kind feelings [you expressed]. For while you care for us in your customary fashion and tell us – as we longed to hear – that you are well too, you both give us an occasion to rejoice and you ask from us what we owe you. May Christ grant plentiful respite[6] for this very piety and benevolence[7] of yours, in which both your elderly men[8] may be strengthened by the gift of your twofold authority[9] and

---

1 The trouble alluded to is unknown. For another allusion to *asperitas* in a festal letter, see *Ep.* 61, p. 87.26.

2 Avitus puns on *asperitas* and *prosperitas*.

3 On Gemellus see *Liber Constitutionum, Constitutiones Extravagantes* 20, where he appears as the inspiration behind an edict of 516 on the subject of foundlings.

4 Perhaps a suggestion that the feast is Christmas.

5 See also *Epp.* 7, 16–18, 75.

6 *Commeatus* here means 'leisure', 'respite', or 'reprieve'. Cf. *Ep.* 66, p. 88.27.

7 Translating *dignatio* which means 'condescension' in a positive sense.

8 *Senes vestri*. The allusion is unclear, but it seems to suggest that Victorius may have been especially charitable to the old.

9 The precise sense of *magisterium geminatum* is unclear, but it seems to be defined by *et per sollicitudinis beneficium* and *et per caritatis exemplum*.

the good offices of your care, and those to come may be taught by the example of your charity.[1]

Epistula 63: Introduction

The circumstances behind this letter are somewhat obscure. It is clearly a Christmas thank-you note, but for what? Not for any gift, because none of the customary vocabulary (*dona, munera, oblatio, expensa*) is present. Instead vaguer language, such as *votiva indicia*, 'news or information we wanted to hear', *visitatio*, 'visit' and *augmentum*, 'addition', suggest that Claudius had agreed to come and see Avitus. See *Ep*. 66 below for a parallel situation where the bishop was prevented from coming by ill health, but sent prayers and a gift.

Avitus the bishop to Claudius the bishop [of Besançon][2] *{88.8 Peiper}*

As you usually do, you increase our longing by the zeal of your piety and by telling us what we hoped to hear. Since you have agreed to visit us, the festivities for the birth of the Lord are doubled by the [anticipated] addition of Your Prosperity.[3] In return for this favour which Your Blessedness multiplies for us with your continuing and frequent acts of kindness, may the Divinity, propitiated, cause you to be among us for many years to come!

Epistula 64: Introduction

Gregorius was ill and unable to visit Avitus for the feast. Instead he sent his prayers and a gift. This letter is Avitus' thank-you note.

---

1 Avitus is wishing Victorius a long life. Cf. *Ep*. 63 for the same sentiment.

2 Claudius of Besançon attended the Councils of Epaon (517) and Lyons (518/23), but see also the comment of Duchesne, *Fastes épiscopaux*, 3, p. 212, n. 6: 'Le catalogue, par la place qu'il lui attribue semble l'identifier avec S. Claude, abbé de Condat au VIIe ou au VIIIe siècle, douzième sur la liste. De cette liste, nous avons deux rédactions l'une en prose, l'autre en vers; la première qualifie Claude d'archiepiscopus et abbas, l'autre ne parle pas de sa qualité épiscopale.' If Claudius did indeed come from Condat, he should be compared with Viventiolus who also seems to have come from the same monastery, and was prior there: see the introductory comments on *Ep*. 19, above pp. 266ff. These two cases may suggest that Condat should be compared to Lérins as a source of bishops, although in numbers of bishops it does not, of course, compete with the southern monastery.

3 Avitus should only be taken to mean that Claudius had promised in his Christmas letter to visit Vienne: Epaon, can. 35, states that the leading citizens should celebrate Christmas and Easter in the presence of a bishop. For similar promises, see *Epp*. 59, 68: Goelzer, p. 594.

Avitus the bishop to Gregorius the bishop [of Langres][1] *{88.14 Peiper}*

I lay it instead to the charge of *my* sins that poor health has prevented you from doing what Your Most Pious Will desired, even though your customary polite respect has kept us company through your prayer[s] and gift. Therefore with this page to act as servant and take upon itself the business of greeting you, discharging my debt, I give you thanks more effectively than I could in speech that, even though you have not been able to make our holiday that is all athirst and longing for you joyful by your presence,[2] you have refreshed us with your [financial] outlay.[3]

[*Epistula* 65 Avitus to bishop Alexandrinus: missing[4]]

---

1 The great-grandfather of Gregory of Tours: see *PLRE* 2, Attalus 1.

2 Lit. 'satisfy our feast day'.

3 *Expensa* (sc. *pecunia*), ablative.

4 L reads *Elexandrinum* (sic), and Sirmond is missing the letter. This must have been an error for *Alexandrinum*. But does Alexandrinus mean 'of Alexandria' or is it a personal name? None of the other festal letters gives the bishop's see, but no local Alexandrinus is known either. One doubts that Avitus sent a five-line Christmas message to the patriarch of Alexandria. For *Alexandrina ecclesia* see *Ep.* 41.

LAYMEN IN BURGUNDIAN TERRITORY

18. HERACLIUS

Contents

Epistula 53 Avitus to Heraclius, *vir illustrissimus*: Avitus congratulates Heraclius, a Catholic lay-orator, on his forceful theological debate before Gundobad. He encourages him to become a bishop.

Epistula 54 Heraclius to Avitus: the answer to *Ep.* 53, a modest disclaimer.

Epistula 95 Avitus to Heraclius, *vir illustrissimus*: Avitus accuses Heraclius of fleeing Vienne, seeking the mountains, and of malingering. He announces sad news: invasions (Godegisel in 500?) and the death of Protadius. He asks Heraclius to keep Ceratius, probably a common relative, with him.

Epistula 96 Heraclius to Avitus: The reply to *Ep.* 95. Heraclius in return accuses Avitus of cowardly conduct in the face of invasion, because he lurked in Vienne.

Epistula 53: Introduction

Heraclius is the recipient of *Epp.* 53 and 95 and author of *Epp.* 54 and 96. He is a talented lay-orator from the senatorial classes who had written royal panegyrics, and has recently successfully defended the Catholic faith before a king, best identified as Gundobad. Avitus would like him to become a bishop, but Heraclius has not agreed to do so yet: he may however later have become bishop of St-Paul-Trois-Châteaux.[1] One might compare Ennodius' words on Rusticus of Lyons in *Vita Epifani* 9: 'Rusticus held the episcopal seat, a man who always prefigured the priest, even in his secular office, and guided the church under the under the cover of the forum' (*Rusticus episcopalem cathedram possidebat, homo qui et in saecularis tituli praefiguratione sacerdotem semper exhibuit, et sub praetexta fori gubernationem gessit ecclesiae*).

Peiper dates this letter to 499/500, but various comments in Heraclius' reply (*Ep.* 54) may place it shortly after the siege of Vienne.[2] If this is the case, the two letters might postdate the rather bitchy *Epp.* 95-96, and suggest that the two men have made their peace.

---

1 *PLRE* 2, Heraclius 5.
2 Greg. Tur. *DLH* 2.33.

Avitus the bishop to Heraclius, vir illustrissimus *{81.29 Peiper}*

Since I am unendingly concerned about the faith and safety of my friends, recently, being worried among the most important things relating to Your Prosperity, I found out something that, I as bishop ought not to be silent about with a Catholic friend: expressions of joy rather than mere words are most appropriate to celebrate the benefit for you of the reward[1] that you have thus finally[2] acquired. Were it not that your extreme modesty prevents you, in your senatorial maturity, from boasting about your own achievement, your own tongue that miraculously convinces your adversaries might perhaps accord deserved praise to the effect of your glorious struggle[3] among your own people.[4]

I hear that you had a debate with the king. In it, as I hear, because you were not seduced, you went †from thresholds†[5] to battle. It was settled by divine fiat:[6] that he who was already known as such for a long time in heaven, now appear to men also as a defender of true belief.[7] Your tongue, accustomed to the ostentation of secular oratory and ever-watered with billowing waves of profound Roman eloquence, seized with all due alacrity the material for a fine disputation that had been sent to it from on high. When your eloquence had been deployed in describing the delights of the world or in praising royal triumphs,[8] when for the first time the better party[9] asked for an advocate,[10] you could not help but be of service in establishing the truth.

1 It is not clear whether Avitus is thinking of the conferment of some office or merely of the Heraclius' theological success.

2 Emending *tamen* (p. 82.1) to *tandem*. An adversative particle makes no sense. *Tandem ... taliter* make a better pair.

3 Is it mere coincidence that this sentence shares three words, *lingua, gloriosi* and *certaminis* with the opening line of Fortunatus, *C.* 2.2.1, *Pange, lingua, gloriosi proelium certaminis,* or do they share some common source?

4 Presumably the Catholics.

5 *Liminibus* is nonsensical and should be obelised.

6 Peiper mispunctuates. A colon is required after *divino*.

7 Although this seems to refer to Heraclius, it could allude to Sigismund openly supporting the Catholic position. The remainder of the letter suggests that it is unlikely to be Gundobad, although he does appear as a Catholic sympathiser elsewhere in the letters, especially *Ep.* 23: see also the comments of Perrat and Audin, 'Alcimi Ecdicii viennensis episcopi homilia', pp. 433–51.

8 An interesting mention of panegyric rhetoric at the royal court. See also *Ep.* 86, p. 282.

9 Rendering *pars melior*. Avitus refers to the Catholics.

10 Peiper inexplicably emends to the feminine *patronam* for L's *patrocinam*. Either the abstract *patrocinium* or the expected *patronum* would be preferable. A/U confusions are common in pre-Carolingian minuscules.

Just as on other occasions you rendered unto Caesar that which was Caesar's by praising the king, so here, in order to render unto God that which was God's, you did not spare Caesar.[1] Therefore the power of the king here has something to admire in you, even if he does not follow it.[2] Since on various occasions he felt that he had been adorned by your declamations, he now feels this all the more clearly; for by standing up to him when it was appropriate, you showed that you were insensible to the lures of [supine] acquiescence. The wisdom of those in power[3] notes that those who put earthly before heavenly things easily change sides in human affairs. Furthermore it is easily known that he who protects the more important causes[4] will also protect those things that are left over.

These things have been said[5] when we speak of the secular sphere. If we come to the affair[s] of bishops – you *still* have not joined their company, yet you already take blame for them, and, about to adorn their fellowship, you first teach them by your example! – which of these, which, I repeat, does not know that you came to the struggle of the spiritual wrestling-ring not unlettered or ignorant of the law, but [exercised] by lengthy training in spiritual meditation? Therefore let it be a new thing for others that you enjoin the necessity of this war because of the perfection of your own virtue:[6] I, however, in whose soul you have long dwelt in a citadel of love, had long recognised without hesitation, once the ardour of your devotion had been proved, that it was not so much that you lacked the *desire* to look into Catholic thought through study and to guard it through your words, as the *time*.[7]

Now that I have offered you my respectful greeting, showing that I too have been fed by the food with which you have satisfied your mind even while the body hungered, whence this small fullness of thanks bursts forth.[8] As for what remains – I beg from God that to him on whom he has already imposed the duty of a preacher, he may give the actual office.[9] Let what you

1 I.e. Gundobad.

2 Gundobad admires the theological reasoning, even if he does not convert to Catholicism.

3 *Potestatum* is *abstractum pro concreto*. For its use to mean 'rulers', see *Ep.* 27, p. 57.27.

4 Goelzer, pp. 592–93, translates *pars* as 'parti, cause'.

5 Taking S's *sunt*. L's perfect passive subunctive, *dicta sint*, must be wrong.

6 I.e. others did not know that Heraclius was so deeply committed to religion as to become involved in religious debate.

7 The plural *tempora*, 'times', as distinct from the singular *tempus*, 'time', is off in this context. It might mean 'opportunities'.

8 I.e. Heraclius' piety, even in his fasts, has sustained Avitus, prompting this letter of thanks.

9 I.e. Avitus is asking God to elevate Heraclius to the episcopate.

exercise in your acts be shown in your attire too. Let the episcopal throne take up not a teachable,[1] but a learned man, not one who is learning, but a teacher. In it, as if to one triumphing adorned with garlands of victorious laurel or myrtle, among the unanimous voices of those acclaiming you with joy, calling out how 'you rise with your shield outstretched',[2] even though he be unwilling, let the enemy who knows agree, because he will never find anything to fault in your merit, but will always have something to fear because of the unequal nature of the battle.[3]

Epistula 54: Introduction

The response to *Ep.* 53. Heraclius deprecates his own part in the doctrinal controversy. He describes the arrival of the heretical document that he had to refute in interesting satirical language.[4] His tongue was sharpened by hearing Avitus' own sermons. Amusingly enough his own style is as bombastic as Avitus'. Various references (*cessantis taedii tranquillitas se publica reddisset: murus nulla obpugnatione quassabitur*) seem to place this after the siege of Vienne in 500,[5] and may thus indicate that this and *Ep.* 53 represent a return to good relations, compared with the bickering between Avitus and Heraclius in *Epp.* 95 and 96.

Heraclius to Avitus the bishop of Vienne {83.1 Peiper}

Would that I could be frequently[6] strengthened in my long-lasting erudition by verbal fecundity like yours! When something like this happens, there is a doubly pleasing effect: lukewarm and fading faith grows hot when addressed by such burning exhortation, and wits that starve in their native poverty grow rich through the wealth of such an outstanding admirer. If you will permit me, I take it upon myself to give you my greatest thanks – along with my greeting – that the speech I made before the king, reported to you by rumour as you indicated, received such fitting praise not from

1 One susceptible to being taught.
2 *Aen.* 11.283. Avitus might also to be drawing a parallel with the practice of raising victorious leaders on a shield. cf. the soldiers' proclamation of Julian in Amm. Marc. 21.5.9. For the treatment of the victorious Clovis see Greg. Tur. *DLH* 2.40. The passage is slightly cryptic in Vergil, and looks as if it means 'towards/into/against his shield'.
3 I.e. the Arian will agree to your elevation because of your merits, even if he fears it because you will defeat him in argument.
4 Compare his language in *Ep.* 96.
5 Greg. Tur. *DLH* 2.33.
6 Heraclius uses *subinde* in its VL sense. Cf. French 'souvent'.

my mouth but from your love.[1] Our excellent ruler, even though he is fiery in his pursuit of material for speeches[2] and fluent in speaking, takes such pains to examine the minds of men that at audiences he invariably turns a very gentle ear. Nonetheless let me stem this tide of prolixity and tell you how my labours went. I say 'labours', because an inexperienced sailor could barely tolerate the storms that rush upon him with their unexpected gusts of wind.[3] Therefore when, thanks to God, the public tranquillity that follows a period of trouble[4] had restored itself, †as if the camp had long been changed†,[5] I found the struggle that awaited me. The most acrimonious conflict invariably seeks out lazy and unwarlike people[6] to attack. At first from another area of its own wrestling[-ground] the speech made some preliminary feints; then, as if from a sudden ambush the vomit from overseas[7] poured forth;[8] then I came upon the document, empty, but yapping out 'Greetings!'[9] It laughed so

1 Heraclius makes a sound-play on *ore* and *amore*.

2 Taking *inventio* in the rhetorical sense.

3 The following sentences are translated by R. Macpherson, *Rome in Involution: Cassiodorus's Variae in their Literary and Historical Setting* (Poznan, 1989), pp. 89–90.

4 Possibly a reference either to the crisis of 500 or to 508.

5 The allusion's grammar is clear (with the apparent substitution of *diu* for *iamdudum*) but the phrase makes little sense: its military imagery, however, is consonant with the rest of the passage and with Heraclius' love of strained metaphor.

6 This might be an ironical allusion to Avitus' accusations of desertion. See *Ep*. 95.

7 The 'vomit' probably came from Byzantium, given that it says 'Chaere'. Although Donatism is ruled out because of the indication that the heresy was Greek, compare *transmarina contagia* in *Ep*. 26.

8 The allusion is unclear, but it might be to the Eutychian problem. It is not clear that the *Bonosiaci* of *Ep*. 31 were foreign, but Photinians, who were often identified with the Bonosiacs (see the commentary on the *Contra Arrianos*, above p. 166), were already known in the Rhône valley: see Sidonius, *Ep*. 6.12.4 praising Patiens of Lyons for his handling of heretics: *teque quodam venatu apostolico feras **Fotinianorum** mentes spiritualium praedicationum cassibus implicare*.

9 An interesting textual problem. Peiper reads *denique incidi chartam, vacuam et chaere oblatrante*. But the syntax is awkward: one would expect an accusative participle (*oblatrantem*) as a minimal correction to parallel *vacuam*. S reads *Denique incidi in chartam vacuam, veteri obliterata* but this is meaningless. L reads *denique incidi chartam vacuam et //aere oblatrante*. Peiper thought the missing letter was a 'k'and emended to 'chaere'. *'Chaere' oblatrantem* might be a satirical allusion to Persius, *prol*. 8: tame parrots were known to call out 'Chaire'. The sense would then be 'empty of content, but yapping out "Greetings!"' The presence of apparent nonsense *veteri **obliterata*** in S is interesting, however. Sirmond made frequent and facile emendations, but this clearly is not one of them. Could it be the case that the text originally read *incidi chartam vacuam chaere obliterato*? 'I came upon a parchment, empty, its salutation-formula erased.' Theological epistles were occasionally circulated without the salutation-formula, cf. Claudianus Mamertus, *De Statu Animae* 1.2: Also *Ep*. 4, above p. 193.

mockingly, drawing its cloak of errors closely around itself, that, saving the liberty of the respondent, because of the wickedness of what was suggested, it had no way out, and brought weapons against its own throat even as it resisted. Need I say more? The page that began to be read [out loud] preferred to remain silent. Let it be clear to all how divided, how facile, how fit for rejection the persuasion was that, even though it had thought out many arguments, was not strong enough to disturb anyone not lacking in divine instruction.

I go over these things in this way so as to cause whatever is decided in God's cause to be ascribed to you beyond a doubt. For it is public knowledge that my conversations with you sharpened[1] my tongue carefully, and that the learning of your sermons enriches us all together. The result is that your episcopal see, to which divine justice brought you, is outstanding for its administrative function,[2] but deserves no less praise for the person of its administrator. Therefore fall upon your knees, home of my affections, and as a steadfast and pious guardian, beg for the help of God as you have been accustomed to, as much for yourself as for all of us. The wall of your faith will not be shaken in any siege.[3] We must see to it that you never cease to protect your children and students[4] with your well-known corrective severity,[5] and that you force them to conquer with you using, as we read, the powerful weapons of learning.

Epistula 95: Introduction

The context this letter and *Ep.* 96 that follows it is a period of war, perhaps even a siege of Vienne. There are three obvious possibilities: the first is the invasion of Clovis in 500: the second is the siege of Vienne by Gundobad, following Clovis' withdrawal from the Burgundian kingdom:[6] the third is the Ostrogothic invasion of 508. The assault on Vienne appears to be coming from west of the Rhône, but this is

---

1 The *lima* or 'file' is a traditional metaphor used of refining literary compositions or speech.

2 Heraclius is perhaps making a point about Vienne being a metropolitan diocese.

3 This appears to be a reference to the siege of Vienne: Greg. Tur. *DLH* 2.33. If the siege is also referred to in *Epp.* 95–96, Heraclius and Avitus are making up after their mutual exchange of acrimony.

4 Perhaps an allusion to the comment on *Ceratius noster* in *Ep.* 95.

5 The Latin is *castigatio*, but the context demands a more positive sense than 'castigation' – perhaps 'correction'. One remembers that Avitus is the *scholasticum bellicosum* of *Ep.* 95. See *Ep.* 28, p. 58.12 for Avitus alluding to his own episcopal severity.

6 For both see Greg. Tur. *DLH.* 2.32–33.

not particularly helpful, in that forces of Clovis, Gundobad and Theodoric might all have approached from that direction: while the main Ostrogothic attack on the Burgundians seems to have been from across the Alps, some troops of Theodoric may have moved towards the Rhône, having retaken the Auvergne. On balance the most likely date for the letters is ca. 500,[1] but the threat could either be from the Franks or from Gundobad. If Avitus had taken refuge in Vienne when the city was controlled by Godegisel, this would surely have affected his relations with Gundobad.

Heraclius must have left Vienne, told Avitus that he had a bad case of gout, and also mentioned that he was writing some sort of poem. Avitus accuses him of malingering and running away. He tells him that a friend Protadius has just died and that he had to attend the obsequies. Avitus asks Heraclius to hold on to a young man called Ceratius. The letter closes with what looks like a nasty sting in the tail – particularly if, as has been suggested, Ceratius is Heraclius' own son.[2] He might have been a relative on his mother's side of Avitus', viz. *nostrum* 'our Ceratius', and the form of the gibe, in which *de meo* seems to be in parallel with *de matris sapientia* and *de vestro* with *de virtute paterna*.[3]

PLRE 2 Heraclius 5 suggests that Heraclius was Protadius' father, presumably on the basis of mistranslating the phrase, 'thus however, even in this [matter] itself, it offers some consolation to a father', *sic tamen vel in hoc ipso patri aliquid consolationis impendat*. This is impossible. Had that been the case, Avitus would never have referred to Protadius as *communis filius noster*. He would have begun his letter with the sad news, and would have employed consolatory rhetoric. It also seems unthinkable, had he been Protadius' father, that Heraclius would not have mentioned his relationship to the young man in the opening of *Ep.* 96. The 'father' (*pater*) in that sentence is clearly some third party. Avitus is excusing himself by saying that he had stayed to attend a funeral and thereby offer consolation to Protadius' father. The communication has much to say about divisions between family members in the face of invasions. A false or cowardly choice seems to have entailed as much *odium* as flight in persecution did among early Christians.

Avitus the bishop to Heraclius, vir illustrissimus *[102.15 Peiper]*

Were I not sorely struck in my spirit mourning the sad death of a friend, I would certainly have a great deal to say![4] For it is an interest in climbing

---

1 Jahn, *Geschichte der Burgundionen*, 2, pp. 125–28, suggested that this letter should be dated to 500, and that the threat across the Rhône was Frankish. Jahn's analysis is questioned by Favrod, *Histoire politique*, pp. 342–43, esp. n. 209.

2 This was suggested by Mathisen, 'PLRE II: Some Suggested Addenda and Corrigenda', p. 369, and accepted by Heinzelmann, 'Gallische Prosopographie (260–527)', Ceratius [Ceretius] 2, p. 578.

3 A version of Shaw's 'your brains and my beauty' quip.

4 Lit. 'would be exaggerating/heaping up many things'.

mountains[1] rather than scanning[2] verses that has got you on the move; even though you are keeping to your bed for fear of a feigned case of gout, you are active and mobile thanks to the customary skill of a doctor, and are putting weight on more than just metrical feet![3] I dictated these words, both sadly and in haste, for I have been summoned to the burial of our common son, the late Protadius: thus, however, even in this [matter] itself, it offers some consolation to his father. If it gives you any pleasure, since a total loss has occurred in our case – to be protected[4] against the dreaded invasions by the Rhone [alone] as boundary, until I return, keep our Ceratius too with you,[5] who has [inherited] some things from my < masculine noun in ellipsis>[6] < in that ... >[7] and not a few from yours,[8] in that he claims to you that I am an irritable schoolman.[9] He (*sc.* Ceratius) inherits from the wisdom of his mother the fact that he willingly flees barbarians,[10] and from the courage[11] of his father that he does not turn his back[12] on literature.

Epistula 96: Introduction

Heraclius has, aside from the first two sentences, sent an extremely ill-tempered response to Avitus, accusing him of cowardice for taking refuge in time of invasion

1 In light of the next letter, it would appear that Avitus is hinting that Heraclius has taken to his heels over the mountains out of Vienne.

2 Avitus puns. In Latin *scando* can mean both 'to climb' and 'to scan'.

3 *Plus quam poeticae pedibus innitentes*. One might suggest an emendation to *poeticis* 'poetic feet', rather than 'the feet of poetry', but it is not necessary, given the early (Ciceronian) attestation of *poetica* as a noun. There is a nice parallel for this sort of punning about feet, scansion and gout in Claudian, *Carm. Min.* 13, *in podagricum qui carmina sua non stare dicebat*. Likewise in Ennod. *Carm.* 2.146.

4 Taking this as an epexegetic infinitive explaining *iactura*.

5 In addition to some other person? Was there a lacuna before this passage?

6 One might guess *pater*, 'father' or *magister*, 'teacher'.

7 There may be a missing clause to parallel *quia ... bellicosum*, 'in that ...' The lacuna may also have included the noun which *meo* and *tuo* modified. At this point the text degenerates so badly that it is close to impossible to reconstruct with any reasonable degree of certainty.

8 Same masculine noun in ellipsis.

9 Translating L's text. The clause from *quia ... bellicosum* is still slightly intrusive, because it is not strictly parallel, i.e. there is no corresponding explanatory clause after *habentem aliqua*. It might be sensible to indicate a lacuna there.

10 Discretion is the better part of valour.

11 Almost certainly sarcastic in tone.

12 *Tergum dare/praebere* means to 'turn tail' in a military sense. Heraclius is clearly every inch the literary man, so a son who fled military trouble (as he did), but never turned his back on letters would match the profile of his *virtus paterna* nicely.

within the walls of Vienne, and for not being present both physically and spiritually for his people. He defends himself against the accusation of having taken to the hills, emphasising that he is exposed to the enemy in wide open spaces. In the inclusion of this letter in the collection we may perhaps see confirmation of the fact that the letters were not selected by Avitus himself.

Heraclius to Avitus, bishop of Vienne {102.26}

You have indicated so great cause of grief to be staunched by written answer, that the wound inflicted by this bitter news compels me to pay service in tears rather than in writing. Nonetheless, since I feared that my silence would be blamed, to the extent that I could, I stole a few words from my sighs. The times therefore are a test of who ought more appropriately to have the stigma[1] of fear ascribed to him, or whose careful foresight committed to cloisters proves rather that *he* is afraid. I, disdaining hiding-places in the city, have exposed the constancy of my heart to testing nearby, in order that I might hold my ground[2] near the flat and open places for a sufficient amount of time for me to show the boldness of my courage[3] by living where I wish to. *You*, however, as soon as you heard the rumour, fled to within the limits of the city like the servants of the winds and [you] whom the countryside has claimed for long periods of time in days of peace, they now cannot lead out from your hiding-place within the walls![4] Indeed, as much as the city used to beg for you before,[5] even though you are now installed within its ramparts,[6] your abandoned possession (i.e. the city)[7] still seeks you to the same extent.

1 Described as if it were a brand-mark of infamy.

2 The MSS read *pervenirem*, 'arrive'. This is odd. *Pervenirem,* which should denote punctual action, 'arriving', is inconsistent with an adverb like *tamdiu* that implies continuous action. One might emend to *permanerem*, 'that I might hold my ground'.

3 Heraclius picks up on Avitus' gibe about *paterna virtus* in *Ep*. 95, p. 102.25.

4 The account of the siege of Vienne in 500 suggests that it was rather more dangerous to remain in the city than outside it: Greg. Tur. *DHL*, 2.32; Marius of Avenches, *s.a.* 500.

5 This might imply that Avitus was an absentee bishop on his country estate (*villa rustica*), a picture that does not fit with the general impression of Avitus' presence in his cathedral city, at least on feast-days and festivals, given by the bishop's other letters.

6 Compare Sidonius' role during the siege of Clermont: Harries, *Sidonius Apollinaris and the Fall of Rome*, pp. 227–29.

7 Perhaps with a vague recollection of Lam. 1.1ff., 'How lonely the city sits that used to be full of people, the mistress of peoples has become like a widow,' etc. *Quomodo sedet sola civitas plena populo: facta est quasi vidua, domina gentium, princeps provinciarum facta est sub tributo… .1.6 facti sunt principes eius quasi arietes non invenientes pascua et abierunt absque fortitudine ante faciem subsequentis.*

19. OTHER LAYMEN

Contents

Epistula 37 Avitus to Aurelianus, *vir illustris*: guarded advice on how Aurelianus should conduct himself in difficult political circumstances.

Epistula 50 Avitus to Arigius, *vir illustrissimus*: Avitus apologises for being unable to attend the dedication of a church that Arigius has restored magnificently – presumably after an enemy invasion.

Epistula 56 Avitus to Messianus, *vir illustrissimus*: a cagey letter asking for news.

Epistula 37: Introduction

An obscure and puzzling letter. In many ways it is a latter-day counterpart of moral epistles such as Horace, *C.* 2.10 *rectius vives, Licini*. The circumstances behind its opaque facade may not be recoverable. Aurelianus[1] has been in some sort of political trouble, and has clearly been led to distrust friends, perhaps even Avitus himself. He must have described his difficulties using the traditional metaphors of storms and shipwreck.[2] The troubles seem to have embittered him, and this may be why Avitus advises him not to think that he can put an end to hostilities by stirring the pot. Instead he advises him to be more cynical and take advantage of momentary respites and changes of allegiance. Avitus ends with an assurance of his own affection for Aurelianus, while recognising the fact that his friend may not be permitted to write to him. The dangerous political circumstances might also indicate that 'in that world instead', *eo magis saeculo*, covertly alludes to the start of a new régime under a new ruler, while apparently talking of the life of the world to come.

If Aurelianus were to be identified with the man who, according to Fredegar,[3] acted as Clovis' double agent at the Burgundian court, facilitating the marriage of Clovis and Chrotechildis, this might explain some of the context of the letter – although it would be difficult to square Avitus' friendship with Aurelianus' anti-Burgundian actions as described by Fredegar.[4] His account, however, also opens up the possibility that Aurelianus was writing from the Frankish kingdom: certainly *si licet, scribite* seems either to imply that there was a frontier between the two men, or

---

1 *PLRE* 2, Aurelianus 7.

2 See Ruricius, *Epp.* 1.12.5 and 2.13.1–3 for similar platitudes. Also Hagendahl, *Correspondance*, pp. 88–89.

3 Fredegar 3.18. The identity of the two men is doubted by Heinzelmann, 'Gallische Prosopographie', Aurelianus 4, 5, p. 564.

4 It is, of course, possible that the two men are one and the same and that Fredegar's account is misleading.

that Aurelianus was under arrest.[1] That Avitus himself was favourable to connections with the Frankish court may be implied by *Ep.* 5, p. 33, 6–8, and can certainly be inferred from *Ep.* 46.

Avitus the bishop to Aurelianus, vir illustrissimus {66.22 Peiper}

It is clear sign of prosperity, however small, that, when the love of friends shines upon us, even though it be but for a little while, we are visited by the semblance[2] of a brief period of peace. Nonetheless that seething flood, which you have compared to natural storms, presses hard on human lives with a flood of persistent turmoil as we sail through the seas of the world. As to the times when we manage to draw breath between the hardships of our times – we should think them a respite from the crises that we suffer rather than an end to them. For this reason this 'peace'[3] seems teasingly only to set a limit to the discomforts of our misfortunes rather than to cure them, in order that future[4] groaning may the more seriously affect minds that have been relaxed by a false sense of security, when cause for fear arises again. Therefore, my dear fellow, stop believing that there is an end to troubles in seething †evils†.[5] When, after the storm has been calmed, some modicum of serenity presents itself instead of the opposite, do not just bask in the variety of benefits, but *take advantage of them.* Do not let good fortune thus raise you up, nor adversity break you in such a way that in your mind the status of your friends changes like the weather. Always remember the affection I offered you. If it is permitted, write; if not, and *that* cannot be prevented – continue to feel affection for me at least. And after the storms that you

---

1 Another contemporary Aurelianus, also living across a frontier, is Ennodius' relative: *PLRE* 2, Aurelianus 7 = Heinzelmann, 'Gallische Prosopographie', Aurelianus 6, pp. 564–65. Although he was bishop by 512, he is thought previously to have been married and to have children. He would have been of the appropriate class for a *v.i.*

2 For this sense of *color*, see *TLL s.v.* 'color', 1721.27–46.

3 Or 'truce': perhaps that between Clovis and Gundobad in 500.

4 *Succiduus = subsequens.*

5 The sentence is both enigmatic and crucial for the interpretation of the letter. L's *in malis ferventibus*, 'in seething evils', is obscure, and unlikely to be sound: 'among seething evils' (the objective external circumstances) or 'in evils on the boil' (a situation that Aurelianus could be perpetuating to achieve a *finis malorum*). *Malis* may well be an *Antizipationsfehler*. S's *mala ferventia* looks like a crude attempt at correction: 'stop believing that seething troubles are the end of trouble'.

describe in your letters, hope for a port in that world[1] instead, where the calm weather you crave will no longer need to fear a shipwreck.

Epistula 50: Introduction

Avitus has been invited to the dedication of a new church by the *dux* Arigius. The dedication will be a great occasion with numerous clergy praising the building.[2] Avitus, however, cannot attend, because the ceremony falls on the Feast of St Peter, which was of special importance to the church of Vienne. The townspeople would, therefore, expect their bishop to be present in his cathedral city.[3] Besides, on this particular occasion a chapel was to be dedicated. Avitus alludes to another reason which he cannot set out, and he also refers to some tragedy requiring commemoration.[4]

Avitus provides an intriguing insight into ceremonies of dedication by describing what he expected to take place, as well as making some comment on the architecture – something which he did in his dedication homily for the baptistery in Vienne.[5] In addition, apart from the insights which Avitus provides on the expectations of his own (rather tetchy) congregation, this letter, parts of which are formidably difficult or, more likely, corrupt, also seems to allude to important events in the history of the Burgundian kingdom.

Arigius is usually identified with the Aridius of Gregory of Tours' *Histories*.[6] According to Gregory he was with Gundobad when the latter took refuge in Avignon during the war of 500, and it was he who, pretending to change sides, negotiated a peace with Clovis that allowed Gundobad to recoup his strength. This information dovetails precisely with what Avitus tells us in the letter about Arigius, and suggests that Arigius had founded a church that was almost ready for dedication when the

---

1 The phrase is no doubt deliberately vague, leaving room for two interpretations: the afterlife or a new regime. *Saeculum*, as used by Avitus elsewhere, is contrasted to the spiritual world (Goelzer, pp. 436 and 451), except where it just means 'time'. Compare Augustine's notion of *saeculum* as discussed by R. A. Markus, *Saeculum. History and Society in the Theology of St Augustine* (Cambridge, 1970).

2 See Wood, 'The Audience of Architecture', pp. 74–79.

3 Compare *Ep.* 67.

4 One might perhaps compare *Ep.* 5, with its possible reference to the death of Fuscina.

5 *Hom.* 18.

6 *PLRE* 2 tentatively identifies him with Aredius (Greg. Tur. *DLH* 2.32; Fredegar 3.18.23; *Lib. Hist. Franc.* 16). The identification is supported by Heinzelmann, 'Gallische Prosopographie', Aredius, p. 559. The identification is phonetically probable. Both 'Arigius' and 'Aridius' would have been trisyllabic in Vulgar Latin: 'Aridyus' and 'Arigyus'. -dy- and -gy- were confused in Gallo-Romance, the result in both cases just being a graphic -i-: cf. Fr. moyen< OFr. meien < *medianus*; Eloi < Elei < Eligius. Eventually both 'Aridius' and 'Arigius' would have turned up as *Aroi.

crisis of 500 struck, that he apparently abandoned his friends, but in doing so saved the day (a point which confirms Gregory's account, which might otherwise be seen as somewhat folkloric), and that, as a result of his actions, he was able to see to the dedication of his church. The possible connection between the information in *Ep.* 50 and Gregory of Tours suggests a date shortly after 500. The letter is, therefore, crucial evidence for the politics as well as for the church of the Burgundian kingdom, revealing a somewhat suspicious world in which the actions of individuals constantly had to be justified.

Avitus the bishop to Arigius, vir illustrissimus *{78.7 Peiper}*

I know how very much you wanted me to go to [our] common[1] celebrations. But you ought to have known that it would have been as someone who would rejoice only with you, not as someone who would be of any use. For while many worthy bishops approach you solemnly and eagerly, I alone am struck by a loss[2] and am not worthy to take part in the joys of your exceptional patronage.

If I had been able to come, as I wished, I would be hearing all of these worthy speakers praising the great work.[3] For after they examined all parts of the lofty structure, they would appropriately ascribe to its builder the elegance of its fittings, the sacrifice[4] involved in its great cost, the harmonious proportion of its dimensions, its size, the height of its roof, the firm solidity of its foundation.[5] They would be able to polish[6] with praise the glory of the marble revetments – only envy of their size would deny them the status of gems! – to praise the daylight collected somehow and enclosed by man's labour,[7] alive with the light of so many precious shining metals, and in all of this pomp and ceremony to praise the relics, which the world barely deserves, ceremoniously laid to rest.[8]

1 I.e. Avitus and Aridius shared a patron saint, Peter.

2 The phrase *ego solus damno percellor* appears also in *Ep.* 45. Here one may wonder whether it relates not just to Avitus not being able to attend the ceremony, but also to the *praeteriti* of the penultimate sentence.

3 Avitus may well have known Sidonius' verse-description of Patiens' church at Lyons. See Sid. *Ep.* 2.10.4ff. Here, as in *Ep.* 46, Avitus recreates the ceremony he could not attend.

4 Lit. 'loss'.

5 Given the antithesis to *culmen*, *humilitas* probably denotes the foundation, though a pun may also be intended, referring to the humility of the founder.

6 The word is chosen with intent.

7 The notion of enclosed light recurs often in Late Antique aesthetics, see Prudentius, *Per.* 3.191–200.

8 *Inferri*. Lit. 'bring brought in'.

I had properly left these things to be praised by others better than myself. But nonetheless my speech had been on the point of claiming its own special reward in remembering that time when without punishment, among fierce storms and disturbances, like a pilot,[1] you conducted the firm and solid finished work, amid the shrieks and crashes of shipwreck, to the [very verge of the][2] safe haven of its dedication. I, as you will remember given our common danger, was weeping instead of rejoicing < ... >[3] †In an access of premature zeal to invoke, after having weighed all the reasons, I persuade him[4] at that time no less to gather[5] him/it[6] together than to weep. †Because, unlike a bride,[7] who had to be joined in whatever way to such a husband, as she was promised,† even though cult-vessels were badly needed, nonetheless it was right to fear the weapons of the plunderers more.[8] Therefore, after you had given due consideration to all the circumstances, brave man[9] as you are, you changed the nature of your steadfastness, and setting aside the boldness of your secular office of *Dux*,[10] in which you are particularly skilled, you overcame, through your fear, whatever danger from the enemy was imminent.[11] Therefore let everyone who sees the occasion for happiness before our eyes, praise your haste in the past. Safety snatched from adversity

1 *Gubernatores invicti* is *pluralis maiestatis* referring to Arigius.

2 *Portus* ought to imply that the dedication has taken place, but from the context it is clear that the it was deferred.

3 There appears to be a gap in the text here. It is completely unclear to what *cui* and *ipsum* refer. *Cui* might be governed by *suadeo*, but even then what is *ipsum*? One could emend to *ipsi* 'to him/her/it itself'

4 *Cui*.

5 Almost certainly corrupt.

6 *Ipsum*, if it is the right reading.

7 *Nuptae should* be dative, continuing the construction in *cui ... suadeo*, but the text is irretrievably garbled. There seem to be two alternatives, either to obelise the whole passage, or else to emend it to *quia non ut nupta tali sponso, cui pacta fuerat, qualitercumque iungenda* so that it is consistently singular and nominative. It could then be attached to the following clause beginning with *etsi* as a negative analogy. It is not the case that the marriage has to take place in any circumstances. The word *nuptae* may refer to the church to be dedicated as the bride of Christ. See *Ep.* 7, p. 37.14ff. It could also refer to an actual bride or to the vessels in the church as figurative 'brides', necessary for the ceremony. The text is too damaged to tell.

8 And hide the *ministeria*, presumably.

9 *Viri fortes*. Again Avitus uses *pluralis maeiestatis* of Arigius. He is addressing one *dux* alone.

10 On *duces* in the Frankish kingdom, see A. R. Lewis, 'The Dukes of the Regnum Francorum, AD 550–751', *Speculum* 51 (1976), pp. 381–410.

11 This seems to be a reference to Aridius' action in retiring with Gundobad to Avignon, thus saving the king and his followers: Greg. Tur. *DLH* 2.33.

was appropriate to your arrangements. It was right that we first gain possession of what it had been your pleasure to adorn in this fashion. Even if nothing be said, you, both as noble patron and fair judge, know why I do not now take full pleasure in the sight of these things.[1] It is because, for your people at Vienne at least, the feast of the Apostles, among the [many] annual celebrations of the martyrs is an occasion of special devotion.[2] I must be present at the time on the day[3] of the passion[4] when the dedication of the little church[5] that you know seems to have been set. Indeed, because there is nothing that Your Affection could not bind me[6] to perform, I would excuse my absence to my beloved little congregation,[7] placing the extraordinary circumstances before routine custom, were it not, as you know, that among our penitents, their zeal, eager to find fault with their neighbours would cause hatred and protest here,[8] since among my people, ambition will motivate some, concern others, and juvenile[9] greed the most.[10] I was afraid that perhaps at the same time eagerness to comply might lead some out of the few who were there[11] to reject other peoples' celebrations and gather instead at their own festival, and that others might be upset – as tends to happen in the event of such a disruption: as if through my absence on that

1 This sentence can be translated (after a fashion) as it stands in Peiper's text. *Advertitis* introduces an indirect question, *quae causa faciat*, on which the result-clause *ut ... perfruar* depends. But the force of the *autem* (p. 78.34) is unclear, as is that of the *et* (before *quae*). The *et* could be bracketed for excision. Given, however, the emphatic pronoun, *ego*, and the *autem* at the beginning of the sentence, one wonders whether there may not instead be a lacuna between *perfruar* and *et*.

2 Taking F's *inter annuos martyrum dies*. One might note that the church of St Peter (i.e. of the Apostles) was the burial place of the bishops of Vienne, notably of Avitus himself: *Vita Aviti* 6. For an argument that some of the surviving fabric may date from Avitus' day, see Wood, 'The Audience of Architecture', pp. 77–8.

3 Taking F's *die*.

4 I.e the Feast of St Peter on 29 June.

5 Following Goelzer, p. 477, and A. Blaise, *Dictionnaire Latin-Française des auteurs chrétiens* (Turnhout, 1967).

6 Lit. 'my spirit'.

7 Compare *Ep.* 68 above p. 274 n. 5.

8 For another problem with penitents, *Ep.* 17.

9 Peiper emends to the rare *gliscentior*. The MS reading *adulescentior*, however, seems acceptable.

10 This presumably refers to the feasts that a bishop might be expected to lay on for his congregation on a major feast day: cf. Greg. Tur. *LVP* 3.

11 *Forent* must be the substantive verb, given the lack of predicate, but 'existed' makes no sense. Is *forent* used for *adforent*? One might suggest an emendation such as *e paucis qui adforent*.

day the routine of our holy worship, through which all kinds of different people were clearly being educated, could be thought to have been omitted. For this reason I deserve to be excused. If you have really understood the reason, forgive me. Recognise the common feast by remembering the dead[1] while a great number [of the living] are present. Celebrate it as much through the offices of those absent as those present. I trust in the mercy of our Lord, that he will also grant me here, at some more opportune moment, a chance to speak to him[2] to whom he has conceded a more lavish double consecration.[3]

Epistula 56: Introduction

An egregiously polite communication, but more than a pure friendship letter. No doubt deliberately elliptical and allusive in content. Avitus never clarifies what precisely it is that Messianus does, though he seems to be someone of importance, given the number of honorifics lavished upon him. The letter was one part of the papyrus, where it appears to have followed *Ep.* 55 and preceded *Ep.* 51, suggesting that the order of letters in Lyons MS and in Sirmond is not original.[4]

Avitus the bishop to Messianus, vir illustrissimus[5] *{85.9 Peiper}*

The crowning touch is added to my desire by eagerly awaited rich joys, if my greedy and concerned prayers find out that Your Magnificent Piety is blooming and flourishing in prosperity. For whatever celestial benefits the kindness of Your Clemency,[6] spread abroad, has bestowed will, without doubt, grow speedily and happily, and enrich us. For we measure the happy increments by which our venture prospers by the extent to which support for what you do continually grows. For this reason, while giving you the polite greeting[7] you deserve, I ask, as we wish, that, if everything is going well for you, Your Greatness so inform us by laying the matter out in an eloquent and fluent page.[8]

---

1 Perhaps an allusion to those who died during the troubles alluded to in this letter.

2 *Quibus* refers to Arigius: *pluralis maiestatis.*

3 Arigius' church is dedicated to the Apostles, not just St Peter.

4 *Scedulae Parisinae,* 5r and 5v: Peiper, p. 154. See Chapter 2.

5 Messianus is otherwise unknown, but see *PLRE* 2, Messianus 2, where it is suggested that he may be the grandson of Messianus 1, who served under the emperor Avitus as *MVM* and *patricius,* and who died at the battle of Placentia. This may imply continuing family connections.

6 *Clementiae vestrae* is genitive.

7 *Honorificum salve,* translated by Goelzer, p. 674, as 'un grand bonjour'.

8 The sentence is adorned by a quadruple p-alliteration in Latin.

20. FESTAL LETTERS TO LAYMEN IN BURGUNDIAN TERRITORY

Contents

Epistula 80 Avitus to Ansemundus, *vir illustrissimus*: festal greetings.
Epistula 81 Avitus to Ansemundus, *vir illustrissimus*: festal greetings.
Epistula 82 Avitus to Valerianus, *vir illustrissimus*: festal greetings for Easter.
Epistula 83 Avitus to Ceretius, *vir illustrissimus*: festal greetings for Lent: Ceretius' presence at court in Chalon calls forth some standard Avitan comments on food (cf. also *Ep.* 76).
Epistula 84 Avitus to Helladius, *vir illustris*: festal greetings.
Epistula 85 Avitus to Ruclo, *vir illustrissimus*: festal greetings for Easter.

Introduction

Epp. 80–85 are all festal letters addressed to laymen and stand together as a group in L and S. Although trite, they give a picture of aristocratic Gallo-Roman society regularly attendant on the king, especially at the great festivals of the church.

Epistula 80: Introduction

This and 81 form a pair. The king was meant to spend Christmas at Vienne, but appears to have been ill; so too Ansemundus. Avitus sends his respects to the latter, who seems to have been *comes* of Vienne,[1] and was clearly attendant on the king, and asks for news. Although a Burgundian, Ansemundus was unquestionably a Catholic: greetings associated with a Christian festival would have caused no difficulty.[2]

Avitus the bishop to Ansemundus,[3] vir illustrissimus {93.27 Peiper}

Our master's[4] recent illness that has not yet – so far as I know – been completely cured has made your servants so alert and worried that, instead of the

---

1 He has been identified with the Aunemundus or one of the Aunemundi who signed the *prima constitutio* of the *Liber Constitutionum*. That he was *comes* of Vienne is implied by the expectation that he would be present on feast-days. See also *Ep.* 55, where Ansemundus also seems to be *comes* of Vienne. See Heinzelmann, 'Gallische Prosopographie', Ansemundus, p. 554.

2 For Ansemundus' involvement in the foundations of St André le Haut and St André le Bas in Vienne, Amory, 'The Textual Transmission of the Donatio Aunemundi', pp. 164–66.

3 L has 'Sigismund', but the reference to *domnus noster* seems to imply that the letter cannot be to him. It is better to take S's 'Ansemundus'.

4 Either Gundobad's or Sigismund's. Given the sickness of the king, it is tempting to

sight of that piety that we have become accustomed to hope for especially on feast[-days], we believe that Your Good Health[1] is sufficient for us in exchange for the joyfulness associated with the solemnities. This is why in paying my customary dutiful and concerned respects after the celebration[2] of the birthday of our Lord I am extremely eager to know whether the shared glory that on this occasion the humble[3] church of Vienne has not been fortunate enough to gain, has perhaps doubled the joys of the people of Lyons.[4] For if you, Christ willing, write back that you have either been able to go on to[5] the church, or have paid the customary devotion, since we will thus have shared in the happiness of our neighbours, we admit that we will feast on the tidings, if we find out that those who were given a chance to meet you were refreshed by the sight.[6]

Epistula 81

Avitus the bishop to Ansemundus, vir illustrissimus *{94.7 Peiper}*

When you keep prayers of your special servants in suspense by staying away,[7] you cause us not fully to achieve what we pray for and not to announce what it is that we want. Now that the holidays associated with the birth of our Lord have been solemnly celebrated to the extent that was possible without you, we are waiting to find out from your worthy lips[8] how our most pious master fares, since we had quite properly longed to see him. You have refreshed that congregation[9] with joy, make this one rich with a letter. May your affection shed light upon it through me, until I meet you and present my respects to you.

---

identify him as Gundobad and to date the letters late in his life.

1 Goelzer, p. 560, takes *commoditas* as 'good health', but Avitus seems to intend some sort of honorific.

2 Taking S's *cultum*.

3 Diminutive *ecclesiola* is presumably used for modesty. Elsewhere they seem to indicate a combination of modesty and affection. Cf. *fabriculae* p. 79.2; *plebeculae* p. 79.3.

4 I.e. whether the king[s] has/have gone to Lyons intead.

5 L has a hapax, *procordare*, printed by Peiper. No translation is offered by Goelzer, p. 461. S reads *procedere*.

6 Lit. 'the gazing'.

7 I.e. by playing hard to get.

8 Lit. 'from such a worthy address' (*alloquio*).

9 The word used is *plebs*. At Lyons. The word *plebs* develops into *plou* (Breton), *plwyf* (Welsh), and *pieve* (Italian), 'parish'. See W. Meyer-Lübke, *Romanisches etymologisches Wörterbuch* (Heidelberg, 1972), 6591.

Epistula 82

Avitus the bishop to Valerianus, vir illustrissimus *{94.14 Peiper}*

Your Piety has maintained its custom of expressing care by visiting us with both favour[1] and letters. You have added to the feast that we celebrated joyfully since God granted it, and, as you were expecting, you supplemented it through the desirable consummation of the cults. To me as I congratulate [you] on what I know about your happiness, it is no less a source of happiness that you have come back after a long period of absence than that you are passing the Easter holiday in a spirit of joy.

Epistula 83: Introduction

Another playful food-letter, one of a fish-sequence comprising *Ep.* 72 (closely related to it in genre) and *Epp.* 66, 74 and 86. Ceretius has been staying too long at Chalon and eating too many fine fish from the Sâone. Avitus offers him a 'revenge' from the Isère: not-so-fine fish. If Ceretius is still in Chalon to receive the present, all is well. If he has left and the package has to wait, he should avoid it. It seems likely that this is another 'fastal' letter joking about episcopal Lenten austerities.[2]

Avitus the bishop to Ceretius,[3] vir illustrissimus *{94.21 Peiper}*

After I had sent the letters that were due to our common master,[4] I also now discharge the debt I always owe Your Sublimity, whom I love. Suggesting, nay rather begging, because you have been so obstinate, that you finally shrink [your] stomach, queasy with the many delights from the Sâone[5] with the more meagre fasts of our[6] Isère.[7] If you do not know how to repay [my] longing – with the result that your absence *still* does not seem sufficiently long to you – compelled by the wrong you do me, this is what I want, and

---

1 Goelzer, p. 589.

2 For a fuller treatment see Shanzer, 'Bishops, Letters'.

3 Cf. *Epp.* 38 and 95, although Heinzelmann, 'Gallische Prosopographie', p. 578, distinguishes between the Ceretius of *Epp.* 38 and 83, and the Ceratius (sic) of *Ep.* 95.

4 Gundobad or Sigismund.

5 Indicating that the royal court has been based at Chalon-sur-Sâone.

6 The sense requires that L's *nostra* be emended to *nostrae* for contrast between Ceretius' location on the Sâone and Avitus' on the Isère. See n. 7 below.

7 Presumably the Isère, which flows into the Rhône at Vienne. Emending L's nonsensical *Iaeriae* to *Iseriae*.

how I revenge[1] myself through the bearer of this imprecation: so that the present state of affairs be altered, let the citizen of Chalon obtain what is plentiful in Vienne. Here we do not have what ought to be sought out; let us send there what it may be your pleasure to reject. And because what I am talking about is already on its way, if you are still delayed on the spot, accept it. If you are already minded to leave, pass it by.[2]

Epistula 84

Avitus the bishop to Helladius,[3] vir illustrissimus *{95.1 Peiper}*

Although my affection is always reason enough to pay my respects to Your Greatness and I rightly owe special devotion to your more than determined kindness, the holiday has now brought upon me the longed-for necessity of coming before Your Kindness through the medium of my letters, even though I would like to be there in person also! Therefore, considering with [all] appropriate respect what holiday you have celebrated and how willingly,[4] I ask, praying the inexhaustible generosity of Our Redeemer that he promote you as he has done up till now under his hundredfold protection, and that he advance your cause and give you every [possible] reward – to redound to *our* credit![5]

Epistula 85

Avitus the bishop to Ruclo, vir illustrissimus *{95.9 Peiper}*

After the feast in which our prayers for the presence and health of our master[6] played a prominent role, and we had sent writings to that effect, it is right that in addition a dutiful letter such as this be offered to you, who hold a special place in our affections. In it,[7] amid all those rumours [rife] about

1 Cf. the identical 'revenge' in *Ep.* 92, p. 90.7.

2 Obviously it will have begun to stink.

3 Mathisen, 'PLRE II: Some Suggested Addenda and Corrigenda', identifies Helladius with Illidius of Greg. Tur. *LVJ* 7–8. See also Heinzelmann, 'Gallische Prosopographie', p. 622, Hillidius, Helladius 2.

4 L's *Et ex voto* is somewhat obscure. S's *ex voto* equally so. As it stands it appears to be a zeugma, but something may be missing

5 Lit. 'to adorn us'. Helladius may be a citizen of Vienne.

6 Compare *Ep.* 80.

7 I.e. the letter. Peiper has mispunctuated. He should have put a full stop not after *offertur*, but after *significo*.

our [evil] circumstances,[1] I inform you that, as it turned out, we spent an happy Easter.[2] I judge[3] that Easter's fulfilment will come to me, thanks to the good effects of the divine gift, in the following fashion: if I am fortunate enough to have the opportunity to speak with you and find out that things have gone well for you too.

Appendix

Post festivitatem in qua de praesentia vel incolumitate domni nostri vota vestra et merita claruerunt, paginis ad ipsum officii destinatis, iure vobis, peculiaribus pectoris mei etiam praesentium litterarum famulatio offertur. Per quam nos inter tantos, ut fieri potuit, rerum rumores Pascha prospere transegisse significo sic mihi eius plenitudine divini muneris beneficiis proventura, si vestri quoque adloquii dignationem cum simili prosperitatis agnitione meruero.

The letter needs repunctuation. Peiper has two sentences: *Post ... offertur* and a second one, *Per quam ... meruero,* where *quam* functions as introductory relative and the main verb is *significo.* But *sic*, 'thus', is not a satisfactory subordinating conjunction for the rest of the second sentence, and it is unclear what *proventura* is doing. As printed it must modify *plenitudine,* but such an ablative absolute is unacceptable. There are two solutions:

1. The letter could be punctuated with a comma after *offertur*, and a full stop (with elegant full periodicity as so often in festal letters) after *significo.* But a main verb is still required for the *sic*-clause. One could emend to an impersonal *proventurum* *<est>*:[4] 'Thus in Easter's[5] fulfilment things will turn out well for me, thanks to the good effects of the divine gift, if I am fortunate enough to have the opportunity to speak with you and find out that things have gone well for you too.'

Post festivitatem in qua de praesentia vel incolumitate domni nostri vota vestra et merita claruerunt, paginis ad ipsum officii destinatis, iure vobis, peculiaribus pectoris mei etiam praesentium litterarum famulatio offertur. Per quam nos inter tantos, ut fieri potuit, rerum rumores Pascha prospere transegisse significo. Sic mihi eius plenitudine divini muneris beneficiis proventurum <est>, si vestri quoque adloquii dignationem cum simili prosperitatis agnitione meruero.

---

1 Presumably bad tidings – perhaps of war, or relating to Avitus' health.

2 *Pascha* (cf. *TLL s.v.* 'Pascha', 586) has variable gender (feminine or neuter) and a correspondingly variable declension. Here *Pascha* (object of *transegisse*) must be neuter accusative singular.

3 Adopting S's reading as in option 2, see appendix below on the text.

4 Reading *proventurum est* (a/u confusion, loss of nasal bar).

5 *Eius* presumably refers to Easter.

2. One could accept S's reading for the *sic* clause: *sic mihi iudicans eius plenitudinem ... proventuram.* In that case the whole letter is one long sentence with partial periodicity, to be translated: 'Judging that Easter's fulfilment will come to me, thanks to the good effects of the divine gift, in the following fashion: if I am fortunate enough to have the opportunity to speak with you and find out that things have gone well for you too.'

Post festivitatem in qua de praesentia vel incolumitate domni nostri vota vestra et merita claruerunt, paginis ad ipsum officii destinatis iure vobis, peculiaribus pectoris mei etiam praesentium litterarum famulatio offertur, per quam nos inter tantos, ut fieri potuit, rerum rumores Pascha prospere transegisse significo, sic mihi iudicans eius plenitudinem divini muneris beneficiis proventuram, si vestri quoque adloquii dignationem cum simili prosperitatis agnitione meruero.

THE VISIGOTHIC KINGDOM

21. APOLLINARIS, *VIR ILLUSTRIS*, AVITUS' KINSMAN

Contents

Epistula 24 Avitus to Apollinaris, *vir illustris*:[1] Avitus gives thanks that Apollinaris is safe and sound after his political contretemps with Alaric (perhaps 507).

Epistula 36 Avitus to Apollinaris, *vir illustris*: Avitus, suffering from an eye infection, writes briefly of his happiness to hear that Apollinaris and his family are safe.

Epistula 43 Avitus to Eufrasius, bishop of Auvergne: Avitus writes to acknowledge receipt of a letter of recommendation for Emeterius. He asks Eufrasius to pass on his copy of *De spiritalis historiae gestis* to Apollinaris, his cousin (date, pre-507).

Epistula 51 Avitus to Apollinaris, *vir illustris*: Avitus expresses his joy to hear that Apollinaris has been restored to Alaric's favour (pre-end of 507).

Epistula 52 Avitus to Apollinaris, *vir illustris*: a continuation of *Ep.* 51: Avitus gives Apollinaris advice on how to handle his return to politics at the Visigothic court (pre-end of 507).

Epistula 24: Introduction

Part of the dossier relating to Apollinaris, *vir illustris*; see also *Epp.* 36, 43, 51 and 52. The latter two mention Apollinaris' political difficulties in the Visigothic kingdom prior to the war of 507. A possible context for this letter is the immediate aftermath of the war,[2] but if so its tone is remarkable, given the disaster that had struck the Visigothic kingdom. If the context is correctly identified it is also extraordinary that Avitus could correspond with his kinsman at that moment, suggesting that Gundobad held off from giving Clovis any support until the outcome of the Visigothic campaign was known.[3]

---

1 *PLRE* 2 Apollinaris 3.

2 On Apollinaris fighting at Vogliacum, See Greg. Tur. *DLH* 2.37.

3 On Gundobad's support for Clovis in 508, see Isidore, *Historia Gothorum, Wandalorum, Sueborum*, 36–37: *Chronicle of 511*, nn. 689–90,

Avitus the bishop to Apollinaris, vir illustris *{56.13 Peiper}*

Your Piety has made worry routine business for me, both by demonstrating yours for me and by believing in mine for you. After I received news of your departure, I hung in suspense for fear and trepidation, because I was receiving information from various quarters stating that you had all alike been mustered to war[1] at the command of the masters[2] whom you serve. My awareness of my own sins brought about the following thought: the fewer people remained to me, the more I should be afraid on their behalf. But thanks be to God who has brought you and yours[3] back safely in happiness to your homeland![4] Furthermore may Christ guard freedom for our common desires, so that it may be possible for us both to console you in your absence and to visit you when you are present.

Epistula 36: Introduction

This letter shows Avitus' concern and affection for his kinsman Apollinaris, son of Sidonius, and for Apollinaris' son Arcadius, on whom the survival of the family depended. Avitus was away from home in Lyons. He appears to have used Domnulus, who seems to have been engaged on an official mission for Gundobad and Sigismund,[5] to find out what had happened to Apollinaris during the period when the latter was under suspicion of treason by Alaric (see *Epp.* 51 and 52). Domnulus, who would seem from his name to have been a member of the senatorial aristocracy, then set off again, presumably on a further round of negotiations, taking with him thanks from Avitus. Thereafter Avitus sent one other message to Apollinaris before the present one. Domnulus' extraordinary to-ing and fro-ing suggests that he was involved in major diplomatic negotiations between Gundobad in Lyons and Alaric II

---

1 Avitus uses *evocare* which can signify either a judicial summons or military muster. Burckhardt, p. 33, took it as the latter, no doubt because of *cunctos* and *pariter* which suggest many people rather than the few who might have been indicted by Alaric in a capital case. That a substantial group of aristocrats from the Auvergne did fight at Vogliacum is clear from Greg. Tur. *DLH* 2.37. Avitus, *Ep.* 24, p. 56.19, *prospero reditu*, likewise supports the military interpretation. If the summons were judicial, then the letter should be compared with *Ep.* 36.

2 The plural may suggest both the Visigothic king and his counsellors.

3 Presumably Arcadius, cf. *Ep.* 36, and perhaps the family retainers.

4 The Auvergne.

5 The name and the use of the word *noster* suggests that he could be a relative of the Domnulus who appears as a correspondent of Sidonius Apollinaris (*Ep.* 4.25): Sidonius' Domnulus may also be Fl. Rusticius Helpidius Domnulus, and Rusticius Helpidius: see *PLRE* 2, Domnulus 1, Domnulus 2 and Helpidius 7: see also Heinzelmann, 'Gallische Prosopographie', p. 593. For another Helpidius who was a correspondent of Avitus, *Ep.* 38.

in Toulouse.[1] The letter is a fine example of cagey writing. Avitus cannot write candidly, and must keep the written record neutral and therefore uncompromising. The result is difficult to translate, replete with circumlocutions and allusions that are discussed in Chapter 3, above, pp. 81ff.

Avitus the bishop of Vienne to Apollinaris, vir illustris *{66.1 Peiper}*

I know that when our Domnulus was on his way back to my beloved lords[2] to tell me things that I did not wish to hear,[3] as I seethed with worry about your Pious Care's parlous situation,[4] he increased,[5] rather than lessened, his haste to return. While I was in Lyons waiting for him, an increasingly severe attack of eye infection made me unable to look at the light.[6] Therefore, since he was not capable of eliciting a written reply, nor I of producing one, I entrusted all the gratitude due to the value of the gifts and the kindness of the givers,[7] as a verbal expression instead to the ears of the messenger. I had little doubt, nonetheless, that in your kind eagerness, the precise order of the instructions would matter little compared to your longing for a letter. But when, once the shadows of my bedroom-prison were dispersed, I first had a chance briefly to arrange my duty, I did not hesitate to pay my debt, and I sent the present messenger[8] on his way. Although[9] he was heavily laden with verbal greetings as far as the *spoken* instructions are concerned, I would estimate that I gave him only a very short *written* message. For lo! God is my witness to how much light our dear friend[10] shed in the night-filled habitation

---

1 He is unaccountably ignored by Heinzelmann, 'Gallische Prosopographie', who only discusses the Fl. Rusticius Helpidius Domnulus who was *quaestor sacri palatii* in c.458. Since he had close links with the emperor Avitus and with Sidonius, a descendent of his would have made a good ambassador between the Burgundian and Visigothic courts.

2 Gundobad and Sigismund.

3 Construing the future participle *relaturus* as expressing purpose and construing *aliter quam volui* with it.

4 See *Ep.* 51 for guarded allusions to Apollinaris' political difficulties.

5 Reading *adceleravit. Adgravavit* makes no sense with *festinationem* as an object.

6 Medical care for eye-infections seems to have been poor in the Burgundian kingdom. See *Ep.* 11 to Caesarius. The topic is known from Ennodius too, see *Ennodius* 267 and 279.

7 Plural: presumably because both Apollinaris and Arcadius (see below) have sent gifts.

8 I.e. the bearer of this letter.

9 *Mandata loquacia* must refer to *spoken* messages, so the *quantum* phrase must be construed with *cui ... onerato.* One would expect some sort of contrast between the copious verbal instructions and the *perbrevis pagina*, so the participle *onerato* has been construed concessively.

10 I.e. Domnulus.

of my beshadowed retreat! After he announced the return[1] of our beloved child[2] (which I had not known about before) he confirmed that our family, had been found reunited – Christ being propitious! – by the man I had sent. Therefore do not now entertain any incomplete[3] information about me. In your company, God willing, my eyes too, as they make amends through the present page, grow <in health>.[4] But they will for certain only receive the grace of joyful day in perfect health, if Your Sweetness, who up till now have so forgiven[5] me [for not writing], now compels me to write back, however ill and anxious I am, in answer to[6] the frequent correspondence that I none-theless[7] long for, while you need only worry about signing letters written now in God's name by Arcadius.[8]

Epistula 43: Introduction

The addressee of this letter was bishop of Auvergne from some time before 506 to 515,[9] and a correspondent of Ruricius.[10] He is to be identified with the friend who snatched away a copy of *De spiritalis historiae gestis* from Avitus, and who later showed Apollinaris' letter praising the work to Avitus. See *Ep.* 51. This information allows us to reconstruct the following context for this *Ep.* 43: Eufrasius has taken a copy of the *SHG* from Avitus' own scribes,[11] and has lent it to Emeterius, who has it with him on a trip to Vienne. There Avitus has learnt about the fate of his work, telling Emeterius to return it to Eufrasius, who is to pass it on to Avitus' cousin Apollinaris. Subsequently (possibly ca. 506) Apollinaris came to be suspected of treason by Alaric II and was unable to write to Avitus to give his reaction to the poem, until he had been cleared.

---

1 *Reditus* is a typo for *reditu*, the subject of the ablative absolute, *reditu ... nuntiato*.

2 Arcadius, son of Apollinaris, see below. For *nostri*, see *Ep.* 52, p. 81.12 *spes reparandae prosapiae*.

3 See above p. 84 n. 1.

4 See above p. 82 n. 1.

5 See above p. 84 n. 2.

6 Construing *ad frequentiam* with *rescribere*.

7 Avitus' eyes are still weak, but he longs to hear from Apollinaris.

8 Arcadius was Apollinaris' son, who had been separated from Apollinaris, the child whose return was alluded to above. He appears in Greg. Tur. *DLH* 3.9.

9 Duchesne, *Fastes épiscopaux*, 2, p. 35, although there is no reason to date his consecration as early as ca. 490. See Greg. Tur. *DLH* 3.2.

10 His letter in *Fausti aliorumque epistulae* 11 in *MGH AA* 8, p. 273, makes polite noises about Ruricius' health. Ruricius' reply to him is 2.22.

11 For another hijacking of a text, Sid. *Ep.* 9.9.6.

Apart from the difficulties presented by the letter in understanding its context, there is also the problem of unravelling the various family relations: in particular does 'brother' (*frater*) refer to a blood relation, or does it define Emeterius as a monk, and does the 'his own' (*sui*) of the second sentence modify 'episcopate' (*pontificatus*) or 'elder brother' (*senioris germani*)? A plausible reading is that Emeterius, who may or may not be a monk, is Eufrasius' brother, and that he is acting on Eufrasius' behalf shortly after the latter's consecration. Certainly Emeterius is unlikely to be the priest who signs the canons of the Council of Arles (524) for bishop Gallicanus of Embrun, simply because he appears to have come from Clermont and to be returning to Clermont: in other words he comes from the Auvergne and not from the Burgundian kingdom.

Avitus the bishop to Eufrasius the bishop {72.27}

I have already sent a letter through my servants to let you know how helpful your recommendation for brother[1] Emeterius was to me. However, I had no doubt that he would, as was only proper, attend to his duties of his elder brother at the start of the latter's episcopate.[2] I have happily added these letters via him.[3] In them I rejoice even more that the thief[4] of my little work, who has now been 'wanted' for a long time, has come into my hands.[5] And because, so far as he has told me, he is taking the book back to you, I beg that, in whatever state it is, previously unpublished, not completely emended, you may please pass it on to that excellent and most pious man, my brother Apollinaris,[6] and make excuses on its behalf. It is little short of sacrilegious that it was not offered to him first out of friendship, were it not again an act of folly for me to provoke the disdain of the son of my lord

1 Possibly 'monk', but more probably blood-brother of Eufrasius.

2 Presumably the *pontificatus* is that of Eufrasius: no bishop called Emeterius is known for the first half of the sixth century. The Latin, however, allows 'the duties of his elder brother at the start of his (i.e. Emeterius') pontificate'.

3 Emeterius.

4 Lit. 'pirate', 'bandit'. Identified as Emeterius by Van de Vyver, 'Victoire contre les Alamans' (1936), p. 885 n. 1, but more probably Eufrasius in the light of *Ep*. 51.

5 I.e. Eufrasius sent Emeterius along with a letter of recommendation for him. Avitus is pleased to meet Emeterius, who has told him that Eufrasius 'lifted' the copy of Avitus' book. The book itself seems to have been the *SHG* referred to in *Ep*. 51, i.e. Avitus, *Carm*. 1–5. If so, Avitus is making a standard display of modesty, for the poems are by no means an *opusculum*.

6 Here Avitus is referring not to his real brother Apollinaris, but to his more distant relation, Sidonius' son, who was to be found in Eufrasius' diocese of Clermont, and who would indeed follow Eufrasius as bishop. On Apollinaris as an arbiter of taste, see Wood, 'Letters and Letter-Collections', p. 31.

Sidonius (i.e. Avitus' cousin Apollinaris) at my presumption *too*: he is a man who among the joys of his father's eloquence will be disgusted at [the mediocrity of] my times. Therefore you must introduce the book without fanfare. If our aforementioned brother [Apollinaris] thinks it right that it be read to the children perhaps, I can find this out whenever His Magnificence [Apollinaris] writes. If, however, after the torrents of his father's [i.e. Sidonius'] eloquence he, as I think is more likely to be the case, rejects the poverty of a vein of inspiration that trickles with the faintest dew, without any shame on my part or lack of respect on his, it will be sufficient for me to understand his disapproval from the fact that he is silent alone.

Epistula 51: Introduction

Avitus has not heard from Apollinaris for a while. Unexpectedly he receives a letter from him which reveals that his kinsman, who has been under a political cloud, has recently been rehabilitated. He writes to congratulate him and to send him a copy of his biblical epic, *SHG*.

This is one of the letters that we know to have been in the now fragmentary papyrus codex of Avitus, currently in Paris (cf. *schedulae Parisinae* 5ᵛ, ed. Peiper, p. 154). There it followed *Epp.* 55 and 56, again indicating that the order of letters in S and L is not that of the earliest collection.

The letter is important because of the light that it sheds on the difficulties faced by the senatorial aristocracy as a result of the creation of frontiers between the newly formed barbarian kingdoms. Apollinaris had been under suspicion of treason: to have been in contact with relatives outside the Visigothic kingdom would have been suicidal: communication had, therefore, to be dropped for a while. In all probability Apollinaris found himself under this political cloud in the build-up of tension prior to the Frankish invasion.[1] Now, however, communication can be resumed. Ruricius, *Ep.* 2.41.4, also to Apollinaris, refers to an easing of difficult times in the Visigothic kingdom making travel possible once more.

The letter is also important for what it says about the production of literary manuscripts. The *SHG*, Avitus' poetic version of Genesis and Exodus, which is to some extent a versification of Augustine's *De Genesi ad Litteram*[2] (and not therefore the light-hearted work one might suppose from this letter), had been copied by a scribe, and awaited revision by the author, when it was seized by bishop Eufrasius. Equally significant, the copy Avitus sends is on parchment, not on papyrus, implying that this is a copy of the work intended to last.

---

1 Greg. Tur. *DLH* 2.37.
2 See Wood, 'Avitus of Vienne, the Augustinian Poet'.

Avitus to Apollinaris, vir illustris *[79.16 Peiper]*

It has been a long time, if you either believe me or reciprocate my feelings about our mutual affection, that, despite my longing to receive a letter from one of you,[1] I wanted nonetheless to do more of my duty, and not always commit for discharge to the casual traveller[2] those obligations that are owed by me to you: first to our affection, then to our family ties, and finally to your rank. Although the very presence of letter-carriers ought to be desirable on account of their frequency, it is nonetheless necessary for that concern which becomes involved of its own accord without external compulsion to prevail. Since I know that I am subject to this duty, I had already for a long time silently been bemoaning the fact that my fair recompense was cut off, all because an unfair stumbling-block got in the way.

The smoke[3] of the carefully laid fire, which, as if from exhausted ashes, the stormy conspiracy, puffing with the the winds of falsehood, had tried in vain to set in motion against Your Sacred and Simple Innocence, had come not only to my attention but also to my grief.[4] Therefore I was hesitant to increase the burden of your worry with a prayer for an offering, and to send to you not consolation, but an increase of sorrow. While things were thus suspended in confused expectation under the cloud of this indecision, God brought me the letter of Your Serenity, endowed with your pristine piety, when I least expected it. There to my great pleasure I recognised your handwriting,[5] the declamatory style that is more than like your father's,[6] the kindness you have most clearly inherited from him. For you wrote that, thanks to the grace of Christ, now that you were back,[7] everything was safe, and that your Lord, King Alaric's high opinion of you was unimpaired and

---

1 Avitus refers to the fact that Arcadius apparently acted as secretary for his father, hence 'one of you'. See *Ep.* 36 p. 66.21.

2 Most letters were probably passed on by such men: on fewer occasions would a messenger be sent to a specific individual.

3 For *fumus* of malicious gossip, see Sid. Ap. *Ep.* 1.11.2 *sinistrae rumor ac fumus opinionis adflavit.*

4 A mannered zeugma.

5 Note how in *Ep.* 36, p. 66.21, Avitus suggested that Apollinaris would only have to sign – hence his pleasure now. This may indicate that personal letters were written by the author and not by the secretary.

6 L reads *quam plus paternam declamationem.* Goelzer, p. 658, takes this as an anomalous formation for *plus quam paternam declamationem*: 'your declamation that is more than like your father's'. But he cites no parallels for *quam plus* instead of *plus quam.* It may well be a textual error, an *Antizipationsfehler* based on *quam maxime.*

7 L's *redux*, despite the number, is to be construed with *scripsistis.*

clean as of old. But I think that, after any sort of *contretemps*, the goodwill of
such people, just as it does not end without danger, so too it is not restored
without being increased. For they wish, as it were, to make amends to
wronged innocence, and they raise it up, when they see that it it has fallen[1]
and thus for them our [good] conscience[2] is sufficient, if their knowledge [of
it] is a witness too. Once, however, I had received the announcement of your,
indeed of *our* safety, – Lo! – I speak with God as my witness – at the
memory of the past I burst into tears mixed with joy. For, as your poet says,
'the image of my dear father came into my mind',[3] as I went over in my
memory how the fate of our common relatives,[4] the fact that we have suffered similarly, is being worked out, because of persecution by the envious,[5]
in our persons – however different our professions[6] may be.

But the same consolation, thank God, is available to us that was available
to them, that – for all the attempts of rivals, with the tooth of envy snapping
around on every side, however often it has seemed to be attacked – our family
was subject only to incriminations, not to actual charges.[7] Therefore, if you
have learnt from *your* father[8] that 'the man acting in this world[9] is at less risk
at war than among detractors',[10] I take an example from *my* [father-figure][11]

---

1 *Credidisse* makes little sense. The opposition to *erigunt* suggests *cecidisse*. Supplying
innocentia (m) as object of *erigunt* as well as subject of *cecidisse*.

2 Or 'that we are party': Avitus plays off *conscientia* and *scientia* in a rhetorical point.

3 Vergil, *Aen.* 2.560. Aeneas thinks of Anchises as he witnesses the murder of Priam.

4 One obvious comparison in Avitus' mind would have been Sidonius' exile after Euric took
over Clermont: Sid. *Ep.* 8.3.2.

5 This is one of Avitus' rare suggestions that he and his relatives had faced danger in Burgundy.

6 Avitus was a churchman, Apollinaris a *vir illustris* involved on occasion in military
matters (see below), and only at the end of his life a bishop.

7 Avitus makes a word-play on *criminatio* and *crimen*.

8 See the appendix below p. 346.

9 *Saeculo militantem*, i.e. not a cleric.

10 Peiper reasonably suggests that this is a precisely quoted *sententia* from Sidonius, but did
not identify the passage. It may, however, not be an exact quotation, but an allusion to some
episode. One good possibility is the satire episode Sidonius tells of in *Ep.* 1.11 where he
suffered the false accusations and whispering campaign of Paeonius, but was generously treated
by the emperor Majorian. See also Sid. *Ep.* 7.9.8 where he mentions his own experiences of the
obloquiorum Scyllas ... linguarum, sed humanarum, latratus he faced in nominating Perpetuus
bishop. For more on *obloquia*, see Claud. Mam. 2.9, p. 137.11 and Avitus, *SHG* 4.500 on the
perils surrounding the church.

11 Apollinaris' Sidonius had undergone trials in his secular career. Avitus' Sidonius underwent difficulties in his religious career too. See Sid. Ap. *Ep.* 7.9.14 for Sidonius' double career:
Sidonius clericatum quia de saeculari professione translatus est ... The point of Avitus'
sententia is that both 'fathers' are one man.

Sidonius, whom I do not dare to call father,[1] of how much a cleric can suffer.[2] Wherefore may God grant this – that just as it is nothing new for us to be assailed, so let no new turn of events cause us rightly to be accused.[3] Let there be a stop to bitternesses at this time of happiness, and, now that there is a chance, a stop also to the constraints imposed upon our speech. How much better that the boldness of one making a poor joke provide an opportunity for laughter!

Several months ago, I saw a letter of Your Magnificence given to a common friend in which you wrote (once the salutation had been made, in the following expository section of the letter) that you had liked the little book in which, in the midst of having to write serious and more pressing things,[4] I had nonetheless disported myself – the one about the events of biblical history also in the form of a poem. Here I now call God as my witness that I am not saying anything falsely, nothing in the spirit of excessive compliance in the face of Your Sincerity. I was as pleased by your judgement as if I had confessed my practice to the ears of my lord, your father, and had been given at his instance some degree of praise. First I was delighted that you weighed out your feelings more generously here than elsewhere; second, because I recognised that you were as prepared to desire something good from your brother's (i.e. my) efforts as to believe good of them. It is quite clear that you supplied for verses that were found to be of disappointing quality through your wishful thinking what you were unable to supply in judgement.

The friend,[5] who I believe sent the book to you, snatched it away not from the booksellers, but from the very hand of the scribe, as yet unproofread and unfinished by me, so that you cannot easily tell whether to be angry at the faults of the author or those of the copyist.[6] So in order not to

---

1 Avitus hints that he does not dare to aspire to Sidonius' literary talents as his true literary 'son'. See the compliment for Apollinaris at p. 79.32 *plus quam paternam declamationem*. This is an expression of modesty.

2 Cf. Sid. Ap. *Ep.* 8. 3.2: Sidonius also faced problems from his own clergy: Greg. Tur. *DLH* 2.23.

3 Sirmond's *nulla* is necessary for the sense.

4 Avitus employs a sound-play involving *seria* and *necessaria*.

5 Eufrasius, see *Ep.* 43.

6 For a similar topos see Solinus' dedicatory letter to Adventus in T. Mommsen, *C. Iulii Solini collectanea rerum memorabilium* (Berlin, 1895), p. 217: *Quoniam quidam inpatientius potius quam studiosius opusculum quod moliebar intercipere properarunt idque etiamtum inpolitum prius in medium dederunt quam incohatae rei summa manus inponeretur, et nunc exemplaribus corruptis quae damnata sunt quasi probata circumferunt praeteritis, quae ad incrementum cognitionis accesserunt cura longiore.*

cause your desire any delay, I have swiftly sent to you my little work, copied onto parchment[1] and still not quite so polished as I should have liked. If indeed it appeals not only to your kindness but also to your critical faculties – because there will perhaps be no lack of people among those outside, whom the boldness of the venture may inspire with envy, I will be more than content that you feel what I hope you will. Because just as the outstanding work of our common Sidonius has redounded no less to my credit than to yours, so too, now that you are flourishing more and more in military[2] matters through the favour of Christ, if my feeble[3] effort will have achieved something something worthwhile to read, it will not disgrace even the old man of Arcadia himself.[4]

Appendix

*Quoniam, si vos a **patre vestro** hoc didicistis virum saeculo militantem minus inter arma quam inter obloquia periclitari, exemplum a Sidonio meo, quem patrem vocare non audeo, quantum clericus perpeti possit adsumo.*

p. 80.12 *patre vestro hoc* Peiper l; *patre vestro Archadio* S Mathisen

The reading of S, *Archadio*, is advocated as a *lectio difficilior* by Mathisen, 'Epistolography', pp. 98–99, who argues that Arcadius was Apollinaris' father-in-law.[5] He assumes a loose use of 'pater' as a term of respect for elderly relatives[6] – here equivalent to 'father-in-law'. *Pater* for *socer* is uncommon, but attested, see *TLL s.v.* 'pater', 675.46–52. *Pater* does not require a possessive, except for emphasis or for clarification. *Vestro* is often used for clarification. Cf. p. 55.14, *domini mei, patris vestri* (Avitus to Sigismund of Gundobad). But it could, according to the traditional interpretation, also have an emphatic function in setting up *Sidonio meo*: your *biological* father, but *my* (respected father-figure) Sidonius. This is supported by p. 81.1 *communis Sollii.* (i.e. yours and mine).

---

1 Parchment is of course used for durability, whereas papyrus was appropriate for letters: Sid. *Ep.* 4.3.1. Also Ruricius, *Ep.* 2.26 and Taurentius *Ep.* to Ruricius.

2 Note, however, that this could also refer to the *militia civilis*. If soldiering is meant, once might take this passage in tandem with Greg. Tur. *DLH* 2.37, to suggest that Apollinaris was the *comes* of Clermont.

3 *Tenuis* is used by Avitus to mean 'feeble' at *SHG* 4.292.

4 Sidonius, see appendix, below. Mathisen, 'Epistolography', p. 99 takes Arcadius to be Apollinaris' father-in-law.

5 The identification is accepted by Heinzelmann, 'Gallische Prosopographie', p. 559 Arcadius 1.

6 See Ruricius, *Ep.* 2.26.3 to Apollinaris where he refers to Sidonius as *nostrum domnum patremque communem.*

With *vester* there to distinguish *your* father from *my* father, then there is a problem in taking the 'marked' *pater vester* as 'socer'. *Pater vester* ought to mean 'your biological father'. If Avitus had alluded to an Arcadius who was his father-*in-law*, he would just have called him *socer* – or to keep up the father-analogy 'patre Arcadio', since it was common knowledge that Apollinaris' real father was Sidonius.

p. 80.35–81.3:

Quia sicut non minus ad meam quam vestram gloriam pervenit communis Sollii opus illustre, ita vobis, favente Christo militari actu magis magisque florentibus, si in me nisus tenuis aliquid dignum lectione confecerit, etiam senem Arcadium non pudebit.

Avitus' sequence of thought seems to be as follows: I hope you approve of my poetry and that you are not just saying so to be kind. There probably will be many outsiders who will be jealous, so I will be happy if *you* like it. For just as our common Sidonius' work reflected no less well on me than on you (i.e. Sollius> Avitus [me] and Sollius > Apollinaris [you]), so too now that you are performing great military deeds and I am not doing too badly in the literary realm, it will reflect well (i.e. 'not shame', *non pudebit*) on the Old Man of Arcadia (Sidonius). There are parallel equations set out in the second half of the sentence. Apollinaris' successes are parallel to those of Sidonius in the previous clause, and the *senex Arcadius* must somehow be an allusion to Sidonius, since Avitus (and his literary success) is clearly present in the *si in me*-clause:

Apollinaris florens militari actu (Apollinaris)>senex Arcadius (Sidonius)
si in me nisus tenuis aliquid dignum lectione confecerit (Avitus)>senex Arcadius (Sidonius)

Thus the net-analysis is: 'Just as *his* work reflects well on both of us, so too our good work (in different spheres) will not embarrass even *him*.' But why is Sidonius called the *Arcadius senex*? The only place that the phrase occurs is in Grattius *Cynegetica* 100:

> **Arcadium** *stat fama* **senem**, *quem Maenalus auctor*
> *et Lacedaemoniae primum vidistis Amyclae*
> *per non adsuetas metantem retia valles,*
> *Dercylon. Haut illo quisquam se iustior egit,*
> *<h>aut fuit in terris divom observantior alter:*
> *ergo illum primis nemorum dea finxit in arvis*
> *auctoremque operi dignata inscribere magno*
> *iussit adire suas et pandere gentibus artes.*

Dercylon, the *Arcadius senex*, is a mysterious figure.[1] He seems to be the virtuous *protos heuretes* of hunting, aided by the goddess Diana herself, and associated with

---

1 See C. Formicola, *Il Cynegeticon di Grattio* (Bologna, 1988), pp. 138–39.

the wilds of Arcadia. He may also be identical with the Vergilian Aristaeus.[1] Note too that Vergil alludes to *Arcadii memoranda inventa magistri* at *Georgics* 4.283. This may be some sort of literary allusion to Sidonius as 'the old man of Arcadia, i.e. of poetry?' himself. We may still be missing the *precise* source-text, but we are not far away from it with Vergil.

Epistula 52: Introduction

A continuation of *Ep*. 51. Avitus' and Apollinaris' letters had crossed. Avitus admonishes Apollinaris to be merciful, but, above all, careful in the wake of his political setback and rehabilitation. He shows no qualms in shamelessly recommending that Apollinaris exploit the moral high ground in forgiving his enemies. By doing so he will heap coals of fire on their heads. As was suggested above (p. 344 n. 10) there seems to be a possibility that Avitus alluded to Sidonius' *contretemps* with Paeonius and the Emperor Majorian (Sid. *Ep*. 1.11) in his discussion of the dangers faced by the *vir saeculo militans*. The end of this letter, describing Apollinaris' triumphant restoration to Alaric's favour, describes a similar reversal of fortune.

Avitus the bishop to Apollinaris, vir illustris *{81.4 Peiper}*

It is a common but true saying, to be sure, that the emotions of souls that are in harmony see one another with the gaze of mutual love.[2] Can our concern for one another be so mutual[3] that, if you measure right, I have answered the letter that the bearer of this one, my son,[4] brought, *before* it arrived?[5] For in that dutiful page I sent to you about this matter[6] through my men, I breathed out both joy derived from your well-being – more in my heart than in my words – and I clutched to my bosom in joy mixed with tears[7] our kinship and that of our common fathers. As far as the rest is concerned, divine pity has placed the hope of repairing our family tree in the honour of your person, and, for the posterity that will follow, although you are the only parent, it has allowed me to be a father too.[8] May it likewise grant that you always successfully trample down the conspiracies of enemies and the envy of

---

1 Formicola, *Cynegeticon*, p. 137.
2 Probably a paraphrase rather than an exact quotation. Source as yet unidentified.
3 Lit. 'one'.
4 *Filius* may well be used in a spiritual sense.
5 Avitus refers to the opening of *Ep*. 51: *illa sollicitudo*.
6 Cf. *Ep*. 51 where Avitus hears that Apollinaris has been restored to royal favour.
7 Cf. *Ep*. 51.
8 Avitus does not have children. Perhaps, apart from any blood relationship, Avitus also implies that he was Arcadius' godfather.

treacherous men.[1] Let the first step of your victory be to restore your integrity to common knowledge;[2] the second, when it is disputed, to prove it in a public hearing; the third, after the sentence, to forgive those who charged you. Let the conquered enemy be tormented in spirit too by the indulgence granted him. And, to our double advantage, in his torture,[3] when he bemoans the fact that you cannot be deceived, let him also regret the fact that you can feel pity. And, once he has been turned over to your power for this reason alone – lest he perish, while he is bitterly angry at your spontaneously granted forgiveness, let him in some fashion be forced to hate his own existence. As for the rest my devout lord brother, care of my soul, adornment of your race, put up with your brother's (i.e. my) hesitant and foolish advice for a while. Watch carefully for evil men and do not trust those who hiss flattery with subterfuges of their biting tongues, but fashion poisonous lies. You know how things are through experience. May your cleverness render you as careful as your innocence renders you safe. For if indeed, now that the opportunity for investigation and harm has been blocked off, perhaps for this reason you have to work less frequently to defeat their attempted coups,[4] namely that in saving them for divine justice, you have always thought it best to forgive the conquered[5] < ... >.[6] Although, as I already said above, whom [your] glory wounds,[7] is not to be considered *totally* unpunished.

Also of importance for Apollinaris is *Ep.* 15 to Contumeliosus of Riez: see above pp. 264ff.

---

1 Peiper mispunctuates, creating a comma splice. We have put a full stop after *livores*.

2 For the use of *conscientia* to mean *scientia*, see Blaise, *s.v.* '*conscientia*' 1.

3 This may imply that Apollinaris' accuser will actually be subjected to torture. In *Cod. Theod.* 9.34 the penalty for defamation is torture or death, and for false accusation (9.39) exile.

4 Or better 'machinations'?

5 *Debellatis* S is clearly right. See *Aen.* 6.853: *parcere subiectis et debellare superbos.*

6 *Siquidem* could be a strong conditional, 'If it is really the case.' It clearly introduces *debetis laborare*. The *quod*-clause is epexegetic, explaining *propter hoc*. But the apodosis of the sentence seems to be missing. What one would have expected is some sort of admonition to watch out for the tongue of his accuser who has not suffered judicial punishment. This in turn explains the allusion to the accuser's psychological *punitio* in the following sentence.

7 Avitus refers to *torqueatur* etc. above. L's *Gloria lacessit* sounds odd, but it might allude to the end of Sidonius, *Ep.* 1.11.17: *fateor exordium contumeliae talis tanti fuisse cui finis gloria fuit.* In both Sidonius' and Apollinaris' case, the accuser was discomfited by the glory accorded the victim by a ruler.

EXTERNAL MATTERS

22. PRISONERS

Contents

Epistula 10: Introduction

This is one of three letters in the Avitus collection dealing with the ransoming of captives.[1] Avitus' most famous involvement in ransoming came in 494/6, when Epiphanius of Pavia undertook negotiations with the Burgundians to gain the release of Italian captives taken by Gundobad.[2] This current letter must, however, deal with a subsequent ransoming of captives, since Eustorgius was not consecrated until 507, 508 or even 511.[3] Given that the prisoners being ransomed by Eustorgius seem to have been Italian, rather than Provençal (*Italiam rigaverit*), it would seem that the Burgundians scored some successes against the Ostrogoths in the fighting that took place following Theodoric's intervention in Gaul after the death of Alaric II. Avitus may be openly acknowledging the benefits that accrue to the aggressors as a result of the payment of ransom (*respergit et Galliam*). But it would appear that he too had some prisoners he needed to ransom from Eustorgius. See p. 44.20, *visitatur opere vestro nostrarum aerumna regionum*, p. 44.10–11, most plausibly an allusion to

---

1 For more on Avitus' interest in captives, see Shanzer, 'Dating the Baptism of Clovis', pp. 42–50.

2 Ennodius, *Vita Epifani* 170, 173–74. Also Shanzer, 'Two Clocks and a Wedding', pp. 225–32.

3 Stein-Palanque, p. 127, n. 1, give 508: the older date of 511 given by F. Savio, *Gli Antichi Vescovi d'Italia dalle origini al 1300* (Milan, 1899), remains the preferred date. Å. J. Fridh, *Cassiodorus, Variae, CCSL* 96 (Turnholt, 1972), p. 19, however, dates Cassiodorus, *Variae* 1.9, to Eustorgius, to 507/11.

returned prisoners, and p. 44.14–15 with its clear implication that *both* bishops have a care and interest in protecting and restoring *libertas*. The operation may well have been one of mutual ransoming. Avitus has lavished the treasures of his eloquence on this epistle including repetitions and puns,[1] a rhyming tricolon,[2] and an elegant chiasmus.[3]

Avitus the bishop to Eustorgius the bishop [of Milan] {44.8 Peiper}

Now that the present messengers have arrived, lo! for a second time gifts have come from Your Desirable and Revered Utterance.[4] They would, however, be even better-omened,[5] if they were more numerous in quantity.[6] But in fact there is twofold reason for rejoicing in your letter. First that you demonstrate to me by your inherited kindness that the same favour for me resides in your spirit, as resided in that of your predecessors.[7] And secondly because you have asked me to be of help in that matter, in which, while you take care to protect and restore liberty, you have judged me too not unworthy of such a role. The sacred and spiritual command of Your Blessedness has been carried out. You have heaped up a reward by your prayer; through your intervention the ransom-money[8] you sent was made yet more precious.[9] Through the harsh barbarian's respect for you, savagery was overcome by humility, cruelty by intercession, and avarice by a gift. We can guess how you tame over-harsh souls there by your preaching, when through your forceful intervention you manage thus to break even[10] stones that are far away from you.[11] The misery of our regions is relieved by your action, and

1 *Secundo ... secunda, vestro ... vestrorum, praecepistis ... praeceptum, pretiosius ... pretium.*

2 *Humilitate ... intercessione ... inlatione.*

3 *Italiam rigaverit, respergit et Galliam.*

4 Taking *affatus* S as an honorific. Cf. *Ep.* 75, p. 91.19, where L likewise shows *affectum*.

5 Avitus is punning on *secunda*, 'of good omen' and *secundo*, 'the second time'.

6 A cryptic phrase: *si fierent numerositate copiosa*. Avitus cannot be complaining that any number of ordinary gifts has not been sufficient. The *dona* here must be the actual captives. Avitus wishes that there had been more of them.

7 'Ancestors' or 'predecessors in office'? If the latter, this sentence may imply that Avitus had dealings with Bishop Laurentius of Milan (486–508).

8 *Pretium.*

9 *Pretiosius.*

10 *Etiam* is probably redundant (it is omitted by S) or else out of place. It would make better sense between *viribus* and *absentia.*

11 Somewhere behind the imagery of this passage lie the pagan figures of Orpheus and Amphion.

the notable abundance of an ever-flowing fountain that emanates from the treasure of your largesse, having watered Italy, now sprinkles Gaul also.[1] Therefore, now that I have paid you the service of an honorific salutation, I hope to insinuate myself especially into your favour and sphere of influence by my abundant prayers of supplication. I desire your letters on all matters, but in these in particular in which it may, thanks to your mercy, come about for you that the fruit of your works touches me also, thanks to my obeying you [i.e. a matter, like the one just completed, where I can show myself useful by obeying you].

Epistula 12: Introduction

This letter may be dated with some certainty to ca. 512.[2] It is one of a number of letters relating to the ransom of captives (or in this case a hostage) taken by Ostrogoths or Burgundians in the course of wars between the two peoples.[3] Avulus had been taken hostage by the Ostrogothic *comes* Betancus, probably in the course of a raid on the Burgundian kingdom. Now a priest, a relative of the boy's father, is trying to buy back Avulus, with Avitus' support. It is perhaps significant that Maximus was bishop of Pavia,[4] and that Avitus had been closely involved in liberating Ostrogothic captives taken by the Burgundians for Maximus' predecessor, Epiphanius in 494/6.[5]

Avitus to Bishop Maximus [of Pavia] {45.26 Peiper}

Although I have not had the honour of receiving any communications from your Apostolic Person[6] that might have incited me to presume to undertake this particular duty, nonetheless you compel me by your reputation, even though you have not ordered[7] it [in writing], to offer the page of humble respect I feel I owe you [i.e. a letter]. Although I am denied the opportunity

---

1 Eustorgius may have commanded the same sort of financial resources as Avitus did, when he was able to help ransom the 6000 Italian captives of the *Vita Epifani*.

2 *PLRE* 2, Betancus: the date is determined by the fact that the recipient of the letter, Maximus of Pavia (following Burckhardt, pp. 45–46), died in ca. 513, and that the most likely period in which a hostage might have been taken from the Burgundian kingdom by an Ostrogoth is 508 or later.

3 See also *Epp*. 10 and 35.

4 Burckhardt, pp. 45–46.

5 Ennodius, *Vita Epiphani* 174. See above p. 350 n. 2.

6 Commonly used by Avitus of bishops' missions. See Goelzer, p. 430.

7 Taking *compellatione* S.

of meeting you face-to-face, I am drawn by your reputation, even while I am constrained by my absence. To this it should be added that you have so relieved the miseries of the unfortunate Gauls by the consolation of your advice and your generosity, that those who hurry to Italy to gain knowledge of their relatives' plight, after a long journey, when under Christ's guidance they have met you,[1] may with reason believe that they are entering their own fatherland,[2] when they encounter the mercy I know of.[3]

For the rest, I recommend to you the priest from my area who is carrying this expression of respect [i.e. letter]. Even though he has entered into this difficult task to buy back the son of one of his relatives, he has been sent [i.e. as a further task] by a certain nobleman from my province (i.e. the Viennensis) with my encouragement to find and bring back – with your help and intercession – Avulus, the son of the aforementioned man. The boy was taken as a hostage about four years ago by Count Betancus.[4] Furthermore I beg that you make it clear in an estimable communication of your own both that freedom can be regained there by those in exile, and those feeling a lack [i.e. myself, wanting letters from you] here have an opportunity to write [to you] that is common to all.

Epistula 35: Introduction

In 508 the Burgundians joined the Franks in plundering what had been the kingdom of Alaric II. Theodoric, however, intervened to protect what had been Visigothic territory, and then appointed Liberius as prefect in Gaul,[5] with Gemellus as his vicar.[6] This letter relates to negotiations at some point ca. 510[7] dealing with the return of captives taken by the Burgundians. As such it is an important witness to episcopal

---

1 Literally 'Deserved to meet your person'.

2 Compare Greg. Tur. *DLH* 4.35, on Avitus of Clermont: *Iam si peregrinus ad eum advenerit, ita diligitur, ut in eodem se habere et patrem recognoscat et patriam.*

3 Maximus' kindness to strangers in distress made Pavia home to them. A variant of this idea appears in *Ep.* 11: no priest is a stranger where there is a Catholic church.

4 The position of *a comite Betanco* is strange, but the phrase must be construed with *adsumptum.* It seems likely that *a comite Betanco* has been transposed from its original position after *nomine Avalum.*

5 For Liberius see *PLRE* 2, Liberius 3. See *PWRE* 13.1 94ff.; *Vita Apollinaris Valentinensis* 10. He was in Gaul in 511 and 512 onwards, and must have written to Avitus to ransom Ostrogothic prisoners. See J. J. O'Donnell, 'Liberius the Patrician', *Traditio* 37 (1981), pp. 44–46, who dates his appointment as *PPO* Galliarum to 510/511.

6 *PLRE* 2, Gemellus 2.

7 Determined by the vicariate of Liberius in 510, and the fact that Gemellus is not attested after that year.

activity in ransoming prisoners.[1] The praetorian prefect, however, also was involved in such negotiations. Liberius was addressed by Ennodius on behalf of his relative Camilla.[2] It is also worth noting that one of the *Variae* addressed to Gemellus, dealing with *postliminium*, may relate to the aftermath of the Burgundian aggression of 508.[3]

The letter is difficult. It starts in a somewhat aggrieved tone complaining about Liberius' failure to write earlier. It then turns into a businesslike statement of episcopal charity.[4] Liberius has sent Gemellus to redeem Gallo-Roman or Visigothic captives taken by Burgundians. Avitus has been asked to negotiate their release. Somehow he either redeemed the captives himself or negotiated their redemption, and eventually returned them. The ransom money proferred by Gemellus, we are told, was not 'accepted' (*recepto*) – apparently by Avitus who seems to have redeemed them himself. This would not be the first time, for he had acted with even greater generosity in paying the ransom for Ostrogothic hostages in 494/6.[5]

The last two sentences are obscure, and Avitus' chain of thought is hard to follow, for the text seems to be corrupt or lacunose. It is important to understand that, following the Roman law of *postliminium*,[6] which was taken over by the Burgundians,[7] ransomed prisoners owed their ransom-price to whoever ransomed them.[8] In this case, therefore, where the captives may have changed hands numerous times, passing from their captors to Avitus and thence to Gemellus, those that Gemellus sought to redeem would ultimately have owed *him* their ransom-price. One cannot be certain about the mechanics of this particular transaction, namely whether Gemellus put up all of the money in advance, or only part of it, or whether Avitus paid all or part of the money and was then to be reimbursed by Gemellus.

p. 65.30 *si aliquid ... debent*: Why should slaves as opposed to free-born captives owe something to Gemellus? A free-born captive once ransomed was free. But a slave captive, even when freed from the barbarians, still needed to be paid in full for by his owner.[9]

The final sentence of the letter seems to imply that if the slave-captives owe

---

1 Ambrose, *De Officiis Ministrorum* 2.15; also Patricius, *Ep.* 14. W. Klingshirn, 'Charity and Power: Caesarius of Arles and the Ransoming of Captives in Sub-Roman Gaul', *JRS* 75 (1985), pp. 183–203; Shanzer, 'Dating the Baptism of Clovis', pp. 42–50. See also Ruricius, *Ep.* 2.8, to Aeonius, on the case of the priest Possessor and his brother. In addition on ransoms in the period see the later *Vita Eptadii* 8–12, *MGH SRM* 3, p. 189.

2 Ennodius 457.4, to Liberius.

3 *Variae* 3.18.

4 For other letters concerned with the ransoming of prisoners, *Epp.* 10 and 12.

5 Ennodius, *Vita Epiphani* 174.

6 *Cod. Theod.* 5.7: *Const. Sirm.* 16, five years of work or the actual price.

7 *Lib. Const.* 56.2, ed. L. R. de Salis.

8 Klingshirn, 'Charity and Power', pp. 184 and 201.

9 *Lib. Const.* 56.1. For the distinction between the ransom of free and servile captives see also *Cod. Theod.* 4.8.5.

anything to Gemellus because of their origins (i.e. the fact that they are slaves), Gemellus should use the money that he offered Avitus, but that Avitus clearly did *not* accept, to redeem further free captives. The clear implication is that in the case of the slave-captives Avitus had charitably waived the ransom offered by Gemellus. In turn he asks Gemellus to regard the refused money as payment in lieu of the sum that the captives would have normally owed him. Thus no money actually changed hands and, Avitus seems to say, Gemellus could therefore use the money to redeem other prisoners, in this case *ingenui*. For the group of letters, see Burckhardt, p. 45.

Avitus to Liberius the prefect {65.15 Peiper}

After the happy arrival of Your Power in the much-troubled Gallic provinces, I have not experienced any response to my desire[1] in the form of letters[2] from you before this moment. Although I believe that I too profit from the benefits that you have been scattering among the provincials for some time, for me, who have up till this moment been thirsting for a letter from you, it is as if it is only just now that you have *really* arrived.[3] The fact is that what caused me not to proffer myself by proffering my dutiful letters without having received one[4] was that I was afraid to make a fuss in the face of the occupations [i.e. your being so busy] by which I thought I was being held back for so long a period from the reading [i.e. of letters from you] that I longed for. But you have written,[5] however belatedly, and I am responding to your distinguished words: thus the rule of alternating exchange has been preserved in our correspondence. You, who have enabled me to reply without embarrassment, [please] make me your debtor by writing frequently! If you are willing, there are in fact good reasons for giving [me] orders; there is an abundance of things you can enjoin on ones [i.e. me] who long to obey.[6] Politesse has more weight than power, and deigning is no less influential than standing on one's dignity.[7] For this very matter, the price of which gave you reason to write to me, has taught us what sort of activities you are most keen to excel in during your official duties [i.e. matters to do with ransoming]. Therefore, I have been glad to do in full, in accordance

---

1 Taking *nullum* LS and *expertus effectum* S. Lit. 'effect of my longing'.
2 Taking *affatibus vestris* S.
3 I.e. in the form of a letter.
4 From you = *ultro*.
5 Rendering *compellentibus*, lit. 'compelling'.
6 This may suggest that the Burgundians have more captives that Avitus can help liberate.
7 Avitus is making a point about *dignatio* and *dignitas*.

with your Highness' order, what was pressed upon me[1] by the *uir specta-bilis*, your Vicar,[2] in the matter of the freeing of certain prisoners. But the price which the messengers had brought I did not take.[3] My motive was that if, because of their [servile] status[4] these people themselves, as a result of their birth, are in some debt to the aforesaid *uir magnificus*, my son Gemellus,[5] he can dole out what he had offered to me, for the redemption[6] of free men. But if you come to find out that these people are free-born, it is enough [for me] that the price [i.e. my paying it] was of benefit.

1 S reads *nobis*, 'us', suggesting that Gemellus commanded Avitus. L's *vobis* implies that Gemellus told *Liberius* what he ought to do. S's reading seems preferable, given the first-person verb *implevi*.

2 For Gemellus, Vicarius of the *PPO* Galliarum, see Cass. *Var.* 3.16, his letter of appointment.

3 Avitus uses *recipio* here in its sense of 'accept' rather than 'receive'.

4 Although *condicio* alone can mean 'servile condition' (see *TLL s.v.* 'condicio', 133.39–51, which cites this passage, and Ennodius 14.5, *populos annexibus violentae condicionis absolvit*, where *condicio* unqualified means slavery) it is awkward to take this as a genitive of description, i.e. 'the individuals themselves of slave condition' in the absence of a qualifying adjective. *Condicio* cannot be construed with *aliquid* either, since it makes little sense to 'owe someone some state of being a slave'. Winterbottom accordingly emends to <*causa*> *condicionis* comparing p. 96.20 for the word-order.

5 Avitus changes his previously neutral reference to Gemellus to the much more full-blown style. *Filius meus* seems to suggest that he knew him.

6 Taking S's *pro redimendis*.

23. A GOOD MEDICAL MAN IS HARD TO FIND

Contents

Epistula 11 Avitus to Caesarius of Arles: a letter of recommendation for a blind bishop, Maximianus, in search of an ophthalmologist in Arles (date post 502).

Epistula 38 Avitus to the Deacon Helpidius, doctor of Theodoric the Great: a complaint that Helpidius allegedly did not receive Avitus' letter, and a referral of a patient, the son of Ceretus.

Epistula 11: Introduction

The one surviving letter of Avitus to his great contemporary, Caesarius, this must be dated after the consecration of the bishop of Arles in 502. It is likely to have been written before the *pallium* was granted to Caesarius by Pope Symmachus in 508,[1] and certainly before the reconfirmation of Caesarius' metropolitan rights in 513.[2] Thereafter tension between the metropolitan sees of Arles and Vienne increased. Moreover, since the Burgundians joined the Franks in the Visigothic wars of 507–508, one might also argue for a *terminus ante quem* of 507. Neither of these arguments, however, can be regarded as absolutely watertight.

Other letters of this period refer to eye-diseases,[3] which could be the subject of miracles. In 556 Venantius Fortunatus undertook a pilgrimage to Tours to thank St Martin for healing his eyes in Ravenna.[4] But Maximianus was apparently not so fortunate. The letter is important for what it implies of the assumed availability of doctors (eye-surgeons?) in Arles, and their apparent scarcity further north. In *Ep.* 36 Avitus himself suffers from a similar complaint. The letter is also important for its casual reference to disruption in Trier, implying that this had been considerable.[5] The reference is all the more suggestive, because it is not contained in a work intent on making moral capital out of destruction by the barbarians, such as Salvian's comments in the *De Gubernatione Dei*.

1 *Epistolae Arelatenses Genuinae*, 2.5.28–29. See G. Morin, 'Maximien, éveque de Trèves dans une lettre d'Avit de Vienne', *RB* 47 (1935), pp. 207–10.

2 Klingshirn, *Caesarius of Arles*, pp. 71 and 129–31.

3 See also Ennodius 24 on Deuterius' eye-infection.

4 Venantius Fortunatus, *Vita S. Martini* 4.687–701.

5 E. Ewig, *Trier im Merowingerreich. Civitas, Stadt, Bistum* (Trier, 1954), pp. 60, 96, cites the Avitus reference as a crucial source for the state of Trier at the start of the sixth century.

Bishop Avitus to Bishop Caesarius {45.1 Peiper}

Even though this venerable letter-bearer may make his way to your kind and fraternal self in person, the holy bishop Maximianus privately asked that this official page from me be sent to you, despite the fact that it is clear from the letter that I ought to be recommended by him rather than he by me.[1] Because he deigned to order <me>[2] to set down out his troubles[3] in my own words, I decided to say nothing of his difficult journey, for however long ago, or however far away he may leave his fatherland, wherever a Catholic church can be found, no ecclesiastic can be called a stranger. Nor need the destruction his area has suffered[4] be exaggerated for you, as if it were unknown. For no place in trouble escapes Your Piety that is always in search of an opportunity to be kind. The main reason he is coming, to the extent that he agrees to state it, is to look for a more experienced doctor to help the weak eyes of his body[5] with whatever skill he has.

Even though the gaze of a devout mind is occupied instead in contemplating spiritual things, and is not excessively alarmed by the blindness of the exterior man, nonetheless he requires this cure to this extent, as far as I know, in order that he may strive to satisfy those who love him in the duress imposed by his work. At the same time, he does not wish his capacity for priestly office to seem reprehensibly lessened – to his discredit – because he is guilty of the crime of neglecting his health. He seeks hope of regaining his sight, as I think, from a biblical example – namely our Tobit, who in darkness as regards earthly things, but gazing at those invisible to the earth, intent on eternal light, and already forgetful of the earthly daylight, was led back by secret cure, concealed in an angelic visitant, through an eye-salve made of gall to the sweetness of health.[6]

---

1 This need not be pure rhetorical fluff. Both the words *sacerdos* and *antistes* by which Maximianus is designated could be used of a bishop. See Goelzer, p. 428 n. 1. The suggestion that Avitus' letter is official may imply that it was regarded as having the same function as an *epistola formata*, that is the episcopal letter of introduction required by any cleric travelling outside his diocese: Epaon, can. 6.

2 Goelzer, p. 70, discusses Avitus' anomalous construction of *iubere*. He employs not only the regular accusative and infinitive, but also a jussive noun-clause. In this sentence L provides no object for *iubere* (S corrected to *ut necessitates … panderem*), but an object needs to be supplied in English.

3 Goelzer, p. 520.

4 Identified with the Frankish invasions by Morin, 'Maximien, éveque de Trèves', p. 209; Ewig, *Trier im Merowingerreich*, pp. 60 and 96.

5 The phrase anticipates the coming contrast to the *mentis intuitus*.

6 Tob. 11.8–13. This letter alone among those in the Avitus collection includes a bit of

Therefore welcome this brother with your usual kindness and with appropriate reverence, and, if he needs consolation in his worry, give it him. A common need will be fulfilled, if any sort of relief for his condition be forthcoming. If not, at least let the eye of the bishop's conscience recognise, in this respect at least no slave to blindness, the incorruptible countenance of our joint good will.

Epistula 38: Introduction

Avitus had written to Helpidius and sent the letter via a major-domo.[1] It never arrived. Helpidius, doctor to Theodoric,[2] must recently have been ill. See p. 67.9, *nuntio tuae incolumitatis*, and p. 67.23, *frequentandae sospitatis*. For Helpidius, see Ennodius 312, 384, 437 and 445, and Cass. *Var.* 4.24, granting him the right to restore a portico in Spoleto. He may have been the author of the *Carmen de Christi Jesu Beneficiis*.[3]

Avitus lavishes elaborate conceits on the mechanical interruption of their correspondence, and only at the end of the letter gets down to brass tacks: he would like Helpidius to treat the son of a friend of his, who is very ill. As to the name of the friend, S reads *Celeri*, L reads *ceriti*. Since the Celer to whom Avitus writes, *Ep.* 48, was in Constantinople, it is better to identify this man with the Ceretius addressed in *Ep.* 83. If *Epp.* 95 and 96 should indeed be dated to ca. 500, and if *Ep.* 83 can be dated to ca. 516, the Ceretius *v. i.* of *Epp.* 38 and 83 might be the boy of *Ep.* 95.[4] He would thus be very closely connected to Avitus. If these identifications are accepted, the letter to Helpidius would have to fall late in Avitus' life, to allow time for Ceretius to marry and have a son. Two letters in the Avitan collection recommend patients to distant physicians: this one and *Ep.* 11 to Caesarius of Arles. Both suggest inadequate medical care or lack of specialists in Vienne.

---

moralising improvisation and a biblical exemplum of the sort so favoured by Ruricius. Compare Greg. Tur. *GC* 39 on Tobit and cures.

1 The *maior domus* in this period was literally the chief organiser of a household. For the activities of major-domos as 'bearers of confidential messages' during the Laurentian schism, see Barnwell, *Emperor, Prefects and Kings*, pp. 141–42. In this case, however, the major-domo seems to have been attached to the household of Helpidius, rather than to that of the ruler. For Helpidius' house, *Vita Caesarii* 1.41; for his use of slaves as messengers, Ennodius, 445.2. On *maiores domus* in other than royal households, Gregory I, *Register* 11, 53.

2 *PLRE* 2, Helpidius 6.

3 *PL* 62, cols. 543–48.

4 This, however, is denied by Heinzelmann, 'Gallische Prosopographie', p. 578.

Avitus the bishop to Helpidius the deacon {67.7}

I have just heard from some priests of the alien religion (i.e. Arians) that you
are in good health: the news came as a gift of God. Just as our Elijah did not
find the food vile that was sent from heaven in the filthy beaks of birds,[1] so
too here the nature of the messengers did not detract from the welcomeness
of the writer. But the fact that you claim that the letter that I wrote you and
sent on its way some time ago did *not* arrive[2] has sprinkled some small
bitterness on the sweetness of your letter, for which I am particularly greedy.
For in my joy to have received your letter through the major-domo – he had
caught up with your commissioner,[3] my master Sigismund, in Vienne when
he had been sent on an embassy by his father[4] – I discharged the duties of my
very bountiful generosity through him (= the major-domo) again, and
cultivated the love that I felt for you and had conceived in my heart, by
writing enthusiastically and committing my affections to the written page.
Your major-domo is bound to know something about how it came about that
you did not receive this letter. I was unhappy about this, and I rejoiced that it
was a source of grief to you that, despite the convenient circumstances, the
gift-exchange of one was lost to both of our desires.[5] But since each side of
our plan to exchange affection is safe, it is sometimes right to forgive and
forget such accidents, in which, once they have stolen our chance for
talking,[6] rather than the desire to do so, a loss can happen to our concern, but
not to the love that motivates it. Whether the chance [to meet] is denied us or
not, there can be no time for neglect in which the longing to increase your
health[7] could grow tepid in me, whatever else I am doing. Therefore I think
that a rather precious thing about the minds of friends, namely that it is clear
that no room is left to chance occurrences, because neither the length of a
journey can dissipate it, nor can forgetfulness frustrate it. I am making a
special effort to pay back kind words in this letter, in case you have
considered my silence a [financial] loss. At the same time, if you will be so
kind, I wish especially to commend a young man to you, the son of Ceretus,

---

1 3 Kgs 17.6: compare *Ep.* 74.

2 Compare the stopping of Sigismund's letters by Theodoric: *Ep.* 94.

3 The Latin word is *mandator*.

4 Gundobad.

5 Avitus uses a conceit: the gift of one (*unius*) is lost to the desires of two (*desideriis
duorum*), i.e. both of them miss the missing letter.

6 The accidents are personified as thieves.

7 *Frequentandae sospitatis* is rather vague. *Sospitas* could refer to health, safety or
prosperity.

vir illustris. You, after God, will make it possible for him to begin to hope[1] for the life of his only child. For he is so shackled by the unfortunate disease of his child that, unsure of what he ought to wish, even while he is compelled to fear his death, he is forced to mourn his life as if he had already lost him. Therefore please join your < ... >[2] to the Divinity that will help. As far as we understand your singular skill,[3] for you to have promised something is partially to have done it. May Christ grant that by exalting[4] and praising your supreme command of this art (i.e. medicine), Italy may owe its fame for medicine and Gaul the health of this child to you.

---

1 Taking S's *sperare*, 'to hope', rather than L's *operiri*, 'to wait for'.

2 An unqualified *tua* cannot be the accusative required by *iunge*. There is also no suitable cursus after a major division. Some words, probably including *vota* or *opem* seem to be missing.

3 Peiper may have mispunctuated. There is probably a gap that included a sentence-ending after *tua*. The *quantum* clause should begin a new sentence, joined to *vestrum promisisse* with a comma.

4 *Exulto*, 'to exult', is intransitive and does not make sense here in a gerundive construction. *Exaltando*, 'to exalt', is correct.

THE FRANKISH KINGDOM

24. THE BAPTISM OF CLOVIS

Contents

Epistula 46 Avitus to Clovis, King of the Franks; congratulations on his baptism and conversion to Catholicism.

Epistula 46: Introduction

Avitus writes to the Frankish king Clovis: he comments on attempts by heretics to mislead the king, and claims his conversion as a victory for Catholicism. He notes that Clovis has not used standard excuses to avoid abandoning his ancestral religion, and he compares the king's religion with that of the Byzantine emperor. He comments on the baptism itself, to which he may have been invited, but did not attend, envisaging the scene in his mind's eye. He then considers what he would have said in praise of the king had he been there: he comments on the king's faith, humility and mercy, which a recently captive people had experienced. He chooses to close with an exhortation in which he challenges Clovis to send missions to the pagans, notably to those pagan peoples whom he has subjected. The end of the letter is missing.

This is the most famous and in many respects the most historically significant letter in the Avitus collection. As the one contemporary reference to and (imagined) description of the baptism of Clovis, it is a key to the christianisation of the Franks, and has, as a result generated an enormous amount of literature.[1] It is the one letter of

---

1 For Clovis' baptism see, for example, A. Angenendt, *Kaiserherrschaft und Königstaufe* (Berlin, 1984), pp. 165–76; W. M. Daly, 'Clovis: How Barbaric, How Pagan?', *Speculum* 69 (1994), pp. 619–64 (pp. 637–41 deal with Avitus, *Ep.* 46); E. Ewig, 'Studien zur merowingischen Dynastie', *Frühmittelalterliche Studien* 8 (1974), pp. 15–59; B. Krusch, 'Die erste deutsche Kaiserkrönung in Tours Weihnachten 508', *SbBerlin. Akad. Wiss.* (1933), pp. 1060–66: L. Levillain, 'La Conversion et le baptême de Clovis', *Revue d'histoire de l'Église de France* 21 (1935), pp. 161–92; F. Lot, 'La Victoire sur les Alamans et la conversion de Clovis', *RBPH* 17 (1938), pp. 63–69; M. McCormick, 'Clovis at Tours, Byzantine Public Ritual and the Origins of Medieval Ruler Symbolism', in *Das Reich und die Barbaren*, ed. E. K. Chrysos and A. Schwarcz (Vienna–Cologne, 1989), pp.155–80; G. Reverdy, 'Note sur l'interprétation d'un passage d'Avitus', *Le moyen âge* 26 (1913), pp. 274–77; Reydellet, *La Royauté dans la littérature latine*; M. Spencer, 'Dating the Baptism of Clovis, 1886–1993', *EME* 3 (1994), pp. 97–116; N. Staubach, 'Germanisches Königtum und lateinische Literatur vom fünften bis zum siebten Jahrhundert', *Frühmittelalterliche Studien* 17 (1983), pp. 1–54, a review article on Reydellet;

Avitus for which a number of translations exist.[1] By contrast the accounts of Clovis' baptism by Nicetius of Trier[2] and Gregory of Tours are secondary constructs, the former made approximately half a century later and latter yet later still.[3] Not surprisingly most discussion has revolved around the importance of the letter for dating the baptism.[4] It cannot be said, however, that Avitus' letter is easily dated. Van de Vyver argued that none of Avitus' letters antedated the siege of Vienne in 500,[5] but the argument that all earlier Avitus' works were destroyed at that time, cannot be proved.

To review all the arguments relating to the baptism would require a book. This is the place to comment on the letter of Avitus and the problems it raises. These include two textual problems, since there are two places in the letter where the text adopted by the editor makes a major difference in the historical interpretation of the passage.[6]

The chief problems of interpretation are as follows:

1. What was Clovis converted from? In formal terms he had clearly been a pagan: he was baptised as a Catholic, and since the Catholics did not rebaptise converts from Arianism, or from most other heresies, he cannot have undergone any previous baptism. Avitus could, thus, reasonably comment on the king's abandonment of paganism, and his breaking with the traditions of his ancestors.[7] Yet Avitus' opening sentence seems to suggest that heretics had very nearly converted the king before he opted for Catholicism.

The beginning of the letter contains a clear allusion to Clovis' interactions with non-orthodox Christians, but only recently has the significance of this passage been realised,[8] and only recently has a deeper textual corruption requiring a supplement

---

G. Tessier, *Le Baptême de Clovis* (Paris, 1964); Von den Steinen, 'Chlodwigs Übergang zum Christentum', pp. 417–501; Van de Vyver, 'La Victoire contre les Alamans' (1936), pp. 859–914; *idem*, 'La Victoire contre les Alamans' (1937), pp. 35–94; Weiss, *Chlodwigs Taufe: Reims 508*; Wood, 'Gregory of Tours and Clovis', pp. 249–72.

1 E.g. J. M. Hillgarth, ed., *Christianity and Paganism, 350–750: The Conversion of Western Europe* (Philadelphia, 1986), pp. 76–78; M. Rouche, *Clovis* (Paris, 1996), pp. 397–400; Murray, *From Roman to Merovingian Gaul*, pp. 261–63. The latter two translations appeared after this one was completed.

2 Nicetius of Trier, *Ep.* to Chlodosuintha: *Epistulae Austrasiacae* 8, *MGH Epp.* 3, p. 118.

3 Greg. Tur. *DLH* 2.30: Wood, 'Gregory of Tours and Clovis', pp. 249–72.

4 See Van de Vyver, 'La Victoire contre les Alamans' (1936), pp. 859–914 and 'La Victoire contre les Alamans' (1937), pp. 35–94; also *idem*, 'L'unique victoire contre les Alamans et la conversion de Clovis en 506', *RBPH* 17 (1938), pp. 793–813, through to Spencer, 'Dating the Baptism of Clovis', pp. 97–116.

5 Van de Vyver, 'La Victoire contre les Alamans' (1936), p. 887.

6 For a fuller discussion of the textual and historical problems, see Shanzer, 'Dating the Baptism of Clovis', pp. 29–57.

7 This was a recurrent issue in conversion: compare *Vita Wulframni* 9, on Radbod's supposed refusal to abandon his ancestors.

8 See Wood, 'Gregory of Tours and Clovis', p. 267 on Clovis' flirtation with Arianism.

been noticed.[1] The Latin text reads:

> *Vestrae subtilitatis acrimoniam quorumcumque scismatum sectatores sen-*
> *tentiis suis variis opinione, diversis multitudine, vacuis veritate Christiani*
> *nominis visi sunt obumbratione velare.*

It is usually translated by some variant of: 'The partisans of the schisms seem to veil and obscure your perspicacity by the variety and number of enunciations and opinions, empty of the name of Christian truth',[2] or 'The followers of Arian error have in vain, by a cloud of contradictory and untrue opinions, sought to conceal from your extreme subtlety the glory of the Christian name.'[3] But *velare* ('to veil', 'to put a cover on') with a direct object *acrimoniam vestrae subtilitatis*, 'keenness of Your Subtlety', is unlikely here in presence of *obumbratione Christiani nominis*.[4] A different direct object is required, something meaning 'lies', 'heresy' or 'lying dogmas'. Accordingly a diagnostic supplement was made: <*detecta mendacia*>, and *acrimoniam* was emended to *acrimonia*. The proposed new text reads:

> *Vestrae subtilitatis acrimonia <detecta mendacia> quorumcumque scisma-*
> *tum sectatores sententiis suis variis opinione, diversis multitudine, vacuis*
> *veritate, Christiani nominis nisi[5] sunt obumbratione velare.*

> 'The chasers after various and sundry schisms, by their opinions, different in nature, many in number, but *all* empty of truth, have tried to conceal, under the cover of the name "Christian", the lies that have been uncovered[6] by the keen intelligence[7] of Your Subtlety.'

At the very least we can conclude from the opening of the letter that Clovis had been influenced by Arianism. And this can be supported by the fact that his own sister, Lenteildis had to convert from Arianism to Catholicism.[8]

---

1 See Shanzer, 'Dating the Baptism', pp. 31–37.

2 An English version of Rouche's French translation (*Clovis*, p. 397).

3 Translated by Hillgarth, *Christianity and Paganism*, p. 77.

4 There is a close but not exact parallel in Greg. Tur. *DHL* 2.3: *Manifestissime autem patuit per huius caecitatem, qualiter haereticorum episcopus oculos cordium misero adsertationis suae velabat amictu, ne veram lucem ulli liceret fidei oculis contemplari.* 'It was utterly clear, through this man's blindness, how the bishop of the heretics used to veil the eyes of their hearts with the wretched covering of his claims, so that no one was allowed to see the light with the eyes of faith.'

5 Taking Labbeus' palmary conjecture for the *visi* of the manuscripts.

6 <*detecta mendacia*>

7 Reading *acrimonia*, abl. for *acrimoniam*.

8 This is clear from the title of the unfortunately lost *Homilia de conversione Lenteildis Chlodovaei sororis* (Avitus, *Hom.* 31), and from Greg. Tur. *DLH* 2.31.

2. The second problem relates to the comparison that Avitus draws between Clovis and the Byzantine emperor. Once again it is necessary to establish what the text actually says.

L reads *Gaudeat equidem Graecia principem legisse nostrum, sed non iam quae tanti muneris donum sola mereatur*: 'As far as I am concerned, let Greece[1] rejoice in having chosen our ruler.' This has been seen as an allusion to the honorary consulship bestowed on Clovis by Anastasius in 508.[2] But Avitus has not used the appropriate language to describe the award of a consulship. Others see here a less specific allusion to Clovis. Weiss, for example, translates the passage: 'Griechenland soll sich freuen, dass unser Fürst (Chlodwig) (sc. Katholizismus) gewählt hat.'[3] But, if Clovis had been intended, it is highly unlikely that Avitus would have called him *princeps noster* – even at a time, such as 507–508, when the Franks and Burgundians were allied against the Visigoths, or after 501 when the Burgundians were the Franks' tributaries. Others have seen here an allusion to Anastasius. Reydellet (p. 111) suggests the following: 'Le prince qu'a choisi la Grèce est qualifié de *noster*, c'est-à-dire qu'il partage notre foi, à nous évêques catholiques d'Occident.' *Principem nostrum* allegedly means 'an orthodox emperor'.[4] But this translation of *principem nostrum* is impossible.

In this case the text provided by S is preferable. S reads *Gaudeat ergo quidem Graecia habere se principem legis nostrae, sed non iam quae tanti muneris dono sola mereatur*: 'Therefore let Greece, to be sure, rejoice that she has a ruler who is orthodox,[5] but she is no longer the only one to deserve to bask in the illumination of such a great gift.' It unlikely to be a conjecture of Sirmond's, because it contains an interesting 'error': Avitus describes Anastasius as orthodox.

This presents an instant problem, since the Emperor Anastasius (491–518) was pro-Monophysite, and throughout his reign Constantinople was in schism with Rome. Either Avitus wished to gloss over the matter for some reason or other, or he did not know about the Acacian schism. The latter explanation is not entirely

---

1 I.e. Byzantium.

2 See Greg. Tur. *DLH* 2.38.

3 Weiss, *Chlodwigs Taufe*, p. 49. The choice for him is Catholicism, according to Weiss.

4 Staubach, 'Germanisches Königtum und lateinische Literatur', p. 20, seems to suggest that. Reydellet, *La Royauté dans la littérature latine*, has combined *legisse nostrum* and *legis nostrae*. This is not clear, for although Reydellet (p. 111 n. 92) cites Courcelle's translation 'qui partage notre foi', he cites the text of L (at p. 109 n. 86), not a composite text like those of the scholars above. It seems instead that he is packing too much meaning into *nostrum*. Von den Steinen, 'Chlodwigs Übergang zum Christentum', p. 479 and Staubach both overstate the case in assuming that *legis nostrae* is an emendation of Sirmond's. It could well be a transmitted correct reading. Reydellet has now been followed by Spencer, 'Dating the Baptism of Clovis', p. 109.

5 For *lex nostra* in this sense, see *Ep.* 8, p. 40.15. For Arianism as the *lex aliena*, see *Ep.* 38, p. 67.8: *clericos legis alienae*.

impossible. In the aftermath of the *Trishagion* riots in 511 Avitus was certainly confused about who was, and who was not, orthodox in Constantinople.[1] He was enlightened to some extent as a result of Vitalian's successful uprising against the emperor in 515.[2] His confusion may have begun during the pontificate of Anastasius (496–98), who was responsible for restoring the metropolitan status of Vienne vis-à-vis Arles,[3] and also attempted to end the Acacian schism by reinstating Acacius.[4] If Avitus was unaware of the breach between Rome and Constantinople between 498 and 511, then the reference to Greece is of no help in dating *Ep.* 46. One letter in the Avitus collection may, however, lead to the conclusion that Avitus was aware of the Acacian schism throughout his episcopate, however confused he may have been about its details: *Ep.* 54, which seems to have been written soon after the siege of Vienne in 500, includes a reference to a 'vomit from overseas' (*vomitus transmarinus*) which appears to have been a Greek heresy of some sort, most plausibly Eutychianism. If Avitus was aware that the Byzantines were in schism with Rome he must have had a very good reason for drawing a parallel between Clovis and the emperor. One possible reason could be Anastasius' conferment of the consulship on the Frankish king in 508.[5]

3. The one other point to note about this part of the letter is that it does not actually say that Clovis was the first Catholic king in the West, although it might be thought to imply that by 'in the West, in the person of a new king, the ray of an age-old light shines forth'. Avitus' failure to make the point, however, is highlighted when one compares *Ep.* 8 on Sigismund's conversion: *adhuc de regibus solus est, quem in bonum transisse non pudeat.*[6] The *argument ex silentio* strongly suggests that Sigismund converted before Clovis.[7] In any case there had been earlier Catholic kings in other barbarian tribes: one should note especially Rechiarius among the Suevi. There may also have been Catholic rulers of the Burgundians before Gundobad.[8]

4. Avitus' letter goes on to envisage the baptism of Clovis: Remigius was quite clearly not the only officiator: a *numerosa pontificum manus* was present, a phrase which is enough on its own to invalidate Gregory of Tours' own imaginative reconstruction of the baptism.[9] One should also note that Avitus describes Clovis as a *competens*, and since he seems to have been kept aware of the king's religious development at this time, it is likely that Clovis underwent the full catechumenate.

---

1 *CE* 1 and 2.

2 See *Epp.* 39–42, 47, 48.

3 *Epp. Arelatenses Genuinae* 23: Klingshirn, *Caesarius of Arles*, p. 71.

4 *Liber Pontificalis* 52.

5 Greg. Tur. *DLH* 2.38.

6 This passage alone does not prove that Sigismund was converted before Clovis, since Avitus is almost certainly thinking only in terms of *Burgundian reges*.

7 See the commentary on *Epp.* 8 and 29 above.

8 Wood, 'Ethnicity and the Ethnogenesis', pp. 58–60.

9 Greg. Tur. *DLH* 1.31.

Also significant for interpreting the context of the baptism is the fact that Avitus seems to have been invited to attend it: *corporaliter non accessi*. Relations between the Franks and the Burgundians must have been extraordinarily good for Avitus to have been invited to, or at the very least kept informed about, the king's baptism, and indeed for him to have written *Ep.* 46. Given the treason accusations faced by others in this period (for instance Caesarius of Arles[1] and Avitus' own cousin Apollinaris)[2] such a letter, sent in response to a message delivered by a messenger of the Frankish king,[3] could hardly have been sent except under very favourable circumstances.

5. The bishop then praises three aspects of the king's behaviour: the fact that he was converted to Catholicism without the help of a preacher; that he had long shown humility to Avitus as bishop – a point which one might compare with Remigius' exhortation to Clovis made in ca. 481, that the king should listen to the advice of bishops;[4] and that he had been merciful to a people who had up until recently been captive. The identity of this *populus* is sadly unclear, but two points can be made: they had been captive up till then (implied by the *adhuc*) and they were Christians: *insinuat lacrimis deo*. Since the Franks are unlikely to have been converted to Catholicism before their king, and since they appear in the next sentence as *gens vester*, the *populus* must, therefore, have been Catholic inhabitants of Gaul, of whom the most likely group are Aquitanians. Avitus would surely not have risked implying that Clovis has in some sense liberated Catholics of the Burgundian kingdom from their masters.

6. The letter concludes with an exhortation to the king telling him to send Catholic missionaries to pagans of *ulteriores gentes*: and he defines these peoples as being about to serve Clovis because of the power of religion: *externi quique populi paganorum pro religionis vobis primitus imperio servituri*. The most obvious pagan people subjected by Clovis are the Alamans. It should be noted, however, that Avitus does not envisage a defeat of pagans as the most recent of Clovis' achievements. More recent was the freeing of the *populus captivus*, or so the word *nuper* implies.

It would be wrong to say that Avitus' letter provides cast-iron clues as to its date: on the other hand the clustering of the subjection of a pagan people (most easily identified with the defeat of the Alamans in 506), the freeing of a Catholic people

---

1 *Vita Caesarii,* ed. B. Krusch, *MGH SRM* 3.1.21, 29–31, 36.

2 *Epp.* 51–2: see more generally, Wood, 'Gregory of Tours and Clovis', p. 25.

3 Van de Vyver, 'La Victoire contre les Alamans' (1936), p. 900, states, 'Il ne remercie point le roi pour une missive, encore moins pour une invitation …' Wrongly. *Nuntius* is not the equivalent of *rumor* or *fama*. A messenger or announcement must have been sent to Avitus, but a discreet one. He did not get the news of Clovis' pending baptism on the grapevine. Clearly he had been in correspondence with Clovis (p. 76.5–6, *humilitatem, quam iam dudum nobis devotione impenditis*), and he was prepared to address Clovis as someone who had shown *humilitas* and did not need further instruction in said virtue. *Humilitas* is almost equivalent to 'tractability' or 'readiness to be guided' in these contexts.

4 *Ep. Austrasiacae* 2.

(most easily linked with the Visigothic war of 507) and a comparison with the Byzantine emperor (which might point to the consulship of 508), can be seen as pointing to a date of 508 for the baptism. One might add that relations between the Burgundians and Franks were particularly good in that year, as both kingdoms joined to dismember Visigothic Aquitaine,[1] and that under such circumstances Avitus' letter would probably not have seemed treasonable.

Ultimately, however, the date of Clovis' baptism is much less significant than is often thought. Clovis had been urged to work with Catholic bishops since the start of his reign, even while a pagan.[2] It is also clear from the collaboration of the Arian Gundobad in the Visigothic campaign of 508 that the king's supposed anti-Arian crusades were not prompted by religion.[3] This is not to deny that Clovis himself used Catholic propaganda at the end of his reign.[4] Nevertheless the anti-Arianism attributed to Clovis is largely a construct of Gregory of Tours.

There are, perhaps, more important issues than chronology to be found in Avitus' letter. First the opening sentence makes it clear that Arianism had made inroads into Clovis' court before the king opted for Catholicism. This can be linked to the evidence of Gregory of Tours, on the conversion from Arianism of Clovis' sister Lenteildis, an event that was recorded in a now lost homily of Avitus.[5] One should also note that another of Clovis' sisters (Audofleda) converted to Arianism, presumably when she married Theodoric the Great.[6] The other side of this coin is that the Burgundians were far less committed to Arianism than is often thought,[7] and indeed that there is little evidence for a major Arian–Catholic conflict in Gaul during Clovis' time.[8]

Finally this letter is exceptional in urging, at so early a date, the christianisation of barbarian peoples outside what had once been the Roman Empire.[9] Popes Celestine and Leo seem to have had similar ideas.[10] Otherwise the first great proponent of the idea appears to have been the seventh-century missionary, Amandus.[11] Avitus,

---

1 Isidore, *Historia Gothorum, Wandalorum, Sueborum* 36–37: *Chronicle of 511*, nos. 689–90.

2 *Ep. Austrasiacae* 2.

3 Isidore, *Historia Gothorum, Wandalorum, Sueborum* 36–37: *Chronicle of 511*, nos. 689–90: also Wood, 'Gregory of Tours and Clovis', pp. 255–57.

4 Wood, 'Gregory of Tours and Clovis', pp. 270–71.

5 *Hom.* 31.

6 Greg. Tur. *DLH* 3.31.

7 Wood, 'Ethnicity and the Ethnogenesis', pp. 58–60.

8 Wood, 'Gregory of Tours and Clovis', pp. 255–58.

9 E. A. Thompson, 'Christianity and the Northern Barbarians', in A. Momigliano, ed., *The Conflict between Paganism and Christianity in the Fourth Century* (Oxford, 1963), pp. 56–78.

10 T. M. Charles-Edwards, 'Palladius, Prosper, and Leo the Great: Mission and Primatial Authority" in D. N. Dumville, ed., *Saint Patrick A.D. 493–1993* (Woodbridge, 1993).

11 W. H. Fritze, 'Universalis gentium confessio. Formeln, Träger und Wege universalmissionarischen Denkens im 7. Jahrhundert', *Frühmittelalterliche Studien* 3 (1969), pp. 79–130.

thus, appears among the early theorists of mission outside the bounds of the Roman Empire.

Avitus the bishop to Clovis the king {75.1 Peiper}

The chasers after various schisms,[1] by their opinions, different in nature, many in number, but *all* empty of truth, tried[2] to conceal, under the cover of the name 'Christian', the lies that have been uncovered[3] by the keen intelligence[4] of Your Subtlety. While we save such things (*sc.* the lies) for eternity, while we reserve for future examination[5] the question of who is right on what, even in our present circumstances a ray of truth has shone through. Divine foresight has found a certain judge for our age. In making a choice for yourself, you judge on behalf of everyone. Your faith is our victory.

Many in this very situation, seeking true belief, if they are moved to the suggestion, encouraged by priests or their friends, usually invoke the custom of their race and the rites of ancestral observance as stumbling-blocks.[6] Thus, to their own detriment, they prefer due reverence[7] to salvation. While they maintain a token respect for their ancestors in continuing to be unbelievers,[8] they demonstrate that they somehow do not know what to choose. Therefore let the dangerous [sense of] shame[9] abandon this excuse after the miracle of your decision![10] You [alone] among your ancient clan,

1 Avitus on occasion uses *schisma* in an imprecise sense as equivalent to heresy. Cf. *Ep.* 31, p. 62.22.

2 Taking Labbeus' *nisi*. *Visi* (as in the MSS) would mean that they had 'appeared' to hide their unorthodoxy under a veil of orthodoxy. An unsuccessful attempt on their part (Clovis had the *acrimonia* to see through the obfuscation) is more in keeping with Avitus' rhetorical point.

3 <*detecta mendacia*>.

4 Reading *acrimonia*, abl. for *acrimoniam*.

5 Presumably the Last Judgement.

6 Avitus also alludes to ancestral religious customs in *Ep.* 6 p. 34.33: *antiquam parentum consuetudinem sive sectam*.

7 Translating *verecundia*.

8 See Wood, *Merovingian Kingdoms*, p. 44: 'For a Merovingian whose dynasty originated with a sea-monster, rejection of previous beliefs must have been particularly hard.' That breaking with the beliefs of ancestors was a genuine problem for Germanic peoples wanting to convert is shown also by *Vita Wulframni*, 9, and Nicholas I, *Ep.* 99.98–100, ed. E. Perels, *MGH Epp.* VI.

9 The Latin phrase used is *noxius pudor*, 'poisonous shame', an oxymoron, given that *pudor* is usually a virtue. Avitus is saying that the sense of respect one feels towards one's ancestors can be poisonous, i.e. dangerous, because it prevents one from converting. The emphatic position of the verb *discedat*, 'let it leave', is reminiscent of the language used in exorcism.

10 This is an early instance of conversion itself being regarded as a miracle, a point of view which was to have considerable importance during the Christianisation of the Germanic peoples.

content with nobility alone,[1] wished whatever could adorn all your lofty ancestry to start from you for the benefit of your race. You have ancestors who did good [deeds], but you wished to be the author of better [ones]. You are the equal[2] of your great-grandfathers in that you reign in the temporal world; for your descendants you have established your rule in heaven.

Therefore let Greece,[3] to be sure, rejoice in having an orthodox ruler[4] but she is no longer the only one to deserve so great a gift.[5] Now her[6] bright glory adorns *your* part of the world also, and in the West, in the person of a new[7] king, the ray of an age-old[8] light shines forth. It is fitting that it began

1 Avitus hints at the idea of the divine origin of German kings. Clovis has given up this idea, and the glory reflected upon his descendants will start from his choice. See Von den Steinen, 'Chlodwigs Übergang zum Christentum', p. 481.

2 Translating *respondetis*.

3 I.e. Byzantium.

4 Taking S's *gaudeat ergo quidem Graecia habere se principem legis nostrae*. See Shanzer, 'Dating the Baptism of Clovis', pp. 37–42. Cf. *Ep.* 8, p. 40.15.

5 Taking L's reading *sed non iam quae tanti muneris donum sola mereatur*.

6 *Sua* is here being used for *eius*, i.e. *Graeciae*. See Goelzer, p. 661.

7 It is clear that *rege* requires a qualifier, and that the simplest and most obvious supplement is Labbeus' supplement to L < *novo*>, 'in a new king, a light shines forth that is not new'. There is a rhetorical point or antithesis here that involves the contrast between the new and the 'not new'. The very presence of the litotes *non novi* presupposes contrast to a form of *novus*. S has a different reading that may likewise be an emendation: *in rege non novo novi iubaris lumen effulgurat*, 'in a king who is not new, a new light shines forth'. If Labbeus' supplement is accepted the sentence means that Clovis is a newly *Christian* king, and that the light that shines in him is some ancient light associated with Christianity. Sirmond's reading implies that although Clovis was already a king (he is not *novus*), a new light (i.e. one new to *him*), Christianity, shines out in him. Labbeus' supplement is preferable because there is probably a secondary allusion here. See n. 8 below. Reydellet, *La Royauté dans la littérature latine*, p. 112 attempts to defend L's *in rege* by suggesting that there is an implied contrast between a barbarian *king* as opposed to a [Roman] emperor. Staubach, 'Germanisches Königtum und lateinische Literatur', p. 27, also defends L's naked *rege*, but really by default: he claims that both Labbeus' and Sirmond's readings are unsatisfactory: 'weil weder *rex novus* noch *rex non novus* eine besonders passende oder ehrenvolle Bezeichnung for Chlodwig wäre'. Staubach fails to allow for the many possible meanings of *novus*. See, for example, the *OLD s.v.* 'novus', which distinguishes seventeen different usages. Both *OLD* 13 'restored, as good as new', *OLD* 14 'modern' would work well in this context.

8 Hillgarth translates 'a rising sun', and fails to render *non novi iubaris*. The passage is far more likely to refer to the Star in the East, for which see Prudentius, *Cath.* 12.1–60 and *Apoth.* 611–49. For an excellent analysis of the trope see Staubach, 'Germanisches Königtum und lateinische Literatur', pp. 26ff. Avitus plays on the idea of the new 'Star in the West'. The Star in Bethlehem was associated with Epiphany, the Magi and hence with the *vocatio gentium*, all themes appropriate for the Christmas baptism of a pagan king. The more standard pagan form of this sort of panegyrical image appears in, for example, *Pan. Lat.* 3.2.3: *hic quasi quoddam*

to shine on the birthday of our Redeemer,[1] so that the vivifying water appropriately gave birth to you in your salvation on the very day when the world received the Lord of Heaven born for its redemption.[2] On the day on which the birthday of our Lord is celebrated, let yours be too – the day on which Christ was born to the world, and you to Christ, the day on which you consecrated your soul to God, your life to those present, and your reputation to posterity.

What can be said about the glorious celebration of your regeneration? Even if I was not present[3] at the rites in the flesh, I was not absent from communion in its joys – above all since divine kindness has added this further cause for thankfulness to our part of the world.[4] Before your baptism a message came to me of the most sublime humility,[5] in which you stated that you were a candidate for baptism. Therefore after this waiting-period,[6] Christmas Eve found me finally[7] sure of you. I was turning things over in my mind, and wondering how it would be when a large company of bishops united, striving in the sacred service, would lap the royal limbs in the life-giving waters, when he would bow before the servants of the Lord the head that should be so feared by pagans,[8] when locks grown long beneath a

---

salutare humano generi sidus exortus <es>. It is also worth noting that *non novi iubaris* allows for there being previous Catholic kings in the West: the phrase thus does not exclude the possibility that Sigismund converted to Catholicism before Clovis. Indeed one might say that the passage studiously avoids saying that Clovis is the first Catholic king, while allowing the reader to think that that is the point of the passage.

1 Easter was the traditional day on which baptism took place, and the Gallic councils condemn baptism on other days: Council of Auxerre (561–605), can. 18: Mâcon II (585), can. 3.

2 Taking *redemptioni* S.

3 For examples of the *praesentia*-topos see *Ep*. 64, p. 88.19; *Ep*. 66, p. 88.25; *Ep*. 72, p. 90.9 and 15; *Ep*. 77, p. 92.18 for spiritual presence; *Ep*. 78, p. 93.2.

4 Taking S's *regionibus nostris*. The sense requires that the news of Clovis' baptism have been a cause of happiness where Avitus was, not just because it happened, but because he knew that it would lead ahead of time.

5 The implication seems to have been that Avitus was invited to the ceremony. Even if one takes the message simply to have been an announcement of the baptism it is difficult to see how it could have been sent to Avitus before 501. In the 490s the Burgundians and Franks were rival peoples. In 501, however, the Burgundians became tributary (Greg. Tur. *DLH* 2.32–3). In 508 they were allies of the Franks, campaigning against the Visigoths. Whereas before 501 Avitus' letter could easily have been seen as treasonable, after that date, and most especially in 508, it might have been less suspect.

6 As *competens*.

7 The *iam* is somewhat sinister, suggesting that Clovis had wavered and that Avitus had been unsure of him up to the last moment.

8 Translating *gentibus*. Perhaps an allusion to Clovis' recent Alamannic victory.

helmet,[1] would put on the helmet of the sacred chrism, when his spotless limbs, the breastplate removed, would shine as white as his baptismal clothes. Have no fear, O most prosperous of Kings! From now on the very softness of that clothing will cause the hardness of your armour to be all the more effective:[2] whatever good luck has offered you in the past, holiness will now provide.

I would like to add some exhortation to my praise of you, were anything escaping either your knowledge or your watchfulness. Certainly I am not going to preach to you the faith that you saw without a preacher[3] *before* your baptism[4] once you have found it. Or should I preach humility perhaps? You had long ago paid it to me by your service,[5] even though only now do you owe it to me through your profession of faith. Or perhaps I should preach the sense of pity that a people, up till[6] recently captive, once released by you, by its joy conveys to the world and by its tears to God?[7]

1 Hillgarth, *Christianity and Paganism*, p. 77, misunderstood the passage and has Clovis being anointed with his helmet on. Avitus' language is purely figurative. He is alluding to 1 Thess. 5.8: *induti loricam fidei et caritatis et galeam spem salutis*. The *crines* of the *reges criniti* are contrasted to the *galea* of salvation. For *nutrire crinem* compare *Statutae Ecclesiae Antiquae*, can. 25, *clericus nec comam nutriat, nec barbam radat*. On long hair as the identifying mark of the Merovingians, see Greg. Tur. *DLH* 2.9 and 6.24.

2 This could well indicate that Clovis' decision to convert did take place in a military context, even if not the one specified by Greg. Tur. *DLH* 2. 30.

3 See Rom. 10.14–15. Clovis surprisingly has done it on his own. We might see here a sign of competition with Remigius to be Clovis' spiritual advisor, or else, perhaps, a sign that Gregory may have exaggerated Remigius' role in the conversion.

4 *Perfectio*.

5 See Remigius' letter of ca. 481: *Epistulae Austrasiacae* 2.

6 Hillgarth, *Christianity and Paganism*, p. 78, translates 'a people once captive, now freed by you'. But *adhuc* modifies *nuper*, which in turn modifies *captivus*. The captivity of this people had continued up till recently. The word-order makes it clear that *nuper* cannot be construed with *solutus*. *Adhuc* then would be nonsensical.

7 According to Reverdy the Franks are the *populus captivus* ('Note sur l'interprétation d'un passage d'Avitus', pp. 274–77). Daly, 'Clovis: How Barbaric, how Pagan?', p. 638 n. 56, follows him, and sees here a reference to the figurative captivity of the pagan Franks. For a possible parallel and example of spiritual *captivitas*, see Symmachus, *Ep.* 12.8 (Thiel, p. 714): *Si enim qui praecessit beatitudinem tuam inter sanctos constitutus Leo archiepiscopus ad Attilam tunc errorem barbarum per se currere non duxit indignum, ut captivitatem corrigeret corporalem, nec tantum Christianorum, sed et Judaeorum, ut credibile est, atque paganorum: quanto magis festinare ad tuam attinet sanctitatem, non ad corporeae, quae bello fit, captivitatis correctionem atque conversionem, sed animarum, quae captivatae sunt vel quotidie captivantur!* For the symbolic use of *captivitas* in Christian contexts, see *TLL s.v.* 'capitivitas', 368.57ff. Avitus alludes to the Gallo-Romans of Aquitaine *per* Wood, 'Gregory of Tours and Clovis', pp. 269–70. Shanzer, 'Dating the Baptism of Clovis', sees here Aquitainian captives

There is only one thing that I would like to be increased. Because God has made your race completely his own through you, please offer the seeds of faith from the treasure-house of your heart to more distant races too: since they still live in their natural ignorance, no seeds of heresy have corrupted.[1] Do not be ashamed or find it troublesome even to take the step of sending missions for this purpose to build up the party[2] of the God who has raised up yours so greatly.[3] To the extent that whatever[4] foreign pagan peoples there are,[5] ready to serve you for the first time because of the rule of your religion, while they still seem to have some other distinctive quality,[6] let them be distinguished by their race rather than through their ruler[7] ... [Here the text of the letter breaks off.]

Appendix

Letter to Remigius, Archbishop of Reims; although no such letter survives in the Avitus corpus, Flodoard in his *History of the Church of Rheims* (3.1) states that Hincmar wrote to Archbishop Ado of Vienne over a letter sent by Avitus to Remigius which the monk Rotfrid said he had read when he was with Ado.[8]

---

after the 507 war. The one thing that is clear about these captives is that they are Christians: they convey their tears to God. That it does not refer to the Franks, however, seems to be indicated by the fact the populus is *solutus a vobis nuper*: *nuper* must refer to time before the moment of Clovis' baptism. While Franks, however, could have been seen as being freed by Clovis' baptism, they could scarcely have been seen as being freed *before*. All historical sources point to the earliest significant baptisms following shortly after Clovis'.

1 For seeds of heresy, cf. *CE* 1, p. 16.171–8; *Hom.* 20, p. 133.21.

2 The word used is *partes*, 'factions, party'. *Nostra pars* is used of Catholicism, see *Ep.* 31, p. 62.9.

3 This is one of the earliest examples of missionary theory extending beyond what had been the boundaries of the Roman Empire. Again it would have seemed treasonable before the subordination of the Burgundian kingdom to Clovis.

4 S's *quoque* is likely to be an emendation of Sirmond's based on the assumption that Clovis was a pagan.

5 This is plausibly a reference to the Alamans: it is difficult to see who else could be defined as *ulteriores gentes/populi pagani* ready to serve Clovis for the first time.

6 Or 'property'.

7 Avitus' argument seems to be moving towards stating that people should be distinguished by their race and not by their religion: it is difficult to see what the word *principe* could have led to.

8 Flodoard of Reims, *Historia ecclesiae Remensis*, 3.21, *PL* 135.202.

TWO HOMILIES

25. TWO HOMILIES

Contents

Homily 25 on the Martyrs of Agaune {145.32 Peiper}

Avitus' homilies present particular problems for the student of his works. Although he is known to have compiled a homiliary, the fragmentary homilies found in the papyrus were almost certainly never part of that collection. They are all occasional pieces, written to commemorate specific events: dedications or the conversion of individuals. It seems significant that they are found alongside Avitus' letters.[1] By contrast, those fragments of homilies that appear to have come from a homiliary could be preached over and over again, on the appropriate church feast. Most of these reusable homilies survive only as passages quoted in later sources, notably in Florus' commentaries on various books of the New Testament. Thus Avitus' homilies, or more often the surviving fragments, for the days running up to Easter and for the following week (*Hom.* 1–5), those for the second and third days of Rogations (*Hom.* 8–9), and for Ascension and Pentecost (*Hom.* 10–11), together with those on the Creed, the Ascension of Elijah, Hezekiah, Jonah, the ordination of a bishop, and the dedication of St Michael's church (*Hom.* 12–17), are transmitted only by Florus. The two complete homilies on Rogations and the first day of Rogations (*Hom.* 6–7) have quite independent transmission. The remainder of the homilies are known from the papyrus codex alone, with the exception of four, the titles of which are recorded, but whose texts have not survived at all (*Hom.* 31–34). Of those homilies excerpted by Florus, only that for the dedication of the church of St Michael is an occasional piece. Since Florus is known to have had access to the papyrus codex,[2] it is perfectly possible that he took the homily on the church dedication from there, where it would have fitted alongside Avitus' other dedication homilies. The other homilies may well have been drawn from the Avitus homiliary, which would have been the appropriate place for them, since they would have been eminently reusable.

Because the majority of Avitus' homilies are fragmentary, many of them so fragmentary as to be impossible to translate,[3] only two examples are included here.

---

1 Wood, 'Letters and Letter-Collections'.

2 Charlier, 'La Compilation augustinienne de Florus sur l'Apôtre', p. 159.

3 For other translations, see Borrel, 'Étude sur l'homélie prêchée par saint Avit' (reprinted in Cabrol-Leclercq, *DACL*, 12, cols. 371–75); Perrat and Audin, 'Alcimi Ecdicii Aviti Viennensis Episcopi Homilia', pp. 433–51.

They are, however, historically the most important, and one, *Homily* 6, has the additional value of being complete. Moreover, since one (*Hom.* 25) is transmitted in the papyrus codex, while the other seems to be derived from the homiliary (*Hom.* 6), the two provide useful examples of the range of Avitus' homiletic output.[1]

Homily 25 is the sermon preached by Avitus on the occasion of the dedication of Sigismund's monastic foundation of Agaune. The site had long been a place of pilgrimage, being the supposed site where the Theban legion was martyred and buried. The legion was thought to have been sent by the emperor Diocletian to kill Christians in Gaul, but to have refused, and as a result to have been annihilated instead.[2] A cult certainly existed at Agaune by the late fifth century, when Eucherius of Lyons wrote a *Passio* of the martyrs.[3] It may be that hermits or monks gathered by the relics. In 515, however, Sigismund decided to reorganise the cult and to found a major monastic community. The new foundation was important in several ways. The cult was a significant one. The new monastery must have attracted considerable comment – not least because Gundobad was still living. On the other hand, any difficulties the monastery might have caused for the Arian king were partially outweighed by the fact that Agaune was on the very edge of the kingdom. In many ways yet more important was the liturgy created for the monastery: despite the fact that one monastic group in Constantinople, the Euchites, had already established a ceaseless liturgy, the *laus perennis,* the endless psalmody of Agaune appears to have been invented specifically for the monastery.[4] It was to become a model for royal foundations under the Franks.[5]

It is possible that Avitus preached a number of dedication homilies in the course of his visit to Agaune. Certainly the title of one other homily (*Hom.* 20), explicitly refers to the bishop's return from the monastery: 'preached on the occasion of the dedication of the basilica which Bishop Maximus founded in the fortress of the city of Geneva, in the field to the left, where a temple had been destroyed. The dedication was celebrated on the return from the dedication of Agaune to Annemasse.'

---

1 It is notable that the volume on *The Sermon,* ed B. M. Kienzle (Turnhout, 2000), in the *Typologie des Sources* entirely ignores the Avitus homilies, thus omitting extremely valuable evidence for the nature of preaching in the immediately post-Roman period.

2 J. M. Theurillat, *L'Abbaye de Saint-Maurice d'Agaune, des origines à la réforme canoniale 515–830* (Sion, 1954), pp. 11–20; F. Masai, 'La Vita patrum iurensium et les débuts du monachisme à Saint-Maurice d'Agaune', in *Festschrift Bernhard Bischoff* (Stuttgart, 1971), pp. 43–69.

3 Eucherius, *Passio Acaunensium Martyrum,* ed. B. Krusch, *MGH SRM* 3 (Hanover, 1896).

4 B. Rosenwein, 'Perennial Prayer at Agaune', in S. Farmer and B. Rosenwein, eds, *Monks and Nuns, Saints and Outcasts* (Ithaca, NY, 2000), pp. 37–56.

5 F. Prinz, *Frühes Mönchtum im Frankenreich* (Munich, 2nd edn, 1988), pp. 102–12.

Homily *25: Delivered in the basilica of the Saints of Agaune on the occasion of the restoration*[1] *of the monastery and on the passion of the martyrs*

According to solemn custom, the order of the passion[2] [just] read has unfolded the praise of the happy army, among whose most blessed company no one perished, though no one escaped,[3] when justice as if of a lot decreed the unjust death of the holy martyrs, so that once it (*sc.* the lot, viz. of decimation) had twice been dispersed over the gentle battle-line, fruit might grow one hundredfold[4] through those decimated,[5] and as hate made the recommendation to good effect, men might be chosen one by one until the elect were all gathered at once[6] ... whose[7] entry is not shut at night, because it has no night;[8] whose doors are always wide open to the just, but inaccessible to the impious. It is not [forcible] exclusion that creates the alternation, but the merits [of those approaching the gates]. Christ is its foundation, faith its frame, a wall its crown, a pearl its gates, gold its street, a lamb its light, its chorus the church. During [the singing of the] divine praises, when it is shut off from the necessity of all work, sincerity of action will be its sole repose. There are many things, most pious protector, junior to some in the seat of justice, ahead of all at the altar,[9] many things, I say among your works, for

1 The Latin word *innovatio* normally carries the implication of restoring or rededicating, and this would be appropriate at a site where there had already been some ascetic organisation. See Rosenwein, 'Perennial Prayer', pp. 48–49.

2 The *Passio* to which Avitus refers is probably that written by Eucherius of Lyons. It would have been read immediately before his sermon to provide a narrative of the martyrs' death.

3 I.e. even though all met death through martyrdom, all were saved: there may be an implicit comparison with a legend such as that of the 40 martyrs of Sebaste in which one soldier apostasised.

4 E.g. Lk. 8.8.

5 Avitus is playing on decimation of soldiers vs. tithing of crops. See Eucherius, *Passio Augaunensium Martyrum* 3 where Maximianus ordered the rebellious legion to be decimated: *decimum quemque ex eadem legione gladio feriri iubet.*

6 In Eucherius' *passio* decimation is enjoined by Maximianus several times (3) until his patience is worn out and he decrees that the whole legion be executed (5).

7 There is a gap in the text, but the relative pronoun must refer to the sanctuary at Agaune.

8 With an implicit contrast to Aen. 6.127: *noctes atque dies patet atri ianua Ditis.* The gates of the Vergilian underworld are open night and day. The allusion might have been especially appropriate, since cliffs quite literally overhang the monastery.

9 The reference is to Sigismund, junior to Gundobad in secular affairs, but senior to his father by virtue of his Catholicism. The phrase contrasts with *Hom.* 24: *qui in tribunali unus prae omnibus, in altari unus ex omnibus.* In *Hom.* 24 the subject appears to be Gundobad, and Avitus appears to be pressing him to make a public confession of Catholicism. See Perrat and Audin, 'Alcimi Ecdicii Aviti Viennensis Episcopi Homilia'.

which we should say that we have hitherto owed thanks. Enriched with gifts, though poor in words, we have received great things, but have paid back few. You have ornamented your churches with a heap of treasures, with a large number of people. You have built at great expense the altars which you have heaped high with gifts. We have never, it is true, paid tribute in words to [your] virtue, but, when it has come to the present solemn psalmody,[1] I think it little if I say my words, namely that today you have surpassed even your own works.[2] For who, meanwhile, denied that, following the emptying of the tabernacles as a result of the change of offices,[3] that glorious [custom] has been instituted, in which the Christian always pours forth sound,[4] Christ is always present, the onlooker is always heard, the hearer always seen. You who are now about to dwell here[5] ... labour in this world invites to the hope of perpetual rest, and all time for sinning is cut off from those occupied in happy action. It is praiseworthy that whatever is sinister has retreated far away from those, because it gives no pleasure, if it cannot <missing verb> the heavenly. You flee the world, to be sure, but you pray for it, even though the *saeculum* has been shut out by you, the act of which ... may your sacred vigil keep watch over all, by which ... May our Gaul flourish: let the world long for what [this] place has brought forth.[6] Today let there begin an eternity for devotion and dignity for the region, with these men praising God in the present world, who will praise him equally in future. May death renew rather than end this action (*sc.* the praise or endless psalmody). May you

---

1 Avitus is referring to the liturgy of Agaune, which was unending, being conducted by squadrons of monks in relay. See Rosenwein, 'Perpetual Prayer', pp. 39–46, which posits an independent origin for the liturgy of Agaune and the *laus perennis* of the sleepless monks of Constantinople. Problems do, however, remain: even though Avitus' confusion over the *Trishagion* riots suggests that the Burgundian church was not au fait with the Euchites in 512/ 3, and indeed that it regarded the Euchites as heretical at that moment (see above, *Contra Eutychianam Haeresim*), it does seem curious that the ceaseless liturgy of Agaune was developed very shortly after Avitus first heard about the Constantinopolitan monks. It may also be relevant here that the *Trishagion* is attested in the Bobbio Missal (25, 32), ed. E. A. Lowe, Henry Bradshaw Society 58 (1920), pp. 14–15, which certainly includes at least one Mass (336–38, pp. 101–102) which must derive from Agaune.

2 Has Peiper mispunctuated here, and should *verba nostra* be read alongside *opera tua* as an object of *vicisti*?

3 Perhaps a reference to the previous community at Agaune, driven out in order to establish the monastery.

4 Again a reference to the *laus perennis*.

5 I.e. the new monks.

6 Perhaps another hint of the innovatory ritual.

rediscover in heaven what customary rewards you will carry from this land. May such great honour follow your perseverance that whatsoever effort you expended on the task be repaid to you as a prize in recognition of your merit.

Homily 6 on Rogations: Introduction

The term Rogations is a confusing one, since it has been applied to two totally different liturgical processions, both of which involved intercessions and prayers asking forgiveness. The Roman Rogations, often called the *litaniae maiores*, were a set of processions, which developed in Rome out of the *Robigalia*, and which are in no way related to those described by Avitus. The Gallican Rogations, which in later sources are sometimes called *litaniae minores*, but also on occasion, and confusingly, *litaniae maiores*, took place on the three days before Ascension,[1] and derived very specifically from the incidents described here, and also in Sidonius, *Epp.* 5.14 and 7.1 (the latter in particular being a clear source for Avitus). There had been, as Sidonius notes, earlier attempts at public litanies, but they have never attracted universal support: it was impossible to please both the potter and the gardener: *figulo pariter hortuloni non opportuit convenire.*[2] The precise year in which Mamertus began the Rogations is uncertain, but it must have been marginally earlier than Sidonius' introduction of the litany into Clermont in 473.[3] Doubtless the period of crisis, with both natural disasters and the Visigothic expansion, helped make popular the Rogation liturgy.

Gregory of Tours, *DLH* 2.34; Ado, *Chron. s.a.* 425. For contemporary homilies on Rogations see Caesarius, *Hom.* 148, 157, 160A, 207, 208, 209, ed. G. Morin, *CCSL* 104 (Turnholt, 1953). This homily was clearly preached on the eve of the three days of Rogation, hence the references to preparation and to the days to come.

Homily *6 on Rogations {108.4 Peiper}*

A certain well-supplied river of rogational observance is flowing in a life-giving course not only through Gaul, but through almost the whole world, and it is purging the land infected with vice with an abundant flow of annual reparation. There is a special cause of religious celebration and joy for us in this liturgical custom, for what now flows to the advantage of all, initially

---

1 The confusion in the terminology is unravelled by J. Hill, 'The *Litaniae maiores* and *minores* in Rome, Francia and Anglo-Saxon England: terminology, texts and traditions', *EME* 9 (2000), pp. 211–46.

2 Sid. Ap. *Ep.* 5.14.2. See, for Rogations in Gaul, Klingshirn, *Caesarius of Arles*, p. 177.

3 Sid. *Epp.* 5.14, 7.1: Harries, *Sidonius Apollinaris and the Fall of Rome*, pp. 190–91.

gushed forth from our fountain.[1] And therefore the origin of this venerable liturgical undertaking is perhaps now relevant to the glory of any privilege.

Besides, when terrible harsh circumstances tamed the rigid hearts of the people of Vienne to humility of this kind, our church, not feeling the cause of its sickness to be related to itself more than to all others, but rather thinking that there was a need for one out of all to institute the present observation, more anxiously took upon herself the remedy rather than the primacy. And I know that many of us recall the causes of the terrors of that time. Thus, frequent fires, continuous earthquakes, nocturnal sounds, portended something prodigious and funereal for the destruction of the whole world.[2] For species of wild animals from the woods joined domestic ones in the populous meeting-places of men:[3] let God see whether it was an optical illusion or the appearance of a portent!

Whichever of these two it was, it was understood as equally monstrous either that the wild hearts of beasts were truly tamed, or that phantasms of false sights could be confected so horribly for the eyes of the terrified. Among all of this, the opinion of the crowd differed as did the views of men of different social status.[4] Some dissimulating what they felt, attributed to accident what they did not wish to make reparation for in weeping. Others with a more healthy spirit, interpreted the new abominations too according to fitting interpretations of the real nature of the evils.[5] For who would not fear the showers of Sodom amid frequent fires?[6] And who would not believe that a collapse of the roofs[7] or the destruction of the earth was imminent amid a trepidation of the spheres?[8] Who seeing, or rather thinking that he really saw, naturally timid deer[9] coming through the narrow gates into the

---

1 I.e. from Vienne.

2 For the same symptoms see Sid. Ap. *Ep.* 7.1.3.

3 Although this looks like a topos, it is in fact the case that in times of famine wild animals do search for food in centres of population in which they would not normally be found: on this see the comments on reservoirs of plague in D. Keys, *Catastrophe. An Investigation into the Origins of the Modern World* (London, 2000), p. 25.

4 For different social classes see Sid. Ap. *Ep.* 7.1.5: *nostri ordinis viris.*

5 The phrase remains obscure. *Proprietatis*, however, modifies *significationibus* and *malorum* modifies *proprietatis.*

6 Gen. 19.24.

7 Sid. Ap. *Ep.* 7.1.3: *caducas culminum cristas.*

8 *Elementa* probably means 'planets' here.

9 Sid. Ap. *Ep.* 7.1.3: *audacium pavenda mansuetudo cervorum.*

open spaces of the forum, would not fear the imminent sentence[1] of desolation?[2]

What more? These things were spun out among public fears and private rumours up till the night before the solemn vigils, on which annual custom demanded that the feast of the Lord's resurrection be celebrated. Thus with one spirit all awaited the wealth of labour, the end of ills, and the security of the fearful. Thus that venerable night had come that opened the way solemnly to the longed-for hope of public absolution. But suddenly a much more violent groan sounded there, with the blow of a whip inflicting a more grievous wound, as if nothing other than chaos could conceivably follow a blow that passing through [all other] grades was already superlative [in degree]. For the city hall[3] which exalted sublimity had set on high atop the summit of the city, began to burn with terrible flames in the twilight. The joy of the solemn feast was thus interrupted by the announcement of disaster. The church was evacuated by people full of terror. For all feared a similar fate for their own property and houses from a certain citadel where the fire blazed on high. But invincible the bishop[4] stood fast at the festive altars and inflaming the warmth of his faith he checked[5] the power allowed to the fires with a river of tears[6] as the fire retreated.

They set their desperation aside and returned to the church and, once the light of the flames had been extinguished, the beauty of lights grew bright. Truly, neither was there any further delay in grasping at the remedy of remorse. For my predecessor and my spiritual father from baptism, Bishop Mamertus (to whom the father of my flesh succeeded not many years ago, after Mamertus had been snatched away,[7] as seemed best to God) conceived

1 *Sententia* is here used in its legal sense of 'judgement'.

2 The colouring may be bliblical. See, for example, Isa. 24.12, *relicta est in urbe solitudo et calamitas opprimet portas*, or Jer. 10.22, *ut ponat civitates Iuda solitudinem et habitaculum draconum*. Likewise Jer. 33.28 and 50.3.

3 *Aedes publica*, glossed by Gregory as *palatium regale*.

4 Mamertus.

5 Sid. Ap. *Ep.* 7.1.4 says that Mamertus stopped the fire by interposing his own body.

6 Sid. Ap. *Ep.* 7.1.5: *aqua potius oculorum quam fluminum retingui posse*. He made this part of Mamertus' injunction. Greg. Tur. *DLH* 2.34, *flumen profluentium lacrimarum*, imitates Avitus.

7 See appendix below, p. 388. Mamertus was almost certainly ordained in 451/2 (R. W. Mathisen, 'Episcopal Hierarchy and Tenure in Office: A Method for Establishing Dates of Ordination', *Francia* 17 [1990], pp. 135 and 137). He was at the council of Arles ca. 470, but Ado says that his successor, the ghostly Hesychius, was bishop 'in the times of Leo and Zeno'. Now Leo only ruled until 474, giving a *terminus ante quem* for Mamertus' death, if we believe

of the whole Rogations in that holy night of the vigils of Easter, as we have described above. And there, silently, with God, he outlined what the world intones today in psalms and prayers. When the solemnity of Easter was over he considered at first in a secret meeting not now *what* should take place, but how or *when* it should. It was thought by some that the senate of Vienne, whose curia then flourished[1] with numerous illustrious men, could not be led to new things, since it scarcely agreed to submit to [long-sanctioned and] legitimate ones.[2] But the pious and caring pastor, generous with the salt of wisdom, first employed prayer to soften the souls of a flock that needed to be tamed, before he used rhetoric to address their hearing.[3] Therefore he set out the arrangements, he indicated the order, he expounded the salubriousness, and to a man of a mind as religious as clever it was meaningless to render the proposition of the institution favourable to the obedient, if he did not seal it with the chain of habit from the start. Therefore since God was inspiring the hearts of the contrite, he was heard, established and exalted by all. The present span of three days was chosen, to be bounded by the feast of holy Ascension and Sunday, as if by a certain border of its own opportunity, with the solemnities surrounding it.[4]

The bishop therefore tested the initial enthusiasm, being particularly concerned to hold the prayer of the first procession at the basilica[5] which was then nearer the walls of the city, so that the observation should not immediately become contemptible at its inception, with few supporting it, on account of the slowness of the people to take it up.[6] It went with great speed, large numbers and the greatest remorse, so that the procession truly seemed short and narrow to the tears and labours of the people. But as soon as the holy bishop saw signs of greater things from the effect of the lesser ones, there was instituted on the following day what we are about to undergo

---

Ado. So that suggests that he died ca. 470/474 at the very outside, and since he is the addressee of a letter from Sidonius (*Ep.* 7.1) apparently in the spring of 473, this gives him a near certain death-date of 473/4. This in turn helps date the death of Claudianus Mamertus, which Loyen dates to either 471–72, 474–75 (Sid. Ap. *Ep.* 4.11). Since Mamertus died before his brother, a death-date of 473/4 for Claudianus would appear to leave the death of Mamertus at 471/2.

1 An implicit contrast with Avitus' own times?

2 Sid. Ap. *Ep.* 7.1.5–7 outlines the differing responses of the different *ordines* in Vienne.

3 Avitus contrasts *orando* (prayer) and *perorando* (rhetoric).

4 Avitus has transposed the days, the Sunday in question being the one before Ascension.

5 The church of St Ferreolus? See Sidonius' reference to the translation of Ferreolus, *Ep.* 7.1, and Greg. Tur. *LVJ* 2.

6 Sid. Ap. *Ep.* 7.1.6 emphasises how the *humilis turba* was immediately *sequax* – a contrast and an example to its betters.

first, i.e. tomorrow, if God assents. The churches of the Gauls subsequently followed the action that set such a pleasing example, but in such a fashion that it was not celebrated among all on the same days on which it had been instituted among us. Furthermore, neither did it make a great difference what three days were chosen provided the performance of the psalms was fulfilled with the annual dues consisting of tears. Nonetheless, as love for Rogations grew along with concord among the priests, a concern for universal observance agreed to a single time, namely the present days. Furthermore it has reached the point that it is appropriate to say these things in advance, so that all, whether by chance we address those who remember or those who are ignorant, may nonetheless take notice that the church, which sets the [prescribed] form of an institution to other [churches], is many times over the one held to[1] the alacrity that must be shown, and she who has become the mother to all by example in so necessary an action, ought to be the first in the duty of compunction.

Whence, if God agrees, we do not point out as if to the ignorant that our extremely taxing feast of Rogations is now at hand, but commend it as if to those who are eager for it. Just as even though the habit of this profession is not to be preserved without work, all the same the harshness of the medicine, in which the hope of salvation has frequently proved to have been found, pleases [us]. 'If we say that we have no sin,' to quote the Apostle 'we deceive ourselves.'[2] And if we ought assiduously to confess that we have sinned, there is a need for the duty of confessing and of the humility of repenting – above all because the compunction of the united populace can thus be combined with the incitement of good works, so that the recalcitrant may blush yet more appropriately, if, contradicting the whole multitude in the solitude of his own mind he does not lament his sins or vice along with the weeping populace. It is therefore necessary to *conspire*[3] in good work. Each takes from the other either an example from humility or solace in confession. Excessively dangerous and for the few is that lonely combat, in which the strength on the other side is tested. But truly, when the approval of the multitude fights against the common enemy, the courage of another man drags along even the timid soldier. When robust warriors fight, infirmity lies hidden, and it becomes an occasion for praise for the weak to be reckoned in the army of the strong by a unified vote. Then when victory has come it is

---

1 See Blaise *s.v. debitrix* 'tenue à', or 'soumise à'.
2 1 John 1.8.
3 Avitus intentionally uses a quasi-paradoxical formulation.

achieved by all, and even though the right hand of the few has fought, the glory of all has triumphed.

I say this about communal weakness, which, if it does not withdraw itself from those praying even when it has done less itself on its own, will not, however, lack profit entirely. In that glorious and rather singular history of the Ninevites,[1] even children[2] were compelled to fight alongside the strengths of seniors against the drawn sword of the aroused divinity. The hunger of animals increased the reward and grace of human fast too.[3] Why even creation lacking in reason, which could not fear displeasure, asked pardon after a fashion. And because men had sinned by living like animals, so in return they forced their animals to fast like men.

< ... >[4] Therefore [it is] on account of this distinction [that] the Lord said in the Gospel, 'Ask, and it shall be given to you; seek, and ye shall find; knock, and it shall be opened unto you.'[5] To ask is for the learned; to seek for the devout. The knowing man asks; he who does not know seeks. When you ask, you wish to receive what you understand; when you seek, you are still trying to find something to ask for. Thus those who are already superior ask by praying; the weaker seek through labour. Furthermore, however, to knock is common to all. No one strikes a blocked entrance with his voice: that is a job for the hand and is an act of the body. Therefore, let knowledge ask, let love seek, let religious observance strike – particularly in this present observance. For this is a festival whose complete delight is in sobriety alone, whose feast is tears, whose nourishment hunger; whose origin is in necessity, perseverance in love, action in rest, rest in labour, since that whole observance is confession of penitence for sin and of appeal for pardon. Indeed, even the present reading from the gospel[6] sets out the use of prayer, when a chorus of disciples, terrified at the sound of the storm, roused the Lord sleeping in the ship. Neither was there any other reason that our profoundly sleeping Lord lay in fearless rest amid such a conflict of wind and sea

1 Cf. Sid. Ap. *Ep.* 7.1.3. Also Jonah 3.

2 Jon. 3.5 does not say so explicitly, but may imply children too. This is certainly the way it is presented by Prudentius *Cath.* 7.155: *iacens harenis et puer provolvitur* and 162–65 *ieiuna mensas pubis omnis liquerat/quin et negato lacte vagientium/fletu madescunt parvulorum cunulae/sucum papillae parca nutrix derogat.*

3 Jon. 3.7.

4 The transition is very abrupt and the following *ergo* inconsequential. The context seems to have required some allusion to, or distinction between, *petere* and *quaerere* to set up the quotation from Matthew. A lacuna seems likely.

5 Mt. 7.7.

6 Mt. 8.25.

fighting against themselves, except for the cause of our fear to take refuge in him among the conflicts that we suffer. That storm strikes us constantly with its blows, the thunder of the temporal world calls out against us with terrible force, the commotion in the world does not shed light with its rays that sparkle to a point,[1] but flashes. The Church is the ship which leads us through various disasters[2] as if between whirlpools in the sea. Although it strikes our ears with detractions and with the hissing of blasphemy, as if 'the structure of the sides had been loosened',[3] what causes damage cannot penetrate a ship built with the solidity of truth. And because Our Lord promised the Church, 'Lo, I am with you alway, even unto the end of the world',[4] he is in the ship in which we are, but he is not able now to fear what we fear. For after his Resurrection and Ascension he is altogether at rest among our dangers. There is rather need for [him to] fear for another so that he who was lying secure may keep watch.

Cry out, therefore, with voices of supplication and, if he does not yet hear as the danger increases, strike with hands [full] of offerings, and say to him, 'Awake, why sleepest thou, O Lord, forgetful of our helplessness and oppression?'[5] He will say when he has arisen, 'Why are ye fearful, O ye of little faith?'[6] Let him give back safety, and upbraid weakness. And even if our faith is small, because we fear things secular, there is, however, some, if we have recourse to God. There would be no fear before him, if he himself were feared. But the slightest knowledge of right is chiefly the greatest cause of fear in our life, for which the continuation of crimes becomes a multitude of crises.[7] Wherefore, if we do not say to Christ, 'Watch with us', we at least say 'Watch on our account'. We have not asked him not to desert us: let us ensure that he return and that he not desert the course of unsteady navigation, until he orders the wind and the sea to be silent, and checks the fury of the raving world with the quickest of ends, and there is a great calm[8] in the retribution of justice that there cannot be in this world. 'If ye were of this world, the world would love his own.'[9] But having overcome the world,

1 Lightning.
2 Vergil, *Aen.* 1.204.
3 Vergil, *Aen.* 1.122.
4 Mt. 28.20.
5 Based on Ps. 44.23–24.
6 Mt. 8.26.
7 Avitus makes a word-play on *criminum* and *discriminum*.
8 Mt. 8.26.
9 Jn 15.19.

may we come to celestial calm, where, since there will be no possibility of dying, neither will a cause of danger be born; where God will always be with us, and we will always be with him, if he has consented, and the man who here sometimes lies asleep with the negligent, will there be perpetually awake with the happy forever.

Appendix

Peiper's text of *Hom.* 6, p. 110.20:

Praedecessor namque meus et spiritalis mihi a baptismo pater Mamertus sacerdos cui ante non (om. GH) paucos annos pater carnis meae accepto, sicut deo visum est, sacerdotii tempore (sacerdotio in tempore GH) successit ...

As it stands, *accepto* has be be construed with *tempore*, because it is not possible for a subject (i.e. *pater carnis meae*) to be sandwiched into a long hyperbaton in the dative. But the resultant ablative absolute, *accepto sacerdotii tempore*, does not make sense. 'My predecessor and my spiritual father from the time of my baptism, Bishop Mamertus to whom, after some time, the father of my flesh (i.e. Hesychius) succeeded, once the time of [his] episcopate had been accepted, as seemed best to God ...' One line of emendation involves moving *pater carnis meae*, so that *accepto* can be construed with *cui*: *cui ante non paucos annos accepto, pater carnis meae, sicut deo visum est, sacerdotii tempore successit.* But the MSS's *accepto* is nonsensical, because it is insufficiently transparent, with no qualification. One might emend to *arrepto*: 'snatched away', or supply some meaningful qualification such as *<in caelum>* before *accepto*.

But both of these emendations still leave the problem of *sacerdotii tempore*. The verb *succedo* often requires both a dative of the one succeeded and some expression of place, be it ablative or accusative. We are talking about succession to a bishopric, and the simplest change is to substitute *loco* for *tempore*.

'My predecessor and my spiritual father from the time of my baptism, Bishop Mamertus to whom, when many years ago he had been snatched away (sc. by death)/received into heaven, the father of my flesh (i.e. Hesychius) succeeded in the bishopric, as seemed best to God ...'

A third question involves the construction of *sicut deo visum est*. As it stands it modifies *successit*. If the subject were postponed, however, one could also leave room for its qualifying *arrepto/<in caelum>* accepto: *Praedecessor namque meus et spiritalis mihi a baptismo pater Mamertus sacerdos cui ante non paucos annos <in caelum> accepto, sicut deo visum est, pater carnis meae sacerdotii loco successit.*

APPENDICES

APPENDIX 1

AVITUS' USE OF HONORIFIC FORMS OF ADDRESS

A database of honorifics was created that listed the honorific, whom it referred to, where it occurred, who used it, and the status of the person to whom it was applied (king, bishop [including pope and patriarchs], other clerics, emperor, lay official, private person, and 'unclear'). Honorifics, however they appeared in the text, were listed with the nominal element first to facilitate comparison, e.g. *clementia vestra* rather than *vestra clementia*. The database permitted more extensive and scientific analysis of Avitus' usage of such title. It should be noted that classification of honorifics is not an exact science and that some cases are doubtful (and may not have not been listed), while others that have been listed may not be true honorifics.[1] All references in this appendix are to the *CA*, *CE* or (unless otherwise noted) Peiper letter number alone.

Clear and predictable patterns emerged: *apostolatus* is used only to bishops (12, 40, 68), the pope (20, 29), the patriarch of Jerusalem (25). The same applies to *affatus* (10, 75), *auctoritas* (16, 17, 88) and *beatitudo* (7, 10, 12, 40, 60, 63), *censura* (18, 72), *sanctitas* (21, 28, 70, 90). *Pontificatus* is used only to the pope (29). The use of *ordinatio* (which should only be used for bishops) is odd: it is used to bishops (19 may be preemptive[2] and 16), but it is also used to Senarius (39).

Celsitudo is used only of kings and emperors (*CA* 30, 44, 48, 78, 93). Likewise *compellatio* (31, 94) and *gloria* (*CA* 30, 6, 45, 78, 79). *Perennitas* applies only to the emperor (78), as does *virtus* (93); *principatus* only to Gundobad (*CE* 1)

Clementia is used to a king (31) and to a private person (56); *dignitas* to Celer (48) and the emperor (93); *prosperitas* to the emperor (78) and to a private person (53); *serenitas* to the emperor (94), and a private person (51). *Culmen* is applied to a king (Sigismund 32) and a lay official (Liberius 35).

---

1 *Dignatio vestra* in *Ep.* 66 illustrates the problem. In this case 'Your Graciousness' is not a fancy equivalent of 'you,' so it has been omitted.

2 I.e. Avitus may know that Viventiolus is about to become bishop of Lyons.

The neutral *dignatio*, as could be expected, has a wider application, and is used of the emperor (94), Gundobad (5), Sigismund (76, 91), and the patriarch of Jerusalem (25). *Pietas*, which appears to be context-specific, has an extremely wide application: to bishops (11, 13, 14, 87, 88), the patriarch of Jerusalem (25), kings (6, 23, 44, 90, 91), and private individuals (24, 50, 56, 82). *Sinceritas* is used to Avitus (17) and to a private person (51). *Magnificentia* is used only to private persons (39, 43, 48, 51); likewise *magnitudo* (56, 84).

Some fairly standard honorifics are used only once: *amplitudo* to Faustus and Symmachus (34), *benignitas* to Gundobad (*CE* 1), *dilectio* to Avitus by Pope Hormisdas (42), *dulcedo* to Apollinaris, *vir illustris* (36), *gratia* to Vitalinus (47), *iudicium* to Vitalinus (47), *iustitia* to Gundobad (44 context-specific),[1] *meritum* to Apollinaris of Valence (14) *potestas* to Liberius (35), *sublimitas* to Ceretius (83).

Some expressions that take the form of honorifics are highly context-specific and occur only once: *acrimonia* (to Gundobad 30),[2] *commendatio* (to Eufrasius 43), *deliberatio* (to Avitus 68), *elegantia* (to Apollinaris of Valence 87) *electio* (to Apollinaris of Valence 88), *eloquentia vestra* (to Gundobad 30), *innocentia* (to Apollinaris, *vir illustris* 51), *inofficiositas* (to Apollinaris of Valence 71), *oblatio* (to Apollinaris of Valence 88), *severitas* (to Sigismund 23), and *subtilitas* (to Clovis 46).

Avitus also uses expressions that have the form of honorifics, but function as self-deprecatory expressions of modesty, incapacity or of concern. These include *curiositas mea* (31), *expectatio nostra* (31), *humilitas mea* (41, 76), *ignavia nostra/ mea* (91, 92), *impossibilitas mea* (67), *indevotio mea* (72), *inertia mea* (15), *sollicitudo nostra* (17, 34, 56),[3] *trepidatio nostra* (91).

Some attention should be devoted to places where Avitus does not use any honorifics. In some theological letters to Gundobad they are missing (4, 22) and in some letters to Sigismund (49, 77, 92), which may indicate his cordial and businesslike relations with both of them. Some people of lesser rank do not seem to rate them: Aurelianus (37) and the deacon Helpidius (38). Serious honorifics are omitted from joke-letters (74, 86). They also seem to be omitted when Avitus (or the author) is angry (55, 57, 69, 95, 96).

---

1 I.e. Avitus is pleading for justice. The word is used deliberately in a very specific context.
2 The word occurs again at the opening of *Ep.* 46.
3 The latter is also used of other people (26, 31, 36).

Festal letters regularly omit them:[1] in the three festal sequences (58–69, 73–74, and 80–86) only 60, 63, 82, 83 and 84 use them seriously or 'straight'. *Ep.* 68 is from Viventiolus, and its honorifics (*apostolatus* and *deliberatio*) are almost certainly over-polite and sarcastic. There are several clear examples of jocular mock-honorifics: *inofficiositas* (71), *indevotio* (72), *censura* (72) and perhaps *sublimitas* (83).[2]

Two cases where they are omitted require special consideration. Is it really plausible that Avitus wrote to the pope and to the patriarch of Constantinople and failed to use appropriate honorifics? Yet there are none in *Epp.* 8 and 9. The former is fragmentary, so they may simply have been lost through damage to the text. but no excuses can be made for *Ep.* 9. Is he being less than polite to the patriarch of a church that had been in schism? *Epp.* 20 and 29 to Pope Symmachus (with whom he had cordial relations) use honorifics. But *Ep.* 40 to Hormisdas does not (although Avitus refers to himself as *humilitas mea*). Avitus was clearly irritated at Hormisdas' apparent failure to respond to his letters, and although the formal headings were used, he omits politesses from the body of a letter where one would expect them. In *Ep.* 42 Hormisdas has to soothe ruffled feathers with *dilectio vestra* and *dilectissime frater*. As was argued in Chapter 2, our extant letters are largely 'file-copies' that lack formal headings or salutations. So it is possible that the beginning of *Ep.* 9 may have supplied the honorifics missing from the body of the letter.

The apparent loss of almost all formal headings from the letters of Avitus leaves us in a quandary when dealing with them. Many individuals addressed are either known only from Avitus' correspondence or have poorly documented careers. Thus, in the case of laymen, it is often impossible to tell whether they are in office or are private persons. It is interesting to note that *magnificentia* (used to Senarius, Celer and Apollinaris of Valence) is in standard use in secular documents of officials,[3] as is *magnitudo* (of the unknown Helladius and Messianus).[4] The titulature used by Avitus may thus suggest that they held some sort of office at the time he wrote to them. Ansemundus (who may have been *comes* of Vienne), however, receives no honorifics other than *pietas vestra* in 50.

---

1 Presumably because they are so short to start with.

2 The joke lies in the use of honorific form for what is not grammatically equivalent to a pronoun, but to a noun-clause, e.g. 'Your Inattention' for 'the fact that you failed to pay attention.'

3 See *TLL s.v.* 'magnificentia' 105.25–49.

4 See *TLL s.v.* 'magnitudo' 120.36–49.

In closing it is worth observing that Avitus modestly avoids using true honorifics of himself. In addition he generally avoids 'honorific-dropping' or 'title-dropping' in allusions to third parties in his letters. The only exceptions occur in letters to Sigismund that refer to Gundobad (e.g. *domini mei, patris vestri* in 23 and *domno patre* in 31) and in letters to the emperor that refer to him (*devotissimi fidelissimique vobis patris mei, proceris vestri* in 94). The pope is often no more than the *papa* (*ad sanctum Hormisdam, seu quicunque nunc ille est, papam* in 39 or *papa Symmacho, sanctum Symmachum papam, papa urbis* in 34).

For more on the use of honorifics, see A. Engelbrecht, *Das Titelwesen bei den spätlateinischen Epistolographen* (Vienna, 1893); Å. J. Fridh, *Terminologie et formules dans les Variae de Cassiodore* (Göteborg, 1956), pp. 169–94 for Cassiodorus' letters; P. Koch, *Die byzantinischen Beamtentitel von 400 bis 700* (Jena, 1903); R. W. Mathisen, 'Imperial Honorifics and Senatorial Status,' in R. W. Mathisen, ed., *Law, Society and Authority in Late Antiquity* (Oxford, 2001); M. B. O'Brien, *Titles of Address in Christian Latin Epistolography to 543 A.D.* (Washington, DC, 1930); H. Zilliacus, *Untersuchungen zu den abstrakten Anredeformen und Höflichkeitstiteln im Griechischen* (Helsinki, 1949) who thinks the transfer of power to Constantinople and Greek influence caused the wide diffusion of the practice in the West.

HONORIFICS LISTED BY TITLE

Title	Addressee	Status of Addressee	Letter	Addresser	Notes
acrimonia vestra	Gundobad	king	30, 46	Avitus	possible honorific
affatus vester	Eustorgius of Milan	bishop	10	Avitus	
affatus vester	Victorius of Grenoble	bishop	75	Avitus	
amplitudo vestra	Faustus and Symmachus	private person	34	Avitus	
apostolatus vester	Avitus	bishop	68	Viventiolus	sarcastic
apostolatus vester	Elias of Jerusalem	bishop	25	Avitus	
apostolatus vester	Maximus of Pavia	bishop	12	Avitus	
apostolatus vester	Peter of Ravenna	bishop	40	Avitus	
apostolatus vester	Pope Symmachus	bishop	20	Avitus	
apostolatus vester	Pope Symmachus	bishop	29	Avitus	
auctoritas vestra	Apollinaris of Valence	bishop	88	Avitus	
auctoritas vestra	Avitus	bishop	16	Victorius of Grenoble	
auctoritas vestra	Victorius of Grenoble	bishop	17	Avitus	
beatitudo tua	Victorius of Grenoble	bishop	7	Avitus	
beatitudo vestra	Claudius of Vaison	bishop	63	Avitus	
beatitudo vestra	Eustorgius	bishop	10	Avitus	
beatitudo vestra	Gemellus	bishop	60	Avitus	
beatitudo vestra	Maximus of Pavia	bishop	12	Avitus	
beatitudo vestra	Peter of Ravenna	bishop	40	Avitus	
benignitas vestra	Gundobad	king	*CE* 1	Avitus	

Title	Addressee	Status of Addressee	Letter	Addresser	Notes
caritas fraterna	Caesarius of Arles	bishop	11	Avitus	
celsitudo sua	Anastasius	emperor	48	Avitus	
celsitudo vestra	Anastasius	emperor	78, 93	Sigismund	
celsitudo vestra	Gundobad	king	*CA* 30, *CE* 2 44	Avitus	
censura vestra	Apollinaris of Valence	bishop	72	Avitus	jocular
censura vestra	Avitus	bishop	18	Victorius of Grenoble	
clementia vestra	Messianus	private person	56	Avitus	
clementia vestra	Sigismund	king	31	Avitus	
commendatio vestra	Eufrasius	bishop	43	Avitus	
commoditas vestra	Ansemundus	lay official	80	Avitus	possible honorific
compellatio augusta	Anastasius	emperor	94	Sigismund	
compellatio vestra	Sigismund	king	31	Avitus	
culmen vestrum	Liberius	lay official	35	Avitus	
culmen vestrum	Sigismund	king	32	Avitus	
curiositas mea	Avitus	bishop	31	Avitus	self
deliberatio vestra	Avitus	bishop	68	Viventiolus	sarcastic
dignatio praecelsa	Sigismund	king	91	Avitus	
dignatio sacra	Anastasius	emperor	94	Sigismund	
dignatio sancta	Gundobad	king	5	Avitus	
dignatio vestra	Elias of Jerusalem	bishop	25	Avitus	
dignatio vestra	Sigismund	king	76	Avitus	
dignitas vestra	Anastasius	emperor	93	Sigismund	
dignitas vestra	Celer	unclear	48	Avitus	
dilectio vestra	Avitus	bishop	42	Hormisdas	*tu, dilectissime frater*
dominus reverentissimus	Avitus	bishop	13	Apollinaris of Valence	

Title	Addressee	Status of Addressee	Letter	Addresser	Notes
dulcedo vestra	Apollinaris, *vir illustris*	private person	36	Avitus	
electio vestra	Apollinaris of Valence	bishop	88	Avitus	one-off
elegantia tua	Apollinaris of Valence	bishop	87	Avitus	one-off
eloquentia vestra	Gundobad	king	30	Avitus	
expectatio nostra	Avitus	bishop	31	Avitus	self
gloria vestra	Anastasius	emperor	78	Sigismund	
gloria vestra	Gundobad	king	*CA* 30, 6	Avitus	
gloria vestra	Sigismund	king	45, 79	Avitus	
gloria vestra	Sigismund	king	79	Avitus	
gloriosissimus princeps	Anastasius	emperor	93	Sigismund	
gratia vestra	Vitalinus	private person?	47	Sigismund	
humilitas mea	Avitus	bishop	41	Avitus	self, to pope
humilitas mea	Avitus	bishop	76	Avitus	self, to Sigismund
ignavia mea	Avitus	bishop	92	Avitus	self
ignavia nostra	Avitus	bishop	91	Avitus	self
impossibilitas mea	Avitus	bishop	67	Avitus	self
indevotio mea	Avitus	bishop	72	Avitus	self, jocular
inertia mea	Avitus	bishop	15	Avitus	
innocentia vestra	Apollinaris, *vir illustris*	private person	51	Avitus	
inofficiositas vestra	Apollinaris of Valence	bishop	71	Avitus	jocular
iudicium vestrum	Vitalinus	private person?	47	Sigismund	
iustitia vestra	Gundobad	king	44	Avitus	
laetitia augusta	Anastasius	emperor	94	Sigismund	
magnificentia vestra	Apollinaris, *vir illustris*	private person	43, 51	Avitus	
magnificentia vestra	Celer	unclear	48	Avitus	

Title	Addressee	Status of Addressee	Letter	Addresser	Notes
magnificentia vestra	Senarius	private person	39	Avitus	
magnitudo vestra	Helladius	private person	84	Avitus	
magnitudo vestra	Messianus	private person	56	Avitus	self
meritum vestrum	Apollinaris of Valence	bishop	14	Avitus	one-off
none	Ansemundus	private person	55	Avitus	?*comes* of Vienne, angry
none	Ansemundus	private person	80	Avitus	? *comes* of Vienne
none	Apollinaris of Valence	bishop	27	Avitus	
none	Arigius	private person	50	Avitus	
none	Aurelianus	private person	37	Avitus	*vir optime*
none	Avitus	bishop	96	Heraclius	angry
none	Gundobad	king	22	Avitus	informal theological
none	Gundobad	king	4	Avitus	
none	Helpidius	other cleric	38	Avitus	deacon, not important enough?
none	Heraclius	private person	95	Avitus	angry
none	patriarch of Constantinople	bishop	9	Avitus	file copy?
none	pope	bishop	8	Avitus	fragmentary
none	'Sapaudus'	private person	86	'Leonianus'	jocular
none	Sigismund	king	49	Avitus	
none	Sigismund	king	77	Avitus	
none	Sigismund	king	92	Avitus	

Title	Addressee	Status of Addressee	Letter	Addresser	Notes
none	Victorius of Grenoble	bishop	75	Avitus	
none	Viventiolus	bishop	57	Avitus	angry
none	Viventiolus	bishop	69	Avitus	angry
oblatio vestra	Apollinaris of Valence	bishop	88	Avitus	
ordinatio vestra	Avitus	bishop	16	Victorius of Grenoble	
ordinatio vestra	Senarius	private person	39	Avitus	
ordinatio vestra	Viventiolus	other cleric	19	Avitus	
ordinatio vestra	Viventiolus	other cleric	19	Avitus	honorific? is he a bishop-elect?
os serenissimum	Anastasius	emperor	78	Sigismund	
perennitas vestra	Anastasius	emperor	78	Sigismund	
pietas sancta	Avitus	bishop	13	Apollinaris of Valence	
pietas vestra	Ansemundus	private person	50	Avitus	
pietas vestra	Apollinaris of Valence	bishop	14	Avitus	
pietas vestra	Apollinaris of Valence	bishop	87	Avitus	
pietas vestra	Apollinaris of Valence	bishop	88	Avitus	
pietas vestra	Apollinaris, *vir illustris*	private person	24	Avitus	
pietas vestra	Caesarius of Arles	bishop	11	Avitus	
pietas vestra	Elias of Jerusalem	bishop	25	Avitus	
pietas vestra	Gundobad	king	6, 44	Avitus	
pietas vestra	Messianus	private person	56	Avitus	
pietas vestra	Sigismund	king	23, 90, 91	Avitus	

Title	Addressee	Status of Addressee	Letter	Addresser	Notes
pietas vestra	Valerianus	private person	82	Avitus	
pontificatus vester	Pope Symmachus	bishop	29	Avitus	
potestas vestra	Liberius	lay official	35	Avitus	
praedicatio vestra	Gundobad	king	*CE* 1	Avitus	
principatus vester	Gundobad	king	*CE* 1	Avitus	
prosperitas vestra	Anastasius	emperor	78	Sigismund	
prosperitas vestra	Heraclius	private person	53	Avitus	
sanctitas tua	Constantius of Martigny	bishop	70	Avitus	
sanctitas vestra	Avitus	bishop	21	Gundobad	
sanctitas vestra	Quintianus of Rodez?	bishop	90	Avitus	
sanctitas vestra	Stephanus of Lyons?	bishop	28	Avitus	
serenitas vestra	Anastasius	emperor	94	Sigismund	
serenitas vestra	Apollinaris, *vir illustris*	private person	51	Avitus	
severitas vestra	Sigismund	king	23	Avitus	
sinceritas vestra	Apollinaris, *vir illustris*	private person	51	Avitus	
sinceritas vestra	Victorius of Grenoble	bishop	17	Avitus	
sinceritas vestra	Victorius of Grenoble	bishop	17	Avitus	
sollicitudo nostra	Avitus	bishop	17	Avitus	
sollicitudo nostra	Avitus	bishop	34	Avitus	self
sollicitudo nostra	Avitus	bishop	56	Avitus	
sollicitudo vestra	Apollinaris, *vir illustris*	private person	36	Avitus	
sollicitudo vestra	Sigismund	king	31	Avitus	
sollicitudo vestra	Stephanus	bishop	26	Avitus	
sublimitas vestra	Ceretius	private person	83	Avitus	jocular
subtilitas vestra	Clovis	king	46	Avitus	
trepidatio nostra	Avitus	bishop	91	Avitus	self
virtus vestra	Anastasius	emperor	93	Sigismund	

HONORIFICS LISTED BY ADDRESSEE

Title	Addressee	Letter	Addresser	Status of Addressee	Notes
celsitudo vestra	Anastasius	78, 93	Sigismund	emperor	
dignitas vestra	Anastasius	93	Sigismund	emperor	
gloria vestra	Anastasius	78	Sigismund	emperor	
gloriosissimus princeps	Anastasius	93	Sigismund	emperor	
perennitas vestra	Anastasius	78	Sigismund	emperor	
prosperitas vestra	Anastasius	78	Sigismund	emperor	
virtus vestra	Anastasius	93	Sigismund	emperor	
celsitudo sua	Anastasius	48	Avitus	emperor	
os serenissimum	Anastasius	78	Sigismund	emperor	
serenitas vestra	Anastasius	94	Sigismund	emperor	
compellatio augusta	Anastasius	94	Sigismund	emperor	
dignatio sacra	Anastasius	94	Sigismund	emperor	
laetitia augusta	Anastasius	94	Sigismund	emperor	
pietas vestra	Ansemundus	50	Avitus	private person	
none	Ansemundus	55	Avitus	private person	?comes of Vienne angry
none	Ansemundus	80	Avitus	private person	? comes of Vienne
commoditas vestra	Ansemundus	80	Avitus	lay official	possible honorific
pietas vestra	Apollinaris of Valence	88	Avitus	bishop	
oblatio vestra	Apollinaris of Valence	88	Avitus	bishop	
pietas vestra	Apollinaris of Valence	14	Avitus	bishop	
none	Apollinaris of Valence	27	Avitus	bishop	
inofficiositas vestra	Apollinaris of Valence	71	Avitus	bishop	jocular
censura vestra	Apollinaris of Valence	72	Avitus	bishop	jocular

Title	Addressee	Letter	Addresser	Status of Addressee	Notes
elegantia tua	Apollinaris of Valence	87	Avitus	bishop	one-off
pietas vestra	Apollinaris of Valence	87	Avitus	bishop	
electio vestra	Apollinaris of Valence	88	Avitus	bishop	one-off
auctoritas vestra	Apollinaris of Valence	88	Avitus	bishop	
meritum vestrum	Apollinaris of Valence	14	Avitus	bishop	one-off
magnificentia vestra	Apollinaris, *vir illustris*	43, 51	Avitus	private person	
sinceritas vestra	Apollinaris, *vir illustris*	51	Avitus	private person	
serenitas vestra	Apollinaris, *vir illustris*	51	Avitus	private person	
dulcedo vestra	Apollinaris, *vir illustris*	36	Avitus	private person	
pietas vestra	Apollinaris, *vir illustris*	24	Avitus	private person	
sollicitudo vestra	Apollinaris, *vir illustris*	36	Avitus	private person	
innocentia vestra	Apollinaris, *vir illustris*	51	Avitus	private person	
none	Arigius	50	Avitus	private person	
none	Aurelianus	37	Avitus	private person	*vir optime*
dominus reverentissimus	Avitus	13	Apollinaris of Valence	bishop	
ordinatio vestra	Avitus	16	Victorius of Grenoble	bishop	
auctoritas vestra	Avitus	16	Victorius of Grenoble	bishop	
deliberatio vestra	Avitus	68	Viventiolus	bishop	sarcastic
pietas sancta	Avitus	13	Apollinaris of Valence	bishop	
inertia mea	Avitus	15	Avitus	bishop	
sollicitudo nostra	Avitus	17	Avitus	bishop	

Title	Addressee	Letter	Addresser	Status of Addressee	Notes
censura vestra	Avitus	18	Victorius of Grenoble	bishop	
sanctitas vestra	Avitus	21	Gundobad	bishop	
curiositas mea	Avitus	31	Avitus	bishop	self
expectatio nostra	Avitus	31	Avitus	bishop	self
sollicitudo nostra	Avitus	34	Avitus	bishop	self
humilitas mea	Avitus	41	Avitus	bishop	self to pope
dilectio vestra	Avitus	42	Hormisdas	bishop	*tu, dilectissime frater*
sollicitudo nostra	Avitus	56	Avitus	bishop	
impossibilitas mea	Avitus	67	Avitus	bishop	self
apostolatus vester	Avitus	68	Viventiolus	bishop	sarcastic
indevotio mea	Avitus	72	Avitus	bishop	self, jocular
humilitas mea	Avitus	76	Avitus	bishop	self, to Sigismund
trepidatio nostra	Avitus	91	Avitus	bishop	self
ignavia nostra	Avitus	91	Avitus	bishop	self
ignavia mea	Avitus	92	Avitus	bishop	self
none	Avitus	96	Heraclius	bishop	angry
pietas vestra	Caesarius of Arles	11	Avitus	bishop	
caritas fraterna	Caesarius of Arles	11	Avitus	bishop	
magnificentia vestra	Celer	48	Avitus	unclear	
dignitas vestra	Celer	48	Avitus	unclear	
sublimitas vestra	Ceretius	83	Avitus	private person	jocular
beatitudo vestra	Claudius of Vaison	63	Avitus	bishop	
subtilitas vestra	Clovis	46	Avitus	king	
sanctitas tua	Constantius of Martigny	70	Avitus	bishop	
apostolatus vester	Elias of Jerusalem	25	Avitus	bishop	
dignatio vestra	Elias of Jerusalem	25	Avitus	bishop	

Title	Addressee	Letter	Addresser	Status of Addressee	Notes
pietas vestra	Elias of Jerusalem	25	Avitus	bishop	
commendatio vestra	Eufrasius	43	Avitus	bishop	
beatitudo vestra	Eustorgius	10	Avitus	bishop	
affatus vester	Eustorgius of Milan	10	Avitus	bishop	
amplitudo vestra	Faustus and Symmachus	34	Avitus	private person	
beatitudo vestra	Gemellus	60	Avitus	bishop	
acrimonia vestra	Gundobad	30, 46	Avitus	king	possible honorific
benignitas vestra	Gundobad	*CE* 1	Avitus	king	
celsitudo vestra	Gundobad	*CA* 30, *CE* 2, 44	Avitus	king	
dignatio sancta	Gundobad	5	Avitus	king	
gloria vestra	Gundobad	*CA* 30, 6	Avitus	king	
iustitia vestra	Gundobad	44	Avitus	king	
pietas vestra	Gundobad	6, 44	Avitus	king	
principatus vester	Gundobad	CE 1	Avitus	king	
none	Gundobad	22	Avitus	king	informal theological
eloquentia vestra	Gundobad	30	Avitus	king	
none	Gundobad	4	Avitus	king	
praedicatio vestra	Gundobad	*CE* 1	Avitus	king	
magnitudo vestra	Helladius	84	Avitus	private person	
none	Helpidius	38	Avitus	other cleric	deacon, not important enough?
prosperitas vestra	Heraclius	53	Avitus	private person	
none	Heraclius	95	Avitus	private person	angry
potestas vestra	Liberius	35	Avitus	lay official	
culmen vestrum	Liberius	35	Avitus	lay official	
apostolatus vester	Maximus of Pavia	12	Avitus	bishop	

Title	Addressee	Letter	Addresser	Status of Addressee	Notes
beatitudo vestra	Maximus of Pavia	12	Avitus	bishop	
pietas vestra	Messianus	56	Avitus	private person	
clementia vestra	Messianus	56	Avitus	private person	
magnitudo vestra	Messianus	56	Avitus	private person	self
none	patriarch of Constantinople	9	Avitus	bishop	file copy?
apostolatus vester	Peter of Ravenna	40	Avitus	bishop	
beatitudo vestra	Peter of Ravenna	40	Avitus	bishop	
none	pope	8	Avitus	bishop	fragmentary
apostolatus vester	Pope Symmachus	20	Avitus	bishop	
apostolatus vester	Pope Symmachus	29	Avitus	bishop	
pontificatus vester	Pope Symmachus	29	Avitus	bishop	
sanctitas vestra	Quintianus of Rodez?	90	Avitus	bishop	
none	'Sapaudus'	86	'Leonianus'	private person	jocular
magnificentia vestra	Senarius	39	Avitus	private person	
ordinatio vestra	Senarius	39	Avitus	private person	
pietas vestra	Sigismund	23, 90, 91	Avitus	king	
gloria vestra	Sigismund	45, 79	Avitus	king	
severitas vestra	Sigismund	23	Avitus	king	
sollicitudo vestra	Sigismund	31	Avitus	king	
clementia vestra	Sigismund	31	Avitus	king	
compellatio vestra	Sigismund	31	Avitus	king	
culmen vestrum	Sigismund	32	Avitus	king	
none	Sigismund	49	Avitus	king	

Title	Addressee	Letter	Addresser	Status of Addressee	Notes
dignatio praecelsa	Sigismund	91	Avitus	king	
dignatio vestra	Sigismund	76	Avitus	king	
none	Sigismund	77	Avitus	king	
gloria vestra	Sigismund	79	Avitus	king	
none	Sigismund	92	Avitus	king	
sollicitudo vestra	Stephanus	26	Avitus	bishop	
sanctitas vestra	Stephanus of Lyons?	28	Avitus	bishop	
pietas vestra	Valerianus	82	Avitus	private person	
affatus vester	Victorius of Grenoble	75	Avitus	bishop	
sinceritas vestra	Victorius of Grenoble	17	Avitus	bishop	
beatitudo tua	Victorius of Grenoble	7	Avitus	bishop	
sinceritas vestra	Victorius of Grenoble	17	Avitus	bishop	
auctoritas vestra	Victorius of Grenoble	17	Avitus	bishop	
none	Victorius of Grenoble	75	Avitus	bishop	
iudicium vestrum	Vitalinus	47	Sigismund	private person?	
gratia vestra	Vitalinus	47	Sigismund	private person?	
ordinatio vestra	Viventiolus	19	Avitus	other cleric	
none	Viventiolus	57	Avitus	bishop	angry
none	Viventiolus	69	Avitus	bishop	angry
ordinatio vestra	Viventiolus	19	Avitus	other cleric	honorific? is he a bishop-elect?

APPENDIX 2

TEXTUAL CHANGES TO PEIPER'S EDITION

Avitus' text is more damaged and corrupt than has been commonly acknowledged. The process of translation brought us face-to-face with all its warts and forced us to commit ourselves to one reading or another. It rapidly became clear, however, that one needs greater leeway for temporary and tentative measures, a greater flexibility to indicate disquiet, doubt, or simply lingering unhappiness than is provided by a conventional apparatus. Like drivers with only right and left turn-signals and a horn, we would have welcomed signs that read 'Sorry!', 'I'm a foreigner', 'I'm lost', or 'Oh, no!'

A TTH volume is not the proper venue for the thorough professional investigation of Avitus' text that is required, yet the translator must translate *some* text. Given that we have had frequently to depart from Peiper, we include the following negative apparatus to our 'virtual' text. Where we are not translating what Peiper printed, we list the letter and page-number, followed by his reading. After the right square bracket comes the reading we have accepted, with acknowledgement (if it is a conjecture) of who made it or (if it is a manuscript variant) where it comes from. All unattributed variants are our emendations. Although we frequently alter Peiper's punctuation, such changes are noted only in the footnotes to the translation, not in this appendix. S is the siglum for Sirmond's 1643 edition; L for the Lyons manuscript.

Many of our suggestions, we emphasise, are not 'hard' conjectures, but diagnostic ones, namely suggestions of what sort of thing ought to be there in situations where something is clearly wrong, but certainty about the text is impossible. A cursory examination of our textual notes will show that we suspect lacunae in many places and have frequently affixed the obelus (†), the sign of condemnation or despair, to words that Peiper considered sound. Pointing out that there is a problem, even if one cannot solve it, is not a waste of time, and we hope that others will be encouraged to return to Avitus with a vigilant eye in the wake of our initial attempt.

Contra Arrianos
p. 4.37 solidata rursus divinitati] rursus solidatum [divinitati] *scripsimus*
p. 7.27 vestrae.] vestrae < ... > *lacunam indicavimus.*
p. 9.30 adoret] adoretur
p. 10.36 †raptos suos monstrat et gratia†] raptus suos *dubitanter suggessimus*

Contra Eutychianam haeresim 1
p. 15.21 praecipuae] praecipua
p. 16.4 adiutorem] auditorem *dubitanter suggessimus*
p. 17.4 duorum] †duorum†
p. 17.30 dei filius ut hominis] dei filius ac hominis
p. 17.33 non intellegenda tantummodo sed contemplanda monstrantur] non contemplanda tantummodo sed intellegenda monstrantur *dubitanter suggessimus*
p. 19.24 quia] qui
p. 19.27 fide] fine
p. 19.32 pertulisse redditurumque perfidiam indignatione] †pertulisse redditurumque perfidiam indignatione†
p. 20.39 contentus] contemptus S
p. 21.8 viribus] veteribus

Contra Eutychianam haeresim 2
p. 22.2 quae] qua Mommsen
p. 22.6 amator trepidus] magis trepidus S
p. 22.14 agitur] actum est igitur S
p. 22.15 meditatione] mediatione
p. 23.31 †sexu carnis] sexu<m> carnis <superante>
p. 24.2 stemmatis] stemmate Peiper *in app.*
p. 26.7 domini necem] dominum necem
p. 27. 28-28 Qui utique ... expertus] [Qui utique ... expertus] *seclusimus*
p. 28.11 Christiano. Qui] Christiano.< ... > Qui
p. 28.14 caecum ire] caecutire Mommsen
p. 29.13 ubi ad eadem clavorum vestigia, quae cernuntur] [ubi] ad eadem clavorum vestigia, quae cernuntur *vel potius* ubi ad eadem clavorum vestigia, quae cernuntur < ... >

Ep. 4
p. 30.2 accusaret; simul etiam qui] accusaret < ... > simul etiam qui *lacunam indicavimus*
p. 31.16 operis] operum

Ep. 5
p. 32.22 concedit] conceditur
p. 33.2 hic nocuit] illic nocuit Mommsen
p. 33.8 misereatur] †misereatur
p. 33.10 ubi diu] ubi <nec> diu

Ep. 6
p. 34.37 cognationi suae voto] cognationis suae onere voto F

Ep. 7
p. 36.13 vivis] vicinis PS
p. 37.4 Id est ille panis, qui dudum sanctus extiterat] [Id est ille panis, qui dudum sanctus extiterat] *tamquam glossa delevimus*
p. 37.17 Post hinc in exitia] Post incesti nexum S
p. 37.27 comparatur] comparat
p. 38.8 emortuo] emortuam

Ep. 10
p. 44.10 affectus] affatus S
p. 44.19 etiam] [etiam] *seclusimus*
p. 44.20 viribus absentia] viribus <etiam> absentia

Ep. 12
p. 45.28-29 appellatione] compellatione S
p. 46.7 a comite Betanco, nomine Avulum] nomine Avulum, a comite Betanco

Ep. 13
p. 46.18 horrorem] honorem
p. 46.25 plus iam iusta] plus quam iusta

Ep. 14
p. 47.2 vestri] vestro S
p. 47.6 dulcis vobis venit a nobis sollicitudo] dulcis nobis venit a vobis sollicitudo

Ep. 16
p. 48.17 a sociis] atrocis S
p. 48.18 proposuit quique] proposuit < ... > quique *lacunam suspicamur*
p. 48.24 nempe] neque *dubitanter*

Ep. 18
p. 50.1 sua] sui S

Ep. 19
p. 50.20 istic] hic
p. 53.2 deferatis] deberetis Winterbottom
p. 53.2 deferatis spiritalis] deferatis < ... > spiritalis *lacunam indicavit* Winterbottom
p. 53.2 conservus Peiper conversus PS conventus L] †conventus† Winterbottom
p. 53.6 ut taliter] qualiter Winterbottom
p. 53.15 de] [de] Winterbottom
p. 53.17 quod] cum Winterbottom
p. 53.18 nec potuit istic] potuisset Winterbottom

Ep. 20
p. 53.28 mundo vel] mundo < ... > vel

Ep. 23
p. 55.14 vestri sensisse] vestri < ... > sensisse *lacunam suspicamur*
p. 55.20 vel] [vel] S

Ep. 25
p. 56.26 cathedra cum persona] cathedramque persona S
p. 57.1 in aetate] a pietate S

Ep. 26
p. 57.23 salvandi] salvari L
p. 57.24 agnoscendi] [agnoscendi] *delevimus*

Ep. 27
p. 57.27 nos] vos
p. 58.1 invitos] invitus

Ep. 28
p. 58.20 aequalitas] inaequalitas
p. 58.24 quisque plus] quisque < ... > plus *lacunam indicavimus*
p. 58. 25 plus mirum est, carere dentibus et furoribus possit] †plus mirum est, carere dentibus et furoribus possit†

Ep. 29
p. 59.21 praeferendam, quia istic] praeferendam < ... > quia *lacunam indicavimus*

p. 59.25 vestri, ubi] vestri < ... > Ubi *lacunam indicavimus*

Ep. 30

p. 60.27 filius datus: natus est nobis] filius datus <ac si diceret deus et homo> natus est *transposuimus*

p. 60.28-29 vocabitur deus fortis: ac si diceret deus et homo] [ac si diceret deus et homo] *seclusimus et transposuimus*

p. 62.2 †ad thorum] ad totum S

Ep. 31

p. 62.7 offerendi officii] †offerendi factum

p. 62.14 insonuit] insinuavit

p. 62.16 acciderit] exciderit Rilliet

p. 62.18 exaratum paulatim] exaratum < ... > paulatim *lacunam posuimus*

Ep. 32

p. 63.1 sitirem] sitiret S

p. 63.4 aequanimiter ferat] aequanimiter <non> ferat

Ep. 34

p. 64.14 exemplaribus sacerdotalis] exemplaribus < e.g. multis... > sacerdotalis

p. 65.1 ecclesiae vestrae] in ecclesia vestra S

Ep. 35

p. 65.17 nullo] nullum LS

p. 65.17 affectibus] affatibus S

p. 65.17 impertitus effectu] expertus effectum S

p. 65.31 condicionis] <causa> condicionis Winterbottom

p. 65.32 redimendis] pro redimendis S

Ep. 36

p. 66.4 adgravavit] adceleravit

p. 66.15 reditus] reditu

p. 66.19 adcrescunt] <valetudine> adcrescunt

Ep. 37

p. 66.32 malis] †malis†

Ep. 38

p. 67. 28 operiri] sperare S

p. 67.31 tua] tua < ... > *lacunam indicavimus*

p. 67.32 exultando] exaltando

Ep. 40
p. 68. sciat] nesciat

Ep. 41
p. 69. 24-25 sola causa] sola hac causa S
p. 70.7 id est Gallicanis] [id est Gallicanis] *seclusimus*

Ep. 42
p. 70.17 a sinceritate] [a] sinceritate *vel* in domino de sinceritate s
p. 71.12 satietate] obscuritate S
p. 71.15 sollicite] solliciti
    p. 72.2 Illyricus] Illyricum

Ep. 44
p. 73.15 inexcusatum] inaccusatum S
p. 73. 19-20 suggerendam, quod] suggerendam, <in eo> quod *supplevit* Winterbottom
p. 73.27 quae ut pii domni dicatis non dubitarit operatione diffiteri] †quae ut pii domni dicatis non dubitarit operatione diffiteri†
p. 73.31 certa] recta Winterbottom

Ep. 45
p. 74.18 pro effectu voluntatum tenente secum] †pro effectu voluntatum tenente secum†
p. 74.28 promissionem] provisionem S

Ep. 46
p. 75. 2 acrimoniam quorumcumque] acrimonia <detecta mendacia> quorum-cumque
p. 75.3 visi] nisi Labbeus
p. 75.17 Gaudeat equidem Graecia principem legisse nostrum] Gaudeat ergo quidem Graecia habere se principem legis nostrae S
p. 75.19 rege] rege <novo> Labbeus
p. 75.21 redemptionis] redemptioni S
p. 75.26 vestris] nostris S

Ep. 47
p. 76.30 fiducia ut] fiducia non convenit ut S
p. 77.6 adicimus famulatum] adicimus <in filio> famulatum S
p. 77.9 ipse commendet] ipse <nos studio suo vobis> commendet

Ep. 49
p. 78.4 in utroque] in neutro S

Ep. 50
p. 78.25 dependente: cui] dependente < ... > cui *lacunam indicavimus*
p. 78.26 congerere] †congerere
p. 78.27 quia non ut nuptae tali sponso, cui pacta fuerat, qualitercumque iungendae] †quia non ut nuptae tali sponso, cui pacta fuerat, qualitercumque iungendae† *vel* quia non ut nupta tali sponso, cui pacta fuerat, qualitercumque iungenda

Ep. 51
p. 79.32 quam plus paternam] plus quam paternam
p. 80.3 credidisse] cecidisse
p. 80.15 ulla] nulla S

Ep. 52
p. 81.27 laborare, quod] laborare < ... > quod *lacunam indicavimus*
p. 81.26 debellantibus] debellatis S

Ep. 53
p. 82.1 tamen] tandem
p. 82.10 patronam] patrocinium *vel* patronum
p. 82.19 sint] sunt S

Ep. 54
p. 83.16 chaere oblatrante] chaere oblatrantem *vel* chaere obliterato

Ep. 57
p. 87.3 minus quam] minus < ... > quam *lacunam indicavimus*

Ep. 72
p. 90.7 ultum isse] ultuisse Klotz
p. 90.14 officiis magis qua] officiis magis quam S

Ep. 74
p. 91.9 rostro ad Heliae] rostro < ... (e.g. devectas) > ad Heliae *lacunam indicavimus*
p. 91.12 animus] manibus S
p. 91.15 circulis] corollis

Ep. 80
p. 93.31 *colum] cultum S

p. 94.3 procordare] procedere S

Ep. 82
p. 94.25 Iaeriae] Iseriae
p. 94. 25 vestrae] nostrae L

Ep. 84
p. 95.6 et ex voto] †et ex voto†

Ep. 85
p. 95.15 sic ... proventura] sic ... proventurum *vel* sic mihi iudicans eius plenitudinem proventuram

Ep. 86
p. 95.18 in cuncta] †in cuncta†
p. 95.28 esuriens querelis] sitiens querelis
p. 95.28 satur lacrimis] satur < vomitans > lacrimis
p. 96.11 medicina] medicamina Koonce
p. 96.11 inopportunitate] importunitate S
p. 96.12 recentes aliis plus] †recentes aliis plus† *vel* tepentes ampullas Tomlin
p. 96.16 ut adesse contingat] ut te deesse contingat S

Ep. 87
p. 96.22 extraxit. Propterea] extraxit < ... > Propterea *lacunam posuimus*
p. 96.27 ferreo] aureo
p. 97.2 ceteris] cereis
p. 97.14-15 fossilis glaebae scrobis, sordibus saeptae] fossilis glaebae < ... > †sordibus saeptae†

Ep. 90
p. 98.6 adsiduitate vel singulos post biennium faceremus] utinam per singula biennia faceremus S
p. 98.25 continendas subscribendasque] sanciendas subscribendasque S
p. 98.25 eligi, sit auctoritas legi] elegisset auctoritas legis L

Ep. 93
p. 100.29 See above p. 148.

Ep. 94
p. 101.21 derelinqueret ad haec] derelinqueret < ... > ad haec
p. 101.29 spectet] †spectet†
p. 101.29 series] species

p. 101.36 discrepat, orant] discrepat < ... > orant *lacunam suspicamur*
p. 102.9 licet] cum

Ep. 95
p. 102.23 aliqua. de vestro] aliqua < ... > de vestro *lacunam indicavimus*

Ep. 96
p.103.3 pervenirem] permanerem

Hom. 6
p. 110.20 See p. 388 above.
p. 111.36 coegerunt. Propter] coegerunt < ... > Propter *lacunam suspicamur*

Prol. SHG
p. 201.16 si] nisi
p. 202.8 ignaviae dabunt] ignaviae <veniam> dabunt
p. 202.8 poetarum, plus] poetarum < ... > *lacunam suspicamur*

APPENDIX 3

LISTING OF LETTERS IN THE ORDER OF PEIPER'S EDITION

BIBLIOGRAPHY

EDITIONS OF AVITUS

Chevalier, Ulysse, *Oeuvres complètes de Saint Avit, Évêque de Vienne* (Lyons, 1890)

Peiper, R., *Alcimi Ecdici Aviti opera quae supersunt, MGH AA* 6.2 (Berlin, 1883)

Sirmondus, Iacobus, *Sancti Aviti Archiepiscopi Viennensis Opera* (Paris, 1643), reprinted in Migne *PL* 59.202–382

Johannes Ferrandus, *Sancti Alcimi Aviti Viennensis Episcopi epistolae quatuor nunc primum in lucem editae et notis illustratae* (Cabilone apud Philippum Tan, 1661)

Borrel, E. L., 'Étude sur l'homélie prêchée par saint Avit, au commencement du VIe siècle dans la basilique de Saint-Pierre de Moutiers en Tarantaise (Savoie), à l'occasion de sa consécration', *Bulletin du Comité des travaux historiques et scientifiques*, Section d'histoire, d'archéologie et de philologie (1883), pp. 46–55

N. Hecquet-Noti, N., *Avit de Vienne. Histoire spirituelle, Tome 1 (Chants i–iii), SC* 444 (Paris, 1999)

Perrat, C. and A. Audin, 'Alcimi Ecdicii Aviti Viennensis Episcopi Homilia Dicta in dedicatione superioris basilicae', in *Studi in onore di A. Calderini e R. Paribeni*, vol. 2 (Milan, 1957), pp. 433–51

PRIMARY SOURCES

Acta Conciliorum Oecumenicorum II, Concilium Universale Chalcedonense, ed. E. Schwartz (Berlin and Leipzig, 1932–38)

Acta Synodi (502), ed. T. Mommsen, *MGH AA* 12 (Berlin, 1894), pp. 444–55

Ado, *Chronicon, PL* 123, cols. 23–138

Ado, *Martyrologium*, ed. J. Dubois and G. Renaud, *Le Martyrologe d'Adon* (Paris, 1984)

Agobard of Lyons, *Liber adversus Felicem Urguellitanum, PL* 104.29–70

Agobard of Lyons, *Liber adversus Legem Gundobadi, PL* 104.113–26

Agobard of Lyons, *Liber contra iudicium dei, PL* 104.249–68

Agobard of Lyons, *Liber de imaginibus sanctorum, PL* 104.199–228

Anthologia Latina, ed. A. Riese (Leipzig, 1894)

Ambrose, *Epistulae, PL* 16, cols. 890–1342

Anonymus Valesianus, ed. I. König, *Aus der Zeit Theoderichs des Großen* (Darmstadt, 1997)

Augustine, *Confessions*, ed. J. J. O'Donnell (Oxford, 1992)

Augustine, *Contra Faustum*, ed. J. Zycha, *CSEL* 25.1 (Vienna, 1891), pp. 249–797

Augustine, *De cura pro mortuis gerenda, PL* 40.591–610

Augustine, *De catechizandis rudibus, PL* 40.309–48; also ed. I. B. Bauer, *CCSL* 46 (Turnhout, 1969), pp. 115–78

Augustine, *De Genesi ad litteram, PL* 34. 245–486; also ed. J. Zycha, *CSEL* 28.1 (Vienna, 1894), pp. 1–456

Augustine, *Epistulae ex duobus codicibus nuper in lucem prolatae*, ed. J. Divjak, *CSEL* 88 (Vienna, 1981)

Baluzius, S., *Miscellaneorum Liber primus, hoc est collectio veterum monumentorum quae hactenus latuerant in variis codicibus et bibliothecis* (Paris, 1678)

Bobbio Missal, ed. E. A. Lowe, *Henry Bradshaw Society* 58 (1920)

Caesarius, *Sermones*, ed. G. Morin, *CCSL* 103–104 (Turnholt, 1953); also G. Morin, and J. Courreau, *Césaire d'Arles, Sermons sur l'écriture, SC* 447 (Paris, 2000)

Cassian, *Contra Nestorium, PL* 50.9–272

Cassiodorus Senator, *Variae*, ed. T. Mommsen, *MGH AA* 12 (Berlin, 1894); trans. S. J. B. Barnish, *The Variae of Magnus Aurelius Cassiodorus Senator ... : being Documents of the Kingdom of the Ostrogoths in Italy*, TTH 12 (Liverpool, 1992)

Cassiodorus Senator, *Variae*, ed. Å. J. Fridh, *CCSL* 96 (Turnholt, 1972)

Chronicle of 511, ed. T. Mommsen, *Chronica Minora* 1, *MGH AA* 9 (Berlin, 1892), pp. 615–66

Claudianus Mamertus, *De Statu Animae*, ed. A. Engelbrecht, *CSEL* 11 (Vienna, 1885)

Codex Theodosianus, ed. T. Mommsen, P. M. Meyer and P. Krüger, *Theodosiani libri XVI cum constitutionibus sirmondianis et leges novellae ad Theodosianum pertinentes* (3 vols) (Berlin, 1905; repr. 1970–71)

Collectio Avellana, ed. O. Günther, *CSEL* 35, 1–2 (Vienna, 1895–98)

Columbanus, *Sancti Columbani Opera*, ed. G. S. M. Walker (Dublin, 1957)

Concilia Galliae A. 314–A. 506, ed. C. Munier, *CCSL* 148 (Turnholt, 1963)

Concilia Galliae A. 511–A. 695, ed. C. de Clercq, *CCSL* 148A (Turnholt, 1963); also J. Gaudemet and B. Basdevant, eds, *Les Canons de conciles mérovingiens (VIe–VIIe siècles)*, *SC* 353–54 (Paris, 1989)

Consentius, *Ars de nomine et verbo* and *Ars de barbarismis et metaplasmis*, in *Grammatici Latini* 5, ed. H. Keil (Leipzig, 1868)

Continuatio Havniensis Prosperi, ed. T. Mommsen, *Chronica Minora* 1, *MGH AA* 9 (Berlin, 1892), pp. 298–339; trans. S. Muhlberger, 'The Copenhagen Continuation: a translation', *Florilegium* 6 (1984), pp. 71–95

Cyril of Scythopolis: The Lives of the Monks of Palestine, trans. R. M. Price (Kalamazoo, 1991)

De Miraculis S. Stephani, *PL* 41.833–54

Ennodius, Magnus Felix, *Opera*, ed. F. Vogel, *MGH AA* 7 (Berlin, 1885); also ed. G. Hartel, *CSEL* 6 (Vienna, 1882)

Epistulae Arelatenses Genuinae, ed. W. Gundlach, *MGH Epp.* 3 (Berlin, 1892), pp. 1–83

Epistulae Austrasiacae, ed. W. Gundlach, *MGH Epp.* 3 (Berlin, 1892), pp. 110–53: reprinted in *CCSL* 117 (Turnholt, 1957), pp. 404–70

Epistolae Romanorum Pontificum Genuinae, ed. A. Thiel, (Brunsberg, 1868)

Eucherius, *Passio Acaunensium Martyrum*, ed. B. Krusch, *MGH SRM* 3 (Hanover, 1896), pp. 20–41

Fasti Vindobonenses Priores, ed. T. Mommsen, *Chronica Minora* 1, *MGH AA* 9 (Berlin, 1892), pp. 274–320

Faustus of Riez, ed. A. Engelbrecht, *CSEL* 21 (Vienna, 1891)

Fredegar, *Chronicon*, ed. B. Krusch, *MGH SRM* 2 (Hanover, 1888)

Gennadius, *Liber de Scriptoribus Ecclesiasticis* (= *De viris inlustribus*), *PL* 58, cols. 1059–1120

Gennadius, *Liber sive definitio ecclesiasticorum dogmatum*, ed. C. H. Turner, 'The *Liber Ecclesiasticorum Dogmatum* Attributed to Gennadius', *JTS* 7 (1906), pp. 78–99

Gildas, *De Excidio Britanniae*, ed. M. Winterbottom, *Gildas, The Ruin of Britain and other works* (Chichester, 1978)

Grattius, *Il Cynegeticon di Grattio*, ed. G. Formicola (Bologna, 1988)

Gregory I, *Register*, ed. P. Ewald and L. Hartmann, *MGH Epp.* 1 and 2 (Hanover, 1887–99)

Gregory of Tours, *Decem Libri Historiarum*, ed. B. Krusch and W, Levison, *MGH SRM* 1.1 (Hanover, 1951)

Gregory of Tours, *Liber in Gloria Confessorum*, ed. B. Krusch, *MGH SRM* 1.2 (Hanover, 1881), pp. 294–370; trans. R. Van Dam, *Gregory of Tours, Glory of the Confessors*, *TTH* 4 (Liverpool, 1988)

Gregory of Tours, *Liber in Gloria Martyrum*, ed. B. Krusch, *MGH SRM* 1.2 (Hanover 1881), pp. 34–111; trans. R. Van Dam, *Gregory of Tours, Glory of the Martyrs*, *TTH* 3 (Liverpool, 1988)

Gregory of Tours, *Liber de Virtutibus Sancti Juliani*, ed. B. Krusch, *MGH SRM* 1.2 (Hanover, 1881), pp. 112–34: trans. R. Van Dam, *Saints and their Miracles in Late Antique Gaul* (Princeton, 1993), pp. 162–95

Gregory of Tours, *Liber de Virtutibus Sancti Martini*, ed. B. Krusch, *MGH SRM* 1.2 (Hanover, 1881), pp. 134–211; trans. R. Van Dam, *Saints and their Miracles in Late Antique Gaul* (Princeton, 1993), pp. 199–303

Gregory of Tours, *Liber Vitae Patrum*, ed. B. Krusch, *MGH SRM* 1.2 (Hanover, 1881), pp. 211–94; trans. E. James, *Gregory of Tours, Life of the Fathers*, *TTH* 1 (Liverpool, 1985)

Hilary of Poitiers, *In Matthaeum*, ed. J. Doignon, *SC* 254 and 258 (Paris, 1978–79)

Hilary of Poitiers, *Hymns*, ed. A. Feder, *CSEL* 65 (Vienna, 1916), pp. 209–16; also *PLS* 1.274–28

Hydatius, *The Chronicle of Hydatius and the Consularia Constantinopolitana*, ed. R.W. Burgess (Oxford, 1993)

Isidore of Seville, *Etymologiae sive Origines*, ed. W. M. Lindsay (Oxford, 1911)

Isidore of Seville, *Indiculus de haeresibus*, in *PL* 81.636–44

Isidore of Seville, *Historia Gothorum, Wandalorum, Sueborum*, ed. T. Mommsen, *Chronica Minora* 2, *MGH AA* 11 (Berlin, 1894), pp. 241–303

John of Antioch, *Fragmenta Historicorum Graecorum*, ed. C. Müller, 4 (Paris, 1868) and 5 (Paris, 1851 and 1870)

Jonas, *Vita Columbani*, ed. B. Krusch, *MGH SRM* 4 (Hanover, 1905), pp. 144–294

Jordanes, *Getica*, ed. F. Giunta and A. Grillone, *Fonti per la Storia d'Italia* 117 (Rome, 1991)

Liber Constitutionum, ed. L. R. De Salis, *Leges Burgundionum*, *MGH Leg.* (Hanover, 1892)

Liber Pontificalis, ed. L. Duchesne (1886–92)

Marcellinus Comes, *Chronicle*, ed. and trans. B. Croke (Sydney, 1995)

Marius of Avenches, *Chronicle*, ed. J. Favrod, *La Chronique de Marius d'Avenches (455–581)* (Lausanne, 1991); also ed. T. Mommsen, *Chronica Minora* 2, *MGH AA* 11 (Berlin, 1894), pp. 226–39

Maximus of Turin, *Sermones*, ed. A. Mutzenbecher, *CCSL* 23 (Turnholt, 1962)

Menander Rhetor, ed. D. A. Russell and N. G. Wilson (Oxford, 1981)

Nicolas I, *Epistolae*, ed. E. Perels, *MGH Epp.* 6 (Berlin, 1892)

Pardessus, J. M., *Diplomata, chartae epistolae, leges aliaque instrumenta ad res Gallo-Francicas spectantia* 1 (Paris, 1843)

Paulinus of Nola, *Carmina*, ed. W. Hartel, *CSEL* 30 (1894)

Pliny the Elder, *Natural History*, ed. and trans. H. Rackham (Cambridge, MA, 1940)

Praeceptio Regis 3, ed. T. Mommsen, *MGH AA* 12 (Berlin, 1894), pp. 419–20

Priscianus, *Ars Grammatica*, in *Grammatici Latini* 2, ed. H. Keil (Leipzig, 1857)

Probus, *Instituta Artium*, in *Grammatici Latini* 4, ed. H. Keil (Leipzig, 1864)

Procopius, *Persian War* (= *Wars* 1–2), ed. and trans. H. B. Dewing (Cambridge, MA, 1914)

Procopius, *Gothic War* (= *Wars* 5–8), ed. and trans. H. B. Dewing (Cambridge, MA, 1919–28)

Prudentius, *Carmina*, ed. M. Cunningham *CCSL* 126 (Turnhout, 1967)

Ruricius of Limoges, *Epistulae*, ed. B. Krusch, *MGH AA* 8 (Berlin, 1887), pp. 299–350; trans. R. W. Mathisen, *Ruricius of Limoges and Friends: A Collection of Letters from Visigothic Gaul*, *TTH* 30 (Liverpool, 1999)

Sidonius Apollinaris, *Sidoine Apollinaire: poèmes et lettres*, ed. A. Loyen (Paris, 1960–1970)

Silvius, Polemius, *Laterculus*, ed. T. Mommsen, *Chronica Minora* 1, *MGH AA* 9 (Berlin, 1892), pp. 511–614

Solinus, G.I., *C. Iulii Solini collectanea rerum memorabilium*, ed. T. Mommsen (Berlin, 1895)

Statuta Ecclesiae Antiquae, ed. C. Munier, *CCSL* 148 (Turnholt, 1963)

Symmachus, Quintus Aurelius, ed. O. Seeck, *MGH AA* 6.1 (Berlin, 1883)

Tertullian, *De exhortatione castitatis*, *PL* 2.913–28; also ed. C. Moreschini and C. J. Frédouille, *SC* 319 (Paris, 1985)

Tertullian, *De Monogamia*, *PL* 2.929–52; also ed. E. Dekkers, *CCSL* 2 (Turnholt, 1954), pp. 1229–53

Venantius Fortunatus, *Carmina*, ed. F. Leo, *MGH AA* 4.1 (Berlin, 1881)

Victor of Vita, *Historia persecutionis Africanae provinciae*, ed. C. Helm, *MGH AA* 2 (Berlin, 1879); trans. J. Moorhead, *Victor of Vita: History of the Vandal Persecution*, *TTH* 10 (Liverpool, 1992)

Vigilius of Thapsus, *Opera*, *PL* 62.93–472

Vita Abbatum Acaunensium, ed. B. Krusch, *MGH SRM* 3 (Hanover, 1896), pp. 171–83

Vita Abbatum Acaunensium absque epitaphiis, ed. B. Krusch, *MGH SRM* 7 (Hanover, 1920), pp. 322–36

Vita Apollinaris Valentinensis, ed. B. Krusch, *MGH SRM* 3 (Hanover, 1896), pp. 194–203

Vita Aviti, ed. R. Peiper, *MGH AA* 6.2 (Berli 1883), pp. 177–81

Vita Caesarii, ed. B. Krusch, *MGH SRM* 3 (Hanover, 1896), pp. 433–501; trans. W. Klingshirn, *Caesarius of Arles: Life, Testament, Letters, TTH* 19 (Liverpool, 1994), pp. 9–65

Vita Clari, *AASS* Jan. 1st, vol. 1 (Brussels, 1863), pp. 54–56

Vita Eptadii, ed. B. Krusch, *MGH SRM* 3 (Hanover, 1896), pp. 184–94

Vita Fuscinulae, *Catalogus codicum hagiographicorum latinorum in Bibliotheca nationali Parisiensi* 3 (Brussels, 1893), pp. 563–65

Vita Genovefae, ed. B. Krusch, *MGH SRM* 3 (Hanover, 1896), pp. 204–38

Vita Marcelli, ed. F. Dolbeau, 'La Vie en prose de Saint Marcel, évêque de Die', *Francia* 11 (1983), pp. 97–130

Vita Patrum Iurensium, ed. F. Martine, *SC* 142 (Paris, 1968)

Vita Wulframni, ed. W. Levison, *MGH SRM* 5 (Hanover, 1910), pp. 661–73

SECONDARY SOURCES

Amory, Patrick, 'The Textual Transmission of the *Donatio Ansemundi*', *Francia* 20 (1993), pp. 163–83

Angenendt, A., *Kaiserherrschaft und Königstaufe*, Berlin, 1984

Arnold, C. J., *Caesarius von Arelate*, Leipzig, 1894

Arweiler, A., *Die Imitation antiker und spät-antiker Literatur in der Dichtung 'De Spiritalis Historiae Gestis,' des Alcimus Avitus*, Berlin, New York, 1999

Bagatti, B., 'Eulogie Palestinesi', *Orientalia Christiana Periodica* 15 (1949), pp. 126–66

Barnwell, P. S., *Emperor, Prefects and Kings: The Roman West 395–565*, London, 1992

Bartlett, R., 'Aristocracy and Asceticism: The Letters of Ennodius and the Gallic and Italian Churches', in *Culture and Society in Late Antique Gaul: Revisiting the Sources*, ed. R. W. Mathisen and D. R. Shanzer, Ashgate, 2001, pp. 201–16

Baudrillart, Alfred, Albert de Meyer and Roger Aubert, *Dictionnaire d'histoire et de géographie ecclésiastiques*, 26 vols., Paris, 1912–99

Bédier, J., *La Tradition manuscrite du Lai de l'Ombre*, Paris, 1970

Besson, M., 'Maxime de Genève', *Anzeiger für schweizerische Geschichte* 9 (1904), pp. 287–99

Binding, K., *Das burgundisch-romanische Königreich I*, 1868 repr., Aalen. 1969

Blaise, A., *Dictionnaire Latin-Française des auteurs chrétiens*, Turnhout, 1967

Blondel, L., 'Le Prieuré Saint-Victor, les débuts du Christianisme et la royauté burgonde à Genève', *Bulletin de la société d'histoire et d'archéologie de Genève* 11 (1958), pp. 211–58

Boissier, G., 'Le *Carmen Paschale* et l'*Opus Paschale* de Sedulius', *Revue de Philologie* 6 (1882), pp. 28–36

Borrel, E. L., 'Étude sur l'homélie prêchée par saint Avit, au commencement du VIe siècle dans la basilique de Saint-Pierre de Moutiers en Tarantaise (Savoie), à l'occasion de sa consécration', *Bulletin du comité des travaux historiques et scientifiques, section d'histoire, d'archéologie et de philologie* (1883), pp. 46–55

Bouvier, Claude, *Saint Avit, poète et orateur*, Vienne, 1883

Brenk, B., 'Mit was für Mitteln kann einem Physisch Anonymen Auctoritas verliehen werden?', in *East and West: Modes of Communication. Proceedings of the First Plenary Conference at Merida*, ed. E. Chrysos and I. N. Wood, Leiden, 1999, pp. 143–72

Brittain, C. F., 'No Place for a Platonist Soul in Fifth-Century Provence? The Case of Claudianus Mamertus', in *Culture and Society in Late Antique Gaul: Revisiting the Sources*, ed. R. W. Mathisen and D. R. Shanzer, Ashgate, 2001, pp. 239–62

Brown, R.E., *The Gospel According to John (I–XII)*, Garden City, NY, 1966

Brundage, James A., *Law, Sex, and Christian Society in Medieval Europe*, Chicago, 1987

Brunhölzl, F., *Histoire de la littérature latine du Moyen Âge*, Louvain-la-neuve, 1990

Burckhardt, Max, *Die Briefsammlung des Bischofs Avitus von Vienne. Abhandlungen zur mittleren und neueren Geschichte*, Vol. 81, Berlin, 1938

Burgess, R. W., *The Chronicle of Hydatius and the Consularia Constantinopolitana*, Oxford, 1993

Cabrol, F., *Dictionnaire d'archéologie chrétienne et de liturgie*, 15 vols, Paris, 1907–53

Cameron, A., *Claudian: Poetry and Propaganda at the Court of Honorius*, Oxford, 1970

Caspar, E., *Geschichte des Papsttums*, 2 vols, Tübingen, 1930

Cavadini, J. C., *The Last Christology of the West. Adoptionism in Spain and Gaul 785–820*, Philadelphia, 1993

Chadwick, H., *Boethius: The Consolations of Music, Logic, Theology and Philosophy*, Oxford, 1981

Chapuis, *Saint Avit, Archévêque de Vienne (455–525)*, Paris, 1898

Charaux, Auguste, *Saint Avit, évêque de Vienne en Dauphiné, sa vie, ses oeuvres*, Paris, 1876

Charles-Edwards, T. M., 'Palladius, Prosper, and Leo the Great: Mission and Primatial Authority', in *Saint Patrick A.D. 493–1993*, ed. D. N. Dumville, Woodbridge, 1993, pp. 1–12

Charlier, C., 'La Compilation augustinienne de Florus sur l'apôtre', *Revue Bénédictine* 57 (1947), pp. 132–67

——, 'Les Manuscrits personnels de Florus', in *Mélanges E. Podechard*, Lyon, 1945, pp. 71–84

——, 'Notes sur les origines de l'écriture dite de Luxeuil', *Revue Bénédictine* 58 (1948), pp. 149–57

Claude, D., 'Untersuchungen zum frühfränkischen Comitat', *Zeitschrift der Savigny-Stiftung für Rechtsgeschichte* germanistische Abteilung 81 (1964), pp. 1–74

Clover, Frank M., *The Late Roman West and the Vandals*, Aldershot, 1993

Costanza, Salvatore, *Avitiana I: I Modelli Epici Del 'De Spiritalis Historiae Gestis'*, Messina, 1968

Courtois, Christian, *Les Vandales et l'Afrique*, Paris, 1955

Coville, Alfred, *Recherches sur l'histoire de Lyon du Vme siècle au IXme siècle (450–800)*, Paris, 1928

Cucheval, Victor, *De Sancti Aviti Viennae Episcopi Operibus Commentarium*, Paris, 1863

Cugusi, Paolo, *Epistolographi Latini Minores*, 2 vols, Turin, 1970

——, *Epistolographi Latini Minores: Commentarium Criticum*, 2 vols, Turin, 1970

D'Achéry, Luc, *Veterum Aliquot Scriptorum ... Spicilegium*, 13 vols, Paris, 1661–87

Dalton, O. M., *Catalogue of the Finger Rings Early Christian, Byzantine, Teutonic, Medieval and Later [in the British Museum]*, London, 1912

Daly, William M., 'Clovis: How Barbaric, How Pagan?', *Speculum* 69 (1994), pp. 619–64

Dando, M., 'Alcimus Avitus (C. 450–C. 518) as the Author of the *De Resurrectione Mortuorum, De Pascha (De Cruce), De Sodoma* and *De Iona*', *Classica et Mediaevalia* 26 (1965), pp. 258–75

Daremberg, Charles, Edmond Saglio, Edmond Pottier, and Georges Lafaye, *Dictionnaire des antiquités grecques et romaines d'après les textes et les monuments*, 5 in 10 vols, Paris, 1877

De Lagrevol, A., *Notice sur saint Avite, évêque de Vienne, lue à l'académie des sciences, belles-lettres et arts de Lyon dans la séance du 12 Mai 1863*, Lyon, 1863

Decret, F., *Aspects du manichéisme dans l'Afrique romaine*, Paris, 1970

Delandine, A. F., *Manuscrits de la bibliothèque de Lyon*, 3 vols, Paris, 1812

Delehaye, H., *Les Origines du culte des martyrs*, Brussels, 1933

Delisle, Léopold V., *Études paléographiques et historiques sur des papyrus de Vième siècle ... renfermant des homélies de saint Avit*, Geneva, 1866

Denkinger, Henri, *Alcimus Ecdicius Avitus, archévêque de Vienne 460–526 et la destruction de l'arianisme en Gaule*, Geneva, 1890

Derichsweiler, H., *Geschichte der Burgunden*, Münster, 1863

Desvernay, Félix, and Auguste Molinier, *Catalogue général des manuscrits des bibliothèques publiques de France. Départements. Lyon*, Vol. 30, Paris, 1890

Dill, Samuel, *Roman Society in Gaul in the Merovingian Age*, London, 1926

——, *Roman Society in the Last Century of the Western Empire*, New York, 2nd rev. edn, 1960

Dolbeau, F., 'La Vie en prose de saint Marcel de Die', *Francia* 11 (1983), pp. 97–129

Dubois, A., *La Latinité d'Ennodius. Contribution à l'étude du Latin littéraire à la fin de l'empire romain d'occident*, Paris, 1903

Dubois, J, and G. Renaud, *Le Martyrologe d'Adon*, Paris, 1984

Duchesne, L., *Fastes épiscopaux de l'ancienne Gaule*, 3 vols, 2nd rev. edn, Paris, 1910

Duchesne, L., *L'église au Vième siècle*, Paris, 1925

Duparc, P., 'La Sapaudia', *Comptes-rendus de l'académie des inscriptions et belles lettres* (1958), pp. 371–84

Durliat, J., 'Les Attributions civiles des évêques mérovingiens: L'exemple de Didier, évêque de Cahors (630–655)', *Annales du Midi* 91 (1979), pp. 237–54

Dvornik, F., *The Photian Schism: History and Legend*, Cambridge, 1948

Engelbrecht, A., *Das Titelwesen bei den spätlateinischen Epistolographen*, Vienna, 1893

——, 'Titel und Titulaturen in den Briefen des Ruricius und seiner Genossen', *Patristiche Analecten* (1892), pp. 48–83

Engemann, J., and B. Rüger, eds, *Spätantike und Frühes Mittelalter*, Bonn, 1991

Ewig, E., 'Die Kathedralpatrozinien im römischen und im fränkischen Gallien', in *Spätantikes und fränkisches Gallien*, ed. E. Ewig, Munich, 1979, vol. 2

——, 'Studien zur Merowingischen Dynastie.' *Frühmittelalterliche Studien* 8 (1974), pp. 15–59

——, *Trier im Merowingerreich. Civitas, Stadt, Bistum*, Trier, 1954

Favrod, J., *Histoire politique du royaume burgonde (443–534)*, Lausanne, 1997

Formicola, C., *Il Cynegeticon Di Grattio*, Bologna, 1988

Fortin, E. L., *Christianisme et culture philosophique au cinquième: La querelle de l'âme humaine en occident*, Paris, 1959

Frantz, Peter Norbert, *Avitus von Vienne (498–512) als Hierarch und Politiker*, Greifswald, 1908

Frend, W. H. C., *The Rise of the Monophysite Movement*, Cambridge, 1972

Fridh, Å. J., *Terminologie et formules dans les Variae de Cassiodore*, Gothenburg, 1956

Fritze, W.H. 'Universalis Gentium Confessio. Formeln, Träger und Wege Universalmissionarischen Denkens im 7. Jahrhundert.' *Frühmittelalterliche Studien* 3 (1969), pp. 79–130

Gasnault, P., 'Fragment retrouvé du manuscrit sur papyrus des homélies de saint Avit', *Comptes-rendus de l'académie des inscriptions et belles lettres* (1994), pp. 315–23

Goelzer, H., *Le Latin de saint Avit*, Paris, 1909

Gordon, C. D., *The Age of Attila*, Ann Arbor, MI, 1960

Gowers, E., *The Loaded Table: Representations of Food in Roman Literature*, Oxford, 1993

Grierson, P., and M. Blackburn, *Medieval European Coinage 1, the Early Middle Ages (5th–10th Centuries)*, Cambridge, 1986

Grimes, W. F., 'Holt: The Works Depot of the Twentieth Legion at Castle Lyons', *Y Cymmrodor* 41 (1930), pp. 24–41

Grossi Gondi, F., *Trattato Di Epigrafia Christiana*, Rome, 1920

Guichard, R., *Essai sur l'histoire du peuple burgonde*, Paris, 1965

Hagendahl, H., *La Correspondance de Ruricius. Acta Universitatis Gothoburgensis*, Vol. 58.3, Gothenburg, 1952

Hannestad, Niels, 'How Did Rising Christianity Cope with Pagan Sculpture?', in *East and West: Modes of Communication. Proceedings of the First Plenary Conference at Merida*, ed. E. Chrysos and I. N. Wood, Leiden, 1999, pp. 173–203

Harries, Jill, *Sidonius Apollinaris and the Fall of Rome, 407–485*, Oxford, 1994

Haupt, M., 'Analecta', *Hermes* 3 (1869), pp. 205–29 at pp. 222–23

Havet, Julien, 'Questions mérovingiennes II: Les découvertes de Jérôme Vignier', *Bibliothèque de l'École des Chartes* 46 (1885), pp. 205–68

Hecquet-Noti, Nicole, *Avit de Vienne, histoire spirituelle: Tome I (chants I– III), SC* 444, Paris, 1999

Heinzelmann, Martin, *Bischofsherrschaft in Gallien. Beiträge der Francia*, Vol. 5, Munich, 1976

——, 'Gallische Prosopographie (260–527)', *Francia* 10 (1982), pp. 531–718

Hill, Joyce, 'The *Litaniae Maiores* and *Minores* in Rome, Francia and Anglo-Saxon England: Terminology, Texts and Traditions', *EME* 9 (2000), pp. 211–46

Hillgarth, J. M., ed., *Christianity and Paganism, 350–750: The Conversion of Western Europe*, Philadelphia, 1986

Hofmann, J. B., and A. Szantyr, *Lateinische Syntax und Stilistik*, Munich, 1972

Jahn, Albert, *Die Geschichte der Burgundionen und Burgundiens bis zum Ende der I Dynastie*, Halle, 1874

James, Edward, 'Beati Pacifici: Bishops and the Law in Sixth-Century Gaul', in *Disputes and Settlements: Law and Human Relations in the West*, ed. John Bossy, Cambridge, New York, 1983, pp. 25–46

——, *The Franks*, London, 1988

Jones, A. H. M., *The Later Roman Empire, 284–602: A Social, Economic and Administrative Survey*, 2 vols, Baltimore, 1986

Jones, A. H. M., J. R. Martindale, and J. Morris, *The Prosopography of the Later Roman Empire*, Cambridge, 1971

Jones, A. H. M., and E. Monroe, *A History of Abyssinia*, Oxford, 1935

Kampers, Gerd, 'Caretena – Königin und Asketin', *Francia* 27 (2000), pp. 1–32

Kelly, J. N. D., *Early Christian Doctrines*, Edinburgh, 4th edn, 1968

Keys, D., *Catastrophe. An Investigation into the Origins of the Modern World*, London, 2000

Kienzle, B. M., ed., *The Sermon, Typologie des Sources*, Turnhout, 2000

Kirkby, Helen, 'The Scholar and his Public,', in *Boethius, his Life, Thought and Influence*, ed. M. Gibson, Oxford, 1981

Klingshirn, William, *Caesarius of Arles: The Making of a Christian Community in Late Antique Gaul*, Cambridge, 1994

——, 'Charity and Power: Caesarius of Arles and the Ransoming of Captives in Sub-Roman Gaul', *JRS* 75 (1985), pp. 183–203

Klotz, A., 'Ultuisse: zu Alcimus Avitus', *ALL* 15 (1908), pp. 418–19

Koch, P., *Die byzantinischen Beamtentitel von 400 bis 700*, Jena, 1903

König, Ingemar, *Aus der Zeit Theoderichs des Grossen*, Darmstadt, 1997

Kramer, J., *Literarische Quellen zur Aussprache des Vulgärlateins*, Meisenheim am Glan, 1976

Krusch, Bruno, 'Chlodovechs Taufe in Tours 507 und die Legende Gregors von Tours (Reims 496)', *Neues Archiv der Gesellschaft für ältere deutsche Geschichtskunde* 49 (1932), pp. 457–69

——, 'Die erste deutsche Kaiserkrönung in Tours Weihnachten 508', *SbBerlin. Akad. Wiss.* (1933), pp. 1060–66

Levillain, L., 'La Conversion et le baptême de Clovis', *Revue d'histoire de l'église de France* 21 (1935), pp. 161–92

Lewis, A. R., 'The Dukes of the Regnum Francorum, A.D. 550–751', *Speculum* 51 (1976), pp. 381–410

Lot, F., 'La Victoire sur les Alamans et la conversion de Clovis', *RBPH* 17 (1938), pp. 63–69

Lowe, E. A., *Codices Latini Antiquiores. France: Paris. Codices Latini Antiquiores*, Vol. 5, Oxford, 1950

Loyen, A., *Sidoine Apollinaire et l'esprit précieux en Gaule aux derniers jours de l'empire*, Paris, 1943

Macpherson, R., *Rome in Involution: Cassiodorus's Variae in Their Literary and Historical Setting*, Poznan, 1989

Malherbe, J., *Ancient Epistolary Theorists*, Atlanta, 1988

Markus, R. A., *From Augustine to Gregory the Great*, Andover, 1983

——, 'The Legacy of Pelagius: Orthodoxy, Heresy and Conciliation', in *The Making of Orthodoxy: Essays in Honour of Henry Chadwick*, ed. R. D. Williams, Cambridge, 1989, pp. 214–34

——, *Saeculum. History and Society in the Theology of St Augustine*, Cambridge, 1970

Marquardt, J., *Das Privatleben der Römer*, 2 vols, Darmstadt, 1980

Marshall, F. H., *Catalogue of the Finger Rings, Greek, Etruscan, and Roman*, London, 1907

Martindale, J. R., *The Prosopography of the Later Roman Empire. A.D. 395–527*, Cambridge, 1980

Martine, F., *Vie des Pères du Jura*: see Primary Sources, *Vita Patrum Iurensium*

Masai, F., 'La *Vita Patrum Iurensium* et les débuts du monachisme à saint-Maurice d'Agaune', in *Festschrift Bernhard Bischoff*, ed. J. Autienrieth and F. Brunhölzl, Stuttgart, 1971, pp. 43–69

Mathisen, Ralph W., *Ruricius of Limoges and Friends: A Collection of Letters from Visigothic Gaul*, *TTH* 30, Liverpool, 1999

——, 'Barbarian Bishops and the Churches "in Barbaricis Gentibus" During Late Antiquity', *Speculum* 72 (1997), pp. 664–97

——, *Ecclesiastical Factionalism and Religious Controversy in Fifth-Century Gaul*, Washington, DC, 1989

——, 'Episcopal Hierarchy and Tenure in Office: A Method for Establishing Dates of Ordination', *Francia* 17 (1990), pp. 125–40

——, 'Epistolography, Literary Circles, and Family Ties in Late Roman Gaul', *TAPA* 111 (1981), pp. 95–109

——, 'Imperial Honorifics and Senatorial Status', in *Law, Society and Authority in Late Antiquity*, ed. R. W. Mathisen, Oxford, 2001, pp. 179–207

——, 'PLRE II: Some Suggested Addenda and Corrigenda', *Historia* 31 (1982), pp. 364–86

——, 'The "Second Council of Arles" and the Spirit of Compilation and Codification in Late Roman Gaul', *Journal of Early Christian Studies* 5 (1997), pp. 511–54

Matthews, J., 'The Letters of Symmachus', in *Latin Literature of the Fourth Century*, ed. J. W. Binns, London, 1974, pp. 58–99

——, *The Roman Empire of Ammianus Marcellinus*, London, 1989

McCormick, M., 'Clovis at Tours, Byzantine Public Ritual and the Origins of Medieval Ruler Symbolism', in *Das Reich und die Barbaren*, ed. E. Chrysos and A. Schwarcz, Vienna–Cologne, 1989, pp. 155–80

——, *Eternal Victory*, Cambridge, 1986

Meyer-Lübke, W., *Romanisches etymologisches Wörterbuch*, Heidelberg, 1972

Mikat, P., 'Die Inzestgesetzgebung der merowingisch-fränkischen Konzilien (511–626/7)', *Rechts- und staatswissenschaftliche Veröffentlichungen der Görres-Gesellschaft*, N.F. 74 (1994)

——, 'Die Inzestverbote des Konzils von Epaon. Ein Beitrag zur Geschichte des fränkischen Eherechts', in *Rechtsbewahrung Und Rechtsentwicklung: Festschrift für H. Lange*, Munich, 1970, pp. 868–88

Mommsen, Theodor, 'Ostgotische Studien', *Neues Archiv* 14 (1889), pp. 225–49 and 453–544

Monceaux, P., 'Le Manichéen Faustus de Milev: Restitution de ses capitula', *Mémoires de l'institut national de France, académie des inscriptions et belles-lettres* (1933), pp. 1–111

Moorhead, John, *Theoderic in Italy*, Oxford, 1992

Morin, G., 'Maximien, éveque de Trèves dans une lettre d'Avit de Vienne', *Revue Bénédictine* 47 (1935), pp. 207–10

Morisi, Luca, *Alcimi Aviti De Mundi Initio*, Bologna, 1996

Munby, A. N. L., ed., *The Phillips Manuscripts*, London, 1968

Murray, Alexander Callander, *From Roman to Merovingian Gaul: A Reader*, Peterborough, 2000

Nodes, Daniel, J., 'Avitus of Vienne's Spiritual History and the Semi-pelagian Controversy: The Doctrinal Implications of Books I–III', *Vigiliae Christianae* 38 (1984), pp. 185–95

——, '*De Subitanea Paenitentia* in Letters of Faustus of Riez and Avitus of Vienne', *Recherches de théologie ancienne et médievale* 55 (1988), pp. 30–40

——, *Doctrine and Exegesis in Biblical Latin Poetry*, Leeds, 1993

Norberg, D., 'Alc. Avit. *Ep.* 9 (Peiper P. 44,1)', *Eranos* 36 (1938), pp. 129–30

Nottarp, H., *Gottesurteilstudien*, Munich, 1956

O'Brien, Mary Bridget, *Titles of Address in Christian Latin Epistolography to 543 A.D.*, Washington, DC, 1930

O'Donnell, James J., 'Liberius the Patrician', *Traditio* 37 (1981), pp. 31–72

Oberhelman, S., 'The Cursus in Late Imperial Prose: A Reconsideration of Methodology', *CP* 83 (1988), pp. 136–49

Otto, A., *Die Sprichwörter und sprichwörtlichen Redensarten der Römer*, Leipzig, 1890

Palanque, J. R., 'Avit', *DHGE* 5 (1931), pp. 1205–08

Parizel, P.. *St. Avit, évêque de Vienne, sa vie et ses écrits*, Louvain, 1859

Perrat, Charles, and Aimable Audin, 'Alcimi Ecdicii Aviti Viennensis Epis-copi Homilia Dicta in Dedicatione Superioris Basilicae', in *Studi in Onore di A. Calderini e R. Paribeni*, Vol. 2, Milan, 1957, pp. 433–51

Perrin, Odet, *Les Burgondes, leur histoire des origines à la fin du premier royaume (534)*, Neuchâtel, 1968

Picotti, G. B., 'I Sinodi Romani nello Scisma Laurenziano', in *Studi Storici in Honore Di G. Volpe*, Florence, 1958, pp. 743–86

Pietri, C., 'Le Sénat, le peuple chrétien, et les partis du cirque à Rome sous le pape Symmaque', *MÉFR* 78 (1966), pp. 123–39

——, *Roma Christiana: Recherches sur l'église de Rome, son organisation, sa politique, son idéologie de Miltiade à Sixte III (311–440)*, 2 vols, Rome, 1976

Pontal, O., *Die Synoden im Merowingerreich*, Paderborn, 1986

——, *Histoire des conciles mérovingiens*, Paris, 1989

Prinz, F., *Frühes Mönchtum im Frankenreich*, Munich, 1988

Rahner, Hugo, *Die gefälschten Papstbriefe aus dem Nachlasse von Jérôme Vignier*, Munich, 1935

Reverdy, G., 'Note sur l'interprétation d'un passage d'Avitus', *Le moyen âge* 17 (1913), pp. 274–77

Reydellet, M., *La Royauté dans la littérature latine de Sidoine Apollinaire à Isidore de Séville*, Rome, 1981

Reynaud, J. F., *Lyon aux premiers temps chrétiens, Guides archéologiques de la France*, Paris, 1986

Rilliet, Albert, *Conjectures historiques sur les homélies préchées par Avitus, évêque de Vienne dans le diocèse de Genève*, Geneva, 1866

Robert, J., and L. Robert, 'Bulletin épigraphique', *Revue des études grecques* 71 (1958), pp. 169–363

Roberts, M., *Biblical Epic and Rhetorical Paraphrase in Late Antiquity*, Liverpool, 1985

——, 'The Prologue to Avitus's *De Spiritalis Historiae Gestis*: Christian Poetry and Poetic License', *Traditio* 36 (1980), pp. 399–407

Roncoroni, Angelo, 'L'epica Biblica di Avito di Vienna', *Vetera Christianorum* 9 (1972), pp. 303–29

——, 'Note Al De Virginitate di Avito di Vienne', *Athenaeum* 51 (1973), pp. 122–34

Rosenwein, Barbara, 'Perennial Prayer at Agaune', in *Monks and Nuns, Saints and Outcasts*, ed. S. Farmer and B. Rosenwein, Ithaca, NY, London, 2000, pp. 37–56

Rouche, Michel, *Clovis*, Paris, 1996

——, *L'Aquitaine: Des Wisigoths aux Arabes 418–781*, Paris, 1979

Savio, F., *Gli Antichi Vescovi D'italia Dalle Origini Al 1300*, Milan, 1899

Schanz, M., C. Hosius, and G. Krüger, *Geschichte der römischen Literatur*, Vol. 4.2, Munich, 1920

Scheibelreiter, G., *Der Bischof in merowingischer Zeit*, Vienna, 1983

——, '*Vester Est Populus Meus.* Byzantinische Reichsideologie und germanisches Selbstverständnis', in *Das Reich und die Barbaren*, ed. E. Chrysos and A. Schwarcz, Vienna, 1989, pp. 203–20

Schmidt, L., *Geschichte der deutschen Stämme bis zum Ausgang der Völkerwanderung: Die Ostgermanen*, Vol. 1, Munich, 1934

——, *Geschichte der deutschen Stämme bis zum Ausgange der Völkerwanderung 1.4 : 1 Abteilung 7. Die Burgunder*, ed. W. Sieglin, Quellen und Forschungen zur alten Geschichte und Geographie 22, Berlin, 1910

Schwartz, E., 'Der Prozess des Eutyches', *SbBAW* phil.-hist. Kl. (1929), pp. 3–93

——, *Publizistische Sammlungen zum acacianischen Schisma*, Munich, 1934

Schwind, Johannes, 'Hieronymus' *Epistula Ad Innocentium* (Epist. 1) – Ein Jugendwerk ?', *Wiener Studien* 110 (1997), pp. 171–86

Shanzer, D. R., 'Bishops, Letters, Fast, Food, and Feast in Later Roman Gaul', in *Culture and Society in Late Antique Gaul: Revisiting the Sources*, ed. R. W. Mathisen and D. R. Shanzer, Ashgate, 2001, pp. 217–36

——, 'Dating the Baptism of Clovis: The Bishop of Vienne vs. the Bishop of Tours', *EME* 7.1 (1998), pp. 29–57

——, 'History, Romance, Love, and Sex in Gregory of Tours' *Decem Libri Historiarum*', in *Gregory of Tours*, ed. K. Mitchell and I. N. Wood, Leiden, 2002, pp. 395–418

——, 'Review of George W. Shea, *The Poems of Alcimus Ecidicius Avitus*', *CR* 49.2 (1999), pp. 404–06

——, 'Two Clocks and a Wedding: Theodoric's Diplomatic Relations with the Burgundians', *Romanobarbarica* 14 (1998), pp. 225–58

Shea, G. W., *The Poems of Alcimus Ecdicius Avitus*, Tempe, 1997

Smith, W., et al., *A Dictionary of Greek and Roman Antiquities*, 2 vols, London, 1890

Solimano, G., *Epistula Didonis ad Aeneam*, Genoa, 1988

Spencer, Mark, 'Dating the Baptism of Clovis, 1886–1993', *EME* 3 (1994), pp. 97–116

Staubach, N., 'Germanisches Königtum und lateinische Literatur vom fünften bis zum siebten Jahrhundert', *Frühmittelalterliche Studien* 17 (1983), pp. 1–54

Stein, Ernest, *Histoire du bas-empire: 476–565*, trans. J. R. Palanque, 2 vols, Paris–Brussels–Amsterdam, 1949

Stowers, S. K., *Letter Writing in Greco-Roman Antiquity*, Philadelphia, 1986

Stroheker, K., *Der senatorische Adel im spätantiken Gallien*, Tübingen, 1948

Strong, D., and D. Brown, eds, *Roman Crafts*, London, 1972

Tessier, Georges, *Le Baptême de Clovis*, Paris, 1964

Teuffel, Wilhelm Sigismund, and Wilhelm Wagner, *A History of Roman Literature*, revised and enlarged Ludwig Schwabe, London, 1891

Theurillat, J.M., *L'abbaye de saint-Maurice d'Agaune, des origines à la réforme canoniale 515–830*, Sion, 1954

Thompson, E. A., 'Christianity and the Northern Barbarians', in *The Conflict between Paganism and Christianity in the Fourth Century*, ed. A. Momigliano, Oxford, 1963, pp. 56–78

Thraede, K., *Grundzüge griechisch-römischer Brieftopik*, Munich, 1970

Timpanaro, S., *Die Entstehung der lachmannschen Methode*, Hamburg, 1971

Tjäder, J.- O., *Die nichtliterarischen lateinischen Papyri Italiens aus der Zeit 445–700*, Lund, 1955

Tomasini, W. J., *The Barbaric Tremissis in Spain and Southern France. Anastasius to Leovigild*, New York, 1964

Turner, C. H., 'The *Liber Ecclesiasticorum Dogmatum* attributed to Gennadius', *JTS* 7 (1906), pp. 78–99

Van de Vyver, A., 'Clovis et la politique méditerranéenne', in *Études dédiées à la mémoire de Henri Pirenne*, Brussels, 1937, pp. 367–87

——, 'La Victoire contre les Alamans et la conversion de Clovis', *RBPH* 16 (1937), pp. 35–94

——, 'La Victoire contre les Alamans et la conversion de Clovis', *RBPH* 15 (1936), pp. 859–914

——, 'L'unique victoire contre les Alamans et la conversion de Clovis en 506', *RBPH* 17 (1938), pp. 793–813

Vinay, G., 'La Poesia di Sant'Avito', *Convivium* 9 (1937), pp. 431–56

Vogel, C., *La Discipline pénitentielle en Gaule des origines à la fin du VIIe siècle*, Paris, 1952

——, *Le Pécheur et la pénitence dans l'église ancienne*, Paris, 1966

Vogel, F., 'Chlodwigs Sieg über die Alamannen und seine Taufe', *Historische Zeitschrift* 56 (1886), pp. 385–403

Von den Steinen, W., 'Chlodwigs Übergang zum Christentum: Eine quellenkritische Studie', *MIÖG* Ergänzungsband 12 (1933), pp. 417–501

Von Moos, P., *Consolatio, Studien über mittellateinischen Trostliteratur*, 4 vols, Munich, 1971

Wagner, Monica, 'A Chapter in Byzantine Epistolography: The Letters of Theodoret of Cyrus', *DOP* 4 (1944), pp. 119–81

Weiss, Rolf, *Chlodwigs Taufe: Reims 508. Geist und Werk der Zeiten*, Vol. 29, Frankfurt, 1971

Wood, I. N., 'The Audience of Architecture in Post–Roman Gaul', in *The Anglo-Saxon Church*, ed. L. A. S. Butler and R. K. Morris, London, 1986, pp. 74–79

——, 'Avitus of Vienne, the Augustinian Poet', in *Culture and Society in Late Antique Gaul: Revisiting the Sources*, ed. D. R. Shanzer and R. W. Mathisen, Ashgate, 2001, pp. 262–77

——, 'Avitus of Vienne: Religion and Culture in the Auvergne and the Rhône Valley, 470–530', unpublished DPhil thesis, Oxford, 1980

——, 'Continuity or Calamity? The Constraints of Literary Models', in *Fifth-Century Gaul: A Crisis of Identity*, ed. J. Drinkwater and Hugh Elton, Cambridge, 1992, pp. 9–18

——, 'Disputes in Late Fifth- and Sixth-Century Gaul: Some Problems', in *The Settlement of Disputes in Early Medieval Europe*, ed. W. Davies and P. Fouracre, Cambridge, 1986, pp. 7–22

——, 'The Ecclesiastical Politics of Merovingian Clermont', in *Ideal and Reality in Frankish and Anglo-Saxon Society*, ed. P. Wormald, Oxford, 1983, pp. 34–57

——, 'Ethnicity and the Ethnogenesis of the Burgundians', in *Typen der Ethnogenese unter besonderer Berücksichtigung der Bayern I*, ed. W. Pohl and H. Wolfram, Vienna, 1990, pp. 53–69

——, 'The Exchange of Gifts among the Late Antique Aristocracy', in M. Almagro-Gorbea, ed., *El Disco De Teodosio*, Madrid, 2000, pp. 301–14

——, 'The Fall of the Western Empire and End of Roman Britain', *Britannia* 18 (1987), pp. 251–62

——, 'Family and Friendship in the West', in *Cambridge Ancient History, 14 Late Antiquity: Empire and Successors, AD 425–600*, ed. A. Cameron, B. Ward-Perkins and M. Whitby, Cambridge, 2000, pp. 416–36

——, 'Gregory of Tours and Clovis', *RBPH* 63 (1985), pp. 249–72

——, 'Incest, Law and the Bible in Sixth-Century Gaul', *EME* 7.3 (1998), pp. 291–303

——, 'Kings, Kingdoms and Consent', in *Early Medieval Kingship*, ed. P. H. Sawyer and I. N. Wood, Leeds, 1977, pp. 6–29

——, 'Letters and Letter-Collections from Antiquity to the Early Middle Ages: The Prose Works of Avitus of Vienne', in *The Culture of Christendom: Essays in Medieval History in Commemoration of Denis L. T. Bethell*, ed. M. A. Meyer, London, 1993, pp. 29–43

——, *The Merovingian Kingdoms 450–571*, London, New York, 1994

——, 'Prelude to Columbanus', in *Columbanus and Merovingian Monasticism*, ed. H. B. Clarke and M. Brennan, Oxford, 1981, pp. 3–32

——, 'The Use and Abuse of Latin Hagiography in the Early Medieval West', in *East and West: Modes of Communication. Proceedings of the First Plenary Conference at Merida*, ed. E. Chrysos and I. N. Wood, Leiden, 1999, pp. 93–109

Zelzer, M., 'Der Brief in der Spätantike. Überlegungen zu einem literarischen Genos am Beispiel der Briefsammlung des Sidonius Apollinaris', *WS* 107–108 (1994–95), pp. 541–45

Zilliacus, Henrik, *Untersuchungen zu den abstrakten Anredeformen und Höflichkeitstiteln im Griechischen*, Helsinki, 1949

MAPS AND GENEALOGIES

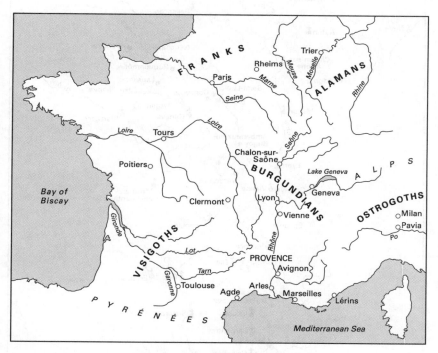

The Burgundians and their Neighbours

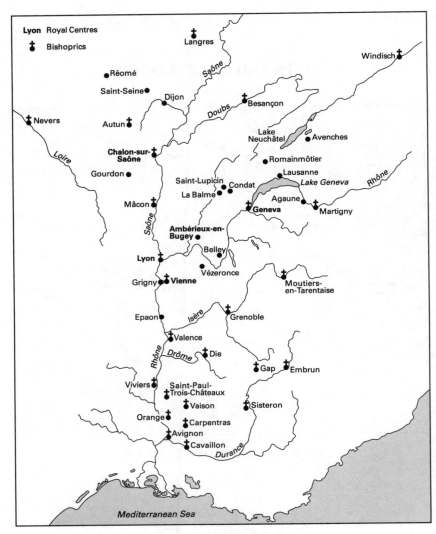

The Burgundian Kingdom

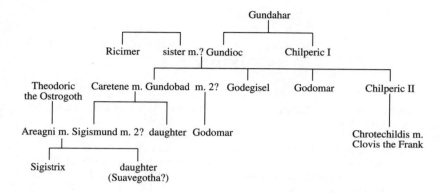

The Burgundian Royal Family

[*Note on the spelling of names*: Given the immense variety in the spelling of Germanic names we have tended to opt for the version used by Avitus, or otherwise by the earliest source. Sigistrix appears in *PLRE* as Sigiric, and Suavegotha as Suavegotho. Areagni is otherwise known as Ostrogotho.]

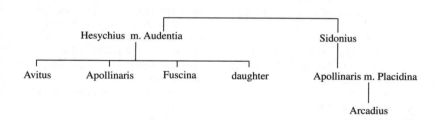

The Family of Avitus of Vienne

INDEX